# ENGINEERING BASICS

## ELECTRICAL, ELECTRONICS AND COMPUTER ENGINEERING

# ENGINEERING BASICS

## ELECTRICAL, ELECTRONICS AND COMPUTER ENGINEERING

### Third Edition

T. THYAGARAJAN
K. P. SENDUR CHELVI
T. R. RANGASWAMY

PUBLISHING FOR ONE WORLD

NEW AGE INTERNATIONAL (P) LIMITED, PUBLISHERS
New Delhi • Bangalore • Chennai • Cochin • Guwahati • Hyderabad
Jalandhar • Kolkata • Lucknow • Mumbai • Ranchi
Visit us at www.newagepublishers.com

Published by New Age International (P) Ltd., Publishers
First Edition: 1994
Third Edition: 2000
**Reprint:** 2015



**BRANCHES**

- **Bangalore** 37/10, 8th Cross (Near Hanuman Temple), Azad Nagar, Chamarajpet Bangalore-560 018, Tel.: (080) 26756823, Telefax: 26756820 **E-mail: bangalore@newagepublishers.com**
- **Chennai** 26, Damodaran Street, T. Nagar, Chennai-600 017, Tel.: (044) 24353401 Telefax: 24351463, **E-mail: chennai@newagepublishers.com**
- **Cochin** CC-39/1016, Carrier Station Road, Ernakulam South, Cochin-682 016 Tel.: (0484) 2377303, Telefax: 4051303 **E-mail: cochin@newagepublishers.com**
- **Guwahati** Hemsen Complex, Mohd. Shah Road, Paltan Bazar, Near Starline Hotel Guwahati-781 008 Tel.: (0361) 2513881, Telefax: 2543669 **E-mail: guwahati@newagepublishers.com**
- **Hyderabad** 105, 1st Floor, Madhiray Kaveri Tower, 3-2-19, Azam Jahi Road, Near Kumar Theater Nimboliadda, Kachiguda, Hyderabad-500 027, Tel.: (040) 24652456 Telefax: 24652457 **E-mail: hyderabad@newagepublishers.com**
- **Kolkata** RDB Chambers (Formerly Lotus Cinema) 106A, 1st Floor, S N Banerjee Road Kolkata-700 014 Tel.: (033) 22273773, Telefax: 22275247 **E-mail: kolkata@newagepublishers.com**
- **Lucknow** 16-A, Jopling Road, Lucknow-226 001, Tel.: (0522) 2209578, 4045297 Telefax: 2204098, **E-mail:lucknow@newagepublishers.com**
- **Mumbai** 142C, Victor House, Ground Floor, N.M. Joshi Marg, Lower Parel Mumbai-400 013, Tel.: (022) 24927869, Telefax: 24915415 **E-mail: mumbai@newagepublishers.com**
- **New Delhi** 22, Golden House, Daryaganj, New Delhi-110 002 Tel.: (011) 23262368, 23262370, Telefax: 43551305 **E-mail: sales@newagepublishers.com**

**ISBN: 978-81-224-1274-1**

**₹ 300.00**

C-16-02-9633

Printed in India at Ajit Printing Press, Delhi.

**PUBLISHING GLOBALLY**
**NEW AGE INTERNATIONAL (P) LIMITED, PUBLISHERS**
7/30 A, Daryaganj, New Delhi - 110002
Visit us at **www.newagepublishers.com**

**To my parents D. Thangavelu,**
**T. Santhakumari, wife Meera**
**and daughter Priyanka** ***—Thyagarajan. T***

**To my parents** ***—Sendur Chelvi. K.P.***

**To my parents** ***—Rangaswamy. T.R.***

# PREFACE TO THE THIRD EDITION

I am happy to bring out the third edition of this book.

I sincerely thank Mr. Thyagarajan for taking care of the second edition and making the book much more useful to the students.

In this third edition, all the authors have made sincere efforts towards revising the book and adding some useful topics. Mr. Thyagarajan, as an academician, has helped a lot in understanding the student requirements and modifying the electrical engineering portion according to the need.

Mr. Rangaswamy is in the industry and with the help of his wider experience both in the academic field and industry, he has presented electronics engineering in a much better way.

I am currently working in the Information Technology (IT) industry. I have been exposed to the Internet/e-commerce related areas. I have modified the integrated circuits and computer engineering sections with much more information on latest technology. The book is expanded now to have rich contents.

I thank all those who helped in making the book very successful. My sincere thanks to New Age International for their constant effort in bringing out this third edition and making it a best seller. We hope to bring out many more editions and introduce the latest technology information to benefit the student community.

**K.P. Sendur Chelvi**
Manager—Technology
Global Software Ltd.
Chennai

# PREFACE TO THE THIRD EDITION

I am happy to bring out the third edition of this book.

I sincerely thank M/s New Age [illegible] for taking care of the second edition and making the book [illegible] to the students.

In the third edition all the authors [illegible] efforts towards revising the book and adding some [illegible] [illegible]

[illegible]

[illegible]

[illegible]

R.K. [illegible]
[illegible] Technology
[illegible]
[illegible]

# CONTENTS

*Chapter 1*

# CONCEPTS OF ELECTRIC CURRENT AND LAWS

In order to understand the basic concepts of electric current, one must understand the **Modern Electron Theory**. Consider the structure of 'matter'. (Substance which is in the form of solid, liquid or gas occupying space and possessing weight.) The smallest particle of 'matter' is called 'molecule'. It is subdivided into 'atoms'. An 'atom' can further be split into electrons, protons etc.

Matter ⟶ Molecule ⟶ Atoms ⟶ Electrons, Protons, etc.

An atom of any element comprises (i) nucleus (at the centre consisting of protons and neutrons) and (ii) electrons (revolving in orbits). It may be recalled here that electrons and protons possess negative and positive charge respectively whereas neutrons have no charge.

## 1.1. ELECTRIC CURRENT

The electrons present in the outermost orbits are called **valence electrons.** In some elements (e.g. metals) the valence electrons are not strongly bound to the nucleus. According to Coulomb's law as the distance between the charges increases, the force between them varies inversely with the square of the distance. Thus the force of attraction between the electrons in the outermost orbit and the protons present in the nucleus is less. Hence these electrons can be easily removed by applying external energy. Such electrons are called **free electrons.** These free electrons move randomly from atom to atom. However, if the random movement of electrons assumes steady flow, it constitutes **electric current.** Thus an electric current is flow of electrons or flow of charge, and is denoted by letter **'I'**.

Current is also defined as the rate of movement of electric charge. If a charge 'Q' is passing across a conductor in time 't', then the current 'I' is given by,

$$I = \frac{Q}{t} \qquad ...(1.1)$$

Where 'Q' is the charge measured in coulombs

't' is the time in seconds

Hence, the current, **'I'** is measured in coulomb/second.

The unit of current is also given by 'ampere'.

Thus, ampere = coulomb/second

The smaller units of current are:

1 Milliampere = 1mA = $1 \times 10^{-3}$ ampere

1 Microampere = 1μA = $1 \times 10^{-6}$ ampere.

The instrument used to measure current is called **ammeter** and it is always connected in series with the circuit. The substances permitting easy flow of their valence electrons through their atoms by offering very little hindrance to their detachment are called **conductors.**

**Direct Current (DC):** It is also called unidirectional current, which always flows in one direction. It is abbreviated as 'D.C.' and is obtained from a D.C. generator or battery or from a rectifier. It is used for electroplating and charging batteries etc. The graphical representation of 'D.C.' is a straight line as shown in Fig. 1.1.

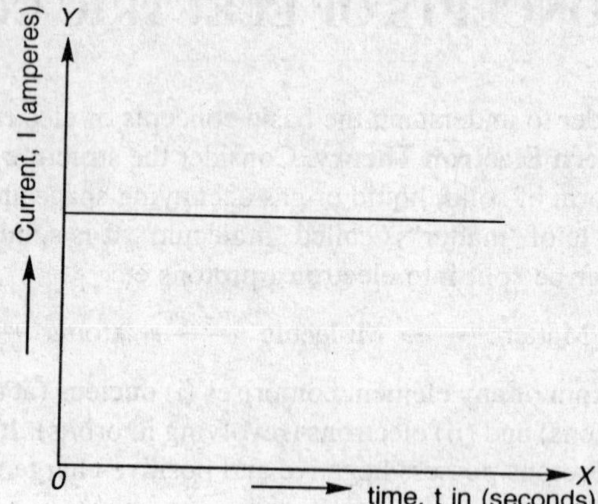


**Fig. 1.1**

**Alternating Current (AC):** An alternating current changes its direction from +ve to –ve & –ve to +ve periodically at regular intervals. It is abbreviated as 'A.C.' It is obtained from A.C. generator. As A.C. is universally generated, it has very wide range of applications. Graphical representation of A.C. is as shown in Fig. 1.2.

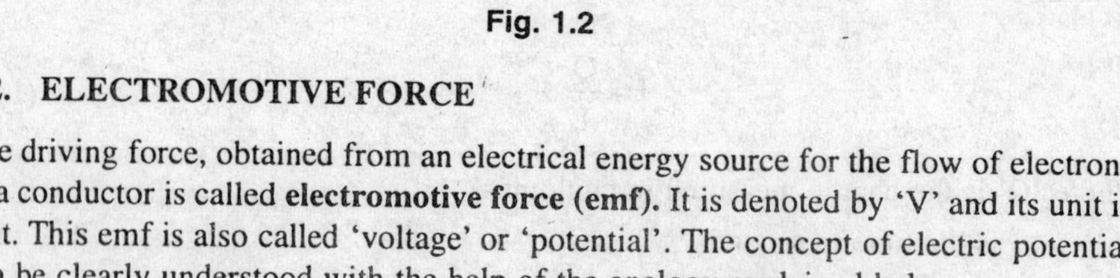


**Fig. 1.2**

## 1.2. ELECTROMOTIVE FORCE

The driving force, obtained from an electrical energy source for the flow of electrons in a conductor is called **electromotive force (emf).** It is denoted by 'V' and its unit is volt. This emf is also called 'voltage' or 'potential'. The concept of electric potential can be clearly understood with the help of the analogy explained below.

To lift an object above the earth's surface, we need to do work against the gravitational force. This work done is stored in the form of potential energy, which is released once the object falls back to the earth. Similarly, since the charges exert force on other charges, work has to be done in moving the charges in the vicinity of other charges (within the substance). If '$W_{MN}$', is the work done in moving a charge 'Q' from the point 'M' to the point 'N', then the potential difference between these two points ($V_{MN}$) is given by the work done per unit charge

$$\therefore \quad V_{MN} = \frac{W_{MN}}{Q} \text{ volts} \quad ...(1.2)$$

$$1 \text{ volt} = \frac{1 \text{ joule}}{1 \text{ coulomb}}$$

The smaller units of voltage are

1 Millvolt = $1 mV = 1 \times 10^{-3}$ volts

1 Microvolt = $1 \mu V = 1 \times 10^{-6}$ volts

1 Picovolt = $1 \mu\mu V = 1 \times 10^{-12}$ volts

The meter used to measure voltage is called **voltmeter** and it is always connected in parallel with the circuit.

## 1.3. RESISTANCE

We know that the flow of current in a substance is due to movement of free electrons (valence electrons). Different substances have different number of free electrons. Hence, for the given applied energy, the substance having more number of free electrons constitute more current than the substance having less number of free electrons. In other words, the latter one is said to offer higher opposition for the flow of current than the former. This property of the conductor by which it opposes the flow of current is called **resistance.** The unit of resistance is 'ohm'. It is denoted by 'Ω'.

**Definition of ohm:** It is the resistance offered by a conductor which, when 1 volt is applied across it, allows a current of 1 ampere.

The resistance of a conductor depends on the following factors:

1. It varies directly with the length of the conductor.
2. It is inversely proportional to the cross-section.
3. It also depends on the material.
4. It is affected by temperature.

If 'R', l, and A are the resistance, length and cross-sectional area of the conductor in ohms, metre and square metres respectively then the resistance of the conductor can be given as

$$R \propto l$$

$$R \propto \frac{1}{A}$$

Fig. 1.2(a)

Thus $$R \propto \frac{l}{A} \Rightarrow R = \rho \frac{l}{A} \quad ...(1.3)$$

where 'ρ' is a constant called **specific resistance** or **resistivity.**

Equation 1.3 can be rewritten as below:

$$\rho = \frac{AR}{l} = \frac{\text{ohm} \times (\text{metre} \times \text{metre})}{(\text{metre})} = \text{ohm - metre } (\Omega - \text{m}) \qquad ...(1.4)$$

**Definition of specific resistance:** It is the resistance offered by unit cube of the material. It is denoted by 'ρ'.

**P. 1.1.** A silver wire of length 12 metres has a resistance of 0.2 Ω. Find the specific resistance of the material. The cross-sectional area of the wire is 0.01 $cm^2$.

**Solution:**

Length of the wire = 12 metre (l)

Area of cross-section = 0.01 $cm^2$

= $0.01 \times 10^{-4}$ $m^2$ (A)

Resistance = 0.2 Ω (R)

Specific resistance = ρ ?

We know that, $R = \frac{\rho l}{A}$

$$\rho = \frac{RA}{l} = \frac{0.2 \times 0.01 \times 10^{-4}}{12}$$

$$= 1.666 \times 10^{-8} \text{ ohm - metre}$$

## 1.4. EFFECT OF TEMPERATURE ON RESISTANCE

| Substance | Effect |
|---|---|
| Metals (copper, iron, etc) | Resistance increases with increase in temperature. |
| Alloys (manganese, eureka) | Resistance increases slightly with increase in temperature. |
| Electrolytes, insulators (glass, rubber, mica) | Resistance decreases with increase in temperature. |
| Gases (argon, neon, helium) | Resistance decreases with increase in temperature. |

**Temperature coefficient of Resistance (α):**

**Definition:** It is defined as the ratio of change in resistance per °C rise of temperature to the resistance at 0°C. It is represented by '$\alpha_0$'. It is also defined as the change in 1 ohm resistance of a material when its temperature is increased from 0°C to 1°C. '$\alpha_0$' is positive for the substances whose resistance increase with increase in temperature and negative for substances whose resistance decrease with increase in temperature. In general, if a material has resistance of '$R_0$' at 0°C, '$R_1$' at $t_1$ °C and $R_2$ at $t_2$ °C, then we can write

$$R_1 = R_0 (1+\alpha_0 t_1) \quad ...(1.5)$$

$$R_2 = R_0 (1+\alpha_0 t_2) \quad ...(1.6)$$

$$\frac{R_1}{R_2} = \frac{(1+\alpha_0 t_1)}{(1+\alpha_0 t_2)} \text{ (or) } \frac{R_2}{R_1} = \frac{(1+\alpha_0 t_2)}{(1+\alpha_0 t_1)} \quad ...(1.7)$$

**P. 1.2.** The resistance of the armature winding of a D.C. machine is 1.5 ohms at 27°C. What will be its resistance at 40°C? The resistance temperature coefficient of copper is 0.0043 per °C at 0°C.

**Solution:**

Given $\alpha_0 = 0.0043$

$t_1 = 27°C$

$t_2 = 40°C$

$R_1 = 1.5\ \Omega$

$R_2 = ?$

$$R_2 = \frac{R_1(1+\alpha_0 t_2)}{(1+\alpha_0 t_1)} = \frac{1.5(1+0.0043\times 40)}{(1+0.0043\times 27)}$$

$= 1.575$ ohm

∴ The resistance of the armature winding at 40°C = 1.575 ohm

## 1.5. ELECTRICAL POWER (P)

Power is the work done per second. It is also defined as the rate of doing work.

$$\therefore \quad \text{Power} = \frac{\text{Work done}}{\text{time}} \quad ...(1.8)$$

From eq. 1.1 and 1.2 we have

Charge = current × time

Work done = voltage × charge

∴ Work done = voltage × current × time

$$\text{Power} = \frac{\text{voltage} \times \text{current} \times \text{time}}{\text{time}}$$

Power = voltage × current ...(1.9)

Power (P) = V × I ...(1.10)

Power is measured in watts. The instrument used to measure power is called wattmeter.

The larger units of power are

1 Kilowatt = 1 kW = $1 \times 10^3$ watts

1 Megawatt = 1 MW = $1 \times 10^6$ watts

## 1.6. ELECTRIC ENERGY

The capacity to do work is called energy and is measured in 'watt-sec'

∴ Energy = Power × time ...(1.11)

Larger unit of energy is

1 Kilowatt hour = 1 Kwh = 1000 × 3600 watt-sec.

## 1.7. INTERNATIONAL SYSTEM OF UNITS

**International ohm:** It is defined as the resistance offered to the flow of current by a column of mercury of length 106.3 cm, 14.452 gm in mass with uniform cross section at 0°C.

**International ampere:** It is defined as that value of steady current when flowing through a solution of silver nitrate in water, deposits silver at the cathode at a rate of 1.118 milligrams per second.

**International volt:** It is defined as that amount of potential difference when applied across a conductor of one international ohm resistance producing a current of one international ampere.

## 1.8. OHM's LAW

In the case of many conducting materials, the voltage applied across them is linearly related to the current passing through them. This law is credited to George Simon Ohm, a German physicist and bears his name, Ohm's Law.

**Statement:** At constant temperature, the current flowing through a conductor is directly proportional to voltage across the conductor.

$$V \propto I$$

$$V = RI \qquad ...(1.12)$$

where 'V' is the voltage in volts

'I' is the current in amperes

'R' is the resistance in ohms

Also we can write $\frac{V}{I} = R$

Thus Ohm's law can also be stated as: temperature remaining constant the ratio of voltage to current is a constant. This law is applicable to both D.C. and A.C. circuits. From Ohm's law we can write the expressions for current, resistance, power and energy. We know that, according to Ohm's Law

$$V = I R \text{ volts}$$

$$\therefore \quad I = \frac{V}{R} \quad \frac{\text{volt}}{\text{ohm}} = \text{ampere} \quad \text{...(1.13)}$$

$$\text{also} \quad R = \frac{V}{I} \quad \frac{\text{volt}}{\text{ampere}} = \text{ohm} \quad \text{...(1.14)}$$

From eq. 1.10 power $= V \times I$

$$= V \times \frac{V}{R}$$

$$\text{Power} \quad = \frac{V^2}{R} \quad \text{...(1.15)}$$

$$\text{also} \quad P = V \times I$$

$$= IR \times I$$

$$\therefore \quad P = I^2 R \quad \text{...(1.16)}$$

From eq. 1.10 we can write

$$I = \frac{P}{V} \text{ ampere} \quad \text{...(1.17)}$$

From eq. 1.16, $$I = \sqrt{\frac{P}{R}} \text{ ampere} \quad \text{...(1.18)}$$

Also from eq. 1.10, $$V = \frac{P}{I} \text{ volts} \quad \text{...(1.19)}$$

From eq. 1.15, $$V = \sqrt{PR} \text{ volts} \quad \text{...(1.20)}$$

$$R = \frac{V^2}{P} \text{ ohms} \quad \text{...(1.21)}$$

From eq. 1.16 $\quad R = \frac{P}{I^2}$ ohms ...(1.22)

$$\text{Energy} = P \times t$$

$$= I^2Rt \quad \text{watt-sec or joule}$$

$$= \frac{V^2}{R}t \quad \text{watt-sec or joule} \qquad ...(1.23)$$

$$= V\,I\,t \quad \text{watt-sec or joule}$$

## 1.9. RESISTORS CONNECTED IN SERIES

When two or more resistors are connected end to end in such a way that the current flowing through each one of them is same, then the resistors are said to be connected in series. In other words there is one and only one path for the flow of current. The expression for total or effective or equivalent resistance (R) of two resistors connected in series is derived below.

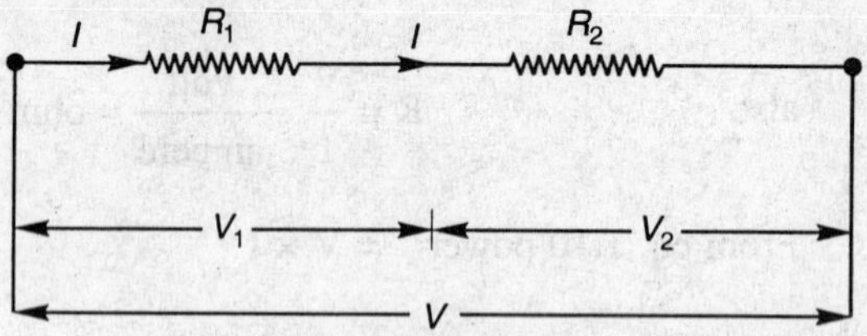

Fig. 1.3

Consider two resistors '$R_1$' and '$R_2$' connected in series across a voltage of 'V' volts as shown in Fig. 1.3

Let '$V_1$' and '$V_2$' be the voltage drops across '$R_1$' and '$R_2$' respectively. Let 'I' be current flowing through the series combination. Let 'R' be the total resistance of series circuit. Since it is a series circuit, the current flowing through $R_1$, $R_2$ is same which is nothing but 'I'.

From Fig. 1.3 it is clear that

$$V = V_1 + V_2 \qquad ...(i)$$

According to Ohm's law

$$V = IR \qquad ...(ii)$$

$$V_1 = IR_1 \qquad ...(iii)$$

$$V_2 = IR_2 \qquad ...(iv)$$

Substituting eq. (ii), (iii), (iv), in eq (i) we get

$$IR = IR_1 + IR_2$$

$$IR = I(R_1 + R_2)$$

$$R = R_1 + R_2 \qquad ...(1.24)$$

Thus, the total resistance of a series combination is equal to the sum of individual resistors connected in series. This holds good for any number of resistors connected in series.

Thus, if we have three resistors in series, then

$$R = R_1 + R_2 + R_3 \qquad \text{...(1.25)}$$

In general, if there are 'n' number of resistors connected in series then

$$R = R_1 + R_2 + R_3 + ..... + R_n.$$

## 1.10. RESISTORS CONNECTED IN PARALLEL

When two or more resistors are connected in such a way that the voltage across each resistor is same, then the resistors are said to be connected in parallel. Here the first terminals of all the resistors are joined together at one junction and the second terminals are joined together at the other junction. The two junctions are connected to a voltage supply, as shown in Fig. 1.4.

Unlike series circuit, in a parallel combination there are more paths for the flow of current.

The expression for total or effective or equivalent resistance (R) of two resistors connected in parallel is derived below.

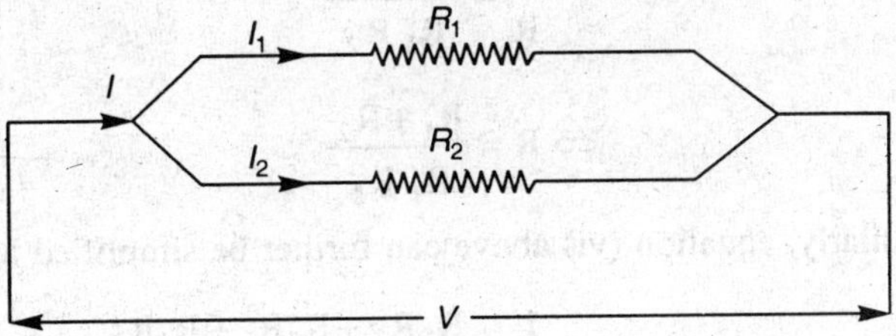

Fig. 1.4

Consider two resistors '$R_1$' and '$R_2$' connected in parallel across a voltage of 'V' volts as shown in Fig. 1.4. Let '$I_1$' and '$I_2$' be the currents flowing through '$R_1$' and '$R_2$' respectively. Let 'V' be voltage applied across the parallel combination. Let 'R' and 'I' be the total resistance and total current of the parallel circuit respectively. Since it is a parallel circuit, the voltage across $R_1$, $R_2$ is same, which is nothing but supply voltage 'V'.

From Fig. 1.4 it is clear that

$$I = I_1 + I_2 \qquad \text{...(i)}$$

According to Ohm's law

$$I = \frac{V}{R} \qquad \text{...(ii)}$$

$$I_1 = \frac{V}{R_1} \qquad \text{...(iii)}$$

$$I_2 = \frac{V}{R_2} \qquad \text{...(iv)}$$

Substituting eq. (ii), (iii), (iv) in eq. (i) we get

$$\frac{V}{R} = \frac{V}{R_1} + \frac{V}{R_2}$$

$$\frac{1}{R} = \frac{1}{R_1} + \frac{1}{R_2} \qquad \text{...(v)}$$

The above equation holds good for any number of resistors connected in parallel. Thus if there are three resistors in parallel,

then, $$\frac{1}{R} = \frac{1}{R_1} + \frac{1}{R_2} + \frac{1}{R_3} \qquad \text{(vi)}$$

In general if there are 'n' number of resistors in parallel,

then, $$\frac{1}{R} = \frac{1}{R_1} + \frac{1}{R_2} + \frac{1}{R_3} + ..... + \frac{1}{R_n}$$

The equation (v) above can be further simplified to find the value of 'R'

$$\frac{1}{R} = \frac{R_2 + R_1}{R_1 R_2} \qquad \text{...(1.26)}$$

$$\Rightarrow R = \frac{R_1 + R_2}{R_1 R_2}$$

Similarly, equation (vi) above can further be simplified as,

$$\frac{1}{R} = \frac{R_2R_3 + R_3R_1 + R_1R_2}{R_1R_2R_3} \qquad \text{...(1.27)}$$

**Application:** In the domestic and power wiring the connections are done in parallel so that the working voltage of the load is equal to the supply voltage.

**Comparison of series and parallel circuits:**

| Series circuits | Parallel circuits |
|---|---|
| 1. The current passing through all the elements connected in series is the same. | 1. Voltage across each element connected in parallel is the same. |
| 2. There is only one path for flow of current. | 2. The paths for flow of current are more than one. |
| 3. The total voltage applied across the series circuit is equal to the sum of the voltage drops across all the elements connected in series i.e. $V = V_1 + V_2 + .....$ | 3. The total current flowing through the parallel combination is equal to sum of all the currents flowing through all the elements connected in parallel i.e. $I = I_1 + I_2 + ....$ |
| 4. The equivalent resistance is greater than the greatest resistance connected in series circuit. | 4. The equivalent resistance in less than that of the least resistance connected in the parallel circuit. |

## 1.11. DIVISION OF CURRENT IN PARALLEL CIRCUIT

Recalling the parallel combination of two resistors arranged in Fig. 1.4, we have if 'R' is the equivalent resistance.

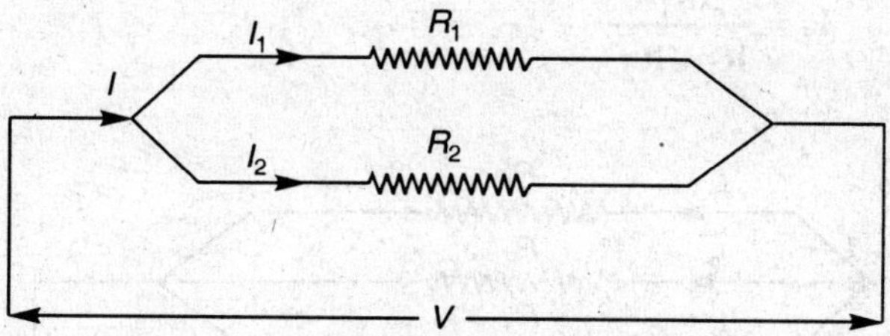


**Fig. 1.4(a)**

then according to Ohm's law,

$$I = \frac{V}{R} \Rightarrow V = IR \qquad \text{...(i)}$$

$$I_1 = \frac{V}{R_1} \Rightarrow V = I_1R_1 \qquad \text{...(ii)}$$

$$I_2 = \frac{V}{R_2} \Rightarrow V = I_2R_2 \qquad \text{...(iii)}$$

From eq. (i) & (ii)

$$I_1R_1 = IR$$

$$I_1 = \frac{IR}{R_1}$$

$$I_1 = \frac{I(R_1 R_2)}{R_1 (R_1 + R_2)} \qquad \text{(from eq. 1.26)}$$

$$I_1 = \frac{IR_2}{R_1 + R_2} \qquad \text{...(1.28)}$$

From eq. (i) & (iii)

$$I_2R_2 = IR$$

$$I_2 = \frac{IR}{R_2}$$

$$I_2 = \frac{I(R_1 R_2)}{R_2 (R_1 + R_2)} \qquad \text{(from eq. 1.26)}$$

$$I_2 = \frac{IR_1}{R_1 + R_2} \qquad (1.29)$$

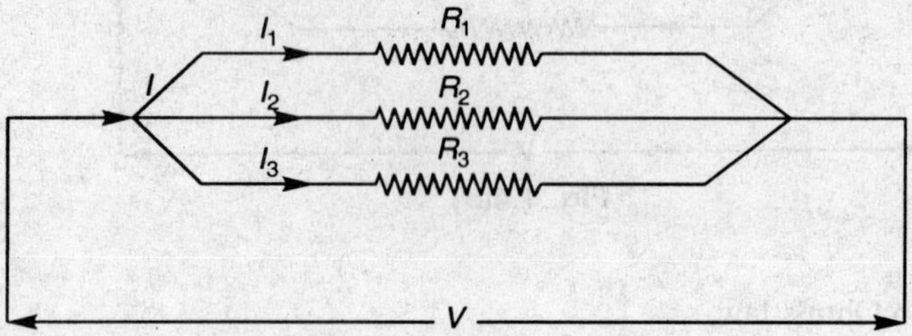


**Fig. 1.5**

If there are 3 resistors connected in parallel as shown in Fig. 1.5 then we have from eq. 1.27 the equivalent resistance given by

$$R = \frac{R_1R_2R_3}{R_1R_2 + R_2R_3 + R_3R_1}$$

Also from Fig. 1.5 we find

$$I = \frac{V}{R} \Rightarrow V = IR \qquad \text{...(i)}$$

$$I_1 = \frac{V}{R_1} \Rightarrow V = I_1R \qquad \text{...(ii)}$$

$$I_2 = \frac{V}{R_2} \Rightarrow V = I_2R_2 \qquad \text{...(iii)}$$

$$I_3 = \frac{V}{R_3} \Rightarrow V = I_3R_3 \qquad \text{...(iv)}$$

From eq. (i) and (ii)

$$I_1R_1 = IR$$

$$I_1 = \frac{IR}{R_1} = \frac{I}{R_1}\left[\frac{R_1R_2R_3}{R_1R_2 + R_2R_3 + R_3R_1}\right]$$

Therefore, $$I_1 = \frac{I R_2 R_3}{R_1R_2 + R_2R_3 + R_3R_1} \quad ...(1.30)$$

From eq. (i) and (iii)

$$I_2R_2 = IR$$

$$I_2 = \frac{IR}{R_2} \Rightarrow I_2 = \frac{I}{R_2}\left[\frac{R_1R_2R_3}{R_1R_2 + R_2R_3 + R_3R_1}\right]$$

Therefore, $$I_2 = \frac{IR_1R_3}{R_1R_2 + R_2R_3 + R_3R_1} \quad ...(1.31)$$

from eq. (i) and (iv)

$$I_3R_3 = IR$$

$$I_3 = \frac{IR}{R_3} \Rightarrow I_3 = \frac{I}{R_3}\left[\frac{R_1R_2R_3}{R_1R_2 + R_2R_3 + R_3R_1}\right]$$

Therefore, $$I_3 = \frac{IR_1R_2}{R_1R_2 + R_2R_3 + R_3R_1} \quad ...(1.32)$$

**P. 1.3.** Three resistors 5Ω, 10Ω, 15Ω are connected in series across 120 volts supply. Find the following:

(i) Total resistance

(ii) Total current

(iii) Voltage across each element

**Solution:**

Given $R_1 = 5\Omega$

$R_2 = 10\Omega$

$R_3 = 15\Omega$

$V = 120$ volts

Since these are connected in series, the circuit is drawn as shown in Fig. 1.6

The equivalent resistance $R = R_1 + R_2 + R_3$

$= 5 + 10 + 15$

$= 30\ \Omega$

Total current $I = \frac{V}{R} = \frac{120}{30} = 4$ amperes

Voltage across $R_1 = V_1 = IR_1 = 4 \times 5 = 20$ volts

Voltage across $R_2 = V_2 = IR_2 = 4 \times 10 = 40$ volts

Voltage across $R_3 = V_3 = IR_3 = 4 \times 15 = 60$ volts

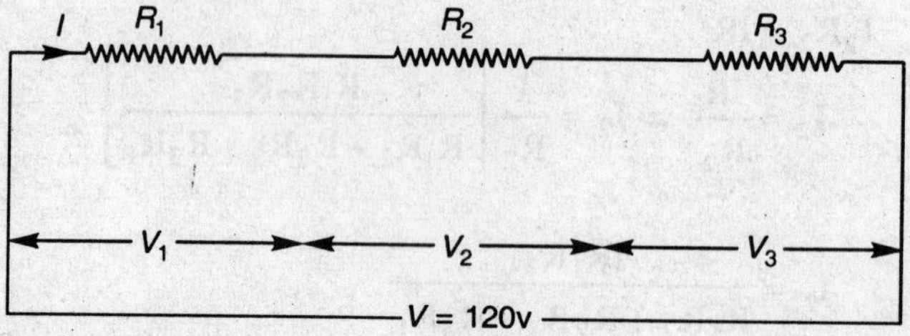


**Fig. 1.6**

**P. 1.4.** Find the equivalent resistance of series parallel combination shown in Fig. 1.7.

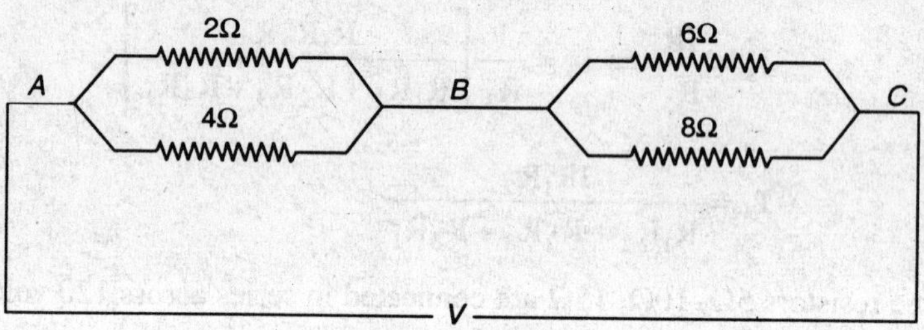


**Fig. 1.7**

**Solution:**

The resistance across AB, $R_{AB} = \dfrac{2 \times 4}{2+4} = 1.33\ \Omega$

The resistance across BC, $R_{BC} = \dfrac{6 \times 8}{6+8} = 3.42\ \Omega$

The resistance across AC $R_{AC} = R_{AB} + R_{BC} = 1.33 + 3.4\ \Omega$

**P. 1.5.** Find the effective resistance of the network shown in Fig. 1.8

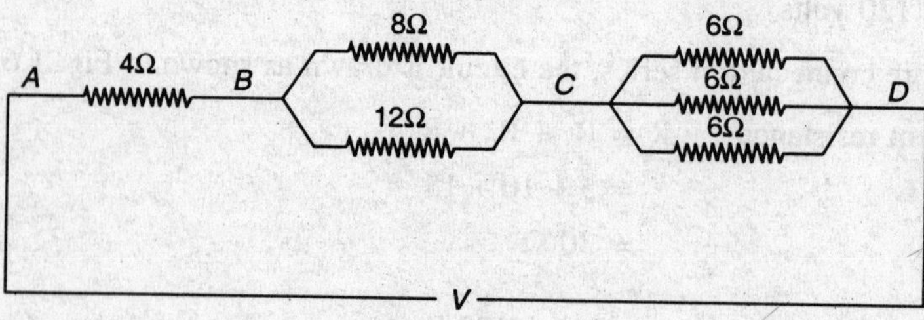


**Fig. 1.8**

**Solution:**

The resistance across AB, $R_{AB} = 4\ \Omega$

The resistance across BC, $R_{BC} = \dfrac{8 \times 12}{8+12} = 4.8\ \Omega$

The resistance across CD, $R_{CD} = \dfrac{6 \times 6 \times 6}{6 \times 6 + 6 \times 6 + 6 \times 6} = 2\ \Omega$

∴ Resistance across AD

$$\text{i.e. } R_{AD} = R_{AB} + R_{BC} + R_{CD}$$
$$= 4 + 4.8 + 2$$
$$= 10.8\ \Omega$$

**P. 1.6.** What resistance must be connected in parallel with the 8Ω resistance of the Fig. 1.9 to give an equivalent resistance of 6Ω?

**Solution:**

Given $R_1 = 8\ \Omega$

$R_2 = ?$

$$R = \frac{R_1 R_2}{R_1 + R_2} = 6\ \Omega$$

$$= \frac{8 \times R_2}{8 + R_2} = 6$$

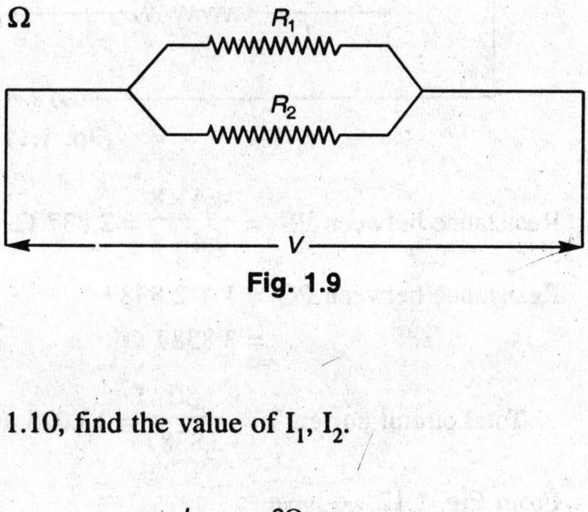

Fig. 1.9

$$8R_2 = (8 + R_2)6$$
$$8R_2 = 48 + 6\ R_2$$
$$8R_2 - 6\ R_2 = 48$$
$$R_2 = 24$$

**P. 1.7.** In the circuit shown in the Fig 1.10, find the value of $I_1$, $I_2$.

**Solution:**

We know that $I_1 = \dfrac{I\,R_2}{R_1 + R_2}$

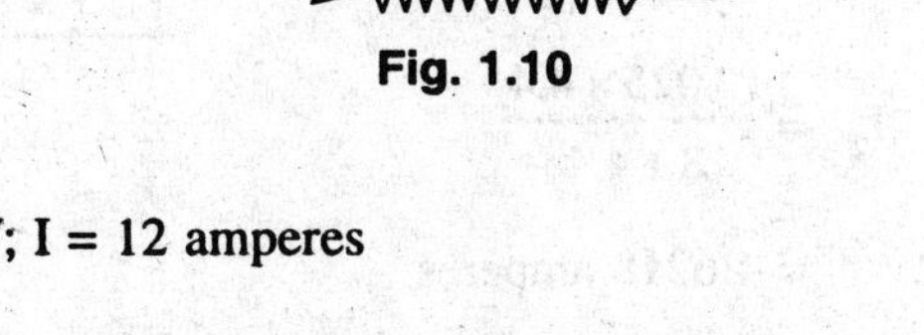

Fig. 1.10

$I_2 = \dfrac{I\,R_1}{R_1 + R_2}$

Given that 1 = 6 W; R2 = 9 W; I = 12 amperes

$$I_1 = \frac{12 \times 8}{6+8} = 6.853 \text{ amperes}$$

$$I_2 = \frac{12 \times 6}{6+8} = 5.14 \text{ amperes}$$

**P. 1.8.** Find the effective resistance of the series-parallel combination of resistances shown in Fig. 1.11 and also the voltage drop across each resistance when the applied voltage is 50V across P and Q.

**Solution:**

Resistances between P and R is $= \frac{4 \times 6}{4+6} = 2.4\ \Omega$

Resistance of the branch PRS $= 2.4 + 2 = 4.4\ \Omega$

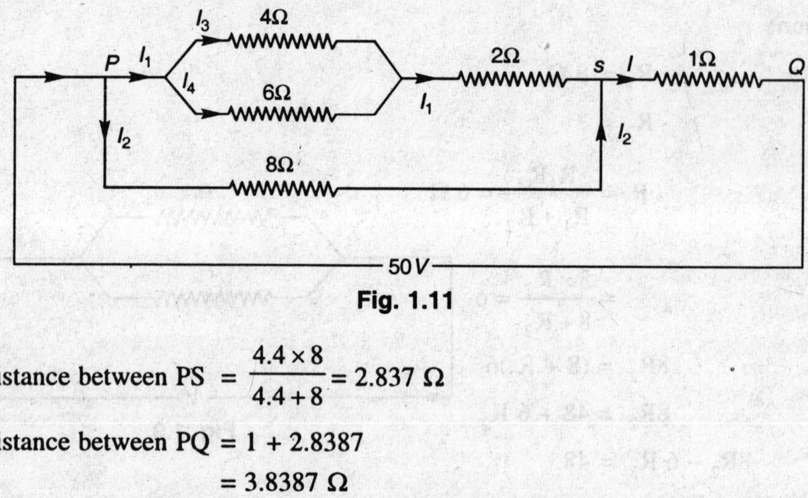


Fig. 1.11

Resistance between PS $= \frac{4.4 \times 8}{4.4+8} = 2.837\ \Omega$

Resistance between PQ $= 1 + 2.8387$

$= 3.8387\ \Omega$

$\therefore$ Total circuit current $I = \frac{50}{3.8387} = 13.025$ amperes

From Fig. 1.12 we have

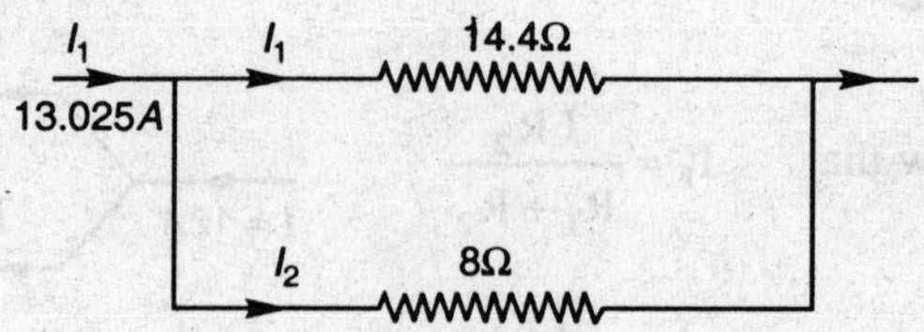


Fig. 1.12

$$I_1 = \frac{13.025 \times 8}{8+4.4}$$

$= 8.403$ amperes

$$I_2 = \frac{13.025 \times 4.4}{8+4.4}$$

$= 4.6218$ amperes

From Fig. 1.13 we have

$$I_3 = \frac{8.403 \times 6}{4+6}$$

$= 5.0418$ amperes

$$I_4 = \frac{8.403 \times 4}{4+6}$$

$= 3.36$ amperes

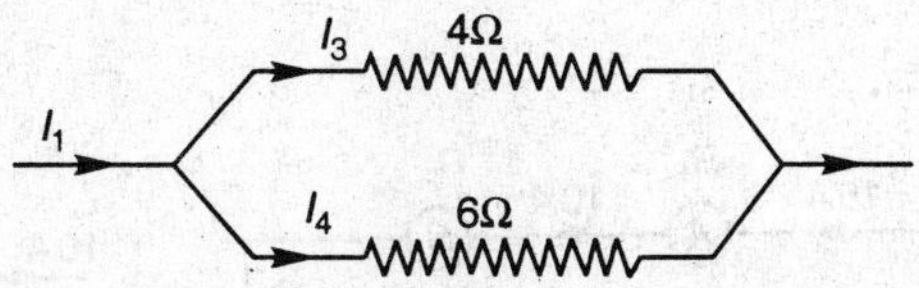


Fig. 1.13

| | | |
|---|---|---|
| Current through 4Ω | = 5.0418 amperes | |
| Current through 6Ω | = 3.36 amperes | |
| Current through 8Ω | = 4.6128 amperes | |
| Current through 2Ω | = 8.403 amperes | |
| Current through 1Ω | = 13.025 amperes | |
| Voltage through 4Ω | = 5.0418 × 4 | = 20.1672 volts |
| Voltage through 6Ω | = 3.36 × 6 | = 20.16 volts |
| Voltage through 8Ω | = 4.6218 × 8 | = 36.97 volts |
| Voltage through 2Ω | = 8.403 × 2 | = 16.806 volts |
| Voltage through 1Ω | = 13.025 × 1 | = 13.025 volts |
| Power dissipated in 4Ω | = 20.1672 × 5.0418 | = 101.678 watts |
| Power dissipated in 6Ω | = 20.1672 × 3.36 | = 67.737 watts |
| Power dissipated in 8Ω | = 36.97 × 4.6218 | = 170.888 watts |
| Power dissipated in 2Ω | = 16.86 × 8.403 | = 141.220 watts |
| Power dissipated in 1Ω | = 13.025 × 13.025 | = 169.650 watts |
| Total power dissipated | | = 651.174 watts |

Total power dissipated is also given by $= VI = 15 \times 13.025$

$= 651.25$ watts.

**P. 1.9.** A current of 10 amps is flowing through two ammeters A and B connected in series. The voltage drop across A and B are 0.2 V and 0.3V respectively. Find how the same current will divide between 'A' and 'B' when they are connected in parallel.

**Solution:**

Let $R_1$ be the resistance of ammeter A, (Fig. 1.14)

$$\therefore \quad R_1 = \frac{0.2}{10}\,\Omega$$

Let $R_2$ be the resistance of ammeter B (Fig. 1.14)

$$R_2 = \frac{0.3}{10}$$

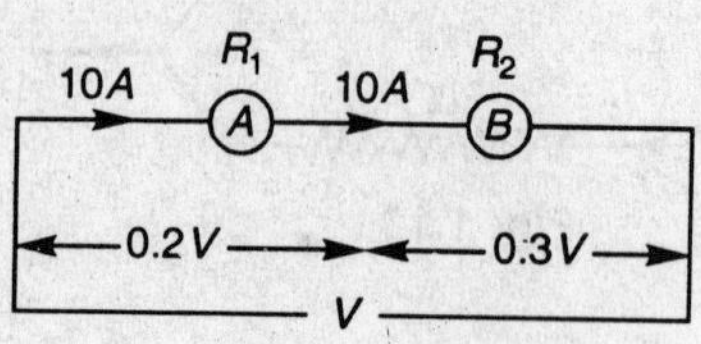


Fig. 1.14

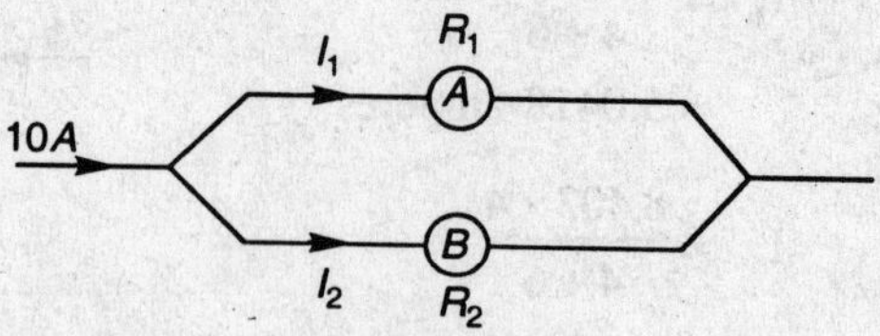


Fig. 1.15

If the same ammeters are connected in parallel (Fig. 1.15)

then the current $I_1$ drawn by ammeter $A_1$ $= \dfrac{10 \times R_2}{R_1 + R_2}$

$$= \frac{10 \times \frac{0.3}{10}}{\frac{0.2}{10} + \frac{0.3}{10}}$$

$$= \frac{0.3 \times 10}{0.5} = 6 \text{ amperes}$$

the current $I_2$ drawn by ammeter $B_1$ $= \dfrac{10 \times R_1}{R_1 + R_2}$

$$= \frac{10 \times \frac{0.2}{10}}{\frac{0.2}{10} + \frac{0.3}{10}}$$

$$= \frac{0.2 \times 10}{0.5} = 4 \text{ amperes}$$

**P. 1.10.** Two coils are connected in parallel and a voltage of 200V is applied across their terminals. The total current drawn is 25 A. The power dissipated in one of the coils is 1500 watts. What is the resistance of each coil?

**Solution:**

Given $V = 200$ V

$I = 25$ amperes

$P_1 = 1500$ W

Resistance of coil 1, $R_1$ is found as below

$$R_1 = \frac{V^2}{P_1} = \frac{200 \times 200}{1500} = \frac{400}{15} = 26.66\ \Omega$$

The total resistance, $R = \frac{V}{I} = \frac{200}{25} = 8\ \Omega$

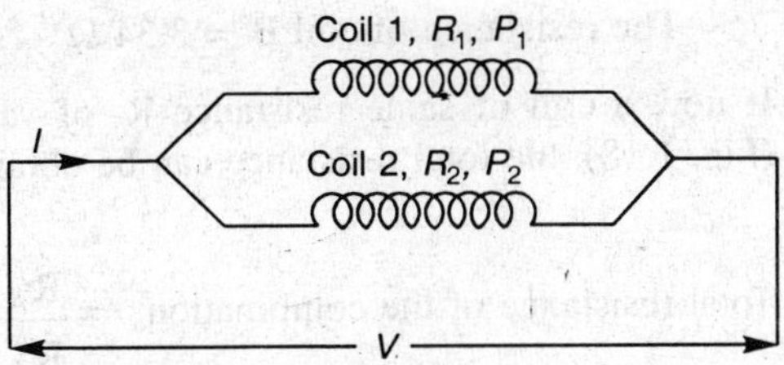


Fig. 1.16

Also we have $\frac{1}{R} = \frac{1}{R_1} + \frac{1}{R_2}$

i.e., $\frac{1}{8} = \frac{1}{\left(\frac{400}{15}\right)} + \frac{1}{R_2}$

$\Rightarrow$ $\frac{1}{R^2} = \frac{1}{8} - \frac{15}{400} = \frac{35}{400}$

$\therefore$ $R_2 = \frac{400}{35}\ \Omega = 11.43\ \Omega$

**P. 1.11.** Two coils A and B of equal resistance are connected in series across 100V supply and the total power dissipated is 1.5 kW. Another coil 'C' of the same resistance is now connected in parallel with coil 'A'. Find the power dissipated in each coil.

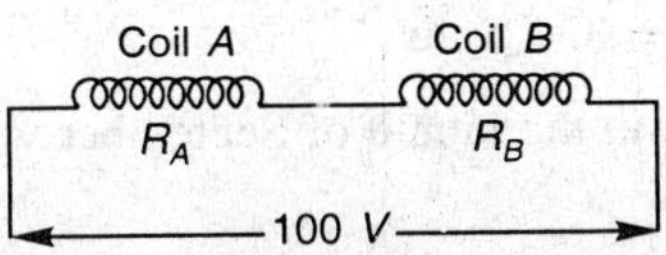


Fig. 1.17

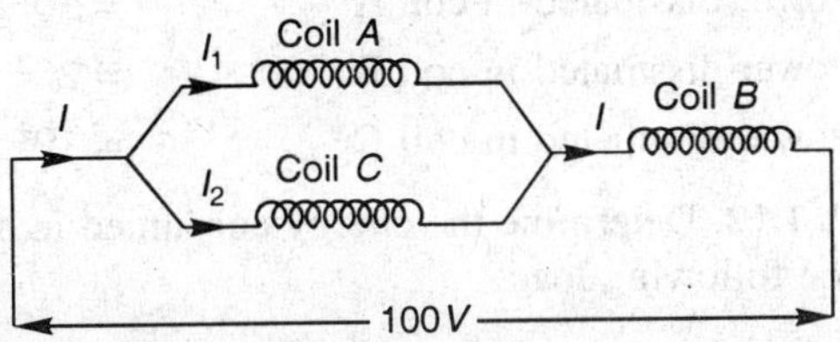


Fig. 1.18

**Solution:**

Given

$$V = 100\ V$$
$$R_A = R_B = R$$
$$P = 1500\ W$$

$\therefore$ Total resistance $= \frac{V^2}{P} = \frac{100 \times 100}{1500} = 6.67\ W$ ...(i)

But $R_A + R_B = 2R$ ...(ii)

From eq. (i) & (ii), 2R = 6.67

$$\therefore \quad R = \frac{6.67}{2} = 3.34\ \Omega$$

∴ The resistance of coil A = 3.34 Ω

The resistance of coil B = 3.34 Ω

If now a coil of same resistance $R_c$ of value, 3.34 Ω is connected across coil A (Fig. 1.18), the total resistance can be obtained as follows.

$$\text{Total resistance of the combination} = \frac{R_A \times R_C}{R_A + R_C} + R_B$$

$$= \frac{3.34 \times 3.34}{3.34 + 3.34} + 3.34$$

$$= 5\ \Omega$$

Total current,
(or)
(Current through coil B)

$$I = \frac{V}{R} = \frac{100}{5} = 20 \text{ amperes}$$

Current through coil A,

$$I_1 = \frac{20 \times 3.34}{3.34 + 3.34} = 10 \text{ amperes}$$

Current through coil C,

$$I_2 = \frac{20 \times 3.34}{3.34 + 3.34} = 10 \text{ amperes}$$

Power dissipated in coil A $= 10^2 \times 3.34 = 334$ watts

Power dissipated in coil B $= 20^2 \times 3.34 = 1336$ watts

Power dissipated in coil C $= 10^2 \times 3.34 = 334$ watts

**P. 1.12.** Determine the energy consumed in a house in the month of September with the following load:

(i) Six lamps of 100 watts each for 6 hours a day

(ii) One heater of 1.5 kW for 2 hours a day

(iii) 1/2 H.P single phase motor used for 2 hours a day

(iv) Four fan points 75W each for 8 hours

Calculate the amount of bill if the cost of energy is 90 paise per unit.

**Solution:**

| Load | (No. × watts × Time) | Watt hour |
|---|---|---|
| (i) Lamps | 6 × 100 × 6 | 3600 |
| (ii) Heater | 1 × 1500 × 2 | 3000 |

| | | |
|---|---|---|
| (iii) 1/2 HP Motor | $1\times\frac{735.5}{2}\times 2$ | 735.5 |
| (iv) Fans | $4 \times 75 \times 8$ | 2400 |
| Total energy consumed in watt hour/day | | 9735.5 |

Total energy consumed kilowatt hour for the month of September (30 days) $= \frac{9735.5\times 30}{1000}$ kWh

$= 292.065$ kWh

1 unit $= 1$ kWh

Total Units $= 292.065$

Cost of energy per unit $= 90$ paise

$\therefore$ Bill amount $= 292.065 \times 0.90$

$= 262.85$

$\approx$ Rs. 263

## 1.12. KIRCHHOFF' LAWS

These laws are used to find current in different branches of an electrical network which may not be easily solved by Ohm's law. These laws are applicable to both D.C. & A.C. There are two Laws

### (1) First Law or point Law or Kirchhoff's current Law or K.C.L.

**Statement:** The algebraic sum of all the currents meeting at a junction of a network is zero.

In other words, the sum of currents flowing towards the junction is equal to the sum of currents flowing away from the junction. Consider the arrangement of four wires connected together at the point 'M' as shown in Fig. 1.19. The arrows indicate the direction of flow of current. The currents $I_1$, $I_3$ are coming towards the junction 'M', and the currents $I_2$, $I_4$ are going away from the junction.

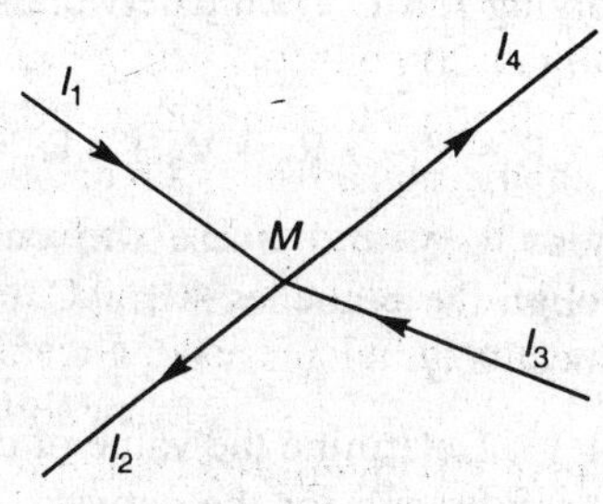

Fig. 1.19

Assume positive sign for incoming currents and negative sign for outgoing currents. According to Kirchhoff's current law,

$$\Sigma I = 0 \qquad ...(1.33)$$

i.e.,

$$(+I_1) + (+I_3) + (-I_2) + (-I_4) = 0$$

$$I_1 + I_3 = I_2 + I_4$$

Sum of incoming currents = Sum of outgoing currents

### (2) Second Law or Mesh Law or Kirchhoff's Voltage Law (K.V.L.)

**Statement**: In any closed network or mesh, the algebraic sum of product of current and resistances in each of the conductor plus the algebraic sum of electromotive forces in that path is zero.

i.e., $$\Sigma IR + \Sigma emf = 0 \quad \text{...(1.34)}$$

Algebraic sum means we have to take 'sign' into consideration. The convention is, a voltage rise is given a + ve sign and a voltage fall is given a –ve sign. We know that current flows from a higher potential to lower potential.

**Determination of sign for emf source:** If we move from +ve terminal of emf source to –ve terminal, there is a fall in potential. Therefore emf is given –ve sign. On the other hand, if we move from –ve terminal of emf source to +ve terminal, then there is rise in potential. Therefore emf is given '+ve' sign.

**Determination of sign for the product of current and resistance:** If we travel through a resistor in the same direction as that of current flowing through it, then there is fall in potential as the current flows from higher potential to lower potential. Therefore a '–ve' sign is assigned for the product. On the other hand if we travel through a resistor in the direction opposite to that of current flowing through it, then there is a rise in potential. Therefore a '+ve' sign is assigned to the product.

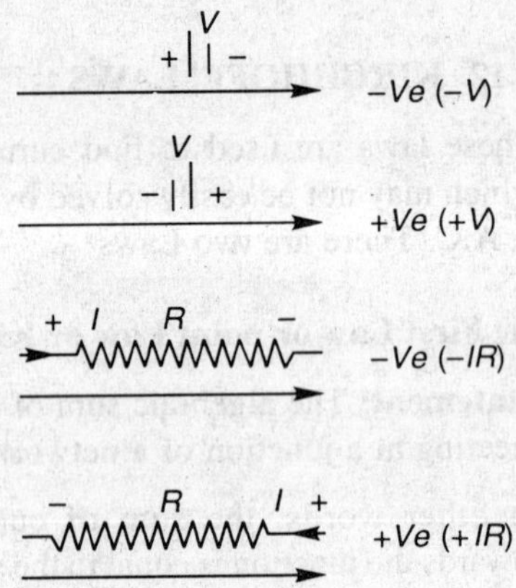


This can be clearly understood by applying K.V.L. for the network shown in Fig. 1.20

$$-x.R_1 - V_1 - z.R_2 + V_2 + y.R_3 = 0$$

where x, y and z are the currents through the branches AB, AC and BC respectively.

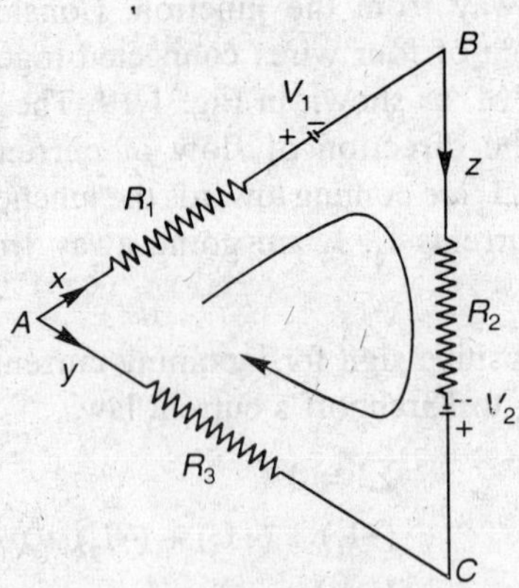


Fig. 1.20

P. 1.13. Determine the value of current in each branch for the network shown in Fig. 1.21 using Kirchhoff's Laws.

**Solution:**

Assume the current in the branches AB, AD, BD, as x, y, z amperes respectively (Fig. 1.22)

The current in branches BC, DC and CA can be written in terms of x,y,z as follows:

Using Kirchhoff's current law, to find the current in branch BC (Fig. 1.23) we get

At junction B

$$P_1 + z = x$$

$$P_1 = x - z$$

∴ Current in BC = y–z

To find the current in Branch DC, (Fig 1.24)

At junction D

$$y + z = P_2$$

∴ Current in branch DC = y + z

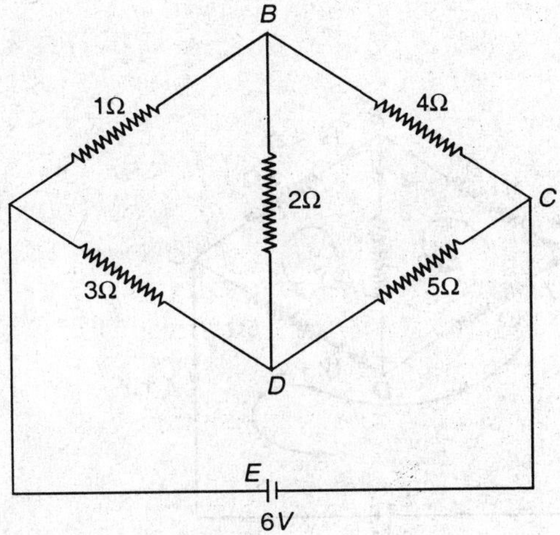


Fig. 1.21

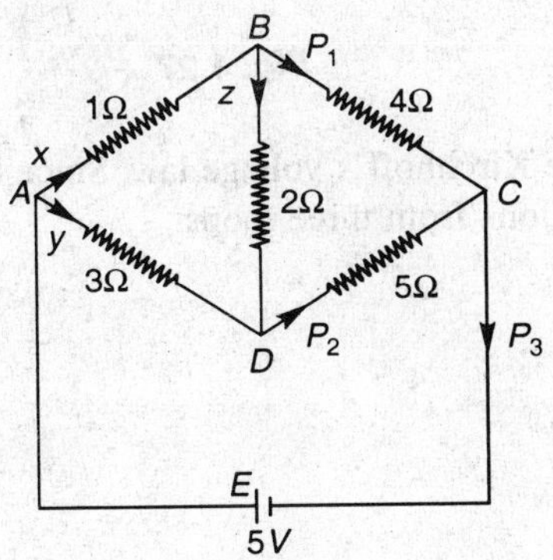


Fig. 1.22

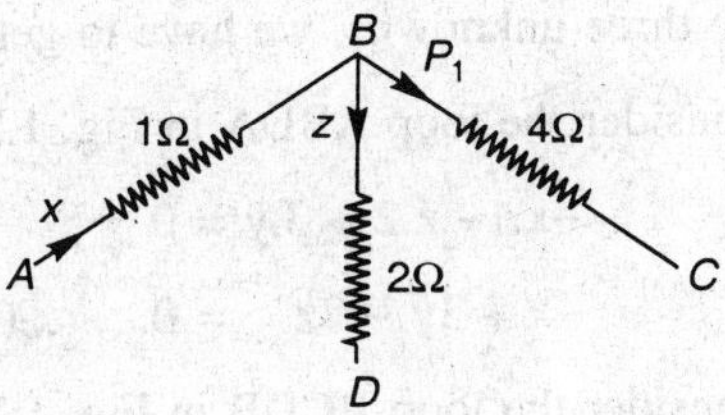


Fig. 1.23

To find the current in branch 'CA' (Fig. 1.25);

At the junction 'C'

$$P_3 = (x - z) + (y + z)$$

$$= x + y$$

∴ Current in CA = x + y

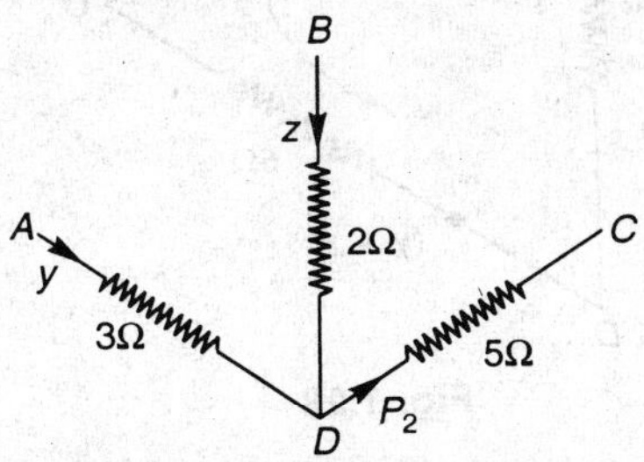


Fig. 1.24

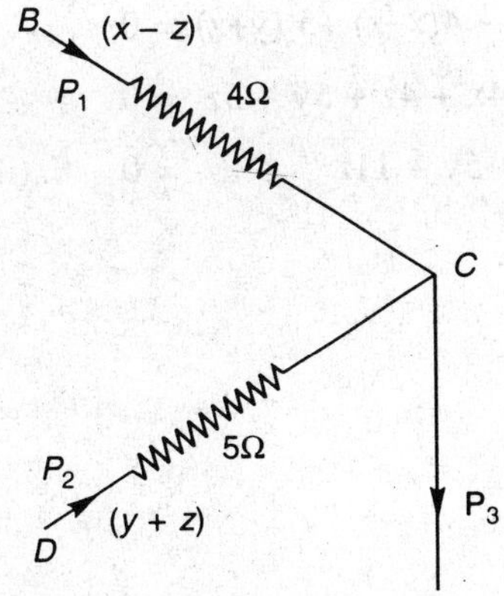


Fig. 1.25

The circuit can be redrawn as shown in Fig. 1.26.

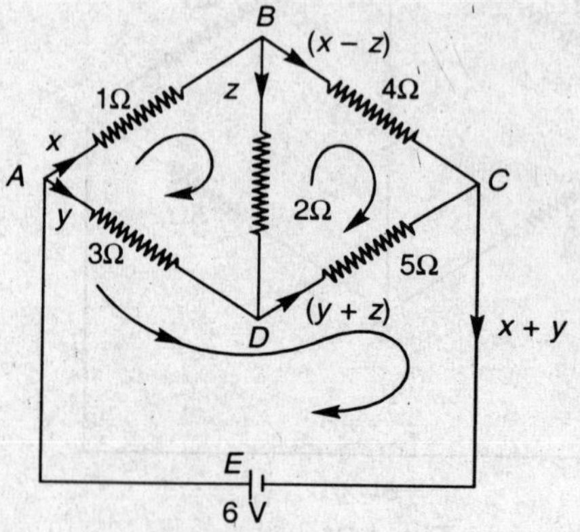


Fig. 1.26

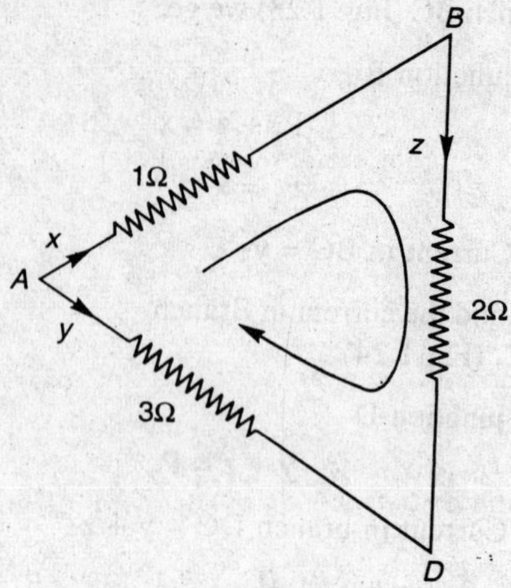


Fig. 1.27

Now to find the values of x, y, z we have to use Kirchhoff's voltage law. Since there are three unknowns, we have to get three equations from three loops.

Consider the loop ABDA in Fig. 1.27

$$-x.1 - z.2 + 3.y = 0$$

$$-x + 3y - 2z \quad = 0 \qquad ...(i)$$

Consider the loop BCDB in Fig. 1.28

$$+ 2.z - 4(x-z) + 5(y+z) = 0$$

$$2z - 4x + 4z + 5y + 5z = 0$$

$$-4x + 5y + 11z \quad = 0 \qquad ...(ii)$$

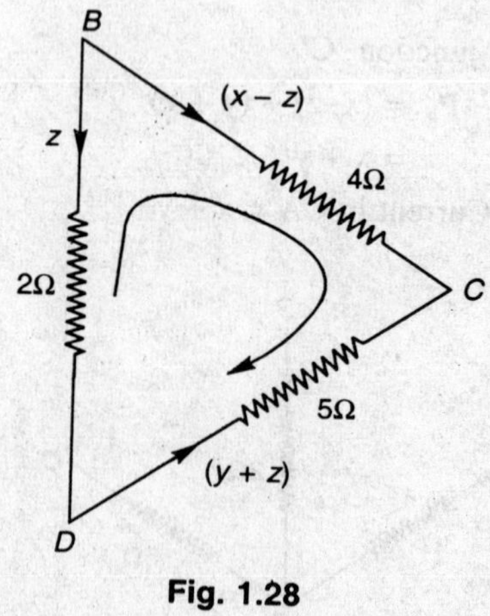


Fig. 1.28

Consider the loop ADCEA in Fig. 1.29

$$-3y - 5(y+z) + 6 = 0$$
$$-3y - 5y - 5z + 6 = 0$$
$$-8y - 5z + 6 = 0 \quad \text{...(iii)}$$

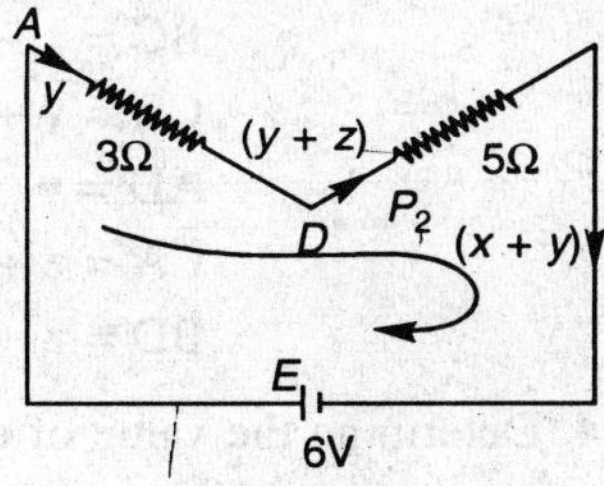


Fig. 1.29

Multiplying eq. (i) by 4 we get

$$-4x + 12y - 8z = 0$$

Subtracting eq. (ii) from the above eq. we get

$$\begin{aligned} -4x + 12y - 8z &= 0 \\ -4x + 5y + 11z &= 0 \\ (+) \quad (-) \quad (-) & \\ \hline 7y - 19z &= 0 \quad \text{...(iv)} \end{aligned}$$

Multiply eq. (iv) by 8 and eq. (iii) by 7 and adding we get

$$\begin{aligned} 56y - 152z &= 0 \\ -56y - 35z &= -42 \\ \hline -187z &= -42 \end{aligned}$$

$$z = \frac{42}{187} = 0.224 \text{ amperes}$$

Substituting the value of 'Z' in eq.(iv) we get

$$7y - 19z = 0$$
$$7y = 19z$$

$$\therefore \quad y = \frac{19 \times 0.224}{7} = 0.6096 \text{ amperes}$$

Substituting the value of 'z' and 'y' in eq.(i) we get

$$-x + 3y - 2z = 0$$
$$x = 3y - 2.z$$
$$x = 3 \times 0.6096 - 2 \times 0.224$$
$$= 1.38 \text{ amperes}$$

∴ current in branch AB = x = 1.38 amperes

" " BC = x − z = 1.156 amperes

" " CD = y + z = 0.8336 amperes

" " AD = y = 0.6096 amperes

" " CA = z + y = 1.9896 amperes

" " BD = z = 0.224 amperes

**P. 1.14.** Determine the value of current in the branch BD for the network shown in Fig. 1.30 using Kirchoff's Laws.

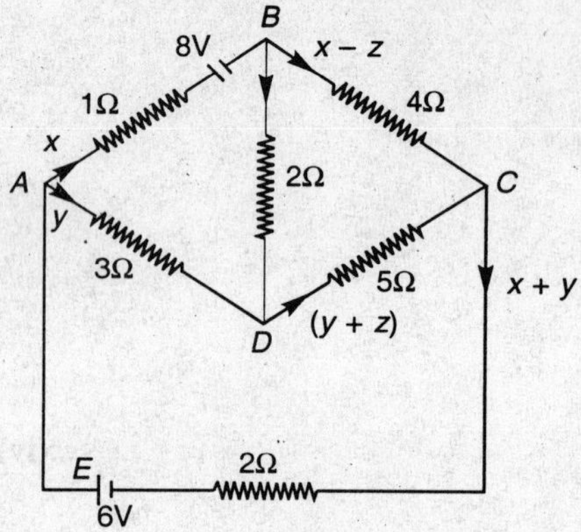


**Fig. 1.30**

**Solution:**

Consider the lpp ABDA

$$-x.1 - 8 - 2z + 3y = 0$$

$$-x + 3y - 2z = 8 \quad \text{...(i)}$$

Consider the loop BCDB

$$-4(x-z) + 5(y+z) + 2z = 0$$

$$-4x + 5y + 11z = 0 \quad \text{...(ii)}$$

Consider the loop ADCEA

$$-3y - 5(y+z) - 2(x+y) + 6 = 0$$

$$-2x - 10y - 5z = -6 \quad \text{...(iii)}$$

Multiplying eq (i) with 4 and subtracting (ii) from (i) we get

$$-4x + 12y - 8z = 32$$

$$-4x + 5y + 11z = 0$$

$$7y - 19z = 32 \quad \text{...(iv)}$$

Multiplying eq. (iii) with 2 and subtracting from eq. (ii) we get

$$-4x + 5y + 11z = 0$$

$$-4x - 20y - 10z = -12$$

$$25y + 21z = 12 \quad \text{...(v)}$$

Multiplying eq. (iv) with 25 and eq. (v) with 7 and subtracting (iv) from (v) we get

$$175y + 147z = 84$$

$$175y - 475z = 800$$

$$622z = -716$$

$$\Rightarrow \quad Z = \frac{-716}{622} \text{ amperes}$$

**P. 1.15.** Determine the value of current in each resistor for the network shown below

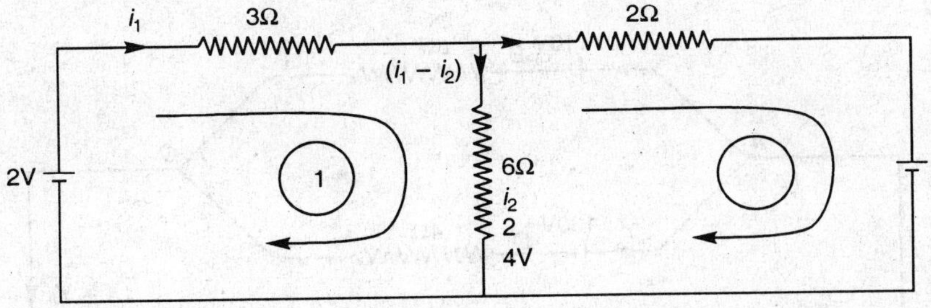


**Fig. 1.31**

**Solution:**

from Loop (1)

$$-3i_1 - 6(i_1 - i_2) + 2 = 0$$

$$-3i_1 - 6i_1 + 6i_2 + 2 = 0$$

$$-9i_1 + 6i_2 + 2 = 0 \quad \text{...(i)}$$

from Loop (2)

$$-2i_2 - 4 + 6(i_1 - i_2) = 0$$

$$6i_1 - 8i_2 - 4 = 0 \quad \text{...(ii)}$$

Multiplying eq. (i) with 6 and eq. (ii) with 9 and adding we get

$$-54i_1 + 36i_2 + 12 = 0$$

$$+54i_1 - 72i_2 - 36 = 0$$

$$-36i_2 - 24 = 0$$

$$i_2 = -2/3 \text{ amperes}$$

Substituting the value of '$i_2$' in eq. (ii) we get

$$6i_1 = 8i_2 + 4$$

$$= 8 \times \left(\frac{-2}{3}\right) + 4$$

$$= \frac{-4}{18} \text{ amperes}$$

**P. 1.16.** Two batteries A and B with internal resistances of 6Ω, 4Ω respectively are connected in parallel. The emf of battery A is 110 V and that of battery B is 130 V. A load of 20Ω is connected across the battery terminals. Using Kirchhoff's laws, determine the magnitude and direction of current flowing in each of the batteries and in the external resistance. Also determine the p.d. across the load resistance.

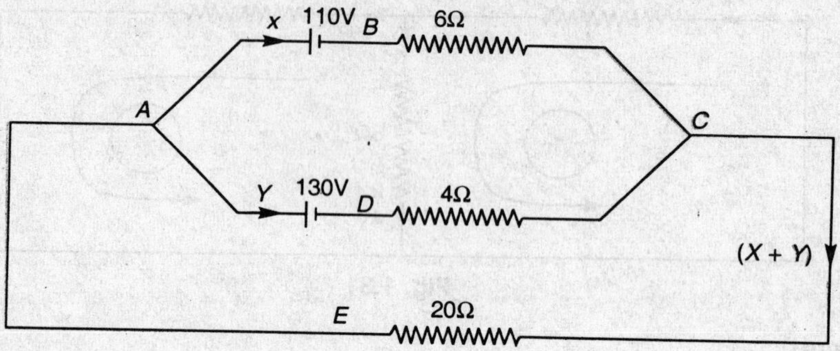


Fig. 1.32

**Solution:**

Take the loop ABCEA

$$-6x - 110 - 20(x+y) = 0$$

i.e. $26x + 20y = -110$

i.e. $13x + 10y = -55$ ...(i)

Take the loop ADCEA

$$-4y - 130 - (x+y)\,20 = 0$$

i.e. $20x + 24y = -130$

i.e. $10x + 12y = -65$ ...(ii)

Multiplying eq.(i) with 12 and eq.(ii) with 10 and subtracting (ii) from (i) we get

$$156x + 120y = -660$$
$$110x + 120y = -650$$

$$56x = -10$$
$$x = -0.1785 \text{ amperes}$$

Since 'x' is –ve its actual direction should be opposite to that shown in Fig. 1.32

Substituting the value of 'x' in eq. (i) we get,

$$13x + 10y = -55$$
$$10y = -55 - 13x$$
$$= -55 + 2.3214$$
$$y = -5.2679 \text{ amperes.}$$

Since 'y' is '–ve' its actual direction should be opposite to that shown in Fig. 1.32

Voltage drop across 20 Ω $= (x + y) \times 20$

$= (5.4464) \times 20$

$= 108.929$ volts

**P. 1.17.** For the circuit shown in Fig. 1.33 determine the value of resistance 'R' and the current through it, when the current through branch BD is zero.

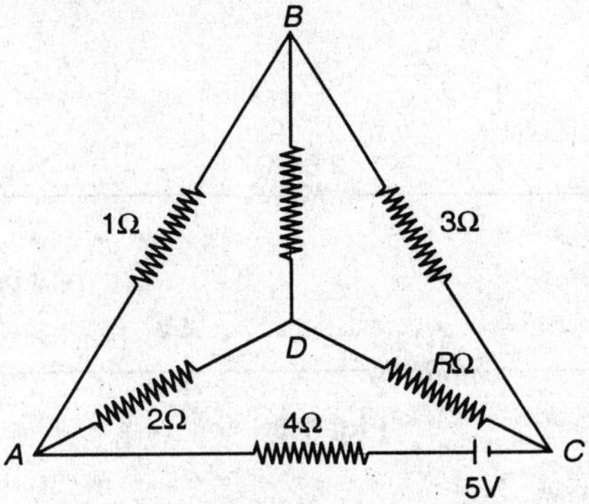


Fig. 1.33

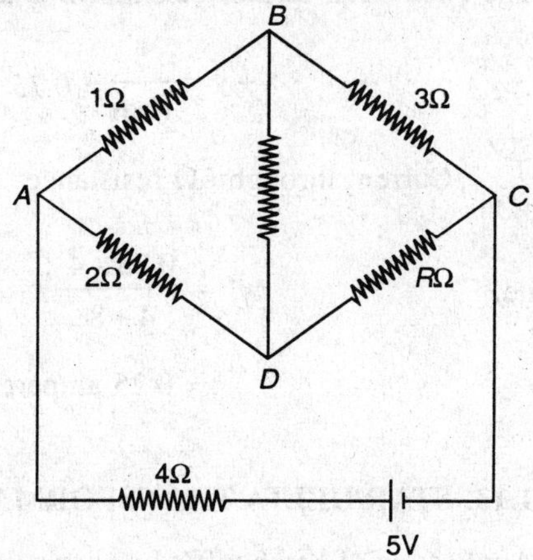


Fig. 1.34

**Solution:**

The circuit in Fig. 1.33 can be redrawn as shown in Fig. 1.34 which is nothing but a wheatstone bridge. When current in Branch BD = 0, The bridge is said to be balanced.

Under balanced conditions

$$1 \times R = 3 \times 2$$

$$R = 6\ \Omega$$

Also when the current in branch BD is zero we can further redraw the Fig. 1.34 as shown in Fig. 1.35.

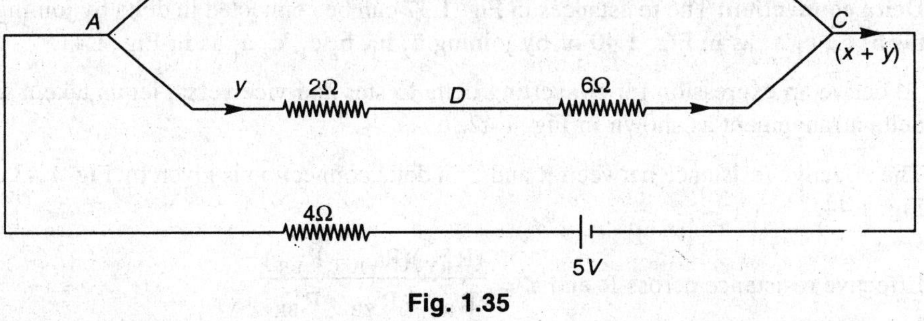


Fig. 1.35

$$R_{ABC} = 1 + 3 = 4\Omega$$

$$R_{ADC} = 2 + 6 = 8\Omega$$

$$R_{AC} = \frac{4 \times 8}{4+8} = 2.661\Omega$$

The circuit can further be simplified as shown in Fig. 1.36.

$$\therefore \quad x + y = \frac{5}{6.66} = 0.75 \text{ amperes}$$

∴ Current through 6Ω resistance

i.e. $$\text{'y'} = \frac{0.75 \times 4}{4+8}$$

$$= 0.25 \text{ ampere.}$$

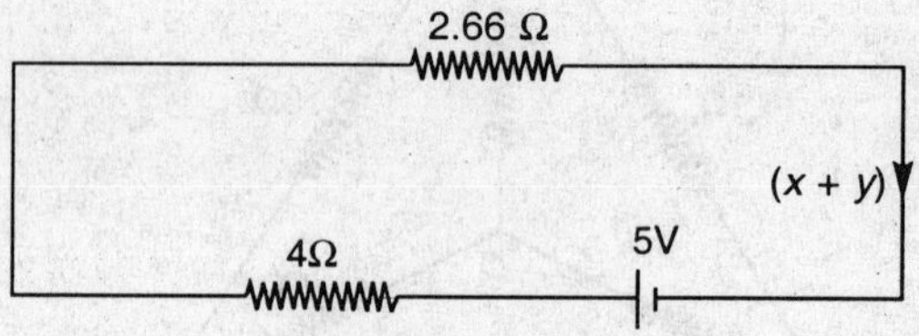

Fig. 1.36

## 1.13. STAR/DELTA TRANSFORMATION

Application of Kirchhoff's Laws in solving complicated networks sometimes consume lot of time in solving the simultaneous equations. However, star-delta transformation can be used to simplify the complicated networks and then Kirchhoff's Law can be applied to solve them.

**Star-connection or Y connection:** Consider three resistances $R_1$, $R_2$, $R_3$ as shown in Fig. 1.37. They can be connected in star by joining terminals $a_1$, $b_1$, $c_1$ and leaving $a_2$, $b_2$ as in Fig. 1.38 or vice versa as in Fig. 1.39.

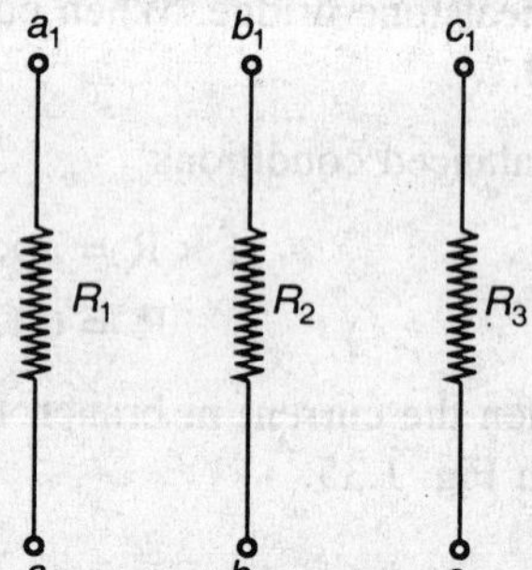

Fig. 1.37

**Delta connection:** The resistances in Fig. 1.37 can be connected in delta by joining $a_1$ $b_2$, $b_1$ $c_2$, $c_1$ $a_2$ as in Fig. 1.40 or by joining $a_2$ $b_1$, $b_2$ $c_1$, $c_2$ $a_1$ as in Fig. 1.41.

To derive an expression for converting delta to star and vice versa, let us take a star-delta arrangement as shown in Fig. 1.42.

The effective resistance between R and Y in delta connection is given by Fig. 1.43 and Fig. 1.44.

$$\text{Effective resistance across R and Y} = \frac{(R_{RY})(R_{YB} + R_{BR})}{R_{RY} + R_{YB} + R_{BR}}$$

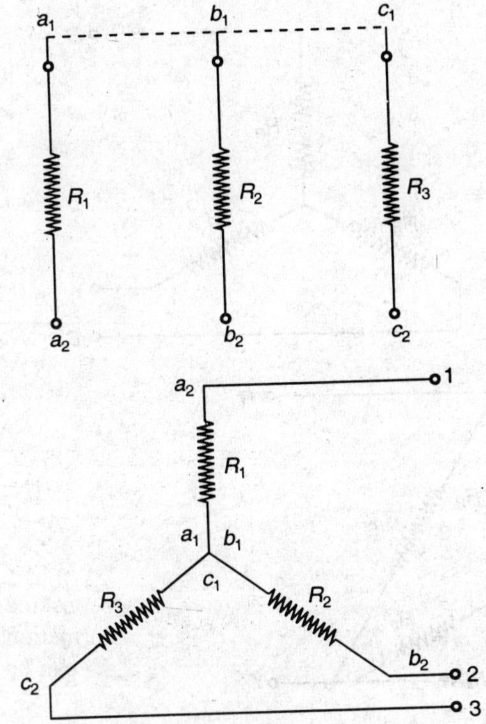


Fig. 1.38

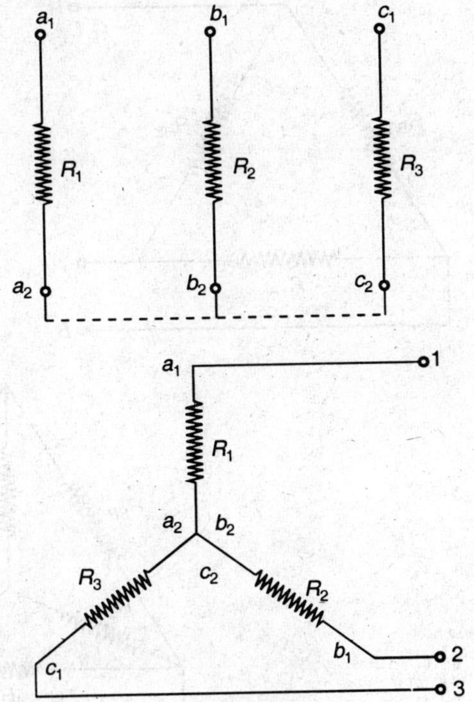


Fig. 1.39

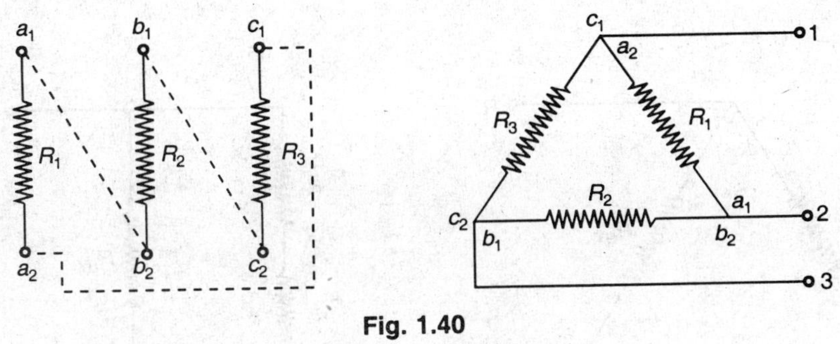


Fig. 1.40

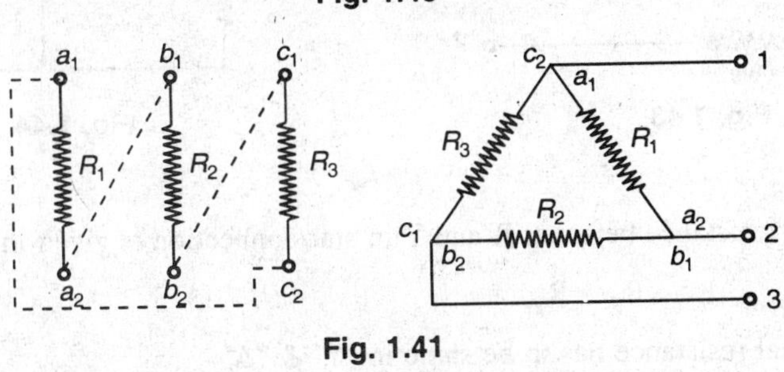


Fig. 1.41

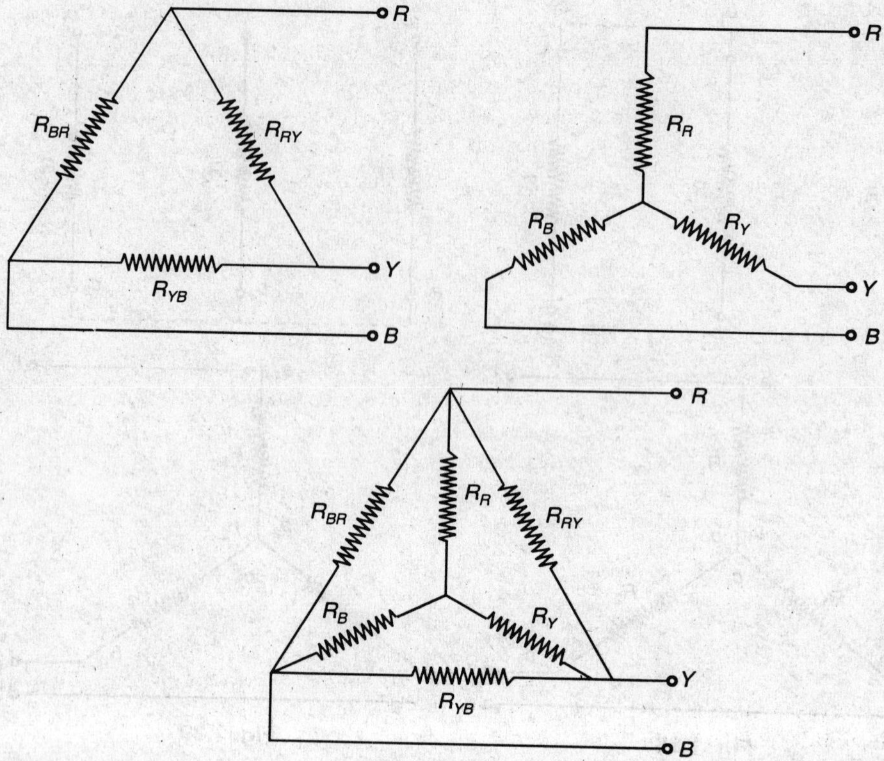


**Fig. 1.42**

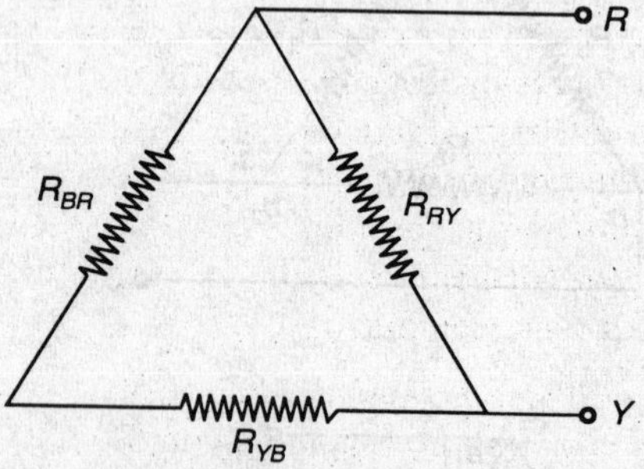


**Fig. 1.43**

=

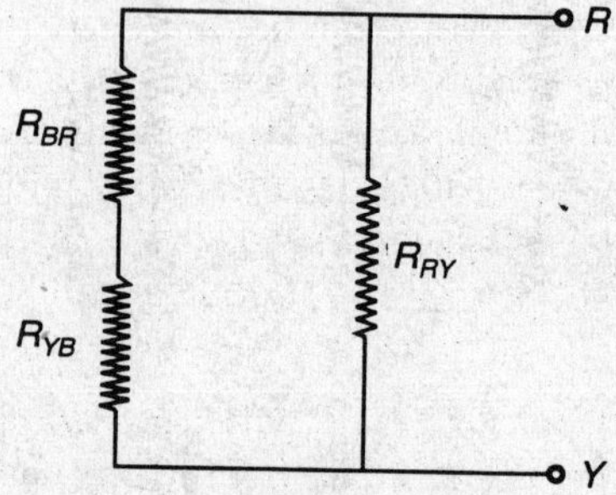


**Fig. 1.44**

The effective resistance between R and Y in star connection is given in Fig. 1.45.

$$R_R + R_Y$$

As the terminal resistance has to be same in 'Y' & 'Δ'

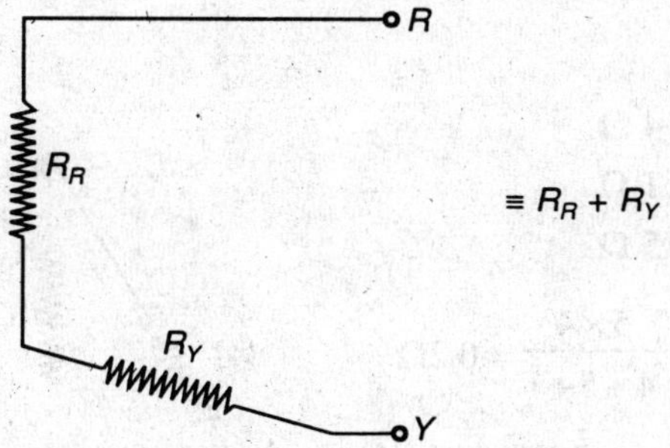


Fig. 1.45

$$\therefore \qquad R_R + R_Y = \frac{(R_{RY})(R_{YB} + R_{BR})}{R_{RY} + R_{YB} + R_{BR}}$$

Similarly, $$R_Y + R_B = \frac{R_{YB}\,(R_{BR} + R_{RY})}{(R_{YB} + R_{BR} + R_{RY})}$$

$$R_B + R_R = \frac{R_{BR}\,(R_{RY} + R_{YB})}{(R_{BR} + R_{RY} + R_{YB})}$$

$$R_R = \frac{R_{RY}\,.\,R_{BR}}{R_{RY} + R_{YB} + R_{BR}} \quad ...(1.35)$$

$$R_Y = \frac{R_{YB}\,.\,R_{RY}}{R_{RY} + R_{YB} + R_{BR}} \quad ...(1.36)$$

$$R_B = \frac{R_{BR}\,.\,R_{YB}}{R_{RY} + R_{YB} + R_{BR}} \quad ...(1.37)$$

Knowing 'star' values, we can easily find the 'delta' values. Thus we have

$$R_{RY} = \frac{R_R R_Y + R_Y R_B + R_B R_R}{R_B} \quad ...(1.38)$$

$$R_{YB} = \frac{R_R R_Y + R_Y R_B + R_B R_R}{R_R} \quad ...(1.39)$$

$$R_{BR} = \frac{R_R R_Y + R_Y R_B + R_B R_R}{R_Y} \quad ...(1.40)$$

**P. 1.18.** Convert the delta circuit of Fig. 1.46 to an equivalent star.

**Solution:**

Given $R_{RY} = 4\ \Omega$

$R_{YB} = 1\ \Omega$

$R_{BR} = 5\ \Omega$

$$\therefore \quad R_R = \frac{5 \times 4}{4+5+1} = 0.2\Omega$$

$$R_Y = \frac{4 \times 1}{4+5+1} = 0.4\Omega$$

$$R_B = \frac{5 \times 1}{4+5+1} = 0.5\Omega$$

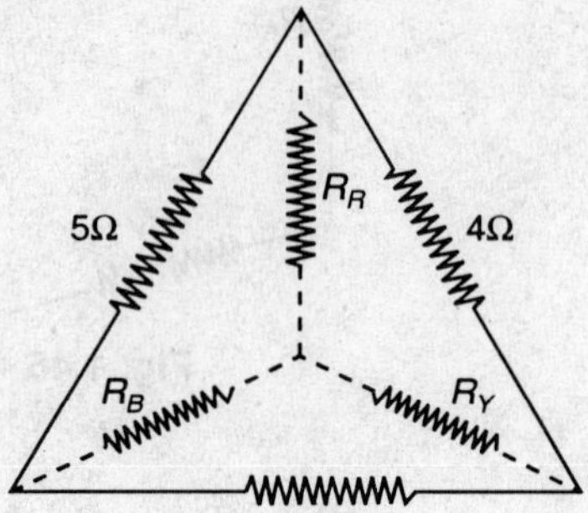


Fig. 1.46

**P. 1.19.** Convert the star circuit of Fig. 1.47 to an equivalent delta.

**Solution:**

Given $R_R = 2\ \Omega$

$R_Y = 0.67\ \Omega$

$R_B = 1\ \Omega$

$$\therefore \quad R_{RY} = \frac{(2 \times 0.67) + (0.67 \times 1) + (1 \times 2)}{1} = 4\Omega$$

$$R_{YB} = \frac{(2 \times 0.67) + (0.67 \times 1) + (1 \times 2)}{2} = 2\Omega$$

$$R_{BR} = \frac{(2 \times 0.67) + (0.67 \times 1) + (1 \times 2)}{0.67} = 6\Omega$$

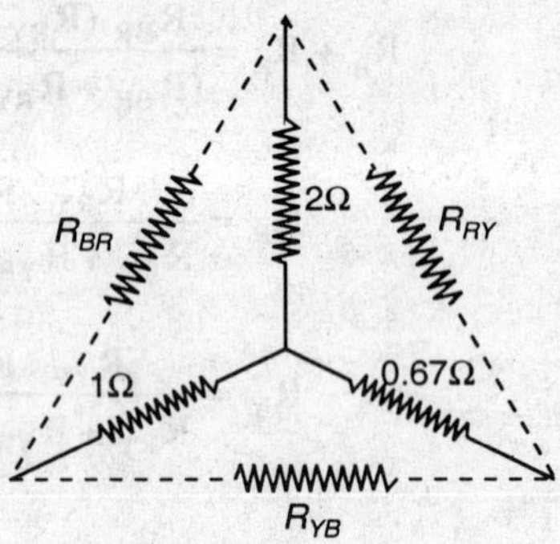


Fig. 1.47

**P. 1.20.** Using star-delta transformation find the equivalent resistance across AB for the circuit shown in Fig. 1.48.

**Solution:**

Given

$R_{RY} = 1$; $R_{YB} = 2$ and $R_{BR} = 3$

$$\therefore \quad R_R = \frac{1 \times 3}{1+2+3} = \frac{3}{6} = \frac{1}{2}$$

$$R_Y = \frac{1 \times 2}{1+2+3} = \frac{2}{6} = \frac{1}{3}$$

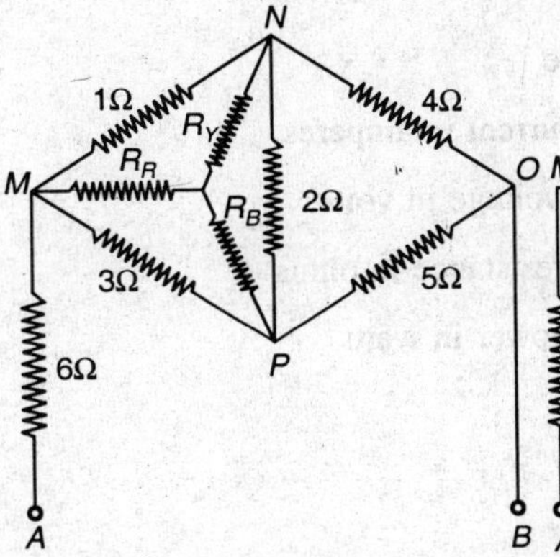


Fig. 1.48

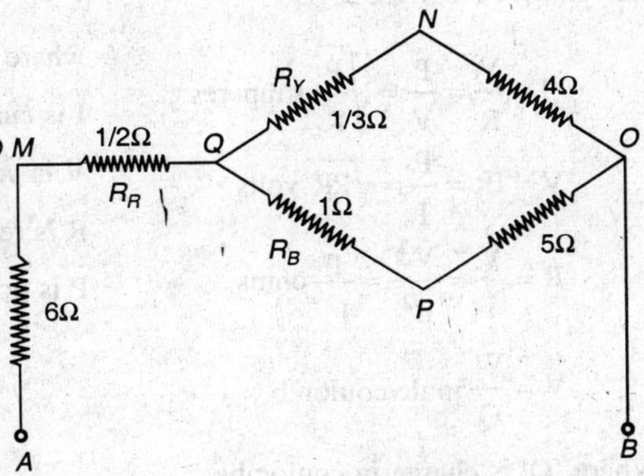


Fig. 1.49

$$R_B = \frac{3 \times 2}{1+2+3} = \frac{6}{6} = 1$$

From Fig 1.50, $R_{QNO} = 4 + \frac{1}{3} = 4.33\ \Omega$

$$R_{QPO} = 1 + 5 = 6\ \Omega$$

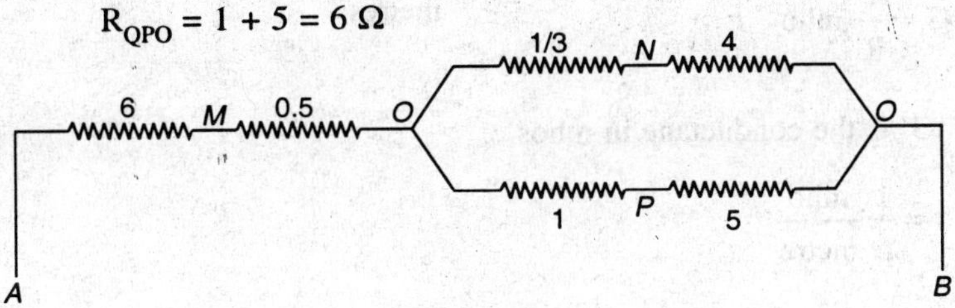


Fig. 1.50

From Fig. 1.51, $R_{QO} = \frac{4.33 \times 6}{4.33 + 6} = 2.51\ \Omega$

$$R_{AB} = 6.5 + 2.51 = 9.01\ \Omega$$

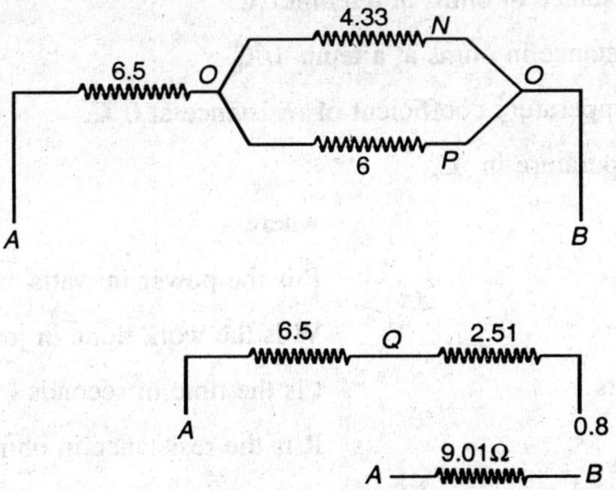


Fig. 1.51

## REVISION FORMULAE

$$I = \frac{V}{R} = \frac{P}{V} = \sqrt{\frac{P}{R}} \text{ Amperes}$$

$$V = IR = \frac{P}{I} = \sqrt{PR} \text{ volts}$$

$$R = \frac{V}{I} = \frac{V^2}{p^2} = \frac{p}{I^2} \text{ ohms}$$

$$V = \frac{W}{Q} \text{ joule/coulomb}$$

where

I is current in amperes

V is voltage in volts

R is resistance in ohms

P is power in watts

Where 'Q' is charge in coulombs
'W' is work done in joules.

$$R = \frac{\rho l}{A} \text{ ohms}$$

$$\rho = \frac{AR}{l} \text{ ohm} - \text{metre}$$

$$G = \frac{1}{R} \text{ mho}$$

where

ρ is the specific resistance

l is the length of the conductor in metre

A is the area of cross section in square metres

Where 'G' is the conductane in mhos

$$\sigma = \frac{1}{\rho} \frac{\text{mho}}{\text{metre}}.$$

where 'σ' is the specific conductance in $\frac{\text{mho}}{\text{metre}}$

$$R_t = R_o (1 + \alpha_o t)$$

Where $R_t$ is the resistance in ohms at a tempt t°C.

$R_o$ is the resistance in ohms at a temp. 0°C.

'$\alpha_o$' is the temperature coefficient of resistance at 0°C.

't' is the temperature in °C.

$$P = \frac{w}{t} \text{ watts}$$

$$P = VI \text{ watts}$$

$$P = I_2 R \text{ watts}$$

$$P = \frac{V^2}{R} \text{ watts}$$

where

P is the power in watts

W is the work done in joules

t is the time in seconds

R is the resistance in ohms

V is the voltage in volts

I is the current in amperes

**In a series circuit**

$R_s = R_1 + R_2$ ohms (for 2 resistors)

$R_s = R_1 + R_2 + R_3$ ohms (for 3 resistors)

**In a parallel circuit**

$$R_P = \frac{R_1 R_2}{R_1 + R_2} \text{ ohms (for 2 resistors)}$$

$$R_P = \frac{R_1 R_2 R_3}{R_1 R_2 + R_2 R_3 + R_3 R_1} \text{ ohms (for 3 resistors)}$$

$R_s$ is the effective resistance of $R_1$,$R_2$,$R_3$, connected in series

$R_p$ is the effective resistance of $R_1$,$R_2$,$R_3$, connected in parallel

**Division of current in parallel circuit**

$$\text{'}I_1\text{'} = \frac{I R_2}{R_1 + R_2} \text{ amperes}$$

$$\text{'}I_2\text{'} = \frac{I R_1}{R_1 + R_2} \text{ amperes}$$

$$\text{'}I_1\text{'} = \frac{I R_2 R_3}{R_1 R_2 + R_2 R_3 + R_3 R_1} \text{ amperes}$$

$$\text{'}I_2\text{'} = \frac{I R_3 R_1}{R_1 R_2 + R_2 R_3 + R_3 R_1} \text{ amperes}$$

$$\text{'}I_3\text{'} = \frac{I R_1 R_2}{R_1 R_2 + R_2 R_3 + R_3 R_1} \text{ amperes}$$

Sign convention for Kirchoff's laws:
(fall in potential) – ve sign for 'V'
(rise in potential) +ve sign for 'V'
(fall in potential) – ve sign for IR product
(rise in potential) + ve sign for IR product
Star – Delta connection (Star values in terms of Delta value)

$$R_R = \frac{R_{RY} \times R_{BR}}{R_{RY} + R_{YB} + R_{BR}} \text{ ohms}$$

$$R_Y = \frac{R_{YB} \times R_{RY}}{R_{RY} + R_{YB} + R_{BR}} \text{ ohms}$$

$$R_B = \frac{R_{BR} \times R_{YB}}{R_{RY} + R_{YB} + R_{BR}} \text{ ohms}$$

(Delta values in terms of star values)

$$R_{RY} = \frac{R_R R_Y + R_Y R_B + R_B R_R}{R_B} \text{ ohms}$$

$$R_{YB} = \frac{R_R R_Y + R_Y R_B + R_B R_R}{R_R} \text{ ohms}$$

$$R_{BR} = \frac{R_R R_Y + R_Y R_B + R_B R_R}{R_{RY} + R_{YB} + R_{BR}} \text{ ohms}$$

**Unit Conversion**

| | |
|---|---|
| 1 milli Amp | $= 10^{-3}$ amperes |
| 1 centimetre | $= 10^{-2}$ metre |
| 1 kiloohm | $= 10^{+3}$ ohm |
| 1 megaohm | $= 10^{+6}$ ohm |
| 1 micro farad | $= 10^{-6}$ farad |
| 1 nano second | $= 10^{-9}$ second |
| 1 pico farad | $= 10^{-12}$ farad |

## REVIEW QUESTIONS

1. What do you understand by electric current, resistance and electromotive force? Give their units.
2. What is the difference between direct current and alternating current?
3. Define the following:
   (a) Specific resistance
   (b) Temperature co-efficient of resistance
   (c) Electrical power
   (d) Electrical energy
4. Define the international system of units for ohm, ampere and volt.
5. State and explain Ohm's Law.
6. Derive an expression for the effective resistance of
   (i) Two resistors connected in series

(ii) Two resistors connected in parallel

7. State and explain Kirchoff's laws.
8. How do you use star delta transformation for simplifying the complicated networks?

## TWO MARKS QUESTIONS AND ANSWERS

1. *Define electric current.*

   Electric current is defined as the flow of electrons in a conductor.

2. *What is electromotive force ?*

   The driving force required for the flow of current in a conductor is called electromotive force.

3. *What is electrical resistance ?*

   The property of the conductor by which it opposes the flow of current is called resistance.

4. *Define specific resistance.*

   The resistance offered by unit cube of the material between its opposite faces is called specific resistance.

5. *What is the difference between power and energy ?*

   Power is defined as the rate of doing work. Energy is defined as the capacity to do the work.

6. *State Ohm's law.*

   At constant temperature, the current flowing through a conductor is directly proportional to the voltage across the conductor.

7. *Define International Ampere.*

   It is defined as that value of steady current when flowing through rotation of silver nitrate in water, deposits silver at the cathode at a rate of 1.18 milligrams per second.

8. *What is a series circuit ?*

   A series circuit is one in which current passing through all the elements is same.

9. *What is a parallel circuit ?*

   A parallel circuit is one in which voltage across each element connected in parallel is same.

10. *State Kirchoff's Laws.*

    Current Law: The algebraic sum of all the currents meeting at a junction is equal to zero i.e., $\Sigma I = 0$

    Voltage Law: In any closed network or mesh, the algebraic sum or product of current and resistances in each of the conductor plus the algebraic sum of electromotive forces in that path is zero, i.e.,

$$(\Sigma IR + \Sigma \text{ e.m.f.} = 0)$$

## EXERCISE PROBLEMS

**P. 1.1:** Find the value of 'I' for the circuit shown in Fig. 1.52.

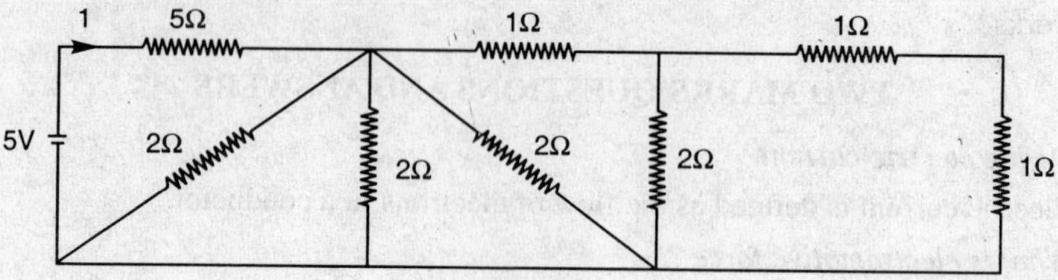


Fig. 1.52

(Ans: I = 5A)

**P. 1.2:** Find the effective value of resistance between AB for the network shown in Fig. 1.53.

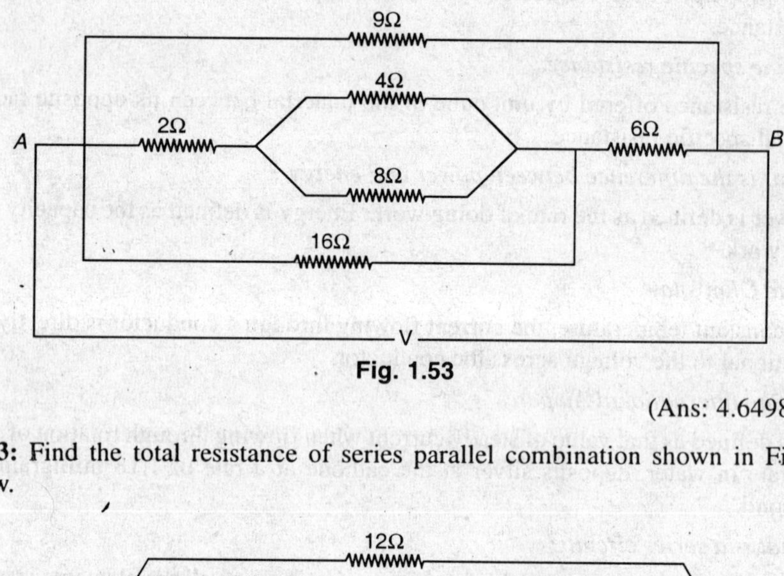


Fig. 1.53

(Ans: 4.6498 ohms)

**P. 1.3:** Find the total resistance of series parallel combination shown in Fig. 1.54 below.

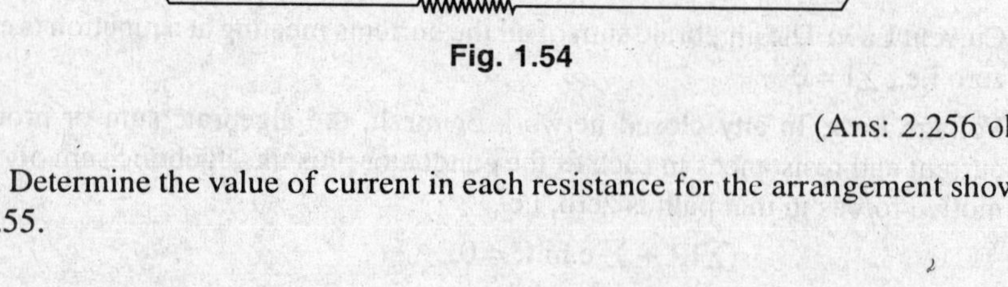


Fig. 1.54

(Ans: 2.256 ohms)

**P. 1.4:** Determine the value of current in each resistance for the arrangement shown in Fig. 1.55.

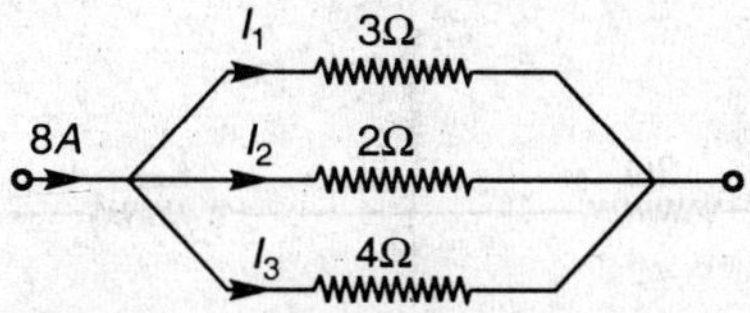


Fig. 1.55

(Ans: $I_1$ = 2.46 A $I_2$ = 3.69 A, $I_3$ = 1.84 A)

**P. 1.5:** The equivalent resistance of three resistors joined in parallel is 15 W. The current flowing through them is 0.8 A, 0.6 A, and 0.3 A respectively. Find the value of each resistor.

(Ans. 31.875 Ω, 42.5 Ω, and 85 Ω)

**P. 1.6:** Two lamps of 80 W and 60 W rated for 200 V supply are connected to 400 V supply mains in series. Find the value of additional resistance to be connected across 60 W lamp to get 200 V on each lamp.

(Ans: 2000 Ω)

**P. 1.7:** A lamp rated 100 V, 75 A is to be connected across 230 V. Find the value of resistance to be connected in series. Also find the power loss occurring in that resistance.

(Ans: 1.73 Ω, 9731 W)

**P. 1.8:** A wheatstone bridge has the following values $R_{AB}$ = 1 Ω; $R_{BC}$ = 4 Ω; $R_{CD}$ = 5 Ω; $R_{DA}$ = 3 Ω; $R_{BD}$ = 2 Ω. A battery of 6 V with internal resistance of 2 ohms is connected across A and C. Find the value of current in branch AB, AD and BD.

(Ans: 0.83 A, 0.37 A, 0.135 A)

**P. 1.9:** Calculate the voltage across 'a' and 'b', and 'c' and 'd' of the circuit shown in Fig. 1.56. The average power across 5 Ω resistor is 20 watts.

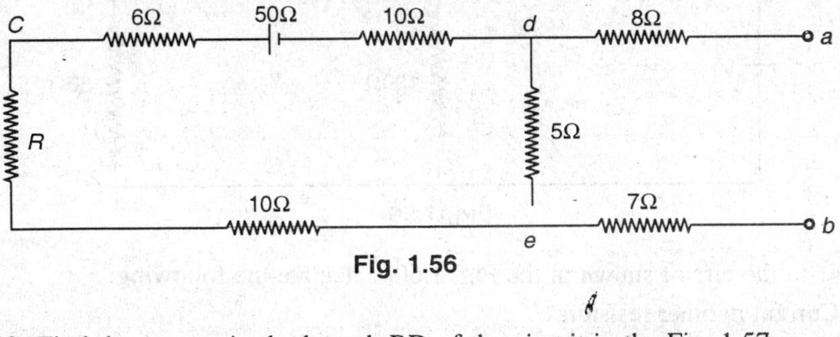


Fig. 1.56

**P. 1.10:** Find the current in the branch BD of the circuit in the Fig. 1.57.

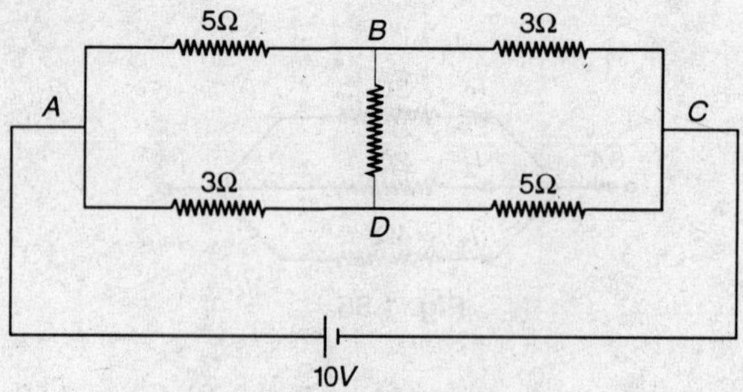


Fig. 1.57

**P. 1.11:** Calculate the current in branch BD of Fig 1.58.

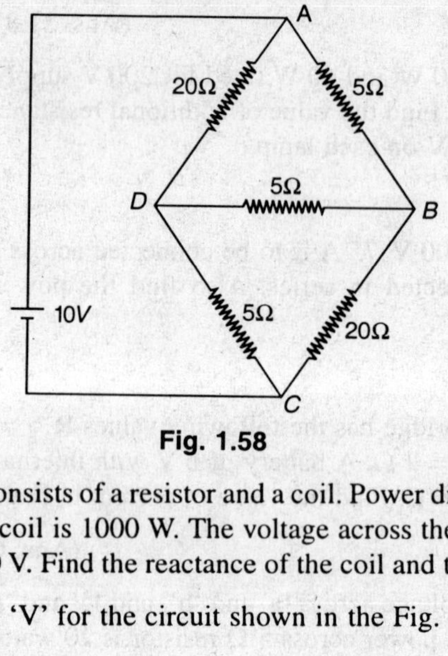


Fig. 1.58

**P. 1.12:** A series circuit consists of a resistor and a coil. Power dissipated in the resistor is 500 W and that in the coil is 1000 W. The voltage across the resistor is 100 V and that across the coil is 200 V. Find the reactance of the coil and the supply voltage.

**P. 1.13:** Find the voltage 'V' for the circuit shown in the Fig. 1.59.

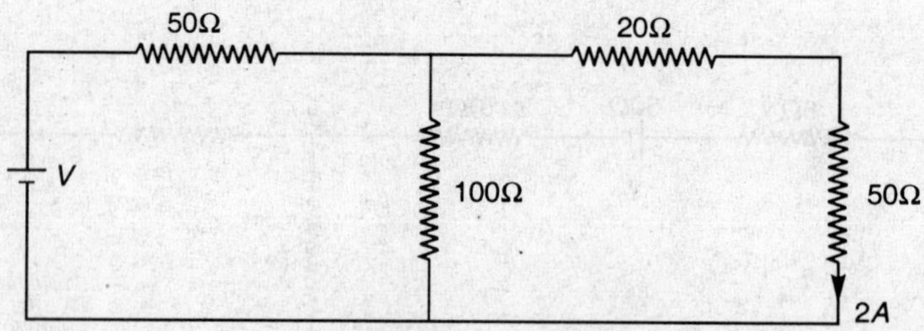


Fig. 1.59

**P. 1.14:** In the circuit shown in the Fig. 1.60, calculate the following:

(i) Current in other resistors

(ii) Value of unknown resistance 'X'

(iii) Equivalent resistance across A B

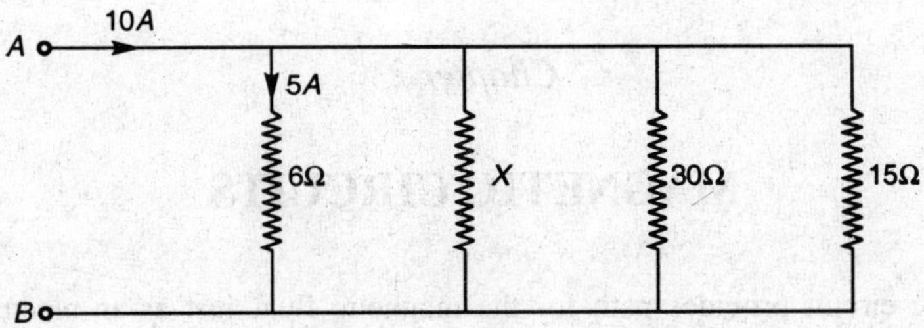


Fig. 1.60

**P. 1.15:** Find the current 'I' in Fig. 1.61.

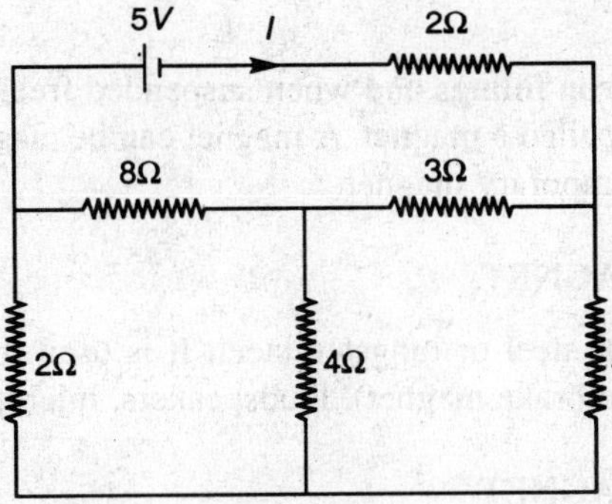


Fig. 1.61

*Chapter 2*

# MAGNETIC CIRCUITS

A magnetic circuit provides path for the magnetic flux, just as an electric circuit provides a path for the flow of current. The knowledge of magnetic circuit concept is useful in the analysis, design and application of electromagnetic devices like rotating machines and transformers etc.

## 2.1. MAGNET

A substance that attracts iron fillings and when suspended freely points in the direction of north and south is called a magnet. A magnet can be classified into two types, namely, permanent and temporary magnet.

## 2.2. PERMANENT MAGNET

This is made up of cobalt, steel or tungsten steel. It is used in moving coil instruments, energy meters (as a brake magnet), loudspeakers, microphones, etc.

## 2.3. TEMPORARY MAGNET

It is also called an electromagnet. The material used here is soft iron of silicon steel. A soft iron piece wound with a coil acts as a magnet as long as current flows through the coil. It is used in electrical machines such as motor and generator.

## 2.4. MAGNETIC LINES OF FORCE

The imaginary magnetic lines (Fig. 2.1) which travel from north pole to south pole outside the magnet, and from south pole to north pole, inside the magnet are called magnetic lines of force.

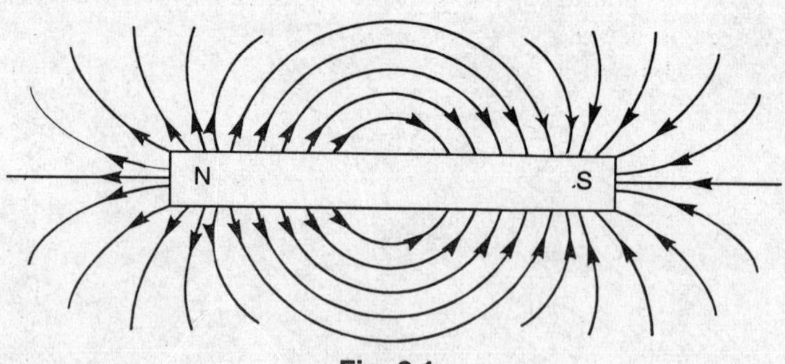


**Fig. 2.1**

## 2.5. MAGNETIC FIELD

The region around which the magnetic lines of force act is called magnetic field.

## 2.6. MAGNETIC FLUX

The total lines of force in the magnetic field is called magnetic flux. It is denoted by '$\Phi$', and its unit is weber.

## 2.7. MAGNETIC FLUX DENSITY (B)

The magnetic flux passing through a unit cross section is called flux density. It is denoted by 'B'.

If '$\Phi$' is magnetic flux in webers

B is flux density is $Wb/m^2$

A is area of cross section in $m^2$

then, $$B = \frac{\Phi}{A} \text{ Wb/m}^2 \qquad \text{...(2.1)}$$

## 2.8. PERMEABILITY

The magnetic conductivity of iron as compared to that of air is called permeability. The absolute permeability '$\mu$' of a medium is given by

$$\mu = \frac{B}{H} \qquad \text{...(2.2)}$$

where B = flux density in $Wb/m^2$

H = magnetic field strength N/Wb.

$\mu$ is also given by the equation

$$\mu = \mu_0 \mu_r \qquad \text{...(2.3)}$$

where $\mu_0 = 4\pi \times 10^{-7}$ H/m and

$\mu_r$ = relative permeability

The relative permeability $\mu_r$ of a medium is given by

$$\mu_r = \frac{B}{B_o} \qquad \text{...(2.4)}$$

where,

B = flux density in the medium under consideration in $Wb/m^2$

$B_0$ = flux density in vacuum.

It can also be defined as the conducting competence of a material for magnetic lines of force as compared with air. The value of $\mu_r = 1$ for air, free space or vacuum.

## 2.9. MAGNETIC FIELD STRENGTH (H)

It is given by the force experienced by unit north pole placed at that point. It is denoted by 'H'.

If 'Φ' is the flux in webers

F is the force in newton (N)

H is the field strength in N/Wb

then $H = \frac{F}{\Phi}$ N/Wb ...(2.5)

H is also given by $B/\mu_0\mu_r$ N/Wb ...(2.6)

## 2.10. MAGNETOMOTIVE FORCE (NI)

It is given by the work done in moving a unit north pole once round the entire magnetic circuit.

It is also given by the driving force required to drive the magnetic flux through a magnetic circuit.

It is given by 'NI' and its unit is ampere turns.

## 2.11. RELUCTANCE (S)

It is the property of a magnetic material by which it opposes the establishment of magnetic flux.

It is denoted by 'S' and its unit is ampere turns/weber.

## 2.12. SIMILARITIES BETWEEN ELECTRIC AND MAGNETIC CIRCUITS

| | **Electric circuit** | **Magnetic circuit** |
|---|---|---|
| 1. | Electric current 'I' in amperes | Magnetic flux F in webers |
| 2. | Electromotive force 'V' in volts | Magneto motive force 'NI' in ampere turns |
| 3. | Resistance 'R' in ohms $= \frac{\rho l}{A}$ | Reluctance 'S' in AT/Wb $\frac{1}{\mu_o\mu_r A}$ |
| 4. | Current density I/A, $A/m^2$ | Magnetic flux density $\frac{\Phi}{A} Wb/m^2$ |
| 5. | Electric intensity 'E' | Magnetic intensity 'H' |
| 6. | Current $= \frac{\text{emf}}{\text{resistance}}$ | Flux = mmf/reluctance |

| | | |
|---|---|---|
| 7. | Conductivity | Permeability |
| 8. | Conductivity is independent of the strength of current. | Permeability depends on the total flux. |

## 2.13. DIFFERENCES

1. In an electric circuit the electric current flows whereas in a magnetic field magnetic flux does not flow.
2. In the magnetic circuit, energy is required only for creating the magnetic flux, not for maintaining it, whereas in the electric circuit current flow involves continuous expenditure of energy.
3. The reluctance of the magnetic material varies with flux density, whereas the resistance remains practically constant with current strength.

## 2.14. ANALYSIS OF MAGNETIC CIRCUIT

**2.14a. Simple Magnetic Circuit:** It consists of a closed iron ring wound with a magnetising coil as shown in Fig. 2.2. The magnetic flux is produced by the coil. Thus the coil acts as a source of mmf and the reluctance for the establishment of magnetic flux is offered by the iron ring.

**Ohm's Law of Magnetism:** Consider a simple magnetic circuit, i.e., a torroidal ring as shown in Fig. 2.2 wound with a coil of 'N' turns. Let 'I' ampere be the current carried by the coil, 'A' be the area of cross section of the ring in $m^2$ and 'l' be length of the magnetic path in metres. Let 'Φ' be flux in weber established in the iron ring.

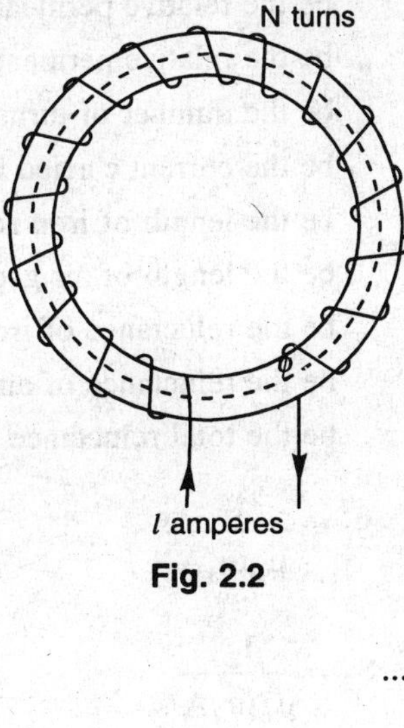

**Fig. 2.2**

The magnetic flux

density 'B' $= \dfrac{\Phi}{A}$ Wb/m²

also $B = \mu_0 \mu_r H$ Wb/m²

where $\mu_r$ = relative permeability of the ring

$\mu_0 = 4\pi \times 10^{-7}$ H/m

$H$ = magnetic field strength in AT/m

But $$H = \frac{NI}{l} \text{ AT/m} \quad ...(2.7)$$

$$\therefore \quad B = \mu_0 \mu_r \frac{NI}{l}$$

$$\therefore \quad \frac{\Phi}{A} = \mu_0 \mu_r \frac{NI}{l}$$

$$\Phi = \frac{NI \mu_o \mu_r A}{l}$$

$$\Phi = \frac{NI}{[l/\mu_o \mu_r A]} \quad ...(2.8)$$

The denominator $\frac{l}{\mu_o \mu_r A}$ is called reluctances 'S' of the circuit.

$$\therefore \quad \Phi = \frac{NI}{l} \quad ...(2.9)$$

Since equation 2.9 resembles the Ohm's law of electricity, namely, $I = \frac{V}{R}$, it is called Ohm's law of magnetism.

### 2.14b. Composite Magnetic Circuit of Iron Ring with Air Gap

An iron ring with small air gap forms a composite magnetic circuit as shown in Fig. 2.3. The reluctance offered by iron ring is different from that offered by air gap. The total reluctance of the magnetic circuit will be the sum of these two reluctances.

Let 'A' be area of cross section of the ring in $m^2$

$\mu r_1$ be the relative permeability of iron ring

$\mu r_2$ be the relative permeability of air gap which is 1

'N' be the number of turns of the coil

I be the current carried by the coil in amperes

$l_1$ be the length of iron ring in metres

$l_2$ be the length of air gap in metres

$S_1$ be the reluctance of iron ring in AT/Wb

$S_2$ be the reluctance of air gap in AT/Wb

S be the total reluctance in AT/Wb

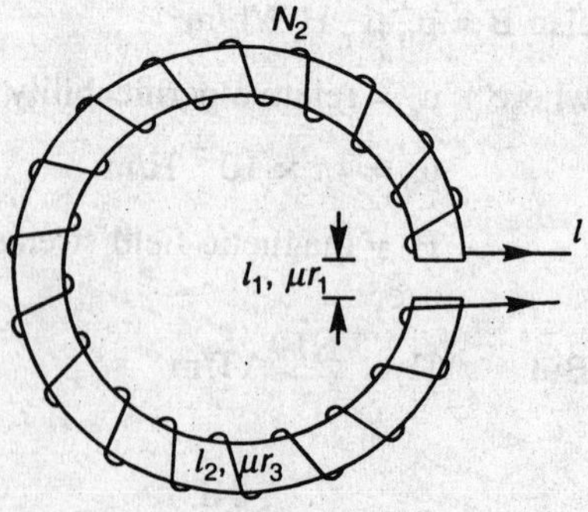

Fig. 2.3

$$\therefore \quad S_1 = \frac{l_1}{\mu_o \mu r_1 A}$$

$$S_2 = \frac{l_2}{\mu_o \mu r_2 A}$$

$$\therefore \quad S = S_1 + S_2 = \frac{l_1}{\mu_o \mu r_2 A} + \frac{l_2}{\mu_o \mu r_2 A}$$

we know that,

$$\text{Flux} = \frac{\text{MMF}}{\text{Reluctance}}$$

$$\therefore \qquad \text{Flux} = \frac{\text{NI}}{\dfrac{l_1}{\mu_o \mu r_1 A} + \dfrac{l_2}{\mu_o \mu r_2 A}} \text{ weber} \qquad ...(2.10)$$

**2.14c. Composite Series Magnetic Circuit:** It consists of different types of iron (or other magnetic materials) with different dimensions and relative permeability as shown in Fig. 2.4. Since they are in series, 'S' the total reluctance can be given by the sum of individual reluctances.,

We know that

$$\text{Flux} = \frac{\text{MMF}}{\text{Total reluctance}}$$

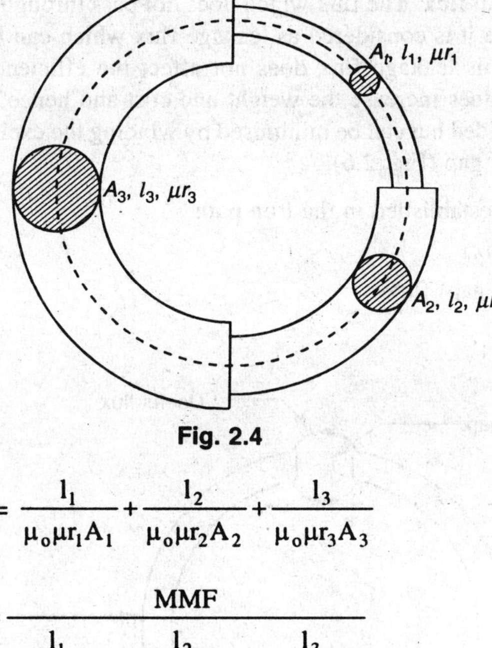


**Fig. 2.4**

where
$$S = \frac{l_1}{\mu_o \mu r_1 A_1} + \frac{l_2}{\mu_o \mu r_2 A_2} + \frac{l_3}{\mu_o \mu r_3 A_3}$$

$$\Phi = \frac{\text{MMF}}{\dfrac{l_1}{\mu_o \mu r_1 A_1} + \dfrac{l_2}{\mu_o \mu r_2 A_2} + \dfrac{l_3}{\mu_o \mu r_3 A_3}}$$

**2.14d. Parallel Magnetic Circuit:** It has more than one path for magnetic flux as shown in Fig. 2.5. Flux is established by the ampere turns provided in the central limb (PQ) and divides into two parts towards PRSQ and PTUQ as $F_1$ and $F_2$ respectively.

Thus the total flux is given by $\Phi = \Phi_1 + \Phi_2$

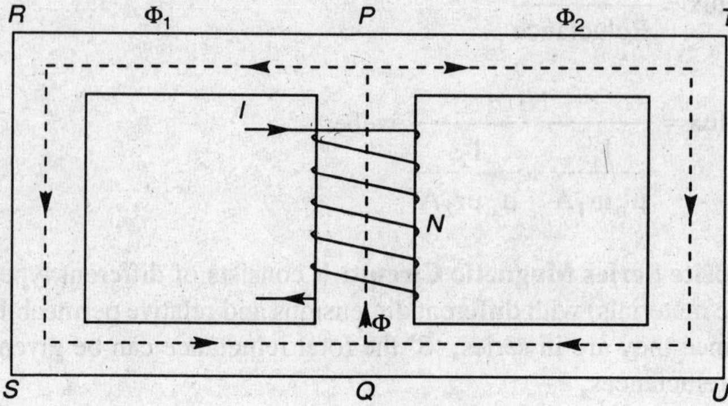


Fig. 2.5

## 2.15. MAGNETIC LEAKAGE

The flux that follows an undesired path is called the leakage flux. To utilize the magnetic flux established by the magnetic material, we provide an air gap. The flux in the air gap is called useful flux. The flux which does not pass through the air gap, cannot be utilised and hence it is considered as leakage flux which can be determined by a compass. Though, this leakage flux does not affect the efficiency of the electrical machine directly, it does increase the weight and cost and hence it is undesirable. It cannot be totally avoided but can be minimised by winding the exciting coils as closely as possible to the air gap (Fig. 2.6).

If $\Phi_t$ – Total flux established in the iron path

$\Phi_l$ – leakage flux.

$\Phi_u$ – useful (air gap) flux

then $\Phi_l = \Phi_t + \Phi_u$ .

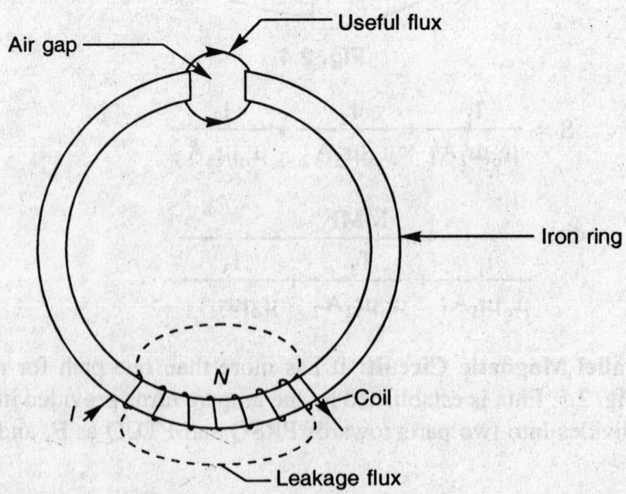


Fig. 2.6

The ratio $\frac{\Phi_l}{\Phi_u}$ is called coefficient of magnetic leakage 'λ'.

'λ' value varies from 1.15 to 1.25.

## 2.16. RETENTIVITY

The retaining capacity of magnetism of a magnetic material after the removal of inducing agency is called retentivity. E.g. Hard steel.

**P. 2.1.** A square cross sectional magnet of side 4 cm has a strength of 0.5 milli webers. Determine the magnetic flux density.

**Solution:**

Given Flux (F) = 0.5 milli webers = $0.5 \times 10^{-3}$ Wb

Cross sectional area (A) = 4 cm × 4 cm = $4 \times 10^{-4}$ m²

$$\therefore \quad \text{Flux density } = B = \frac{\Phi}{A} = \frac{0.5 \times 10^{-3}}{4 \times 10^{-4}}$$

$$= 1.25 \text{ Wb/m}^2.$$

**P. 2.2.** A solenoid is wound with a coil of 100 turns. The coil is of length 50 cm and is carrying a current of 2 amperes. Determine the magnetic field strength at the centre of the solenoid (Fig. 2.7).

**Solution:**

Given $I = 2$ A

$l = 50$ cm

$= 50 \times 10^{-2}$ m

$N = 100$ turns

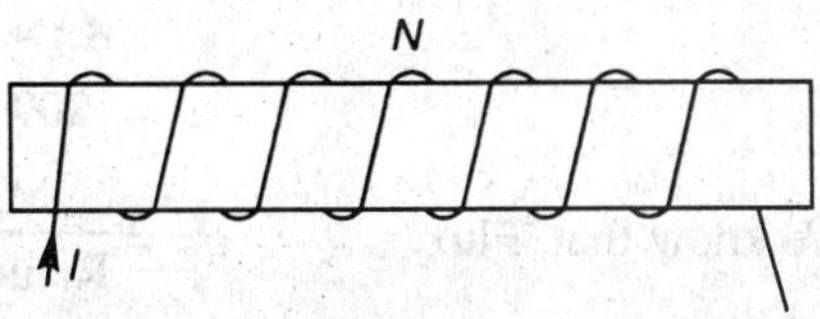


Fig. 2.7

∴ Magnetic field strength

$$H = \frac{NI}{l} \text{ AT/m}$$

$$= \frac{100 \times 2}{50 \times 10^{-2}}$$

$$= 400 \text{ AT/m}.$$

**P. 2.3.** A mild steel ring of mean circumference 50 cm and cross sectional area of 5 cm² has a coil of 250 turns wound uniformly around it.

(i) calculate the reluctance and

(ii) the current required to produce a flux of 700 μ Wb in the ring.

Take $\mu_r$ of mild steel as 380

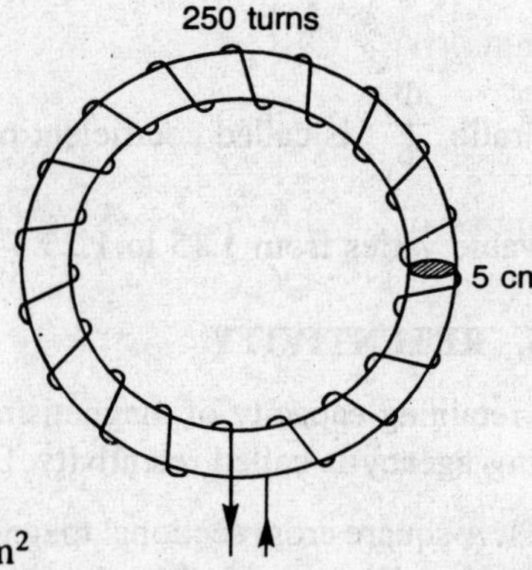


Fig. 2.8

**Solution:**

Given

Cross sectional area of ring (A) $= 5\ cm^2$

$= 5 \times 10^{-4}\ m^2$

Number of turns of coil (N) = 250

Length of the magnetic path (l) = Circumference of the ring

$\therefore$ (l) = 50 cm

$= 50 \times 10^{2}$ m

Flux established $\Phi = 700\ \mu wb$

$= 700 \times 10^{-6}$ Wb

Relative permeability $\mu_r = 380$

(i) Reluctance $S = \dfrac{1}{\mu_o \mu_r A}$ AT/Wb

where $\mu_0 = 4\pi \times 10^{-7}$ H/m

$$\therefore \quad S = \frac{50 \times 10^{-2}}{4\pi \times 10^{-7} \times 380 \times 5 \times 10^{-4}}$$

= 2094144 AT/Wb

(ii) We know that, Flux $= \dfrac{MMF}{Reluctance}$

$$\Phi = \frac{NI}{S}$$

$$\frac{\Phi S}{N} = I$$

= 5.86 amperes.

**P. 2.4.** An iron ring of mean diameter 15 cm is uniformly wound with 450 turns of wire. A current of 2 amperes when passed through the coil, establishes a flux density of 1.2 Wb/m² in the iron ring. Determine the value of relative permeability of iron.

**Solution:**

Given mean diameter (D) = 15 cm

Length (l) = Mean circumference $= \pi D$

$= \pi \times 15$ cm

$= \pi \times 15 \times 10^{-2}$ m

Number of turns (N) = 450

Current passing through the coil (I) = 2 amperes

Flux density (B) = 1.2 $wb/m^2$

$\mu_0 = 4\pi \times 10^{-7}$ H/m

Relative permeability = ?

We know that, $B = \mu_0 \mu_r H$

$$\frac{B}{\mu_o H} = \mu_r$$

where H is magnetic field strength

$$H = \frac{NI}{l} AT/m$$

$$= \frac{450 \times 2}{\pi \times 15 \times 10^{-2}} AT/m$$

$$\therefore \quad \mu_r = \frac{1.2}{4\pi \times 10^{-7} \times 450 \times 2 / \pi \times 15 \times 10^{-2}}$$

$$= 500$$

**P. 2.5.** A flux density of 1.2 $Wb/m^2$ is required in the 1mm air gap of an electromagnet having an iron path of 1.5 metre long. Calculate the mmf required. Given relative permeability of iron = 1600. Neglect leakage.

**Solution:**

*Iron path*

Given length ($l_{iron}$) = 1.5 m

$\mu_r$ of iron = 1600

Flux density (B) = 1.2 $Wb/m^2$

$\mu_0 = 4\pi \times 10^{-7}$ H/m

We know that, $H = \frac{NI}{l_{iron}}$

$\Rightarrow \quad lH = NI$

Where $$H = \frac{B}{\mu_o \mu_r} = \frac{1.2}{4\pi \times 10^{-7} \times 1600}$$

$$\therefore \text{Ampere turns required in iron path} = \frac{1.5 \times 1.2}{4\pi \times 10^{-7} \times 1600} \text{AT}$$

$$= 895.24 \text{ AT}$$

*Air gap* $(l_{air})$

Given length of air gap $= 1\text{mm}$

$= 1 \times 10^{-3}$ m

$\mu_r$ of air $= 1$

$\mu_0 = 4\pi \times 10^{-7}$ H/m

Flux density (B) $= 1.2$ Wb/M$^2$ (Neglecting leakage)

Ampere turns required $$= \frac{l_{air} \times B}{\mu_o \mu_r}$$

$$= \frac{1 \times 10^{-3} \times 1.2}{4\pi \times 10^{-7} \times 1} = 954.93 \text{ AT}$$

Total ampere turns = Ampere turns in iron path + Ampere turns in air gap

$= 895.24 + 954.93 = 1850.17$ AT

**P. 2.6.** A magnetic circuit has a uniform cross sectional area of 5 cm$^2$ and a length of 25 cm. A coil of 100 turns is wound uniformly over the magnetic circuit. When the current in the coil is 2 amperes, the total flux is 0.3 milli weber and when the current in the coil is 5 A, the total flux is 0.58 milli weber. For each value of current calculate,

(i) Magnetising force
(ii) Relative permeability
(iii) Magnetic flux density.

**Solution: (1st case)**

Given, cross sectional area (A) $= 5 \text{ cm}^2 = 5 \times 10^{-4} \text{ m}^2$

Length (l) $= 25 \text{ cm} = 25 \times 10^{-2}$ m

Number of turns (N) $= 100$

Current in the coil (I) $= 2$A

Total flux established ($\Phi$) $= 0.3$ mWb

$= 0.3 \times 10^{-3}$ Wb

Magnetic force (H) $= \dfrac{NI}{l} AT/m$

$$= \frac{100 \times 2}{25 \times 10^{-2}}$$

$$= 800 \text{ AT/m}$$

Total relative permeability $\mu_r = ?$

we have, $\Phi = \dfrac{NI}{l/\mu_o \mu_r A}$

$$\Phi = \frac{NI\mu_o\mu_r A}{l}$$

$$\frac{\Phi \times l}{NI\mu_o A} = \mu_r$$

$$= \frac{0.3 \times 10^{-3} \times 25 \times 10^{-2}}{100 \times 2 \times 4\pi \times 10^{-7} \times 5 \times 10^{-4}}$$

$$\mu_r = 596.83 \approx 597$$

∴ Flux density B $= \mu_0 \mu_r H$

$$= 4\pi \times 10^{-7} \times 597 \times 800 \text{ Wb/m}^2$$

$$= 0.6 \text{ Wb/m}^2$$

2nd case

$$A = 5 \times 10^{-4} \text{ m}^2$$

$$l = 25 \times 10^{-2} \text{ m}$$

$$N = 100$$

$$I = 5A$$

$$\Phi = 0.58 \times 10^{-3}$$

$$H = \frac{NI}{l}$$

$$= \frac{100 \times 5}{25 \times 10^{-2}}$$

$$= 2000 \text{ AT/m}$$

$$\mu_r = \frac{\Phi \times l}{NI\mu_o A}$$

$$= \frac{0.58 \times 10^{-3} \times 25 \times 10^{-2}}{100 \times 5 \times 4\pi \times 10^{-7} \times 5 \times 10^{-4}}$$

$$\mu_r = 461.55 \approx 462$$

$$B = \mu_0 \, \mu_r \, H \text{ Wb/m}^2$$

$$B = 4\pi \times 10^{-7} \times 462 \times 2000 \text{ Wb/m}^2$$

$$= 1.16 \text{ Wb/m}^2$$

**P. 2.7.** A magnetic ring has a mean circumference of 150 cm, area of cross section of 0.01 $m^2$ and is wound with 200 turns. A saw cut of 2 mm is made in the ring. Calculate the magnetising current required to produce a flux of 800 milli webers in the air gap. Assume relative permeability of iron as 600 and leakage factor as 1.2.

**Solution:**

Given

Area of cross section (A) $= 0.01 \text{ m}^2$

Length of air gap ($l_{air}$) $= 2\text{mm} = 2 \times 10^{-3}$ m

Relative permeability ($\mu_r$) = 1 (for air gap)

$\mu_0 = 4\pi \times 10^{-7}$ H/m

Magnetic flux in the air gap ($\Phi$) = 800 μWb

$= 800 \times 10^{-6}$ Wb.

Flux density in the air (B) $= \frac{\Phi}{A} = \frac{800 \times 10^{-6}}{0.01} = 0.08 \text{Wb/m}^2$

Magnetising force in the air gap (H) $= \frac{B}{\mu_o \mu_r} = \frac{0.08}{4\pi \times 10^{-7} \times 1} = 63661.9$ AT/m

Ampere turns for air gap $= H \times l_{air}$

$= 63661.9 \times 2 \times 10^{-3}$

$= 127.32$ AT

Ampere turns for iron path $= \frac{\Phi_i \times l_{iron}}{A \mu_o \mu_{r\,iron}}$

Where $\Phi_{iron} = (800 \times 10^{-6}) \times 1.2 = 9.6 \times 10^{-4}$ Wb.

$\mu_{r\,iron} = 600$

$l_{iron} = 150 \times 10^{-2}$ m

$$\therefore \text{ Ampere turns for iron path} = \frac{(800 \times 10^{-6}) \times (1.2) \times (150 \times 10^{-2})}{0.01 \times 4\pi \times 10^{-7} \times 600}$$

$$= 190.98$$

$$= 191 \text{ ampere turns}$$

Total ampere turns = Ampere turns for air + Ampere turns for iron path

$$= 127.32 + 191 = 318.32$$

Total No. of turns = 200

$$\therefore \text{ Magnetising current} = \frac{\text{Total ampere turns}}{200} = 1.59 \text{ A}$$

**P. 2.8.** An electromagnet is made of iron of square cross section with 5 cm side. A flux of 1.2 milli webers is required in the air gap. Find the number of ampere turns required. Take $\mu_r = 2000$. Neglect leakage and fringing. For further dimensions see Fig. 2.9.

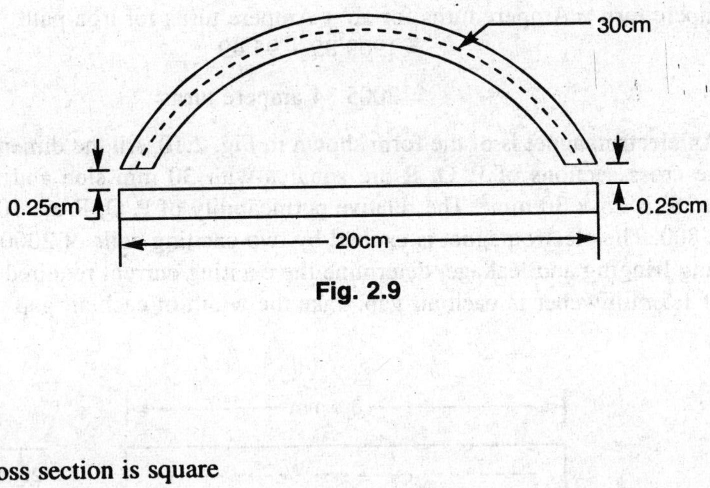


Fig. 2.9

**Solution:**

Given

Area of cross section is square

$\therefore \quad A = 5 \times 5 \text{ cm}^2$

$= 25 \text{ cm}^2$

$= 25 \times 10^{-4} \text{ m}^2$

$\Phi = 1.2$ milliweber

$= 1.2 \times 10^{-3}$ Wb

for air $\mu_r = 1$ ; $\mu_o = 4\pi \times 10^{-7}$

$l_{\text{air gap}} = 0.25 \times 10^{-2}$

Ampere turns in the air gap $= \dfrac{\Phi \times l_{air\ gap}}{\mu_o \times \mu_r \times A}$

$$= \frac{1.2 \times 10^{-3} \times 0.25 \times 10^{-2}}{4\pi \times 10^{-7} \times 1 \times 25 \times 10^{-4}} = 954.92$$

For two air gaps $= 2 \times (954.92) = 1909.85$ AT

For iron path $\mu_r = 2000$ ; $\mu_o = 4\pi \times 10^{-7}$

$$l_{iron} = (30 \times 10^{-2} + 20 \times 10^{-2}) = 50 \times 10^{-2}$$

Ampere turns in the iron path $= \dfrac{\Phi \times l_{iron}}{\mu_o \mu_r \times A}$

$$= \frac{1.2 \times 10^{-3} \times (50 \times 10^{-2})}{4\pi \times 10^{-7} \times 2000 \times 25 \times 10^{-4}} = 95.49$$

Total ampere turn = Ampere turns for air + Ampere turns for iron path

$= 1909.85 + 95.49$

$= 2005.34$ ampere turns

**P. 2.9.** An electromagnet is of the form shown in Fig. 2.10. All the dimensions are in mm. The cross sections of P, Q, R are squares with 30 mm side and that of iron armature 'S' is $25 \times 30$ mm$^2$. The relative permeability of P, Q, R are 1000 and that of 'S' is 800. The electromagnet is excited by two exciting coils of 2000 turns each. Neglecting fringing and leakage, determine the exciting current required to establish a flux of 1.5 milliweber in each air gap. Take the width of each air gap as 2 mm.

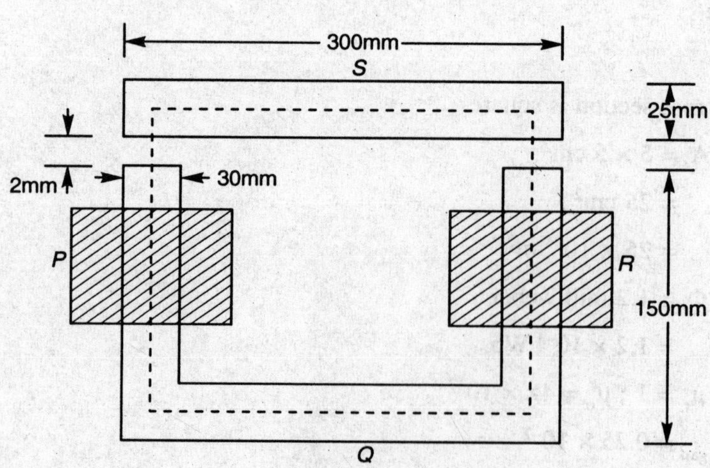


Fig. 2.10

**Solution:**

The mean flux path is shown by dotted line.

for air gap $\mu_r = 1$

$\Phi = 1.5 \times 10^{-3}$ Wb

$A = 30 \times 30 \times 10^{-6}$

$= 900 \times 10^{-6}$

$= 9 \times 10^{-4}$ m$^2$

$$B = \frac{\Phi}{A} = \frac{1.5 \times 10^{-3}}{9 \times 10^{-4}} = 1.67 \text{ Wb/m}^2$$

$$H = \frac{B}{\mu_o \mu_r} = \frac{1.67}{4\pi \times 10^{-7} \times 1} = 1328943.8$$

Ampere turns in the air gap = $H \times l_{air}$

where $l_{air\ gap} = (2 + 2) \times 10^{-3}$

∴ Ampere turns in air gap $= (1328943.8)\ (4 \times 10^{-3})$ ...(i)

$= 5315.77$

For iron armature ; $\mu_r = 800$

$\Phi = 1.5 \times 10^{-3}$ Wb

$A = (25 \times 30) \times 10^{-6}$ m$^2$ $= 750 \times 10^{-6}$

$$B = \frac{\Phi}{A} = \frac{1.5 \times 10^{-3}}{750 \times 10^{-6}} = 2 \text{ Wb/m}^2$$

$$H = \frac{B}{\mu_o \mu_r} = \frac{2}{4\pi \times 10^{-7} \times 800} = 1989.936 \text{ AT/m}$$

But, ampere turns $= H \times l_s$

where $l_s = 300 - (2 \times 15)$ mm

$= 270$ mm $= 270 \times 10^{-3}$

Ampere turns in the portion 'S' = $(1989.936) \times 270 \times 10^{-3}$ ...(ii)

$= 537.15$ AT

For the portion P,Q,R ; $\mu_r = 1000$

$\Phi = 1.5 \times 10^{-3}$

$A = 30 \times 30 \times 10^{-6}$

$$= 9 \times 10^{-4} \text{ m}^2$$

$$B = \frac{\Phi}{A} = \frac{1.5 \times 10^{-3}}{9 \times 10^{-4}} = 1.67 \text{ Wb/m}^2$$

$$H = \frac{B}{\mu_o \mu_r}$$

where, $\mu_r = 1000$

$$\therefore \quad H = \frac{1.67}{4\pi \times 10^{-7} \times 1000} = 1326.29 \text{ AT/m}$$

$\therefore$ Ampere turns $= H \times (I_P + I_Q + I_R)$

Where $I_P = 150 - 15 = 135 \text{ mm} = 135 \times 10^{-3} \text{ m}$

$I_Q = 300 - 30 = 270 \text{ mm} = 270 \times 10^{-3} \text{ m}$

$I_R = 150 - 15 = 135 \text{ mm} = 135 \times 10^{-3} \text{ m}$

$\therefore$ Ampere turns $= (1326.29) \times (135 + 270 + 135) \times 10^{-3}$

$= 716.197 \cong 716.2$ ...(iii)

Total ampere turns = (i) + (ii) + (iii) = 5315.77 + 537.15 + 716.2

= 6569.12

Total number of turns = 2 × 2000

$$\text{Exciting current} = \frac{6569.12}{2 \times 2000} \text{ amperes}$$

= 1.642 amperes

**P. 2.10.** A Magnetic core has the dimensions shown in Fig. 2.11.

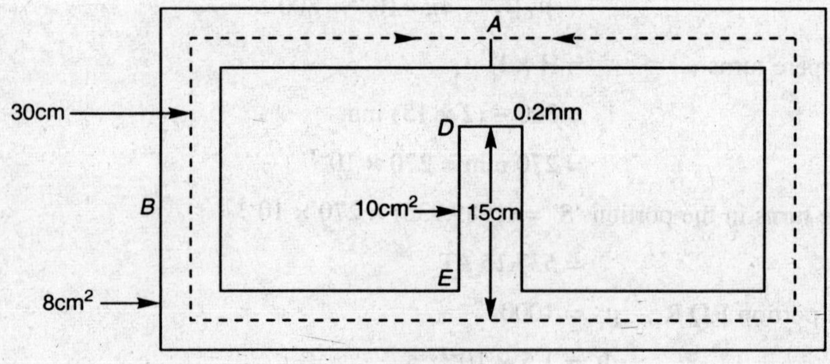


**Fig. 2.11**

| | |
|---|---|
| The length of portion DE | = 15 cm |
| Area of cross section | = 10 $cm^2$ |
| Length of portion ABE | = 30 cm |
| Area of cross section | = 8 $cm^2$ |
| Length of portion ACE | = 30 cm |
| Area of cross section | = 8 $cm^2$ |
| Length of air gap | = 0.2 mm |
| Air gap flux | = 1.2 m Wb |

The central limb is wound with 500 turns.

Calculate total ampere turns and the current required in the coil to produce the above flux.

The Data for B - H current for the core is

| B $Wb/m^2$ | 0.45 | 0.75 | 1.0 | 1.2 |
|---|---|---|---|---|
| H AT/m | 90 | 140 | 230 | 450 |

**Solution:**

For air gap $\mu_r = 1$ ; $\mu_0 = 4\pi \times 10^{-7}$

Length of air gap (l) $= 0.2 \times 10^{-3}$ m

Area of cross section (A) $= 10 \times 10^{-4}$ $m^2$

Flux ($\Phi$) $= 1.2 \times 10^{-3}$ Wb

$$B = \frac{\Phi}{A} = \frac{1.2 \times 10^{-3}}{10 \times 10^{-4}} = 1.2 \text{ Wb/m}^2$$

$$H = \frac{B}{\mu_o \mu_r} = \frac{1.2}{4\pi \times 10^{-7} \times 1} = 954929.66$$

∴ Ampere turns required in air gap $= H \times l = 190.985$ AT

$\approx 191$ ...(i)

For the central limb DE, $l = 15 \times 10^{-2}$ m

$\Phi = 1.2 \times 10^{-3}$

$A = (10) \times 10^{-4}$

$= 1 \times 10^{-3}$

$$B = \frac{\Phi}{A} = \frac{1.2 \times 10^{-3}}{1 \times 10^{-3}} = 1.2 \times 10^{-3} \text{ Wb/m}^2$$

'H' corresponding to $1.2 \times 10^{-3}$ $Wb/m^2$ from the table = 450 AT/m

$\therefore$ AT required = $450 \times 15 \times 10^{-2} = 67.5$ AT ...(ii)

For the portion ABE and portion ACE,

AT point 'A' the flux is divided into two equal parts

$\therefore$ Flux through each portion $= \dfrac{1.2 \times 10^{-3}}{2} = 0.6 \times 10^{-3}$ Wb

Area of cross section of each portion $= 8 \times 10^{-4}\ m^2$

$\therefore$ Flux density $= \dfrac{0.6 \times 10^{-3}}{8 \times 10^{-4}} = 0.75\ Wb/m^2$

The 'H' corresponding to $0.75\ Wb/m^2$ from the table = 140 AT/m

Length of portion ABC or ACE $= 30 \times 10^{-2}$ m

$\therefore$ Ampere turns required $= 140 \times 30 \times 10^{-2}$

= 42 AT ...(iii)

Total ampere turns = (i) + (ii) + (iii)

= 190 + 67.5 + 42

= 300.5 AT

Total number of turns = 500

$\therefore$ Exciting current = 0.601 A

## 2.17. MAGNETIC HYSTERESIS

Hysteresis means lagging. The lagging of flux density (B) behind the magnetising force (H) is called magnetic hysteresis. We know that the substances are generally classified as diamagnetic ($\mu < 1$ e.g. silver), paramagnetic ($\mu > 1$, e.g. aluminium, platinum) and ferromagnetic ($\mu >>> 1$, for eg. iron, cobalt, Nickel). The magnetisation characteristic curve of ferromagnetic substance is non-linear as shown in Fig. 2.12 below. Initially (Portion 0A), the curve raises rapidly, indicating rapid change in 'B' with relatively small change in 'H'. At portion AB, we can notice gradual decrease in the slope of the characteristic. At saturation, the slope of the curve becomes constant.

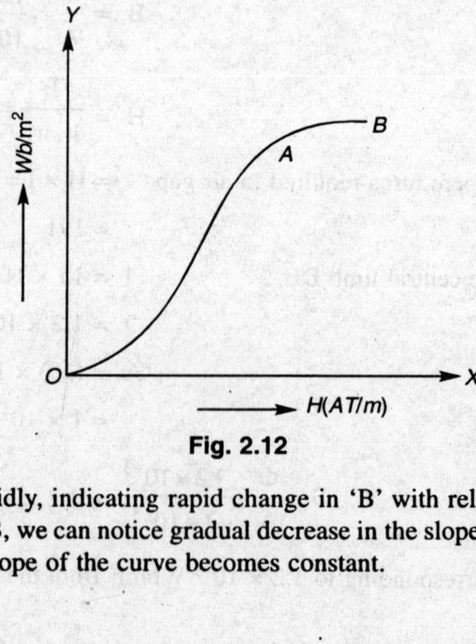


Fig. 2.12

## 2.18. MAGNETISATION CYCLE

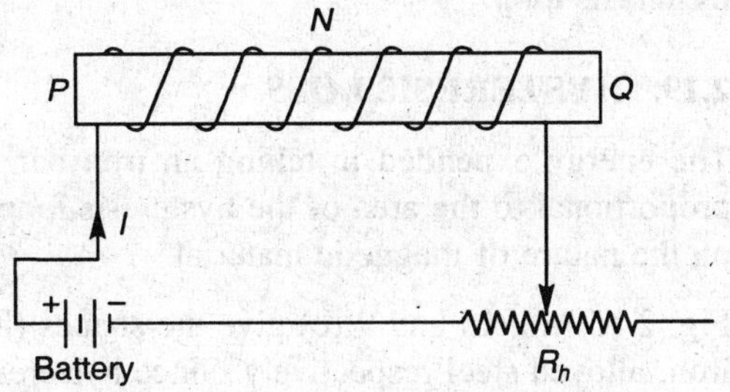


Fig. 2.13

Consider an unmagnetised iron bar 'PQ'. It can be magnetised by placing it in the magnetising force 'H' produced by the solenoid. This 'H' can be varied from zero to maximum value by varying the current with the help of the rheostat (Fig. 2.13) and corresponding B values can be noted. The relation between 'B' and 'H' can be plotted as shown in Fig. 2.14. The bar becomes saturated at 'E'. In other words when 'H' becomes $H_{max}$, the corresponding flux density will be $B_{max}$. If now 'H' is decreased to zero by decreasing the current with the help of the rheostat, 'B' will not decrease along EO but will decrease along EC. Also when 'H' is zero, 'B' is not becoming zero, instead it has a definite value OF. This value of 'B' is the measure of residual magnetism or remanence. This indicates that even on removing the magnetising force 'H', the bar is not getting completely demagnetised.

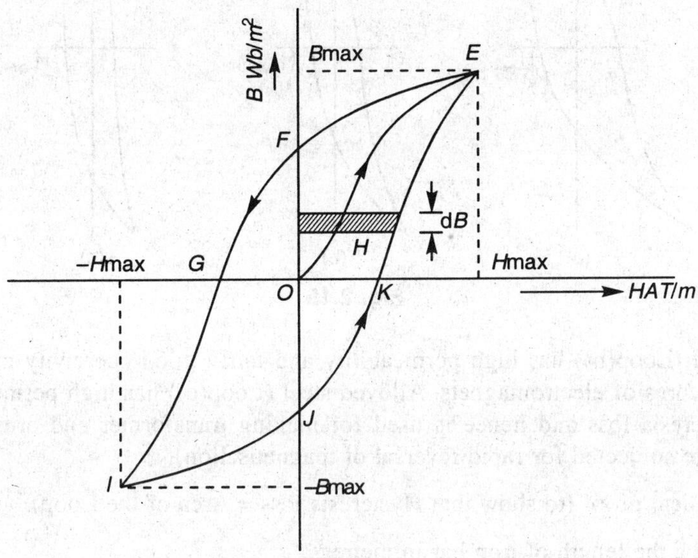


Fig. 2.14

To remove this residual magnetism, 'H' has to be applied in the reverse direction. When this value of 'H' becomes equal to 'OG', the flux density becomes zero at 'G'. This value of 'H' is called coercive force. If 'H' is further increased in the reverse direction, it reaches maximum value at 'I'. Plotting corresponding 'B' and 'H' values we get the curve'GI'. If we reduce 'H' to zero again, B-H plot will be given by the curve 'IJ'. When H = 0, B = OJ = the residual magnetism. If we reverse 'H' and gradually increase it to the same maximum, we will get the curve JKE.

Thus it is seen that 'B' always lags behind 'H'. This lagging of flux density 'B' with respect to magnetising force 'H' is called 'Hysteresis' and the complete loop is called hysteresis loop.

## 2.19. HYSTERESIS LOSS

The energy expended in taking an iron bar through one cycle of magnetization is proportional to the area of the hysteresis loop. The shape of hysteresis loop depends on the nature of magnetic material.

Fig. 2.15 (a), (b) and 9 (c) give the shapes (hysteresis loops) of hard steel, wrought iron, alloyed steel respectively. Since hysteresis loop measures the energy dissipated in the form of heat due to hysteresis, hard steel (Loop (a)) is not suitable for applications where rapid reversal of magnetisation takes place. Due to its high retentivity and coercivity, hard steel is used for making permanent magnets.

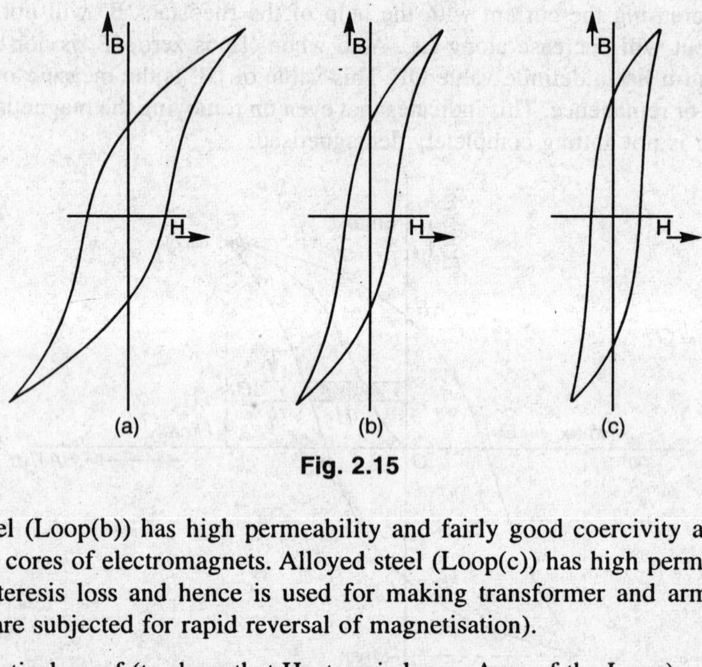


**Fig. 2.15**

Cast steel (Loop(b)) has high permeability and fairly good coercivity and hence is used for cores of electromagnets. Alloyed steel (Loop(c)) has high permeability and low hysteresis loss and hence is used for making transformer and armature cores (which are subjected for rapid reversal of magnetisation).

Mathematical proof (to show that Hysteresis loss = Area of the Loop).

Let 'l' be the length of iron bar in metres.

A be the area of cross section in square metres.

'N' be number of turns of the wire.

'B' be flux density in $Wb/m^2$

'$\Phi$' be flux in weber

'e' be induced emf in volts

'H' be magnetising force in AT/m

'W' be work done in joules.

When the current through the coil changes, flux also changes inducing an emf whose value is given by

$$e = \frac{N.d\Phi}{dt} \text{ volts (Neglect '–ve' sign)}$$

But $$B = \frac{Q}{A} \Rightarrow \Phi = B.A$$

$\therefore$ $$e = N.\frac{d(BA)}{dt}$$

$$e = NA.\frac{dB}{dt} \text{ volts}$$

Also we have $H = \frac{NI}{l} \Rightarrow I = \frac{H.l}{N}$

The electrical power = Rate of energy expended to maintain a current of 'i' amperes against the emf,e'

$$= e.i. \text{ watts}$$

$$= N.A. \frac{dB}{dt} \times \frac{Hl}{N} \text{ watts}$$

We know that

$$\text{Energy} = \text{Power} \times \text{Time}$$

$\therefore$ Energy in joules, (dw) spent in a time 'dt' = $A.l.H. \frac{dB}{dt} \times dt$ joules

$\therefore$ $$dw = A.l.H \text{ db joules.}$$

Thus the total workdone during

one complete cycle of hysteresis $= W = \int dw = \int A.l.H.dB$

$$= A.l \int HdB \text{ joules}$$

But $\int$ HdB is the area of complete Hysteresis Loop (Fig. 2.14)

$\therefore$ W = A.l. (Area of loop) joules.

But A.l = Volume of the magnetic material in $m^3$

$\therefore$ Work done/cycle/$m^3$ = (Area of loop) joules.

### 2.20. STEINMETZ's LAW

Steinmetz experimentally found that hysteresis loss can be approximately expressed as below.

Hysteresis loss = $\eta \; B^{k}_{max} \; f \; v$ watts

where $\eta$ is a constant called steinmetz 's' hysteresis coefficient which depends upon the magnetic material.

K = 1.6 for $0.1 < B_{max} \; 1.2 \; Wb/m^2$

K > 1.6for $B_{max} < 0.1 \; Wb/m^2$

$B_{max} > 1.2 \; Wb/m^2$

when 'V' is volume of the magnetic material in $m^3$

'f' is frequency of magnetic reversal in reversals/second.

Hysteresis loss can be reduced by selecting material for core such as special silicon steels which have a low hysteresis coefficient and high electrical resistivity.

## 2.21. EDDY CURRENT LOSS

Whenever a conducting material moves in a magnetic field, the material cuts the magnetic flux. According to the laws of electromagnetic induction, an emf is induced in the conductor. This emf sets up large currents throughout the solid mass of the material. These currents resemble the eddy currents.

The heat liberated by eddy currents is considered as a loss as it does not serve any purpose. In a solid core, a direct path is offered for the flow of eddy current whereas a laminated core offers broken path. As the laminated core has much less cross section, it offers higher resistance for the flow of eddy current. Thus eddy current loss can be minimised by using a laminated core.

P. 2.11. A magnetic material has the following data:

Area of hysteresis loop = $50 cm^2$

X-axis scale 1cm = 200 AT/m

Y-axis scale 1cm = $0.2 \; Wb/m^2$

Frequency (f) = 50Hz

Density of the material = $10 \; g/cm^3$

Calculate the hysteresis loss in joules/s

**Solution:**

We know that the hysteresis loss = Area of hysteresis loop $J/m^3$/cycle

$= 50 \times 200 \times 0.2 \; J/m^3/\text{cycle}$

Volume of 1kg of material $= \dfrac{\text{Mass}}{\text{Density}} = \dfrac{1000 \text{ gm}}{10 \text{ gm}/\text{cm}^3} = \dfrac{1000}{10} \text{cm}^3$

$= \dfrac{1000}{10} \times 10^{-6} \; m^3$

$= 10^{-4} \; m^3$

∴ Hysteresis loss = $(50 \times 200 \times 0.2) \times 10^{-4}$ J/cycle

Also hysteresis loss = $(50 \times 200 \times 0.2) \times 10^{-4} \times 50$ J/s

= 10 J/s

## REVISION FORMULA

$B = \frac{\Phi}{A}$ Wb/m²; f = B.A webers

where B is Flux density in weber/metre²

Φ is Flux in webers

A is area of cross section in metre²

$B = \mu_o \mu_r H$ Wb/m² ; $H = \frac{B}{\mu_o \mu_r}$

Where 'H' is magnetic field strength in newton/weber

$\mu_r$ = relative permeability

$\mu_0 = 4\pi \times 10^{-7}$ H/m

$H = \frac{F}{\Phi}$ N / Wb

where F is the force in newtons

$H = \frac{NI}{l} \frac{AT}{M}$

where 'NI' is the magneto motive force in ampere turns

$\Phi = \frac{NI}{S}$ webers

where 'S' is the reluctance in AT/Wb

$S = \frac{1}{\mu_o \mu_r A}$ AT/Wb

where 'A' is the area of cross section

For composite magnetic circuit

$$\Phi = \frac{NI}{\frac{l_1}{\mu_o \mu_{r1} A_1} + \frac{l_2}{\mu_o \mu_{r2} A_2} + \frac{l_3}{\mu_o \mu_{r3} A_3}} \text{ Wb}$$

$W_b = \eta B_{max}^{1.6}$ f.v. watts

where $W_h$ = hysteresis loss in watts

$B_{max}$ = maximum flux density in $Wb/m^2$

f = frequency of magnetic reversals in reversals/second

$\eta$ = steinmetz's hysteresis coefficient.

## REVIEW QUESTIONS

1. Define the following:
   (a) Magnetic field (b) Magnetic flux
   (c) Permeability (d) Magnetic field strength
   (e) Magnetic force (f) Reluctance
2. What are the similarities and differences between electric and magnetic circuits ?
3. Derive an expression for Ohm's law of magnetism.
4. What do you understand by magnetic leakage?
5. Explain the following:
   (a) Hysteresis loss
   (b) Eddy current loss
6. Prove that the hysteresis loss is equal to the area of hysteresis loop.

## TWO MARKS QUESTIONS AND ANSWERS

1. *What is magnetic field ?*

   The region around which the magnetic lines of force act is called magnetic field.

2. *Define Magnetic flux density.*

   The magnetic flux passing through unit cross section is called flux density. It is denoted by 'B'. Its unit is weber/$m^2$.

3. *Define Magnetic field strength.*

   The force experienced by unit north pole placed at that point is called magnetic field strength. It is denoted by 'H'. Its unit is newtons/weber.

4. *Define magnetomotive force.*

   It is given by the work done in moving a unit north pole once round the entire magnetic circuit.

5. *What is reluctance ?*

   It is the property of a magnetic material by which it opposes the establishment of magnetic flux.

6. *What is leakage flux and useful flux ?*

   The flux that follows an undesired path is called leakage flux. To utilise the magnetic flux established by the magnetic material, we provide an air gap. The flux in the air gap is called useful flux. The flux which does not pass through air gap cannot be utilised hence it is considered as leakage flux.

7. *What is retentivity ?*
   The retaining capacity of magnetism of a magnetic material after the removal of inducing agency is called retentivity.
8. *Write the expression for Ohm's law of magnetism.*

$$\Phi = \frac{NI}{S}$$

   where $\Phi$ is the magnetic flux in webers
   NI is the magnetomotive force in ampere turns
   S is the reluctance in AT/Wb
9. *Write two similarities between magnetic and electric circuits.*

| *Magnetic circuit* | *Electric circuit* |
|---|---|
| 1. Magnetomotive force | Electromotive force |
| 2. Reluctance | Resistance |

10. *Write two differences between magnetic and electric circuits*
    1. In the electric circuit, electric current flows whereas in a magnetic circuit the magnetic flux does not flow.
    2. The reluctance of the magnetic circuit varies with flux density, whereas the resistance remains practically constant with current strength.

## EXERCISE PROBLEMS

**P. 2.1:** A iron magnetic circuit has a uniform cross sectional area of 5 $cm^2$ and a length of 25 cm. A coil of 120 turns is wound uniformly over the magnetic circuit. When the current in the coil is 5 A and total flux is 9.6 milli weber calculate

(i) Magnetic field strength
(ii) Relative permeability.

(Ans: 2400 AT/m ; 6366.19)

**P. 2.2:** A circular iron ring of relative permeability 650 and diametre 20 cm is wound with a coil of 300 turns. An air gap 1mm width is cut in it. The area of cross section of the iron is 3.6 $cm^2$. Calculate the current required in the coil to send a flux of 0.5 milliweber through the air. Neglect ringing.

(Ans: 8.8 A)

**P. 2.3:** An iron ring 100 cm mean circumference and of circular cross section 5 $cm^2$ has a saw cut of 2 mm length. It is wound with 500 turns of wire. If 0.5 milliweber. flux exists across the air gap, what will be the value of the exciting current? Take coefficient of leakage as 1.26 and relative permeability of iron as 500.

(Ans: 7.1937 A)

**P. 2.4:** The hysteresis loss of a transformer at a flux density of 1.2 $w/m^2$ is 150 watts at 50H. What will be the loss when flux density is reduced to 1wb/$m^2$ at 45 Hz ?

(Ans: 199.84 W)

**P. 2.5:** The flux in the air gap of mild still frame is 1300 Wb., with an exciting coil of 100 turns wound on central limb. The cross sectional area of central limb is 8 $cm^2$ and that of each outer limb is 5 $cm^2$. The air gap is 1mm and mean length of various paths are shown in Fig. 2.16. Calculate the exciting current. The data given are

H for B = 1.625 $wb/m^2$ is 3800 AT/m

H for B = 1.3 $wb/m^2$ is 850 AT/m

(Ans: I = 2.1 A)

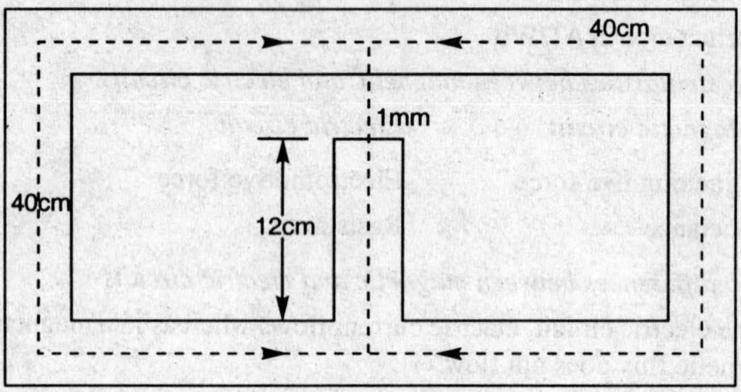


Fig. 2.16

*Chapter 3*

# ELECTROMAGNETISM

In 1831 Faraday discovered that the emf can be produced by electromagnetic induction. This principle is widely used in commercial generation of power.

## 3.1. ELECTROMAGNETIC INDUCTION

Whenever magnetic flux linking with the coil changes, an emf is induced in the coil. The phenomenon is called electromagnetic induction. The change in flux linkage is obtained by three methods.

**Method 1**

Consider a coil wound for a few number of turns of copper wire. When a magnet is moved towards the coil, (Fig. 3.1), we can observe the deflection in the galvanometer connected across the coil, indicating flow of current. This current is due to the induced emf in the coil.

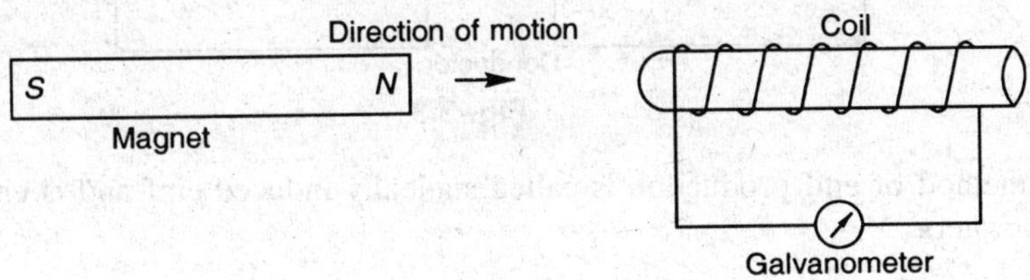


**Fig. 3.1**

If now the magnet movement is stopped, the pointer (of the galvanometer) will show zero-deflection. Thus, even though the flux is still linking with the coil, since there is no change in the value of flux, the emf induced in the coil is zero. If the magnet moves with higher speed, or if the number of turns of coil is increased or if we use a stronger magnet; in all the three cases we can observe greater deflection of the pointer.

**Method 2**

The emf can also be induced in the coil, by moving the coil and keeping the magnet stationary (Fig. 3.2).

These two methods of producing emf are called dynamic methods and are employed in generators. The induced emf is called dynamically induced emf.

**Method 3**

Here both conductor and magnet are kept stationary. The magnetic lines of force are varied with the help of the arrangement shown in Fig. 3.3.

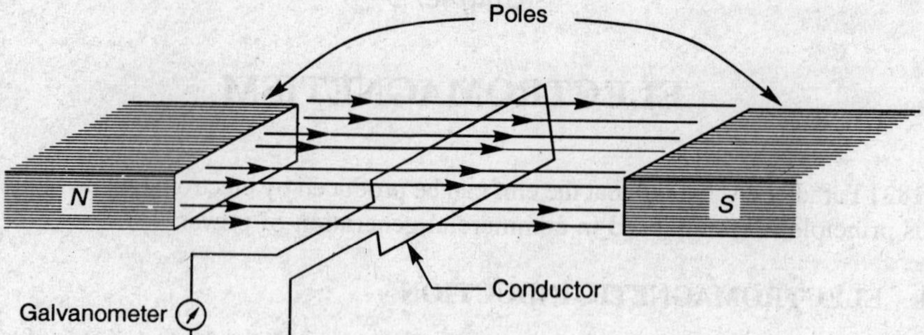


**Fig. 3.2**

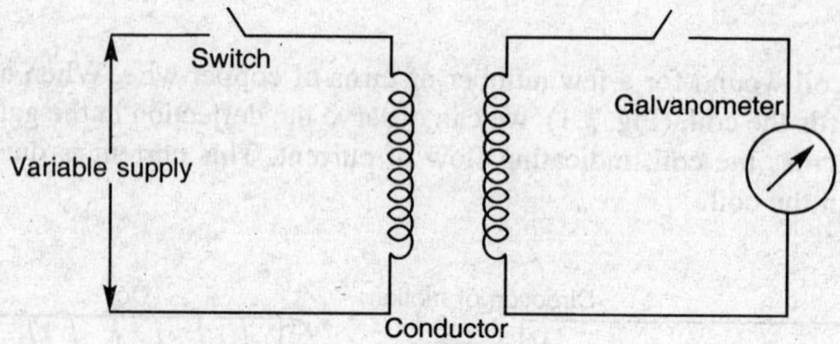


**Fig. 3.3**

This method of emf production is called statically induced emf and is employed in transformers.

Thus we can sum up that

1. Mere magnetic flux linkage cannot induce emf. There must be change in the magnetic flux linking with the coil to induce emf.
2. The magnitude of emf induced depends upon relative motion between coil and field strength of magnetic field and also on the number of turns of the coil.

## 3.2. LAWS OF ELECTROMAGNETIC INDUCTION

**Faraday's laws of electromagnetic induction**

There are two laws.

**First Law:** Whenever magnetic flux linking with the coil changes an emf is induced in the coil (or) whenever a conductor cuts magnetic flux, an emf is induced in the conductor.

**Second Law:** The magnitude of the induced emf is equal to the product of number of turns of the coil and the rate of change of flux.

Consider a coil of 'N' turns.

Let the initial value of flux be '$\Phi_1$' Wb.

and the final value of flux be '$\Phi_2$' Wb

Let 'e' emf induced in volts and let 't' be time during which the change in flux takes place. According to Faraday's Laws of electromagnetic induction.

$$e = \frac{N(\Phi_2 - \Phi_1)}{t} \text{ volts}$$

The above equation can also be written in the differential form as below:

$$e = N.\frac{d\Phi}{dt} \text{ volts} \quad ...(3.1)$$

**LENZ'S LAW**

This gives the direction of induced emf. According to this law, the direction of emf induced is such that, it opposes the very cause of production of it.

$$\therefore \quad e = -N\frac{d\Phi}{dt} \text{ volts} \quad ...(3.2)$$

**P. 3.1.** Calculate the emf induced in a coil of 200 turns, when the flux linking with it changes from 1 milli weber in 0.1 second.

**Solution:**

Given number of turns (N) = 200

Initial value of flux ($\Phi_1$) = 1 milli weber

= $1 \times 10^{-3}$ weber

Final value of flux ($\Phi_2$) = $3 \times 10^{-3}$ Wb

$\therefore$ $d\Phi = \Phi_2 - \Phi_1 = 2 \times 10^{-3}$ weber

Time for the change in value of flux = 0.1 s

$$\therefore \quad e = -N.\frac{d\Phi}{dt} = -200 \times \frac{2 \times 10^{-3}}{0.1}$$

= 4 volts (neglecting negative sign)

**The expression for dynamically induced emf** can also be given as below.

In Fig. 3.2 consider a condition where the conductor of length 'l' metres cuts the magnetic flux at right angles. Let 'dx' be the distance moved by the conductor in a time 'dt'.

Then the area swept by it = l. dx

If 'B' is the flux density in Wb/m$^2$

Then the flux cut by the conductor = l. dx. B

From equation 3.1 (for a single turn coil, N = 1) we have

$$e = l.\frac{d\Phi}{dt} = l.\frac{B.I.dx}{dt} = B.l\left(\frac{dx}{dt}\right) = B.l.v$$

Where $\frac{dx}{dt} = v =$ velocity

If the conductor moves at an angle 'θ' with the direction of magnetic lines of flux, the value of induced emf can be written as follows

$$e = B.l.v.\ \text{Sin}\ \theta \text{ volts} \qquad ...(3.3)$$

where e = emf induced in volts

B = flux density in $Wb/m^2$

l = length of the conductor in metres

v = velocity of the conductor m/s

θ = angle between conductor and magnetic lines of force in degrees

**P. 3.2.** Calculate the emf induced in 2 metre long straight conductor when it is moved at a velocity of 4 m/s at right angles to a uniform magnetic flux of $1.2 Wb/m^2$.

**Solution:**

Given

Flux density (B) = 1.2 $Wb/m^2$

Velocity of the conductor (V) = 4 m/s

Length of the conductor (l) = 2 m

Angle between conductor and lines of force (θ) = 90°

∴ emf induced (e) = B.l.V. sin θ

= 1.2 × 2 × 4 × sin 90°

= 1.2 × 2 × 4 × 1

= 9.6 volts

## 3.3. FLEMING'S RULES

**Fleming's Right hand rule"** is used to determine the direction of emf induced (current). According to this rule, if we keep our thumb, first finger (or) (forefinger) and middle finger of the right hand at right angles to one another (Fig. 3.4) and if the first finger represents the direction of magnetic lines of flux, the thumb indicates the direction of motion of the conductor, then the middle finger will indicate the direction of induced emf. (current). This rule is used in generators.

**Fleming's Left hand rule:** This is used to determine the direction of the force acting on current carrying conductor placed in a magnetic field. We know that, whenever a conductor of length 'l' metres carrying a current of 'I' ampere is placed in a magnetic

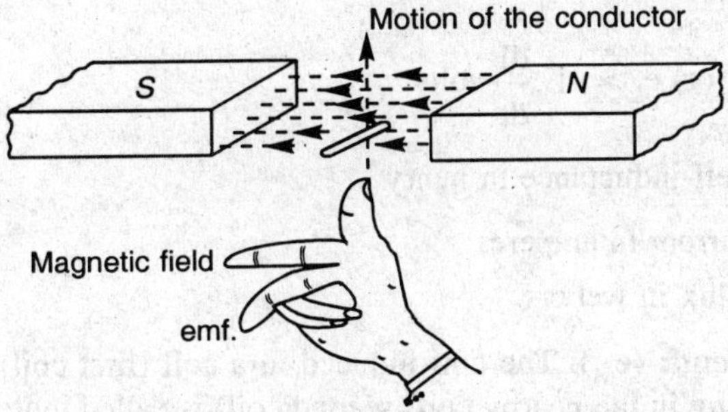


Fig. 3.4

field of flux density B Wb/m$^2$, a force 'F' is exerted on the conductor (F = BIl sinθ N where 'θ' is the angle between the conductor and field). The direction of this force can be found using Fleming's left hand rule. According to this rule if we keep our thumb, first finger (or) (forefinger) and middle finger of left hand at right angles to one another (Fig. 3.5) and if the first finger represents direction of magnetic field, the middle finger indicates the direction of current, then the thumb will indicate the direction of force acting on the conductor (or) (direction of motion of the conductor due to this force). This rule is used in motor.

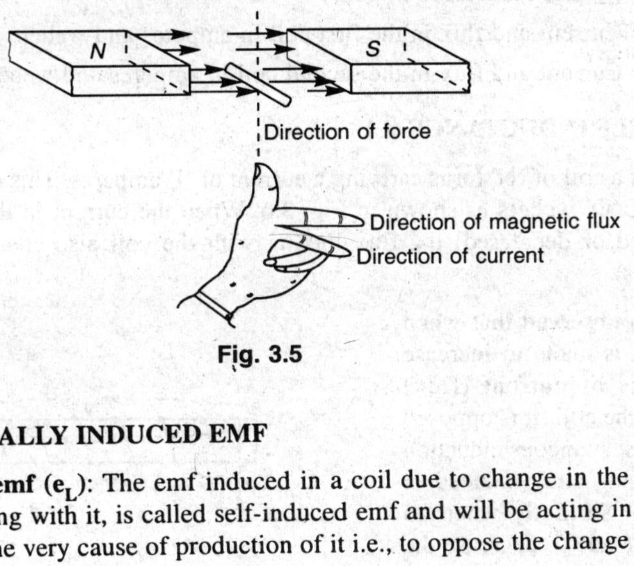


Fig. 3.5

### 3.4. STATICALLY INDUCED EMF

**Self induced emf ($e_L$)**: The emf induced in a coil due to change in the value of its own flux linking with it, is called self-induced emf and will be acting in such a way as to oppose the very cause of production of it i.e., to oppose the change in the value of flux.

It is denoted by '$e_L$' and is measured in volts

$$e_L = -N.\frac{d\Phi}{dt} \text{ volts} \quad ...(3.5)$$

$$\text{(or) } e_L = -L.\frac{dI}{dt} \text{ volts} \quad ...(3.6)$$

where 'L' is the self-inductance in henry

'I' is the current in amperes

'Φ' is the flux in webers.

**Mutual induced emf: ($e_M$):** The emf induced in a coil (first coil) due to change in value of flux linking in the nearby coil (second coil) is called mutually induced emf. Vice versa also holds good.

$$e_{M1} = -M.\frac{dI_2}{dt} = -N_1\frac{d\Phi_2}{dt} \quad ...(3.7)$$

$$e_{M2} = -M.\frac{dI_1}{dt} = -N_2\frac{d\Phi_1}{dt} \quad ...(3.8)$$

$e_{M1}$ = Mutual emf induced in the first coil in volts

$e_{M2}$ = Mutual emf induced in the second coil in volts

M = Mutual inductance in henry

$I_1$, $\Phi_1$ = Current and flux in the first coil in amperes and webers respectively

$I_2$, $\Phi_2$ = Current and flux in the second coil in amperes and webers respectively

## 3.5. SELF INDUCTANCE (L)

Consider a coil of 'N' turns carrying a current of 'I' amperes. This current establishes a flux of 'Φ' webers as shown in Fig. 3.6. When the current in the coil is changed (increased or decreased) the flux linking with the coil also changes (increases or decreases).

It is also observed that when an effort is made to increase the value of current (flux) through the coil, it is opposed by the instantaneous induction of opposing emf (induced in the coil). Similarly when an effort is made to decrease the value of current (flux) through the coil, it is also opposed by the instantaneous induction of opposing emf (induced in the coil).

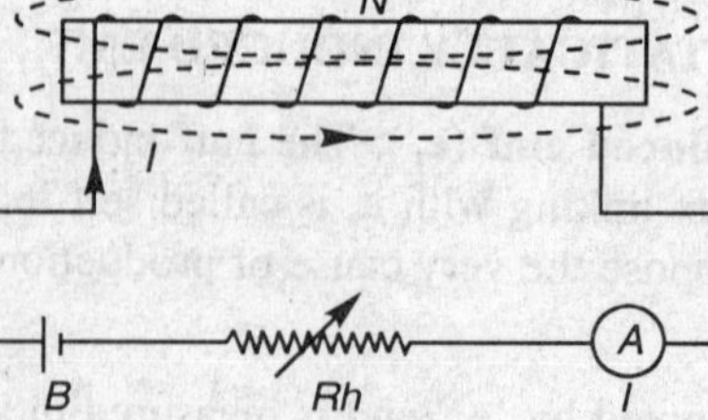


Fig. 3.6

This property of the coil by which it opposes change in value of current or flux through it due to the production of self-induced emf is called self inductance and is measured in terms or coefficient of self-inductance (L). Its unit is henry. This property is analogous to electrical inertia.

**Definition of 'L':** A coil is said to have one Henry of self inductance if a current of one ampere flowing through it produces 1 Wb-turn flux linkage.

Thus $$L = \frac{N\Phi}{I} \text{ henry} \qquad \text{...(3.9)}$$

We know that $$\Phi = \frac{NI}{S}$$

$$\therefore \quad L = \frac{N}{I}\frac{(NI)}{S} = \frac{N^2}{S}$$

$$\therefore \quad L = \frac{N^2}{S} \qquad \text{...(3.10)}$$

where S = Reluctance given by $S = \dfrac{l}{\mu_o \mu_r A}$ AT/Wb

Expression for self-induced emf ($e_L$)

We have $$L = \frac{N\Phi}{I}$$

$$\Rightarrow \quad LI = N\Phi$$

$$\Rightarrow -LI = -N\Phi$$

Differentiating the above eq. on both sides with respect to 't'

$$-L\frac{dI}{dt} = -N.\frac{d\Phi}{dt}$$

But according to Faraday's laws of electromagnetic induction

$$-N.\frac{d\Phi}{dt} = \text{induced emf} \quad \text{(from eq. 3.5)}$$

$\therefore$ The self-induced emf $$e_L = -L\frac{dI}{dt} \text{ volts} \qquad \text{...(3.11)}$$

$$\Rightarrow \quad L = -\frac{e_L}{\frac{dI}{dt}} \text{ henry} \qquad \text{...(3.12)}$$

If $e_L = 1$ volt and $\frac{dI}{dt} = 1$, then L = 1 henry

Thus a coil is said to have a self inductance of 1 henry, if current through it changes at the rate of 1 A/sec. inducting an emf of 1 volt in it.

**P. 3.3.** A coil of 1500 turns carries a current of 10 amperes, establishing a flux of 0.5 milli webers. Find the inductance of the coil.

**Solution:**

Given

No. of turns (N) $= 1500$

Current through the coil (i) $= 10$ amperes

Flux established ($\Phi$) $= 0.5 \times 10^{-3}$ Wb

Inductance (L) $= \frac{N\Phi}{I}$

$$= \frac{1500 \times 0.5 \times 10^{-3}}{10}$$

$= 0.075$ henry.

**P. 3.4.** An air cored solenoid of length is 30 cm has a cross sectional area of 5 cm$^2$. It is wound with 400 turns of coil. Calculate its self inductance.

**Solution:**

Given

aircored solenoid ⇒ $\mu_r = 1$

No. of turns (N) $= 400$

length (l) $= 30$ cm

$= 30 \times 10^{-2}$ m

Cross sectional area (A) $= 5$ cm$^2$

$= 5 \times 10^{-4}$ m$^2$

Self inductance $= L = \frac{N^2}{S}$

where $s = \frac{l}{\mu_o \mu_r A} = \frac{30 \times 10^{-2}}{4\pi \times 10^{-7} \times 1 \times 5 \times 10^{-4}}$ AT/m

$= 4.77 \times 10^8$ AT/m

$$\therefore \qquad L = \frac{400 \times 400}{4.77 \times 10^8}$$

$$= 3.35 \times 10^{-4} \text{ henry.}$$

**P. 3.5.** An air cored torroidal ring with mean diameter of 25 cm and a circular cross sectional diameter of 4 cm is wound uniformly with 500 turns of copper wire of 1mm diameter. Calculate the inductance of the coil. Also calculate the emf induced in it when the current of 5A is reversed in 50 milli seconds.

**Solution:**

Given

Air cored torroidal ring $\Rightarrow \mu_r = 1$

Mean dia (D) $= 25 \times 10^{-2}$ m

$\therefore$ length (l) $= \pi D$

$= \pi \times 25 \times 10^{-2}$

$= 0.785$ m.

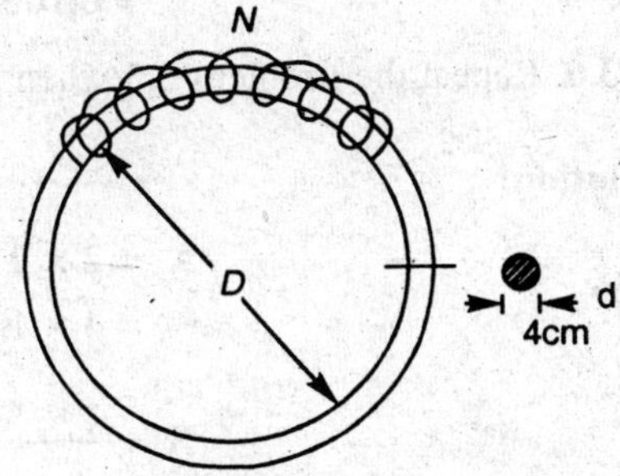


Fig. 3.7

No. of turns (N) $= 500$

Cross sectional diameter (d) $= 4 \times 10^{-2}$

Cross sectional area (A) $= \pi\,(d^2/4)$

$$= \frac{\pi \times 4 \times 10^{-2} \times 4 \times 10^{-2}}{4} = 1.256 \times 10^{-3} \text{ m}^2$$

Self inductance (L) $= \dfrac{N^2}{s}$

Where $s = \dfrac{1}{\mu_o \mu_r A}$

$$= \frac{0.785}{4\pi \times 10^{-7} \times 1 \times 1.256 \times 10^{-3}}$$

$$= 49.71 \times 10^7 \text{ AT/Wb}$$

$$\therefore \qquad L = \frac{500 \times 500}{49.71 \times 10^7} \text{ henry}$$

$$L = 5.029 \times 10^{-4} \text{ henry}$$

given $\qquad dI = 5 - (-5) = 10$ A

$$dt = 50 \times 10^{-3} \text{ s}$$

$$\frac{dI}{dt} = \frac{10}{50 \times 10^{-3}} = 200 \text{ A/s}$$

∴ Induced emf $e_L = L\frac{dI}{dt}$ (Neglecting –ve sign)

$$= 5.29 \times 10^{-4} \times 200$$

$$= 0.1005 \text{ volts.}$$

**P. 3.6.** Repeat the problem 3.5 when the cross section is a square of side 2 cm.

**Solution:**

∴ $A = 2 \times 2 \times 10^{-4} \text{ m}^2$

$$= 4 \times 10^{-4} \text{ m}^2$$

$$S = \frac{0.785}{4\pi \times 10^{-7} \times 1 \times 4 \times 10^{-4}} = 1.56 \times 10^9 \text{ AT/m}$$

$$L = \frac{500 \times 500}{1.56 \times 10^9} = 1.6 \times 10^{-4} \text{ henry}$$

∴ $e_L = 1.6 \times 10^{-4} \times 200$

$$= 0.032 \text{ volts.}$$

**P. 3.7.** Repeat the problem 3.5 when the current in the coil

(i) rises from 0 to 5 amperes in 0.05 seconds.

(ii) increasing at the rate of 400 A/second.

**Solution:**

(i) From P. 3.5 we have L = $5.029 \times 10^{-4}$ henry

Induced emf $= e_L = L\frac{dl}{dt}$

Given

$$dl = 5\text{-}0 = 5 \text{ A}$$

$$dt = 0.05 \text{ s}$$

∴ $\frac{dl}{dt} = \frac{5}{0.05} = 100 \text{ A/s}$

∴ $e_L = 5.029 \times 10^{-4} \times 100$

$$= 0.05029 \text{ volts.}$$

(ii) From P. 3.5 we have L = $5.029 \times 10^{-4}$ henry

Induced emf $e_L = L\dfrac{dl}{dt}$

Given $\dfrac{dI}{dt} = 400$ A / s

$\therefore$ $e_L = 5.029 \times 10^{-4} \times 400$

$= 0.2012$ volts.

### 3.6. MUTUAL INDUCTANCE (M)

Consider two coils 'A' and 'B' having $N_1$ and $N_2$ number f turns respectively placed close to each other as shown in Fig. 3.8. Let $I_1$ be the current in amperes carried by coil A establishing a flux of '$\Phi_1$' webers in it.

Now since coil 'B' is closer to coil 'A', some of the flux established by coil 'A' will be linking with coil 'B'. Thus, a change in current or flux in coil 'A' will cause a change in the flux linking with the coil 'B'. This change in the value of flux or current in coil 'A' will not only produce an emf in the coil 'A' itself (due to property of self inductance) but also produce an emf in coil 'B'. This emf induced in the coil 'B' is called mutually induced emf.

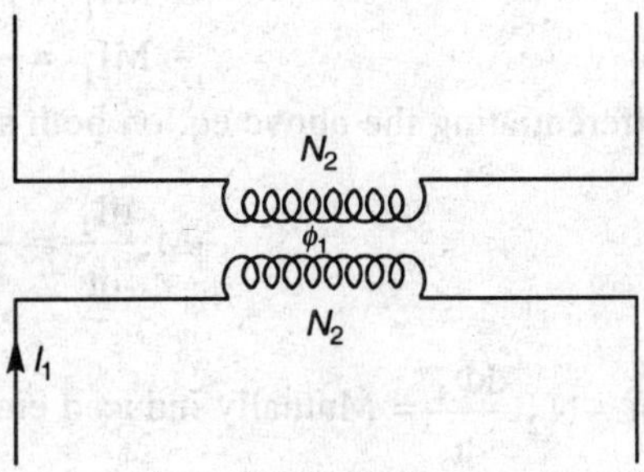


Fig. 3.8

Thus mutual inductance (M) is the ability of the first coil to produce an emf in the nearby coil (second coil) due to change of current or flux in the first coil. The reciprocal action also holds good, i.e. whenever the current or flux in the second coil changes, an emf is induced in the first (nearby coil). This ability is measured in terms of coefficient of mutual inductance (M). Its unit is henry.

The coefficient of mutual inductance between two coils is defined as the weber turns in one coil due to a current of one ampere in the other coil.

Thus $$M = \frac{N_2\Phi_1}{I_1} \qquad ...(3.13)$$

If $N_2 \Phi_1 = 1$ Wb turn and $I_1 = 1$ ampere then M = 1 henry. Hence two coils are said to have a mutual inductance of 1 henry, if one ampere current flowing in the first coil produces 1 Wb turn flux linkage in the second coil.

We know that $\Phi = \dfrac{NI}{S} \Rightarrow \Phi_1 = \dfrac{N_1 I_1}{S}$

Substituting this in eq. 3.13 we get

$$M = \frac{N_2}{I_1}\left(\frac{N_1 I_1}{s}\right)$$

$$\therefore \quad M = \frac{N_1 N_2}{s} \text{ henry} \qquad ...(3.14)$$

where $s = \text{Reluctance} = \dfrac{l}{\mu_o \mu_r A}$ AT/Wb

**Expression for Mutual induced emf ($e_M$)**

We have $M = \dfrac{N_2 \Phi_1}{I_1}$

$$MI_1 = N_2 \Phi_1$$

$$-MI_1 = -N_2 \Phi_1$$

Differentiating the above eq. on both sides with respect to 't'

$$-M.\frac{dI_1}{dt} = -N_2 \frac{d\Phi_1}{dt}$$

But $-N_2 \dfrac{d\Phi_1}{dt}$ = Mutually induced emf in the second coil ($e_{M2}$)

$$\therefore \quad e_{M2} = M.\frac{dI_1}{dt} \qquad ...(3.15)$$

If $\dfrac{dI_1}{dt} = 1$ A/s and $e_{M2} = 1$ volt then M = 1 henry

Hence, two coils are said to have a mutual inductance of one henry, if current through the one coil changes at the rate of 1 A/s inducing an emf of 1 volt in the other.

From eq. 3.13 we have, $M = \dfrac{N_2 \Phi_1}{I_1}$

Here the assumption is that the entire flux '$\Phi_1$' produced by coil 'A' is linking with coil 'B'. If it is not the case then the above equation can be modified as:

$$M = \frac{N_2 K_1 \Phi_1}{I_1}$$

where '$K_1$' is percentage of '$\Phi_1$' linking with coil 'B'.

Similarly we can write,

$$M = \frac{N_1\Phi_2}{I_2} \text{ or } \frac{N_1K_2\Phi_2}{I_2} \text{ henry} \quad ...(3.17)$$

and $$e_{M1} = -M\frac{dI_2}{dt} \text{ volts} \quad ...(3.18)$$

where '$I_2$' is the current carried by coil 'B' establishing a flux of '$\Phi_2$' webers in it and '$e_{M1}$' is mutually induced emf in the coil 'A' due to the change of current or flux in the coil 'B'.

P. 3.8 Two coils having 50 and 400 turns respectively are wound side by side on a closed iron circuit of cross section of area 150 cm$^2$ and mean length 200 cm.

(i) Calculate the mutual inductance between the two coils. Take relative permeability of iron as 2500.

(ii) If the current in the first coil changes from + 12 to −12 ampere in 0.03 second, determine the emf induced in the second coil.

**Solution:**

Given

Number of turns of 1st coil ($N_1$) = 50

Number of turns of 2nd coil ($N_2$) = 400

Area of cross section (A) = $150 \times 10^{-4}$ m$^2$

Mean length (l) = $200 \times 10^{-2}$ m

Relative permeability ($\mu_r$) = 2500

Mutual inductance between the two coils is given by

(i) $$M = \frac{N_1N_2}{S}$$

where $$S = \frac{l}{\mu_o\mu_rA}$$

where $\mu_0 = 4\pi \times 10^{-7}$ H/m

$$\therefore \quad S = \frac{200 \times 10^{-2}}{4\pi \times 10^{-7} \times 2500 \times 150 \times 10^{-4}}$$

$$= 42441.32 \text{ AT/Wb}$$

$$\therefore \quad M = \frac{50 \times 400}{42441.32}$$

$$= 0.4712 \text{ henry}$$

(ii) $dI_1 = +12 - (-12) = 24$ A

$dt = 0.03$ s

$$\therefore \quad \frac{dI_1}{dt} = \frac{24}{0.03} = 800 \text{ A/second}$$

$\therefore$ Mutual induced emf in the 2nd coil = $e_{M2} = M\dfrac{dI_1}{dt}$

$= 376.99$ volts

## 3.7 ENERGY STORED IN THE MAGNETIC FIELD

Consider a coil of inductance 'L' henry. Let the current in the coil be raised from 0 to 'i' ampere. This rise in the value of current establishes a self induced emf in the coil which opposes the very cause of production of it (namely, the rise in value of current). Any increase in the value of current in the circuit can be achieved only by doing certain work against the self induced emf. This work done provided through a source is stored in the magnetic field.

The self induced emf in the coil is given by, $e = L\dfrac{di}{dt}$

We know that power = e.i

Also energy = power × time

$\therefore$ Energy supplied during time dt = e.i.dt

$$= L.\frac{di}{dt}.i.dt$$

$$= L.i.di$$

The total energy supplied to the system to establish a current of 'I' ampere from '0' value $\Bigg\}$ $= \displaystyle\int_0^I L.i.di$

$$= L\left[\frac{i^2}{2}\right]_0^I$$

$\therefore$ Energy stored in the magnetic field $= \dfrac{1}{2}\,LI^2$ joules ...(3.19)

## 3.8 STORED ENERGY PER UNIT VOLUME OF MAGNETIC FIELD

We know that $L = \dfrac{N^2}{s}$

where 'L' = Self inductance of the coil in henry

N = Number of turns of the coil

S = Reluctance given by $\frac{l}{\mu_o \mu_r A}$ AT/Wb

Also $H = \frac{NI}{l}$ AT/m

where H = Magnetic field strength

The eq. 3.19 can be rewritten as below

$$\therefore \quad E = \frac{1}{2} \times \frac{N^2}{\frac{l}{\mu_o \mu_r A}} \times I^2$$

$$E = \frac{1}{2} \frac{N^2 I^2 \mu_o \mu_r A}{l}$$

Divide both numerator and denominator by 'l'.

$$E = \frac{1}{2} \frac{N^2 I^2}{l^2} \mu_o \mu_r A.l$$

$$= \frac{1}{2}.H^2 \mu_o \mu_r.V \text{ joules}$$

where 'V' is the volume.

$$\therefore \quad \text{Stored energy/m}^3 = \frac{1}{2}.H^2 \mu_o \mu_r. \qquad ...(3.20)$$

But, $B = \mu_0 \mu_r H \Rightarrow H = \frac{B}{\mu_o \mu_r}$

$$\text{Stored energy/m}^3 = \frac{1}{2}.\frac{B^2}{\mu_o^2 \mu_r^2} \mu_o \mu_r$$

$$\therefore \quad \text{Stored energy/m}^3 = \frac{1}{2} \frac{B^2}{\mu_o \mu_r} \qquad ...(3.21)$$

$$\text{Stored energy/m}^3 = \frac{1}{2} \frac{B^2}{\mu_o} \text{ (for air)} \qquad ...(3.22)$$

## 3.9. LIFTING POWER OF A MAGNET

Consider the arrangement of two poles as shown in Fig. 3.9. Let 'P' be the force of attraction between the two poles in newtons.

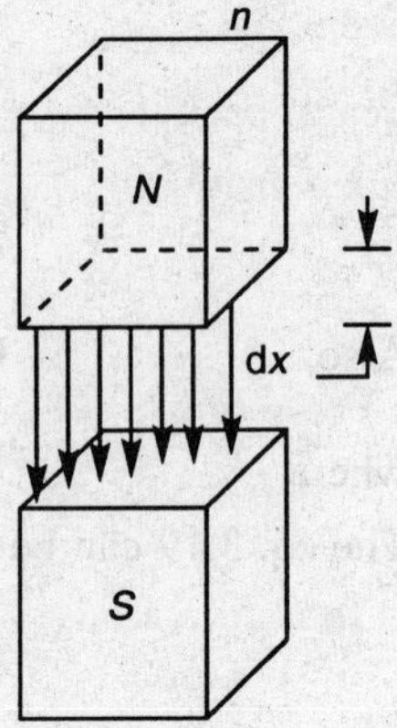


Fig. 3.9

Let 'A' be the area of the magnet. **Keeping 'S' pole fixed,** let the 'N' pole be pulled upwards through a distance 'dx' against the force of attraction.

The work done $= P \,.\, (dx)$ joules, ...(3.23)

This work done is stored in magnetic field, which is given by equation 3.22

i.e., Stored energy/m³ $= \frac{1}{2}\frac{B^2}{\mu_o}$

$\therefore$ Stored energy $= \frac{1}{2}\frac{B^2}{\mu_o} \times A \,.\, \partial x$ ...(3.24)

From equations 3.23 and 3.24 we have

$$\therefore \quad P.dx = \frac{B^2}{2\mu_o} A.dx$$

$$\therefore \quad P = \frac{B^2}{2\mu_o} A.dx \text{ newton} \qquad ...(3.25)$$

**P. 3.9.** The inductance of a coil carrying a current of 2 A is 0.5 henry. Find the energy stored in it.

**Solution:**

Given

Inductance of the coil (L) = 0.5 henry

Current (I) = 2 A

$\therefore$ Energy stored $= \frac{1}{2} LI^2$ joules

$= \frac{1}{2} \times 0.5 \times 2 \times 2$

= 1 joule.

**P. 3.10.** A horse-shoe magnet has two poles each of area 1.5 cm². Determine the pull between the poles and keeper when the flux density of the contact surface is 1.2 Wb/m².

**Solution:**

Given

Area of each pole (A) $= 15 \times 10^{-4}\ m^2$

Flux density (B) $= 1.2\ Wb/m^2$

$\mu_r = 1$

$\therefore$ Force of attraction on each pole $= \dfrac{B^2 A}{2\mu_o}$

$\therefore$ Total force on both the poles $= 2\times\dfrac{B^2 A}{2\mu_o}$

$$= \frac{2\times(1.2)^2\times 15\times 10^{-4}}{2\times 4\pi\times 10^{-7}}$$

$= 1718.8$ N.

## REVISION FORMULAE

$$e = N\frac{d\Phi}{dt}\ \text{volts}$$

where e is emf induced in volts

N is number of turns of coil

$\dfrac{d\Phi}{dt}$ is rate of change of flux in weber / second

$e = Blv \sin\theta$ volts

where B is flux density in weber/metre$^2$

l is length of conductor in metres

V is the velocity of the conductor in metre / second

θ is angle between conductor and magnetic lines of force.

$$e_L = -L\frac{dI}{dt}\ \text{volts}$$

where $e_L$ is self induced emf in volts

L is the self inductance in henry

$\dfrac{dI}{dt}$ rate of change of current in ampere/seconds.

$$e_{m1} = -M\frac{dI_2}{dt} \text{ volts}$$

$$e_{m2} = -M\frac{dI_1}{dt} \text{ volts}$$

where $eM_1$ is the Mutual induced emf in the first coil in volts

$eM_2$ is the Mutual induced emf in the second coil in volts

M is the Mutual inductance in henry

$\frac{dI_2}{dt}$ = rate of change of current in second coil in ampere/second

$\frac{dI_1}{dt}$ = rate of change of current in first coil in ampere/second

$$L = \frac{N\Phi}{I} \text{ henry}$$

$$L = \frac{N^2}{S} \text{ henry}$$

where L is the self inductance in henry

N is the number of turns of the coil

'Φ' is the flux linking with the coil in weber

I is the current flowing through the coil in amperes

S is the reluctance in amperes turns/weber.

$$M = \frac{N_2 k_1 \Phi_1}{I_1} \text{ henry}$$

$$M = \frac{N_1 k_2 \Phi_2}{I_2} \text{ henry}$$

$$M = \frac{N_1 N_2}{S} \text{ henry}$$

where

M is mutual inductance in henry

$N_1$ & '$N_2$' are number of turns of first and second coils respectively

$K_1$ is percentage of $\Phi_1$ linking with second coil

$K_2$ is percentage of $\Phi_2$ linking with first coil

$\Phi_1$ & $\Phi_2$ are fluxes in first and second coils respectively (in webers)

$I_1$ & $I_2$ are currents in first and second coils respectively (in amperes)

Energy stored in the magnetic field $\frac{1}{2} L I^2$ joules

where L is self inductance in henry

I is current in amperes

Energy stored in the magnetic field per unit volume $\frac{1}{2} \frac{B^2}{\mu_o \mu_r}$ joules / $m^3$

where B is flux density in weber / metre$^2$, $\mu_r$, is relative permeability

$\mu o = 4\pi \times 10^{-7}$ H/m

Lifting power of a magnet $\frac{B^2}{\mu_o \mu_r} A\, dx$ newton

'A' is the area of the magnet in metre$^2$

'dx' is the distance in metres.

## REVIEW QUESTIONS

1. Explain the phenomena of electromagnetic induction.
2. State and explain Faraday's laws of electromagnetic induction.
3. What is Lenz's law?
4. Derive an expression for dynamically induced emf.
5. What is meant by
   (a) Dynamically induced emf
   (b) Statically induced emf
6. Explain Flemings rules
7. Explain the following terms
   (a) Self inductance
   (b) Mutual inductance
8. Derive an expression for energy stored in a magnetic field.
9. Derive an expression for lifting power of a magnet.

## TWO MARKS QUESTIONS AND ANSWERS

1. *State Faraday's Laws of electromagnetism.*

   **First law:** Whenever magnetic flux linking with the coil changes an emf is induced in the coil.

   **Second law:** The magnitude of the induced emf is equal to the product of number of turns of the coil and the rate of change of flux.

2. *What is Fleming's left hand rule ?*

   This is used to determine the direction of the force acting on a current carrying conductor placed in the magnetic field. According to this rule, if we keep our thumb, first finger or forefinger and middle finger of the left hand at right angles to one another and if the first finger represents the direction of magnetic field, the middle finger indicates the direction of current then the thumb will indicate the direction of force acting on the conductor.

3. *What is Fleming's right hand rule ?*

   This is used to determine the direction of emf induced. According to this, if we keep our thumb, first finger (or) forefinger and middle finger of the right hand at right angles to one another and if the first finger represents the direction of magnetic lines of flux, the thumb indicates the direction of motion of the conductor, then the middle finger will indicate the direction of induced emf.

4. *What is self inductance ?*

   The property of a coil by which it opposes the change in the value of current or flux through it due to the production of self induced emf is called self inductance.

5. *What is mutual inductance ?*

   The ability of one coil to produce an emf in the nearby coil due to change of current or flux in the first coil is called mutual inductance.

6. *What is self induced emf ?*

   The emf induced in a coil due to change in the value of its own flux linking with it, is called self induced emf.

7. *What is mutual induced emf ?*

   The emf induced in one coil due to change in value of flux linking in nearby coil is called mutual induced emf.

8. *How do you produce dynamically induced emf ?*

   The dynamically induced emf is produced by moving the coil and keeping the magnet stationary or vice versa.

9. *The inductance of a coil carrying a current of 1 A is 0.25 henrys. Find the energy stored in it.*

   Given Inductance (L) = 0.25 henry

   Current (I) = 1 amperes

   Energy stored = $(1/2)\ LI^2$

   $= (1/2) \times 0.25 \times 1 \times 1$

   = 0.125 joules

10. *A coil of inductance 0.075 henry carrying a current of 10 amperes is wound with 1500 turns. Find the flux established in the coil.*

    Given Inductance (L) = 0.075 henry

    Current (I) = 10 amperes

    No. of turns (N) = 1500 turns

$$\text{Flux established (F) } (\phi) = \frac{LI}{N} = \frac{0.075 \times 10}{1500}$$

$$= 0.5 \text{ m Wb}$$

## EXERCISE PROBLEMS

**P. 1:** A coil of 500 turns is uniformly wound on a ring of non-magnetic material of mean diameter 25 cm. The cross sectional area of the coil is 5 cm$^2$. A current of 3 A is flowing through the coil. Find the inductance of the coil.

(Ans: $2 \times 10^{-4}$ H)

**P. 2:** An aircored solenoid 50 cm long and 5 cm in radius is wound with 1000 turns. Determine (i) the inductance and also (ii) the energy stored in the magnetic field when a current of 5 A flows through it.

(Ans: $19.7 \times 10^{-3}$ H, 0.2467 J)

**P. 3:** Two coils A and B have 600 and 1000 turns respectively. If a current of 4 A in coil A, establishes a flux of 5mWb in coil A and 2.5 mWb in coil B, determine (i) Self inductance of coil A (ii) Mutual inductance.

(Ans: 0.75 H, 0.625 H)

**P. 4:** Two coils have mutual inductance of 0.4 henry. If the current in one coil is reduced from 5 A to 1 A in 0.01 s, find the emf induced in the second coil. Assume that whole flux set up by first coil is linking with second coil.

(Ans: 160 V)

**P. 5:** The self inductance of a coil of 600 turns is 0.35 H. If 50% of the flux is linking with a second coil of 8000 turns, calculate the mutual inductance between the two coils.

(Ans: 2.33 H)

*Chapter 4*

# A.C. CIRCUITS

## 4.1. GENERATION OF ALTERNATING EMF

Alternating emf can be generated by rotating a coil in a magnetic field (Fig. 4.1) or by rotating a magnetic field in a stationary coil (Fig. 4.2).

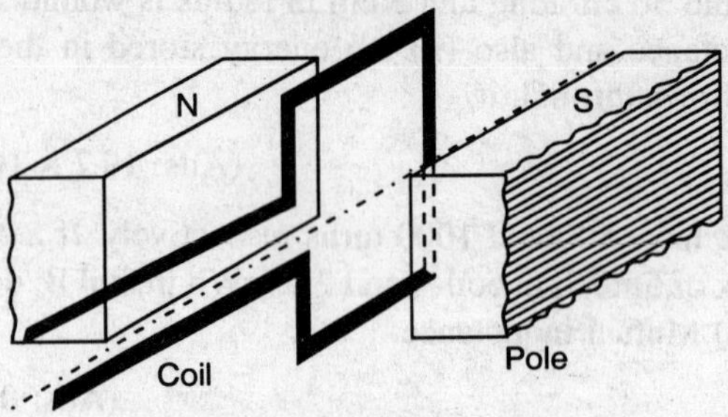


**Fig. 4.1**

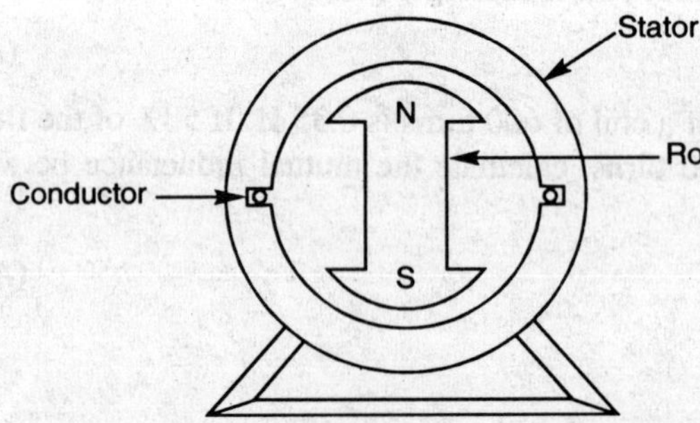


**Fig. 4.2**

The magnitude of emf generated depends on the position of the coil. In the Fig. 4.3, the coil is stationary. The magnitude of voltage induced is 0 volts. In the Fig. 4.4, the coil rotates through an angle of 90° generating maximum voltage, corresponding to position B in the waveform of Fig. 4.8. In Fig. 4.5, the coil has rotated through 180° generating 0 volts, corresponding to position C in the waveform (Fig. 4.8).

Similarly points D, E correspond to 270° and 360° rotation of the coil respectively generating maximum value and zero value of voltage.

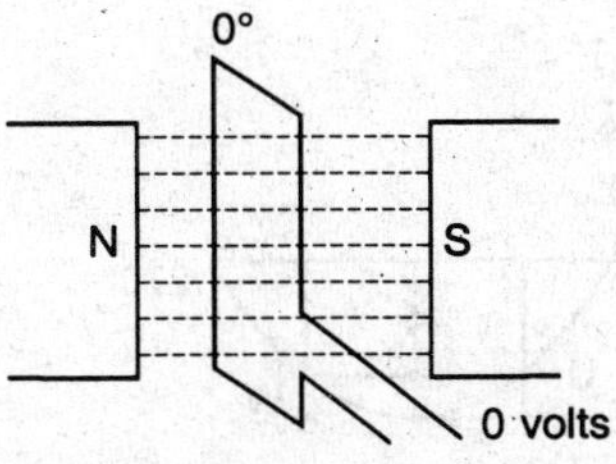


Fig. 4.3

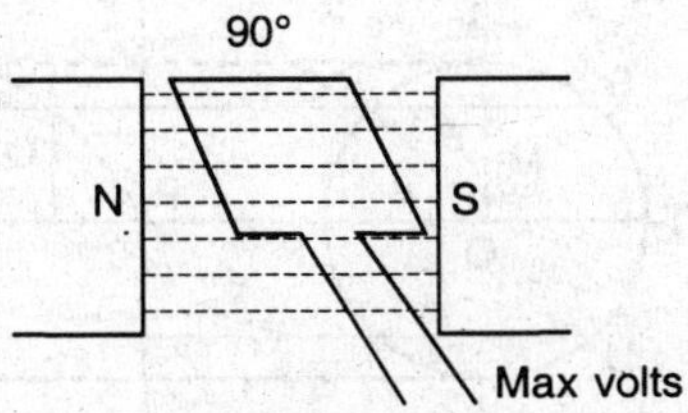


Fig. 4.4

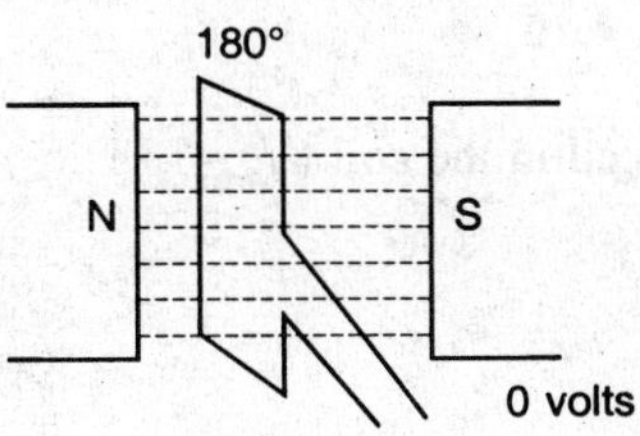


Fig. 4.5

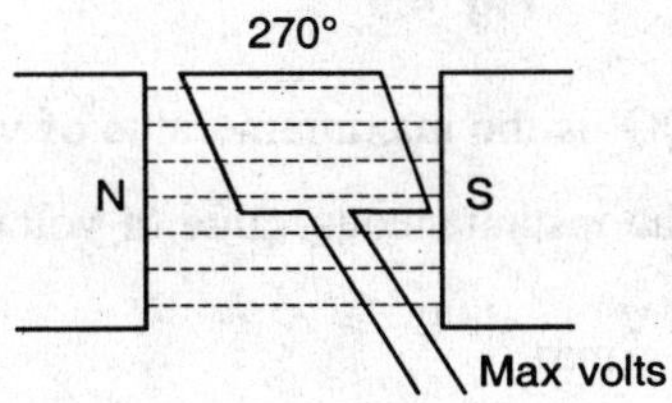


Fig. 4.6

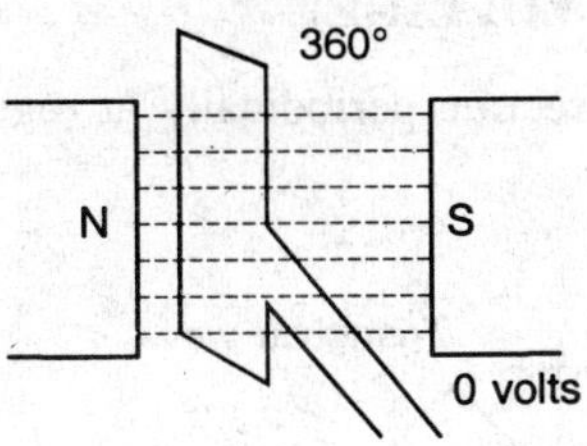


Fig. 4.7

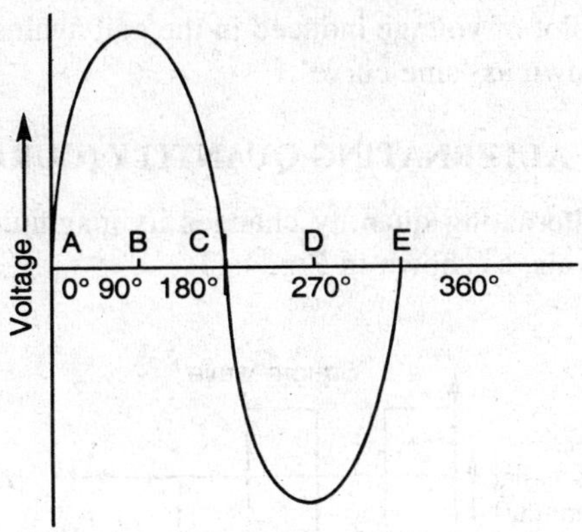


Fig. 4.8

## 4.2. EQUATION OF ALTERNATING VOLTAGE

Consider a rectangular coil (of coil side OP) rotating in a magnetic field in the counter clockwise direction with an angular speed of 'ω' as shown in Fig. 4.9. The instantaneous value of emf is given by the projection of vector (showing maximum value of voltage generated) on the Y-axis. As 'OP' moves through an angle 'θ', i.e. in counter clockwise direction it takes the position OQ. The line 'OM' gives the projection of 'OQ' on Y-axis. Now 'OMQ' is a right angled triangle.

Thus, $\dfrac{OM}{OQ}$ sin θ ; OM = OQ sin θ

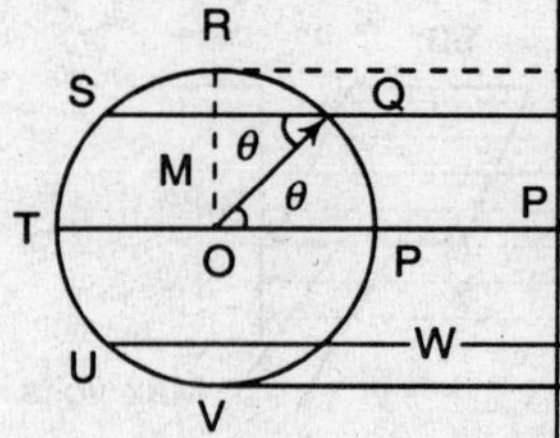


Fig. 4.9

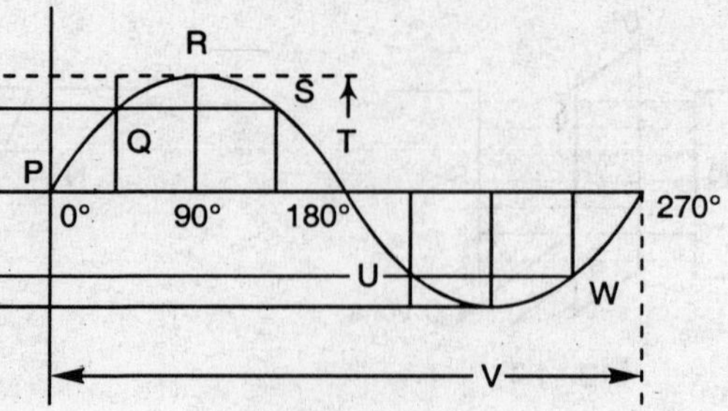


Fig. 4.10

where, 'OQ' is the maximum value of voltage induced in the coil ($V_{max}$).

'OM' is the instantaneous value of voltage (v)

$$\therefore \quad v = V_{max} \sin \theta \qquad ...(4.1)$$

Similarly, the instantaneous value of current is given by

$$I = I_{max} \sin \theta \qquad ...(4.2)$$

The plot of voltage induced in the coil against time is shown in Fig. 4.10. This curve is known as 'sine curve'.

## 4.3. ALTERNATING QUANTITY (CURRENT or VOLTAGE)

An alternating quantity changes its magnitude and direction periodically at regular intervals, as shown in Fig. 4.11.

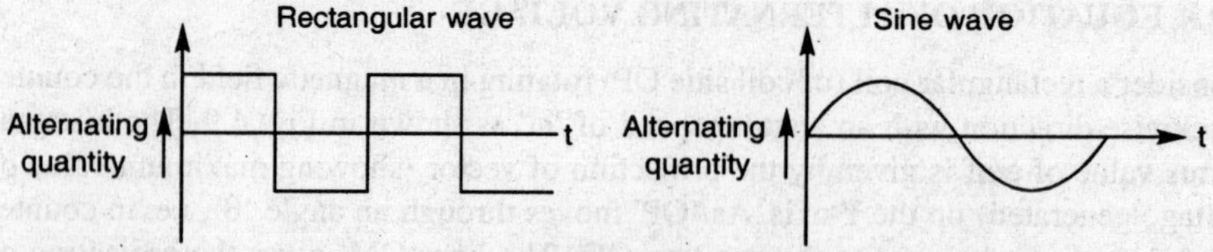


Fig. 4.11

## 4.4. CYCLE

One complete set of positive and negative values of an alternating quantity constitutes one cycle.

## 4.5. TIME PERIOD (T)

It is the time taken by an alternating quantity to complete one cycle.

For example, a 50Hz alternating quantity has a time period of 1/50 second or 20 milliseconds.

## 4.6. FREQUENCY (F)

The number of cycles complete per second is known as the frequency. Its unit is cycles/sec or Hertz and is denoted by 'f'.

Thus we have, $$f = \frac{1}{T} \quad \Rightarrow \quad T = \frac{1}{f} \qquad ...(4.3)$$

## 4.7. MAXIMUM VALUE or PEAK VALUE or AMPLITUDE

The maximum value (positive or negative) of an alternating quantity is called amplitude.

The above definitions can be understood with the help of Fig. 4.12.

From equation 4.1 we have,

$$v = V_{max} \sin \theta$$

Where, $V_{max}$ is the amplitude.

The same equation can be rewritten as follows:

$$v = V_{max} \sin \omega t \qquad \text{where } \theta = \omega t$$

$$= V_{max} \sin 2\pi ft \qquad \text{where } \theta = 2\pi f$$

$$= V_{max} \sin\left(\frac{2\pi}{T}\right)t \qquad \text{where } f = \frac{1}{T}$$

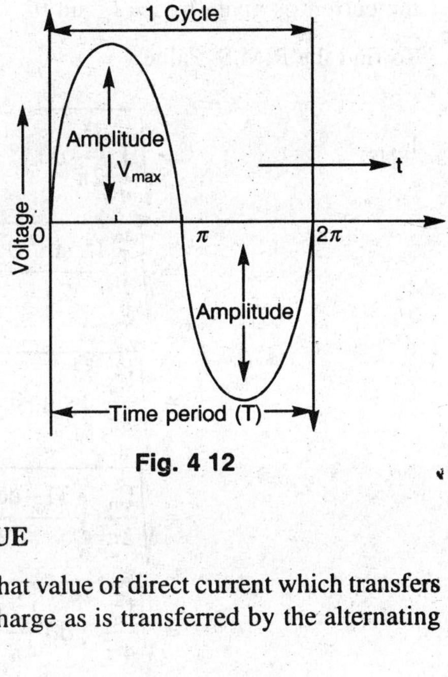


Fig. 4 12

## 4.8. AVERAGE VALUE or MEAN VALUE

The average value of an alternating current is that value of direct current which transfers across any circuit in a given time the same charge as is transferred by the alternating current in the same circuit.

## 4.9. ROOT MEAN SQUARE VALUE (R.M.S. VALUE)

It is also called **virtual value** or **effective value**. The R.M.S value of an alternating current is given by that value of direct current which when flowing through a given circuit for a given time produces the same heating effect as that produced by an alternating current when flowing through the same circuit for the same time.

Note: Moving coil meter reads the average value, and moving iron meter reads the R.M.S. value.

## 4.10. FORM FACTOR

Form factor ($K_f$) is given by the ratio of R.M.S. value to average value,

$$K_f = \frac{\text{R.M.S. value}}{\text{Average value}} \quad ...(4.4)$$

## 4.11. PEAK or CREST or AMPLITUDE FACTOR

Peak factor ($K_a$) is given by the ratio of maximum value to R.M.S. value.

$$Ka = \frac{\text{Maximum value}}{\text{R.M.S. value}} \quad ...(4.5)$$

## 4.12. EXPRESSION FOR R.M.S. VALUE, AVERAGE VALUE, FORM FACTOR and PEAK FACTOR of a SINUSOIDAL ALTERNATING QUANTITY

The sinusoidal alternating current is shown in Fig. 4.13. The instantaneous value of the current is given by $i = I_m \sin\theta$

To find the R.M.S. value

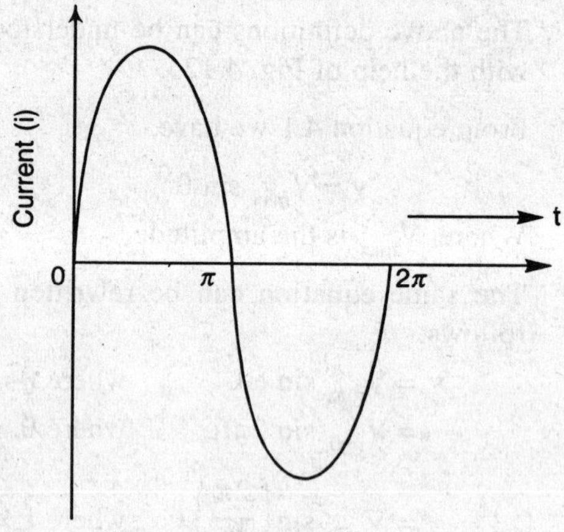


Fig. 4.13

$$I_{RMS} = \sqrt{\int_0^{2\pi} \frac{i^2}{2\pi} d\theta}$$

$$= \sqrt{\int_0^{2\pi} \frac{I_m^2 \sin^2\theta}{2\pi} d\theta}$$

$$= \sqrt{\frac{I_m^2}{2\pi} \int_0^{2\pi} \sin^2\theta \, d\theta}$$

$$= \sqrt{\frac{I_m^2}{2\pi} \int_0^{2\pi} \frac{(1-\cos 2\theta)}{2} d\theta}$$

$$= \sqrt{\frac{I_m^2}{4\pi} \int_0^{2\pi} d\theta - \frac{I_m^2}{4\pi} \int_0^{2\pi} \cos 2\theta \, d\theta}$$

$$= \sqrt{\frac{I_m^2}{4\pi} [\theta]_0^{2\pi} - \frac{I_m^2}{4\pi} \left[\frac{\sin 2\theta}{2}\right]_0^{2\pi}}$$

$$= \sqrt{\frac{I_m^2}{4\pi}[2\pi - 0] - \frac{I_m^2}{8\pi}[\sin 4\pi - \sin 0]}$$

$$= \sqrt{\frac{I_m^2}{4\pi} \times 2\pi - 0} = \sqrt{\frac{I_m^2}{2}}$$

$$\therefore \quad I_{R.M.S.} = \frac{I_m}{\sqrt{2}} \qquad \text{...(4.6)}$$

**To find the average value**

(since it is a symmetrical wave we have to consider only half cycle)

$$\therefore \quad I_{av} = \int_0^\pi \frac{i d\theta}{\pi} = \frac{1}{\pi}\int_0^\pi I_m \sin\theta d\theta$$

$$= \frac{I_m}{\pi}\int_0^\pi \sin\theta \, d\theta$$

$$I_{av} = \frac{-I_m}{\pi}[\cos\theta]_0^\pi$$

$$= \frac{I_m}{\pi}[\cos\pi - \cos\theta]$$

$$= \frac{-I_m}{\pi}[-1-1]$$

$$I_{av} = \frac{2I_m}{\pi}$$

$$\therefore \quad I_{av} = \frac{I_m}{\pi/2} \qquad \text{...(4.7)}$$

$$\therefore \quad \text{Form factor} = \frac{\text{R.M.S. value}}{\text{Average value}} = \frac{I_m/\sqrt{2}}{I_m/\pi\sqrt{2}} = 1.11 \qquad \text{...(4.8)}$$

$$\text{Peak factor} = \frac{\text{Maximum value}}{\text{R.M.S. value}} = \frac{I_m}{I_m/\sqrt{2}} = 1.414 \qquad \text{...(4.9)}$$

## 4.13. EXPRESSION for R.M.S. VALUE, AVERAGE VALUE, FORM FACTOR and PEAK FACTOR of HALF WAVE RECTIFIED A.C.

The half wave rectified a.c. is shown in Fig. 4.14.

**To find the R.M.S. value**

$$i = I_m \sin\theta \qquad 0 < \theta \le \pi$$

$i = 0 \qquad\qquad \pi < \theta \le 2\pi$

To find the average value

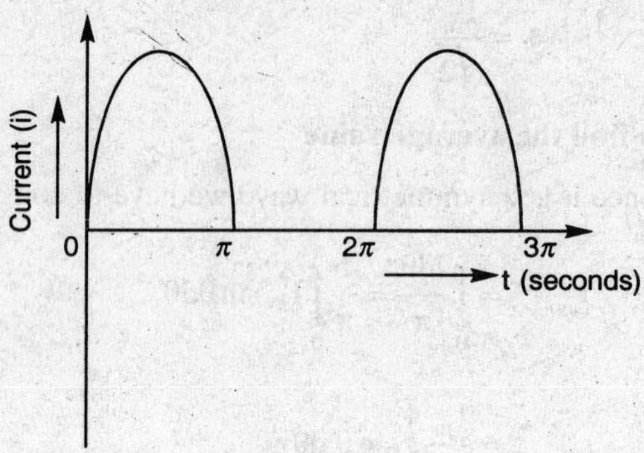


Fig. 4.14

$$I_{R.M.S.} = \sqrt{\int_0^{2\pi} \frac{i^2 d\theta}{2\pi}}$$

$$= \sqrt{\int_0^{\pi} \frac{i^2 d\theta}{2\pi} + \int_0^{2\pi} \frac{i^2 d\theta}{2\pi}}$$

$$= \sqrt{\int_0^{\pi} \frac{I_m^2 \sin^2 \theta d\theta}{2\pi} + 0}$$

$$= \sqrt{\frac{I_m^2}{2\pi} \int_0^{\pi} \sin^2 \theta d\theta}$$

$$= \sqrt{\frac{I_m^2}{2\pi} \int_0^{\pi} \frac{1 - \cos 2\theta d\theta}{2}}$$

$$= \sqrt{\frac{I_m^2}{4\pi} \int_0^{\pi} d\theta - \frac{I_m^2}{4\pi} \int_0^{\pi} \cos 2\theta d\theta}$$

$$= \sqrt{\frac{I_m^2}{4\pi} [\theta]_0^{\pi} - \frac{I_m^2}{4\pi} \left[\frac{\sin 2\theta}{2}\right]_0^{\pi}}$$

$$= \sqrt{\frac{I_m^2}{4\pi} [\pi - 0] - 0} = \sqrt{\frac{I_m^2}{4}}$$

$$\therefore \quad I_{RMS} = \frac{I_m}{2}$$

**To find the average value**

$$I_{av} = \int_0^{2\pi} \frac{i d\theta}{2\pi}$$

$$= \int_0^{\pi} \frac{i d\theta}{2\pi} + \int_{\pi}^{2\pi} \frac{i d\theta}{2\pi}$$

$$= \int_0^{\pi} \frac{I_m}{2\pi} \sin\theta d\theta + 0$$

$$= \frac{I_m}{2\pi} \int_0^{\pi} \sin\theta d\theta$$

$$= \frac{-I_m}{2\pi} [\cos\theta]_0^{\pi}$$

$$= \frac{-I_m}{2\pi} [\cos\pi - \cos\theta]$$

$$= \frac{I_m}{2\pi} [-1-1] = \frac{I_m}{\pi}$$

$$\therefore \quad I_{av} = \frac{I_m}{\pi}$$

$$\text{Form factor} = \frac{\text{R.M.S. value}}{\text{Average value}} = \frac{I_m / 2}{I_m / \pi} = \frac{\pi}{2} \qquad ...(4.12)$$

$$\text{Peak factor} = \frac{\text{Maximum value}}{\text{R.M.S. value}} = \frac{I_{max}}{I_{max} / 2} = 2 \qquad ...(4.13)$$

**P. 4.1.** The equation of an alternating current is given by

i = 40 sin 314t

Determine the following:

(i) Maximum value of current, (ii) Average value of current (iii) R.M.S. value of current (iv) Frequency and angular frequency (v) From factor (vi) Peak factor.

**Solution:**

Given, i $= 40 \sin 314\, t$ ...(i)

we have, i $= I_m \sin \omega\, t$ ...(ii)

Comparing (i) and (ii) we get

Maximum value of current $I_m$ = 40 A

Angular frequency $\omega$ = 314 rad/second

Average value ($I_{av}$) $= \frac{I_{max}}{\sqrt{2}} = 25.464$ A

R.M.S. value ($I_{R.M.S.}$) $= \frac{I_{max}}{\pi / 2} = 28.288$ A

Frequency (f) $= \frac{\omega}{2\pi} = \frac{314}{2\pi} \approx 50$ Hz

Form factor $= \frac{\text{R.M.S. value}}{\text{Average value}} = \frac{28.288}{25.464} = 1.11$

Peak factor $= \frac{\text{Maximum value}}{\text{R.M.S. value}} = \frac{40}{28.288} = 1.414$

**P. 4.2.** What is the equation of a 50Hz voltage sine wave with an R.M.S. value of 50 volts?

**Solution:**

Given $f = 50$ Hz

$V_{R.M.S.} = 50V$

we have, $v = V_{MAX} \sin \omega t$

where $V_{MAX} = V_{R.M.S.} \times \sqrt{2}$ and $\omega = 2\pi f$

$\therefore$ $V_{MAX} = 50 \times \sqrt{2} = 70.7$ volts

$\omega = 2\pi \times 50$

$= 314$ rad/s

$\therefore$ Voltage equation is given by

$v = 70.7 \sin (314)t.$

**P. 4.3.** An alternating voltage of frequency 50Hz has an R.M.S. value of 200 volts. Find the instantaneous value of voltage after 2.5 milliseconds. Also determine the time taken to reach the instantaneous voltage of 150V.

**Solution:**

Given,

Frequency $= 50$ Hz

$V_{R.M.S.} = 200$ V

$\therefore$ $V_{MAX} = 200 \times \sqrt{2}$

$= 282.2$ volts

The equation for voltage is given by

$v = V_{MAX} \sin \omega t$

$= 282.8 \sin (2\pi \times 50t)$
$= 282.8 \sin 314t$

To find the instantaneous value of voltage after 2.5 milliseconds

$$v = 282.8 \sin 314 \times (2.5 \times 10^{-3})$$
$$= 282.8 \sin (0.785) \quad \text{(Note: angle 0.785 is in radians)}$$
$$= 199.89 \text{ volts}$$

or

$$v = 282.8 \sin (2\pi \times 50)\, t$$
$$= 282.8 \sin (2 \times 180 \times 50) \times 2.5 \times 10^{-3}$$
$$= 282.8 \sin (45°) \quad \text{(Note: angle 45° is in degrees)}$$

To find the time to reach the instantaneous voltage of 150 V

we have, $v = V_m \sin (2\pi f)t$

$$150 = 282.8 \sin (2 \times 180 \times 50) \times t$$

$$\frac{150}{282.8} = \sin (18000\, t)$$

$$18000\, t = \sin^{-1}\left(\frac{150}{282.8}\right)$$

$$t = \frac{32.033}{18000}$$

$$t = 1.779 \times 10^{-3} \text{ seconds}$$

**P. 4.4.** Calculate the R.M.S. value and the average value for the voltage wave shown in Fig. 4.15.

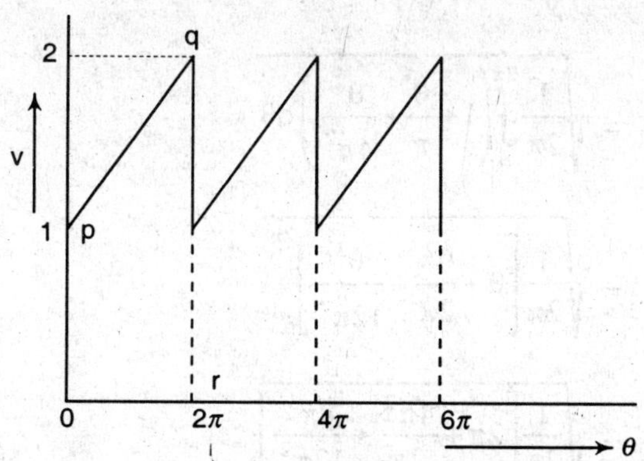


**Fig. 4.15**

**Solution:**

**Note:** The equation of a straight line passing through $(x_1, y_1)$, $(x_2, y_2)$ is given by

$$\frac{x - x_1}{y - y_1} = \frac{x_2 - x_1}{y_2 - y_1}$$

In this case the variable on Y-axis is 'v' (voltage) and the variable on X-axis is 'θ' (angle).

The coordinates of the point 'p' are (0, 1) $\Rightarrow x_1 = 0; y_1 = 1$

The coordinates of point 'q' are (2π, 2) $\Rightarrow x_2 = 2\pi; y_2 = 2$

∴ The equation of straight line 'pq' is given by

$$\frac{\theta - 0}{v - 1} = \frac{2\pi - 0}{2 - 1}$$

$$\frac{\theta}{v - 1} = \frac{2\pi}{1}$$

$$\theta = 2\pi (v - 1)$$

$$\frac{\theta}{2\pi} = v - 1$$

$$\Rightarrow v = 1 + \frac{\theta}{2\pi}$$

Now, we know that

$$V_{R.M.S.} = \sqrt{\int_0^{2\pi} \frac{v^2 . d\theta}{2\pi - 0}} = \sqrt{\frac{1}{2\pi}\int_0^{2\pi}\left(1 + \frac{\theta}{2\pi}\right)^2 . d\theta}$$

$$= \sqrt{\frac{1}{2\pi}\int_0^{2\pi}\left(1 + \frac{\theta}{\pi} + \frac{\theta^2}{4\pi^2}\right) d\theta}$$

$$= \sqrt{\frac{1}{2\pi}\left[\theta + \frac{\theta^2}{2\pi} + \frac{\theta^3}{12\pi^2}\right]_0^{2\pi}}$$

$$= \sqrt{\frac{1}{2\pi}\left[2\pi + \frac{4\pi^2}{2\pi} + \frac{8\pi^3}{12\pi^2}\right]}$$

$$= \sqrt{\frac{1}{2\pi}\left[2\pi + 2\pi + \frac{2\pi}{3}\right]}$$

$$V_{R.M.S.} = \sqrt{\frac{7}{3}} \text{ volts}$$

$$V_{Average} = \frac{1}{2\pi}\int_0^{2\pi} v d\theta$$

$$= \frac{1}{2\pi}\int_0^{2\pi}\left(1 + \frac{\theta}{2\pi}\right) d\theta$$

$$= \frac{1}{2\pi}\left[\theta + \frac{\theta^2}{2\pi}\right]_0^{2\pi}$$

$$= \frac{1}{2\pi}\left[2\pi + \frac{4\pi^2}{4\pi}\right]$$

$$= \frac{1}{2\pi}[3\pi] = 1.5 \text{ volts}$$

**P. 4.5.** Determine the average value and the R.M.S. value of the triangular wave form shown in Fig. 4.16.

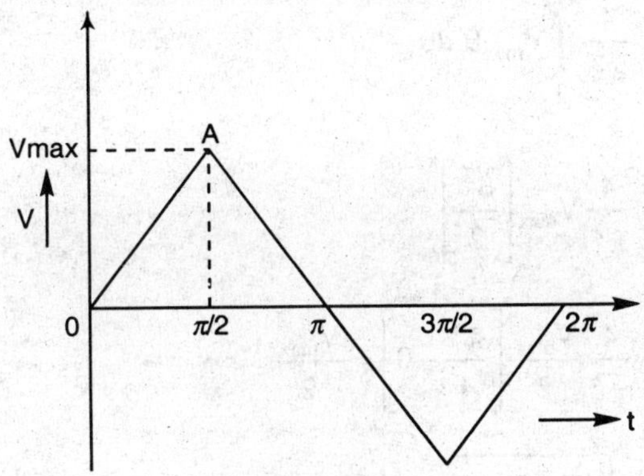


**Fig. 4.16**

**Solution:**

The coordinates of 'O' are

$$O(0,0) \Rightarrow x_1 = 0; y_1 = 0$$

The coordinates of 'A' are

$$A(\pi/2, V_{MAX}) \Rightarrow x_2 = \pi/2; y_2 = V_{MAX};$$

'v' is on Y-axis

'θ' is on X-axis;

we have $\dfrac{x - x_1}{y - y_1} = \dfrac{x_2 - x_1}{y_2 - y_1}$

The equation of the straight line '0A' is given by

$$\frac{\theta - 0}{v - 0} = \frac{\pi/2 - 0}{V_{max} - 0}$$

$$\frac{\theta}{v} = \frac{\pi/2}{V_{max}}$$

$$\theta . v_{MAX} = v.\pi/2$$

$$\therefore \quad Vav = \int_0^{\pi/2} \frac{v.d\theta}{\pi/2 - 0}$$

$$= \frac{2}{\pi}\int_0^{\pi/2} \frac{V_{max}}{\pi/2}.\theta d\theta$$

$$= \frac{4}{\pi^2}\int_0^{\pi/2} V_{max}\theta.d\theta$$

$$= \frac{4}{\pi^2}V_{max}\left[\frac{\theta^2}{2}\right]_0^{\pi/2}$$

$$= \frac{4}{\pi^2}\frac{V_{max}}{2}\left[\frac{\pi^2}{4} - 0\right] = \frac{V_{max}}{2}$$

$$\text{R.M.S. value} = \sqrt{\int_0^{\pi/2} \frac{v^2.d\theta}{\pi/2 - 0}}$$

$$= \sqrt{\frac{2}{\pi}\int_0^{\pi/2}\left(\frac{V_{max}.\theta}{\pi/2}\right)^2.d\theta}$$

$$= \sqrt{\frac{2}{\pi}\frac{4}{\pi^2}.V_{max}^2 \int_0^{\pi/2} \theta^2 d\theta}$$

$$= \sqrt{\frac{8}{\pi^3}.V_{max}^2 \left[\frac{\theta^3}{3}\right]_0^{\pi/2}}$$

$$= \sqrt{\frac{8V_{max}^2}{\pi^3 \times 3}\left[\frac{\pi^3}{8} - 0\right]}$$

$$= \sqrt{\frac{V_{max}^2}{3}}$$

$$\therefore \quad V_{R.M.S.} = \frac{V_{max}}{\sqrt{3}}$$

## 4.14. PHASOR REPRESENTATION of ALTERNATING QUANTITY

In Fig. 4.2 we have shown that alternating current or voltage can be represented by a vector rotating in counter clockwise direction with the same frequency as that of alternating quantity. Also we have said that the length of the vector projection (OM) should be equal to maximum value of alternating quantity (Fig. 4.9 and Fig. 4.10). This vector representation of alternating quantity simplifies the complexity of the problems in the AC circuits.

## 4.15. PHASE

The phase of an alternating quantity at point 'P' in Fig. 4.17 is 3π/2. This implies that the phase is nothing but a fraction of time period that has elapsed from reference position (in this case zero position). Two alternating quantities are said to be in phase, if they reach their zero value or maximum value) at the same time.

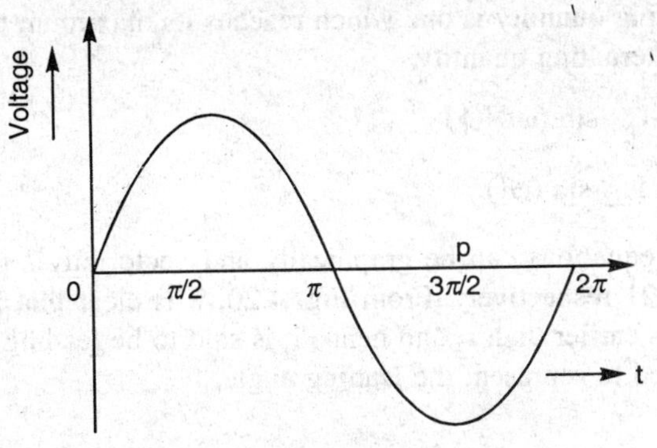


Fig. 4.17

For example the two alternating quantities, namely,

$$i_1 = I_{m1} \sin \theta$$
$$i_2 = I_{m2} \sin \theta$$

can be graphically represented as shown in Fig. 4.18 and vectorially represented as in Fig. 4.19. From Fig. 4.18, it is clear that both $i_1$ and $i_2$ reach their zero or maximum values at the same time and hence are said to be in phase. Note that the phase difference is 0°.

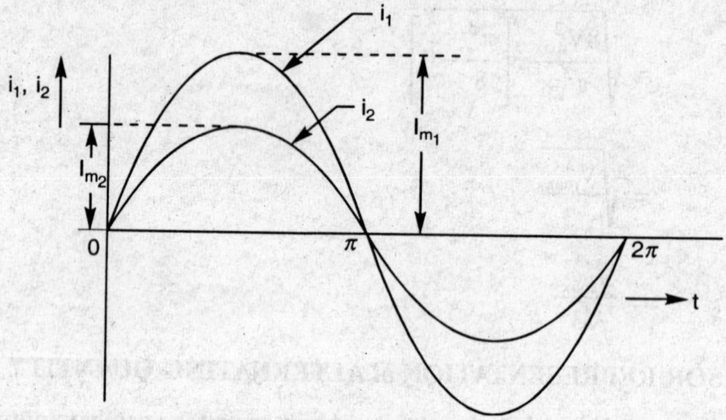


Fig. 4.18

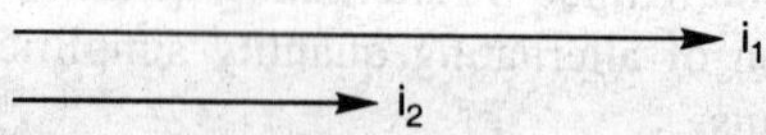


Fig. 4.19

## 4.16. OUT OF PHASE or PHASE DIFFERENCE

When the two alternating quantities do not reach their zero or maximum value at the same time, then they are said to be out of phase. This phase differences is measured in electrical degrees or in radians. It is given in terms of 'lead' or 'lag'.

Leading alternating quantity is one which reaches its maximum or zero value earlier than the other alternating quantity.

If $$i_1 = I_{m1} \sin (\omega t + \phi)$$

$$i_2 = I_{m2} \sin (\omega t)$$

Then these two equations can be graphically and vectorially represented as in Fig. 4.20 and Fig. 4.21 respectively. From Fig. 4.20, it is clear that $i_1$ reaches zero and maximum values earlier than $i_2$ and hence $i_1$ is said to be leading $i_2$ by an angle $\phi$. A 'plus' sign is used to represent the leading angle.

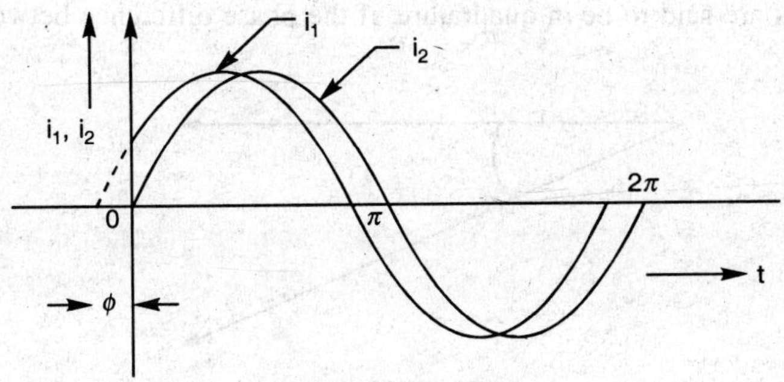


Fig. 4.20

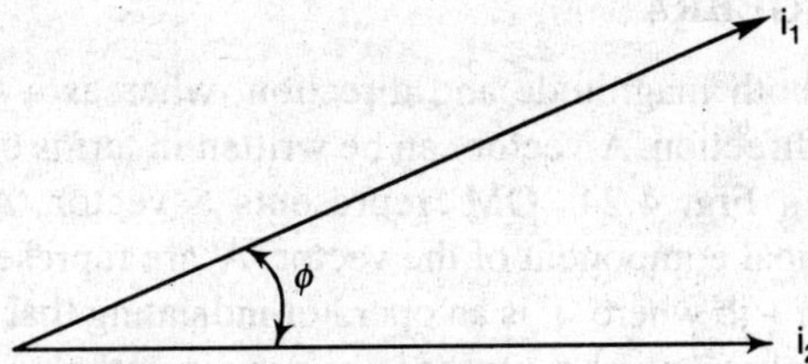


Fig. 4.21

Lagging alternating quantity is one which reaches its maximum value and zero value later than that of the other alternating quantity.

If $$i_1 = I_{m1} \sin (\omega t - \phi)$$

$$i_2 = I_{m2} \sin (\omega t),$$

Then these two equations can be graphically and vectorially represented as in Fig. 4.22 and Fig. 4.23 respectively.

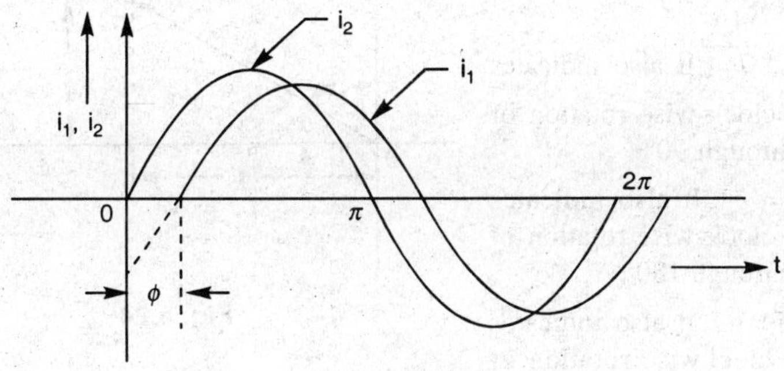


Fig. 4.22

From Fig. 4.22, it is clear that, $i_1$ is reaching the zero value and maximum value later than i2. Hence $i_1$ is said to be lagging $i_2$ by an angle '$\phi$'. A 'minus' sign is usually given to represent the lagging angle.

Note: 1. Two vectors are said to be in antiphase if the phase difference between them is 180°.

2. Two vectors are said to be in quadrature, if the phase difference between them is 90°.

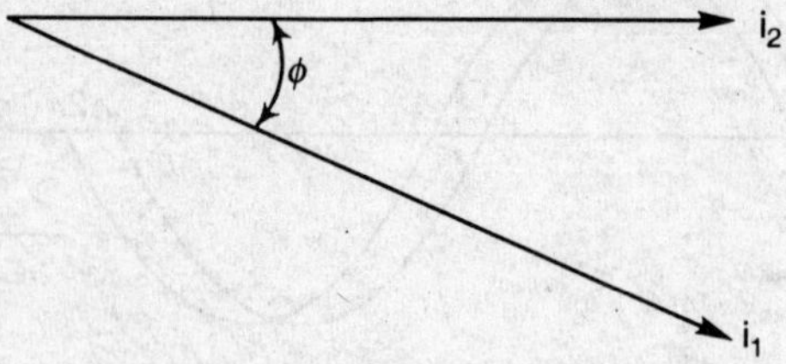


Fig. 4.23

## 4.17. COMPLEX ALGEBRA

A vector quantity has both magnitude and direction, whereas a scalar quantity has only magnitude but no direction. A vector can be written in terms of its horizontal and vertical components. In Fig. 4.24 'OM' represents a vector 'A'. The horizontal component and the vertical component of the vector 'A' are represented by 'a' and 'b' respectively. Thus $A = a + jb$ where 'j' is an operator indicating that 'b' is in quadrature with 'a'. This form of representing a vector is known as complex form.

'a' is the in phase or active component of vector A.

'b' is the quadrature or reactive component of vector A.

The magnitude of vector A is given by $(A) = \sqrt{a^2 + b^2}$ . The angle ($\alpha$) made by the vector 'A' with x-axis is given by $\tan^{-1}\left(\frac{b}{a}\right)$.

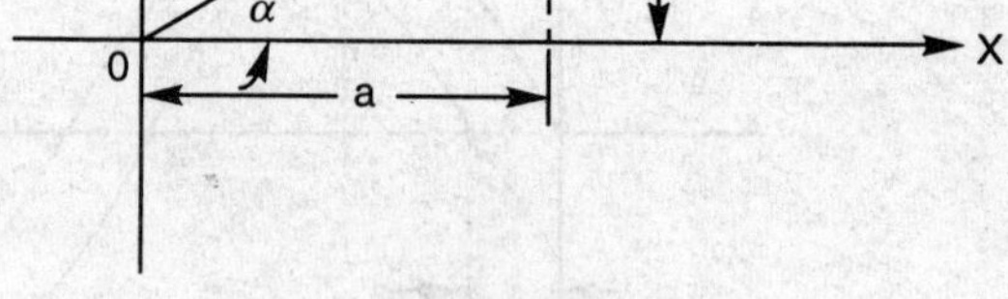


Fig. 4.24

Note: (1) $j = \sqrt{-1}$. It also indicates counter clock-wise rotation of vector through 90°

(2) $j^2 = j.j = -1$. It also indicates counter clock-wise rotation of vector through 180°

(3) $j^3 = j.j.j = -j$. It also indicates counter clockwise rotation of vector through 270°

(4) $j^4 = j.j.j.j = 1$. It also indicates counter clockwise rotation of vector through 360°

(5) $\frac{1}{j} = \frac{1.j}{j.j} = \frac{j}{j^2} = \frac{j}{-1} = -j$

(6) '-j' indicates clockwise rotation of vector through 90°

A vector 'A' written in the form 5 + j7 is known as rectangular form.

The magnitude of A = $|A| = \sqrt{5^2 + 7^2} = 8.6$

The angle $\alpha = \tan^{-1}(7/5) = 54°.46$

The same vector can be rewritten as

$$A = |A| \angle \alpha°$$

i.e., $$A = 8.6 \angle 54°.46.$$

This form of representation of vector is known as polar form.

Note:

1. Addition and subtraction of vectors can be easily done in rectangular form
2. Multiplication and division of vectors can be easily done in polar form.

**P. 4.6.** Add the following vectors and hence find the magnitude and slope of the resultant vector.

A = 3 + j5  B = 8 − j6

**Solution:**

$$\begin{aligned} A + B &= 3 + j5 + 8 - j6 \\ &= 11 - j1 \end{aligned}$$

Magnitude $= |A+B| = \sqrt{(11)^2 + (-1)^2} = 11.045$

Slope of (A + B) $= \tan^{-1}\left(\frac{-1}{11}\right) = -5°.19$

**P. 4.7.** Subtract the above vectors and hence find the magnitude and slope of the resultant vector.

Solution:

Given
$$\begin{aligned} A &= 3 + j5 \\ B &= 8 - j6 \\ A - B &= 3 + j5 - (8 - j6) \\ &= 3 + j5 - 8 + j6 \\ &= -5 + j11 \end{aligned}$$

∴ Magnitude $= |A - B| = \sqrt{(-5)^2 + (11)^2} = 12.08$

Slope of (A − B) $= \tan^{-1}\left(\frac{11}{-5}\right) = -65°.55$

**P. 4.8.** Given the following two vectors

A = 60 ∠20° ; B = 30 ∠15°

Determine (i) $\frac{A}{B}$ (ii) A × B

**Solution:**

Given A = 60 ∠20°

B = 30 ∠15°

$$\therefore \quad \frac{A}{B} = \frac{60\angle 20^\circ}{30\angle 15^\circ} = 2\angle(20^\circ - 15^\circ) = 2\angle 5^\circ$$

Also A × B = 60 ∠ 20° × 30 ∠ 15° = 1800 ∠(20° + 15°)

= 1800 ∠35°

**P. 4.9.** Perform the following operations for the data given below

A = 12 ∠–10° B = 16 + j8 C = 0–j20 D = 2 + j0

(i) A.B (ii) B.C (iii) C.D (iv) $\frac{A}{B}$ (v) $\frac{B}{C}$

(vi) $\frac{C}{D}$ (vii) ABCD (viii) $\frac{AB}{CD}$ (ix) $\frac{CD}{AB}$ (x) $\frac{BC}{AD}$

(xi) A + B (xii) C + D (xiii) A – B

**Solution:**

Given A = 12 ∠–10°

∴ Rectangular form of A = 11.81 – j2

B = 16 + j8

Polar form of B = 17.88 ∠ 26°.56

C = 0 – j20

Polar form of C = 20 ∠– 90°

D = 2 + j0

Polar form of D = 2 ∠ 0°

Note: Addition and subtraction can be easily done in rectangular form and multiplication and division can be easily done in polar form.

(i) A.B = 12 ∠–10° × 17.88 ∠ 26°.56 = 12× 17.88 ∠ (-10° + 26°.56)

= 214.56 ∠ 16°.5

(ii) B.C = 17.88 ∠ 26°.56 × 20 ∠ -90° = 17.88 × 20 ∠ (26°.56-90°)

= 357.6 ∠ -63°.44

(iii) C.D = 20 ∠-90° × 2 ∠ 0° = 20 × 2 ∠ -90° + 0°) = 40 ∠-90°

$$\text{(iv)} \quad \frac{A}{B} = \frac{12\angle -10^\circ}{17.88\angle 26^\circ.56} = \frac{12}{17.88}\angle(-10^\circ - 26^\circ.56) = 0.671\angle -36^\circ.56$$

(v) $\frac{B}{C}=\frac{17.88\angle 26°.56}{20\angle -90°}=\frac{17.88}{20}\angle(26°.56+90°)=0.894\angle 116°.56$

(vi) $\frac{C}{D}=\frac{20\angle -90°}{2\angle 0°}=\frac{20}{2}=\angle(-90°-0°)\;=10\angle -90°$

(vii) $ABCD = 12\angle -10° \times 17.88\angle 26°.56 \times 20\angle -90° \times 2\angle 0°$

$= 12 \times 17.88 \times 20 \times 2\angle(-10° + 26°.56 - 90° + 0°$

$= 858.24\;\angle -73°.44$

(viii) $\frac{AB}{CD}=\frac{214.56\angle 16°.5}{40\angle -90°}=5.364\angle(16.5°+90)=5.364\angle 106°.5$

(ix) $\frac{CD}{AB}=\frac{40\angle -90°}{214.56\angle 16°.5}=0.1864\angle(-90°-16°.5)=0.1864\angle -106°.5$

(x) $\frac{BC}{AD}=\frac{357.6\angle -63°.44}{12\angle -10°\times 2\angle 0°}=14.9\angle(-63°.44+10°)=14.9\angle -53°.44$

(xi) $A + B = (11.81 - j2) + (16 + j8)$

$= 11.81 - j2 + 16 + j8$

$= 27.81 + j6$

(xii) $C + D = (0 - j20) + (2 + j0)$

$= 2 - j20$

(xiii) $A - B = (11.81 - j2) - (16 + j8)$

$= 11.81 - j2 - 16 - j8$

$= - 4.14 - j10$

**P. 4.10.** Find the magnitude and phase of Z

where $Z=\frac{10+j3}{6+j12}$

**Solution:**

Given $Z=\frac{10+j3}{6+j12}$

$10 + j3$ in polar form $= 16.44\angle 16°.7$

$6 + j12$ in polar form $= 13.41\angle 63°.4$

$\therefore\quad Z=\frac{10.44\angle 16°.7}{13.41\angle 63°.4}=0.7785\angle 46°.7$

$\therefore$ Magnitude of Z i.e. $|Z| = 0.7785$

Phase angle of $Z = -46°.7$

**P. 4.11.** Determine the resultant of the two vectors

$$i_1 = 5 \sin \omega t$$
$$i_2 = 10 \sin \omega t + 60°$$

**Solution:**

Draw OA = 5A along X-axis
Draw OD = 10A at 60° to X-axis } (with suitable scale)
Draw AC = 10A parallel to 'OD' at 'A'
join 'O' and 'C'
OC gives the resultant ($i_R$) of $i_1$ and $i_2$
$\therefore$ $i_R$ = Vector sum of $i_1$ and $i_2$ = OC
Referring to the vector diagram of Fig. 4.25

The magnitude of OC = $\sqrt{OB^2 + BC^2}$

$$\alpha = \tan^{-1}\left(\frac{BC}{OB}\right)$$

Also from the triangle ABC

$$\sin 60° = \frac{BC}{AC}$$

$$\Rightarrow BC = AC \sin 60°$$

$$\therefore \quad BC = 10 \sin 60° = 8.66 \text{ A}$$

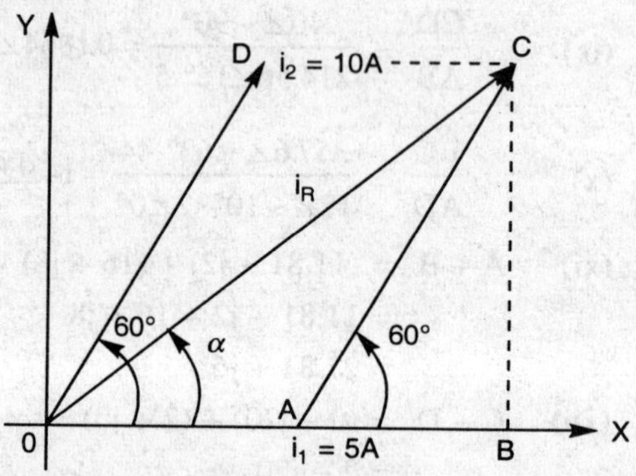


**Fig. 4.25**

Now to find the value of 'OB' we have to consider the triangle ABC

$$\cos 60° = \frac{AB}{AC}$$

$$\therefore \quad AB = (AC) \cos 60° = 10 \times 0.5 = 5$$

$$\therefore \quad OB = OA + AB = 5 + 5 = 10$$

$$\therefore \quad (OC) = \sqrt{(10)^2 + (8.66)^2} = 13.228$$

$$\alpha = \tan^{-1}\left(\frac{8.66}{10}\right) = 40°.89$$

$\therefore$ The resultant current ($i_R$)

$$= |OC| \sin (\omega t + \alpha)$$

$$i_R = 13.228 \sin (\omega t + 40°.89)$$

## 4.18. BEHAVIOUR of A.C. THROUGH PURE RESISTANCE

A pure resistive circuit is one which has no inductance and capacitance but only resistance as shown in Fig. 4.26 (e.g. of pure resistance circuits are filament lamps and water heaters etc.)

When an a.c. voltage of

$$v = V_m \sin\theta$$

or $$v = V_m \sin\omega t \quad ...(4.14)$$

is applied across such a circuit, a current will flow through it. The value of this current is given by Ohm's law.

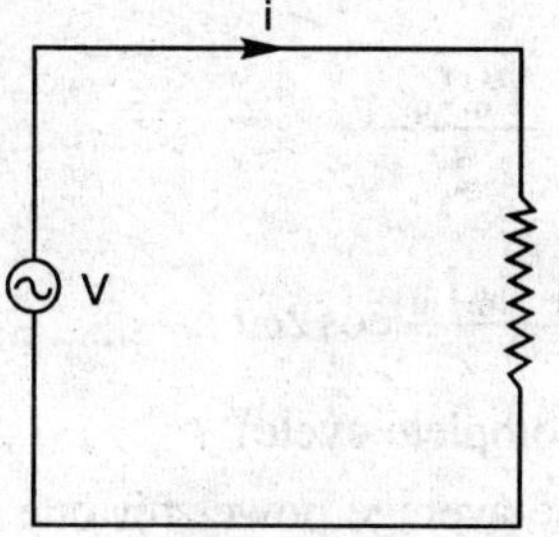


Fig. 4.26

Accordingly $i = = \frac{v}{R}$

$$\Rightarrow i = \frac{V_m}{R}\sin\omega t$$

$$i = I_m \sin\omega t \quad ...(4.15)$$

where $Im = \frac{V_m}{R}$ because `i' is maximum where $\sin\omega t = 1$

Comparing (4.14) and (4.15) we find that the v and i are in phase. The graphical and vectorial representation of these two quantities are shown in Fig. 4.27 (a) and Fig. 4.27 (b) respectively.

Instantaneous Power P = v × i

$$= (V_m \sin\omega t)\,(I_m \sin\omega t)$$

$$= V_m I_m \sin^2\omega t$$

$$= \frac{V_m I_m}{2}(1 - \cos\omega t)$$

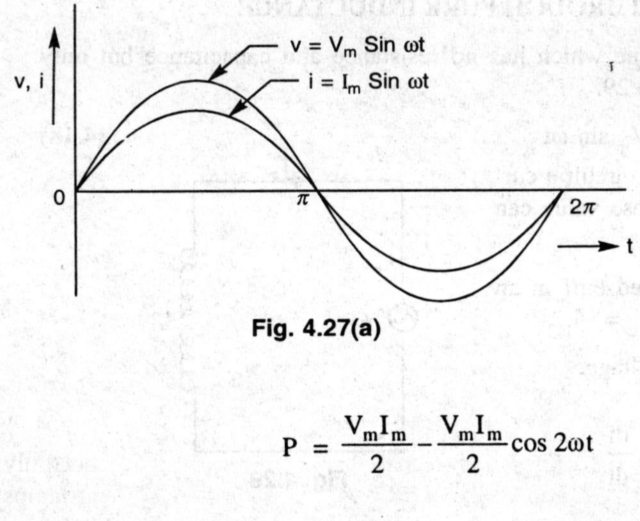


Fig. 4.27(a)

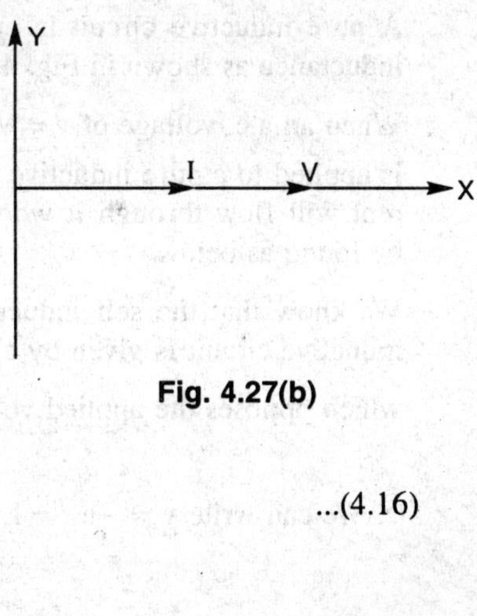


Fig. 4.27(b)

$$P = \frac{V_m I_m}{2} - \frac{V_m I_m}{2}\cos 2\omega t \quad ...(4.16)$$

Thus the power consists of two parts

$$\frac{V_m I_m}{2} \quad \text{............ constant part}$$

and $\frac{V_m I_m}{2}\cos 2\omega t$ ............ fluctuating part (whose average value will be 0 for one complete cycle)

∴ The average power for one complete cycle

$$P_{av} = \frac{1}{2\pi}\int_0^{2\pi} V_{max} I_{max} \sin^2 \theta d\theta$$

$$= \frac{1}{2\pi}\int_0^{2\pi} \frac{V_m I_m (1-\cos 2\theta)}{2} d\theta$$

$$= \frac{V_m I_m}{4\pi}\int_0^{2\pi} d\theta - \frac{V_m I_m}{4\pi}\int_0^{2\pi} \cos 2\theta d\theta$$

$$= \frac{V_m I_m}{4\pi}[\theta]_0^{2\pi} - \frac{V_m I_m}{4\pi}\left[\frac{\sin 2\theta}{2}\right]_0^{2\pi}$$

$$= \frac{V_m I_m}{4\pi}[2\pi - 0] - 0$$

$$P_{av} = \frac{V_m I_m}{2}$$

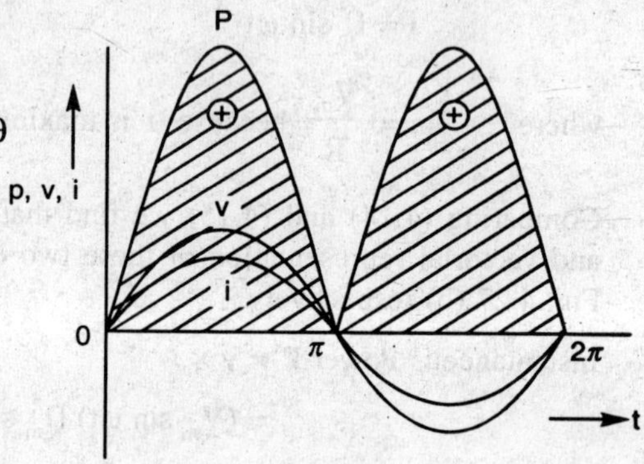


Fig. 4.28

Thus in pure resistive circuit, the average power is never equal to zero [Fig. (4.28)].

## 4.19. BEHAVIOUR of A.C. THROUGH PURE INDUCTANCE

A pure inductive circuit is one which has no resistance and capacitance but only inductance as shown in Fig. 4.29.

When an a.c. voltage of $v = V_m \sin \omega t$ ...(4.18)

is applied to a pure inductive circuit a current will flow through it whose value can be found as below.

We know that the self induced emf in an inductive circuit is given by $e_L = -L$.

which opposes the applied voltage.

∴ We can write $v = -e_L = L\frac{di}{dt}$

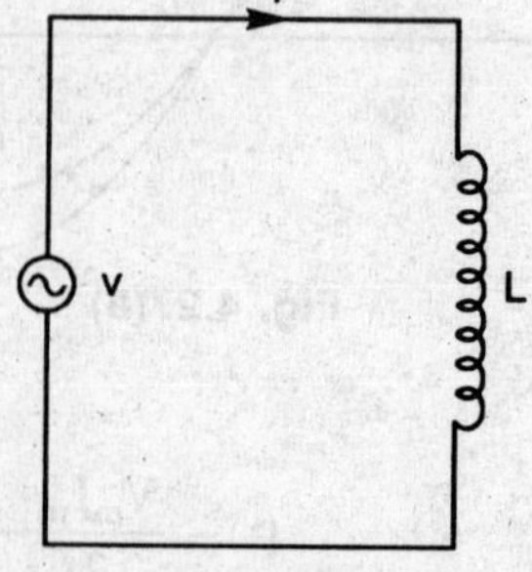


Fig. 4.29

$$v = L\frac{di}{dt}$$

$$\Rightarrow \quad \frac{v}{L}.dt = di$$

$$\Rightarrow \quad di = \frac{V_m}{L}\sin \omega t.dt$$

Integrating both sides we get

$$i = \frac{V_m}{L}\int \sin \omega t.dt$$

$$= \frac{-V_m}{\omega L}[-\cos \omega t]$$

$$= \frac{V_m}{\omega L}[-\cos \omega t]$$

$$= \frac{V_m}{\omega L}[\sin(\omega t - \pi/2)]$$

$$i = I_m \sin(\omega t - \pi/2)$$

where $$I_m = \frac{V_m}{\omega L} \qquad ...(4.20)$$

From equations 4.18 and 4.19 it is clear that current lags behind the applied voitage by 90°. This can be shown in Fig. 4.30 and Fig. 4.31.

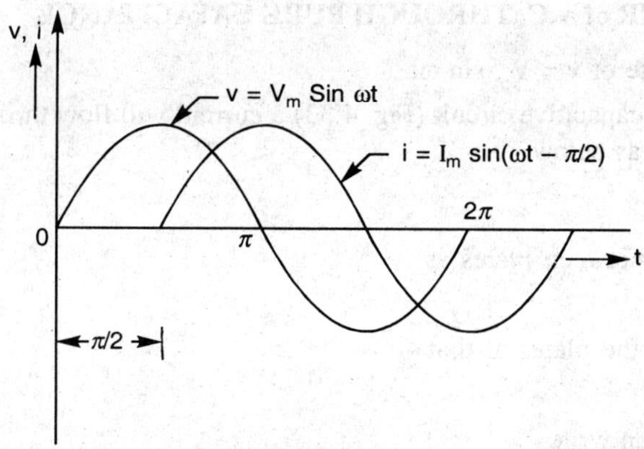


**Fig. 4.30**

In the equation 4.20 '$\omega L$' is called inductive reactance, denoted by '$X_L$' and its unit is also ohms.

$$\therefore \quad I_m = \frac{V_m}{X_L} \qquad ...(4.21)$$

Instantaneous power

$$P = v \times i$$

$$= V_m \sin \omega t \times I_m \sin(\omega t - \pi/2)$$

$$= -V_m I_m \sin \omega t . \cos \omega t$$

$$= \frac{-V_m I_m}{2} \sin 2\omega t \qquad ...(4.22)$$

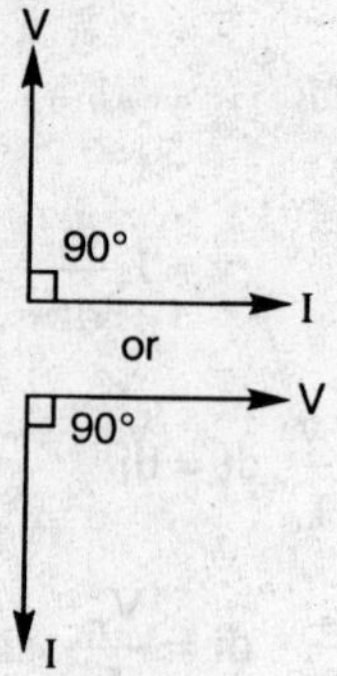


Fig. 4.31

$\therefore$ The average power over one complete cycle =

$$P_{av} = \frac{-V_m I_m}{2} \int_0^{2\pi} \sin 2\theta d\theta$$

$$= \frac{V_m I_m}{2} \left[ \frac{\cos 2\theta}{2} \right]_0^{2\pi}$$

$$= \frac{V_m I_m}{4} [\cos 4\pi - \cos 0].$$

$$= \frac{V_m I_m}{4} [1 - 1]$$

$$\therefore \quad P_{av} = 0$$

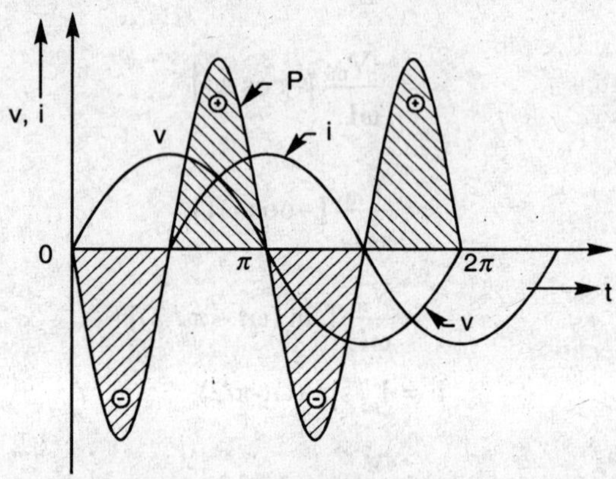


Fig. 4.32

$\therefore$ In a pure inductive circuit, the average power over one complete cycle = zero (Fig. 4.32).

## 4.20. BEHAVIOUR of A.C. THROUGH PURE CAPACITANCE

When an a.c. voltage of $v = V_m \sin \omega t$ ...(4.23)

is applied to a pure capacitive circuit (Fig. 4.33) a current will flow through it whose value can be found as below.

We know that $q = cv$

where $v$ = voltage between plates at any instant of time

and $q$ = charge on the plates at that instant of time

equation 4.23 we can write

$$q = C.V_{max} \sin \omega t$$

Also we know that

$$i = \frac{dq}{dt}$$

$$\therefore \quad i = \frac{d}{dt}(C.V_{max} \sin \omega t)$$

$$= C.V_{max}. \cos \omega t.\omega$$

$$= \omega C.V_{max}. \cos \omega t$$

$$= \left[\frac{V_{max}}{1/\omega C}\right] \sin\left(\frac{\pi}{2} + \omega t\right)$$

$$= \left[\frac{V_{max}}{X_c}\right] \sin\left(\frac{\pi}{2} + \omega t\right)$$

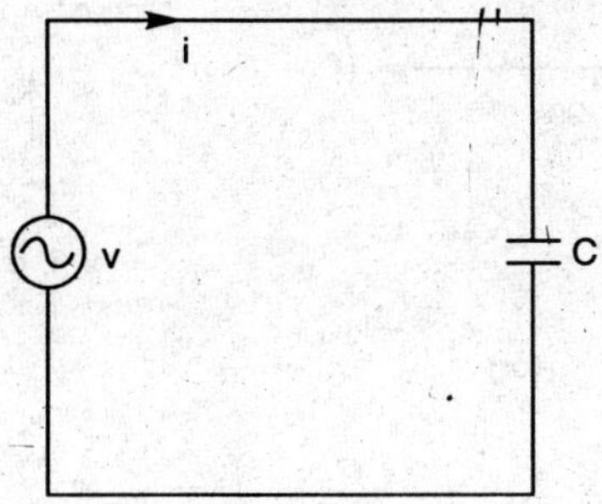


Fig. 4.33

$$i = I_m \sin(\pi/2 + \omega t) \qquad \text{...(4.24)}$$

$$\text{where } I_m = \frac{V_m}{1/\omega C} = \frac{V_m}{X_c} \qquad \text{...(4.25)}$$

because 'i' becomes $I_{max}$ when $\sin\left(\frac{\pi}{2} + \omega t\right) = 1$

$Xc = \frac{1}{\omega c}$ is called capacitive reactance and its unit is also ohm.

From equations 4.23 and 4.24, it is clear that current leads voltage by 90°. This is shown in Fig. 4.34 and Fig. 4.35.

The instantaneous power $P = v \times i$

$$= V_m \sin \omega t . I_m \sin(\omega t + 90)$$

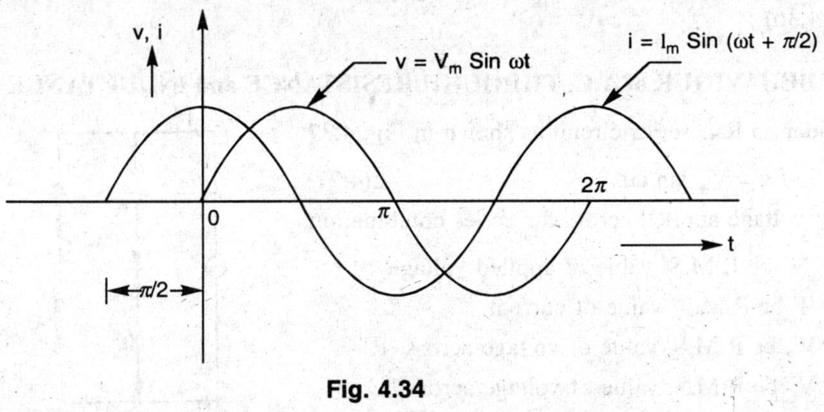


Fig. 4.34

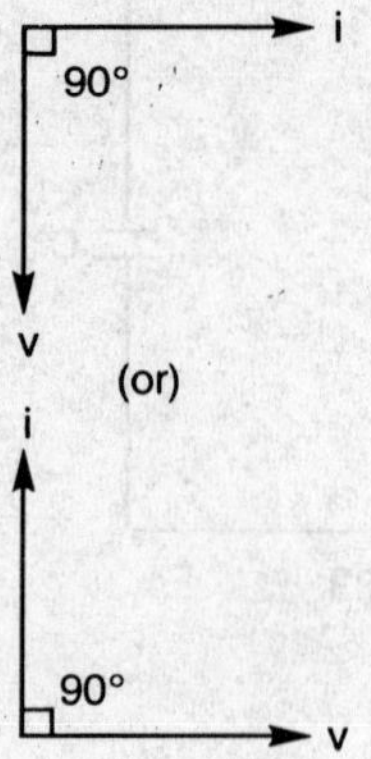


Fig. 4.35

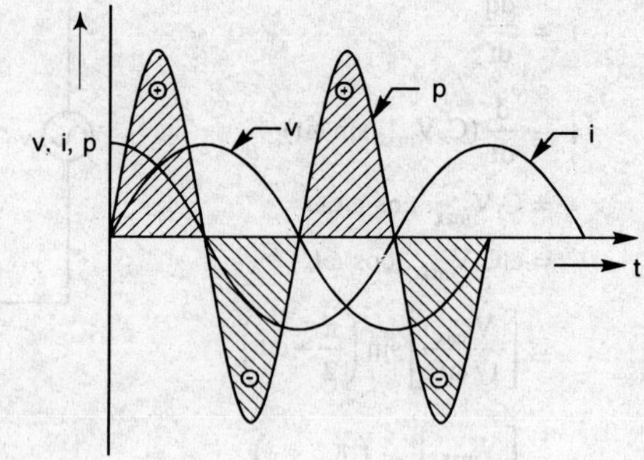


Fig. 4.36

$$= V_m I_m \sin \omega t . \cos \omega t$$

$$P = \frac{V_m I_m}{2} \sin 2\,\omega t \qquad ...(4.26)$$

The average power over one complete cycle =

$$P_{av} = \int_0^{2\pi} \frac{V_m I_m}{2} \sin 2\theta\, d\theta$$

$$= \frac{-V_m I_m}{2} \left[ \frac{\cos 2\theta}{2} \right]_0^{2\pi}$$

$$= \frac{-V_m I_m}{4} [\cos 4\pi - \cos 0]$$

$$= \frac{-V_m I_m}{4} [1 - 1]$$

$$P_{av} = 0$$

∴ In a pure capacitive circuit, the average power over one complete cycle = zero (Fig. 4.36)

## 4.21. BEHAVIOUR of A.C. THROUGH RESISTANCE and INDUCTANCE

Consider an R-L series circuit as shown in Fig. 4.37

Let $v = V_m \sin \omega t$ ...(4.27)

be the voltage applied across the series combination.

Let 'V' be R.M.S. value of applied voltage

'I' be R.M.S. value of current

$V_R$ be R.M.S. value of voltage across 'R'

$V_L$ be R.M.S. value of voltage across 'L'

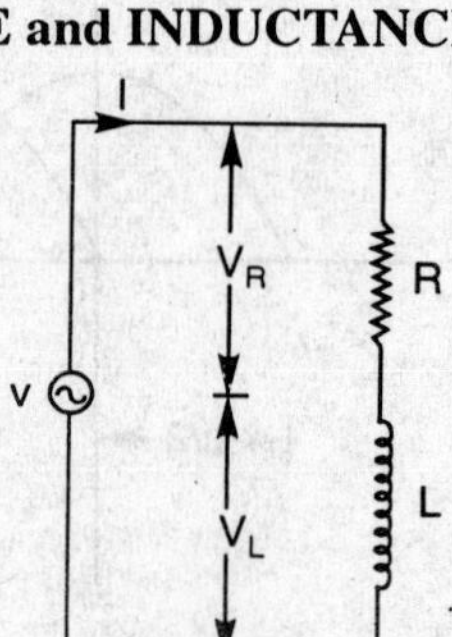


Fig. 4.37

Using Fig. 4.27 and Fig. 4.31 we can draw the vector diagram of Fig. 4.37 as below (Fig. 4.38). In Fig. 4.38 'OP' represents the current vector 'OM' represents $V_R$ (voltage drop across resistance), 'MN' represents $V_L$ (voltage drop across inductance) and 'ON' represents applied voltage V.

Thus $$ON = \sqrt{(OM)^2 + (MN)^2}$$

$$V = \sqrt{(V_R)^2 + (V_L)^2}$$

but $$VR = I \cdot R$$

$$VL = I.X_L$$

$$V = \sqrt{(IR)^2 + (IX_L)^2}$$

$$= I\sqrt{(R^2 + X_L)^2}$$

$$\frac{V}{\sqrt{R^2 + X_L^2}} = 1$$

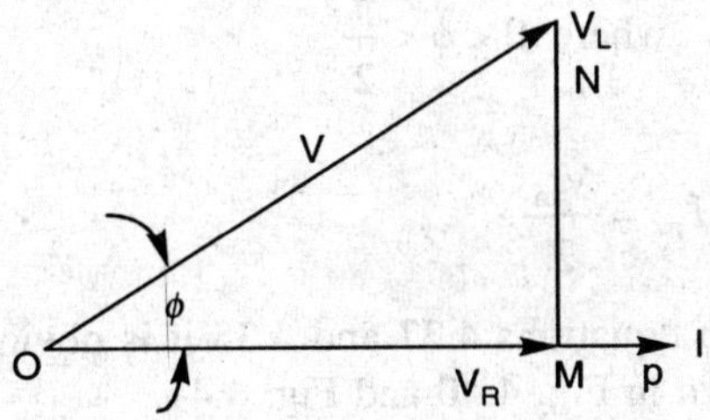

Fig. 4.38

The quantity $\sqrt{R^2 + X_L^2}$ is known as impedance and is denoted by "Z". Its unit is ohm.

$$\therefore \qquad I = \frac{V}{Z} \qquad ...(4.28)$$

From Fig. 4.39, we have

$$Z^2 = R^2 + X_L^2$$

This triangle is called impedance triangle.

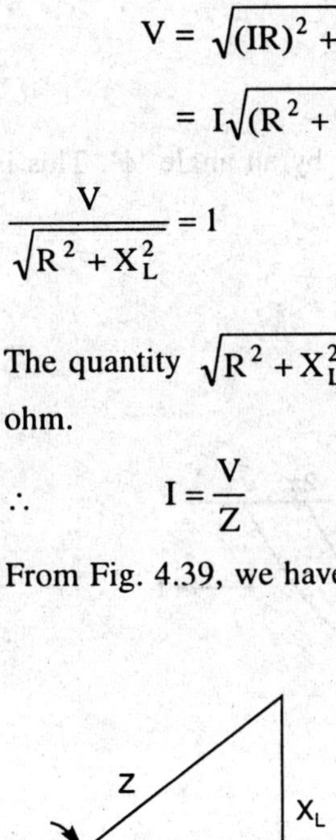

Fig. 4.39

Also we can write $$\tan\phi = \frac{X_L}{R} \qquad ...(4.29)$$

$$\phi = \tan^{-1}\left(\frac{X_L}{R}\right) \qquad ...(4.30)$$

and $$\cos\phi = \frac{R}{Z} \qquad ...(4.31)$$

$$\phi = \cos^{-1}\left(\frac{R}{Z}\right) \qquad ...(4.32)$$

$$\sin\phi = \frac{X_L}{Z} \qquad ...(4.33)$$

$$\phi = \sin^{-1}\left(\frac{X_L}{Z}\right) \qquad \text{...(4.34)}$$

Thus in an R-L circuit

if $v = V_m \sin \omega t$ is the applied voltage then the current flowing through it is given by

$$i = I_m \sin(\omega t - \phi) \qquad \text{...(4.35)}$$

$$\text{where } 0 < \phi < \frac{\pi}{2}$$

$$\text{and } I_m = \frac{V_m}{Z}$$

From equations 4.27 and 4.35 it is obvious that 'i' lags 'v' by an angle '$\phi$'. This is shown in Fig. 4.40 and Fig. 4.41.

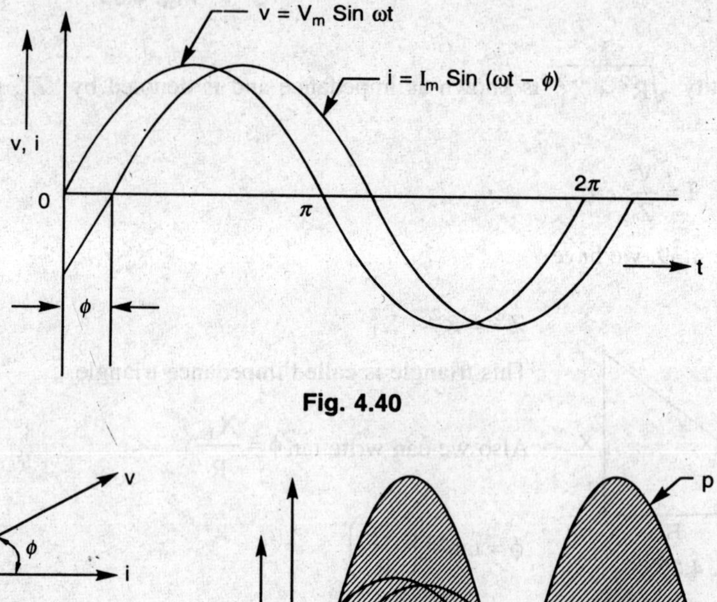


Fig. 4.40

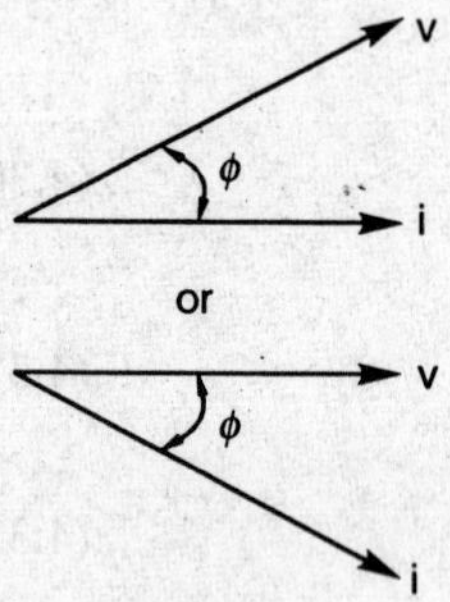


Fig. 4.41

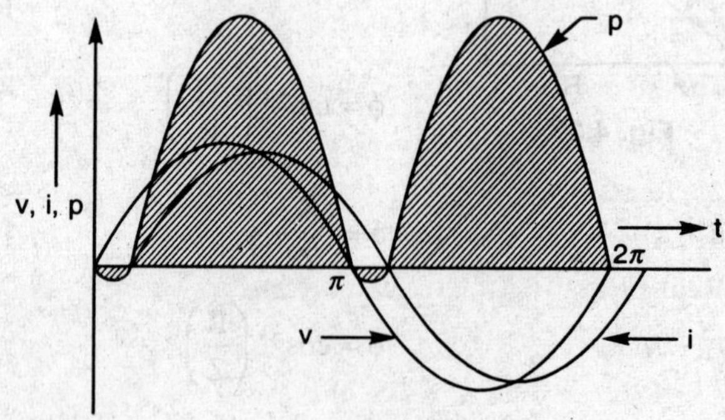


Fig. 4.42

The instantaneous power = v × i

$$P = V_m \sin \omega t \times I_m \sin(\omega t - \phi)$$

$$= V_m I_m . \sin \omega t . \sin (\omega t - \phi)$$

$$= \frac{V_m I_m}{2} [\cos \phi - \cos(2\omega t - \phi)]$$

$$P = \frac{V_m I_m}{2} \cos \phi - \frac{V_m I_m}{2} \cos (2\omega t - \phi)$$

Average power consumed $P_{av} = \int_0^{2\pi} V_m I_m \sin \omega t . \sin (\omega t - \phi) dt$

After simplification we get

$$P_{av} = \frac{V_m I_m}{2} \cos \phi$$

$$= \frac{V_m}{\sqrt{2}} . \frac{I_m}{\sqrt{2}} \cos \phi$$

$$P_{av} = V_{R.M.S.} \cdot I_{R.M.S.} \cos \phi \quad \text{...(4.37)}$$

Note: In general $P = I^2 R$

$$= I \times I \times R$$

$$= I \times \frac{V}{Z} \times R \quad \text{(from equation 4.28)}$$

$$= I \times V \times \left(\frac{R}{Z}\right)$$

$$= I \times V \times \cos \phi \quad \text{(from equation 4.31)}$$

$\therefore$ $P = VI \cos \phi$

## 4.22. POWER in A.C. CIRCUIT

The three powers in a.c. circuits are:

1. Real power or active power
2. Reactive power
3. Apparent power

**Real Power:** The actual power consumed in an a.c. circuit is called real power.

If 'V' is the R.M.S. value of voltage

'I' is the R.M.S. value of current

'$\phi$' is the phase angle between

Then real power = VI cos $\phi$ ...(4.38)

Its unit is watts.

**Reactive Power:** The power absorbed by a pure reactance ($X_L$ or $X_c$) in a circuit is called reactive power. It is given by product of VI and sine of angle between 'V' and 'I'.

$\therefore$ Reactive power = V.I sin $\phi$ ...(4.39)

The unit of reactive power in VAR $\rightarrow$ (Voltampere reactive)

**Apparent Power:** It is given by the product of voltage and current.

Thus apparent power = V $\times$ I Voltampere ...(4.40)

From eq. 4.38, 4.39, 4.30, we have

$$\sqrt{(\text{activepower})^2 + (\text{reactivepower})^2} = \text{Apparent power} \quad ...(4.41)$$

## 4.23. POWER FACTOR (COS $\phi$)

It may be defined as the cosine of angle between voltage and current.

It is also given by the ratio of resistance to impedance

Thus $$\cos \phi = \frac{R}{Z} \quad ...(4.42)$$

It is also given by ratio of real power to apparent power

Thus $$\cos \phi = \frac{VI \cos \phi}{VI} \quad ...(4.43)$$

**Note:**

1) The power factor of a system has to be as high as possible
2) The maximum value of power factor is 1

## 4.24. BEHAVIOUR of A.C. THROUGH RESISTANCE and CAPACITANCE

Consider an R-C circuit as shown in Fig. 4.43.

Let $v = V_m \sin \omega t$ ...(4.44)

be the applied voltage across the series combination

Using Fig. 4.27 and Fig. 4.35 we can draw the vector diagram of Fig. 4.43 as above [Fig. (4.44)].

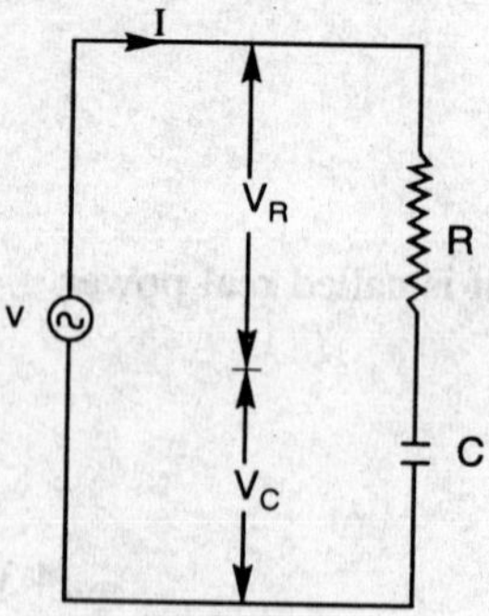


Fig. 4.43

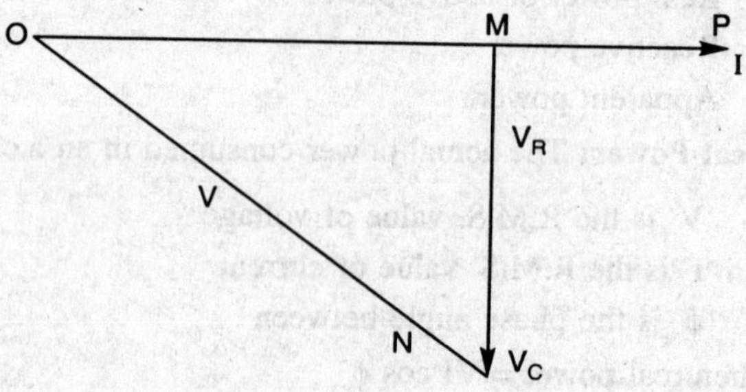


Fig. 4.44

In Fig. 4.44

OM represents $V_R$ (drop across R)

OP represents I

ON represents V (supply voltage)

MN represents $V_C$ (drop across C)

Thus we have

$$ON = \sqrt{V_R^2 + V_C^2} \qquad \text{but } V_R = I_R$$

$$= \sqrt{(IR)^2 + (IX_C)^2} \qquad V_C = I.X_C$$

$$V = I\sqrt{R^2 + (X_C)^2}$$

$$\frac{V}{\sqrt{R^2 + (X_C)^2}} = I = \frac{V}{Z} \qquad ...(4.45)$$

where $Z = \sqrt{R^2 + (X_C)^2}$ is called impedance of the circuit

The impedance triangle can be drawn as shown in Fig. 4.45

$$\cos\phi = \frac{R}{Z} \qquad ...(4.46)$$

$$\angle\phi = \cos^{-1}(R/Z) \qquad ...(4.47)$$

$$\tan\phi = \left(\frac{X_C}{R}\right) \qquad ...(4.48)$$

$$= \tan^{-1}\left(\frac{X_C}{R}\right) \qquad ...(4.49)$$

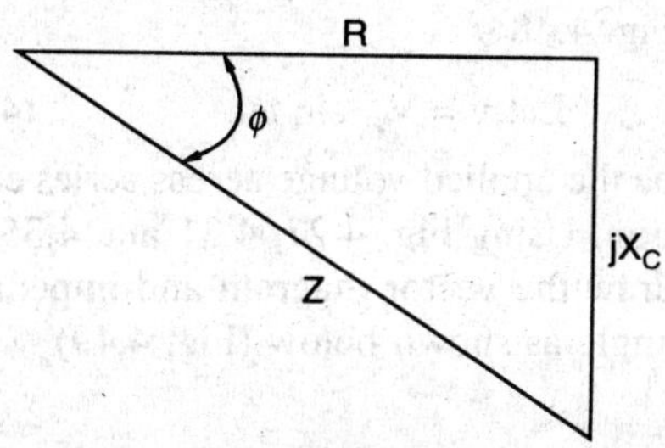


Fig. 4.45

Thus in an R-C series circuit

if $v = V_m \sin \omega t$ is applied voltage

then the current flowing through it is given by

$$i = I_m \sin(\omega t + \phi) \qquad ...(4.50)$$

$$\text{where} \quad 0 < \phi < \frac{\pi}{2}$$

From equations 4.44 and 4.50 we can see that 'i' leads 'V' by an angle $\phi$. This is shown in Fig. 4.46 and Fig. 4.47

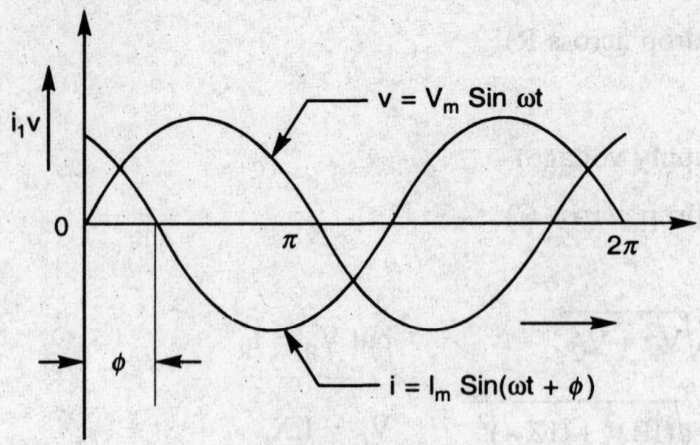


Fig. 4.46

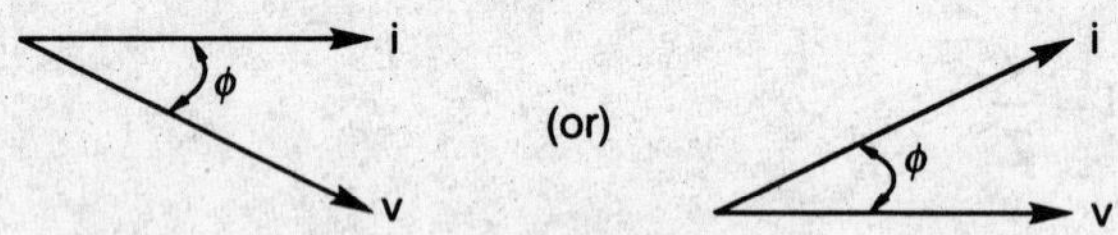


Fig. 4.47

## 4.25. BEHAVIOUR of A.C. THROUGH RESISTANCE, INDUCTANCE and CAPACITANCE

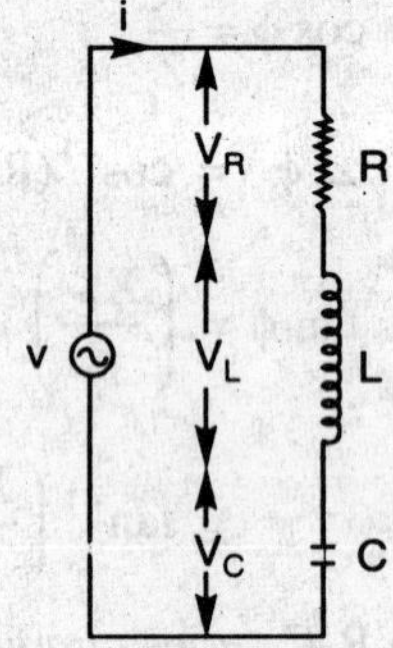


Fig. 4.48

Consider R-L-C series circuit as shown in Fig. 4.48

Let $v = V_m \sin \omega t$ ...(4.51)

be the applied voltage across series combination. Using Fig. 4.27, 4.31 and 4.35 we can draw the vector diagram and impedance triangle as shown below (Fig. 4.49)

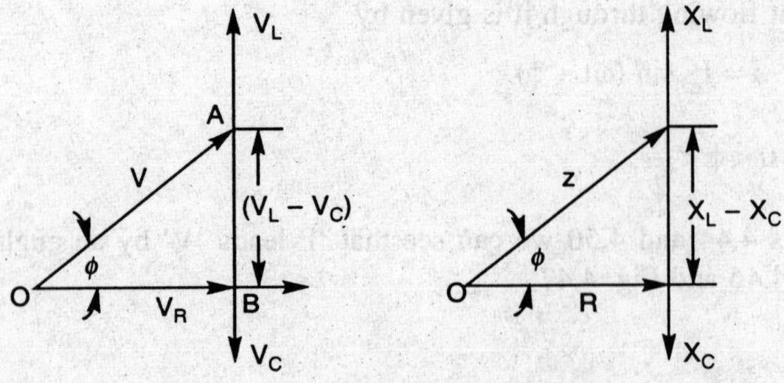


Fig. 4.49

On the other hand if $V_C > V_L$ and $X_C > X_L$ the same can be redrawn as below in Fig. 4.50.

From Fig. 4.49

$$(OA)^2 = (OB)^2 + (AB)^2$$

$$OA = \sqrt{(OB)^2 + (AB)^2}$$

where $OA = V$ (resultant voltage)

$OB = V_R$ (voltage across resistance) $= IR$

$AB = (V_L - V_C)$ [net reactive drop] $= I(X_L - X_C)$

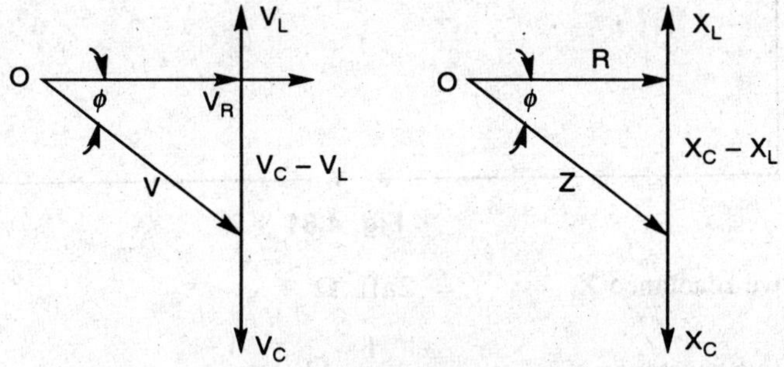


**Fig. 4.50**

$$OA = \sqrt{(IR)^2 + [I(X_L - X_C]^2}$$

$$V = I\sqrt{R^2 + (X_L - X_C)^2}$$

$$\frac{V}{\sqrt{R^2 + (X_L - X_C)^2}} = I$$

The quantity $\sqrt{R^2 + (X_L - X_C)^2}$ is called impedance of the circuit. It is denoted by 'Z' and its unit is ohm.

$$\therefore \quad I = \frac{V}{Z} \text{ where } Z = \sqrt{R^2 + (X_L - X_C)^2} \quad \text{...(4.52)}$$

from the impedance triangle (Fig. 4.49)

$$\cos\phi = \frac{R}{Z} \quad \Rightarrow \quad \phi = \cos^{-1}(R/Z) \quad \text{...(4.53)}$$

$$\tan\phi = \frac{(X_L - X_C)}{R} \quad \Rightarrow \quad \phi = \tan^{-1}\frac{(X_L - X_C)}{R} \quad \text{...(4.54)}$$

Thus in an R-L-C series circuit,

if $v = V_m \sin \omega t$ is the applied voltage then the current flowing through it is given by

$$i = I_m \sin(\omega t \pm \phi)$$

where $0 < \phi < \frac{\pi}{2}$

and $+\phi$ for $X_C > X_L$

$-\phi$ for $X_L > X_C$

## 4.26. R-L-C SERIES RESONANCE

Consider an R-L-C series circuit as shown in Fig. 4.51

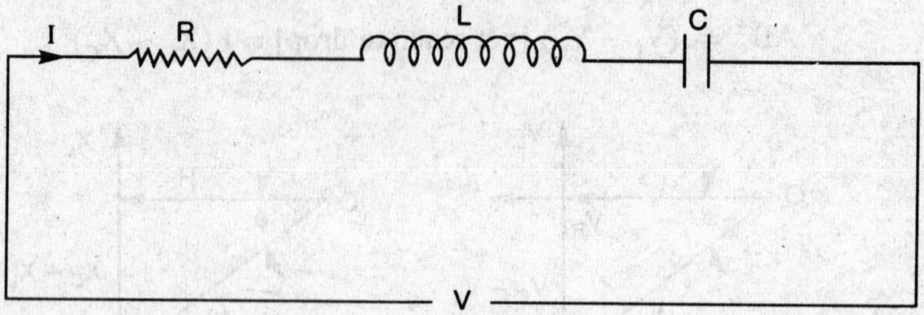


**Fig. 4.51**

The inductive reactance $X_L$ $= 2\pi fL\ \Omega$

The capacitive reactance $X_C$ $= \frac{1}{2\pi fC}\Omega$

The resistance $= R\ \Omega$

The net reactance X $= X_L - X_C$

The impedance of the circuit $= Z = \sqrt{R^2 + X^2}$

$$= \sqrt{R^2 + (X_L - X_C)^2}$$

**A circuit of the type shown in Fig. 4.51 is said to be at resonance, when net reactance of the circuit is zero.**

i.e. $X = 0$

$\Rightarrow$ $X_L - X_C = 0$

$\Rightarrow$ $X_L = X_C$

Also when $X_L = X_C$; the impedance $Z = \sqrt{R^2 + O^2}$

$$= R$$

Thus circuit current becomes maximum

The power factor is given by $(\cos\phi) = \frac{R}{Z} = \frac{R}{R} = 1$

i.e., the power factor becomes unity.

To find the frequency at resonance '$f_0$'

We have at resonance

$$X_L = X_C$$

$$2\pi f_0 L = \frac{1}{2\pi f_0 c}$$

$$(2\pi f_0)^2 = \frac{1}{LC}$$

$$(2\pi f_0) = \frac{1}{\sqrt{LC}}$$

$$\therefore \quad f_0 = \frac{1}{2\pi\sqrt{LC}} \text{Hz} \qquad ...(4.55)$$

Thus at series resonance

(i) Net reactance 'X' = 0

(ii) $X_L = X_C$

(iii) Impedance of the circuit Z = R (Minimum)

(iv) Current becomes maximum $I = \frac{V}{R}$

(v) Power factor becomes unity.

## 4.27. RESONANCE in PARALLEL CIRCUIT

A circuit of the type shown in Fig. 4.52 is said to be at resonance, when the net reactive component of current is zero.

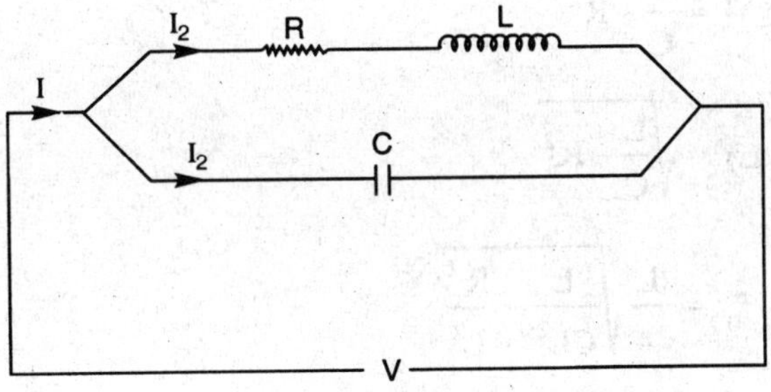


Fig. 4.52

The vector diagram of the circuit Fig. 4.52 can be drawn as Fig. 4.53.

From Fig. 4.53, the net reactive component of current is given by $(I_2 - I_1 \sin \phi_1)$

$\therefore$ at resonance $(I_2 - I_1 \sin \phi_1) = 0$

$$I_2 = I_1 \sin \phi_1$$

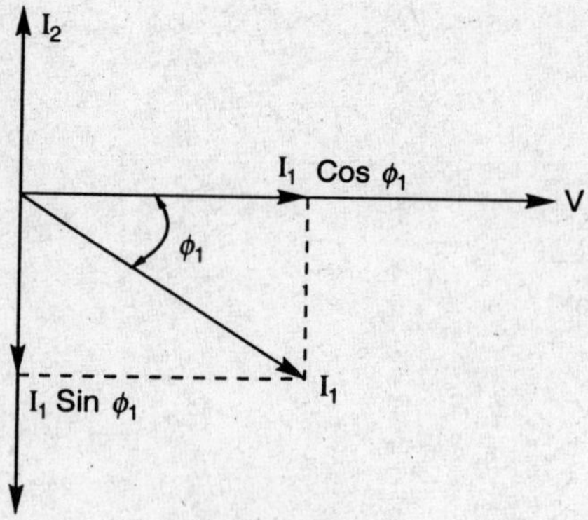


**Fig. 4.53**

From equations 4.25, 4.28 and 4.33 we get

$$\frac{V}{X_C} = \frac{V}{\sqrt{R^2 + X_L^2}} \cdot \frac{X_L}{\sqrt{R^2 + X_L^2}}$$

$$\frac{1}{X_C} = \frac{X_L}{R^2 + X_L^2}$$

$$R^2 + X_L{}^2 = X_L \cdot X_C$$

$$R^2 + (\omega L)^2 = (\omega . L)\left(\frac{1}{\omega C}\right)$$

$$(\omega L)^2 = \frac{L}{C} - R^2$$

$$(2\pi f_0 L)^2 = \frac{L}{C} - R^2$$

$$(2\pi f_0 L) = \sqrt{\frac{L}{C} - R^2}$$

$$f_0 = \frac{1}{2\pi}\sqrt{\frac{L}{CL^2} - \frac{R^2}{L^2}}$$

$$f_0 = \frac{1}{2\pi}\sqrt{\frac{1}{LC} - \frac{R^2}{L^2}} \text{ Hz} \qquad ...(4.56)$$

**P. 4.12.** A pure resistive circuit is excited with a voltage of v = 200 sin 314t. The current flowing through it is found to be i = 50 sin 314t. Determine the power dissipated in the resistance.

**Solution:**

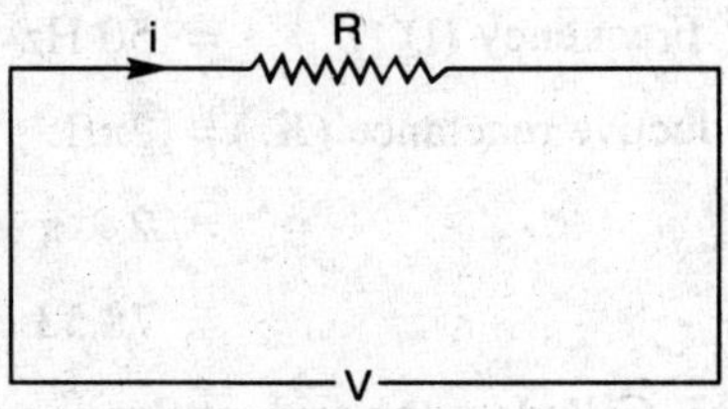


Fig. 4.54

Given $v = 200 \sin 314\, t$

but we have $v = V_m \sin \omega t$

$\Rightarrow \quad V_m = 200$

$\omega = 314t$

also $i = 50 \sin 314t$

but $i = I_m \sin \omega t$

$\Rightarrow \quad I_m = 50$

$\omega = 314$

$$\therefore \quad R = \frac{V_m}{I_m} = \frac{200}{50} = 4\Omega$$

$\therefore$ Power dissipated in the resistance $= I^2_{R.M.S.} \times R$

$$= \left(\frac{50}{\sqrt{2}}\right)^2 \times 4$$

$= 5000$ watts.

**P. 4.13.** The power dissipated in a pure resistive circuit is 200 watts. The current flowing through the circuit is $i = 5 \sin \omega t$. Find a similar expressions for voltage.

**Solution:**

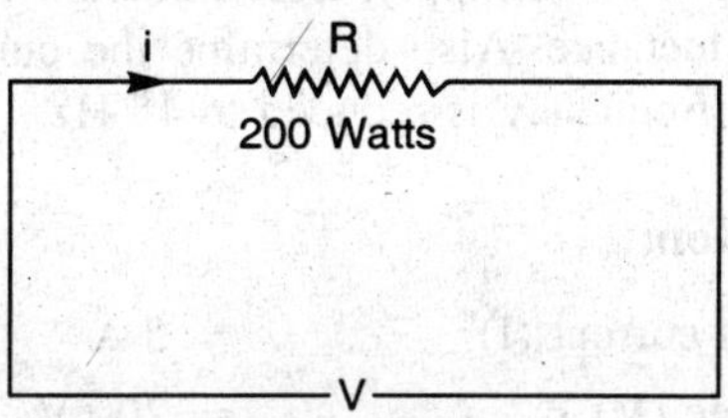


Fig. 4.55

Given $i = 5 \sin \omega t$...(i)

Power dissipated = 200 watts = $I^2_{R.M.S.} R$

From equation (i) we have

$I_{max} = 5$ A

$$I_{R.M.S.} = \frac{5}{\sqrt{2}}$$

$$\Rightarrow \quad 200 = \left(\frac{5}{\sqrt{2}}\right)^2 \times R$$

$\therefore \quad R = 16$ ohms

$\therefore \quad V_m = I_{max} \times R = 5 \times 16 = 80$ volts

$\therefore \quad v = 80 \sin \omega t$ volts.

**P. 4.14.** Determine the inductive reactance of a coil of inductance 0.25 henry, if the frequency is 50 Hz.

**Solution:**

Given, Inductance (L) = 0.25 H

Frequency (f) = 50 Hz

$\therefore$ Inductive reactance ($X_L$) = $2\pi fL$

$= 2 \times \pi \times 50 \times 0.25$

$= 78.53$ ohms.

**P. 4.15.** Calculate the current flowing through a coil of inductance 0.05 H when it is connected to a 230V, 60Hz supply.

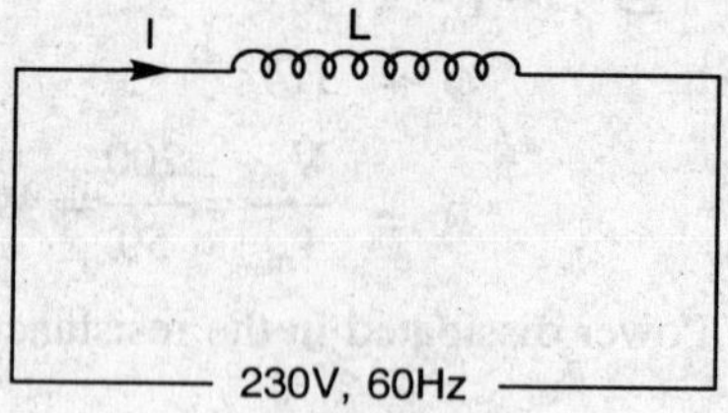


Fig. 4.56

**Solution:**

Given inductance (L) = 0.05H

Supply voltage ($V_{R.M.S.}$) = 230V

Supply frequency (f) = 60 Hz

Inductive reactance ($X_L$) = $2\pi fL$

$= 2 \times \pi \times 60 \times 0.05$

$= 18.85\ \Omega$

$\therefore$ Current through coil (I) = $\dfrac{V}{X_L}$ A

$= 12.2$ A

**P. 4.16.** A choking coil of negligible resistance takes a current of 5 A when connected to 200V, 50Hz supply. Determine the value of inductance. Also determine the current when frequency is reduced to 45 Hz.

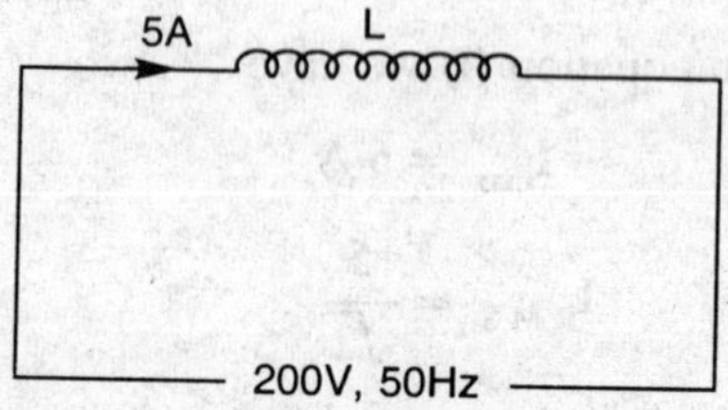


Fig. 4.57

**Solution:**

Given current (I) = 5 A

Voltage (V) = 200 V

Frequency (f) = 50 Hz

Inductive reactance ($X_L$) = $2\pi fL$

$= 2\pi \times 50 \times (L)$ ...(i)

For coil of negligible resistance $X_L = \dfrac{V}{I} = \dfrac{200}{5} = 40\Omega$ ...(ii)

From (i) and (ii)

$2\pi \times 50 \times (L) = 40$

$$L = \frac{40}{2\pi \times 50} = 0.1273 \text{ henry}$$

Now when the frequency is reduced to 45 Hz

$$I = \frac{V}{X_L}$$

where $XL = 2\pi fL$

given $f = 45$ Hz

$L = 0.159$

$V = 200V$

$$\therefore \quad I = \frac{200}{2 \times \pi \times 45 \times 0.159} = 4.444 \text{ A}$$

**P. 4.17.** A voltage of 150V, 50 Hz is applied to a coil of negligible resistance and inductance 0.2 H. Write the time equation for voltage and current.

**Solution:**

Given, $V_{R.M.S.} = 150V \Rightarrow V_{max} = 2\sqrt{2} \times V_{R.M.S.} = 212.132$ volts

Supply frequency = 50 Hz

Inductance (L) = 0.2 H

Inductive reactance ($X_L$) = $2\pi fL$

$= 2 \times \pi \times 50 \times 0.2$

$= 62.83$ ohms

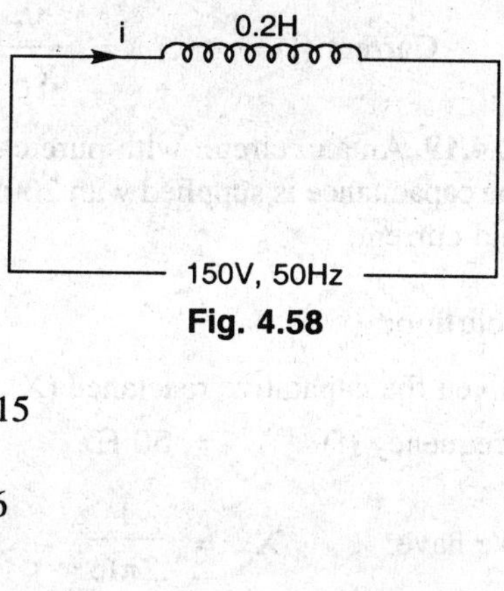

Fig. 4.58

In a pure inductive coil

if $v = V_m \sin \omega t$

then $i = I_m \sin (\omega t - \pi/2)$

where $\omega = 2\pi f = 2\pi \times 50 = 314.15$

$$I_m = \frac{V_{max}}{X_L} = \frac{212.13}{62.83} = 3.376$$

$\therefore$ $v = 212.13 \sin 314\, t$

and $i = 3.376 \sin (314t - \pi/2)$

**P. 4.18.** Calculate the current drawn by a pre capacitive circuit of 25μF when connected to a 200V, 60 Hz supply. Also calculate the current through it when

(i) frequency is doubled

(ii) frequency is halved

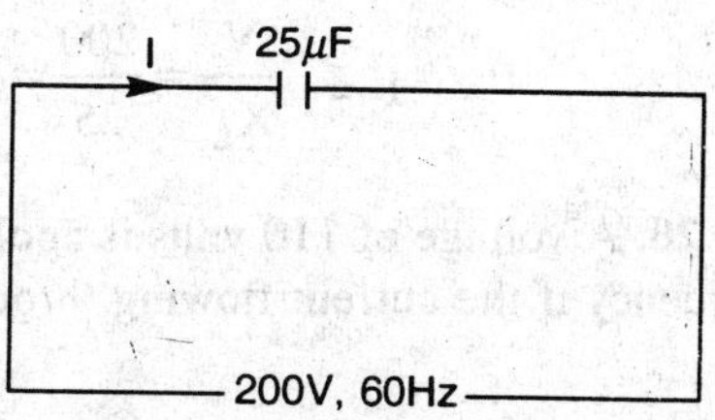

Fig. 4.59

**Solution:**

Given capacitance (C) = 25μF

$= 25 \times 10^{-6}$ F

Supply voltage (V) = 200 V

Supply frequency (f) = 60 Hz

$$\text{Capacitive reactance } (X_C) = \frac{1}{2\pi fc} = \frac{1}{2\pi \times 60 \times 25 \times 10^{-6}}$$

$$= 106.1033\ \Omega$$

$$\text{Current drawn (I)} = \frac{V}{X_C} = \frac{200}{106.103} = 1.88\ \text{A}$$

when the frequency is doubled

$$X_C = \frac{1}{2\pi \times 120 \times 25 \times 10^{-6}} = 53.051\ \Omega$$

$$\therefore \quad \text{Current} \quad (I) = \frac{V}{X_C} = \frac{200}{53.051} = 3.769\ \text{A}$$

when the frequency is halvled

$$X_C = \frac{1}{2\pi \times 30 \times 25 \times 10^{-6}} = 212.206\ \Omega$$

$$\therefore \quad \text{Current (I)} = \frac{V}{X_C} = \frac{200}{212.206} = 0.9424\ \text{A}$$

**P. 4.19.** An a.c. circuit with pure capacitance has a reactance of 25W at 50Hz. When the capacitance is supplied with 200V, 50Hz supply determine the values of capacitance and current.

**Solution:**

Given the capacitive reactance ($X_C$) = 25 Ω

Frequency (f) = 50 Hz

We have, $$X_C = \frac{1}{2\pi fc}$$

$$\Rightarrow \quad C = \frac{1}{2\pi f X_C} = \frac{1}{2\pi \times 50 \times 25}$$

$$= 1.273 \times 10^{-4}\ \text{F}$$

$$I = \frac{V}{X_L} = \frac{200}{25} = 8\ \text{A}$$

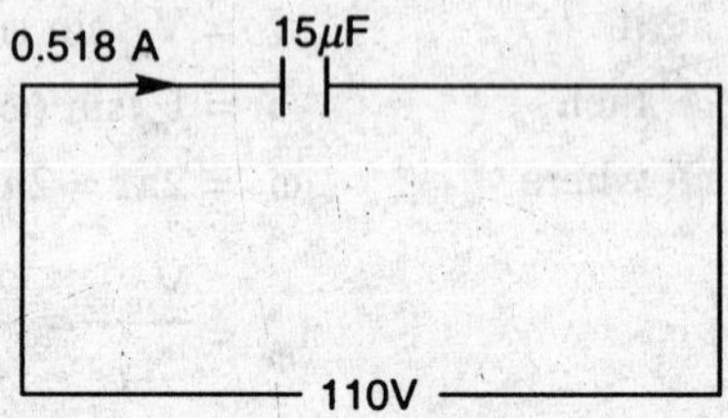

Fig. 4.60

**P. 4.20.** A voltage of 110 volts is applied to a capacitance of 15μF. What must be the frequency if the current flowing through it is 0.518 A?

**Solution:**

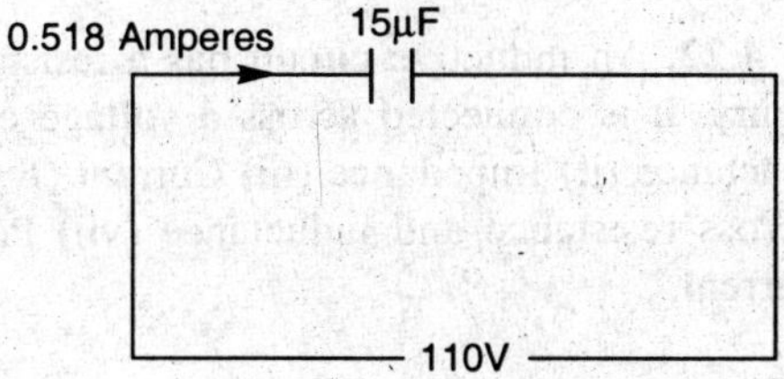

**Fig. 4.61**

Given $V_{R.M.S.} = 110V$

Capacitance (C) $= 15 \times 10^{-6}$ F

Current (I) $= 0.518$ A

We have $\frac{V}{I} = X_C$

$$\therefore X_C = \frac{110}{0.518} = 212.206\ \Omega$$

But, $X_C = \frac{1}{2\pi fc}$

$$f = \frac{1}{2\pi(X_C).C} = \frac{1}{2\pi \times 212.206 \times 15 \times 10^{-6}}$$

$$= 50 \text{ Hz.}$$

**P. 4.21.** Calculate the current flowing through a coil of resistance 10 Ω and inductance 0.02 henry when supplied with a voltage of 250V, 50 Hz. Also determine the phase angle between voltage and current.

**Solution:**

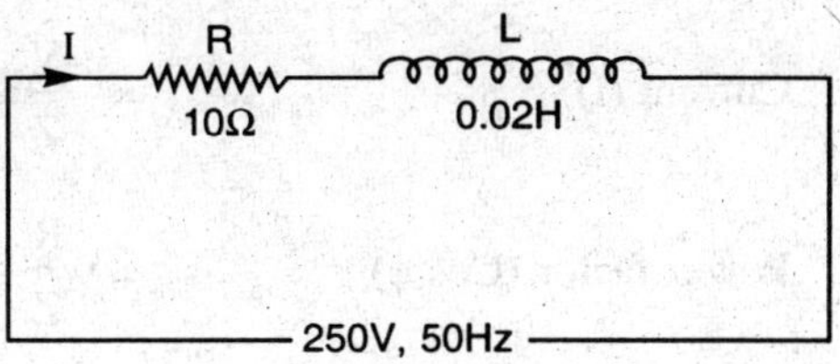

**Fig. 4.62**

Given Resistance of coil (R) = 10 Ω

Inductance of the coil (L) = 0.02 H

Supply voltage ($V_{R.M.S.}$) = 250 V

Supply frequency (f) = 50 Hz

Inductive reactance $(X_L) = 2\pi fL$

$= 2 \times \pi \times 50 \times 0.02$

$= 6.28\ \Omega$

Impedance $(Z) = \sqrt{R^2 + X_L^2} = 11.8\ \Omega$

Current $I = \frac{V}{Z} = \frac{250}{11.8} = 21.168$ A

Power factor (cos φ) $= \frac{R}{|Z|} = \frac{10}{11.8} = 0.847$

∴ Phase angle (φ) $= \cos^{-1}\left(\frac{R}{Z}\right)$

$= 30°.06$

**P. 4.22.** An inductive circuit has a resistance of 50 ohms and an inductance of 0.5 henry. It is connected across a voltage of 200 V, 50 Hz supply. Find (i) Inductive reactance (ii) Impedance (iii) Current (iv) Power factor (v) Phase angle (vi) Voltage across resistance and inductance (vii) Power (viii) Time equation for voltage and current.

**Solution:**

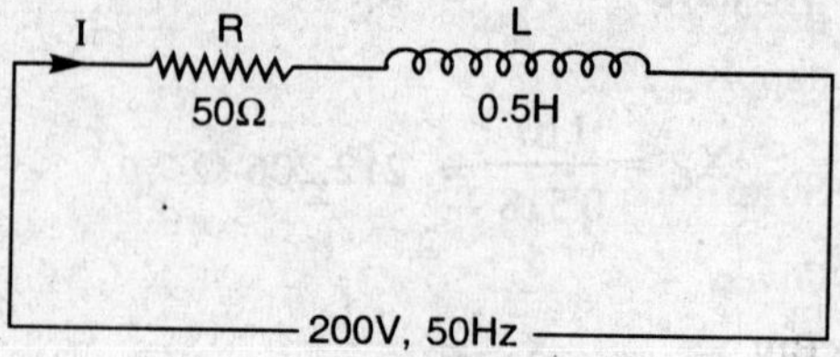


**Fig. 4.63**

Given

Resistance (R) $= 50\ \Omega$

Inductance (L) $= 0.5$ H

Voltage ($V_{R.M.S.}$) $= 200$ V

Frequency (f) $= 50$ Hz

Inductive reactance ($X_L$) $= 2\pi fL$

$= 2 \times \pi \times 50 \times 0.5$

$= 157.1\ \Omega$

Impedance (Z) $= \sqrt{R^2 + X_L^2} = 164.85\ \Omega$

Current (I) $= \frac{V}{Z} = \frac{200}{164.8} = 1.21$ A.

Power factor (Cos $\phi$) $= \frac{R}{Z} = \frac{50}{164.8} = 0.3034$

Phase angle ($\phi$) $= \cos^{-1}\left(\frac{R}{Z}\right) = 72°.34$

Voltage across resistance ($V_R$) $= I \times R$

$= 1.21 \times 50 = 60.5$ volts

Voltage across inductance ($V_L$) $= I \times (X_L)$

$= 1.21 \times 157.1 = 190.9$ volts

Active power $= VI \cos \phi$

$= 73.42$ watts

Reactive power $= VI \sin\phi$

$= 230.5$ VARs

Apparent power $= VI$

$= 242$ volt A

Time equation for voltage

$$v = V_m \sin \omega t$$

$$= (200)\sqrt{2} \sin (2\pi 50)t$$

$$v = 282.8 \sin 314\, t$$

Time equation for current

$$i = I_m \sin(\omega t - \phi)$$
$$= (1.21)\sqrt{2} \sin(314t - 72°.34)$$
$$i = 1.711 \sin(314\, t - 72°.34)$$

**P. 4.23.** An inductive circuit of resistance 15 ohms and inductance of 0.15 henry draws a current of 20 amperes. Determine the supply voltage if the frequency of the supply is 50Hz.

**Solution:**

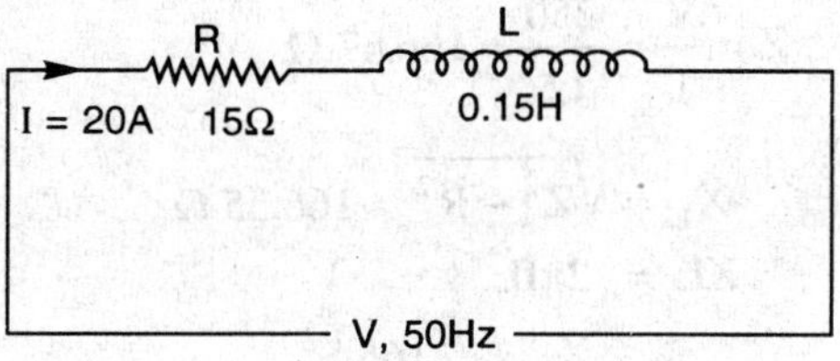


**Fig. 4.64**

Given

$$R = 15\ \Omega$$
$$L = 0.15\ H$$
$$I = 20\ A$$
$$f = 50\ Hz$$
$$X_L = 2\pi fL$$
$$= 2\pi \times 50 \times 0.15 = 47.124\ \Omega$$
$$Z = \sqrt{R^2 + X_L^2} = 49.45\ \Omega$$

$$\text{Supply voltage } (V) = IZ$$
$$= 20 \times 49.454$$
$$= 989.07 \text{ volts}$$

**P. 4.24.** An inductive circuit has an inductance of 0.4 henry and takes a current of 0.5 A when connected to 200V, 50Hz supply. Determine the resistance of the circuit.

**Solution:**

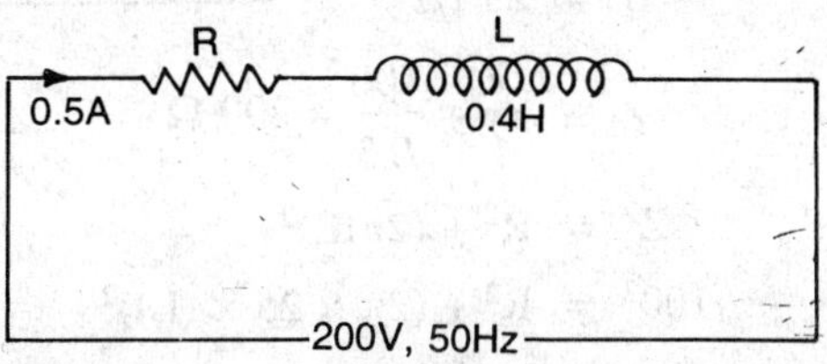


**Fig. 4.65**

$$V = 200V$$
$$I = 0.5\ A$$
$$\therefore \quad Z = \frac{V}{I} = \frac{200}{0.5} = 400 \text{ ohms}$$
$$L = 0.4\ H$$
$$f = 50\ Hz$$
$$X_L = 2\pi fL$$
$$= 2 \times \pi \times 50 \times 0.4 = 125.66\ \Omega$$
$$Z^2 = R^2 + X_L^2$$
$$\therefore \quad R = \sqrt{Z^2 + X_L^2} = 379.748 \text{ ohms.}$$

**P. 4.25.** A coil has a resistance of 6 ohms and takes a current of 1.5 A when connected across 250V, 60 Hz supply. What is the value of inductance of the coil?

**Solution:**

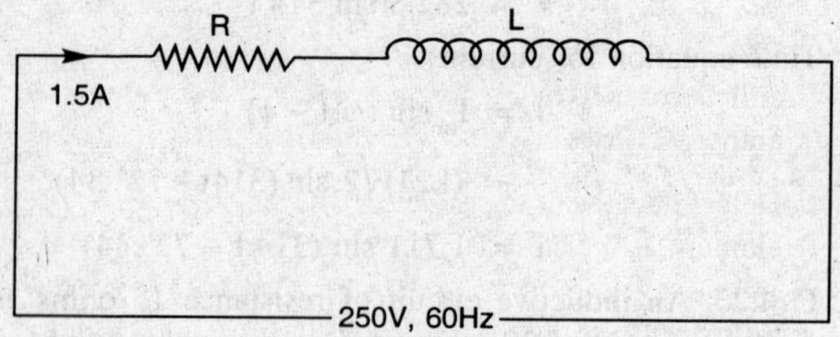

**Fig. 4.66**

Given $R = 6\ \Omega$

$L = ?$

$V = 250\ V$

$I = 1.5\ A$

$f = 60\ Hz$

$$Z = \frac{V}{I} = \frac{250}{1.5} = 166.67\ \Omega$$

$$X_L = \sqrt{Z^2 - R^2} = 166.55\ \Omega$$

But $XL = 2\pi fL$

$$\therefore \quad L = \frac{X_L}{2\pi f} = \frac{166.55}{2 \times \pi \times 60} = 0.4418 \text{ henry}$$

**P. 4.26.** An RL series circuit carries a current of 1 A at 100V, 25Hz supply. Same circuit when supplied with 100V, 75Hz carries a current of 0.5 A. Determine the value of 'R' and 'L'

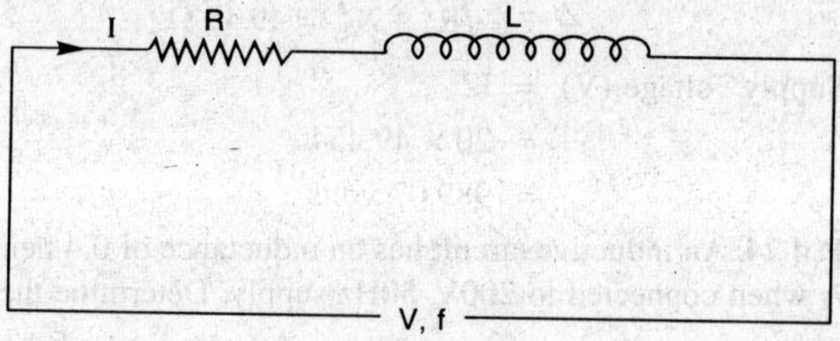

**Fig. 4.67**

**Solution:**

Given **1st case**

$I = 1\ A$

$V = 100\ V$

$f = 25\ Hz$

$$Z = \frac{V}{I} = \frac{100}{0.5} = 200\ \Omega$$

$$Z^2 = R^2 + (2\pi fL)^2$$

$$100^2 = R^2 + (2\pi \times 25 \times (L))^2 \qquad ...(i)$$

**2nd Case**

$I = 0.5\ A$

$V = 100\ V$

$f = 75\ Hz$

$$Z = \frac{V}{I} = \frac{100}{0.5}\ 200\Omega$$

$$Z^2 = R^2 + (2\pi f^2 L)$$

$$200^2 = R^2 + (471.23L)^2 \qquad ...(ii)$$

Solving (i) and (ii) we get

$L = 0.3898$ henry

$R = 79.05$ ohms

**P. 4.27.** A non-inductive resistance of 10 ohms is connected in series with a choking coil across 200V, 50Hz supply. The current drawn by the series combination is 7 amperes. The resistance of choking coil is 1.5 ohms.

Determine the inductance of the choking coil. Also determine voltage across each element and across the choking coil.

**Solution:**

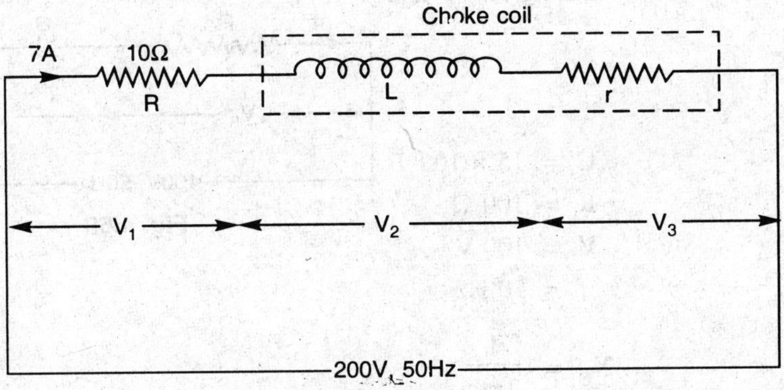


**Fig. 4.68**

Given $I = 7$ A

$V = 200$V

$f = 50$ Hz

$R = 10\ \Omega$

$r = 1.5\ \Omega$

$\therefore \quad V_1 = 1 \times R$

$= 7 \times 10$

$= 70$ Volts

$\therefore \quad V_3 = I \times r$

$= 7 \times 1.5$

$= 10.5$ V

$$V_2 = \sqrt{V^2 - (V_1 + V_3)^2}$$

$$= \sqrt{200^2 - (70 + 10.5)^2}$$

$= 183.084$ volts

$$X_L = \frac{V_2}{I} = \frac{183.084}{7} = 26.154\ \Omega$$

But $X_L = 2\pi fL$

$$L = \frac{X_L}{2\pi f} = \frac{26.154}{2 \times \pi \times 50} = 0.0832 \text{ henry}$$

Voltage across choking coil $= \sqrt{V_2^2 + V_3^2}$

$= \sqrt{(183.084)^2 + (10.5)^2}$

$= 183.384$ volts.

**P. 4.28.** A capacitor of 15 μF is connected in series with a non inductive resistance of 100 Ω across 100V, 50 Hz supply. Calculate the following (i) Capacitive reactance (ii) Impedance (iii) Current (iv) Power factor (v) Phase angle (vi) Voltage across R and C (vii) Power (viii) Time equating for 'v' and 'i'

**Solution:**

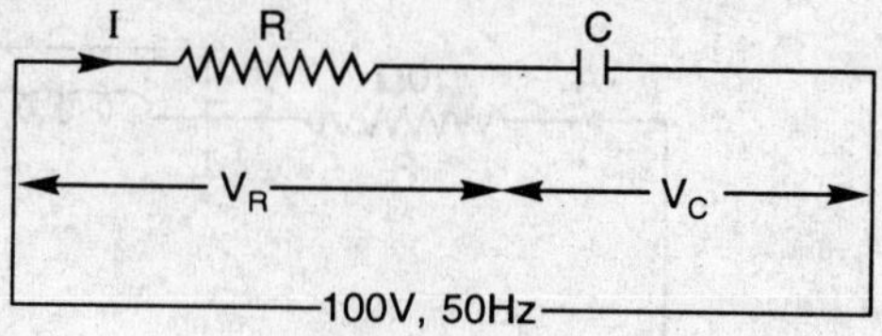

**Fig. 4.69**

Given

$$C = 15 \times 10^{-6} \text{ F}$$
$$R = 100\ \Omega$$
$$V = 100 \text{ V}$$
$$f = 50 \text{ Hz}$$

$$X_C = \frac{1}{2\pi fc}$$

$$= \frac{1}{2 \times \pi \times 50 \times 15 \times 10^{-6}}$$

$$= 212.206\ \Omega$$

$$Z = \sqrt{R^2 + (-X_C)^2} = 234.58\ \Omega$$

$$I = \frac{V}{Z}$$

$$= 0.426 \text{ A}$$

$$\cos\phi = \frac{R}{Z}$$

$$= 0.4263$$

$$\phi = \cos^{-1}\left(\frac{R}{Z}\right)$$

$$= 64^\circ.76$$

$$V_R = I \times R$$

$$= 42.6 \text{ volts}$$

$$V_C = I \times (X_C)$$

$$= 90.399 \text{ volts}$$

Active power $= VI \cos \phi$

$= 18.173$ watts

Reactive power $= VI \sin \phi$

$= 38.53$ VARs

Apparent power $= V$

The time equation for 'v' and i is given by

if $v = V_m \sin \omega t$

$i = I_m \sin (\omega t + \phi)$

i.e. $v = (100)\sqrt{2}\sin (314t)$

$i = (0.426)\sqrt{2} \sin (314t + 64°.76).I$

**P. 4.29.** In an RL series circuit, determine the current flowing through it, if the applied voltage is 100 ∠30° at 50 Hz. Take R = 30 Ω and L = 0.5 H.

**Solution:**

Given $R = 30\ \Omega$

$L = 0.5$

$f = 50$ Hz

$X_L = 2\pi fL$

$= 2 \times \pi \times 50 \times 0.5$

$= 157.07\ \Omega$

$Z = R + j X_L$

$= 30 + j\ 157.07$

$= 159.9 \angle 79°.18$

Given, $V = 100 \angle 30°$

$\therefore$ $I = \dfrac{V}{Z}$

$$= \frac{100\underline{|30°}}{159.9\underline{|79°.18}}$$

$$= \frac{100}{159.9}\angle 30° - 70°.18)$$

$= 0.625 \angle -49°.18$ A

or $I = 0.4085 - j\ 0.4729$ A

**P. 4.30.** An RC series circuit consists of R = 300 Ω and C = 10 μF. The current flowing through it is given by i = 2 sin 314 t. Find the equation for instantaneous value of voltage across R and C and also for the voltage across entire circuit.

**Solution:**

Given
$$R = 300$$
$$C = 10\ \mu F = 10 \times 10^{-6}\ F$$
$$i = 2 \sin 314t$$
$$= I_m \sin \omega t$$
$$\Rightarrow \quad \omega = 314$$
$$2\pi f = 314$$
$$f = 50\ Hz$$

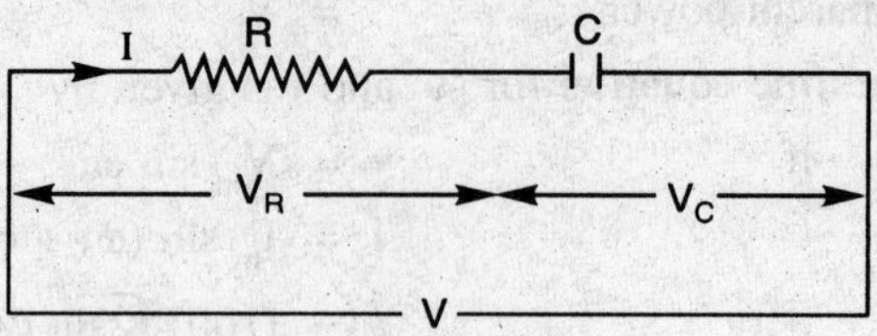


**Fig. 4.70**

$$\therefore \quad X_C = \frac{1}{2\pi fc} = \frac{1}{2 \times \pi \times 50 \times 10 \times 10^{-6}} = 318\ \Omega$$

$$Z = \sqrt{R^2 + X_C^2} = \sqrt{(300)^2 + (318)^2} = 437.17\ \Omega$$

$$\cos\phi = \frac{R}{Z} = \frac{300}{437.17} = 0.6862$$

$$\phi = \cos^{-1}\left(\frac{R}{Z}\right) = 46°.66$$

$$I_{max} = 2$$
$$V_{max} = 2 \times Z = 874.34 \text{ volts}$$

If $\quad i = I_{max} \sin \omega t$

then, $\quad v = V_{max} \sin(\omega t - \phi)$ (for RC circuit voltage lags current)

$$\therefore \quad v = \sin\ (314t - 46°.66)$$
$$V_{Rmax} = I_{max} \times (R) = 2 \times 300 = 600V$$
$$\therefore \quad V_R = V_{Rmax} \sin \omega t = 600 \sin 314t$$
$$V_{Cmax} = I_{max} \times (Xc) = 2 \times 318 = 636 \text{ volts}$$
$$\therefore \quad V_C = V_{Cmax} \sin(\omega t - \pi/2)$$
$$V_C = 636 \sin(\omega t - \pi/2)$$

**P. 4.31.** An R-C Series circuit is supplied with 150V, 50 Hz supply. The current drawn by it is 2.5 amperes. The power dissipated in the resistor is 100 watts. Calculate the values of 'R' and 'C' neglecting the power loss in the capacitor.

**Solution:**

Given
$$I = 2.5 \text{ amperes}$$
$$V = 150\ V$$
$$f = 50\ Hz$$

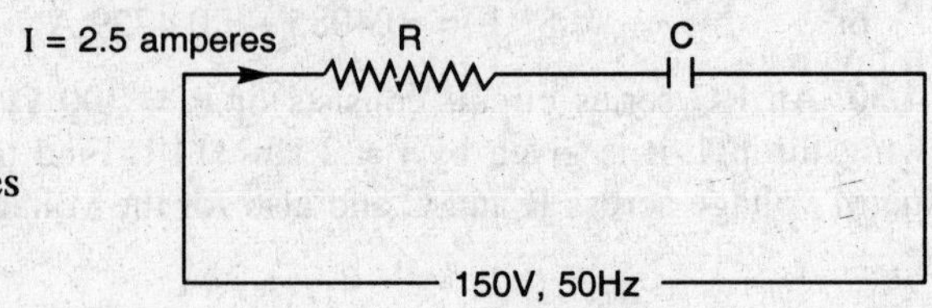


**Fig. 4.71**

$$\therefore \quad Z = \frac{V}{I} = \frac{150}{2.5} = 60\Omega$$

also given that power dissipated in the resistor = 100 watts

$$\Rightarrow \quad I^2R = 100$$

$$\therefore \quad R = \frac{100}{2.5 \times 2.5} = 16\Omega$$

But $\quad Z = \sqrt{R^2 + (-X_C)^2}$

$$\Rightarrow X_C = \sqrt{Z^2 - R^2} = \sqrt{60^2 - 16^2} = 57.83\Omega$$

but $\quad X_C = \dfrac{1}{2\pi fc}$

$$\Rightarrow C = \frac{1}{2\pi f x_C} = \frac{1}{2 \times \pi \times 50 \times 7.83} = 5.5 \times 10^{-5} \text{ farads}$$

**P. 4.32.** A lamp rated 500W - 100v is connected in series with a capacitor across 250V, 50 Hz supply. Determine the value of the capacitance.

**Solution:**

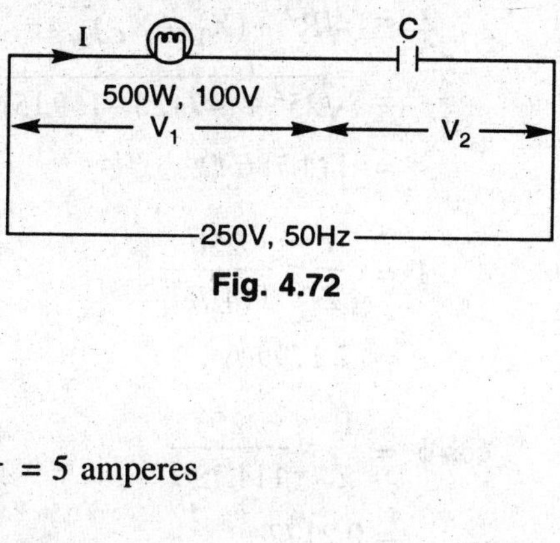

**Fig. 4.72**

Given

$V_1 = 100V$

$V = 250V$

$f = 50$ Hz

Power rating of the bulb (P) = 500 (W)

Voltage rating of the bulb (V) = 100V

$\therefore$ Current rating of the bulb (I) $= \dfrac{P}{V} = \dfrac{500}{100} = 5$ amperes

$$V_2 = \sqrt{V^2 - V_1^2} = \sqrt{250^2 - 100^2} = 229.12 \text{ volts.}$$

$$\therefore X_C = \frac{V_2}{I} = 45.825\ \Omega \cdot \text{But } X_C = \frac{1}{2\pi fc} \Rightarrow C = \frac{1}{2\pi f X_C} = 6.9 \times 10^{-5}\text{ F}$$

**P. 4.33.** A R - L - C series circuit has the following data:

$R = 25\ \Omega$

$C = 20\ \mu F$

$L = 150$ mH

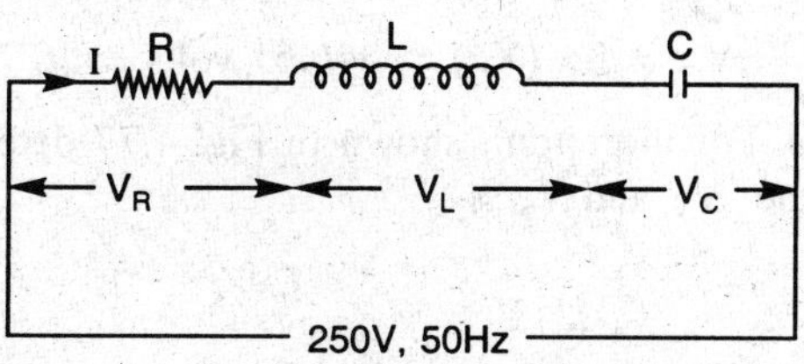

**Fig. 4.73**

V = 250 V

f = 50 Hz

Determine the following

(a) Inductive reactance, (b) Capacitve reactance (c) Impedance (d) Current (e) Power factor (f) Phase angle (g) Voltage across R, L, C. Also draw the vector diagram.

Given

$R = 25\ \Omega$

$C = 20 \times 10^{-6}$ F

$L = 150 \times 10^{-3}$ H

V = 250 V

f = 50 Hz

$X_L = 2\pi fL = 2 \times \pi \times 50 \times 150 \times 10^{-3}$

$= 47.123\ \Omega$

$X_C = \dfrac{1}{2\pi fc} = \dfrac{1}{2 \times \pi \times 50 \times 20 \times 10^{-6}}$

$= 159.15\ \Omega$

$\therefore \quad Z = \sqrt{R^2 + (X_L - X_C)^2}$

$= \sqrt{25^2 + (47.123 - 159.15)^2}$

$= 114.786\ \Omega$

$I = \dfrac{V}{Z} = \dfrac{250}{114.786}$

$= 2.1799$ A

$\cos\phi = \dfrac{R}{Z} = \dfrac{25}{114.786}$

$= 0.2177$

Phase angle $(\phi) = \cos^{-1}\left(\dfrac{R}{Z}\right) = 77°.42$

$V_R = I \times R \quad = 54.44$ volts

$V_L = I \times (X_L) = 102.62$ volts

$V_C = I \times (X_C) = 346.61$ volts

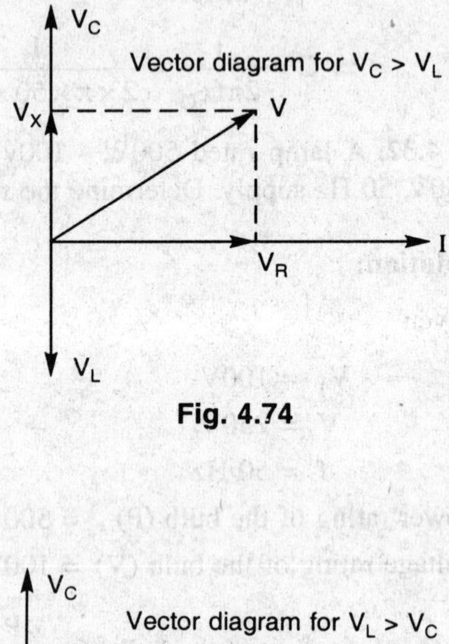


Fig. 4.74

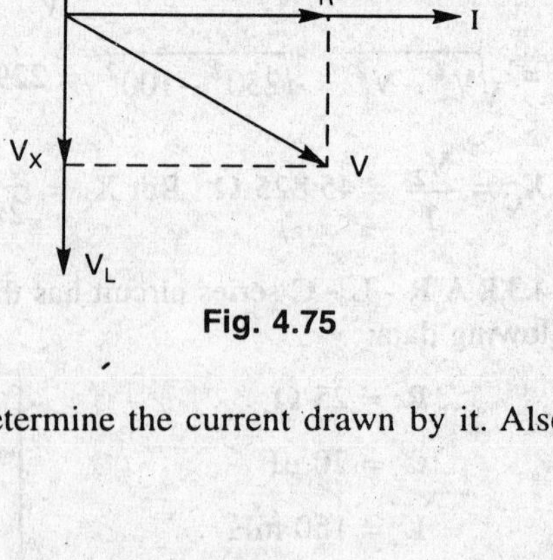


Fig. 4.75

**P. 4.34.** For the circuit shown in Fig. 4.77 determine the current drawn by it. Also calculate `$V_1$' and $V_2$.

**Solution:**

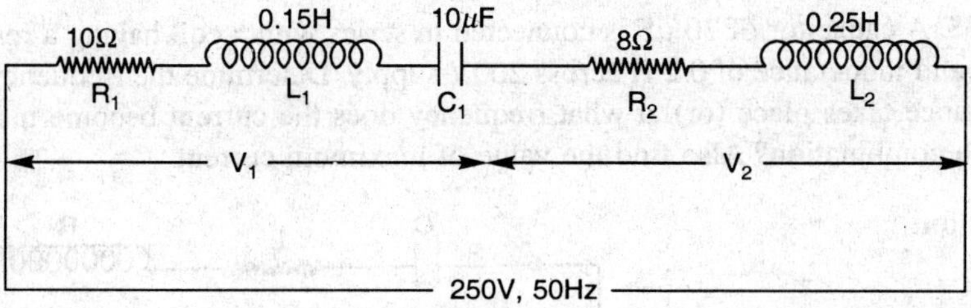


**Fig. 4.76**

Given

$$V = 250 \text{ V}$$

$$f = 50 \text{ Hz}$$

$$R_1 = 10\ \Omega$$

$$L_1 = 0.15 \text{ H}$$

$$\therefore \quad X_{L1} = 2 \times \pi \times 50 \times\ 0.15 = 47.123\ \Omega$$

$$C_1 = 10 \times 10^{-6} \text{ F}$$

$$X_{C1} = \frac{1}{2 \times \pi \times 50 \times 10 \times 10^{-6}}$$

$$= 318.309\ \Omega$$

$$R_2 = 8\ \Omega$$

$$L_2 = 0.25 \text{ H}$$

$$X_{L2} = 2 \times \pi \times 50 \times 0.25$$

$$= 78.539\ \Omega$$

$$\therefore \text{ Total impedance (Z)} = \sqrt{(R_1 + (R_2)^2 + [(X_{L1} + X_{L2}) - X_{C1}]^2}$$

$$= \sqrt{(10+8)^2 + (125.66 - 318.309)^2}$$

$$= 193.48\ \Omega$$

$$\therefore \quad I = \frac{V}{Z} = \frac{250}{193.48} = 1.292 \text{ A}$$

$$V_1 = I \times Z_1$$

where $$Z_1 = \sqrt{R_1^2 + (X_{L1} - X_{C1})^2}$$

$$= \sqrt{10^2 + (47.123 - 318.309)^2} = 271.37\ \Omega$$

$$\therefore \quad V_1 = 1.292 \times 271.37 = 350.6 \text{ volts}$$

$$V_2 = IZ_2$$

Where $\quad Z_2 = \sqrt{R_2^2 + (X_{L2})^2} = \sqrt{8^2 + (78.539)^2} = 78.945\ \Omega$

$\therefore \quad V_2 = 1.292 \times 78.945 = 101.99$ volts

**P. 4.35.** A capacitor of 30 μF is connected in series with a coil having a resistance of 12 Ω and inductance of 0.2 H across 200V supply. Determine the frequency at which resonance takes place (or) at what frequency does the current become maximum in such a combination? Also find the value of maximum current.

**Solution:**

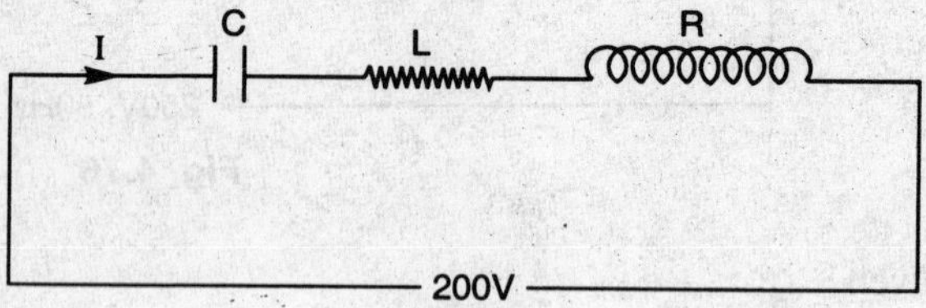


Fig. 4.77

Given

$C = 30 \times 10^{-6}$F

$R = 12\ \Omega$

$L = 0.2$ H

$V = 200$V

Note : At resonance the current in the circuit will be maximum

The frequency at series resonance = $f = \dfrac{1}{2\pi\sqrt{LC}}$ Hz

$$= \frac{1}{2\pi\sqrt{0.2 \times 30 \times 10^{-6}}}$$

$= 64.97$ Hz.

The maximum current at resonance = $I = \dfrac{V}{R} = \dfrac{200}{12} = 16.66$ A

**P. 4.36.** A resonance circuit consists of a capacitance 30 μF in parallel with an inductor of 0.2 H having a resistance of 12 Ω. Calculate the frequency at resonance.

**Solution:**

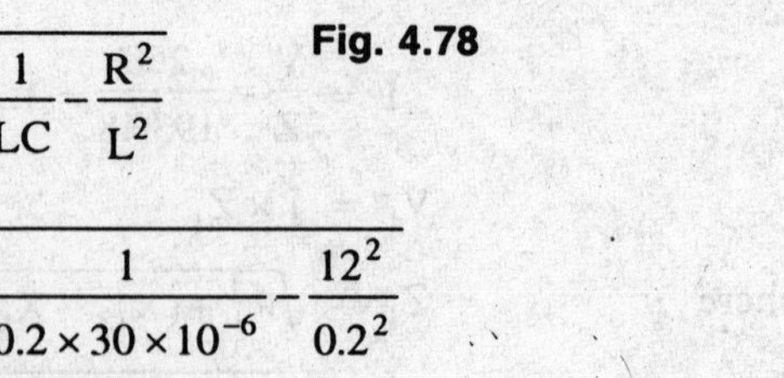


Fig. 4.78

Given

$C = 30 \times 10^{-6}$F

$L = 0.2$ H

$R = 12\ \Omega$

The frequency at resonance = $f = \dfrac{1}{2\pi}\sqrt{\dfrac{1}{LC} - \dfrac{R^2}{L^2}}$

$$= \frac{1}{2\pi}\sqrt{\frac{1}{0.2 \times 30 \times 10^{-6}} - \frac{12^2}{0.2^2}}$$

$= 64.269$ Hz.

**P. 4.37.** A coil resistance 30W and inductance 0.2 henry is connected in parallel with a coil of resistance 40 ohms and inductance of 0.12 henry. The parallel combination is connected across 200V, 50 Hz supply.

Determine

(i) Total impedance (ii) Total current (iii) Total power factor (iv) Total power (v) Current, power and the power factor of each branch.

**Solution:**

Given

$$R_1 = 30\Omega$$
$$L_1 = 0.2 \text{ H}$$
$$\therefore \quad X_{L1} = 2 \times \pi \times 50 \times 0.2$$
$$= 62.83 \ \Omega$$
$$\therefore \quad Z_1 = R_1 + j X_{L1}$$
$$= 30 + j\ 62.83$$
$$= 69.63\angle 64°.47$$

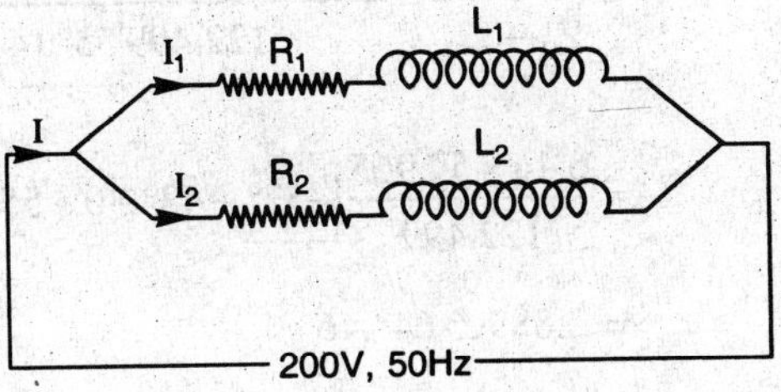


Fig. 4.79

$$R_2 = 40\ \Omega$$
$$L_2 = 0.12 \text{ H}$$
$$X_{L2} = 2 \times \pi \times 50 \times 0.12$$
$$= 37.699\ \Omega$$
$$Z_2 = R_2 + jX_{L2}$$
$$= 40 + j\ 37.699$$
$$= 54.965\ \angle 43°.30$$
$$V = 200 + j0$$
$$V = 200\ \angle 0°$$

$$Z = \frac{Z_1 Z_2}{Z_1 + Z_2} = \frac{69.63\underline{|64°.47} \times 54.965\underline{|43°.30}}{70 + j100.529}$$

$$= \frac{69.63\underline{|64°.47} \times 54.965\underline{|43°.30}}{122.499\underline{|55°.14}}$$

$$= \frac{69.23 \times 54.965}{122.499}\underline{|64°.47 + 43°.30 - 55°.14)}$$

$$Z = 31.06\angle 52°.620$$
$$\therefore \quad Z = 18.858 + j\ 24.683$$

$$I = \frac{V}{Z} = \frac{200\underline{|0°}}{31.06\underline{|52°.62}} = 6.44\angle -52°.62$$

$$\cos\phi = \frac{R}{Z} = \frac{18.858}{31.06} = 0.607$$

$$P = I^2R = (6.44)^2 \times 18.858$$

$$= 782.109 \text{ watts}$$

$$I_1 = \frac{IZ_2}{Z_1 + Z_2} = \frac{6.44\underline{|-52°.62} \times 54.965\underline{|43°.3}}{122.499\underline{|55°.14}}$$

$$= \frac{6.44 \times 54.965}{122.499}\underline{|-52° + 43°.30 - 55°.14)}$$

$$= 2.889\angle{-64°.46}$$

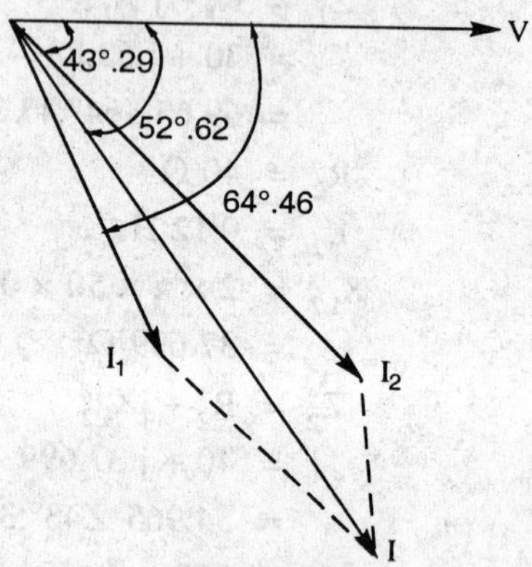


Fig. 4.80

**Vector Diagram**

$$I_2 = \frac{IZ_1}{Z_1 + Z_2} = \frac{6.44\underline{|-52°.62} \times 69.63\underline{|64°.47}}{122.499\underline{|55°.14}}$$

$$= 3.66\angle{-43°.29}$$

$$\cos\phi_1 = \frac{R_1}{Z_1} = \frac{30}{69.63} = 0.4308$$

$$P_1 = I_1^2R_1 = (2.889)^2 \times 30 = 250.38 \text{ watts}$$

$$\cos\phi_2 = \frac{R_2}{Z_2} = \frac{40}{54.965} = 0.7277$$

$$P_2 = I_2^2R_2 = (3.66)^2 \times 40 = 535.824 \text{ watts}$$

**P. 4.38.** A circuit having resistance of 10 Ω inductive reactance of 12 Ω is connected in parallel with another circuit consisting of a resistance of 15 Ω in series with a capacitive reactance of 20 Ω. Find the following, if this combination is excited by 200V, 50 Hz supply.

(i) Total impedance (ii) Total current (iii) Total p.f (iv) Total power (v) Current, power and power factor in each branch.

**Solution:**

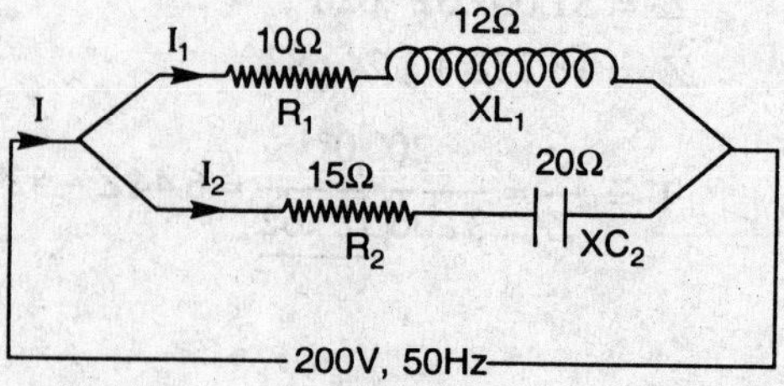


Fig. 4.81

Given

$$Z_1 = R_1 + j\,X_{L1}$$

where, $R_1 = 10\Omega$

$$X_{L1} = 12\Omega$$

$\therefore \quad Z_1 = 10 + j\,12$

$= 15.6 \angle 50.19$

$Z_2 = R_2 - j\,X_{C2}$

where, $R_2 = 15\ \Omega$

$X_{C2} = 20\Omega$

$\therefore \quad Z_2 = 15 - j\,20$

$= 25 \angle -53°.13$

$\therefore Z_1 + Z_2 = 25 - j8 = 26.25 \angle -17°.7$

$V = 200 + j0$

$= 200 \angle 0°$

$$Z = \frac{15.6\angle 50°.19 \times 25\angle -53°13}{26.25 - 17.7}$$

$Z = 14.857\angle 14°.80$

$Z = 14.36 + j\,3.791$

$$I = \frac{V}{Z} = \frac{200\angle 0°}{14.857\angle 14°.80} = 13.46\angle -14°.80$$

$$I_1 = \frac{IZ_2}{Z_1 + Z_2} = \frac{13.46\angle -14°.80 \times 25\angle -53°13}{26.25 - \angle 17.7} = 12.819 \angle -50°.23$$

$$I_2 = \frac{IZ_1}{Z_1 + Z_2} = \frac{13.46\angle -14°.80 \times 15.6\angle 50°19}{26.25\angle -17.7} = 7.999 \angle 53°.23$$

$$\cos\phi = \frac{R}{Z} = \frac{14.36}{14.857} = 0.9665$$

$P = I^2R = (13.46)^2 \times 14.36 = 2602.26$ watts

$$\cos\phi_1 = \frac{R_1}{Z_1} = \frac{10}{15.6} = 0.641$$

$P_1 = I_1^2 R_1 = (12.819)^2 \times 10 = 1643.27$ watts

$$\cos\phi_2 = \frac{R_2}{Z_2} = \frac{15}{25} = 0.6$$

$P_2 = I_2^2 R_1 = (7.999)^2 \times 15 = 959.78$ watts

**Vector Diagram is drawn as shown in Fig. 4.82**

**P. 4.39.** For the circuit shown in Fig. 4.84 below find the values of

(i) Total current, power, power factor

(ii) Current, power, power factor of each branch

(iii) Draw the vector diagram

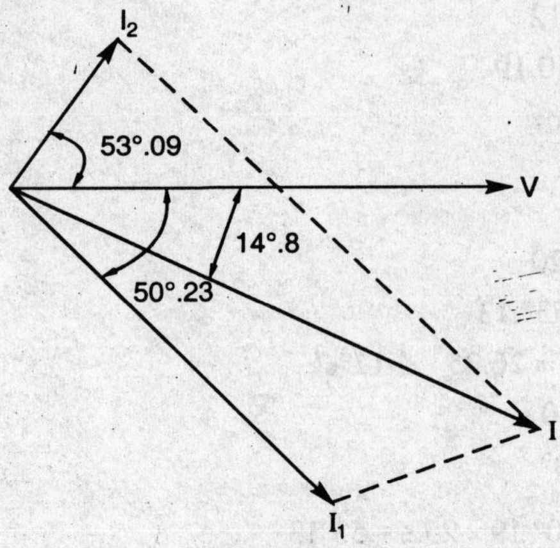


Fig. 4.82

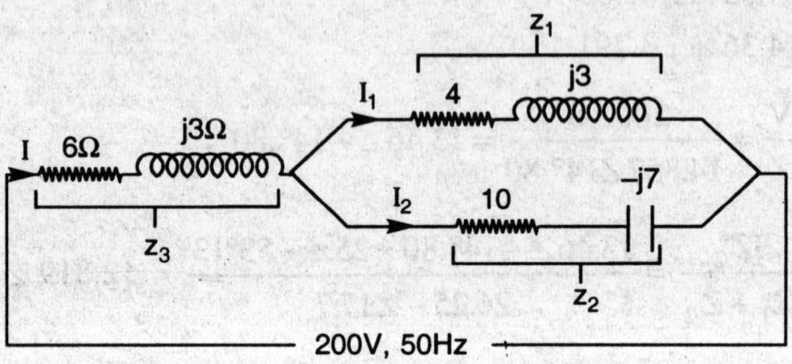


Fig. 4.83

**Solution:**

Given

Let $Z_1 = 4 + j3 = 5 \angle 36°.86$

$Z_2 = 10 - j7 = 12.21 \angle -35°$

$Z_3 = 6 + j3 = 6.71 \angle 26°.56$

$V = 200 + j0 = 200 \angle 0°$

$$Z = \frac{Z_1 Z_2}{Z_1 + Z_2} + Z_3$$

$Z_1 Z_2 = 5\angle 36°.86 \times 12.2 \angle -35° = 61\angle 1°.86$

$Z_1 + Z_2 = 14 - j4 = 14.56 \angle -15°.95$

$$\frac{Z_1 Z_2}{Z_1 + Z_2} = \frac{61\angle 1°.86}{14.56\angle -15°.95} = 4.189 \angle 17°.8$$

$= 3.98 + j\,1.28$

$$Z_3 + \frac{Z_1Z_2}{Z_1+Z_2} = 6 + j3 + 3.98 + j\,1.28$$

$$= 9.98 + j\,4.28$$

$$= 10.859 \angle 23°.217$$

$$I = \frac{V}{Z} = \frac{200\angle 0°}{9.98 + j4.28} = \frac{200\angle 0°}{10.859\angle 23°.217} = 18.41 \angle -23°.217$$

$$I_1 = \frac{IZ_2}{Z_1+Z_2} = \frac{(18.41\angle -23°.217)(12.2\angle -35°)}{14.56\angle -15°.95}$$

$$= 15.43 \angle -42°.267$$

$$I_2 = \frac{IZ_1}{Z_1+Z_2} = \frac{(18.41\angle -23°.217)(5\angle 36°.86)}{14.56\angle -15°.95}$$

$$= 6.322 \angle 29°.593$$

Total power factor $= \frac{R}{Z} = \frac{9.98}{10.859} = 0.919$

Power factor of branch 1 $= \frac{R_1}{Z_1} = \frac{4}{5} = 0.8$

Power factor of branch 2 $= \frac{R_2}{Z_2} = \frac{10}{12.21} = 0.819$

Power factor of branch 3 $= \frac{R_3}{Z_3} = \frac{6}{6.71} = 0.894$

Total power dissipated $= I^2R$

$= (18.41)^2 \times 9.98 = 3382.30$ watts

Power dissipated in branch 1 $= I_1^2 R_1$

$= (15.43)^2 \times 4 = 952.3396$ watts

Power dissipated in branch 2 $= I_2^2 R_2$

$= (6.322)^2 \times 10 = 399.676$ watts

Power dissipated in branch 3 $= I_3^2 R_3$

$= (18.41)^2 \times 6 = 2033.56$ watts

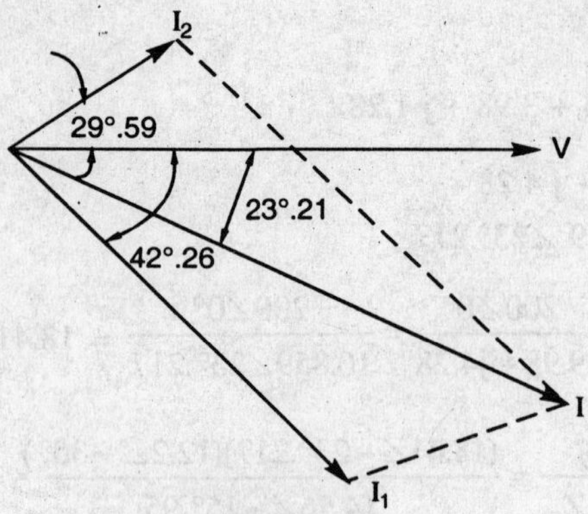


Fig. 4.84

Vector Diagram

## 4.28. THREE PHASE CIRCUITS

We know that coil rotating in an uniform magnetic field generates alternating emf. In a three-phase system three coils which are kept 120° apart are made to rotate on the same shaft in the magnetic field as shown in Fig. 4.85. The emfs induced in the coils are vectorially represented in Fig. 4.86 and are given by

$$E_R = E_{max} \sin \omega t \quad ...(4.57)$$

$$E_Y = E_{max} \sin (\omega t - 120°) \quad ...(4.58)$$

$$E_B = E_{max} \sin (\omega t - 240°) \quad ...(4.59)$$

or $$E_B = E_{max} \sin (\omega t - 120°) \quad ...(4.60)$$

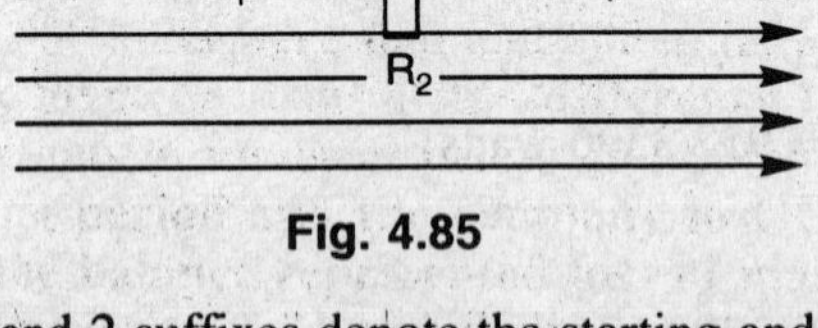


Fig. 4.85

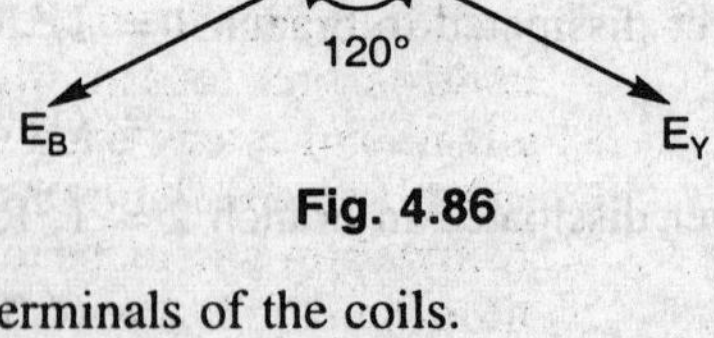


Fig. 4.86

1 and 2 suffixes denote the starting and ending terminals of the coils.

From equations 4.57 to 4.59, it is clear that '$E_y$' lags '$E_R$' by 120° and '$E_B$' lags '$E_R$' by 240°.

The graphical representation of the three emfs is shown in Fig. 4.87.

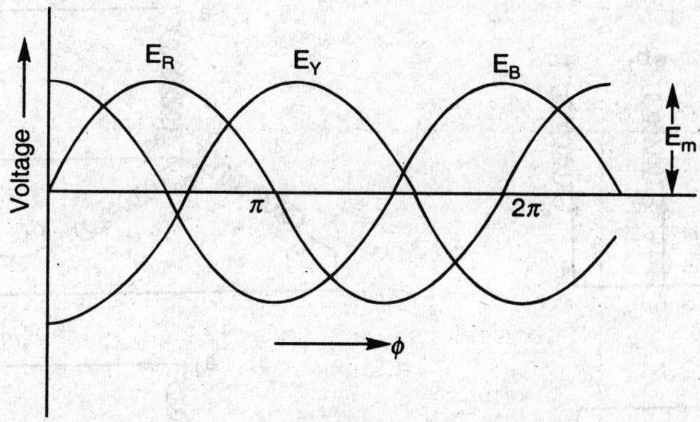


Fig. 4.87

The current flowing in different phases depends upon the nature of the load.

## 4.29. PHASE SEQUENCE

It is the sequence through which the induced emf reaches zero value or maximum value. In the Fig. 4.87 it is clear that the phase sequence is R - Y - B. If the phase sequence is changed, the direction of rotation of motor also changes.

The general methods of interconnection of the three phases are listed.

(i) Star or wye connection (Y)

(ii) Delta or mesh connection (Δ)

## 4.30. STAR CONNECTION

Here the similar ends i.e., the 'starting ends' of three coils or finishing end of three coils are joined together at point 'N' called neutral as shown in Fig. 4.88.

## 4.31. DELTA CONNECTION

Here dissimilar ends of the three phase windings are joined together i.e, 'starting end' of one coil is joined to 'finishing end' of the other and so on as shown in Fig. 4.89.

## 4.32. PHASE VOLTAGE

It is the voltage induced in each winding and is represented by $E_{ph}$ or $V_{ph}$

## 4.33. PHASE CURRENT

The current flowing through any of the phase winding is called phase current and is represented by $I_{ph}$.

## 4.34. LINE VOLTAGE

It is given by the voltage between any two lines of the supply system and is represented by $V_L$.

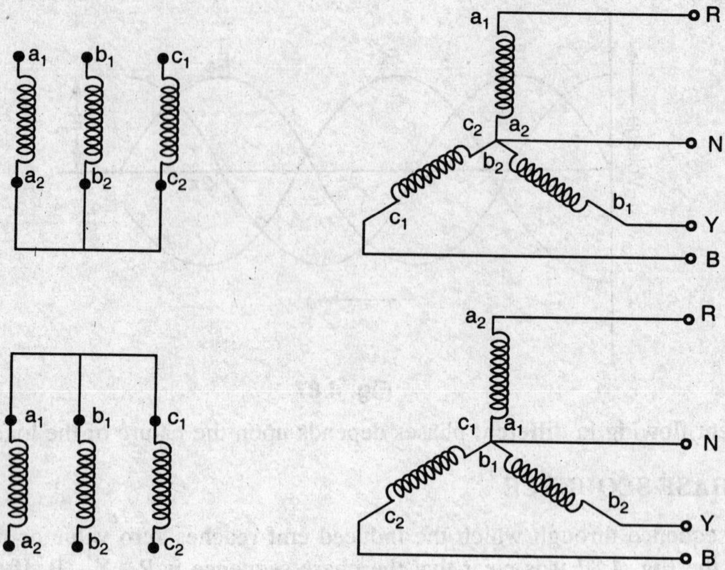


Fig. 4.88

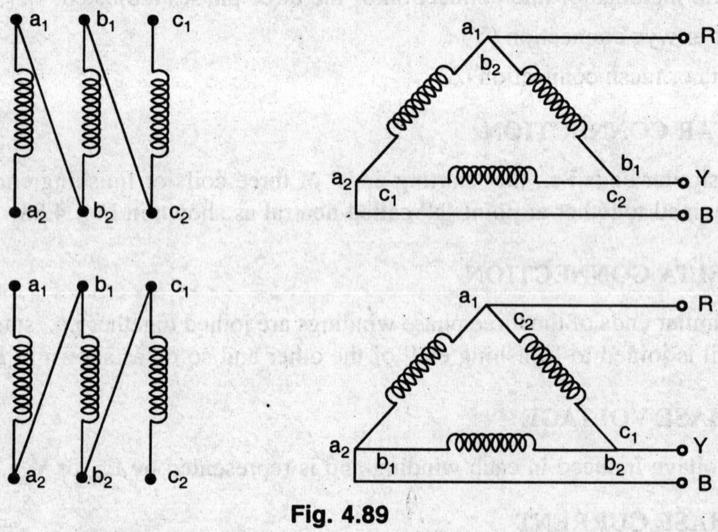


Fig. 4.89

## 4.35. LINE CURRENT

The current flowing in each line is known as line current '$I_L$'.

## 4.36. BALANCED SYSTEM

A balance system is one in which the currents in the three phases are equal in magnitude and are displaced from one another by equal angles and also the voltages in all phases are equal in magnitude and are displaced from one another by equal angles.

## 4.37. BALANCED LOAD

A balanced load is one in which the loads connected across all the three phases are equal in magnitude and phase. In other words, a load is said to be a balanced load, if the power factors and phase currents of the three phases of the three-phase system are equal.

## 4.38. UNBALANCED LOAD

If the three phases have different power factors and phase currents, then the load is said to be an unbalanced load.

## 4.39. RELATION BETWEEN LINE VOLTAGE and PHASE VOLTAGE and LINE CURRENT and PHASE CURRENT in STAR CONNECTION (Fig. 4.90)

Let $I_R, I_Y, I_B$ be the phase currents

$E_R, E_Y, E_B$ be the phase voltages

$I_{L1}, I_{L2}, I_{L3}$ be the line currents

$V_{Ry}, V_{yB}, V_{BR}$ be the line voltages

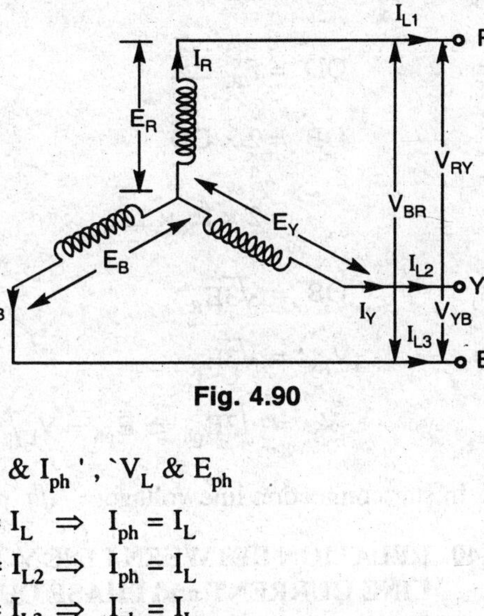


Fig. 4.90

Since it is a balanced system

$$I_R = I_Y = I_B = I_{ph}$$
$$I_{L1} = I_{L2} = I_{L3} = I_L$$
$$E_R = E_Y = E_B = E_{ph}$$
$$V_{Ry} = V_{YB} = V_{BR} = V_L$$

Our aim is to find the relation between `$I_L$ & $I_{ph}$ ' , `$V_L$ & $E_{ph}$

From the Fig. 4.90 it is clear that $I_R = I_L \Rightarrow I_{ph} = I_L$

$$I_Y = I_{L2} \Rightarrow I_{ph} = I_L$$
$$I_B = I_{L3} \Rightarrow I_{ph} = I_L$$

Thus in a star connection

**Line current ($I_L$) = phase current ($I_{ph}$)** ...(4.61)

Also we have line voltage

$$V_{Ry} = E_R + (-E_Y)$$
$$V_{yB} = E_y + (-E_B)$$
$$V_{BR} = E_B + (-E_R)$$

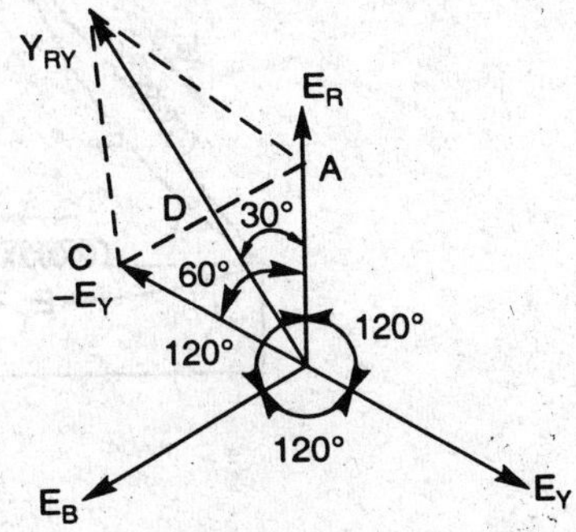


Fig. 4.91

From the vector diagram Fig. 4.91

$$OA = E_R$$
$$OC = -E_Y$$

OA + OC (vector sum) = OB = $V_{Ry}$

$$\angle AOC = 60°$$
$$\angle AOD = 30°$$

OCBAO is a rhombus

$\therefore \quad \angle ODA = 90°$

Also $\quad OD = DB$

$\therefore \quad OB = OD + DB$

$= OD + OD$

$= 2 \times (OD)$

From triangle ODA (right angled triangle)

$$\cos 30° = \frac{OD}{OA}$$

$$OA.\ \cos 30° = OD$$

$$E_{R.}\ \cos 30° = OD$$

$$\Rightarrow \quad OD = E_{R.} \frac{\sqrt{3}}{2}$$

$$OB = 2 \times OD$$

$$= 2 \times E_R \times \frac{\sqrt{3}}{2}$$

$$\therefore \quad OB = \sqrt{3} E_R$$

i.e., $\quad V_{Ry} = \sqrt{3} E_R$

$$V_L = \sqrt{3} E_{ph} \Rightarrow E_{ph} = V_L / \sqrt{3} \qquad \text{...(4.62)}$$

$\therefore$ In star connection line voltage = $\sqrt{3}$ phase voltage.

## 4.40. RELATION BETWEEN LINE VOLTAGE and PHASE VOLTAGE and LINE CURRENT and PHASE CURRENT in DELTA CONNECTION

From Fig 4.92 it is clear that

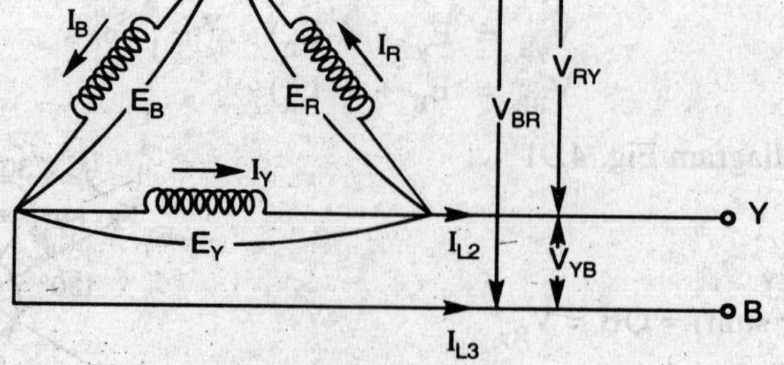


Fig. 4.92

$$E_R = V_{Ry} = E_{ph} = V_L$$
$$E_y = V_{yB} = E_{ph} = V_L$$
$$E_B = V_{BR} = E_{ph} = V_L$$

Thus in delta connection

**Line voltage ($V_L$) = Phase voltage ($E_{ph}$)** ...(4.63)

Also from the Fig. 4.93 we have

$$I_{L1} = I_R + (-I_B)$$
$$I_{L2} = I_y + (-I_R)$$
$$I_{L3} = I_B + (-I_y)$$

From the vector diagram Fig. 4.93, we have

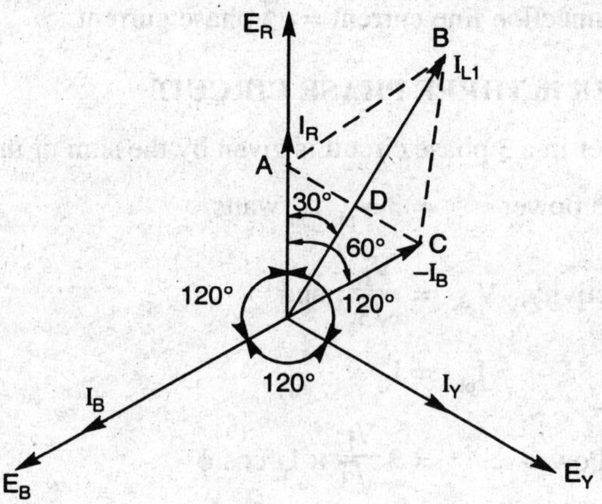


**Fig. 4.93**

$$OA = I_R$$
$$OC = -I_B$$

OA + OC (vector sum) = OB = $I_{L!}$

$$\angle AOC = 60°$$
$$\angle AOD = 30°$$

OCBAO is a rhombus

$$\therefore \angle ODA = 90°$$

Also OD = DB

$$\therefore OB = OD + DB$$
$$= OD + OD$$
$$= 2 \times OD$$

Triangle ODA is a right angled triangle

$$\therefore \cos 30° = \frac{OD}{OA}$$

OA, cos 30° = OD

$I_R \cos 30° = OD$

$\therefore \quad OB = 2 \times OD$

$= 2 \times I_R \times \cos 30°$

$= 2 \times I_R \times \frac{\sqrt{3}}{2}$

$OB = \sqrt{3} I_R$

$I_{L1} = \sqrt{3} I_R$

$$I_L = \sqrt{3} I_{ph} \quad \text{...(4.64)}$$

$\therefore$ In delta connection line current $= \sqrt{3}$ phase current.

## 4.41. POWER in THREE PHASE CIRCUIT

The total power in a 3 phase circuit is given by the sum of the powers in three phases.

$\therefore$ Total active power $= 3\, V_{ph}\, I_{ph}$ watts

In star connectivity, $V_{ph} = \frac{V_L}{\sqrt{3}}$; and

$I_{ph} = I_L$

$\therefore$ Active Power $= 3 \frac{V_L}{\sqrt{3}} \times I_L \cos \phi$

$$= \sqrt{3}\, V_L\, I_L \cos \phi \quad \text{...(4.65)}$$

In delta connection $V_{ph} = V_L$ ; $I_{ph} = \frac{I_L}{\sqrt{3}}$

$\therefore$ Active Power $= 3\, V_L . \frac{I_L}{\sqrt{3}} \cos \phi$

$$= \sqrt{3}\, V_L\, I_L \cos \phi \text{ watts} \quad \text{...(4.66)}$$

Similarly

Reactive Power $= 3.\, V_{ph} I_{ph} \sin \phi$

$$= \sqrt{3}\, V_L\, I_L \sin \phi \text{ VARs} \quad \text{...(4.67)}$$

Apparent power $= 3. V_{ph} I_{ph}$ volt ampere

$$= 3\, V_L . I_L \quad \text{...(4.68)}$$

The equations 4.67 and 4.68 holds good for both Y & Δ connection.

## 4.42. THREE-PHASE POWER MEASUREMENT

The three-phase power can be measured by using one watt meter in each phase and the algebraic sum of their readings will give us the total three-phase power. But the difficulty in this method is to get the neutral point in star connection.

It is interesting to note that, the three phase power can be measured by using only two watt meters with the help of the circuit shown in Fig. 4.94.

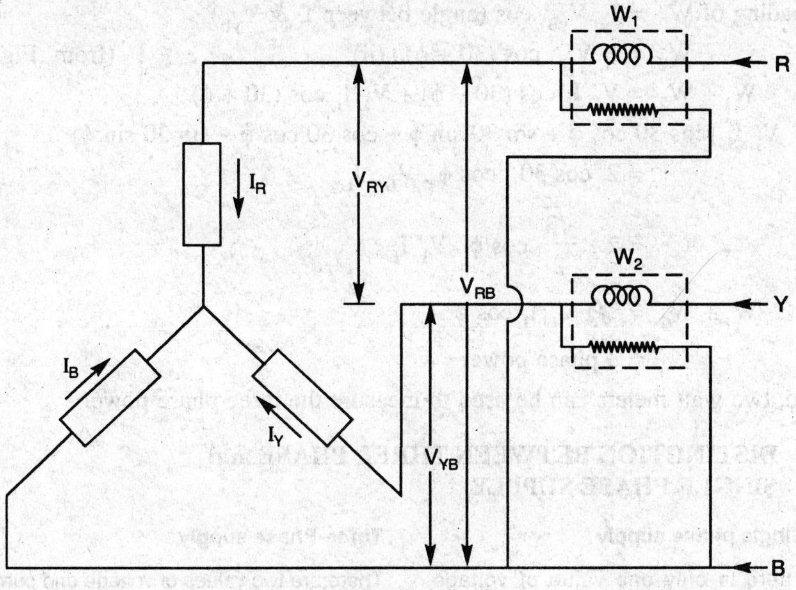


Fig. 4.94

Since it is a balanced system

$$E_R = E_Y = E_B = E_{ph}$$

$$V_{Ry} = V_{YB} = V_{BR} = V_L$$

$$I_R = I_Y = I_B = I_{ph}$$

$$I_{L1} = I_{L2} = I_{L3} = I_L$$

Also, since it is star connection

$$V_L = \sqrt{3}\, E_{ph}$$

and

$$I_L = I_{ph}$$

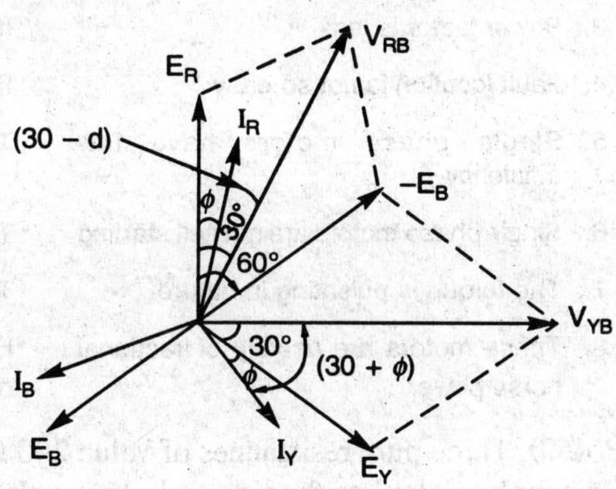


Fig. 4.95

Now current through the watt meter

$$W_1 = I_{L1} = I_L$$

But $I_{L1} = I_R$

Voltage across $W_1 = V_{RB} = E_R + (-E_B)$

But, $V_{RB} = V_L$

$\therefore$ Reading of $W_1 = I_R . V_{RB} .\cos$ (angle between $I_R$ & $V_{RB}$)

$W_1 = I_L V_L \cos(30 - \phi)$ ...(i) (from Fig. 4.95.)

Similarly current through $W_2 = I_{L2} = I_2$

But $\quad I_{L2} = I_y$

Voltage across $W_2 = V_{yB} = E_y + (-E_B)$

But, $\quad V_{yB} = V_L$

$\therefore$ Reading of $W_2 = I_y . V_{yB} .\cos$ (angle between $I_y$ & $V_{yB}$)

$W_2 = I_L V_L . \cos (30 + \phi)$...(ii) (from Fig. 4.95)

$\therefore \quad W_1 + W_2 = V_L I_L \cos (30 - \phi) + V_L I_L \cos (30 + \phi)$

$W_1 = V_L I_L [\cos 30 \cos \phi + \sin 30 \sin \phi + \cos 30 \cos \phi - \sin 30 \sin \phi)$

$= 2. \cos 30 . \cos \phi . V_L . I_L$

$$= 2 . \frac{\sqrt{3}}{2} .\cos \phi . V_L I_L$$

$$W_1 + W_2 = \sqrt{3}\, V_L I_L \cos \phi$$

= 3 phase power

Hence, two watt meters can be used to measure the three phase power.

## 4.43. DISTINCTION BETWEEN THREE PHASE and SINGLE PHASE SUPPLY

| | Single phase supply | Three-Phase supply |
|---|---|---|
| 1. | There is only one value of voltage and current. | There are two values of voltage and current, namely, line values and phase values. |
| 2. | Losses are more | Losses are less |
| 3. | Power factor is less | It has better power factor |
| 4. | Fault location is not so easy | Fault location is easy |
| 5. | Single phase motors have low efficiency | Three phase motor have good efficiency |
| 6. | Single phase motors are not self starting | Three phase motors are self starting |
| 7. | The torque is pulsating in nature | They have uniform torque |
| 8. | These motors are usually of fractional horse power. | Here it is possible to manufacture higher outputs. |

**P. 4.40.** Three pure resistances of value 200 Ω each are connected to 3 phase 440V, 50 Hz supply. Calculate the line and phase values of current and voltage in both star and delta connection.

**Solution:**

Given

$R_{ph} = 200\ \Omega$

$V_L = 440$ V

$f = 50$ Hz

**Star connection:**

$V_L = V_L/\sqrt{3} = 254.04$ volts

$I_{ph} = \frac{V_{ph}}{R_{ph}} = \frac{440}{200} = 1.270A$

$I_L = I_{ph} = 1.270A$

Power factor = 1 (pure resistive circuit)

3 phase active power = $3.\ V_{ph}I_{ph} \cos\phi = 3 \times 254.04 \times 1.27 \times 1$

= 968.05 watts

or 3 phase active power = $\sqrt{3}\, V_L\, I_L \cos\phi = \sqrt{3} \times 440 \times 1.27 \times 1$

= 968.05 watts

**Delta connection**

$V_{ph} = V_L = 440V$

$I_{ph} = \frac{V_{ph}}{R_{ph}} = \frac{440}{200} = 1.270A$

$I_L = \sqrt{3}\, I_{ph} = 3.8104A$

Power factor = 1

3 phase active power = $3\ V_{ph}I_{ph} \cos\phi$

= $3 \times 440 \times 2.2 \times 1$

= 2903.8 watts

= $\sqrt{3}\, V_L\, I_L \cos\phi = \sqrt{3} \times 440 \times 3.8104 \times 1$

= 2903.8 watts

**P. 4.41.** Three similar coils each of resistance 15 Ω and inductance of 0.25 H are connected in star and then in delta to a three phase 400V, 50 Hz supply. Calculate line and phase values of current in both the cases. Also calculate the total power absorbed.

**Solution:**

Given

$R_{ph} = 15\ \Omega$

$L_{ph} = 0.25$ H

$f = 50$ Hz

$X_{Lph} = 2 \times \pi \times 50 \times 0.25$

$= 78.539\ \Omega$

$$Z_{ph} = \sqrt{R_{ph}^2 + X_{Lph}^2} = \sqrt{(15)^2 + (78.539)^2}$$

$$= 79.959\ \Omega$$

$$V_L = 400\ V$$

**In star connection**

$$V_{ph} = \frac{400}{\sqrt{3}} = 230.946 \text{ volts}$$

$$I_{ph} = \frac{V_{ph}}{Z_{ph}} = \frac{230.946}{79.959} = 2.888A$$

$$I_L = I_{ph} = 2.888\ A$$

$$\cos\phi = \frac{R_{ph}}{Z_{ph}} = \frac{15}{79.959} = 0.1875$$

Total power absorbed $= 3\ V_{ph} I_{ph} \cos\phi$

$= 3 \times 230.946 \times 2.888 \times 0.1875$

$= 375.36$ watts

**In delta connection**

$$V_L = V_{ph} = 400\ V$$

$$Z_{ph} = 79.959\ \Omega$$

$$I_{ph} = \frac{V_{ph}}{Z_{ph}} = 5.0025A$$

$$I_L = \sqrt{3}\, I_{ph} = 8.664A$$

$$\cos\phi = \frac{R_{ph}}{Z_{ph}} = \frac{15}{79.959} = 0.1875$$

Total power absorbed $= 3\ V_{ph} I_{ph} \cos\phi$ watts

$= 3 \times 400 \times 5.0025 \times 0.1875$ watts

$= 1125.56$ watts.

**P. 4.42.** Three identical impedances are connected in star to a three phase supply of 400V. The line current is 35 amperes and the total power absorbed is 15 kW calculate the resistance and reactance of the circuit.

**Star connection**

**Solution:**

Given

$$V_L = 400\text{ V} \Rightarrow V_{ph} = \frac{V_L}{\sqrt{3}} = \frac{400}{1.732} = 230.94 \text{ volts}$$

$$I_L = 35\text{ A} = I_{ph}$$

$$Z_{ph} = \frac{V_{ph}}{I_{ph}} = \frac{230.94}{35} = 6.598\Omega$$

$$\sqrt{3}\, V_L\, I_L \cos\phi = 15 \times 10^{-3} \text{ watts}$$

$$\cos\phi = \frac{15\times 10^3}{\sqrt{3}\times 400\times 35} = 0.6186$$

But $\cos\phi = \frac{R_{ph}}{Z_{ph}}$

$$\therefore \quad R_{ph} = Z_{ph} \,.\, \cos\phi = 6.598 \times 0.6186 = 4.0815\ \Omega$$

$$X_{ph} = \sqrt{Z_{ph}^2 - R_{ph}^2}$$

$$= 5.184\ \Omega$$

**P. 4.43.** In a two wattmeter method of measuring three phase power, one of the watt meter readings is 5 kW and that of the other is 3 kW. Calculate the power factor.

**Solution:**

Given

$$W_1 = 5 \times 10^3 \text{ watts}$$

$$W_2 = 3 \times 10^3 \text{ watts}$$

$$\Rightarrow W_1 + W_2 = 8 \times 10^3 \text{ watts}$$

$$W_1 - W_2 = 2 \times 10^3 \text{ watts}$$

We have $W_1 + W_2 = \sqrt{3}\, V_L\, I_L \cos\phi$ ...(i)

where $W_1 = V_L\, I_L \cos(30 + \phi)$

and $W_2 = V_L\, I_L \cos(30 - \phi)$

$\therefore \quad W_1 - W_2 = V_L\, I_L \sin\phi$ ...(ii)

$$\frac{(ii)}{(i)} \Rightarrow \tan\phi = \frac{\sqrt{3}(W_1 - W_2)}{(W_1 + W_2)} \text{ ( for lag p.f)} \quad ...(iii)$$

$$\tan\phi = \frac{\sqrt{3}(W_1 - W_2)}{(W_1 + W_2)} \qquad \text{(for lead p.f)}$$

From equation (iii)

$$\tan\phi = \frac{\sqrt{3}(W_1 - W_2)}{(W_1 + W_2)}$$

$$\tan\phi = \sqrt{3}\left(\frac{2\times10^3}{8\times10^3}\right)$$

$$= \sqrt{3}\times\frac{2}{8} = 0.433$$

$$\phi = \tan^{-1}(0.433) = 23°.41$$

## REVISION FORMULA

A sisusodial alternating voltage is given by

$$v = V_{max}\sin\theta$$

where v is instantaneous value or voltage in volts

$V_{max}$ is maximum value of voltage in volts

where $\theta = wt$

$= 2\pi ft$

$= \frac{2\pi}{T}t$

where T is the time period in seconds

f is the frequency in hertz

ω is the angular frequency in radians

$$\text{Form factor} = \frac{\text{R.M.S value}}{\text{Average value}}$$

$$\text{Peak or crest or amplitude factor} = \frac{\text{Maximum value}}{\text{R.M.S value}}$$

| For full sinusoidal wave | For half sinusoidal wave |
|---|---|
| $I_{RMS} = \frac{I_{max}}{\sqrt{2}}$ | $I_{RMS} = \frac{I_{max}}{\sqrt{2}}$ |
| $I_{aw} = \frac{I_{max}}{\pi/2}$ | $I_{av} = \frac{I_{max}}{\pi}$ |

Form factor = 1.11

Peak factor = 1.414

Form factor = $\pi/2$

Peak factor = 2

For triangular wave

$$I_{RMS} = \frac{I_{max}}{\sqrt{3}}$$

$$I_{av} = \frac{I_{max}}{2}$$

j operator

$$j = \sqrt{-1}$$
$$j^2 = -1$$
$$j^3 = -j$$
$$j^4 = 1$$

For pure resistor circuit

$$v = V_m \sin \omega t$$

$$i = \text{'I'}_m \sin \omega t \qquad \text{where } I_m = \frac{V_m}{R}$$

$$\text{Average power} = \frac{V_m I_m}{2} \text{ watts}$$

where $V_m$ is the max value of voltage in volts.

'I'$_m$ is the max value of current in amperes.

v and i are in phase

For pure inductive circuit

$$v = V_m \sin \omega t$$

$$i = \text{'I'}_m \sin\left(\omega t - \frac{\pi}{2}\right);$$

$$\text{where 'I'}_m = \frac{V_m}{X_L} = \frac{V_m}{\omega . L}$$

$X_L$ is the inductive reactance in ohms

L is the inductance in henry

Average power = 0

'i' lags behind 'v' by $\frac{\pi}{2}$

For pure capacitive circuit

$$v = V_m \sin \omega t$$

$$i = 'I'_m \sin(\omega t - \frac{\pi}{2});$$

where $'I'_m = \frac{V_m}{X_c} = \frac{V_m}{1/wc}$

where $X_C$ is the inductive reactance in ohms

C is the inductance in henry

'i' lags 'v' be $\frac{\pi}{2}$

Average power = 0

For R-L series circuit

$$v = V_m \sin \omega t$$

$$i = 'I'_m \sin(\omega t - \phi) \qquad '0' < \phi < \frac{\pi}{2}$$

$$I_m = \frac{V_m}{Z} A$$

where $Z = R + j\, x_L$ ohms

where '$Z$' is the impedance in ohms

$$|Z| = \sqrt{R^2 + X_L^2}$$

'i' lags 'v' by '$\phi$'

(power factor) $\cos\phi = \frac{R}{Z}$

$$\cos\phi = \frac{X_L}{Z}$$

$$\tan\phi = \frac{X_L}{R}$$

Active power (P) $= VI \cos\phi$ watts

Reactive power (Q) $= VI \sin\phi$ VARs

Apparent power (S) $= VI$ Volt amperes

$$S = \sqrt{P^2 + Q^2}$$

Power factor ($\cos\phi$) $= \frac{R}{Z}$

$$\cos \phi = \frac{\text{Active power}}{\text{Apparent power}}$$

For R-C series circuit:

$$v = V_m \sin \omega t$$

$$i = \text{'I'}_m \sin (\omega t \pm \phi) \qquad \text{'0'} < \phi < \frac{\pi}{2}$$

+ ve sign for $X_C > X_L$

– ve sign for $X_L > X_C$

$$\text{'I'}_m = \frac{V_m}{Z} A$$

where $Z = R + j X_L \sim X_C)$ ohms

$$(Z) = \sqrt{R^2 + (X_L \sim X_C)^2}$$

$$\cos \phi = \frac{R}{Z}$$

$$\sin \phi = \frac{X_L \sim X_C}{Z}$$

$$\tan \phi = \frac{X_L \sim X_C}{R}$$

Frequency at series resonance $f_o = \frac{I}{2\pi\sqrt{LC}}$ Hz

where L is the inductance in henry.
C is the capacitance in Farads

Frequency at parallel resonance $f_o = \frac{1}{2\pi}\sqrt{\frac{1}{LC} - \frac{R^2}{L^2}}$ Hz

In star connection,

$$V_L = \sqrt{3} V_{ph} \text{ volts;} = \frac{V_L}{\sqrt{3}} \text{ volts}$$

$$I_L = I_{ph} A$$

3 phase active power $= 3\, V_{ph}\, I_{ph} \cos\phi$

$= \sqrt{3} V_L I_L \cos \phi$ watts

3 phase apparent power = 3 Vph Iph VA

$$= \sqrt{3} V_L I_L \text{ VA}$$

3 phase reactive power $= 3V_{ph} I_{ph} \sin\phi$ VARs

$$= \sqrt{3} V_L I_L \sin\phi \text{ VARs}$$

In Delta connection

$$V_L = V_{ph} \text{ volts}$$

$$I_L = \sqrt{3} I_{ph} ; I_{ph} = \frac{I_L}{\sqrt{3}} \text{ A}$$

The power equations remains same

where $V_L$ – Line voltage in volts.

$I_L$ – Line current in A.

$V_{ph}$ – Phase voltage in volts.

$I_{ph}$ – Phase current in A.

## REVIEW QUESTIONS

1. Explain the method of generating alternating emf.
2. Define the following terms
   a) Alternating quantity b) Cycle
   c) Time period d) Frequency
   e) Amplitude f) Average value
   g) Root mean square value h) Form factor
   i) Peak factor
3. Derive an expression for r.m.s value, average value, form factor and peak factor of
   i) Sinusoidal alternating quantity
   ii) Half wave rectified current
   iii) Lagging vector
5. Explain the behaviour of alternating current through
   a) R b) L c) C
   d) R-L c) R-C d) R-L-C circuits.
6. Derive an expression for power in a.c. circuit.
7. What do you understand by power factor?
8. Explain the following
   a) Series resonance b) Parallel resonance
9. Explain the following terms with respect to 3 phase circuits
   a) Phase sequence b) Star and Delta connection

c) Phase voltage d) Phase current

e) Line voltage f) Line current

g) Balanced system h) Balanced and unbalanced load

10. Establish the relation between line and phase values of voltage and current in

i) Star connection ii) Delta connection.

11. Prove that the three phase power can be measured using two voltmeters.

12. Write the distinction between single phase and three phase supply.

## TWO MARKS QUESTIONS AND ANSWERS

1. *What is an alternating quantity ?*

It is one in which the magnitude and direction changes periodically at regular intervals.

2. *What is cycle ?*

One complete set of positive and negative values of an alternating quantity constitutes one cycle.

3. *What is time period ?*

It is the time taken by an alternating quantity to complete one cycle. It is denoted by 'T'. Its unit is second.

4. *What is frequency ?*

The number of cycles completed per second is known as frequency. It is denoted by 'f' and its unit is hertz.

5. *What is amplitude ?*

The maximum value either positive or negative of an alternating quantity is called amplitude.

6. *What is average value ?*

The average value of an alternating current is that value of direct current which transfers across any circuit in a given time the same charge as is transferred by the alternating current in the same circuit.

7. *What is R.M.S. value ?*

R.M.S. value of an alternating current is given by that value of direct current which when flowing through a given circuit for given time produces the same heating effect as that produced by an alternating current when flowing through the same circuit for the same time.

8. *Define Form factor and Peak factor.*

$$1.\ \text{Form factor} = \frac{\text{R.M.S. value}}{\text{Average value}}$$

$$2.\ \text{Peak factor} = \frac{\text{Maximum value}}{\text{R.M.S. value}}$$

9. *What is meant by balanced system ?*

   It is one in which currents in the three phases are equal in magnitude and are displaced from one another by equal angles and also the voltages in all phases are equal in magnitude and are displaced from one another by equal angles.

10. *Give the. relation between line and phase values of voltage and current in star connection.*

    Line voltage = $\sqrt{3}$ × phase voltage

    Line current = phase current

    In delta connection

    Line voltage = $\sqrt{3}$ × phase current

    Line voltage = phase current

## EXERCISE PROBLEMS

**P. 4.1:** For the circuit given in Fig. 4.96, calculate the current, power, power factor and voltage across each element.

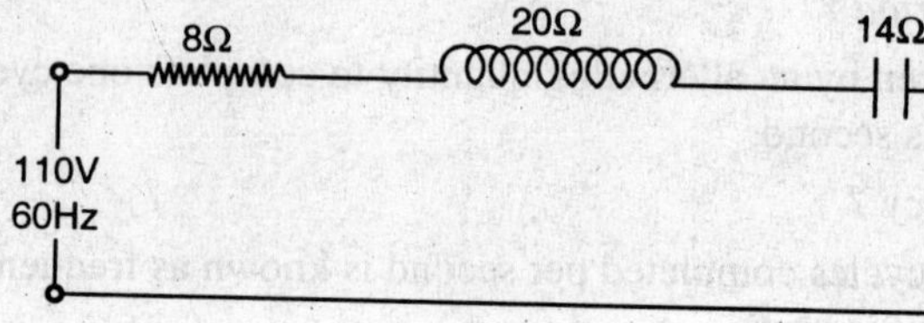


**Fig. 4.96**

(Ans: 11A, 968 W, 0.8, 88 V, 220 V, 154 V)

**P. 4.2:** A series circuit with R = 10 W and L = 20 mH has a current of i = 2 Sin 500t. Obtain the total voltage across the series circuit and angle by which the current lags the voltage.

(Ans: 20V, 45°)

**P. 4.3:** Calculate the current, power and power factor for each impedance shown in Fig. 4.97 below. Also calculate the total current, power and power factor of the whole combination.

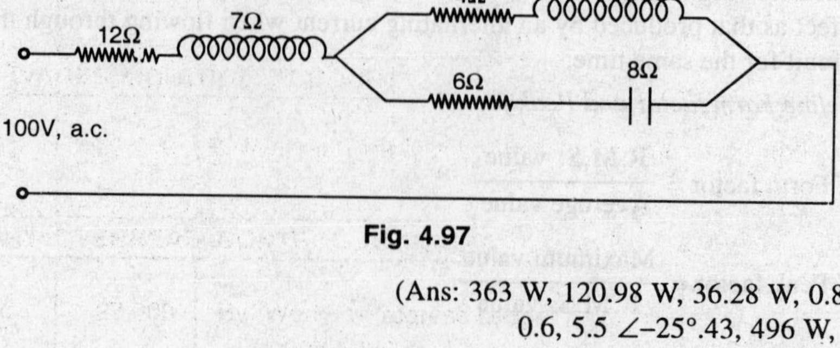


**Fig. 4.97**

(Ans: 363 W, 120.98 W, 36.28 W, 0.86, 0.8, 0.6, 5.5 ∠−25°.43, 496 W, 0.903)

**P. 4.4:** Find the value of the capacitor 'C' at which the power factor is unity for the circuit given in Fig. 4.98. Also draw the vector diagram.

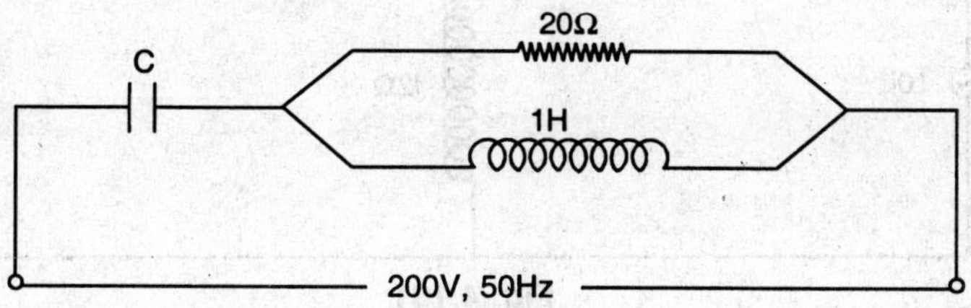


Fig. 4.98

(Ans: $2.5 \times 10^{-3}$ F)

**P. 4.5:** Find the average value and r.m.s. value of the wave form shown in Fig. 4.99.

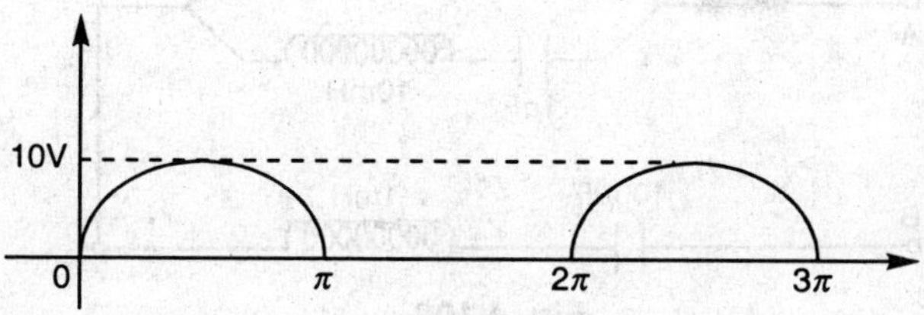


Fig. 4.99

$$\left(\text{Ans: } \frac{I_m}{\pi}, \frac{I_m}{2}\right)$$

**P. 4.6:** Find the impedance, current, power factor and power in the circuit shown in Fig. 4.100.

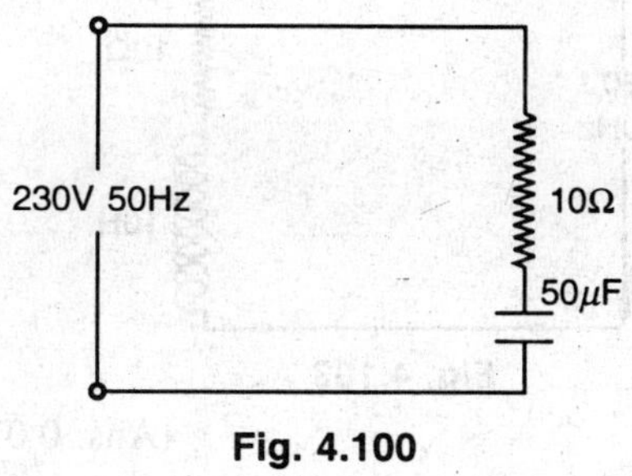


Fig. 4.100

(Ans: 64.44 Ω, 3.569 A, 0.155, 127.38 W)

**P. 4.7:** Find the power dissipated in each resistor for the circuit shown in Fig. 4.101.

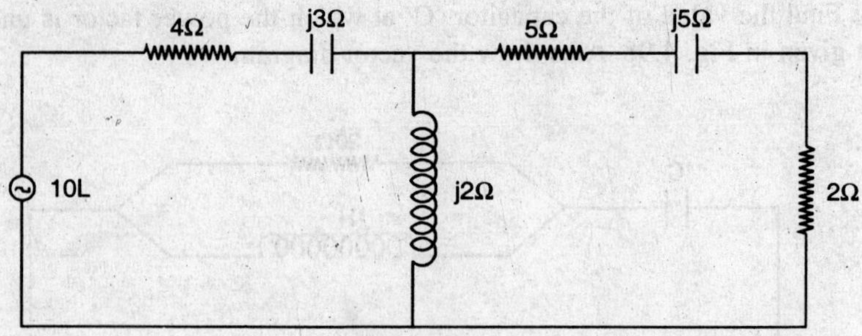


Fig. 4.101

(Ans: 19.36 W, 1.669 W, 0.6677 W)

**P. 4.8:** Find the impedance across the terminals AB for the circuit given in Fig. 4.102. The frequency of operation is 50 Hz.

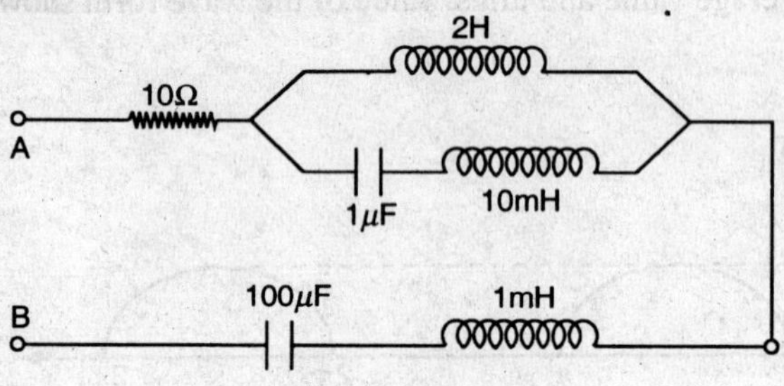


Fig. 4.102

(Ans: 10 + j 751.495 Ω)

**P. 4.9:** Find the current 'I' and the power factor of the circuit shown in Fig. 4.103.

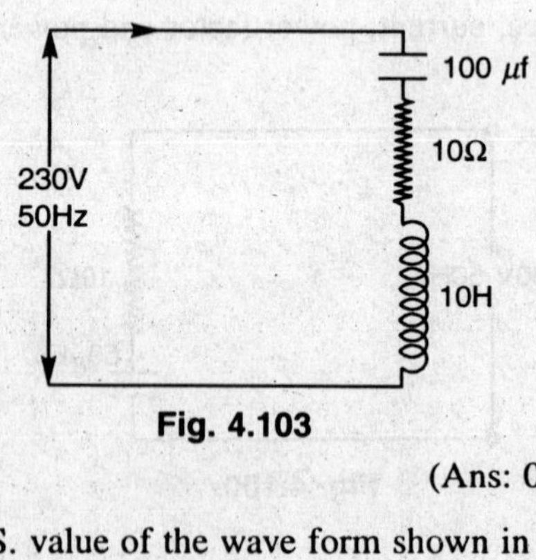


Fig. 4.103

(Ans: 0.0739 -89°.31 A, 0.0032)

**P. 4.10:** Find the R.M.S. value of the wave form shown in Fig. 4.104.

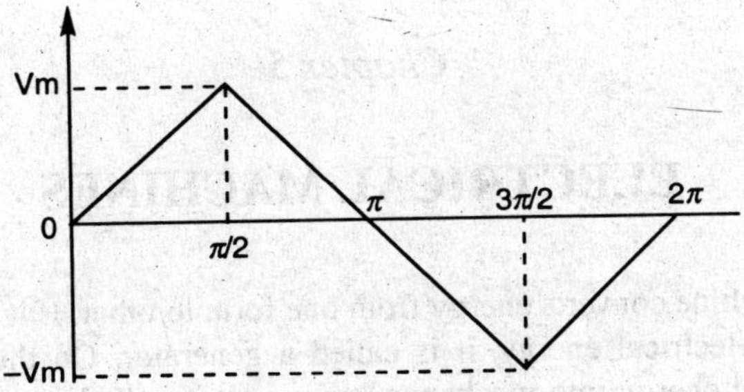


Fig. 4.104

**P. 4.11:** For the circuit shown in Fig. 4.105 find the current drawn from the source.

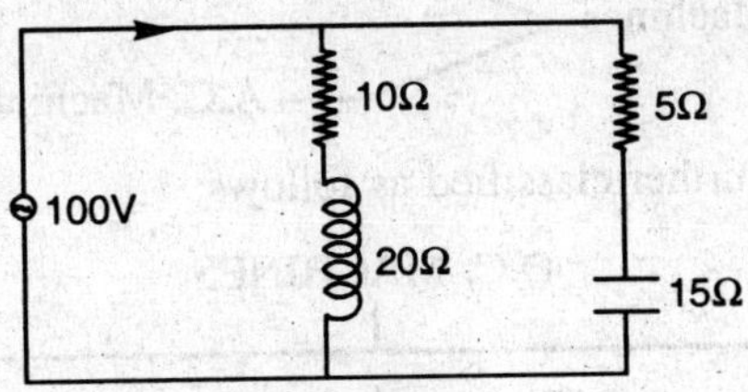


Fig. 4.105

**P. 4.12:** Three similar resistors of 10 Ohms each are connected in delta to a 3 phase 50 Hz line. The line voltage in 400V. Calculate line and phase values of current and also the power absorbed.

*Chapter 5*

# ELECTRICAL MACHINES

An electrical machine converts energy from one form to other. If it converts mechanical energy into electrical energy, it is called a generator. On the other hand, if it converts electrical energy into mechanical energy, it is called a motor.

The broad classification of electrical machines can be made as follows:

- Electrical Machines
  - D.C. Machines
  - A.C. Machines

The d.c. machines are further classified as follows:

- D.C. MACHINES
  - Generator
    - Separately excited
    - Self excited
      - Compound
        - Long Shunt
          - Cumulative
          - Differential
        - Short Shunt
          - Cumulative
          - Differential
      - Series
      - Shunt
  - Motor
    - Shunt
    - Series
    - Compound
      - Long shunt
        - Cumulative
        - Differential
      - Short shunt
        - Cumulative
        - Differential

## 5.1. PRINCIPLE OF D.C. GENERATOR

A generator is one which converts mechanical energy into electrical energy. It works on Faraday's laws of electromagnetic induction principle. Accordingly, whenever a conductor cuts a magnetic flux, an emf is induced in the conductor causing a current to flow through it, when the circuit is closed. The direction of the emf induced is given by Fleming's right hand rule.

The essential parts of the generator are: (i) Conductor, (ii) Magnetic field.

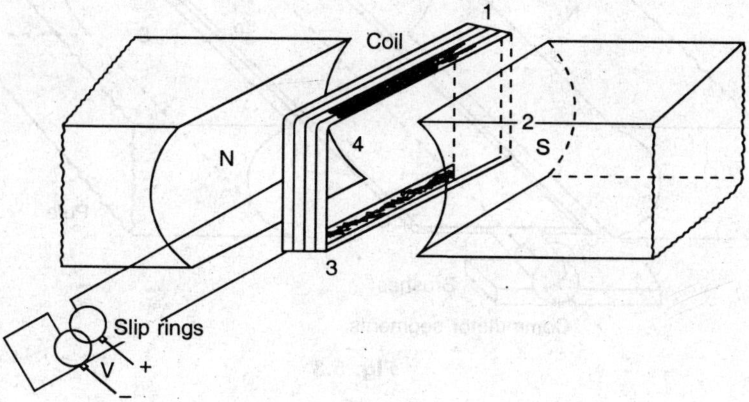


Fig. 5.1

The principle of the operation can be clearly understood with the help of the arrangement shown in Fig. 5.1. A single turn coil is allowed to rotate in an uniform magnetic field at a constant speed. As the coil takes different positions in the magnetic field, the flux linking with the coil changes and hence the magnitude of emf induced in it also changes. When the coil is at the position 1 as shown in Fig. 5.1, the rate of change of flux linkage is minimum and hence the emf induced is also minimum. At position 2, the emf induced is maximum because the rate of change of flux linkages is maximum. Again in position 3, the emf is minimum due to minimum rate of change of flux linkages. This process repeats in the next half cycle. Thus even in a D.C. generator, the emf induced in the coil is alternating as shown in the Fig. 5.2.

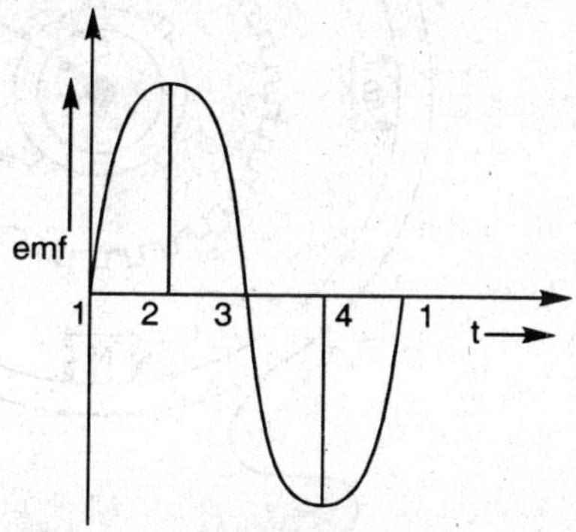


Fig. 5.2

In order to obtain an unidirectional voltage at the coil terminals, the slip rings (Fig. 5.1) are to be replaced by commutator segments as shown in Fig. 5.3.

## 5.2. PARTS OF D.C. GENERATOR

The DC generator consists of: (i) Yoke, (ii) Pole core and pole shoe, (iii) Pole coil, (iv) Armature, (v) Commutator, (vi) Brushes and (vii) Bearings as shown in Fig. 5.4.

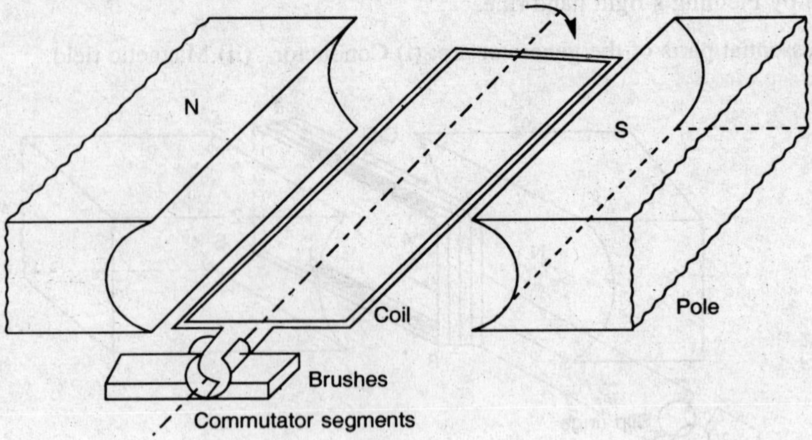


Fig. 5.3

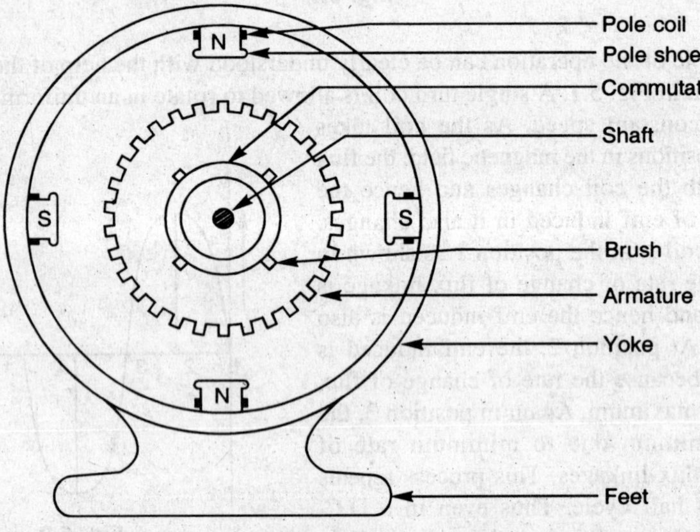


Fig. 5.4

**Yoke:** It is made of magnetic material. In smaller machines, where cost is the main consideration rather than the weight, cast iron is used. For larger machines where weight and efficiency are the main considerations, cast steel is used. The feet and terminal boxes are welded to the yoke. The purpose of the yoke is to provide support to the armature and field windings and also to carry the magnetic flux produced by the pole.

**Pole core and pole shoe:** Pole core is made up of cast iron or cast steel as shown in Fig. 5.5. For small machines the poles are cast with the yoke, whereas for large machines they are screwed with the yoke. The pole shoe not only supports the pole coil but also spreads the flux in the air gap. Both pole core and pole shoe are laminated to reduce the eddy current loss.

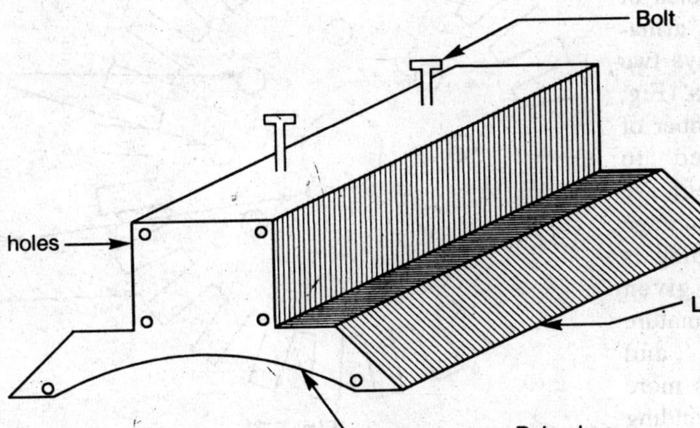


Fig. 5.5

**Pole coil:** This is also called field coil or exciting coil. It consists of copper wire usually former wound and placed over the pole. Whenever they carry current, the poles are electromagnetised which produce the magnetic flux.

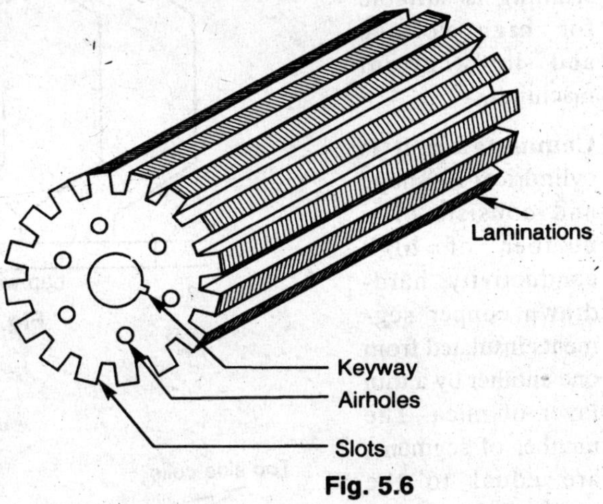


Fig. 5.6

**Armature:** It is a cylindrical drum (Fig. 5.6) consisting of thin circular stampings of silicon steel (Fig. 5.7). These discs or stampings are insulated from one another by a shellac varnish or paper or oxide film coating. The thickness of these stamping varies from 0.35 to 0.5 mm. This is done to reduce the eddy current loss. On its periphery it has slots to accommodate the armature conductors. The stampings are held firmly by a key and are mounted on the shaft. The purpose of armature is to (i) house the armature conductors (ii) rotate them in the magnetic field (iii) provide a very low reluctance path.

**Armature windings:** Mainly there are two types of armature windings, namely, lap winding and wave winding.

**Lap winding:** The number of parallel paths are equal to the number of poles and the total current is equally divided among them (Fig. 5.8). The number of brushes are equal to the number of poles. Lap winding is suitable for large current and low voltage requirements. Whenever lap winding is employed, equaliser rings are used to avoid unequal distribution of current at the brushes.

**Wave winding:** Here irrespective of the number of poles of machine, the armature has always two parallel paths (Fig. 5.9). The number of brushes used to collect current are two. The advantage of wave winding is that, for a given number of armature conductors and poles, it gives more emf than lap winding hence wave winding is suitable for small generators. Equaliser ring is not used in wave winding. Wave winding is suitable for high voltage and low current machines.

**Commutator:** It is cylindrical in shape and consists of a number of high conductivity, hard-drawn copper segments insulated from one another by a thin layer of mica. The number of segments are equal to the number of armature coils. A copper lug (riser) is used to connect commutator segment to the armature conductor (refer Fig. 5.10). The function of commutator is to convert the alternating current

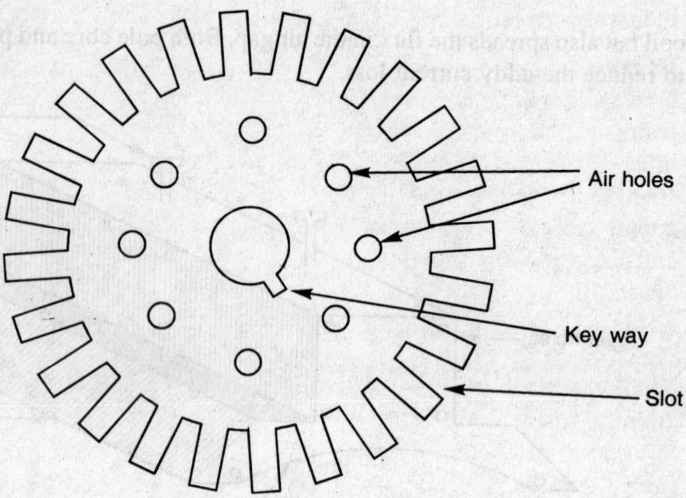


Fig. 5.7

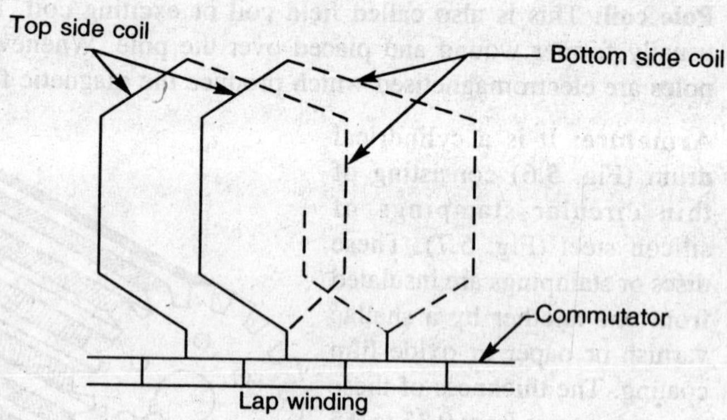


Fig. 5.8

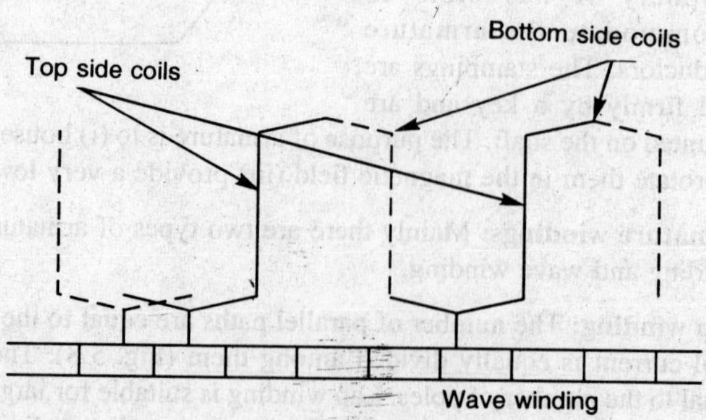


Fig. 5.9

induced in the armature into unidirectional current in the external circuit.

**Brushes:** The function of brushes is to collect current from the commutator. The brushes are made of carbon (for small machines) or copper (for large machines) and are placed in hollow brass bars called brush holders as shown in Fig. 5.11. The brushes rest on the commutator segments against spring tension. A lever is used to adjust the spring tension. The pigtail made of copper wire connects the brush with the outside circuit.

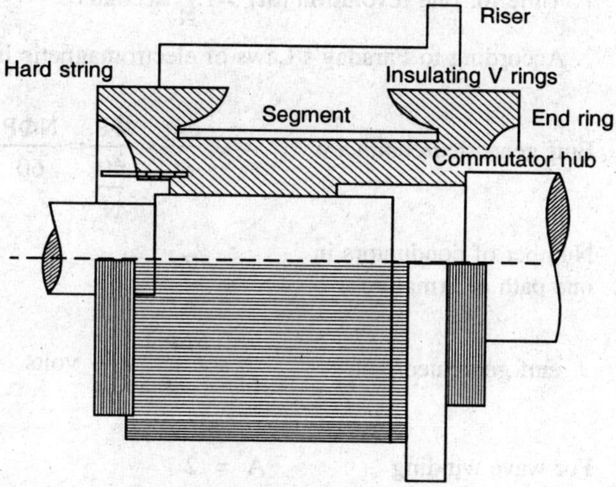


Fig. 5.10

**Bearings:** The bearings are fitted inside the cover and their purpose is to provide free and smooth rotation to the armature. The different types of bearings used are bush bearings, ball bearings and roller bearings. Because of their reliability ball bearings are frequently used. However for heavy duties roller bearings are used.

## 5.3. EMF EQUATION

Let P = Number of poles

$\Phi$ = Flux/pole in weber

N = Speed of armature in r.p.m.

$\frac{N}{60}$ = Speed of armature in RPS

Z = Total number of armature conductors

A = Number of parallel paths

E = emf induced in any parallel path in the armature in volts.

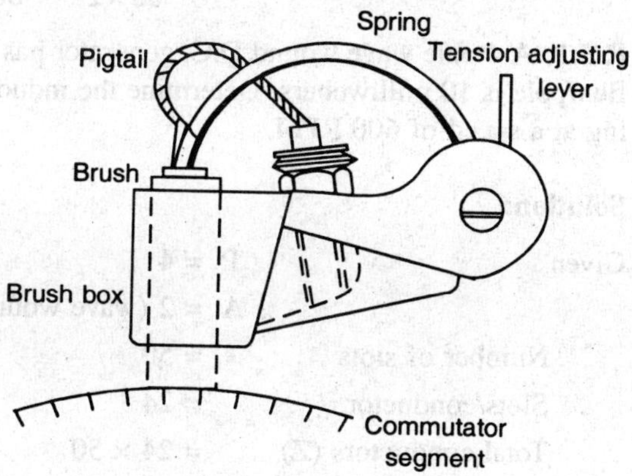


Fig. 5.11

Average emf generated/conductor $= \frac{d\Phi}{dt}$

But, flux cut/conductor during one revolution $(d\Phi) = \Phi \times P$ weber.

Number of revolutions per second $= \frac{N}{60}$ seconds

$\therefore$ Time for one revolution (dt) $= \dfrac{60}{N}$ seconds

$\therefore$ According to Faraday's Laws of electromagnetic induction

Emf generated/conductor $= \dfrac{d\Phi}{dt} = \dfrac{\Phi P}{\frac{60}{N}} = \dfrac{N\Phi P}{60}$ volts

Number of conductors in one path of armature $= \dfrac{Z}{A}$

$\therefore$ emf generated/path $= \dfrac{\Phi PN}{60} \times \dfrac{Z}{A}$ volts ...(5.1)

For wave winding A = 2

$\therefore$ Emf generated/path $= \dfrac{\Phi ZNP}{60 \times 2} = \dfrac{\Phi ZNP}{120}$ volts ...(5.2)

For lap winding A = P

$\therefore$ emf generated/path $= \dfrac{\Phi ZNP}{60 \times 2} = \dfrac{\Phi ZN}{60} =$ volts ...(5.3)

**P. 5.1.** A 4 pole wave wound D.C. generator has 50 slots and 24 conductors/slot. The flux/pole is 10 milliwebers. Determine the induced emf in the armature, if it is rotating at a speed of 600 RPM.

**Solution:-**

Given P = 4

A = 2 (wave wound)

Number of slots = 50

Slots/conductor = 24

$\therefore$ Total conductors (Z) = 24 × 50

Flux/pole ($\Phi$) = $10 \times 10^{-3}$ Wb.

Speed of armature (N) = 600 r.p.m.

emf induced E $= \dfrac{\Phi ZNP}{60\ A} = \dfrac{(10 \times 10^{-3}) \times (24 \times 50) \times 600 \times 4}{60 \times 2}$

= 240 volts.

**P. 5.2.** Repeat the above problem 5.1 for lap connection.

**Solution:**

For lap winding $A = P = 4$

$$\therefore \quad E = \frac{\Phi ZNP}{60\ A} = \frac{(10\times10^{-3})\times(24\times50)\times600\times4}{60\times4}$$

$$= 120 \text{ volts.}$$

**P. 5.3.** A 6 pole wound armature has 780 conductors and a flux of 12 milliwebers. Find the speed of the armature when the generated emf is 400 V. What will be the speed when it is lap wound?

**Solution:**

Given $P = 6$

Wave wound $A = 2$

Armature conductors (Z) $= 780$

Flux/pole ($\Phi$) $= 12\times10^{-3}$ Wb

$E = 400V$

Speed $N = ?$

we know that, $$E = \frac{\Phi ZNP}{60\ A}$$

$$\frac{E\ 60\ A}{\Phi\ ZP} = N$$

$$\frac{400\times60\times2}{12\times10^{-3}\times780\times6} = N = 854.70 \text{ rpm}$$

when it is lap wound $A = P = 6$

$$\therefore \quad N = \frac{400\times60\times6}{12\times10^{-3}\times780\times6}$$

$$= 2564.1 \text{ rpm}$$

## 5.4. TYPES OF GENERATORS (Fig. 5.12)

Generators are classified according to the manner in which their fields are excited. Accordingly, they are classified into:

(i) Separately excited generator (field is excited by an external source)

(ii) Self excited generator (field is excited by the emf induced in the generator itself).

The self excited generators are further classified into shunts, series, compound (long shunt, short shunt) depending upon the manner in which their field windings are connected with their armature.

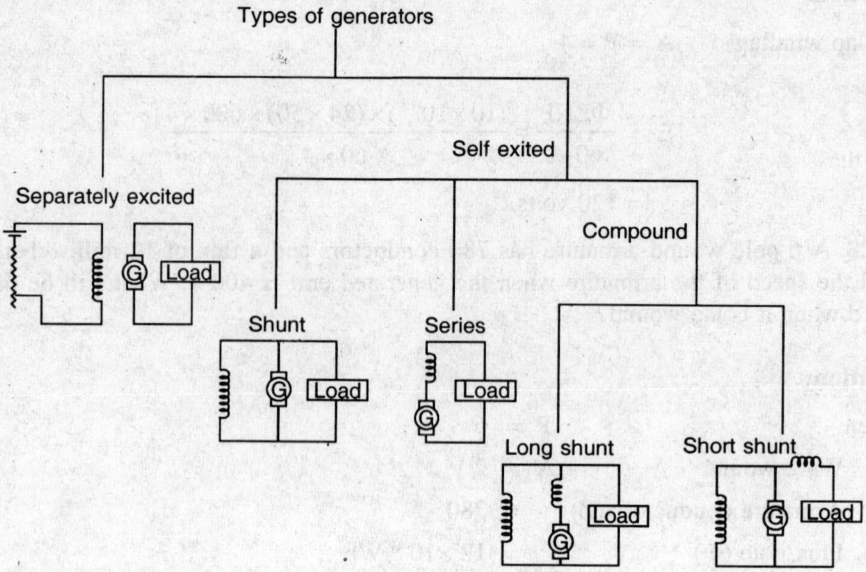


Fig. 5.12

**Shunt Generator** (Fig. 5.13)

Let $I_a$, $I_{sh}$, $I_L$ be armature, shunt field, and load currents respectively. Let $R_a$, $R_{sh}$, $R_L$ be armature, shunt field, and load resistances respectively.

A-AA—Armature terminals

G – Generator

f-ff – Shunt field terminals

$P_L$ – Load (power) in watts

$V_L$ – Terminal voltage

B.C.D. – Brush contact drop in volts

Eg – Generated emf in volts

$R_L$ – Load resistance in ohms

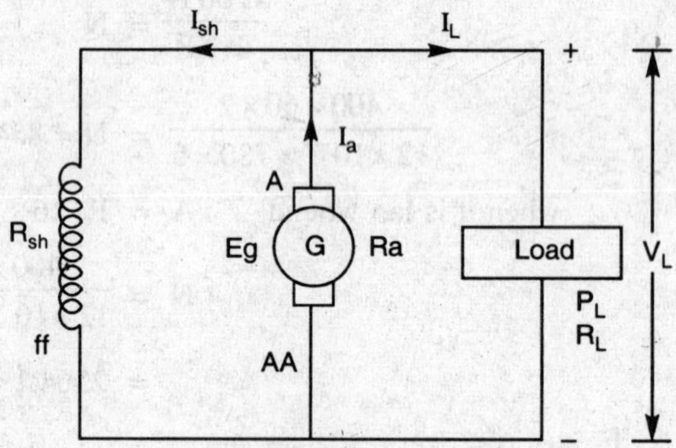


Fig. 5.13

From Fig. 5.13 it is clear that

$$I_a = I_L + I_{sh} \qquad ...(5.4)$$

$$\text{Also, } I_L = \frac{P_L}{V_L} = \frac{V_L}{R_L} \qquad ...(5.5)$$

$$\text{and } I_{sh} = \frac{V_L}{R_{sh}} \qquad ...(5.6)$$

$\therefore$ Eg (generated emf) = $V_L + I_a R_a$ + B.C.D. volts

**Series Generator** (Fig. 5.14)

Let $R_a$, $R_{se}$, $R_L$ be the armature, series field and load resistances respectively. Let $I_a$, $I_{se}$, $I_L$ be the armature, series field and load current respectively.

Let $V_L$ be the terminal voltage
$P_L$ be the load (power) in watts
A-AA—Armature terminals
y-yy—series field terminals.

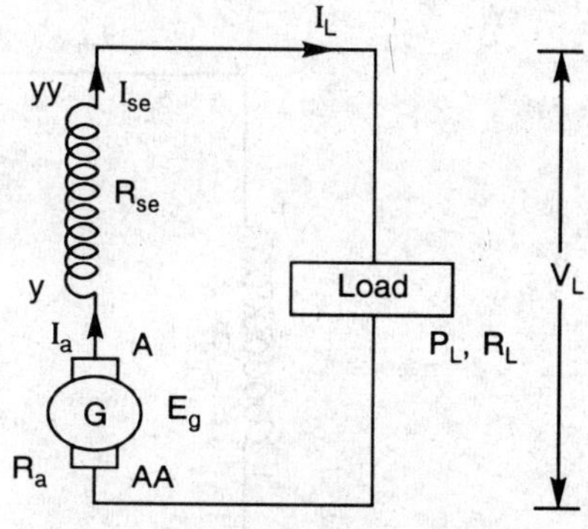

Fig. 5.14

From Fig. 5.14 it is clear that

$$I_a = I_{se} = I_L = \frac{P_L}{V_L} \qquad ...(5.8)$$

$$Eg = V_L + I_a R_a + I_{se} R_{se} + \text{B.C.D. volts} \qquad ...(5.9)$$

**Long shunt compound generator:** (Fig. 5.15)

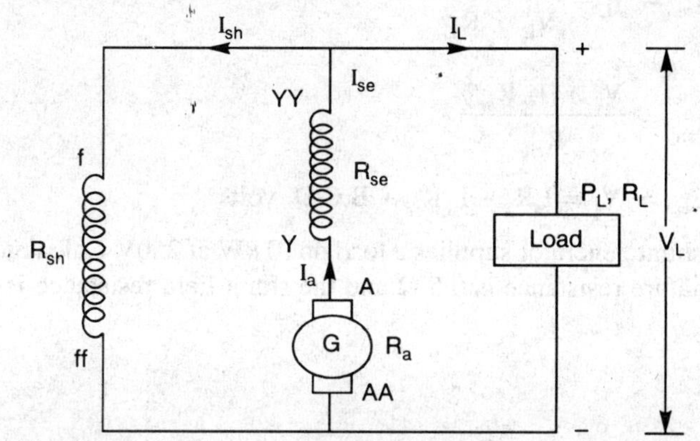

Fig. 5.15

From Fig. 5.15 it is clear that,

$$I_{se} = I_L + I_{sh} \qquad ...(5.10)$$

$$I_{se} = I_a \qquad ...(5.11)$$

$$I_L = \frac{P_L}{V_L} = \frac{V_L}{R_L} \qquad ...(5.12)$$

$$I_{sh} = \frac{V_L}{R_{sh}} \qquad ...(5.13)$$

$$Eg = V_L + I_a R_a + I_{se} R_{se} + \text{B.C.D. volts} \qquad ...(5.14)$$

**Short shunt generator:**

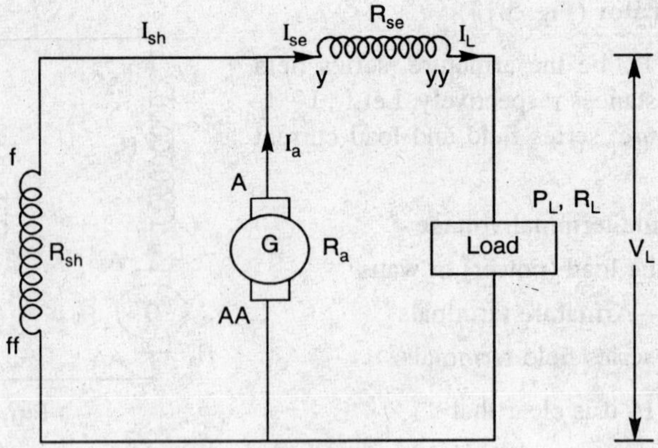


Fig. 5.16

From Fig. 5.16 we have

$$I_a = I_{sh} + I_{se} \qquad ...(5.15)$$

$$I_{se} = I_L = \frac{P_L}{V_L} = \frac{V_L}{R_L} \qquad ...(5.16)$$

$$I_{sh} = \frac{V_L + (I_{se} R_{se})}{R_{sh}} \qquad ...(5.17)$$

$$Eg = V_L = I_a R_a + I_{se} R_{se} + \text{B.C.D. volts} \qquad ...(5.18)$$

**P. 5.4.** A D.C. shunt generator supplies a load of 10 kW at 250V. Calculate the induced emf, if the armature resistance is 0.5 Ω and the shunt field resistance is 100 Ω.

**Solution:**

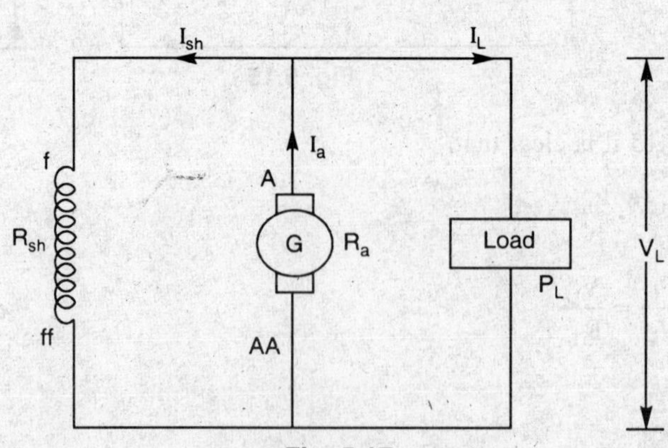


Fig. 5.17

Given,

$R_a = 0.05\ \Omega$

$R_{sh} = 100\ \Omega$

$V_L = 250V$

$P_L = 10 \times 10^3$ watts

$$I_L = \frac{10 \times 10^3}{250} = 40 \text{ amperes}$$

$$I_{sh} = \frac{V_L}{R_{sh}} = \frac{250}{100} = 2.5 \text{ amperes}$$

$\therefore \quad I_a = I_L + I_{sh} = 40 + 2.5 = 42.5$ amperes

$\therefore \quad Eg = V_L + I_a R_a$

$= 250 + (42.5) \times 0.5$

$= 271.25$ volts.

**P. 5.5.** A D.C. long shunt compound generator delivers a load current of 200 amperes at 500 volts. The resistance of the armature, series field and shunt field are 0.03 Ω, 0.015 Ω and 150 Ω respectively. Calculate the emf induced in the armature. Allow a brush contact drop of 1V/Brush.

**Solution:**

Given,

$I_L = 200$ amperes

$V_L = 500$ V

$R_a = 0.03\ \Omega$

$R_{se} = 0.015\ \Omega$

$R_{sh} = 150\ \Omega$

B.C.D. = 1V/brush

$= 1 \times 2$

$= 2$ volts.

Eg = ?

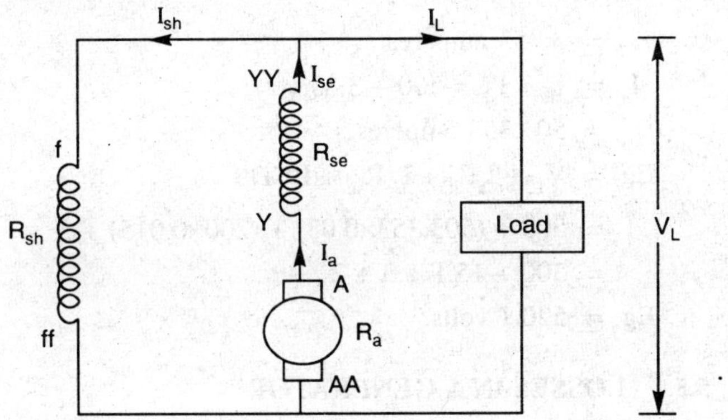


Fig. 5.18

$$I_{sh} = \frac{V_L}{R_{sh}} = \frac{500}{150} = 3.33 \text{ amperes}$$

$I_a = I_L + I_{sh} = 200 + 3.33 = 203.33$ amperes

$I_a = I_{se} = 203.33$ amperes

$Eg = V_L + I_a R_a + I_{se} R_{se} + BCD$

$= 500 + (203.33 \times 0.03) + (203.33 \times 0.015) + 2$

$= 500 + 6.1 + 3.05 + 2$

$Eg = 511.15$ volts.

**P. 5.6.** Repeat the problem 5.5 for a short shunt compound generator.

**Solution:**

Given

$I_L = 200$ amperes

$V_L = 500$ V

$R_a = 0.03\ \Omega$

$R_{se} = 0.015\ \Omega$

$R_{sh} = 150\ \Omega$

$BCD = 1 \times 2 = 2V.$

$Eg = ?$

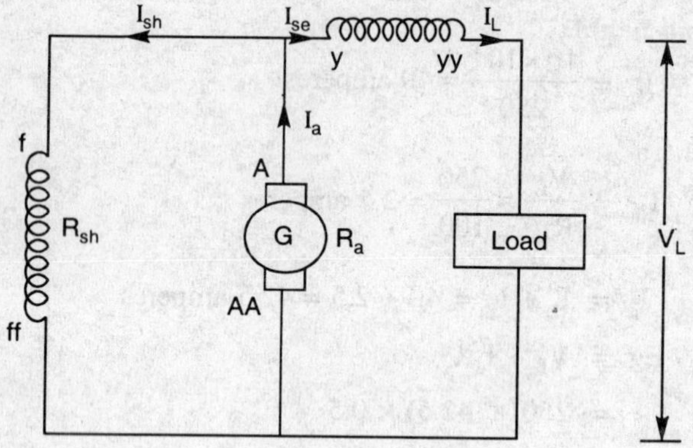


**Fig. 5.19**

We know that for a short shunt compound generator

$I_L = I_{se}$

$\therefore\ I_L = I_{se} = 200$ amperes

$$I_{sh} = \frac{V_L + I_{se}R_{se}}{R_{sh}} = \frac{500 + (200 \times 0.015)}{150}$$

$= 3.353$ amperes

$I_a = I_L + I_{sh} = 500 + 3.353$

$= 503.353$ amperes

$\therefore\ Eg = V_L + I_aR_a + I_{se}R_{se} + BCD$

$= 500 + (503.353 \times 0.03) + (200 \times 0.015) + 2$

$= 500 + 15.1 + 3 + 2$

$Eg = 520.1$ volts.

## 5.5. LOSSES IN A GENERATOR

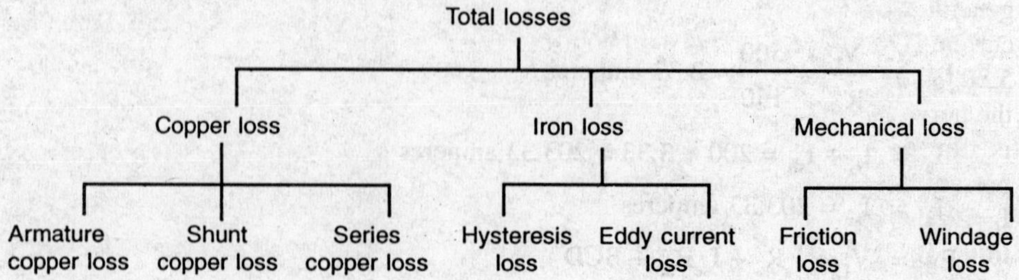

**Note:** Iron loss is also called core loss or magnetic loss. Armature copper loss is also called variable loss. Iron loss and mechanical loss are together called stray loss. The shunt field copper loss and stray loss together are called constant loss.

**Copper loss:** It is due to the resistance of armature, shunt and series field windings.

The armature copper loss $= I_a^2 R_a$ watts

Shunt field loss $= I_{sh}^2 R_{sh}$ watts

Series field copper loss $= I_{se}^2 R_{se}$ watts

The armature copper loss is about 30 to 40% of full load loss whereas the field copper loss is about 20 to 30% of full load loss.

**Iron loss:** It consists of eddy current loss and hysteresis loss.

Eddy current loss is due to eddy currents induced in the core and is given by

$$W_e = KB^2_{max} f^2 t^2 \text{ watts} \quad ...(5.19)$$

where 't' is the thickness of lamination. This loss can be minimised by using a laminated core.

Hysteresis loss is due to the magnetic reversal and is given by

$$W_h = B^{1.6}_{max} \times f \times V \text{ watts.} \quad ...(5.20)$$

The hysteresis loss can be minimised by selecting a material for the core which has low hysteresis coefficient, for example, silicon steel. Iron loss is about 20 to 30% of full load loss. For shunt and compound generator these losses practically remain constant.

**Mechanical loss:** Mechanical loss consists of friction loss at the bearings and the windage loss of rotating armature. This loss is about 10 to 20% of full load loss.

## 5.6. CHARACTERISTICS OF A GENERATOR

There are three characteristics, namely:

(i) Open circuit characteristics or O.C.C. or magnetic characteristic.

(ii) Total or internal characteristics.

(iii) External characteristics or voltage regulation curve.

**Magnetic characteristics of D.C. shunt generator**

It is a curve drawn by taking no load generator emf '$E_o$' on Y-axis and field current ($I_f$) on X-axis as shown in Fig. 5.20. From Fig. 5.20 it is clear that the curve is not starting from zero. It is due to the residual magnetism present in the poles. Thus even when $I_f = 0$, there is some voltage 'OA' due to the residual flux.

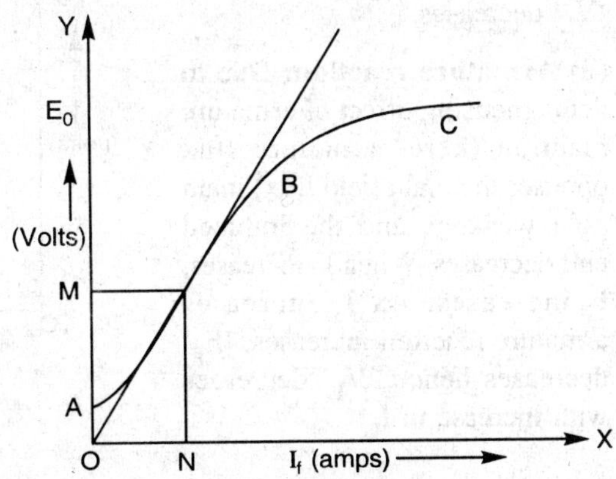


Fig. 5.20

The portion AB is practically a straight line. It is due to the fact that at low flux densities, the reluctance offered by iron path is negligible. Hence the total reluctance is only due to air gap which is constant. Thus as '$I_f$' increases, '$E_o$' increases. In other words $E_o$ μ $I_f$ (or) $E_o = kI_f$ which is the equation of straight line passing through origin, hence the portion AB. The portion BC refers to saturation i.e. at higher flux densities iron path reluctance becomes appreciable and hence '$E_o$' will no more be proportional to '$I_f$'.

**Critical Resistance ($R_c$)**

It is the slope of the tangent drawn to the linear portion of the O.C.C from origin. It is the value of field resistance where the generator will just excite.

From Fig. 5.20 $R_C = \frac{OM}{ON}$

**Conditions for build up of a self excited shunt generator**

1. There must be some residual magnetism.
2. For the given direction of rotation, shunt field coils should be properly connected to the armature terminals.
3. Shunt field resistance should be less than the critical–resistance (when excited on open circuit).

**External characteristics of D.C. shunt generator**

It is a curve drawn by taking terminal voltage ($V_L$) on Y-axis and load current ($I_L$) an X-axis as shown in Fig. 5.21.

It is clear from Fig. 5.21 that as the load current increases, the terminal voltage decreases. There are three reasons for the decrease in the terminal voltage.

**(i) Armature resistance drop:** As '$I_L$' increases, $I_a$ increases because $I_a = I_L + I_{sh}$. Therefore '$I_aR_a$' drop increases. For shunt generator $V_L = E_g - I_aR_a$. Hence '$V_L$' decreases.

**(ii) Armature reaction:** Due to demagnetising effect of armature reaction (here armature flux opposes the main field flux) main pole weakens and the induced emf decreases. When $I_L$ increases, $I_a$ increases. As $I_a$ increases armature reaction increases. '$E_g$' decreases hence '$V_L$' decreases with increase in $I_L$.

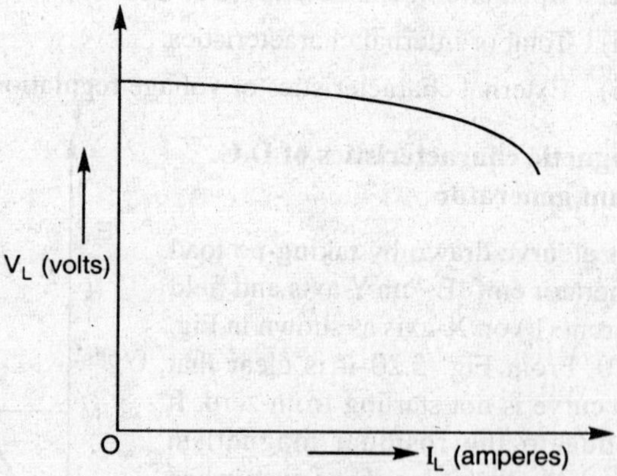


Fig. 5.21

**(iii) Due to the above two reasons** field current decreases causing decrease in '$E_g$', therefore '$V_L$' decreases.

**Internal characteristics of a shunt generator**

It is a curve drawn by taking '$E_g$' (= $V_L + I_aR_a$) on Y-axis and '$I_a$' (= $I_L + I_{sh}$) on X-axis as shown in Fig. 5.22.

$E_g$ – generated emf

$I_a$ – Armature current

The argument made for external characteristics holds good for internal characteristics also.

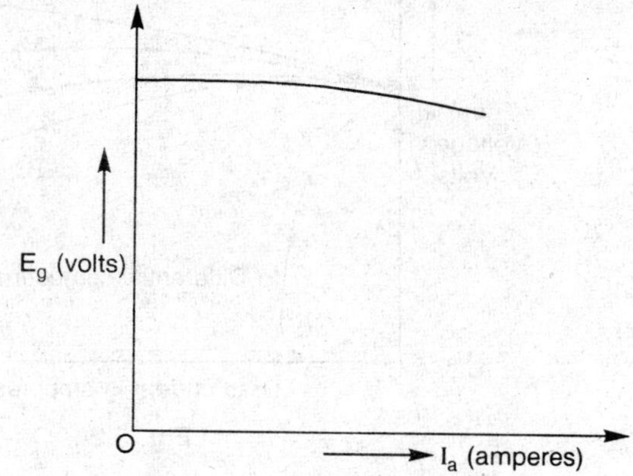


Fig. 5.22

**Series generator Characteristics:**

In Fig. 5.23, curve 1 represents O.C.C. of a series generator ($E_o I_f$). The curve 2 represents the internal characteristics i.e. $E_g/I_a$ and the curve 3 represents the external characteristics i.e. $V_L/I_L$.

It is seen from Fig. 5.23 that the series generator has a rising characteristic, i.e., the voltage increases with increase in load. However at high loads due to demagnetising effect of armature reaction, the voltage starts decreasing with increase in load.

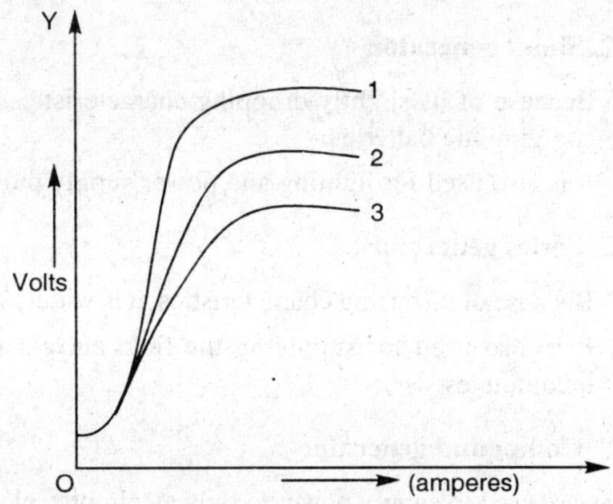


Fig. 5.23

**Compound generator characteristics (Fig. 5.24)**

Note1: An over compound generator is one whose terminal voltage increases with the load (or) full load voltage is greater than no load voltage.

2. A flat compound generator is one whose full load voltage is equal to no load voltage.
3. An under compound generator is one whose full load voltage is less than no load voltage.
4. When the series field mmf helps the shunt field mmf, it is called cumulative compound generator.

5. When the series field mmf opposes the shunt field mmf, it is calied different compound generator.

The external load voltage characteristics of compound generator are shown in Fig. 5.24.

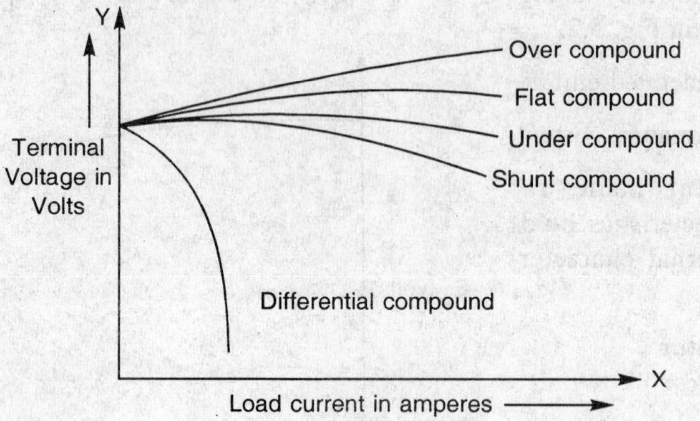


**Fig. 5.24**

## 5.7. APPLICATIONS OF A D.C. GENERATOR

### D.C. Shunt generator

(i) Because of its slightly drooping characteristics, the shunt generator is suited for charging the batteries.

(ii) It is also used for lighting and power supply purposes.

### D.C. Series generator

(i) Because of its raising characteristics, it is widely used as boosters (railway service).

(ii) It is also used for supplying the field current for regenerative braking of D.C. locomotives.

### D.C. Compound generator

They are used to supply power to railway circuits, elevator motors, incandescent lamps etc. Differentially compound generator is used as an arc welding generator.

## D.C. MOTOR:

## 5.8. PRINCIPLE OF A D.C. MOTOR

A motor is one which converts electrical energy into mechanical energy. Whenever a current carrying conductor is placed in a magnetic field, a force (F) acts on the conductor whose magnitude is given by the equation 5.21.

$$F = B.I.l.\sin\theta \text{ newtons} \qquad ...(5.21)$$

where 'B' is the flux density in $Wb/m^2$.

'I' is the current in amperes.

'l' is the length of conductor in metres.

'θ' is the angle between the conductor and the field.

The direction of the force is given by Fleming's left hand rule.

Note: 1. We know that, whenever a conductor carries a current it establishes its own magnetic flux whose direction is given by using either Right hand Rule (hold the wire or conductor in the right hand with the thumb pointing in the direction of the current, the fingers then curl round in the direction of the lines of force) or Maxwell's cork-screw rule (when a right handed corkscrew is held such that its axis is parallel to the conductor and pointing in the direction in which the current is flowing, then the direction of magnetic lines of force will be same as that in which corkscrew must be rotated to cause it to advance in the direction of the current).

2. A 'dot', '•' indicates that the current in the conductor is flowing in the direction towards the observer and a 'cross', '⊕' indicates that the current in the conductor is flowing in the direction away from the observer. With the above points in mind, we can easily understand the 'Motoring action'.

Consider a current carrying conductor placed in the magnetic field established by two poles as shown in Fig. 5.25.

In Fig. 5.25 (i) the direction of the current flowing through the conductor is in the direction away from the observer, hence the flux set up by it will be in the clockwise direction. In Fig. 5.25 (ii) the direction of flux lines set up by the pair of poles will be from 'N' to 'S'. The resultant of these two fluxes is given in Fig. 5.25 (iii) which is strengthened on the right side and weakened on the left side. Since the flux lines, aligned in the same direction, repel each other, the conductor will experience a force in the direction shown in Fig. 5.25 (iv) (which is just similar to the force exerted by the bent elastic rubber band of catapult on the stone piece). If number of such conductors are placed, the force exerted on them will cause rotation. This is called 'Motoring-Action.'

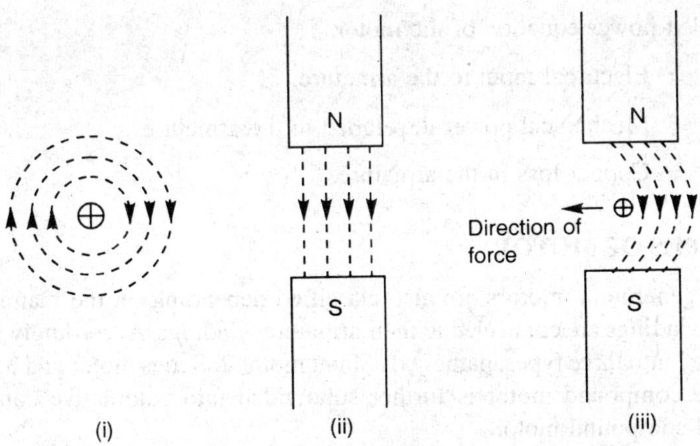


Fig. 5.25

## 5.9. PARTS OF A D.C. MOTOR

A D.C. machine whether generator or motor have the same parts namely, yoke, pole core and pole shoe, field coil, armature winding, commutator etc. Constructionally there is no difference between motor and a generator. We can use the same machine as a motor as well as a generator. The function of a commutator in a motor is to develop a continuous and unidirectional torque.

## 5.10. BACK EMF($E_b$)

When the motor rotates i.e., the conductors housed in the armature rotates, the magnetic flux is being cut by these conductors. Hence, according to Faraday's Laws of electromagnetic induction, an emf is induced in the conductors, whose direction will be given by Fleming's Right hand Rule. When we apply this rule, the direction of the emf induced in the armature conductor is found to be acting opposite to the applied voltage and hence it is called back emf '$E_b$' whose value is given by

$$E_b = \frac{\Phi ZNP}{60A} \text{ volts} \qquad \text{...(5.22)}$$

This back emf is always less than the applied voltage. When it becomes equal to applied voltage 'V' the motor action will stop because no current will flow through the armature.

$$\therefore \text{ The current flowing through the armature } (I_a) = \frac{V - E_b}{R_a} \qquad \text{...(5.23)}$$

$$\Rightarrow E_b = V - I_a R_a \qquad \text{...(5.24)}$$

$$\Rightarrow V = E_b + I_a R_a \qquad \text{...(5.25)}$$

where '$R_a$' is the armature resistance in ohms

Multiply equation 5.25 by '$I_a$' we get

$$VI_a = E_b I_a + I_a^2 R_a \qquad \text{...(5.26)}$$

This is called power equation of the motor.

where $VI_a$ = Electrical input to the armature.

$E_b I_a$ = Mechanical power developed in the armature

$I_a^2 R_a$ = Copper loss in the armature.

## 5.11. TYPES OF MOTOR

Similar to generators, motors are also classified depending on the manner in which their field windings are connected to their armature windings. Accordingly D.C. motors are classified into three types, namely, 1. Shunt motor 2. Series motor and 3. Compound motor. The compound motor is further subdivided into cumulative compound and differential compound motor.

**Shunt Motor:** (Fig. 5.26)

$P_L$ = Input power

$V_L$ = Applied voltage

$I_L$ = Input current

$I_a$ = Armature current

$R_a$ = Armature resistance

$R_{sh}$ = Shunt field resistance

$I_{sh}$ = Shunt field current

$E_b$ = Back emf

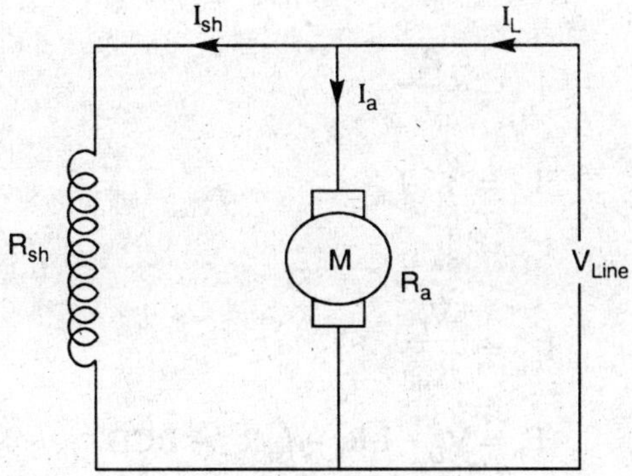


**Fig. 5.26**

Thus we have, $$I_L = \frac{P_L}{V_L} \quad \text{...(5.27)}$$

$$I_{sh} = \frac{V_L}{R_{sh}} \quad \text{...(5.28)}$$

$$I_a = I_L - I_{sh} \quad \text{...(5.29)}$$

$$E_b = V_L - I_a R_a - \text{BCD} \quad \text{...(5.30)}$$

where, BCD = Brush contact drop

**Series Motor** (Fig. 5.27)

$$I_L = I_{se} = I_a \quad \text{...(5.31)}$$

where, $I_{se}$ = Series field current

Let $R_{se}$ = Series field resistance

$$I_L = \frac{P_L}{V_L} \quad \text{...(5.32)}$$

$$E_b = V_L - I_a R_a - I_{se} R_{se} - \text{BCD} \quad \text{...(5.33)}$$

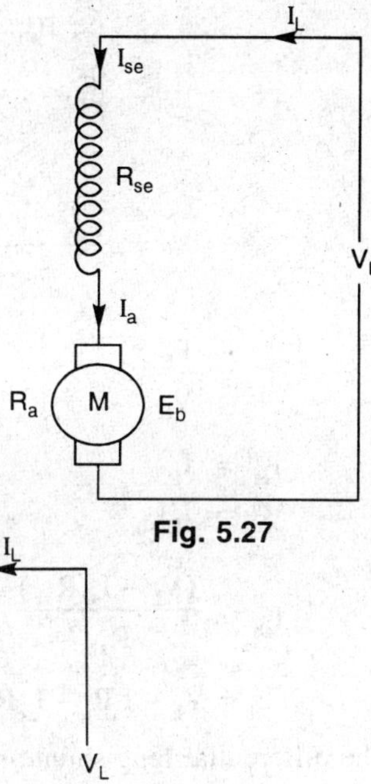


**Fig. 5.27**

**Long shunt motor (cumulative)** (Fig. 5.28)

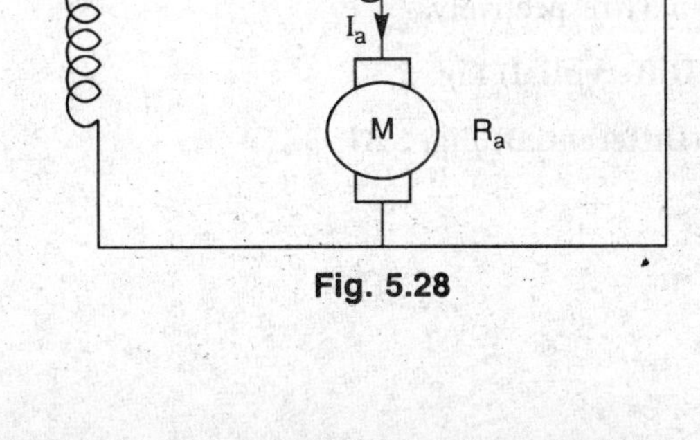


**Fig. 5.28**

$$I_L = \frac{P_L}{V_L} \quad \text{...(5.34)}$$

$$I_a = I_L - I_{sh} \quad \text{...(5.35)}$$

$$I_{se} = I_a \quad \text{...(5.36)}$$

$$I_{sh} = \frac{V_L}{R_{sh}} \quad \text{...(5.37)}$$

$$E_b = V_L - I_a R_a - I_{se} R_{se} - BCD \quad \text{...(5.38)}$$

**Short shunt motor (cumulative)** (Fig. 5.29)

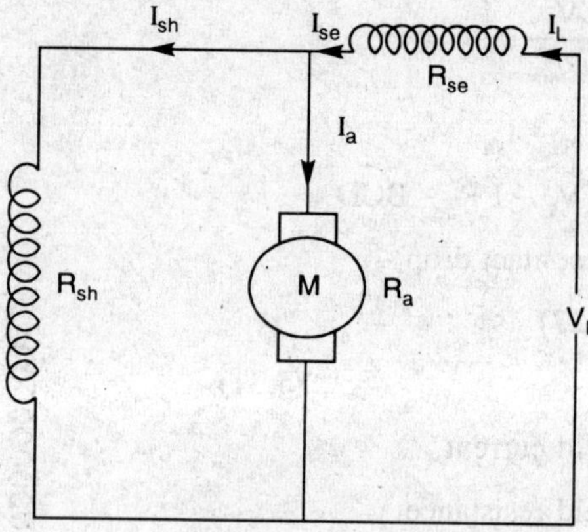


**Fig. 5.29**

$$I_L = \frac{P_L}{V_L} \quad \text{...(5.39)}$$

$$I_{se} = I_L \quad \text{...(5.40)}$$

$$I_a = I_L I_{sh} \quad \text{...(5.41)}$$

$$I_{sh} = \frac{(V_L - I_{se} R_{se})}{R_{sh}} \quad \text{...(5.42)}$$

$$E_b = V_L - I_a R_a - I_{se} R_{se} - BCD \quad \text{...(5.43)}$$

The differential long shunt and differential short shunt compound motors are shown in Fig. 5.30 and Fig. 5.31 respectively.

**Long shunt motor (Differential)** Fig. 5.30

**Short shunt motor (Differential)** Fig. 5.31.

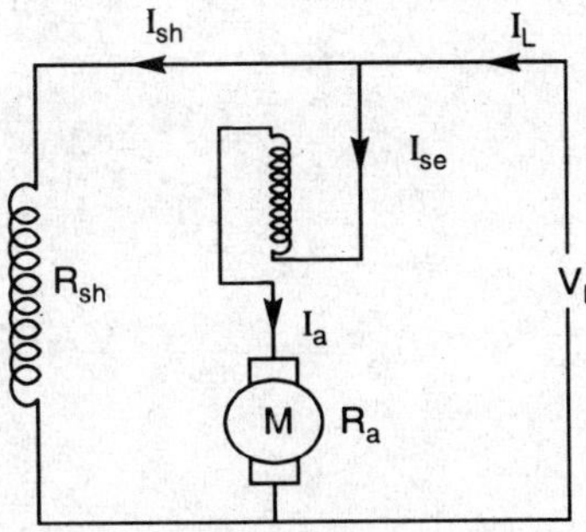


Fig. 5.30

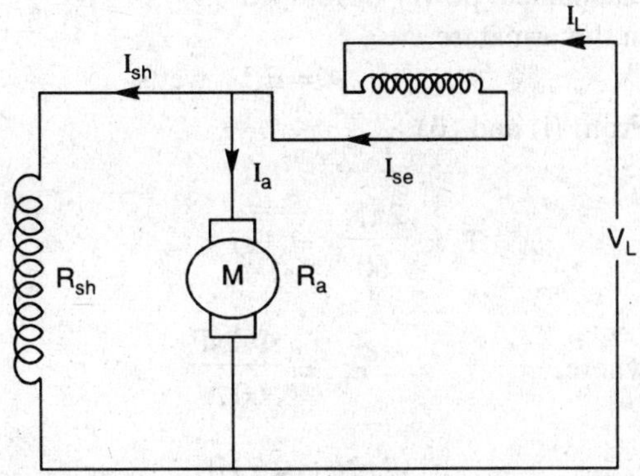


Fig. 5.31

## 5.12. ARMATURE TORQUE OF A MOTOR ($T_a$)

Let '$T_a$' be the torque developed by the motor armature in Nw-m.

'N' be speed of rotation of armature in R.P.M.

$\frac{N}{60}$ be speed in RPS

$E_b$ the back emf in volts

$I_a$ be the armature current in amperes.

'$\Phi$' be the flux/pole in weber

P be the number of poles

Z be the number of armature conductors

A be the number of parallel paths

We know that the torque is the twisting moment of a force about an axis and is given by the product of the force and the radius at which the force acts.

$\therefore$ Torque = Force × distance $= F \times R \text{ N} - \text{m}$

Also, Workdone/second $= \text{Force} \times (2\pi R) \times \frac{N}{60}$

$$= (F \times R) \times 2\pi \frac{N}{60}$$

$\therefore$ Workdone/second or power developed $= T_a \times 2\pi \frac{N}{60}$ joules or watts ...(i)

Also the electrical equivalent of mechanical power developed in the armature

$$= E_b I_a \text{ watts} \quad \text{...(ii)}$$

From (i) and (ii)

$$T_a \times \frac{2\pi N}{60} = E_b I_a$$

where,

$$E_b = \frac{\Phi ZNP}{60\,A}$$

$$\therefore \quad T_a \times \frac{2\pi N}{60} = \frac{\Phi ZNP}{60\,A} \times I_a$$

$$T_a \times 2\pi = \frac{\Phi ZP}{A} \times I_a$$

$$T_a = \frac{1}{2\pi} \frac{\Phi ZPI_a}{A}$$

$$\therefore \quad T_a = 0.159\ \Phi\ ZPI_a/A \quad \text{...(5.44)}$$

We can rewrite equation 5.44 as

$$T_a = \left(\frac{0.159\ ZP}{A}\right)\Phi I_a$$

$$\Rightarrow T_a \propto \Phi I_a \quad \text{...(5.45)}$$

**Note:** 1. For a shunt motor, 'Φ' is practically constant

$$\therefore \quad T_a \propto I_a$$

2. For a series motor, before saturation, as the field winding carries armature current, $\Phi \propto I_a$

$$\therefore \quad T_a \propto I_a \cdot I_a \Rightarrow T_a \propto I_a^2$$

## 5.13. SPEED OF A D.C. MOTOR

From equation 5.25 we have

$$V = E_b + I_a R_a$$

$$\Rightarrow \quad E_b = V - I_a R_a \quad \text{...(i)}$$

Also from equation 5.22 we have

$$E_b = \frac{\Phi ZNP}{60\,A} \quad \text{...(ii)}$$

From (i) & (ii)

$$\frac{\Phi ZNP}{60\ A} = V - I_a R_a$$

$$\therefore \quad N = \frac{(V - I_a R_a)60A}{\Phi ZP}$$

But $V - I_a R_a = E_b$

$$\therefore \quad N = \frac{E_b 60\ A}{\Phi ZP}$$

$$\Rightarrow \quad N = \frac{60\ A}{ZP}\frac{E_b}{\Phi}$$

$$\Rightarrow \quad N = K\frac{E_b}{\Phi} \qquad \text{i.e., } N \propto \frac{E_b}{\Phi} \qquad ...(5.46)$$

Equation 5.46 shows that the speed is directly proportional to the back emf and inversely proportional to the flux.

**For shunt motor**

Let $N_1$, $I_{a1}$, $\Phi_1$ be the speed (RPM), armature current (amperes), flux (weber) in the first case and

Let $N_2$, $T_{a2}$, $\Phi_2$ be that of the second case

From equation 5.46 we can write

$$N_1 \propto \frac{E_{b1}}{\Phi_1} \qquad \text{where } E_{b1} = V - I_{a1} R_a$$

$$N_2 \propto \frac{E_{b2}}{\Phi_2} \qquad \text{where } E_{b2} = V - I_{a2} R_a$$

$$\therefore \quad \frac{N_2}{N_1} = \frac{E_{b2}}{E_{b1}} \times \frac{\Phi_1}{\Phi_2}$$

But for the shunt motor flux is constant ie $\Phi_1 = \Phi_2 = \Phi$

$$\therefore \quad \frac{N_2}{N_1} = \frac{E_{b2}}{E_{b1}} \qquad ...(5.46)$$

**For series motor**

From equation 5.46 we can write

$$N_1 \propto \frac{E_{b1}}{\Phi_1}$$

$$N_2 \propto \frac{E_{b2}}{\Phi_2}$$

$$\therefore \quad \frac{N_2}{N_1} = \frac{E_{b2}}{E_{b1}} \times \frac{\Phi_1}{\Phi_2}$$

For a series motor before saturation, $\Phi \propto I_a$

$$\therefore \quad N_1 \propto \frac{E_{b1}}{I_{a1}}$$

and $$N_2 \propto \frac{E_{b2}}{I_{a2}}$$

$$\therefore \quad \frac{N_2}{N_1} = \frac{E_{b2}}{E_{b1}} \times \frac{I_{a1}}{I_{a2}} \qquad \text{...(5.47)}$$

**P. 5.7.** A 250 V D.C. shunt motor takes 40 amperes at full load. The resistance of the armature and shunt field windings are 0.5 Ω and 250 Ω respectively. Determine the back emf on full load.

**Solution:** (Refer Fig. 5.26)

Given

$$R_a = 0.5\ \Omega$$

$$R_{sh} = 250\ \Omega$$

($V_L$) Line voltage = 250V

($I_L$) Line current = 40 amperes

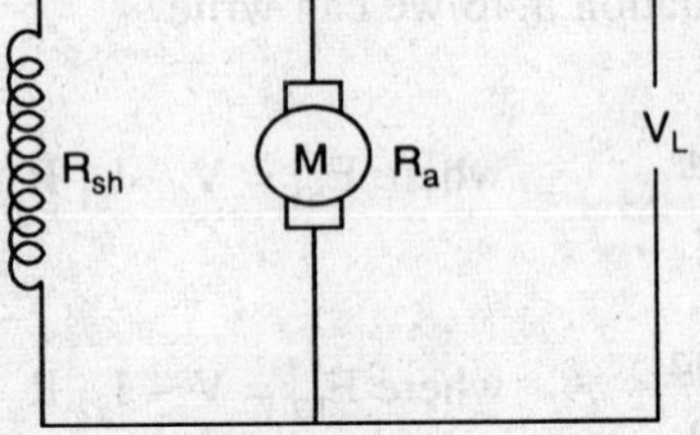


Fig. 5.31A

$$I_{sh} = \frac{250}{250} = 1 \text{ ampere}$$

$$I_a = I_L - I_{sh} = 40 - 1 = 39 \text{ amperes}$$

$$\therefore E_b = V_L - I_a R_a$$

$$= 250 - 39 \times 0.5$$

$$E_b = 230.5 \text{ volts}$$

**P. 5.8.** A 20 kW, 200V D.C. shunt generator has armature and field resistance of 0.05Ω and 150Ω respectively. Determine the total armature power developed when working as a generator delivering 20 kW output and when working as a motor taking 20 kW.

**Solution:**

When the machine acts as a D.C. shunt generator. (Refer the Fig. 5.13)

Given for D.C. shunt generator

$$P_L = 20 \times 10^3 \text{ watts}$$

$$V_L = 200V$$

$$R_a = 0.05\Omega$$

$$R_{sh} = 150\Omega$$

$$I_{sh} = \frac{V_L}{R_{sh}} = \frac{200}{150} = 1.33 \text{ amperes}$$

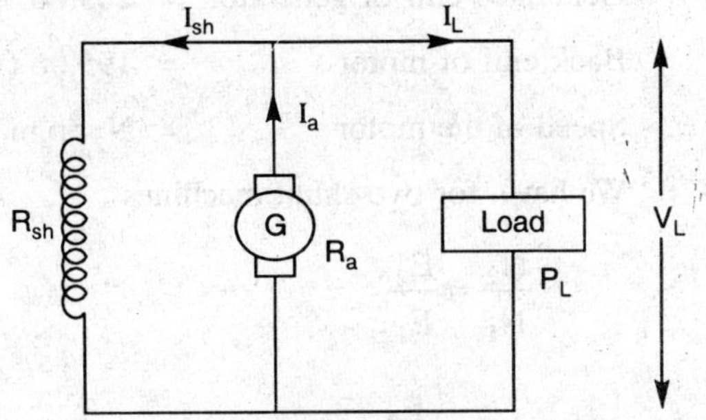


Fig. 5.31B

$$I_L = \frac{P_L}{V_L} = \frac{20\times10^3}{200} = 100 \text{ amperes}$$

$$I_a = I_L + I_{sh} = 101.33 \text{ amperes}$$

$$E_g = V_L + I_a R_a$$

$$= 200 + (101.33\times0.05) = 205.06\text{volts}$$

$\therefore$ Armature power developed $= E_g \times I_a$

$= 205.06 \times 101.33$

$= 20779.388$ watts

When same machine is running as a D.C. shunt motor (Refer Fig. 5.26)

$P_L$ (Input power) $= 20\times10^3$

$V_L$(Input voltage) $=$ 200V

$$I_L \text{ (Input current)} = \frac{20\times10^3}{200}$$

$= 100$ amperes

$$I_{sh} = \frac{V_L}{R_{sh}} = \frac{200}{150}$$

$= 1.33$ amperes

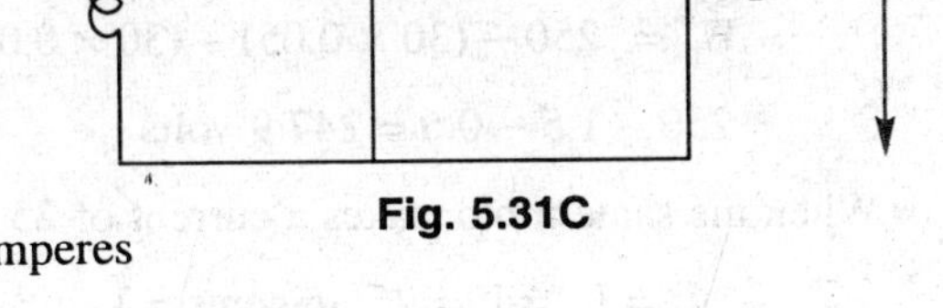


Fig. 5.31C

$$I_a = I_L \times I_{sh} = 98.67 \text{ amperes}$$

$$E_b = V_L - I_a R_a = 200-(98.67 \times 0.05)$$

$= 195.06$ volts

$\therefore$ Armature power developed = 19247.2 watts

**P. 5.9.** In the above problem 5.8, if the D.C. shunt generator runs at a speed of 1000 r.p.m. Calculate the speed of the machine when running as a motor all the data remaining same.

**Solution:**

Given speed of generator = 1000 r.p.m. ($N_1$)

Generated emf of generator = 205.06 volts ($E_1$)

Back emf of motor = 195.06 (volts) $E_2$

Speed of the motor = $N_2$ r.p.m.

We have, for two shunt machines

$$\frac{N_2}{N_1} = \frac{E_2}{E_1}$$

$$N_2 = \frac{E_2}{E_1} N_1$$

$$= \frac{195.06}{205.00} \times 1000$$

$$N_2 = 951.23 \text{ r.p.m.}$$

**P. 5.10.** A 250 D.C. series motor has an armature resistance of 0.05Ω and series field resistance of 0.02Ω. It is running at a speed of 900 r.p.m. taking a current of 30 amperes. Determine its speed when it takes a current of 25 amperes.

**Solution:**

Given $V_L$ = 250V

$R_a$ = 0.05 Ω

$R_{se}$ = 0.02 Ω

$I_L = I_{se}$ = 30 amperes = $I_1$

$N_1$ = 400 r.p.m.

$E_1 = V_L - I_a R_a - I_{se} R_{se}$

$E_1$ = 250 – (30 × 0.05) – (30 × 0.02)

250 – 1.5 – 0.6 = 247.9 volts

When the same motor takes a current of 25 amperes

$I_L = I_{se} = I_a$ = 25 amperes = $I_2$

∴ $E_2$ = 250 – (25 × 0.05) –25 × 0.02)

250 – 1.25 – 0.5 = 248.25V

We have $\frac{N_2}{N_1} = \frac{E_2}{E_1} \times \frac{I_1}{I_2}$

$$\therefore \quad N_2 = N_1 \times \frac{E_2}{E_1} \times \frac{I_1}{I_2}$$

$$= 400 \times \frac{248.25}{247.9} \times \frac{30}{25}$$

$$N_2 = 480.67 \text{ r.p.m.}$$

**P. 5.11.** A 4 pole wave wound 200V shunt motor has 700 armature conductors. The resistance of the armature is 0.02Ω and that of shunt field is 50Ω. Find the torque developed when it takes a current of 60 amperes. The flux/pole is 30 milliwebers.

**Solution:**

Given

$$V_L = 200\text{V}$$

$$I_L = 60 \text{ amperes}$$

$$R_{sh} = 50\ \Omega$$

$$\therefore \quad I_{sh} = \frac{V_L}{R_{sh}} = \frac{200}{50} = 4 \text{ amperes}$$

$$I_a = I_l - I_{sh} = 60 - 4 = 56 \text{ amperes.}$$

$$\Phi = 30 \times 10^{-3}$$

$$Z = 700$$

$$P = 4$$

$$A = 2$$

$$\therefore \quad T = 0.159 \times \Phi \times Z \times I_a \times P/A \text{ N–m}$$

$$= \frac{0.159 \times 30 \times 10^{-3} \times 700 \times 56 \times 4}{2}$$

$$= 373.96 \text{ N–m.}$$

## 5.14. CHARACTERISTICS OF MOTOR

There are three characteristics

1. Armature torque versus armature current $T_a/I_a$. This is also called electrical characteristics.
2. Speed versus armature current ($N/I_a$).
3. Speed versus armature torque ($N/T_a$). This is also called mechanical characteristics.

The following relations are to be recalled while discussing the above characteristics.

(i) $T_a \propto \Phi I_a$

(ii) $N \propto \frac{E_b}{\Phi}$

(iii) '$\Phi$' is constant for shunt motor

(iv) $\Phi$ is proportional to '$I_a$' for a series motor, before saturation.

**Characteristics of series motor:**

**1. $T_a I_a$ characteristic** (Fig. 5.32)

We know that $T_a \propto \Phi I_a$

But, before saturation $\Phi \propto I_a$

$\therefore \quad T_a \propto I_a.I_a$

$\therefore \quad T_a \propto I_a^2$

$\Rightarrow \quad T_a = KI_a^2$

In Fig. 5.32, '$T_a$' is taken on Y-axis and '$I_a$' on X-axis. Therefore, prior to saturation, equation (i) resembles $y = mx^2$ which is the equation of a parabola, as shown in Fig. 5.32. Thus, a series motor is used where very high starting torque is required for accelerating heavy masses quickly as in case of cranes, hoists, electric trains.

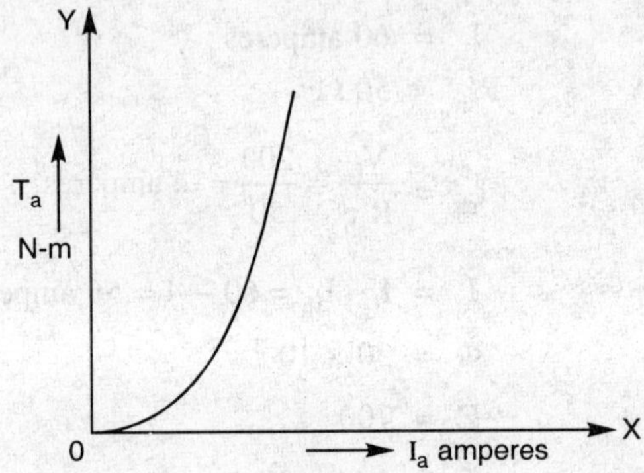


**Fig. 5.32**

However after saturation, '$\Phi$' is independent of '$I_a$'

$\therefore \quad T_a \propto I_a$ only

i.e., $T_a = K^1 I_a$.

Since '$T_a$' is on Y-axis and '$I_a$' on X-axis equation (ii) resembles $y = mx$, which is the equation of a straight line passing through origin, this curve becomes a straight line, after saturation.

**$N/I_a$ characteristic**

we know that $N \propto \frac{E_b}{\Phi}$

where $E_b = V - I_a R_a - I_{se} R_{se}$ (for a series motor).

Since, $R_a$, $R_{se}$ are very small, $I_a R_a$, $I_{se} R_{se}$ drops does not change much with variation of load. Hence '$E_b$' is approximately constant. Therefore $N \propto 1/\Phi$ also in a series motor since $\Phi \propto I_a$ ; we can write $N \propto 1 / I_a$.

Thus as load increases, $I_a$ increases and hence speed decreases as shown in Fig. 5.33.

Note: However when the load is completely removed, the armature current falls to a very small value and the speed becomes dangerously high. Therefore, the series motors should never be started on no load. From the characteristics (Fig. 5.33), it is clear that a series motor is a variable speed motor which adjusts its speed according to load.

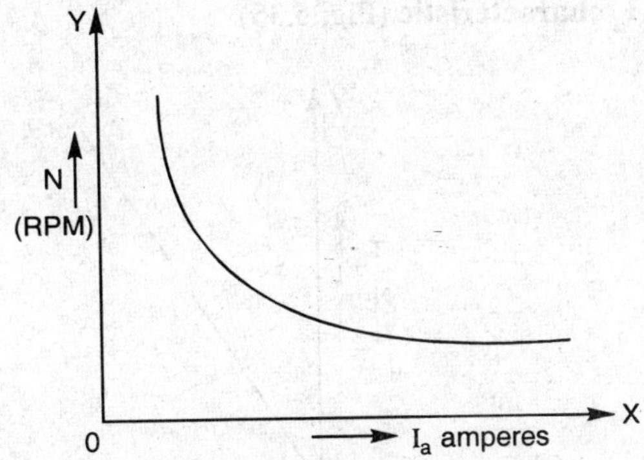


Fig. 5.33

**$N/T_a$ characteristic**

We have the mechanical power developed in the armature $= \dfrac{T_a \times 2\pi N}{60}$

i.e. the output of the motor $= \dfrac{T_a \times 2\pi N}{60}$

$$\frac{\text{output of the motor} \times 60}{2\pi N} = T_a$$

For a given load, the term '$\left(\dfrac{\text{output of the motor} \times 60}{2\Pi}\right)$' is a constant.

$$\therefore \quad T_a \propto \frac{1}{N} \Rightarrow N \propto \frac{1}{T_a}$$

$\therefore$ For a constant load, if the speed is increased, torque decreases and vice versa. Hence the '$N/T_a$' characteristic is shown in Fig. 5.34.

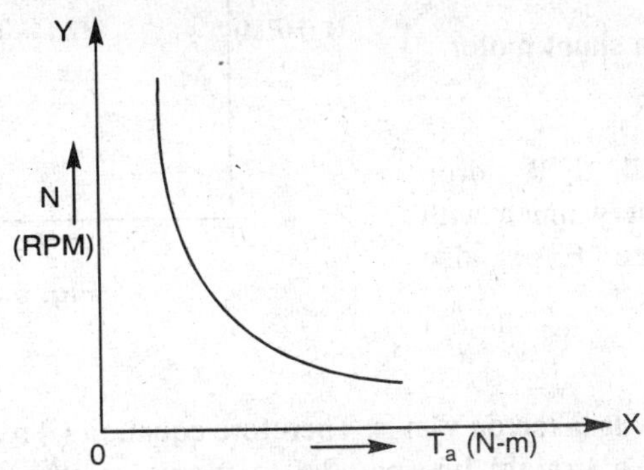


Fig. 5.34

**Characteristics of shunt motor:**

**$T_a I_a$ characteristic** (Fig. 5.35)

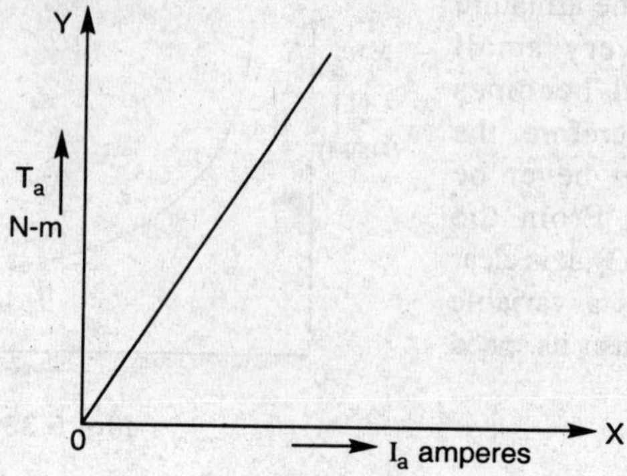


**Fig. 5.35**

We know that $T_a \propto \Phi I_a$

But, for a shunt motor '$\Phi$' is constant

$\therefore \quad T_a \propto I_a$

$T_a = KI_a$ ...(i)

In Fig. 5.35, '$T_a$' is taken on y-axis and '$I_a$' on x-axis. Therefore equation (1) resembles '$y = mx$' which is the equation of a straight line passing through origin. Shunt motors are never started on heavy load, because, a heavy load needs a heavy starting current which may affect the voltage regulation of the supply and also the electrical installation.

**$N/I_a$ characteristic** (Fig. 5.36)

We know that, $N \propto \frac{E_b}{\Phi}$, but for a shunt motor, '$\Phi$' is constant

$\therefore \quad N \propto E_b$

Also we have for a shunt motor

$E_b = V - I_a R_a$

Since '$R_a$' is small, '$I_a R_a$' drop does not change very much with the load and hence '$E_b$' is also constant.

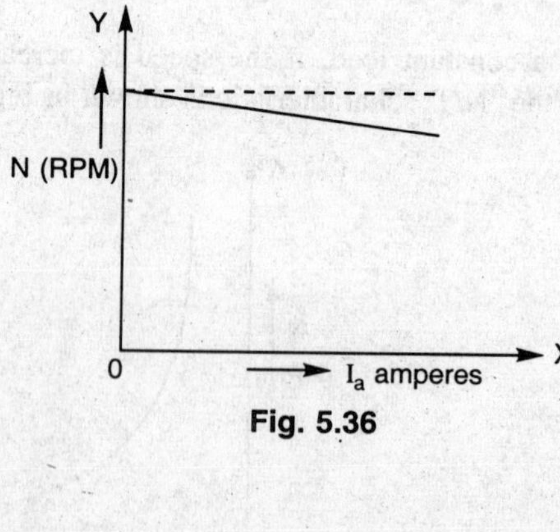


**Fig. 5.36**

$\therefore \quad N = K$ ...(i)

In the Fig. 5.36, 'N' is taken on y-axis. Therefore equation (i) resembles $y = K$, which is the equation of a straight line parallel to x-axis as shown by the dotted line. (Fig. 5.36)

Hence shunt motors are used for constant speed applications (lathes, water pumps etc.). However, strictly speaking, both 'Φ' and '$E_b$' decrease with the load. In fact, decrease in '$E_b$' is slightly more than that of decrease in the value of 'Φ'. Hence the speed of the motor decreases slightly with increase in load Fig. 5.36.

**N/$T_a$ characteristic** (Fig. 5.37)

This characteristic can be easily obtained from the above two characteristics $T_a/I_a$ and N/$I_a$. When the load is increased, motor speed falls slightly. When 'N' decreases slightly '$E_b$' also does the same. 'V' dominates over '$E_b$' and hence more current flows through the armature ($I_a$). But $T_a \propto I_a$. Hence 'N' decreases (slightly) when $T_a$ increases and vice versa.

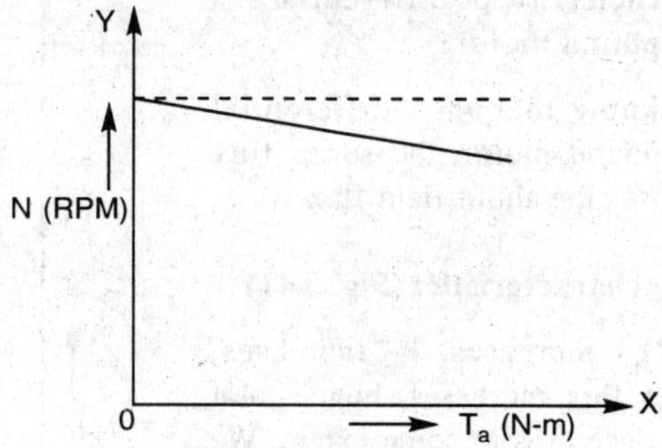


**Fig. 5.37**

**Characteristics of cumulative compound motor:**

**$T_a/I_a$ characteristic**

We know that in a cumulative compound motor, the series flux helps the shunt field flux. As '$I_a$' increases, $I_{se}$ increases, series flux increases. Hence the total flux increases. We have '$T_a$'$\propto I_a$. Therefore '$T_a$' also increases hence the characteristic is drawn as shown in Fig. 5.38.

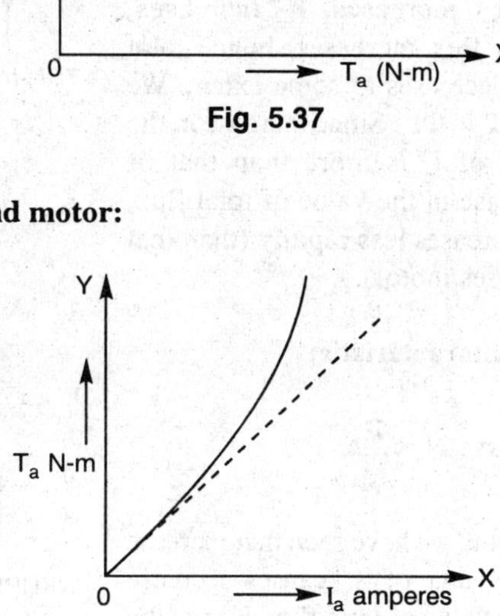


**Fig. 5.38**

**N/$I_a$ characteristic**

We have $N \propto \dfrac{E_b}{\Phi}$

As $I_a$ increases $I_{se}$ increases series flux increases and hence total flux increases (because cumulative compound). Thus, speed decreases with increase in '$I_a$' as shown in Fig. 5.39. However the decrease in speed is less rapid than that of series motor and more rapid than that of shunt motor.

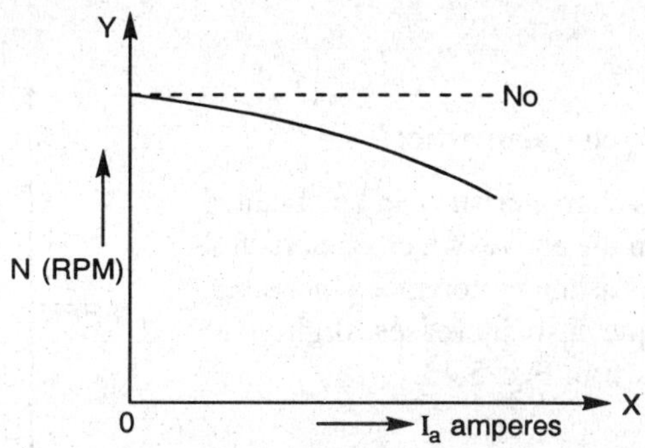


**Fig. 5.39**

**$N/T_a$ characteristic:**

From the above two characteristics we can obtain the $N/T_a$ characteristic as shown in Fig. 5.40.

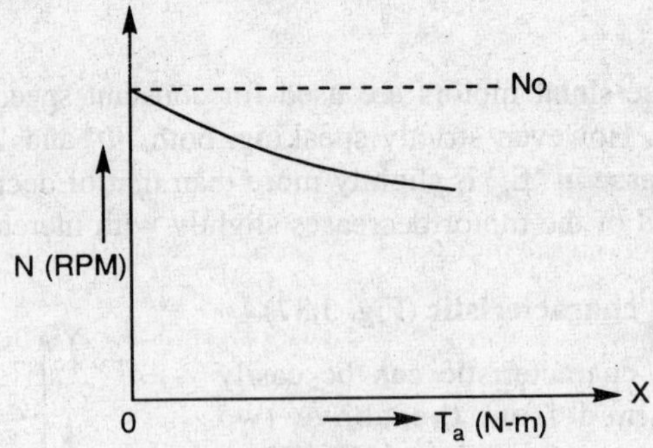


Fig. 5.40

**Characteristic of differential compound motor:**

We know that in a differential compound motor, the series flux opposes the shunt field flux.

**$T_a/I_a$ characteristic:** (Fig. 5.41)

As '$I_a$' increases, $I_{se}$ increases, series flux increases, hence total flux decreases to some extent. We have $T_a \propto \Phi I_a$. Since increase in the value of $I_a$ is more than that of decrease in the value of total flux, $T_a$ increases less rapidly (than that of series motor).

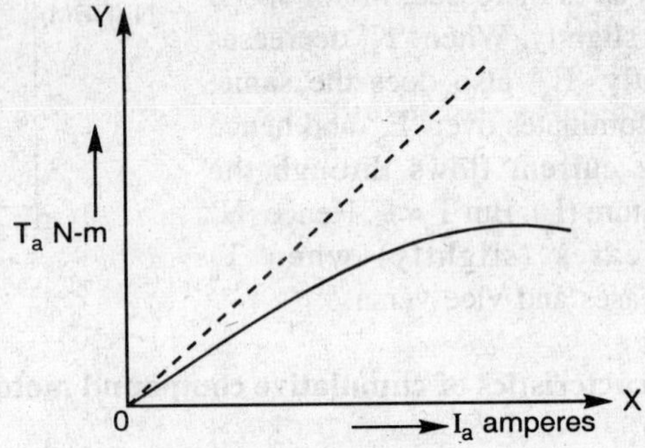


Fig. 5.41

**$N/I_a$ characteristic:**

We have $N \propto \frac{E_b}{\Phi}$.

Just now we have seen that increase in the value of '$I_a$' causes decrease in the value of total flux. Hence the speed increases slightly as shown in Fig. 5.42.

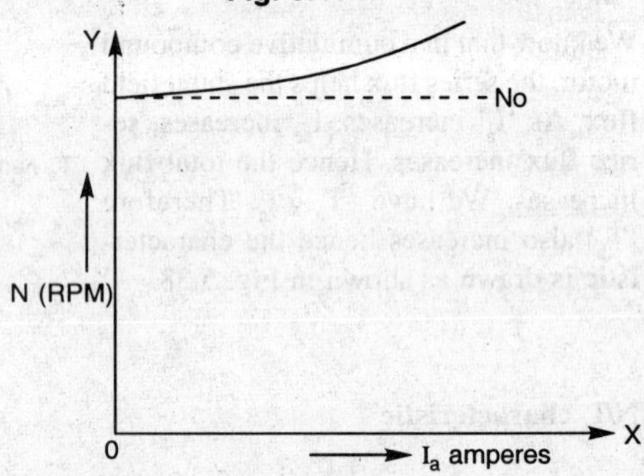


Fig. 5.42

**$N/T_a$ characteristic:**

This characteristic can be obtained from the above two characteristics. Thus as the motor speed increases, torque also increases slightly as shown in Fig. 5.43.

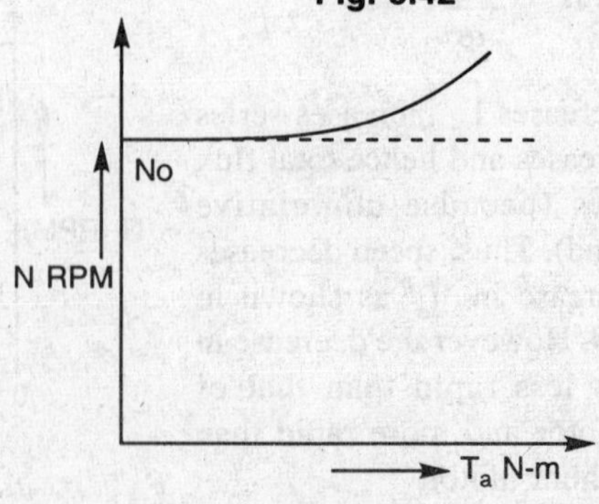


Fig. 5.43

## 5.15. APPLICATION OF D.C. MOTOR

### Shunt motor applications

Since shunt motor has approximately constant speed it can be used for lathes line-shaft drives, centrifugal pumps, reciprocating pumps, machine tools, blowers, fans, grinders, shapers, wood working machines, small printing presses etc.

### Series Motor Applications

Since series motor has high starting torque, it can be used for electric traction, tram cars and railway cars, cranes, hoists, elevators, winches, conveyors, etc.

### Cumulative compound motor applications

Since this motor has high starting torque it can be used for shears, punches, heavy planers, rolling mills, elevators, conveyors, stamping presses, large printing presses, mine hoists, haulage gears, power fans etc.

## TRANSFORMER

## 5.16. PRINCIPLE OF TRANSFORMER

Transformer is a static machine which transforms electric power from one circuit to another circuit. It does so without change in frequency. It can increase or decrease the voltage in a circuit with a corresponding decrease or increase in current. If it delivers energy at higher voltage, it is called a step up transformer and if it delivers energy at lower voltage, it is called step down transformer (Fig. 5.44). It works on mutual induction principle. It consists of two coils which are magnetically coupled through a core. The coil to which alternating voltage is supplied is called primary winding (Fig. 5.45) and the coil to which load is connected is called secondary winding.

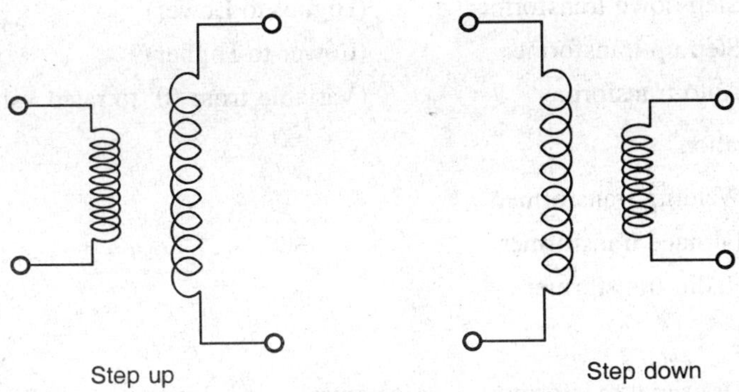


**Fig. 5.44**

Whenever the primary winding is given an alternating supply, the alternating flux established in it also links with secondary winding. According to Faraday's law of electromagnetic induction, an emf is induced in the secondary winding which is called mutually induced emf.

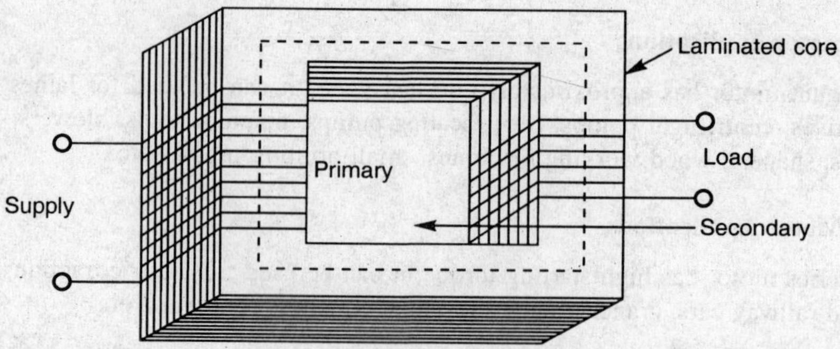


Fig. 5.45

## 5.17. CLASSIFICATION OF TRANSFORMERS

Transformers are classified on the basis of

(i) Duty they perform

1. Power transformer – for transmission purposes and distribution
2. Current transformer – Instrument transformer
3. Potential transformer – Instrument transformer

(ii) Construction

1. Core type transformer
2. Shell type transformer
3. Berry type transformer

(iii) Voltage output

1. Step down transformer (Higher to Lower)
2. Step up transformer (Lower to Higher)
3. Auto transformer (Variable from '0' to rated value)

(iv) Application

1. Welding transformer
2. Furnace transformer
3. Radio transformer

(v) Cooling

1. Dry type transformer (Air natural or Air last)
2. Oil immersed
   (a) Self cooled
   (b) Forced air cooled
   (c) Water cooled
   (d) Forced oil cooled

(vi) Three phase transformers

1. Star-Star
2. Star-Delta
3. Delta-Delta
4. Delta-Star
5. Open-Delta
6. Scott connection

## 5.18. CONSTRUCTIONAL DETAILS

**Parts of Transformer:**

1. **Primary winding:** The winding which is connected to supply is called primary winding.
2. **Secondary winding:** The winding which is connected to load is called secondary winding.
3. **Transformer core:** The two windings of the transformer are magnetically coupled through the core. The core is made up of silicon steel to reduce the hysteresis loss. It is also made up of laminated stampings which are insulated from each other by core varnish or oxide layer to reduce eddy current loss. The thickness of the lamination varies from 0.35 mm to 0.5 mm. The two types of transformer cores are (a) Core type (b) Shell type.

(a) **Core type transformer**: Here the winding surrounds a considerable part of core as shown in Fig. 5.46 and has only one magnetic path. It has two limbs for the windings and is made up of two L-type stamping (Fig. 5.47). The coils used are of cylindrical type and are usually form wound. For transformers of higher rating stepped core with circular cylindrical coils are used. For transformers of smaller rating, rectangular coils with core of square or rectangular cross section is used. Insulating cylinders are used to separate windings from the core and from each other.

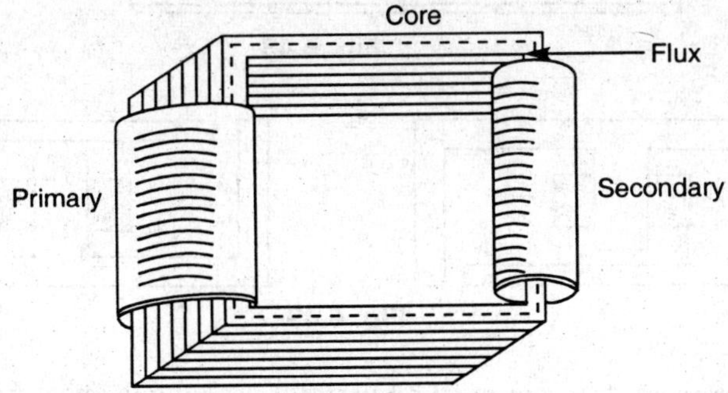


Fig. 5.46

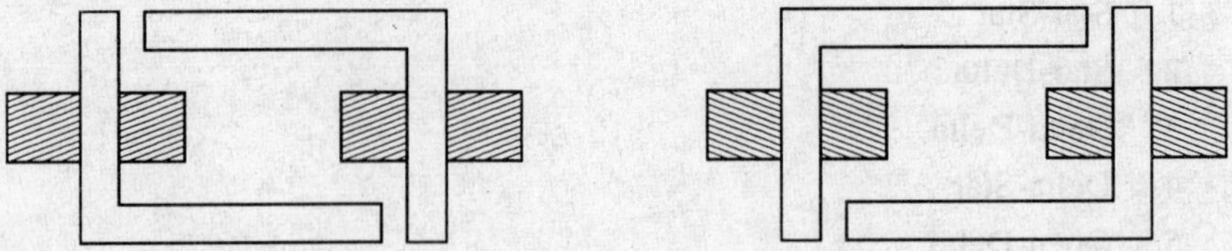

Fig. 5.47

(b) **Shell Type Transformer**: Here the core surrounds a considerable part of windings as shown in Fig. 5.48. The two windings are carried by central limb. The core is made up of E and I stampings (Fig. 5.49) and has three limbs. It has two parallel paths for magnetic flux.

The coils used are of multilayer disc type and are former wound in the form of pan-cakes. Each layer is insulated from each other by paper.

4. **Transformer Tank**: It is a metallic container used for accommodating assembled core and windings. For better cooling, the surface area of the tank is increased by providing corrugated sheets.

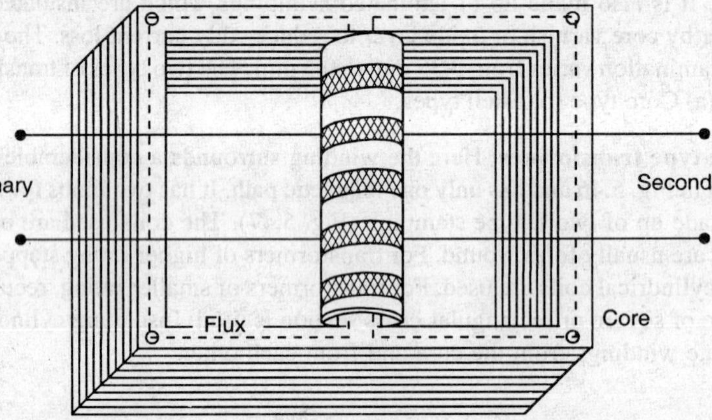


Fig. 5.48

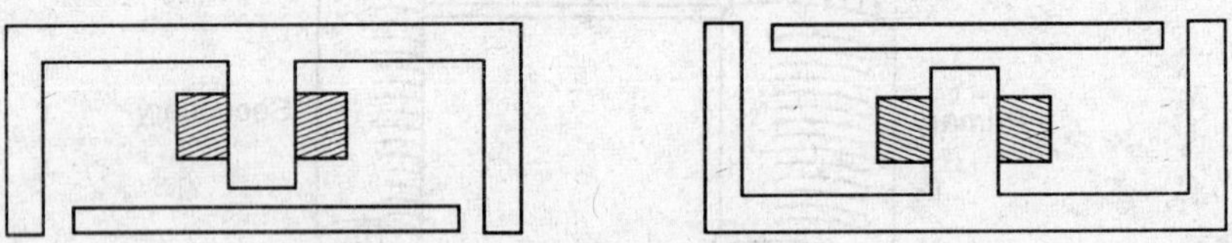

Fig. 5.49

5. **Transformer oil**: It is a mineral oil used for carrying the heat from the core and coils. It also provides additional insulation. It is obtained by refining crude petroleum. High dielectric strength, high flash point, low viscosity are some of the essential properties of the transformer oil.

6. **Conservator**: It is a drum mounted on the top of transformer tank and contains transformer oil. The conservator is connected to the transformer tank by means of a pipe. The main purpose of the conservator is to provide space for contraction and expansion of the oil without exposing it to come in contact with outside atmosphere.

7. **Breather**: A breather is a cylindrical tube containing silica gel impregnated with cobalt. The purpose of breather is to extract moisture from the air coming inside the transformer during breathing.

## 5.19. E.M.F. EQUATION OF TRANSFORMER

Consider a transformer arrangement as shown in Fig. 5.50.

Let $N_1$ – Primary number of turns

$N_2$ – Secondary number of turns

$\Phi_m$ – Maximum value of flux in the core in Wb.

$B_m$ – Maximum value of flux density in the core in Wb/$m^2$

A – Area of the core in $m^2$

f – Frequency of the a.c. supply in hertz

$V_1$ – Supply voltage across secondary in volts

$V_2$ – Terminal voltage across secondary in volts

$I_1$ – Full load primary current in amperes

$I_2$ – Full load secondary current in amperes

$E_1$ – emf induced in the primary in volts

$E_2$ – emf induced in the secondary in volts

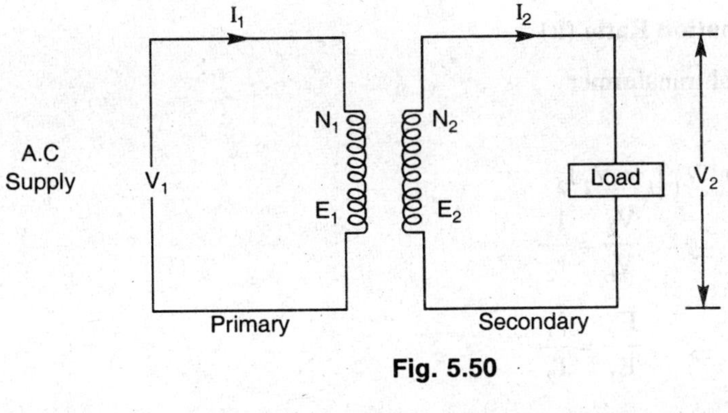


**Fig. 5.50**

Since applied voltage is alternating in nature, the flux established is also alternating as shown in Fig. 5.51. From Fig. 5.51 it is clear that the flux is attaining its maximum value in one quarter of the cycle i.e., in T/4 where 'T' is the time period in seconds.

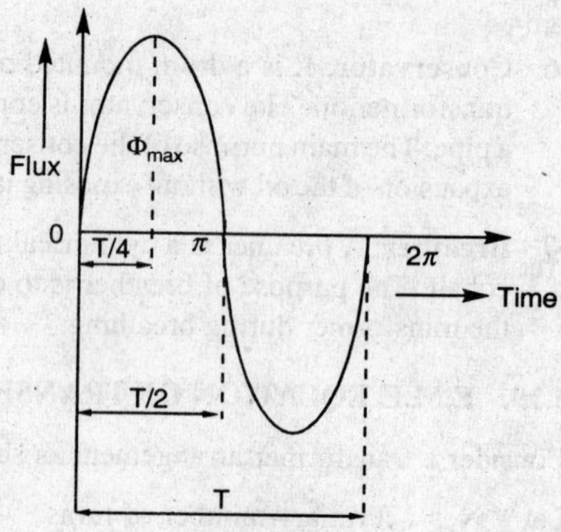

Fig. 5.51

We know that $T = \dfrac{1}{f}$

where 'f' is the frequency in hertz.

$\therefore$ Average rate of change of flux $= \dfrac{\Phi_m}{1/4f}$

$= 4f \times \Phi_m$ Wb/s.

If we assume single turn coil then according to Faraday's laws of electromagnetic induction

The average value of emf induced/turn = $4f \times \Phi_m$ volts.

But, form factor $= \dfrac{\text{R.M.S value}}{\text{Average value}} = 1.11$ (since $\Phi_m$ is sinusoidal)

$\therefore$ R.M.S. Value = Form factor × Average value

$\therefore$ R.M.S. Value of emf induced/turn $= (1.11) \times (4f \times \Phi_m)$

$= 4.44f\,\Phi_m$ volts

$\therefore$ R.M.S. Value of emf induces in the entire primary winding $E_1 = 4.44f\,\Phi_m \times N_1$ ...(5.48)

$E_1 = 4.44f\,B_m A N_1$ volts ...(5.49)

Similarly R.M.S. value of emf induced in the secondary $E_2 = 4.44f\,\Phi_m \times N_2$ volts ...(5.50)

(or) $E_2 = 4.44f\,(B_m A)\,N_2$ ...(5.51)

**Transformation Ratio (k)**

For an ideal transformer

$V_1 = E_1$

$V_2 = E_2$ and $V_1 I_1 = V_2 I_2$

$$\Rightarrow \frac{V_2}{V_1} = \frac{I_1}{I_2}$$

$$\Rightarrow \frac{E_2}{E_1} = \frac{I_1}{I_2} \qquad ...(5.52)$$

From equations 5.48 and 5.50 we have,

$$\frac{E_2}{E_1} = \frac{N_2}{N_1} \qquad ...(5.53)$$

From equations 5.52 and 5.53 we have,

$$\frac{E_2}{E_1} = \frac{N_2}{N_1} = \frac{I_1}{I_2} = K \qquad ...(5.54)$$

where 'K' is called transformation ratio.

**Note:** If $N_2 > N_1$, ie $K > 1$, then the transformer is a step up transformer. If $N_2 < N_1$, ie $K < 1$ then the transformer is a step down transformer.

## 5.20. TRANSFORMER ON NO LOAD

If the primary winding is connected to an alternating voltage and secondary winding is left open, then the transformer is said to be on no load (Fig. 5.52). Let the supply voltage be '$V_1$' volts. This causes a flow of alternating current through the primary. Since secondary is open, this current is called no load primary current ($I_o$). This '$I_o$' establishes a flux '$\Phi$' weber in the core. '$I_o$' has two components: (i) Active or working or iron loss or wattful component ($I_W$) which is in phase with '$V_1$'. and supplies the iron loss and negligible amount of primary copper loss.

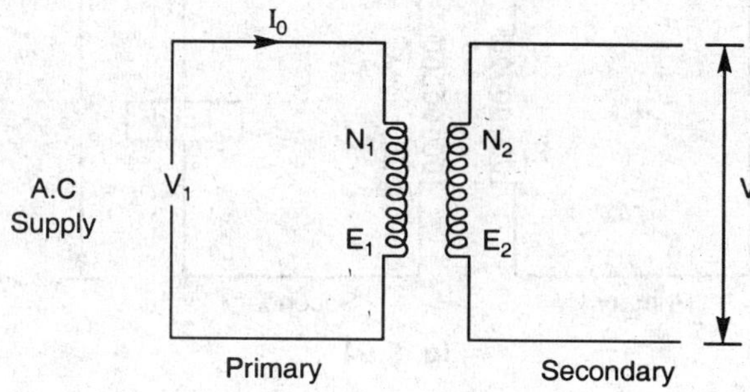


Fig. 5.52

$$I_W = I_o \cos \phi_o$$

where $\cos \phi_o$ = No load power factor

(ii) Reactive or magnetising or wattless component ($I_\mu$) which is in quadrature with $V_1$, and its function is to sustain the flux in the core.

$$I\mu = I_o \sin \phi_o \qquad ...(5.56)$$

From equations 5.55 and 5.56 we have

$$I_0 = \sqrt{I_w^2 + I_\mu^2} \qquad ...(5.57)$$

The no load vector diagram is shown in (Fig. 5.53)

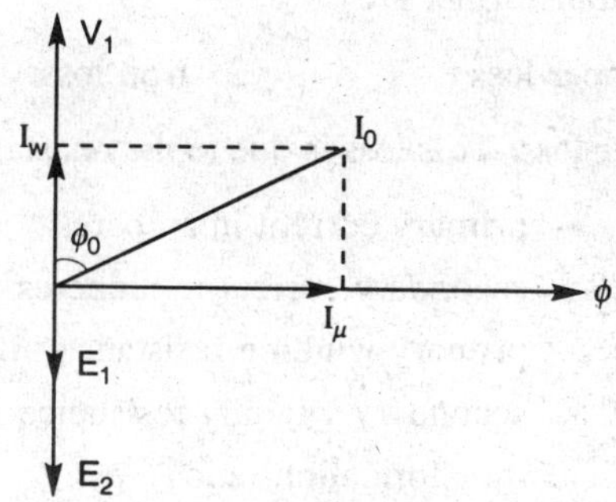


Fig. 5.53

## 5.21. TRANSFORMER ON LOAD

When the secondary winding is connected to a load, then the transformer is said to be on load (Fig. 5.54). The phase angle between '$V_2$' and '$I_2$' depends on the type of the load. When the load is resistive '$I_2$' will be in phase with '$V_2$'. When the load is inductive '$I_2$' will lag behind '$V_2$' and when the load is capacitive, '$I_2$' will lead '$V_2$'. When the secondary circuit is closed, a current '$I_2$' will flow through the secondary establishing a flux '$\Phi_2$' in it. This $\Phi_2$ opposes '$\Phi_o$' (flux established by $I_o$ and weakens it momentarily. Hence E, reduces and '$V_1$' dominates over $E_1$ and hence causes additional current '$I_2^1$' to flow through the primary. '$I_2^1$' establishes a flux '$\Phi_2$' which is equal in magnitude to $\Phi_2$ but opposite in direction. Hence '$\Phi_2^1$' and $\Phi_2$ cancel each other. Thus when the transformer is loaded.

(i) The flux through the core is same as that at no load.

(ii) The total primary current ($I_1$) will be vector sum of $I_o$ and $I_2^1$.

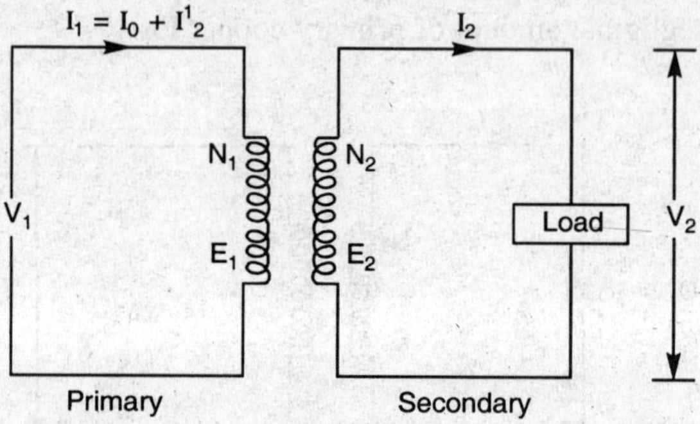


**Fig. 5.54**

## 5.22. TRANSFORMER LOSSES

Since a transformer is a **static device**, it has no rotational losses. The losses that occur in the transformer are

1. Copper loss 2. **Iron** loss

**Copper loss:** This loss is **due to the** resistance of the primary and secondary winding.

If $I_1$ – primary current in amperes.

$I_2$ – secondary current in amperes.

$R_1$ – primary winding resistance in ohms.

$R_2$ – secondary winding resistance in ohms.

K – transformation ratio

Then the total copper loss in the transformer

$$= I_1^2 R_1 + I_2^2 R_2 \quad ...(5.58)$$

$$= I_1^2 R_{01} \quad ...(5.59)$$

$$= I_2^1 R_{02} \quad ...(5.60)$$

where $$R_{01} = R_1 + \frac{R_2}{K^2} \quad ...(5.61)$$

$$R_{02} = R_2 + R_1 K^2 \quad ...(5.62)$$

Then from the equations (5.58 to 5.60) it is clear that copper loss is a variable loss and varies with square of the current or output. Thus copper loss at quarter load is 1/16th of that at full load.

Copper loss can be found by conducting short circuit test on the transformer. If this loss is high it will damage the insulation.

**Iron loss:** It consists of hysteresis loss and eddy current loss.

**Hysteresis loss:** Since the supply to the primary is alternating the core gets alternately magnetised and demagnetised causing loss of energy. This loss is given by equation (5.63).

$$W_h = \eta B^{1.6}_{max} \times f \times V \text{ watts} \quad ...(5.63)$$

where, $W_h$ = Hysteresis loss in watts

$B_{max}$ = Maximum value of flux density in Wb/m$^2$.

$f$ = Frequency of magnetic reversal in Hz.

$V$ = Volume of the core in m$^3$.

$\eta$ = Steinmetz constant.

This loss can be minimised by selecting a material for the core which has low hysteresis coefficient e.g. silicon steel.

**Eddy current loss:** This loss is due to eddy current induced in the transformer core and is seen in the form of heat in the core. This loss is given by equation (5.64)

$$W_e = KB^2_{max} f^2 t^2 \text{ watts} \quad ...(5.64)$$

where 't' is the thickness of lamination.

This loss can be minimised by using laminated core. Iron loss remains almost constant for all loads. This is also called core loss or magnetic loss and can be found by conducting O.C. test on the transformer.

## 5.23. EFFICIENCY

It is given by the ratio of output to input. Transformer has high efficiency since it has no friction and windage loss (static device).

$$\therefore \text{Efficiency} = \frac{\text{Output}}{\text{Input}} \quad ...(5.65)$$

But, input = output + total losses ...(5.66)

where total losses: (Iron loss) + $x^2$ (copper loss) ...(5.67)

where $x$ = fraction of the load

$$\therefore \text{ Efficiency} = \frac{\text{Output}}{\text{Input} + \text{Total loss}} \quad ...(5.65)$$

Also, output = Input – Total losses ...(5.68)

Also, output in watts = (Rated KVA) × 1000 × P.f. × (x) ...(5.69)

Where (i) x = 1 full load

(ii) x = 0.75 for 3/4th full load

(iii) x = 0.5 for 1/2 full load

(iv) x = 0.25 for 1/4 full load

$$\therefore \text{ Efficiency} = \frac{\text{Input} - \text{Total loss}}{\text{Input}} = 1 - \frac{\text{Total loss}}{\text{Input}}$$

$$\% \text{ Efficiency} = \frac{\text{Output}}{\text{Input}} \times 100 \quad ...(5.70)$$

## 5.24. APPLICATION OF TRANSFORMER

Transformers are used:

(i) in electrical power engineering for transmission and distribution

(ii) in communication engineering for impedance transformation etc.

(iii) as an instrument transformer for measuring current (Current Transformer, CT) and measuring voltage (Potential Transformer, PT)

(iv) as a step down and step up transformer to get reduced or increased output voltage.

(v) in radio and TV circuits, telephone circuits, control and instrumentation circuits.

(vi) in furnaces and welding.

**P. 5.12.** A 50 KVA 6000/250 volts transformer has 52 turns on the secondary. Determine the primary number of turns. Also calculate primary and secondary currents.

**Solution:**

Given

Rated KVA = 50

Primary voltage $E_1$ = 6000V

Secondary voltage $E_2$ = 250 V

Secondary number of turns $N_2$ = 52

We know that $\frac{E_2}{E_1} = \frac{N_2}{N_1}$

$$\Rightarrow N_1 = N_2 \times \frac{E_1}{E_2} = \frac{52 \times 6000}{250} = 1248 \text{ turns}$$

$$\text{secondary current } (I_2) = \frac{\text{Rated KVA} \times 1000}{E_2}$$

$$= \frac{50 \times 1000}{250} = 200 \text{ amperes}$$

$$\text{Primary current } (I_1) = \frac{\text{Rated KVA} \times 1000}{E_2}$$

$$= \frac{50 \times 1000}{6000} = 8.33 \text{ amperes}$$

**P. 5.13.** A single phase 50 Hz transformer has 350 turns on the primary and 800 turns on the secondary. The primary voltage is 400V and the cross section area of the core in 75 cm$^2$. Determine the emf induced in the secondary and the maximum value of flux density.

**Solution:**

Given

$f = 50$ Hz

$N_1 = 350$

$N_2 = 800$

$E_1 = 400$

$$\frac{E_2}{E_1} = \frac{N_2}{N_1} \Rightarrow E_2 = \frac{N_2}{N_1} E_1 = \frac{800}{350} \times 400 = 914.2 \text{ volts}$$

Also, $E_1 = 4.44 \times f \times B_m A \times N_1$

Given, $A = 75 \times 10^{-4} \text{m}^2$.

$$\therefore \quad B_m = \frac{E_1}{4.44 \times f \times A \times N_1} \text{ Wb/m}^2$$

$$= \frac{400}{4.44 \times 50 \times 75 \times 10^{-4} \times 350} = 0.686 \text{ Wb/m}^2$$

**P. 5.14.** A 440/200V transformer takes a current of 0.2 amperes on open circuit at a p.f. of 0.18. Find the magnetising and iron loss component of current.

**Solution:**

Given

$E_1 = 440$V

$$E_2 = 200V$$

$$I_o = 0.2A$$

$$\cos\phi_o = 0.18 \Rightarrow \sin\phi_o = \sqrt{1-\cos^2\varphi_0}$$

$$= 0.9836$$

$$\therefore \quad I_w = I_o \cos\phi_o = 0.036 \text{ amperes}$$

$$I_\mu = I_o \sin\phi_o = 0.1967 \text{ amperes}$$

**P. 5.15.** Determine the % efficiency of single phase 20KVA, 2200/200V transformer at full load 0.8 pf and half full load 0.4pf. Take full load copper loss = 400 watts and iron loss = 350 watts.

**Solution:**

Given

Rated KVA = 20

Iron loss = 350 W

Full load copper loss = 400 W

To find % efficiency at F.L, 0.8 pf,

Fraction of the load (x) = 1

$$\therefore \text{Output} = \text{Rated KVA} \times 1000 \times \text{p.f.} \times (x)$$

$$= 20 \times 1000 \times 0.8 \times 1$$

$$= 16000 \text{ watts.}$$

$$\text{Total loss} = (\text{Iron loss}) + x^2 (\text{Copper loss})$$

$$= 350 + (1)^2 \times 400 = 750 \text{ watts.}$$

$$\text{Input} = \text{Output} + \text{Total loss}$$

$$= 16000 + 750 = 16750 \text{ watts}$$

$$\therefore \quad \%\,\eta = \frac{\text{Output}}{\text{Input}} \times 100 = \frac{16000}{16750} \times 100$$

$$= 95.52.$$

To find % efficiency at half load, 0.4 pf

Fraction of the load (x) = 0.5

$$\text{Output} = 20 \times 1000 \times 0.4 \times 0.5$$

$$= 4000 \text{ watts}$$

$$\text{Total loss} = 350 + (0.5)^2 \times 400$$

$$= 450 \text{ watts}$$

$$\text{Input} = 4000 + 450$$

$$= 4450 \text{ watts}$$

$$\% \eta = \frac{\text{Output}}{\text{Input}} \times 100$$

$$= 89.88.$$

The classification of A.C. machines are presented below:

A.C. MACHINES

- Generator (or) Alternator
  - Salient Pole
  - Smooth Cylindrical
- Motor
  - Synchronous
  - Asynchronous
    - Three Phase Induction Motor
      - Squirrel Cage
        - Single Cage
        - Double Cage
      - Slip Ring
    - Commutator Motor
      - Series
      - Repulsion
      - Induction
        - Single phase Induction Motor
          - Split Phase
          - Capacitor
          - Shaded Pole

## THREE PHASE INDUCTION MOTOR

Three phase induction motor is a work horse of the modern industry. It has a very wide range of applications. It has specific advantages like simple construction, low capital cost, ruggedness and absence of commutator problems, reasonably good power factor, sufficiently high efficiently, simple starting arrangement, minimum maintenance etc. However its starting torque is somewhat less and as the load increases the speed decreases.

## 5.25. PRINCIPLE OF OPERATION OF THREE PHASE INDUCTION MOTOR

A three phase induction motor consists of stator (stationary part) and rotor (rotating part). Whenever three phase supply is given to three phase winding of stator, a magnetic flux of constant magnitude but rotating with certain speed is obtained. This speed of stator magnetic flux is called synchronous speed ($N_s$) given by

$$N_s = \frac{120\,f}{P} \text{ RPM} \qquad \text{...(5.71)}$$

where $N_s$ = Synchronous speed or
Speed of the stator magnetic flux

p = Number of stator poles

f = Frequency of the supply in Hz.

This rotating flux when passes through the air gap is being cut by the stationary rotor conductors. According to Faraday's laws of electromagnetic induction, the relative speed between the stator (rotating) magnetic flux and rotor (stationary) conductors, induces an emf in the rotor conductors. The magnitude of induced emf depends on the relative speed between the stator flux and the rotor conductors. The direction of emf is given by Fleming's right hand rule. Since rotor conductors form a closed circuit, the induced emf causes a current to flow through the rotor conductors whose direction (given by Lenz's law) will be in such a way as to oppose the very cause of production of it. The cause of production is the relative speed between the stator flux and the rotor conductor i.e. ($N_s$ – N) where 'N' is the speed of the rotor. For a 50 Hz, 4 pole 3 phase induction motor

$$N_s = \frac{120\,f}{P} = \frac{120 \times 50}{4} = 1500 \text{ RPM}$$

Initially rotor is stationary i.e., N = 0

∴ Relative speed = $N_s$ – N = 1500 – 0 = 1500 RPM

If the relative speed is opposed by the induced rotor current, then ($N_s$ – N) value has to decrease. For a given motor and supply, 'P' and 'f' are fixed, hence '$N_s$' is fixed. Therefore to reduce ($N_s$ – N) 'N' has to increase. Thus rotor starts rotating in the same direction as that of stator flux.

## 5.26. CONSTRUCTIONAL DETAILS

The main parts of induction motor are (i) Stator and (ii) Rotor

**Stator:** The stator is built up of sheet steel laminations of 0.4 to 0.5 mm thickness. Each lamination is insulated from one another by means of varnish (or) oxide coating. In the outer periphery of hollow cylindrical stator, slots are made to accommodate the stator conductors. The stator is wound for 3 phase supply and its connections are brought out to terminal box to the frame. For cooling purpose, radial ventilating ducts are also provided. A typical stator stamping is shown in Fig. 5.55.

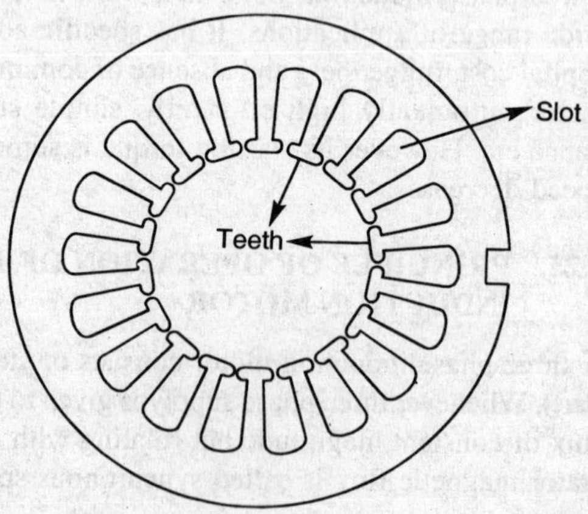


Fig. 5.55

**Rotor:** There are two types of rotors. 1. Squirrel cage rotor 2. Phase wound or wound or slip ring motor.

**Squirrel Cage Rotor:** (Fig. 5.56): It is cylindrical in shape and is built up of sheet steel laminations. The number of ventilating ducts provided is equal to that of stator. It has slots to accommodate rotor conductors. These rotor conductors or bars are short circuited at the ends of the rotor by brazing the copper rings resembling the cage of a squirrel and hence the name squirrel cage rotor. Since the rotor conductors are permanently short circuited, it is not possible to add any external resistance in series with the rotor. This type of rotor is cheap and has simple and rugged construction.

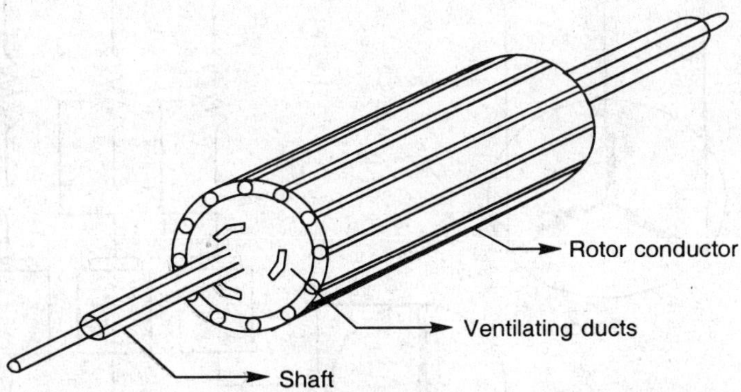


Fig. 5.56

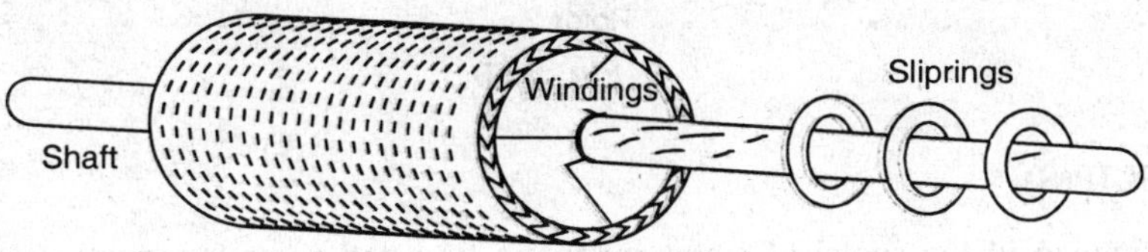


Fig. 5.57

**Slip Ring Rotor** (Fig. 5.57) : The rotor winding is wound for the same number of poles and phases as that of stator winding. For a three phase winding, the three phases start at one junction and the other three ends are connected to slip rings mounted on the shaft. To increase the starting torque and to reduce the starting current, starting resistances can be connected in star through carbon brushes (which are placed on the sliprings). As soon as the motor

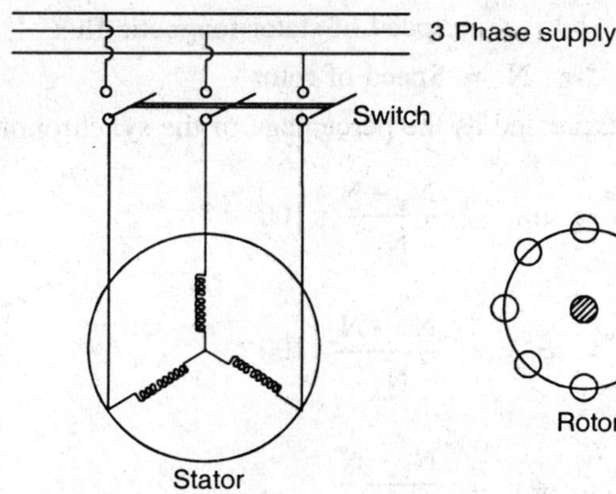


Fig. 5.58

achieves its rated speed, the starting resistances can be removed gradually from the rotor circuit and finally slip rings are short circuited. But the disadvantage is, slipring rotors are more costlier than squirrel cage rotors. Stator and rotor of a squirrel cage and slipring induction motor are shown in Fig. 5.58 and Fig. 5.59 respectively.

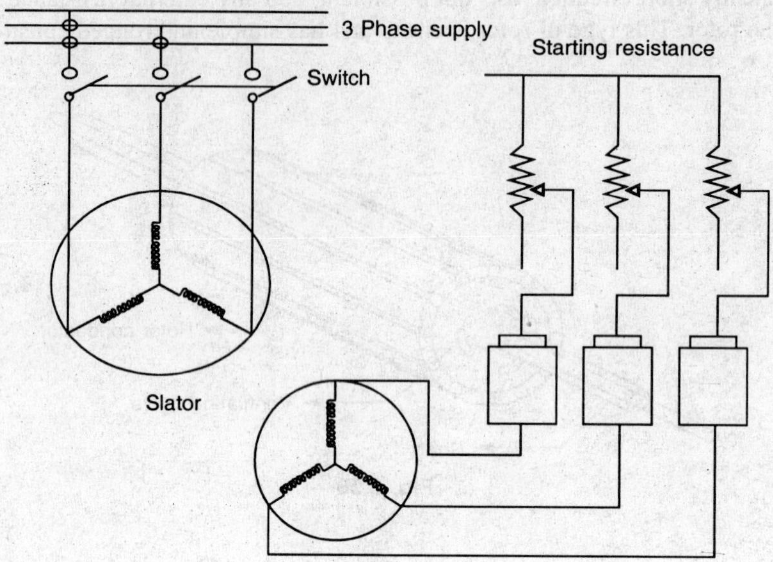


**Fig. 5.59**

## 5.27. SLIP(S)

The difference in the speed of stator magnetic flux and rotor (conductor) is called slip.

$\therefore$ Slip = $N_s - N$ ...(5.72)

where, $N_s$ = Synchronous speed or speed of stator magnetic flux

$N$ = Speed of rotor

It is expressed as the percentage of the synchronous speed

$$\therefore \quad \% \text{ Slip} = \frac{N_s - N}{N_s} \times 100$$

$$\% \text{ s} = \frac{N_s - N}{N_s} \times 100 \quad ...(5.73)$$

$$\text{or s} = \frac{N_s - N}{N_s} \quad ...(5.74)$$

$$\Rightarrow \quad s = 1 - \frac{N}{N_s}$$

$$\Rightarrow \quad N = N_s(1 - s) \qquad ...(5.75)$$

## 5.28. FREQUENCY OF ROTOR CURRENT ($f^1$)

When the rotor is stationary the frequency of the rotor current is the same as the supply frequency (f). But, when the rotor starts rotating, the frequency of rotor current depends upon the relative speed. Let the frequency of rotor current be '$f^1$

We have, relative speed = $N_s - N$

$$\text{where,} \quad N_s = \frac{120\,f}{P} \qquad ...(i)$$

According to definition of '$f^1$'

$$N_s - N = \frac{120\,f^1}{P} \qquad ...(ii)$$

$$\frac{(ii)}{(i)} \text{ gives } \frac{N_s - N}{N_s} = \frac{f^1}{f}$$

$$\therefore \quad s = \frac{f^1}{f}$$

$$\Rightarrow \quad f^1 = s.f. \qquad ...(5.76)$$

**P. 5.16.** A 3 phase 50 Hz 4 pole induction motor runs at 1460 RPM calculate the following at this speed.

(i) Synchronous speed

(ii) Slip

(iii) Frequency of rotor induced emf

**Solution:**

Given,

supply frequency (f) = 50Hz

Poles (p) = 4

$$\therefore \text{ Synchronous speed } (N_s) = \frac{120\,f}{P}$$

$$= \frac{120 \times 50}{4}$$

$$\therefore \quad N_s = 1500 \text{ RPM}$$

Also given, speed of the motor (N) = 1460 RPM

$$\therefore \quad \text{Slip} = s = \frac{N_s - N}{N_s} = \frac{1500 - 1460}{1500} = 0.026$$

$\therefore$ % Slip = 2.66

The frequency of the rotor induced emf ($f^1$) $= s \times f$

$= 0.026 \times 50$

$= 1.3\text{Hz}$

**P. 5.17.** A 6 pole, 50Hz 3 phase induction motor has frequency of rotor induced emf = 1.5Hz. Determine the value of slip and speed of the motor.

**Solution:**

Given

$P = 6$

$f = 50\text{Hz}$

$$\therefore \quad N_s = \frac{120\,f}{P}$$

$$= \frac{120 \times 50}{6}$$

$= 1000$ RPM

Given

$f^1 = 1.5\text{Hz}$

But $f^1 = sf$

$$\therefore \quad s = \frac{f^1}{f} = \frac{1.5}{50} = 0.03$$

$\therefore$ Slip = 0.03

The speed of the motor (N) $= N_s (1 - s)$

$= 1000\,(1 - 0.03)$

$= 970$ RPM.

**P. 5.18.** A 3 phase induction motor runs almost at 1000 RPM on no load and 960 RPM on full load when supplied with 50 Hz 3 phase. Calculate the following:

(i) Number of poles

(ii) Slip at full load

(iii) Frequency of rotor emf

(iv) Speed of the motor at 8% slip.

**Solution:**

Given

$$N_s = 1000$$
$$N = 960$$
$$f = 50\text{Hz}$$

$$\text{Synchronous speed } (N_s) = \frac{120\,f}{P}$$

$$\text{Number of poles(P)} = \frac{120\,f}{N_s} = \frac{120 \times 50}{1000} = 6$$

$$\text{Full Load slip (s)} = \frac{N_s - N}{N_s} = \frac{1000 - 960}{1000} = 0.04$$

Frequency of rotor emf ($f^1$) = s × f = 0.04 × 50 = 2Hz.

Speed of the motor at 8% slip is given by

$$N = N_s(1-s) \qquad \text{where } N_s = 1000$$
$$= 1000\,(1 - 0.08) \qquad s = 0.08$$
$$= 920 \text{ RPM}$$

## 5.29. EXPRESSION FOR TORQUE

The rotor of a 3 phase induction motor has two states

(i) Standstill condition (ii) Running condition.

Accordingly its parameters under standstill condition are given by

- $f$ – Rotor current frequency
- $R_2$ – Rotor resistance/phase
- $X_2$ – Rotor reactance/phase
- $Z_2$ – Rotor impedance/phase
- $E_2$ – Rotor emf/phase

The same parameters under running condition are given by

- $f^1$ – Rotor current frequency
- $X_r$ – Rotor reactance/phase
- $Z_r$ – Rotor impedance/phase
- $E_r$ – Rotor emf/phase
- $R_2$ – Rotor resistance/phase (remains same under both conditions)

We have proved in art 5.28 that

$f^1 = s.f$, where 's' is the slip

Similarly we can write

$$X_r = sX_2 \quad ...(5.77)$$

$$E_r = sE_2 \quad ...(5.78)$$

$$Z_r = \sqrt{R_2^2 + X_r^2} \quad ...(5.79)$$

We know that in a D.C. motor, the expression for torque is given by $T_a \propto \Phi I_a$.

In the case of induction motor the expression for torque is given by equation 5.80

$$T \propto \Phi I_r \cos \phi_r \quad ...(5.80)$$

where $I_r$ – Rotor current/phase under running condition

$\Phi$ – Stator flux/pole

But $I_r = \dfrac{E_r}{Z_r}$

$\cos \phi_r = \dfrac{R_2}{Z_r}$ (from impedance triangle 5.60)

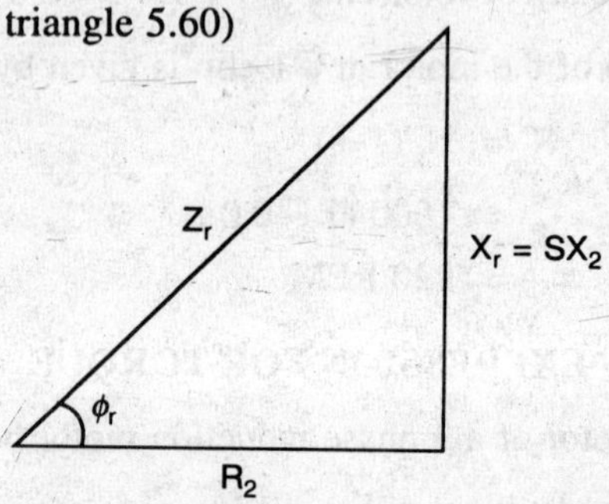

Fig. 5.60

$$\therefore \quad T = K.\Phi.\frac{E_r}{Z_r}.\frac{R_2}{Z_r}$$

$$= \frac{K.\Phi\, E_r \cdot R_2}{Z^2 r}$$

From that impedance triangle

$$Z_r^2 = (R_2)^2 + (sX_2)^2$$

Also we have $E_r = sE_2$ (from eq. 5.78)

$$\therefore \quad T = \frac{K\Phi.s.E_2.R_2}{R_2^2 + (sx_2)^2} \quad ...(5.81)$$

The equation (5.81) is the expression for torque.

## 5.30. TORQUE-SLIP CHARACTERISTICS

The torque slip characteristics of 3 phase induction motor is as shown in the Fig. 5.61. From the figure it is clear that the curve starts from origin. In other words when s = 0; T should be equal to zero. This can be easily verified as follows.

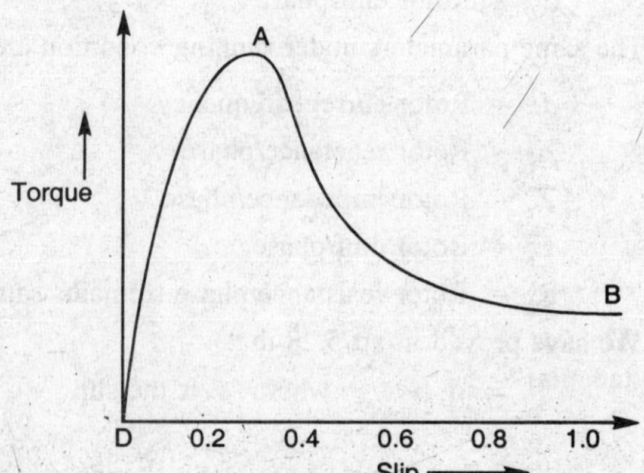

Fig. 5.61

From the equation 5.81, we have

$$T = \frac{K\,\Phi s\, E_2 R_2}{R_2^2 + (sx_2)^2}$$

Put s = 0, we get

$$T = \frac{0}{R_2^2 + 0} = 0$$

Thus, when s = 0; T = 0. Hence the curve starts from origin.

The portion 'AB' is a straight line passing through the origin. This can be verified as follows. At speeds close to synchronism, 's' will be small. Therefore $(sX_2)$ is very small compared to $R_2$ hence can be neglected.

Thus, the equation 5.81 can be written as follows

$$T = \frac{K\Phi s E_2 R_2}{R_2^2 + (sx_2)^2}$$

$$= \frac{K.\Phi.sE_2\,R_2}{R_2^2} \qquad sX_2 \lll R_2$$

$$T = \frac{K\Phi E_2 R_2}{R_2^2}.s$$

$$T \propto s$$

$$\Rightarrow \quad T = K^1 s \qquad \text{...(i)}$$

This is the equation of straight line passing through the origin and hence the portion AB. The shape of the portion BC can be explained as follows. When 'N' is not very close to $N_s$, 's' will be large when compared $R_2$. Hence '$R_2$' can be neglected when compared to '$sX_2$'. In other words, $sX_2 \ggg R_2$.

∴ The equation 5.81 can be rewritten as follows.

$$T = \frac{K\Phi s E_2 R_2}{(sx_2)^2}$$

$$= \frac{K\Phi E_2 R_2.s}{(x_2)^2.s^2}$$

$$T = \left(\frac{K\Phi E_2\,R_2}{(x_2)^2}\right)\frac{1}{s}$$

$$\Rightarrow T \propto \frac{1}{s}$$

Thus as slip increases, torque decreases. Thus the torque slip, characteristic is a rectangular hyperbola. The important points to be noted are given below

(i) At low values of slip, the torque slip characteristic is a straight line.

(ii) As slip increases with increase in the load, the torque also increases and becomes maximum when $s = \frac{R_2}{x_2}$

(iii) Beyond the point of $T_{max}$, when the load further increases, the torque starts decreasing.

## 5.31. APPLICATIONS OF 3 PHASE INDUCTION MOTOR

**Slipring induction motor:** These motors are used in places where high starting torque is required (also starting currents should be low) such as pumps, fans, conveyors, hoists, compressors, lifts, etc.

**Squirrel cage induction motor:**

When the requirement is

(i) Low starting torque, with normal starting current e.g., fans and centrifugal pumps.

(ii) High torque with low starting current e.g., conveyors, compressors, crushes, agitators, reciprocating pumps.

(iii) High torque with medium and high slip e.g., sheers, punches, die stamping etc.

(iv) Normal torque with normal starting current e.g., fans, blowers, centrifugal pumps, line shafting etc.

## ELECTRICAL MACHINES

## 5.32. SINGLE PHASE INDUCTION MOTORS

Single phase induction motors operate on single phase supply. They find wide variety of applications in industries, workshops, offices, space vehicles as well as for domestic purposes. Depending on the method of starting, single phase induction motors may be classified as

(i) Split-phase induction motor.

(ii) Capacitor-start, capacitor-start-and-run and two-valve capacitor motors.

(iii) Shaded pole motors.

The construction of a single phase induction motor is almost similar to a poly phase induction motor. However the stator of single phase induction motor has two windings namely (i) main winding and (ii) auxiliary or starting winding. The rotor is of squirrel cage type.

Single phase induction motor is not a self-starting motor. To make it self-starting, the 'starting winding' is spaced 90° electrically apart with the stator main winding. The starting torque can be made high by keeping large phase difference (ideally 90°) between the currents in the main winding and the starting winding.

## 5.33. SPLIT-PHASE INDUCTION MOTOR

The split-phase induction motor is shown in the Fig. 5.62. its stator has two windings, namely (i) Main winding with low resistance and high reactance and (ii) Auxiliary or starting winding with high resistance and low reactance. This is done to achieve time displacement of the currents flowing through the two windings. Since the starting torque is proportional to 'sin α [where α is the angle between main winding current ($I_m$) and starting winding current ($I_s$)], the phase angle between $I_s$ and $I_m$ is made as large as possible (Fig. 5.63). The centrifugal switch 's' connected in series with the starting winding from the supply, when once the motor reaches 80 percent of its rated speed.

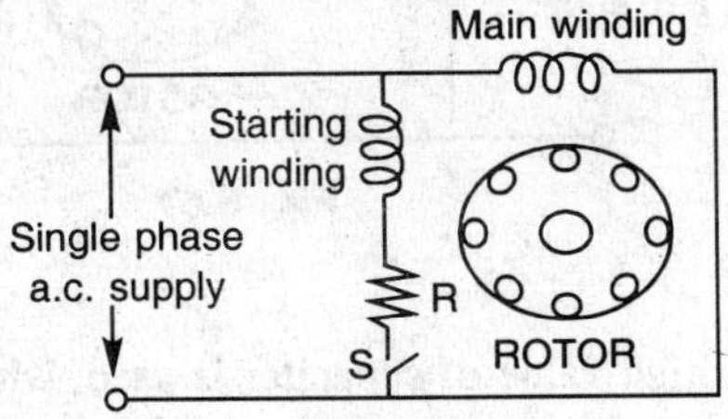

Fig. 5.62

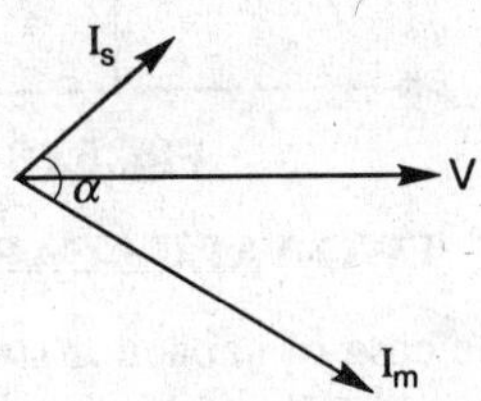

Fig. 5.63

### Applications

Split-phase motors are used in washing machines, domestic refrigerators, duplicating machines, fans, blowers and centrifugal pumps.

## 5.34. CAPACITOR-START MOTOR

The torque developed by a split-phase motor is less (α is around 30°C, sin α is small and hence the torque). This could be overcome by replacing the resistor with a capacitor in the starting winding as shown in the Fig. 5.64. The capacitor used is of electrolytic type and is generally mounted on the surface of the motor. The phase angle α between current in the starting winding ($I_s$) and the main winding ($I_m$) is around 80° as shown in the Fig. 5.65 and hence the starting torque developed by the capacitors start motor is nearly double that of the torque developed by a split-phase motor. The purpose of the centrifugal switch is same as that in the previous case.

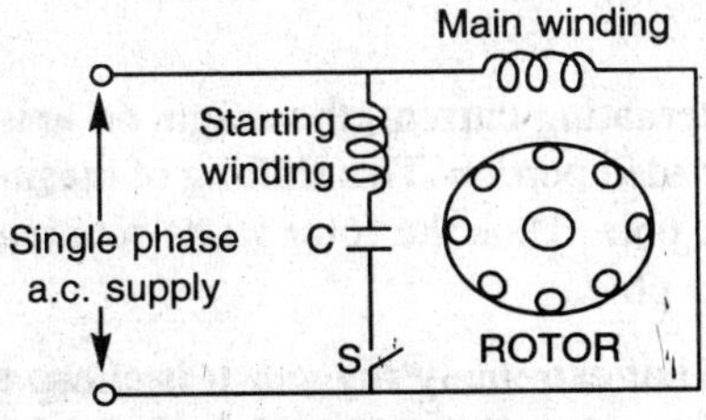

Fig. 5.64

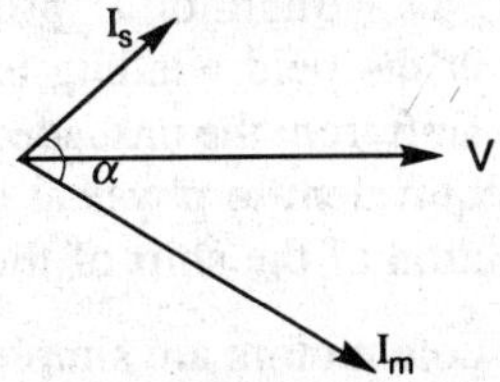

Fig. 5.65

## 5.35. CAPACITOR-START-AND-RUN MOTOR

The arrangement of capacitor-start-and-run motor is as shown in the Fig. 5.66. Here the capacitor (c) and the starting winding is connected throughout the operation of the motor. This leads to (i) Higher power-factor (ii) higher efficiency (iii) noise-free operation of the motor and (iv) increased over-load capacity of the motor.

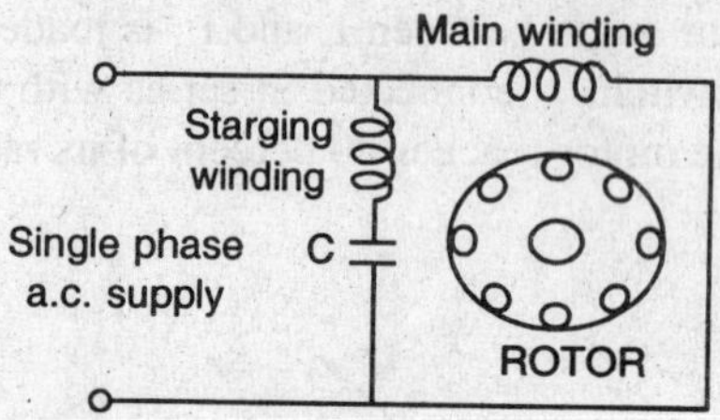


Fig. 5.66

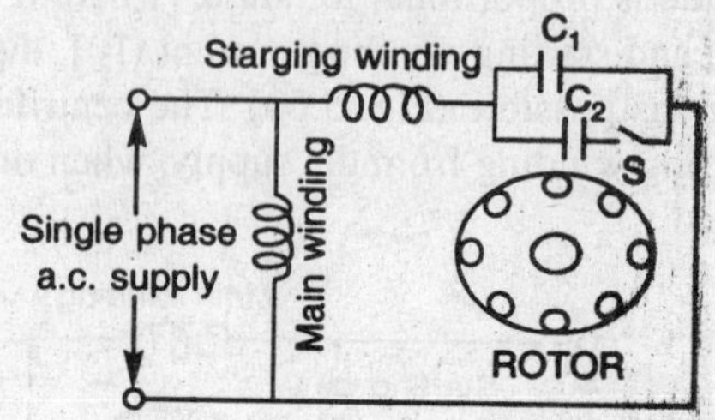


Fig. 5.67

## 5.36. TWO-VALUE CAPACITY MOTOR

In the case of capacitor-start-and-run motor, high value of capacitor is used, when it is desired to have high starting torque as well as high power factor, which increases the cost of the capacitor. This could be avoided by using a two-value capacitor motor, where a high capacitor is used in series with the starting winding during starting. A low value capacitor is substituted by means of centrifugal switch (S) during running as shown in the Fig. 5.67. The two-value capacitor motor has (i) very quiet operation (ii) higher efficiency and power factor (iii) ability to start at heavy loads. These motors are preferred in compressors and fire strokes.

## 5.37. SHADED—POLE MOTOR

In a shaded pole motor, the phase-split is obtained by induction. A short-circuited copper coil known as 'Shaded ring' is placed around the small portion of the poles as shown in Fig. 5.68. The motor is of squirrel cage type. The portion of the pole where the shaded ring is placed, is known as shaded portion and the remaining portion of the pole is known as 'unshaded portion'. Whenever the field winding is excited with alternating current, the magnetic axis of the pole shift from the unshaded portion to the shaded portion. This shifting of magnetic axis is equivalent to physical movement of the pole. Thus the rotor starts rotating in the direction of the shift of the magnetic of the pole.

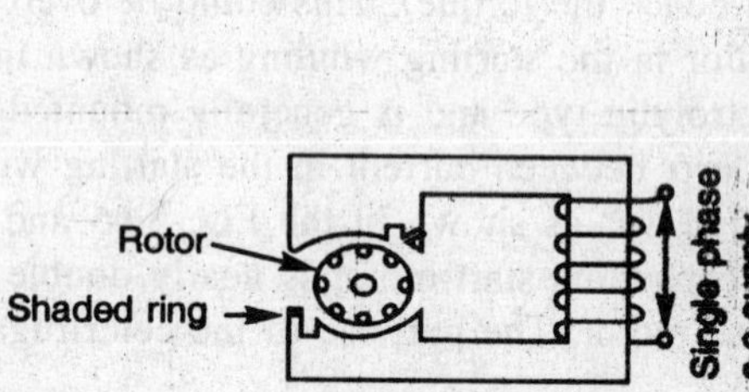


Fig. 5.68

Shaded pole motors are simple in construction but extremely rugged. It is cheap and reliable the disadvantages are (i) low overload capacity (ii) poor efficiency and (iii) low starting torque. These motors are generally used in hair driers, ventilators, toys, small fans and circulators.

## ALTERNATOR

### 5.38. PRINCIPLE OF OPERATION

Alternator or a.c. generator operates on the fundamental principle of electromagnetic induction. It consists of armature winding and a magnetic field. The alternator may be of revolving-armature type or revolving-field type.

### 5.39. REVOLVING –ARMATURE TYPE ALTERNATOR

This type of alternator is used for relatively small capacity and low voltage rating. It has stationary field poles and revolving armature as shown in the Fig. 5.69. The voltage generated in the armature is collected through slip-rings.

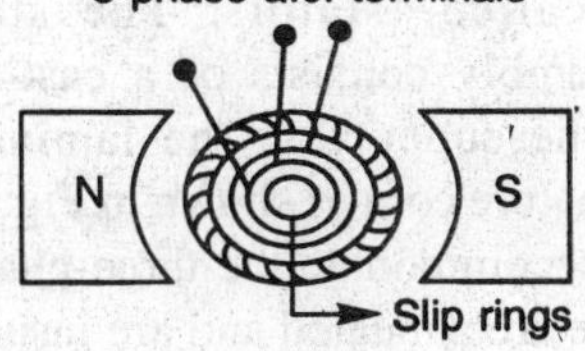


Fig. 5.69

### 5.40. REVOLVING-FIELD TYPE ALTERNATOR

This type of alternator is the most commonly used alternator, where the field pole rotates in a stationary armature as shown in the Fig. 5.70. When the field poles rotate in the stationary armature, the stationary armature conductors are cut by the magnetic flux. According to the electromagnetic induction principle, an emf is induced in the armature conductor.

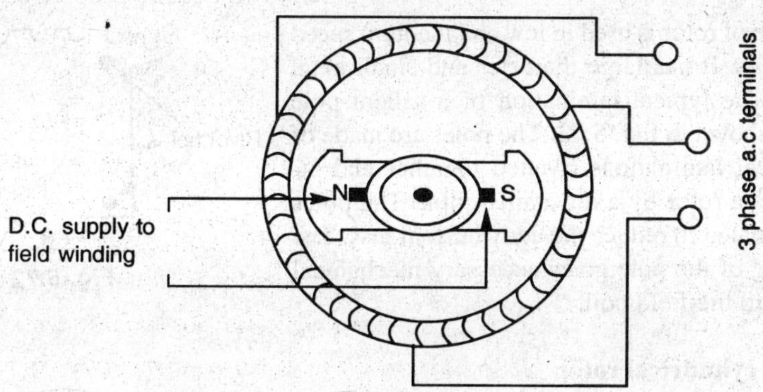


Fig. 5.70

The advantages of revolving field (or starting armature)

(1) The output current can be directly taken from the fixed terminals of the stator to the load without any brushes.

(2) Insulating the stationary armature winding for high a.c. voltage is easy.

(3) The bracing of armature windings can be done easily.

(4) The slip-rings are transferred to low voltage d.c. field circuit, which can be easily insulated.

## 5.41. CONSTRUCTIONAL DETAILS (of revolving field type alternator)

The two major parts of an alternator are (i) Stator and (ii) Rotor.

### Stator

The stationary part of the alternator is called 'stator'. In the revolving-field type alternator, the armature is the stationary element hence it is called 'stator'. The stator assembly consists of a cast-iron frame supporting the laminated armature core as shown in Fig. 5.71. The armature core has slots on its inner periphery to accommodate the three-phase armature winding. The laminations of the armature core are annealed and are insulated from each other by a thin coating of oxide and an enamel. The 'open slots' are used which permit easy installation of armature coils. Ventilating holes are provided for cooling the machine.

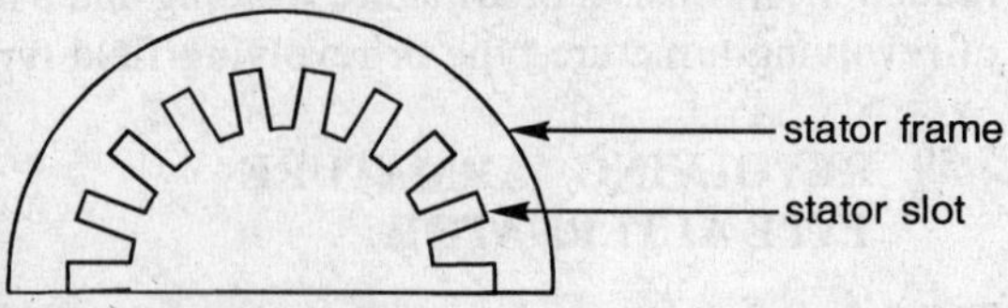


Fig. 5.71

### Rotor

The revolving field structure is called 'rotor'. The rotors are of two types, namely, (i) Salient pole rotor and (ii) Smooth cylindrical type rotor.

### Salient pole rotor

This type of rotor is used in low and medium speed alternators. It has large diameter and small axial length. The typical lamination of a salient pole rotor is shown in Fig. 5.72. The poles are made of thick steel laminations rivetted together and attached to a rotor by a dovetailed joint. The poles are laminated to reduce the eddy current loss. The overhang of the pole gives necessary mechanical support to the field coil.

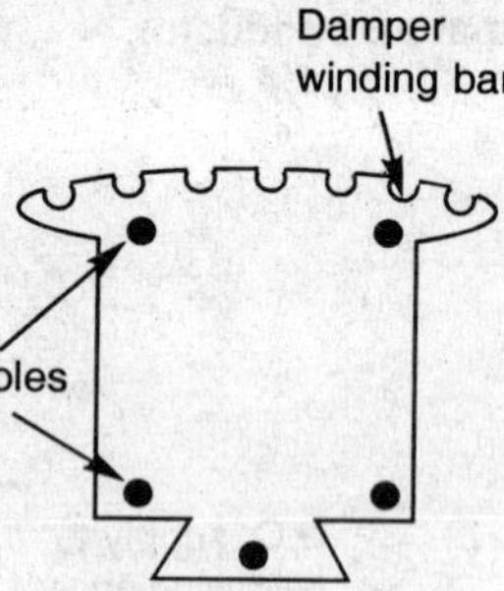


Fig. 5.72

### Smooth cylindrical rotor

This type of rotor is used in high speed alternators. To reduce the peripheral speed, the diameter of the rotor is reduced (whereas axial length is increased). Usually, the number of poles of the rotor are 2 or 4. The rotor is made of solid forging of alloy steel. Slots are provided on the outer periphery to accommodate the field winding as shown in the Fig. 5.73.

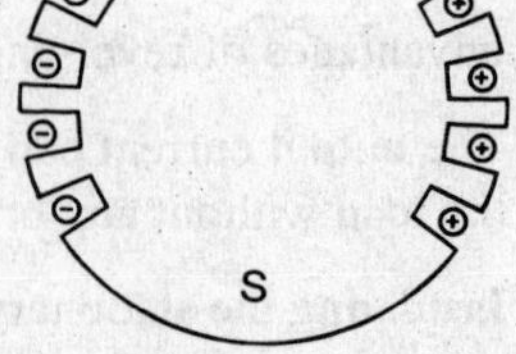


Fig. 5.73

The smooth cylindrical rotors are used in stream turbine-driven alternators.

## 5.42. EMF EQUATION OF AN ALTERNATOR

When the rotor rotates in the stator, the stator windings are cut by the magnetic flux of rotor. Thus an emf is induced in the stator conductors. The expression for the emf induced is obtained as follows.

Let 'Z' number of armature conductors per phase

'T' be the number of turns per phase (Thus $T = \frac{Z}{2}$)

'P' be the number of rotor poles

'Φ' be the flux/pole in webers

'N' be the speed of rotation of rotor in RPM

'f' be the frequency of induced emf in hertz.

The number of rotations per second $= \frac{N}{60}$

Time taken by the rotor for one revolution $= \frac{60}{N}$

The flux cut by the conductor = ΦP webers in one revolution of rotor

Thus, $d\Phi = \Phi P$ and $dt = \frac{60}{N}$ seconds

$\therefore$ Average emf induced per conductors $= \frac{d\Phi}{dt} = \frac{\Phi P}{60/N} = \frac{N\Phi P}{60}$ volts

But we have $f = \frac{PN}{120}$

$\Rightarrow \quad N = \frac{120\,f}{P}$

$\therefore$ Average emf induced per conductor $= \frac{120\,f}{P} \times \frac{\Phi P}{60} = 2\,f\,\Phi P$

Average emf induced in all the 'Z' conductor per phase $= 2f\,\Phi\,Z$ volts

$T = 4f\,\Phi\,T$ volts

RMS value of emf induced per phase $= 1.11 \times 2f\,\Phi Z$

$= 2.22f\,\Phi Z$ volts

$= 4.44f\,\Phi T$ volts

**P. 5.19.** A 3 phase 50Hz, 16 pole alternator has 160 slots in the stator. Each slot consists of 6 conductors. The flux per pole is 20 milliwebers and is sinusoidally distributed. Calculate the induced emf per phase.

**Solution:**

Given

$$f = 50\text{Hz}$$

$$P = 16$$

Number of slots $= 160$

Conductor/slots $= 6$

Total number of conductor $= 160 \times 6 = 960$

Total number of conductors/phase $= \frac{960}{3} = 320 \quad (Z)$

Flux/pole $= 25$ milli Wb

$= 25 \times 10^{-3}$ Wb $(\Phi)$

RMS value of emf induced/phase $= 2.22 f \Phi Z$ volts

$= 2.22 \times 50 \times 25 \times 10^{-3} \times 320$ volts

$= 888$ volts

## SYNCHRONOUS MOTOR

### 5.43. PRINCIPLE OF OPERATION

**The synchronous motor consists of a 'stator' wound for 3 phase and a 'rotor' with electromagnetic poles. Whenever a 3 phase supply is given to 3 phase stator winding, a magnetic field of constant magnitude but rotating with synchronous speed is obtained. In the first half cycle this field can be considered as north pole ($N_s$) and south pole ($S_s$) rotating in space at synchronous speed in a clock-wise direction as shown in Fig. 5.74. (a) Let rotor pole be represented by '$N_r$' and '$S_r$'. Since the like poles $N_s$ and N and $S_s$ and $S_r$ repel each other, the rotor begins to rotate in the anti-clockwise direction as shown in the Fig. 5.74(a). In the second half cycle, the position of the stator pole are interchanged as shown in the Fig. 5.74(b). Here '$N_s$' attracts '$S_r$' and '$S_s$' attracts '$N_r$'. Hence rotor begins to rotate in the clock-wise direction [Fig. 5.74(b)]. Due to the large inertia of the rotor, the rotor cannot respond instantaneously to such quick-reversing torque. Hence rotor remains stationary. Therefore the synchronous motor is not a self-starting motor.**

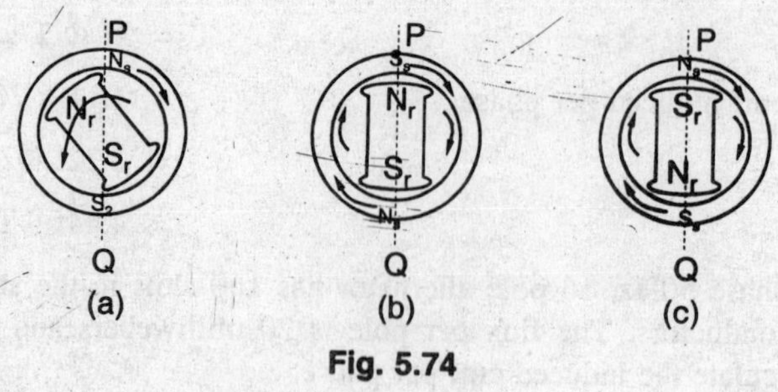


**Fig. 5.74**

On the other hand, if the rotor is not stationary (initially), but is rotating clockwise near about synchronous speed by means of an external source, then at a particular instant, stator and rotor poles attract each other as shown in Fig. 5.74 (c). Thus, by this magnetic coupling, the motor will continue to run exactly at synchronous speed.

## 5.44. METHODS OF STARTING SYNCHRONOUS MOTOR

There are four different methods used for starting the synchronous motor. The method of starting the synchronous motor as a squirrel cage induction motor with the help of 'damper winding' is described here. In this method, the motor starts as an ordinary squirrel cage induction motor and later on operates as a synchronous motor. The damper winding provided on the rotor of the synchronous motor, acts as a squirrel cage motor. The damper winding consists of thick copper bars placed in the slots of the rotor as shown in Fig. 5.75.

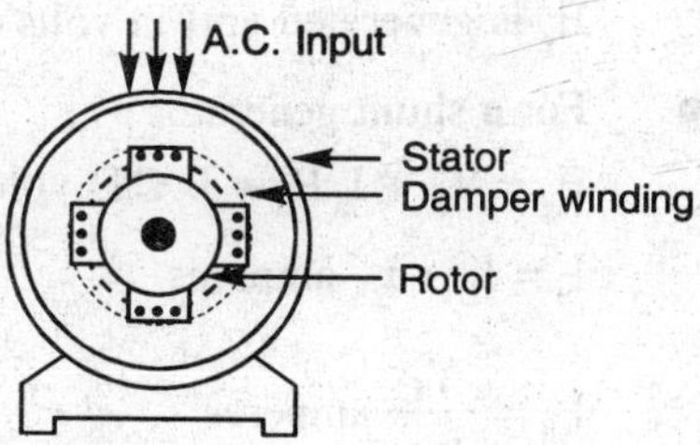

Fig. 5.75

Initially, d.c. supply to the field winding is kept disconnected. The field winding is short-circuited through an external resistor during the starting period. The three-phase a.c. supply is given to the stator. The synchronous motor then starts as a squirrel cage induction motor with 'damper winding' acting as a squirrel cage rotor. When the motor is switched on for the field excitation. Now the rotor and stator poles get magnetically coupled with each other and hence the motor now acts as a synchronous motor.

## 5.45. HUNTING

The synchronous motor is very sensitive to fluctuations in the load. A sudden increase in load on the synchronous motor causes the rotor poles to fall behind the stator poles. On the other hand if the load is suddenly decreased, then the rotor poles pull upwards or get advanced. Thus the rotor will oscillate about the final stable position. This oscillation of rotor is known as hunting or phase swinging.

Hunting can be reduced by using damper windings. When hunting occurs, the difference in speed of stator and rotor poles develops an induced emf in the damper winding bars, which acts in such a way as to suppress the rotor oscillation.

## 5.46. APPLICATIONS OF SYNCHRONOUS MOTOR

(1) It is used in power houses and substations to improve the power factor.

(2) It is used to improve power factor in industries where large number of induction motors are operating at lagging power factor.

(3) It can also be used in textile mills, cement industries and rubber mills for power applications.

## REVISION FORMULA

- $E_g = \dfrac{\Phi ZNP}{60A}$ volts

  $\Phi$ is flux per pole in webers
  N is speed of armature in R.P.M.
  P is number of poles
  Z is number of armature conductors
  A is number of parallel paths
  $E_g$ is generated emf in volts

- For a shunt generator

  $E_g = V_L + I_a R_a + \text{B.C.D}$ volts

  $I_a = I_L + I_{sh}$ amperes

  $I_{sh} = \dfrac{V_L}{R_{sh}}$ amperes

  $I_L = \dfrac{P_L}{V_L} = \dfrac{V_L}{R_L}$ amperes

- For a series generator

  $E_g = V_L + I_a R_a + I_{se} R_{se} + \text{B.C.D}$ volts

  $I_a = I_L = I_{se} = \dfrac{P_L}{V_L}$ ampere

- For a Long shunt compound generator

  $E_g = V_L + I_a R_a + I_{se} R_{se} + \text{B.C.D}$ volts

  $I_L = \dfrac{P_L}{V_L}$; $I_{sh} = \dfrac{V_L}{R_{sh}}$ amperes

  $I_a = I_{se} = I_L + I_{sh}$

- For a short shunt compound generator

  $E_g = V_L + I_a R_a + I_{se} R_{se} + \text{B.C.D}$ volts

  $I_{se} = I_L = \dfrac{P_L}{V_L}$ ampere

  $I_a = I_L = I_{sh}$

Where $I_a$ and $R_a$ are armature current in amperes and armature resistance in ohms.

$I_{sh}$, $R_{sh}$ are shunt field current in amperes and shunt field resistance in ohms.

$I_L$, $R_L$, $P_L$, $V_L$ are load current in amperes, load resistance in ohms, load in watts and load voltage in volts.

$I_{se}$, $R_{se}$ are series field current in amperes and series field resistance in ohms.

$E_g$ is generated voltage in volts.

B.C.D is brush contact drop in volts.

- $$E_b = \frac{\Phi ZNP}{60\ A} \text{ volts}$$

  where $E_b$ is back emf in volts.

- For shunt motor

  $E_b = V_L - I_a R_a - \text{B.C.D volts}$

  $$I_L = \frac{P_L}{V_L} \text{ ampere}$$

  $$I_{sh} = \frac{V_L}{R_{sh}} \text{ ampere}$$

  $I_a = I_L - I_{sh}$ ampere

- For series motor

  $E_b = V_L - I_a R_a - I_{se} R_{se} - \text{B.C.D volts}$

  $$I_L = I_{se} = I_a = \frac{P_L}{V_L} \text{ ampere}$$

- For long shunt motor

  $E_b = V_L - I_a R_a - I_{se} R_{se} - \text{B.C.D volts}$

  $$I_L = \frac{P_L}{V_L}; I_{se} = I_a = I_L - I_{sh}; I_{sh} = \frac{V_L}{R_{sh}} \text{ amperes}$$

- For short shunt motor

  $E_b = V_L - I_a R_a - I_{se} R_{se} - \text{B.C.D volts}$

  $$I_{se} = I_L = \frac{P_L}{V_L}; \; I_{sh} = \frac{V_L - I_{se} R_{se}}{R_{sh}}$$

  where $I_L$ is line current in amperes

  $P_L$ is the power input in watts

  $V_L$ is the voltage input in volts.

- $$T_a = \frac{0.159\ ZP}{A} \Phi\, I_a \quad \text{N} - \text{m}$$

  where $T_a$ = armature torque

  For two shunt machines

$N_1$, $E_1$ are speed in RPM and emf induced in volts for the first machine.

$N_2$, $E_2$ are speed in RPM and emf induced in volts for the machine.

- For two series motors

$$\frac{N_2}{N_1} = \frac{E_2}{E_1} \times \frac{I_2}{I_1}$$

$I_1$, $I_2$ are the input currents in ampere of first and second motor

$E_1 = 4.44f\ \Phi_m N_1$ volts

$E_1 = 4.44f\ B_m AN_1$ volts

$E_2 = 4.44f\ \Phi_m N_2$ volts

$E_2 = 4.44f\ B_m AN_2$ volts

$$\frac{N_2}{N_1} = \frac{E_2}{E_1} = \frac{I_1}{I_2} = K = \text{transformation ratio}$$

where $E_1$, $E_2$ are induced emfs in volts in the primary and secondary windings

$N_1$, $N_2$ are primary and secondary number of turns

$\Phi_m$ is maximum value of flux in webers

$B_m$ is maximum value of flux in density in weber/meter$^2$

$I_1$ and $I_2$ full load primary and secondary currents in amperes

$I_o = \sqrt{I_W^2 + I_\mu^2}$

$I_w = I_o \cos \phi_o$

$I_\mu = I_o \sin\phi_o$

$I_o$ = No load primary current in amperes

$I_w$ = Active component of current in amperes

$I_\mu$ = Reactive component of current in amperes

$$R_{01} = R_1 + \frac{R_2}{K^2};\ R_{02} = R_2 + R_1K^2 \text{ ohms}$$

where $R_{01}$ is equivalent resistance referred to primary in ohms.

$R_{02}$ is equivalent resistance referred to secondary in ohms.

$R_1$, $R_2$ are the resistance of primary and secondary windings in ohms.

- Efficiency $= \dfrac{\text{Output}}{\text{Input}}$

Output = Input – Total losses

Input = Output – Total losses

$$\text{Efficiency} = \frac{\text{Output}}{\text{Output + Total losses}}$$

$$= \frac{\text{Input} - \text{Total losses}}{\text{Output}}$$

Output = Rated KVA × 1000 × Power factor × (x)

where x = fraction of the load

x = 1 for full load or 100% load

x = 0.75 for $\frac{3}{4}$ full load or 75% load

x = 0.5 for $\frac{1}{2}$ full load or 50% load

x = 0.25 for $\frac{1}{4}$ full load or 25% load

- $$N_s = \frac{120f}{P} \text{ RPM}$$

Where $N_s$ is synchronous speed in RPM

f is supply frequency in hertz

P is number of poles of stator

- $$\text{slip}(S) = \frac{N_s - N}{N_s}$$

where N is the speed of induction motor in RPM

$N = N_s(1-s)$ RPM

$f^1 = sf$ Hz

Where '$f^1$' is the frequency of the rotor emf

$$T = \frac{K\Phi SE_2R_2}{R_2^2 + (SX_2)^2} \text{ N-m}$$

where T is torque in newton-metre

$R_2$ is rotor resistance at standstill in ohms

$X_2$ is rotor reactance at standstill in ohms

$E_2$ is rotor emf in volts standstill per phase

$\Phi$ is stator flux per pole in weber.

## REVIEW QUESTIONS

1. Explain the working principle of a d.c. generator.
2. Explain the constructional details of a d.c. generator with neat sketches.
3. Derive an expression for emf induced in a d.c. generator.
4. Explain the following
   (i) Types of generators (ii) Losses in d.c. machines.
5. Explain the open circuit characteristics of a d.c. shunt generator.
6. What do you understand by critical resistance?
7. What are the conditions required for the voltage build up of a self-excited d.c. shunt generator?
8. Explain the internal and external characteristics of d.c. shunt generator.
9. What are the applications of d.c. shunt, series and compound generators?
10. Explain the working principle of a d.c. motor.
11. What is the significance of back emf?
12. What are the types of d.c. motors?
13. Derive an expression for
    (i) Torque equation (ii) Speed equation for a d.c. motor
14. Explain the three characteristics of
    (i) D.C. shunt motor (ii) D.C. series motor
    (iii) D.C compound motor
15. What are the applications of a d.c. shunt, series and compound motors?
16. Explain the working principle of single phase transformer.
17. Write the constructional details of single phase transformer.
18. Derive an expression for emf induced in a transformer.
19. Explain the behaviour of a transformer when it is
    (i) On no load (ii) On load
20. What are the losses in a transformer?
21. What are the applications of a transformer?
22. Explain the principle of operation of 3 phase induction motor.
23. With neat sketches explain the constructional details of 3 phase induction motor.
24. What is meant by slip?
25. Derive an expression for torque equation of a 3 phase induction motor.
26. Explain the torque slip characteristics of 3 phase induction motor.
27. What are the applications of 3 phase induction motor?
28. What are the different types of single phase induction motors? How do you make them self-starting?
29. Explain the principle of operation of split-phase induction motor.

30. Explain the principle of operator of capacitor-start induction motor.
31. Write short notes on
    (a) Capacitor-start-and-run motor.
    (b) Two-value capacitor motor.
32. Explain the working principle of shaded pole motor.
33. Give various applications of single phase induction motor.
34. Explain the principle of operation of an alternator.
35. Describe the constructional details of an alternator.
36. Derive an expression for emf induced in an alternator.
37. Explain the principle of operation of a synchronous motor.
38. Explain any one method of starting a synchronous motor.
39. What is hunting in a synchronous motor? How do you reduce it?
40. What are the applications of synchronous motor?

## TWO MARKS QUESTIONS AND ANSWERS

1. *What is the principle of electric generator ?*

   It is an electrical machine which converts mechanical energy into electrical energy.

2. *What are the parts of a D.C. machine ?*

   Yoke, pole core, pole shoe, pole coil, armature, armature winding, commutator, brushes and bearings are the parts of a D.C. machine.

3. *What is the function of commutator ?*

   The function of commutator is to convert the alternating emf induced in the armature into unidirectional current in the external circuit.

4. *What are the types of D.C. generators ?*

   The generators are classified into separately excited and self-excited generators. The self-excited generators are further classified into shunt, series, long shunt (cumulative and differential) and short shunt (cumulative and differential).

5. *What are the various losses in a D.C. machine ?*

   The total losses in a D.C. machine are

   1. Copper loss (includes armature copper loss, shunt field copper loss and series field copper loss).
   2. Iron loss (includes hysteresis loss and eddy current loss).
   3. Mechanical loss (includes friction loss and windage loss).

6. *Name the three characteristics of D.C. generator.*

   1. Open circuit characteristics or magnetic characteristics (emf generated under no load versus field current).
   2. Total or internal characteristics (generator emf versus armature current).

3. External characteristics or voltage regulation curve (terminal voltage versus load current).

7. *What is critical resistance ?*

It is the slope of the tangent drawn to the linear portion of the open circuit characteristics from origin.

It is the value of resistance in the field circuit where the generator will just excite.

8. *What are the conditions for build up of a shunt generator ?*

1. There must be some residual magnetism.
2. For given direction of rotation, shunt field coils should be properly connected to the armature terminals.
3. Shunt field resistance should be less than the critical resistance (when excited on open circuit.)

9. *What are applications of D.C. generators ?*

D.C. shunt generator – for lighting, power supply and for charging batteries.

D.C. series generator – as boosters.

D.C. compound generator – as power supply unit to railway circuits, elevators motors and incandescent lamps.

10. *What is the principle of electric motor ?*

It is an electrical machine which converts electrical energy into mechanical energy.

11. *What is back emf ?*

When the motor rotates i.e., the conductors housed in the armature rotates, the magnetic flux is being cut by these conductors. Hence according to Faraday's Laws of electromagnetic induction, an emf is induced in the conductors acting in a direction opposite to the applied voltage and hence it is called back emf:

$$E_b = \Phi \frac{zNP}{60A} \text{ volts}$$

This back emf is always less than the applied voltage.

12. *What are the characteristics of D.C. motor ?*

There are three characteristics

1. Armature torque versus armature current. This is also called electrical characteristics.
2. Speed versus armature current.
3. Speed versus armature torque. This is also called mechanical characteristics.

13. *Write the applications of a D.C. shunt motor.*

Since D.C. shunt motor has approximately constant speed, it can be used for lathes, line-shaft drives, centrifugal pumps, reciprocating pumps, machine tools, blowers, fans, grinders, shapers, wood working machines, small printing presses etc.

14. *Write the applications of a D.C. series motor.*

Since series motor has high starting torque, it can be used for electric traction, tram cars, railway cars, cranes, hoists, elevators, winches, conveyors etc.

15. *What are the applications of a D.C. compound motor ?*

Since this motor has high starting torque it can be used for shears, punches, heavy planners, rolling mills, elevators, conveyors, stamping presses, large printing presses, mine hoists, haulage gears and power fans etc.

16. *What is the principle of a transformer ?*

A transformer works on mutual induction principle. Whenever the primary winding is given an alternating supply, the alternating flux established in it also links with secondary winding. According to Faraday's laws of electromagnetic induction, an emf is induced in the secondary winding which is called mutually induced emf.

17. *List the parts of a transformer.*

Primary and secondary winding, core, tank, transformer oil, conservator and breather.

18. *What are the types of transformer core ?*

The two types of transformer core are

1. **Core type:** Here the windings surround the considerable part of the core.
2. **Shell type:** Here the core surrounds a considerable part of the winding.

19. *What are the losses in a transformer? Why the efficiency of a transformer is high ?*

The losses that occur in the transformer are:

1. Copper loss (due to resistance of the transformer winding)
2. Iron loss (includes hysteresis and eddy current loss)

Since transformer is a static device it has no rotational losses. Hence the efficiency of the transformer is high.

20. *Why do we use silicon steel for transformer core ?*

The hysteresis loss in the transformer core can be minimised by selecting a material for the core which has low hysteresis coefficient like silicon steel. Hence silicon steel is used for transformer core.

21. *Write applications of transformer.*

Transformers are used in transmission and distribution of electric power, (as step-down and step-up transformer) measuring current (current transformer), measuring voltage (potential transformer), furnaces, welding, radio and TV circuits, control and instrumentation circuits etc.

22. *What are the main parts of 3 phase induction motor ?*

The main parts are

1. Stator (Stationary part)
2. Rotor (Rotating part) — Squirrel cage rotor / Slip ring rotor

23. *What is slip ?*

It is the difference in speed of stator magnetic flux and rotor (conductor).

24. *What are the applications of squirrel cage induction motor ?*

Squirrel cage induction motors are used in fans, conveyors, compressors, crushes, agitators, sheers, punches, die stamping, blowers, line shafting etc.

25. *What are the applications of slip ring induction motor ?*

Slip ring induction motors are used in pumps, fans, conveyors, hoists, compressors, lifts etc.

26. *List the different types of single phase induction motors.*

(a) Split-phase motor

(b) Capacitor-start-induction run motor

(c) Capacitor-start-and-run motor

(d) Two-value capacitor motor

(e) Shaded pole motor

27. *Mention any four applications of single phase induction motors.*

The single phase induction motors are used in

(a) Washing machines

(b) Domestic refrigerators

(c) Centrifugal pumps

(d) Fans

28. *What are the two types of rotors used in an alternator ?*

(a) Salient-pole rotor (b) Smooth cylindrical type rotor

29. *Where do you use a salient pole rotor ?*

Salient pole rotor is used in low and medium speed alternators.

30. Where do you use a smooth cylindrical type rotor?

Smooth cylindrical type rotor is used for high speed applications (turbo-alternators).

31. *What is the expression for emf induced in an alternator ?*

E = 2.2f $\Phi$ z volts

32. *How a synchronous motor can be operated at the desired power factor ?*

A synchronous motor can be operated at the desired power factor by changing the d.c. excitation to the motor.

33. *What are the uses of damper winding ?*

Damper windings are used to (i) develop necessary starting torque and to (ii) reduce hunting

34. *What is 'hunting' ?*

The oscillation of rotor at its new position of equilibrium corresponding to new load is called hunting.

35. *What is a synchronous capacitor ?*

The over-excited synchronous motor is called a synchronous capacitor. It acts like a capacitor taking leading current.

## EXERCISE PROBLEMS

**P. 5.1:** Determine the terminal voltage of lap wound D.C. shunt generator with the following name plate details: poles = 4, FWX/pole = 0.05 Wb, number of armature conductors = 400, armature resistance = 0.5 ohms, speed of rotations = 900 RPM, armature current = 40 amperes.

(Ans: 280V)

**P. 5.2:** A 6 pole long shunt compound generator delivers a load current of 200 amperes at a terminal voltage of 500V. Calculate the generated emf if armature, series field and shunt field resistances are 0.02Ω, 0.05Ω, 125Ω respectively. Allow a brush contact droop of 2V/brush.

(Ans: 518.28V)

**P. 5.3:** A 250V D.C. shunt motor runs at 1200 RPM at no load and takes 9 amperes. The armature and shunt field resistance are 0.2Ω and 200Ω respectively. Calculate the speed when it is loaded and drawing a current of 60 amperes.

(Ans: 1150.73 RPM)

**P. 5.4:** A 400V D.C. motor has an armature rotating at 700 RPM drawing an armature current of 50A. The armature resistance is 0.3 ohms. Calculate the torque developed by the motor.

(Ans: 262.6 N–m)

**P. 5.5:** A single phase 50KVA transformer has iron loss of 400 watts and full load copper loss of 750 watts. Determine the % efficiency at half full load 0.8 pf.

(Ans: 97.14)

**P. 5.6:** A 20KVA, 2200/200V transformer has 60 turns in the secondary. Calculate the primary number of turns and also full load primary and secondary currents.

(Ans: 660 turns, 9.09A, 100A)

**P. 5.7:** A 6 pole 3 phase induction motor is connected to a 50 HZ supply. Determine the percentage slip when it is running at 980 RPM.

(Ans: 2)

**P. 5.8:** A 4 pole 3 phase 50Hz induction motor has a full load slip of 3%. Determine the synchronous speed, speed of rotor and the frequency of rotor emf.

(Ans: 1500 RPM, 1455 RPM, 1.5 Hz)

*Chapter 6*

# MEASURING INSTRUMENTS

Measurement of electrical quantities is done with the help of (i) Indicating instruments (ii) Integrating instruments and (iii) Recording instruments.

Indicating instruments indicate the magnitude of the quantity under measurement on a graduated scale with the help of a pointer. Integrating instruments keep a record of the quantity to be measured from the time they are connected to the supply. Recording instruments keep a record of the readings on a graph sheet.

## 6.1. INDICATING INSTRUMENTS

As already mentioned, it indicates the magnitude of the quantity being measured on a graduated scale. A pointer moves over the scale to indicate the reading. The essential requirements of these instruments are (i) they should not load the circuit to which they are connected (ii) they should draw minimum power for their operation (iii) the moving system should be light.

For satisfactory operation of the measuring instruments, the following torques are employed:

(i) Deflecting torque (to move the pointer)

(ii) Controlling torque (to act as an opposite torque)

(iii) Damping torque (to prevent the oscillation of the moving system).

## 6.2. DEFLECTING TORQUE ($T_D$)

The deflecting torque is necessary to produce a deflecting force to move the pointer from zero position. This deflecting torque can be obtained with the help of any one of the effects listed below:

(i) Magnetic effect (for ammeters and voltmeters)

(ii) Thermal effect (for ammeters and voltmeters)

(iii) Electromagnetic effect (for ammeters, voltmeters, watthourmeters, wattmeters)

(iv) Electrodynamic effect (for ammeters, voltmeters and particularly wattmeters).

## 6.3. CONTROLLING TORQUE ($T_C$)

The controlling torque acts as an opposing torque and serves two purposes: (i) to make pointer to deflect to a definite position, which will take place when $T_D = T_C$. (In the absence of '$T_C$' the deflection of the pointer will be indefinite.) (ii) to bring the moving system to zero position when the instrument is disconnected from the circuit. The controlling torque is obtained from (i) Spring control and (ii) Gravity control.

**Spring control**: In the spring control the moving system is attached to two phosphor bronze spiral hair springs as shown in Fig. 6.1. When the pointer deflects, the springs get twisted and the combined twist produces the controlling torque which is proportional to angle of twist 'θ'

i.e., $T_C \propto \theta$

But, $T_D \propto I$.

Since the angle of twist of the spring is proportional to deflection of the pointer, $T_c$ can be made equal (and opposite) to $T_D$. At this instant, the pointer achieves a steady deflected position. At final steady deflected position $T_C = T_D$, therefore $\theta \propto I$. The spring used for providing '$T_C$' should

(i) be non magnetic
(ii) not be affected by fatigue
(iii) have low specific resistance
(iv) have low temperature co-efficient resistance.

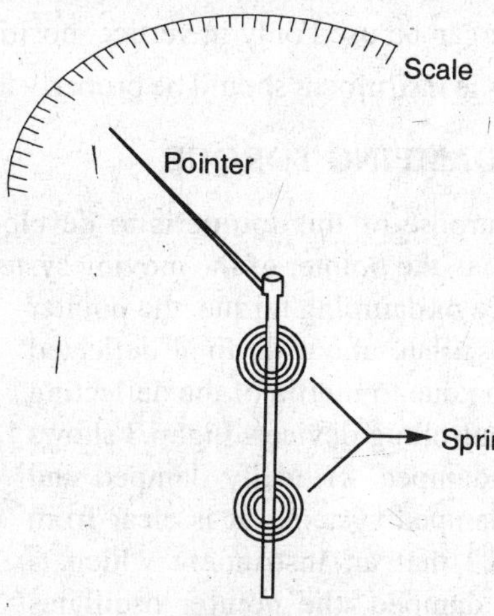

Fig. 6.1

**Gravity Control** (Fig 6.2)

In the case of gravity control, small adjustable weight is attached to the moving system. When the pointer is at zero position, $T_D$ is zero. Here the weight will remain vertically downwards. When the pointer moves due to $T_D$, this weight goes up and it exerts a force in the downward direction. As the position of this weight is in a direction opposite to the movement of pointer, a controlling torque ($T_C$) is developed, which is proportional to 'sin θ', where 'θ' is the angle of deflection. Hence gravity controlled instruments have cramped scales (instead of uniform scales).

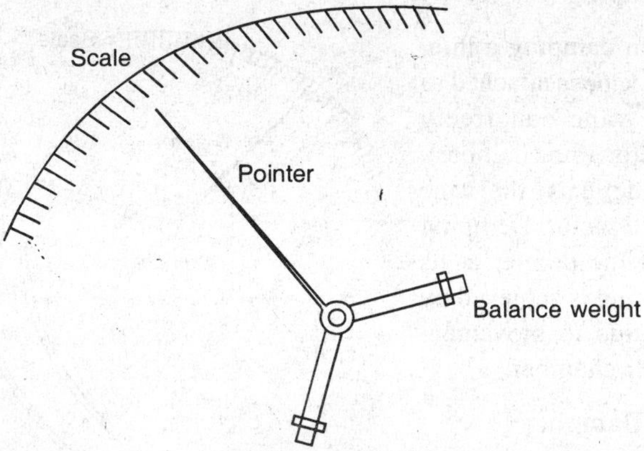

Fig. 6.2

The advantages of gravity control compared to spring control are listed below:

(i) It is cheap

(ii) It does not get affected by temperature.

However it has the following disadvantages:

(i) Scale is cramped

(ii) It can be used only in vertical position

(iii) The instrument should be properly levelled before being used, to avoid zero error.

## 6.4. DAMPING TORQUE

The purpose of this torque is to develop a damping force of sufficient magnitude, such that, the pointer of the moving system comes to final steady value quickly. In the absence of damping torque, the pointer may oscillate about its final deflected position due to inertia of the deflecting and controlling devices. Fig. 6.3 shows under-damped, critically damped and over damped systems. It is clear from Fig. 6.3 that an instrument which is under damped, the pointer oscillates before reaching steady value. The instrument which is critically damped, the pointer reaches its steady position quickly and smoothly whereas the pointer moves slowly to its final steady value, if the instrument is over damped.

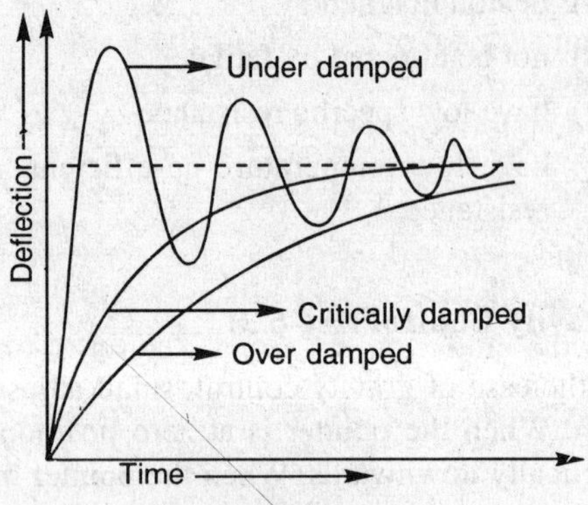


**Fig. 6.3**

Damping torque can be produced by the following methods:

(i) Air friction damping (ii) Eddy current damping and (iii) Fluid friction damping.

**Air friction damping** (Fig. 6.4)

In the air friction damping a thin, light aluminium vane is attached to a spindle. The vane can freely move in the sector (air chamber). As the pointer deflects, the vane also moves in the sector. Damping of oscillation of the pointer at its final steady position is achieved by the air friction due to movement of vane in the air chamber.

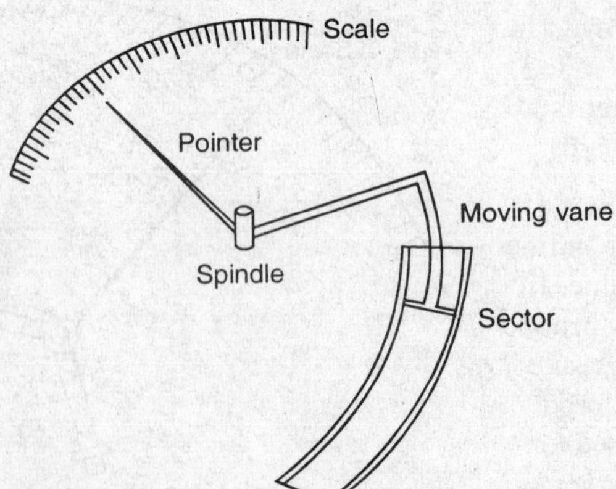


**Fig. 6.4**

**Eddy Current Damping** (Fig. 6.5)

Eddy current damping is the most

efficient and effective form of damping. Damping torque is produced due to the eddy current. Two essential parts of eddy current damping are (i) Disc and (ii) Magnet. The disc used may be made up of aluminium or copper which is fixed to the spindle. The magnet is a permanent magnet. As the pointer deflects, the spindle causes the thin disc to move between the poles of a permanent magnet. This movement of the disc under the influence of magnetic field induces eddy current in the disc producing the essential damping torque. The direction of the torque developed will be opposite to the motion of the disc.

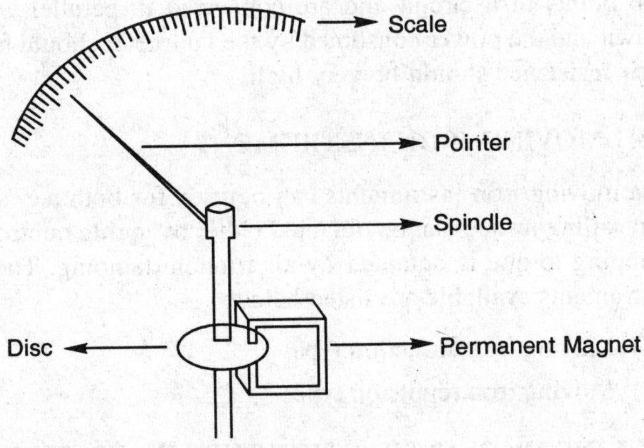


**Fig. 6.5**

**Fluid Friction Damping** (Fig. 6.6)

In the case of fluid friction damping, the moving vanes attached to the lower end of the spindle are dipped in the oil. Greater the viscosity of oil, greater is the opposition for the motion of the vanes. The disadvantages of this method are listed below:

(i) Since creeping of oil is undesirable, the instruments are to be always kept in vertical position.

(ii) This damping method cannot be used for portable instruments.

Hence fluid friction damping is employed in instruments which are to be fixed at one place, e.g., instruments which are used in panel boards.

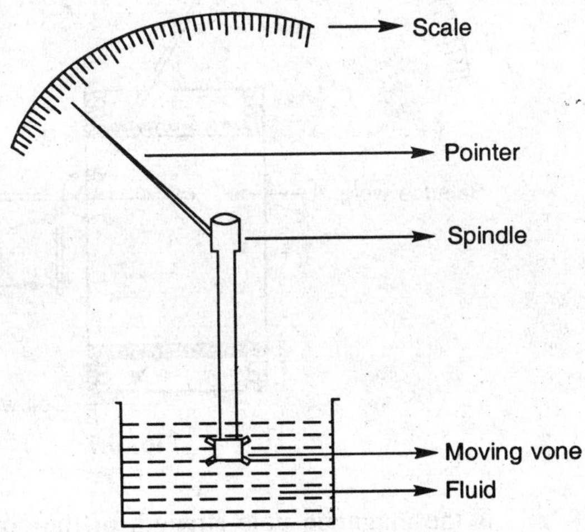


**Fig. 6.6**

**Note:** 1. The principle of operation of ammeters and voltmeters are same. In the case of ammeter '$T_D$' is produced by the current to be measured, whereas in a voltmeter, $T_D$ is produced by the current proportional to voltage to be measured. 2. Ammeters are used to measure current and are connected in series with the circuit. Voltage drop and power consumed by the ammeter should be as small as possible hence their resistance should be as small as possible. 3. Voltmeters are used to measure voltage across any two points in a circuit and are connected in parallel with the circuit. The current drawn and the power consumed by the voltmeter should be as small as possible hence their resistance should be very high.

## 6.5. MOVING IRON INSTRUMENT

The moving iron instruments can be used for both a.c. and d.c. measurements. The controlling torque can be obtained either by spring control or by gravity control. The damping torque is obtained by air friction damping. The two types of moving iron instruments available are listed below:

(i) Moving iron attraction type.

(ii) Moving iron repulsion type.

## MOVING IRON ATTRACTION TYPE INSTRUMENT

The arrangement of a moving iron attraction type instrument is shown in Fig. 6.7. A flat soft iron disc is fitted to the spindle. Whenever the instrument is connected to the circuit, the magnetic field produced by the current through the coil drags the disc inside. As the disc moves, the pointer moves on the scale.

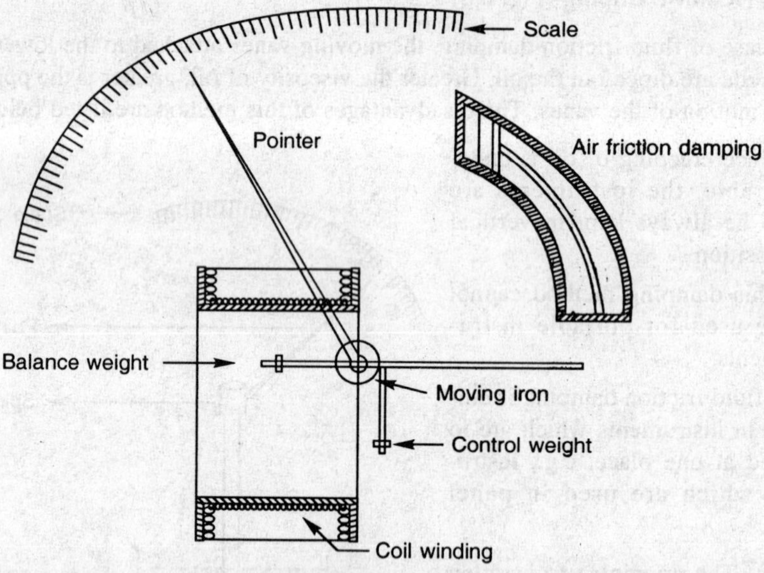


Fig. 6.7

If '$m_1$' is the magnetic pole strength of the coil and if '$m_2$' is the magnetic pole strength of disc, then the force of attraction is given by

$$F \propto \frac{m_1 m_2}{d^2}$$

where 'd' is the distance between the two plates.

But $m_1$ and $m_2$ are proportional to 'I' amperes.

$\therefore \quad F \propto I^2.$

Thus '$T_D$' is directly proportional to '$I^2$' and hence the scale is not uniform. Since the deflection of the pointer does not depend on direction of current, it can be used for both a.c. and d.c. measurements.

**Moving iron repulsion type instruments** (Fig 6.8)

The moving iron repulsion type instrument consists of a hollow cylindrical fixed coil. Two soft iron rods P, Q are placed inside the coil. 'Q' is fixed, whereas 'P' is a movable one which also carries the pointer that moves over the scale. When the current to be measured, is passed through the fixed coil, the two rods are magnetised to same polarity and experience a force of repulsion which moves the pointer against the controlling torque produced by spring or gravity control. The '$T_D$' is due to repulsive force between 'P' and 'Q'. The repulsive force is proportional to $m_1$ $m_2$, where '$m_1$' and '$m_2$' are the pole strengths, which are proportional to 'H' which itself is proportional to 'I'.

$\therefore \quad T_D \propto I^2.$

Thus the scale is not uniform. Since the deflection of pointer does not depend on direction of current flow, it can be used for both a.c. and d.c. measurements. The damping system employed is air friction damping. The eddy current damping cannot be used because the presence of permanent magnet would affect the deflection of the pointer. These instruments are robust and cheap however they are less accurate. The scale is cramped.

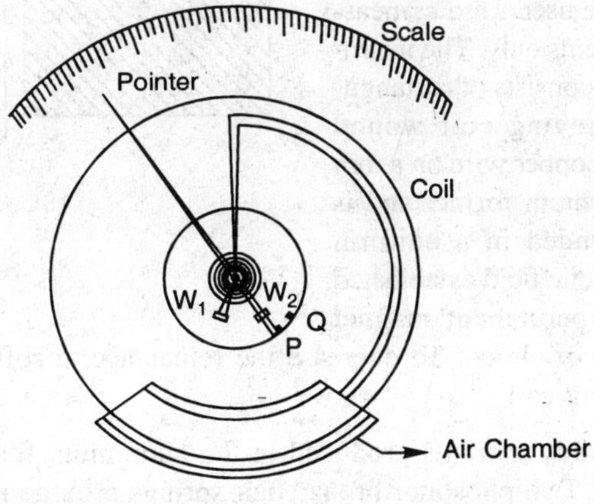


$W_1$ - $W_2$ – weight
P – Moving iron
Q – Fixed iron

**Fig. 6.8**

## 6.6. MOVING COIL INSTRUMENT (PERMANENT MAGNET TYPE) (Fig. 6.9)

We know that whenever a current carrying conductor is placed in a magnetic field, a force acts on the coil, which is given by

$$F = BIl \text{ newtons}$$

where B = Flux density in $Wb/m^2$

I = Current passing through the moving coil in amperes

'l' = Length of the conduction in meters
F = Force acting on the coil in newtons.
θ = Angle between conductor and plane of the magnetic field

Since 'B' and 'l' are constant, we have

$$F \propto I$$

M, M – Permanent Magnet
C – Rectangular coil
S – Spring
I – Soft iron cylinder

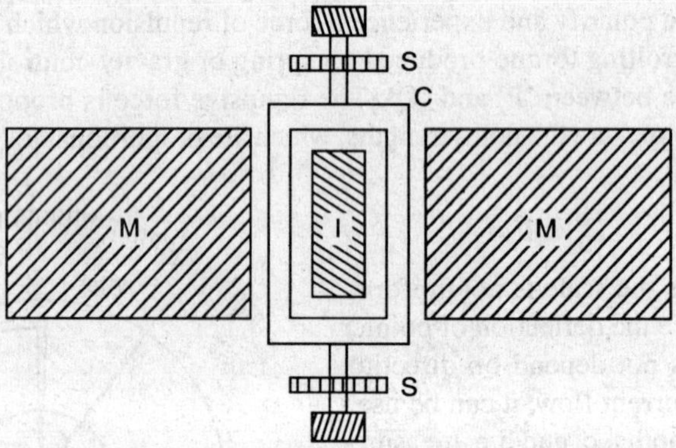


Fig. 6.9

Thus the deflection of the instrument is proportional to current and hence the scale is uniform. The deflection of pointer depends upon the direction of current flow hence it can be used for d.c. measurements only. The instrument consists of rectangular moving coil wound with copper wire on a thin aluminium former and is suspended in a uniform magnetic field established by a permanent magnet made of alnico. To decrease the reluctance, a soft iron core is kept in between the moving coil.

The eddy currents produced in the aluminium former, develops sufficient damping force. Two phosphor bronze hair springs provide the necessary control torque. They also serve the purpose of leading the current in and out of the coil.

**Advantages and Disadvantages:**

**Advantages:**

The power consumption is low.
Hysteresis loss is not present.
Eddy current damping is very effective.
Performance is unaffected by stray magnetic fields.
Scale is uniform.
Extension of ranges is possible.

**Disadvantages:**

It can be used for d.c. measurements only.

Costlier than moving iron instruments.
Errors in the reading due to ageing (of magnet and spring).

**Comparison of Moving Iron and Moving Coil Measurements**

| Moving Iron | Moving Coil |
|---|---|
| Robust in construction | Delicate |
| Not sensitive | Very sensitive |
| Scale is cramped | Scale is uniform |
| Air friction damping is used | Eddy current damping is used |
| Cheaper | Costly |
| Less accurate | More accurate |

## 6.7. DYNAMOMETER TYPE WATTMETER

Dynamometer type wattmeter is as shown in Fig. 6.10. It has two coils (i) Fixed coil (ii) Moving coil.

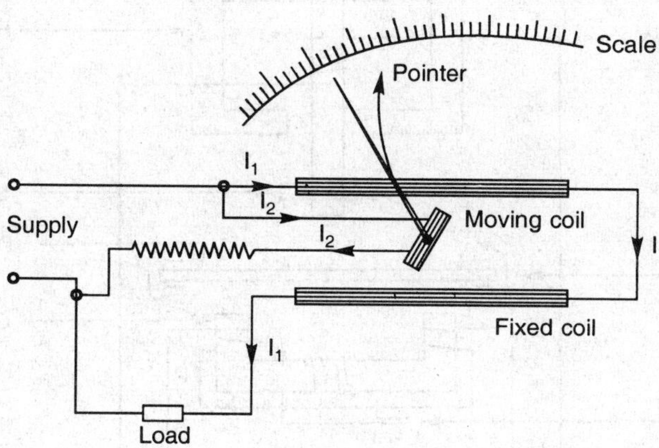


**Fig. 6.10**

**Fixed Coil**: It is also called current coil and is connected in series with the load. It is made of few turns of thin wire and is wound on an aluminium former. This aluminium former gives eddy current damping. The spiral phosphor bronze provides the controlling torque.

**Moving Coil**: It is also called pressure coil. It is pivoted centrally and carries a current '$I_2$. The high resistance connected in series with this coil drops a large voltage across it, enabling free movement of moving coil.

The deflecting torque is proportional to the product of voltage and current in the two coils.

$\therefore$ Deflecting torque $T \propto V \times I$

$$T = KV \times I$$

But '$V \times I$' is the power in watts

Thus the deflection of the pointer directly gives the power in watts.

## 6.8. SINGLE PHASE INDUCTION TYPE ENERGY METER

The single phase induction type energy meter is shown in Fig. 6.11. The single phase energy meter consists of two coils, namely, current coil and pressure coil. The current coil is made of few turns of thick wire and is connected in series with the load. Pressure coil is made of many turns of thin wire and is connected in parallel with the supply. The current (flux) in the pressure coil lags behind the voltage by 90°. This displacement of exact 90° can be achieved with the help of shaded ring. An aluminium disc mounted on a spindle is placed between the two coils. The two fluxes produced by the two coils interact with aluminium disc and produce eddy currents in the disc, hence disc starts rotating. The braking is obtained from a pair of brake magnets. The speed of the disc is proportional to energy consumed by the load. The register mechanism is either of pointer type or cyclometer type.

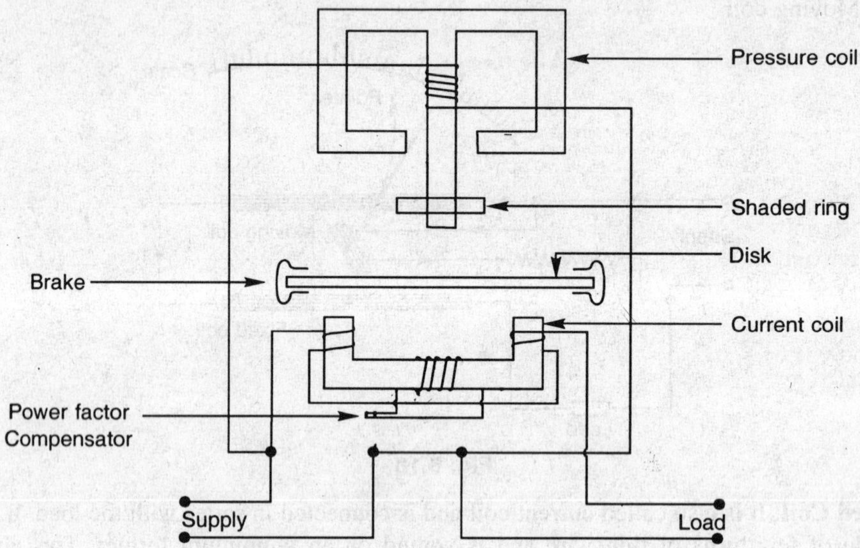


Fig. 6.11

## 6.9. MEGGER

Megger is basically a resistance measuring instrument used for measuring high resistance of cables. It is a simple, robust and portable instrument. It consists of two main parts: (i) Generating part (ii) Resistance measuring circuit.

**Generating Part**: The megger has a permanent magnet hand driven D.C. generator which is capable of generating either 250V or 500V at full speed.

**Resistance measuring circuit**: It consists of two coils (i) Control coil or Voltage coil (ii) Deflecting coil or the Current coil which are fixed at right angles to each other to a spindle. The spindle is free to move in the magnetic field produced by two permanent magnet poles. A needle moving over a graduated scale (zero to infinity) is also fixed to the spindle as shown in Fig. 6.12.

PC – Pressure coil or voltage coil
CC – Current coil

$R_1$, $R_2$ are the current limiting resistances connected in series with PC and CC respectively.

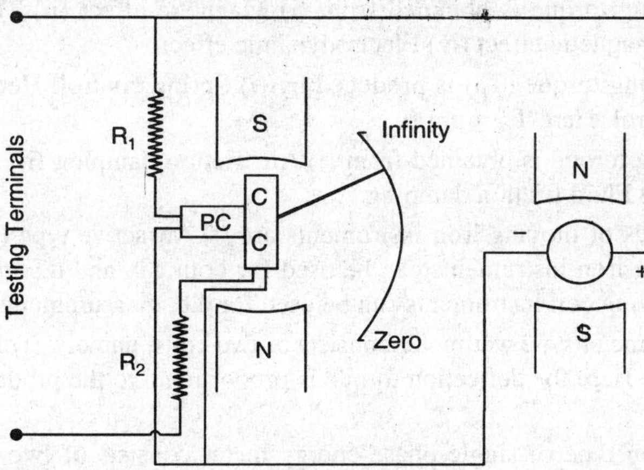


Fig. 6.12

When the megger terminals are short circuited, current in the current coil will be maximum and hence the pointer will show, 'zero' position on the scale. On the other hand, if the megger terminals are kept open, no current will flow through the current coil. The pointer will show 'infinity' position on the scale under the effect of voltage coil alone. If any unknown resistance is connected the pointer will show a reading in between zero and infinity.

## 6.10. ARRANGEMENT OF MEASUREMENTS

To get a general idea of connecting the measuring instruments an arrangement of ammeter, voltmeter, wattmeter, energy meter to measure current, voltage, power, energy in a single phase circuit with lamp load is as shown in Fig. 6.13.

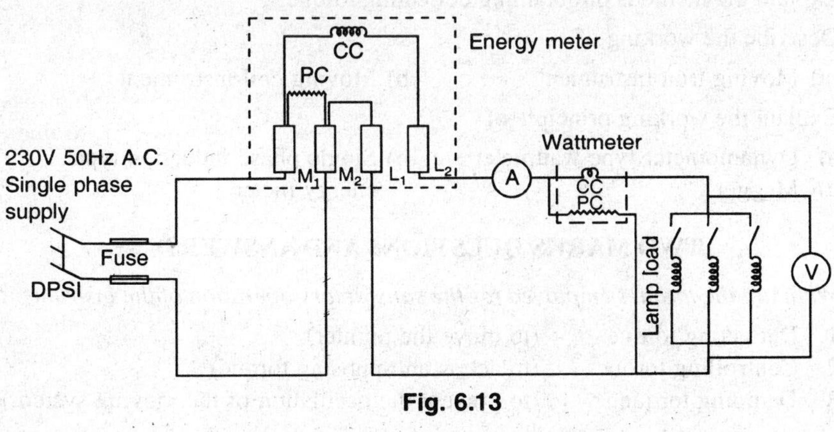


Fig. 6.13

## HIGHLIGHTS

- Measuring instruments are classified into (i) Indicating instruments (ii) Intregrating instruments (iii) Recording instruments.
- The torques employed in measuring instruments are (i) Deflecting torque (ii) Controlling torque (iii) Damping torque.
- The deflecting torque is obtained from (i) Magnetic effect (ii) Thermal effect (iii) Electromagnetic effect (iv) Electrodynamic effect.
- The controlling torque ($T_C$) is produced by (i) Spring control. Here $T_C \propto \theta$ (ii) Gravity control. Here $T_C \propto \sin\theta$.
- The damping torque is obtained from (i) Air friction damping (ii) Eddy current damping (iii) Fluid friction damping.
- The two types of moving iron instruments are (i) Attractive type (ii) Repulsion type. Moving iron instruments can be used for both a.c. and d.c. measurements whereas moving coil instruments can be used for d.c. measurements only.
- The dynamometer type wattmeter consists of two coils, namely, (i) Fixed coil (ii) Moving coil. Here the deflection torque is proportional to the product of voltage and current.
- The induction type of single phase energy meter consists of two coils namely current coil and potential coil. The two fluxes produced by the coils, namely, current coil and potential coil. The two fluxes produced by the two coils interact with aluminium disc and produce eddy currents in the disc, thus making the disc to rotate.
- The main parts of megger are (i) Voltage generating part and (ii) Resistance measuring circuit.
- Megger is used for measuring very high resistance.

## REVIEW QUESTIONS

1. What are the torques that are employed in the measuring instruments for their satisfactory operation?
2. Explain the methods of obtaining controlling torque.
3. Explain the methods of obtaining deflecting torque.
4. Describe the working of
   a) Moving iron instrument  b) Moving coil instrument
5. Explain the working principle of
   a) Dynamometer type wattmeter  b) Single phase induction type energy meter
   c) Megger

## TWO MARKS QUESTIONS AND ANSWERS

1. *What are the torques employed for the satisfactory operation of the instruments ?*

   1. Deflecting torque (to move the pointer)
   2. Controlling torque (to act as an opposing torque)
   3. Damping torque (to prevent the oscillation of the moving system)

2. *How the deflecting torque is produced ?*

   The deflecting torque is obtained from

   1. Magnetic effect
   2. Thermal effect
   3. Electromagnetic effect
   4. Electrodynamic effect

3. *How the controlling torque is obtained ?*

   The controlling torque is obtained from

   1. Spring control
   2. Gravity control

   In spring control, controlling torque is proportional to deflection angle '$\theta$' whereas in the gravity control, the controlling torque is proportional to '$\sin \theta$'.

4. *What are the advantages and disadvantages of gravity control compared to spring control ?*

   **Advantages:**

   1. It is cheap.
   2. It does not get affected by temperature.

   **Disadvantages:**

   1. Scale is cramped.
   2. It can be used in vertical position only.

5. *How the Damping torque is produced ?*

   Damping torque is produced by

   1. Air friction damping
   2. Eddy current damping
   3. Fluid friction damping.

6. *What are the disadvantages of fluid friction damping ?*

   1. Since creeping of oil is undesirable, the instruments are to be always kept in vertical position.
   2. This damping method cannot be used for portable instruments.

7. *What are the two types of moving iron instruments ?*

   1. Moving iron attraction type
   2. Moving iron repulsion type

8. *What are the features of moving coil instruments ?*

   1. The power consumption is low
   2. Hysteresis loss is absent
   3. Scale is uniform
   4. Used for d.c. only.

9. *What are the features of moving iron instruments ?*

   1. The scale is not uniform.

2. Used for both a.c. and d.c.
3. Less accurate.
4. Cheap and robust.

10. *What are the parts of single phase induction type energy meter ?*

1. Current coil
2. Pressure coil
3. Brake magnet
4. Shaded ring
5. Disc
6. Power factor compensator.

# *Chapter 7*

# DOMESTIC WIRING

The selection of wiring system for domestic wiring depends on the type of installation, cost of the installation, future expansion etc. The commonly used wiring system for domestic wiring is 'two wire system' or three phase four wire system.

## 7.1. WIRING MATERIAL AND ACCESSORIES

Irrespective of the type of wiring system, the following are some of the accessories, one should get acquainted with. Switches, main switches, distribution board, fuse, socket outlet, flexible chords, plug, ceiling rose, lamp holders and cables etc.

**Switch:** The 'ON' and 'OFF' i.e. the 'make' and 'break' of electrical connection to the load (fan, lamp etc.,) is done with the help of a switch. When the switch is 'on', the circuit is alive and when the switch is 'off', the circuit is dead. The usual ratings of the switches used for domestic purposes are 5A and 15A. There are certain special switches like two-way switches, three-way switches available for stair-case wiring. Depending on the shape and appearance they can be classified into tumbler switch (project out of the wall) and flush switch (does not project out of the wall).

**Main switch**: The purpose of this switch is to control all the sub-circuits provided in the building. It is enclosed in an iron box and is called Iron Clad Switch.

There are three types of Iron Clad Switches available. They are listed below:

(i) Double pole iron switch (DPIC). Its function is to control single phase 2 wire circuits.

(ii) Triple pole iron clad switch (TPIC). Its function is to control 3 phase power with 3 wire system.

(iii) Triple pole iron clad switch with neutral link (TPNIC). Its function is to control 3 phase power with 4 wire system.

### DISTRIBUTION BOARD (DB)

The output of the main switch is given to DB where the consumer's load branches into smaller ones forming subcircuits. The maximum number of points connected to one subcircuit should not exceed ten. Each subcircuit is electrically isolated from the other inside the DB (refer Fig. 7.11).

### Fuse

The main purpose of the fuse is to isolate the circuit in the event of any short-circuit or overloading or fault. It is always provided in the phase or live wire (not on neutral) and is held in fuse carrier (porcelain). Whenever excessive current flows or a fault occurs, the fuse wire gets heated, it melts and breaks the circuit. Hence fuse should have low melting point. The materials used for fuse are copper, zinc, lead, tin, aluminium and alloys of tin and lead. Once fuse melts it has to be replaced.

**Socket outlet**

These are of either two pin or three pin type and have 2A, 5A, 15A ratings. These are used for temporary electrical connections like tape recorder, table lamp etc.

**Flexible cords**

These are used as connecting wires for connecting radio, tape recorder, lamps etc., and consists of large number of fine wires to form the conductor. Plastic can be used to insulate these cords. The advantage of cords is that they are flexible.

**Plug**

Supply to the appliances like radio, table fan etc., can be fed from socket outlets through plugs and flexible cords. The plugs are available in two types, namely, (i)Two pin types (ii)Three pin plugs (the third pin is used to earth the appliance). The available current rating of plugs are 5A and 15A.

**Ceiling rose**

Ceiling rose consists of two parts, namely, base and cover, both made of porcelain or bakelite. The tubelight, ceiling fan etc. are connected to supply through flexible cords and ceiling rose. The normal voltage rating of ceiling rose is 250V.

**Lamp holder**

The lamp holder not only connects the lamps to the supply but also gives support to them. Lamp holders are normally available with bakelite exterior and porcelain interior or brass exterior with porcelain interior.

These lamp holders are of four types. They are listed below:

(i) Batten holder (ii) Pendant holder (iii) Angle holder (iv) Bracket holder

**Cables**

The various cables commonly used for domestic wiring are as follows:

1. Vulcanised Indian Rubber (VIR) insulated cables.
2. Polyvinyl Chloride insulated cables (PVC).
3. Tough Rubber Sheathed cable (TRS).
4. Cab Tyre Sheathed Cable (CTS).
5. Lead Sheathed Cable.
6. Weather Proof Cable.

These cables are made of copper or aluminium surrounded by insulation and a sheath. The cross sectional area of the cable conductor is determined by the current the

carrying capacity and the thickness of insulation is determined by the operating voltage.

## 7.2. RATINGS OF WIRING MATERIALS

| | |
|---|---|
| 1. Sockets | 15A, 3 pin, 250V<br>5A, 3 pin, 250V |
| 2. Single pole switches | 5A, 250V<br>15a, 250V |
| 3. Two way switches | 5A, 250V |
| 4. Holders | Batten holder<br>Pendent holder<br>(Made of brass or bakelite) |
| 5. Ceiling Roses (5A, 250V, 2 plate) | |
| 6. Wooden round blocks | |
| 7. Screws and wooden plugs | |
| 8. ICDB (Iron clad Distribution Box) | 15A, 250V, one way<br>15A, 250V, two way. |
| 9. DPIC switch (Double Pole Iron Clad) | 250V, 5A<br>250V, 15A |
| 10. Earth wire | 14 SWG (copper, aluminium or G.I. wire) |

The above mentioned accessories are used in all the types of wiring system. However the following accessories are used for particular type of wiring system only.

11. For the conduit wiring systems the additional accessories used are listed below:
    1. Junction boxes (1 to 4 ways)
    2. Cast iron boxes covered with bakelite
    3. Elbows, bends and tees
    4. Saddles
    5. Earth clips
    6. Hooks
    7. Back entry terminal box
    8. GI conduit

**Cables:** VIR cables and PVC cables are used for all types of wiring except for lead sheathed wiring system. For TRS wiring system, TRS cables are used. For CTS, wiring system, CTS cables are used. For lead sheathed wiring system, lead sheathed cables are used.

In addition to above, porcelain cleats are used for cleat wiring, wooden casing is used for casing wiring, wooden boards and wooden hexagonal blocks are used for all types of wiring systems except conduit wiring systems. TW battens and joint clips are used for lead sheathed, tough rubber sheathed or cab tyre sheathed wiring.

**Abbreviations used:**

| | | |
|---|---|---|
| ICDB | – | Iron Clad Distribution Box |
| DPIC | – | Double Pole Iron Clad |
| G.I. | – | Galvanised Iron |
| SWG | – | Standard Wire Gauge |
| VIR cable | – | Vulcanised Indian Rubber |
| PVC cable | – | Polyvinyl Chloride |
| TRS | – | Tough Rubber Sheathed |
| CTS | – | Cab Tyre Sheathed |
| TW | – | Teak Wood |
| MS | – | Mild Steel |

## 7.3. TYPES OF WIRING

The following are the different types of wiring system used for domestic electrical installation.

1. Cleat wiring system
2. Wooden casing-capping wiring system
3. PVC wiring or CTS or TRS wiring system
4. Lead sheathed wiring system
5. Conduit wiring system.

### Cleat wiring system

The cleat wiring system is very cheap and can be laid very easily. The disadvantage of this wiring system is that its life is short as there is no continuous base for the wires. It is not used for domestic wiring. Instead it is used in industries and workgroups for temporary wirings. This type of wiring uses porcelain cleats. The base of the cleat is grooved to accommodate the cables and the cap is placed on it. The base and cap assembly is screwed with wooden plugs (which are already cemented in the wall). The distance between the cleats vary from 0.3 m to 0.6 m. The arrangement is shown in Fig. 7.1.

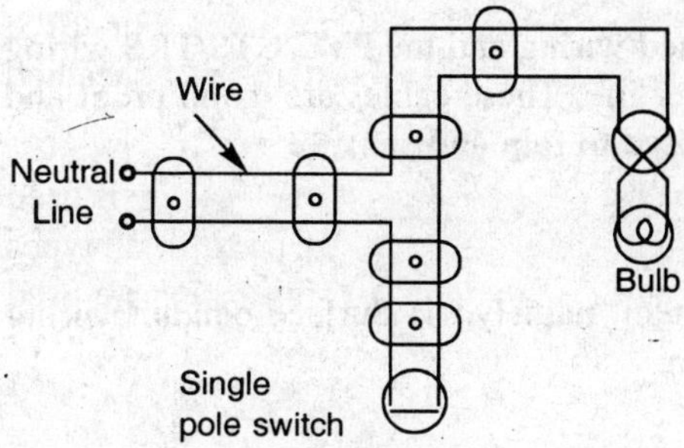


Fig. 7.1

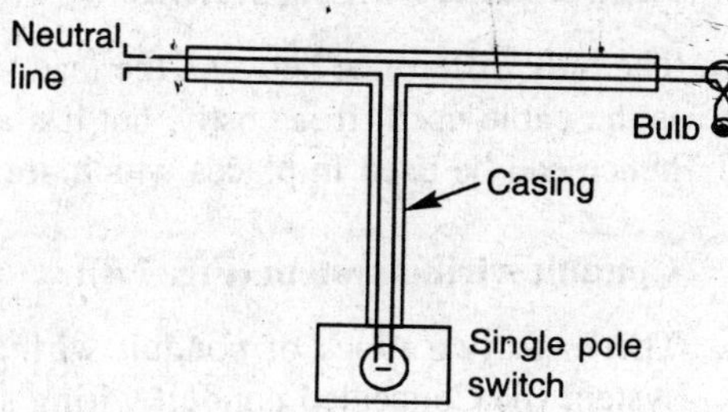


Fig. 7.2

**Wooden casing capping wiring system**

The arrangement of wooden casing capping wiring system is shown in Fig. 7.2. This wiring is widely used for domestic purposes as it has longer life due to covered cables. The disadvantage is that it is costly. The cables are housed in casing. The casing is screwed to the wooden plugs which are cemented in the wall. The cables used are either PVC or VIR. After placing the cable in the casing it is covered with the help of rectangular wooden strip called capping.

To keep the back of casing dry, it is usually placed about 0.4 cm above the wall with the help of porcelain pieces.

**PVC wiring or CTS or TRS wiring**

The PVC or CTS or TRS wiring system is also called batten wiring system as it employs teak wood batten. Depending upon the type of cable used, for example if PVC cable is used it is called PVC wiring system; if cab tyre sheathed or tough rubber sheathed cable is used it is called CTS or TRS wiring system. The battens are fixed with the clips and then screwed to the walls with the help of wooden plugs and screws. The distance between the clips usually vary from 6 to 15 cm. The arrangement is as shown in Fig. 7.3.

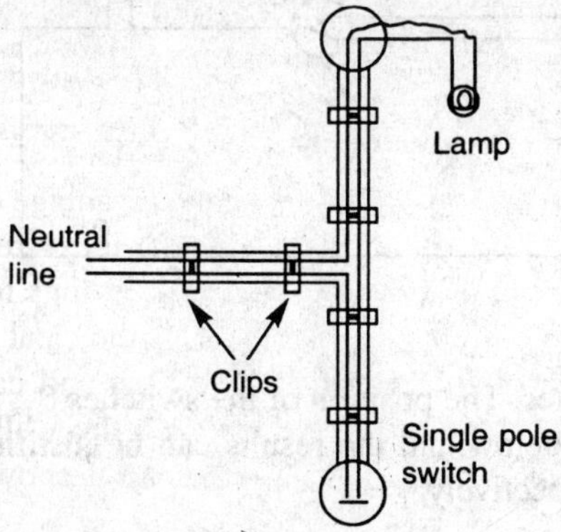


Fig. 7.3

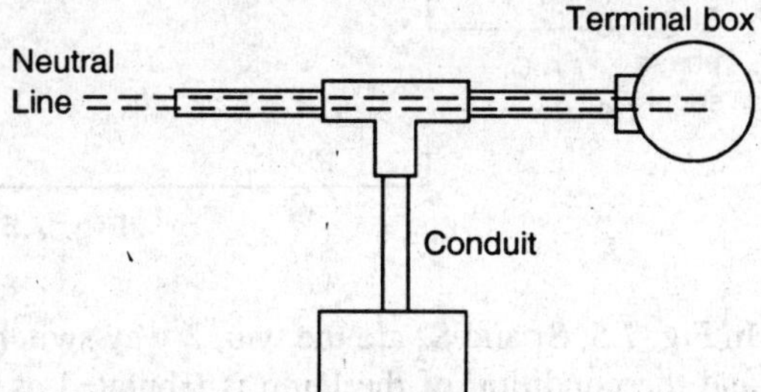


Fig. 7.4

**Lead sheathed wiring system**

The only difference between the lead sheathed wiring and the PVC/CTS/TRS wiring is the cable used. It is costly, but has a better life. These cables are damp proof and hence can be used in places which are exposed to rain and sun.

**Conduit wiring system (Fig. 7.4):**

There are two types of conduit wiring system, namely, (i) Surface conduit wiring system (ii) Concealed conduit wiring system.

**Surface conduit wiring system**

Surface conduit wiring system is very costly. Since it is safer wiring (conduit gives protection against mechanical damage, fire or dampness) and has longer life, it is preferred in factories and important buildings. Since the conduit is made of conducting material earthing is essential. The cables used are either PVC or VIR. The GI conduit is fixed on the wall with the help of saddles and gutties. A snake wire (thin steel or GI wire) is used to draw the cables inside the conduits.

**Concealed conduit wiring system:**

Concealed conduit wiring system is the same as that of the surface conduit wiring system. The only difference is that the conduits are kept inside the ceiling and the walls (during the construction of building before plastering). Once the plastering is done, the conduit will not be visible hence the name is given as concealed conduit wiring system. Though it is very costly, it is still preferred for posh appearance.

## 7.4. STAIR CASE WIRING

The purpose of stair case wiring is, to enable the user to switch on and switch off lights from more than one point. This can be achieved by using two, 2-way switches. the arrangement of control of lamp using two, 2-way switches is as shown in Fig. 7.5.

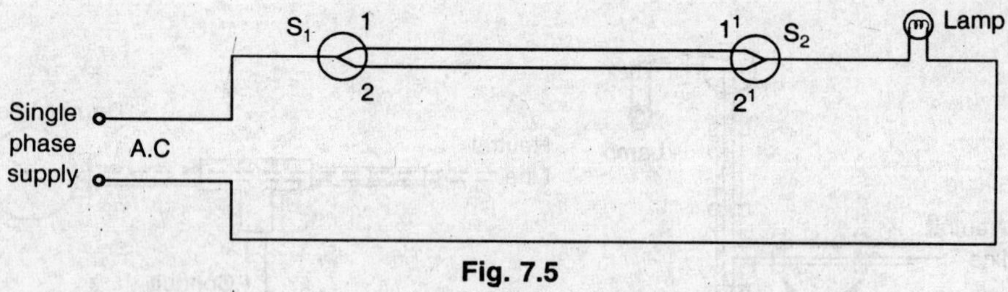


**Fig. 7.5**

In Fig. 7.5, $S_1$ and $S_2$ are the two, 2-way switches. The position of the switches $S_1$, $S_2$ and the condition of the lamp is tabulated as below and the results can be justified with the help of Figs. 7.6, 7.7, 7.8 and 7.9 respectively.

| *Position of '$S_1$'* | *Position of '$S_2$'* | *Condition of Lamp* |
|---|---|---|
| 1 | $1^1$ | ON |
| 1 | $2^1$ | OFF |
| 2 | $2^1$ | ON |
| 2 | $1^1$ | OFF |

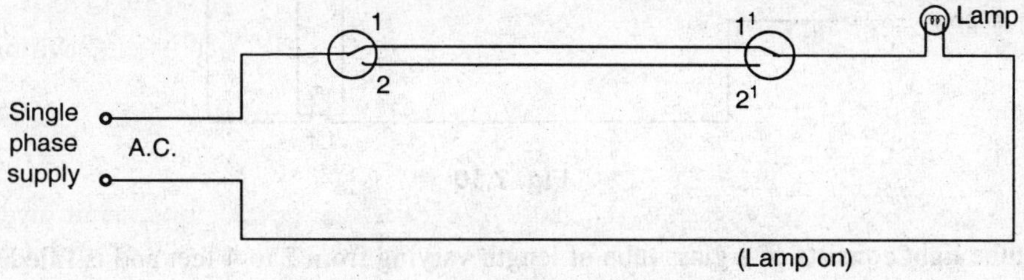


Fig. 7.6

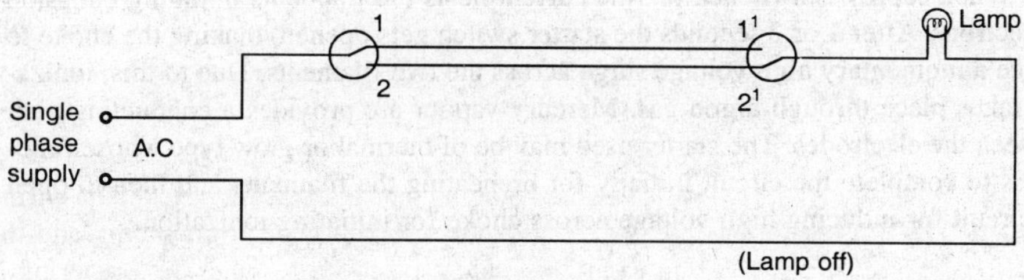


Fig. 7.7

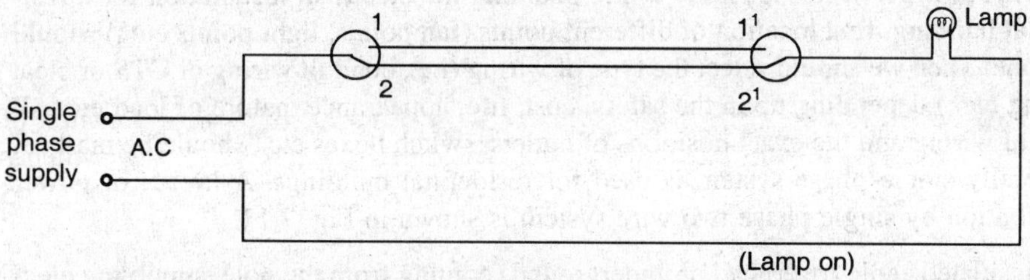


Fig. 7.8

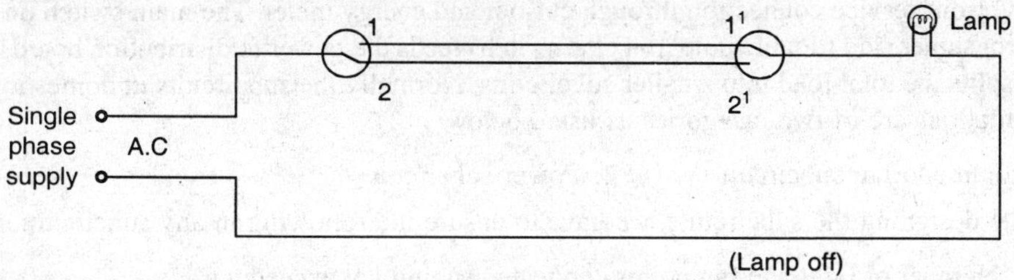


Fig. 7.9

## 7.5. FLUORESCENT TUBE WIRING

The circuit is shown in Fig. 7.10

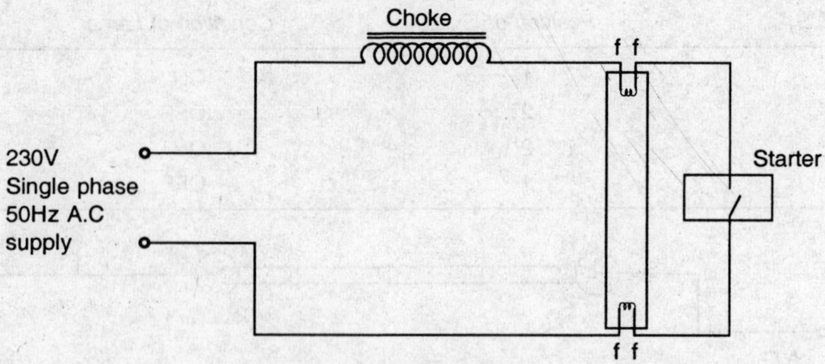


Fig. 7.10

The tube light consists of a glass tube of length varying from 2 to 4 feet and is filled with low pressure argon gas and a drop of mercury. Initially, starter is in closed position. When supply is switched on, the current heats the filaments initiating emission of electrons. After 1 or 2 seconds the starter switch gets opened, making the choke to induce a momentary high voltage surge across the two filaments. Due to this, ionization takes place through argon gas. Mercury vapour arc provides a conducting path between the electrodes. The starter used may be of thermal or glow type whose function is to complete the circuit initially for preheating the filaments and then to open the circuit for inducing high voltage across choke for initiating ionization.

## 7.6. SIMPLE DOMESTIC WIRING LAYOUT (Fig. 7.11)

The layout is given in Fig. 7.11. While planning the electrical installation for a residential building, first location of different points (fan points, light points etc.,) should be done. Then we should select the type of wiring (i.e., conduit wiring or CTS or cleat wiring etc.,) depending upon the safety, cost, life, appearance, nature of load etc. All runs of wiring and the exact positions of outlets, switch boxes etc., should be marked. Generally single phase system is used for residential buildings. A layout of power distribution by single phase two wire system is shown in Fig. 7.11.

The insulated cable (overhead or underground) coming from the pole, supplying electrical power to the consumer's terminal is called 'service connection'. Power is fed to DPIC from service connection through cut-out and energy meter. The main switch on the consumer side (double pole iron clad switch) feeds the power to distribution board. DB splits the total load into smaller subcircuits. Normally the subcircuits in domestic installations are of two categories as listed below:

1. Light and fan subcircuit
2. Power subcircuit

While designing the subcircuits, we have to ensure the following in any subcircuit:

(i) Number of light and fan points connected should not exceed ten.
(ii) The total load connected should not be more than 800 watts.
(iii) The switches used for fans and light points should be of 5Amp rating.
(iv) Socket outlets used should also be of 5Amp rating.

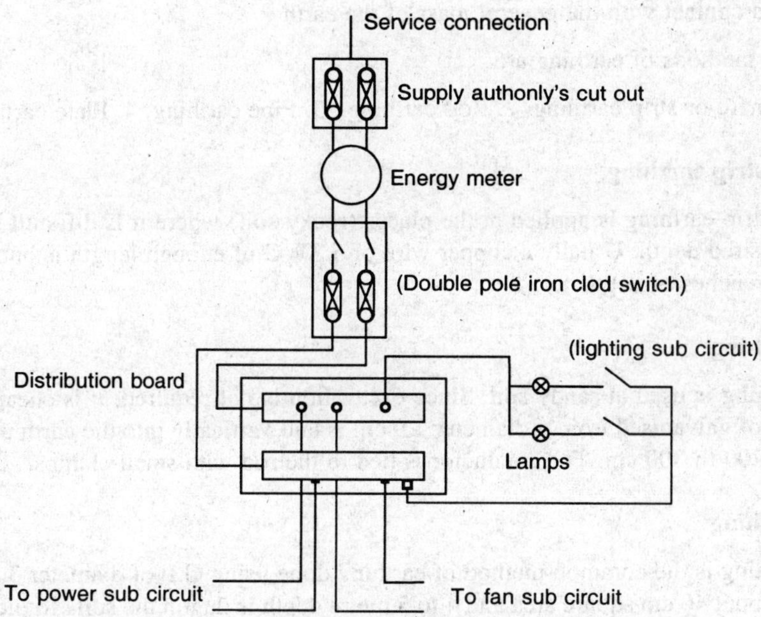


Fig. 7.11

## 7.7. EARTHING

The purpose of earthing is to avoid electric shock to human body. Technically, it is to ensure that all parts of the system other than live parts shall be at earth potential.

According to Indian Electricity Rule No.61 the following equipments are to be connected to earth.

(i) Metal frame of motors, generators and other metallic parts of equipment are to be earthed.

(ii) Earth terminals of the three pin lighting and power plug socket should be earthed.

(iii) The metal casing of the portable apparatus like heater, electric iron, refrigerator, hair drier etc., should be earthed.

(iv) All metal parts of the electrical installation such as metal conduits, light fittings, iron clad main switches, iron clad distribution, cable sheathes etc., should be earthed.

The conductors used for earthing purposes are copper or galvanised iron wire. However since the conductor used for earthing must have high conductivity, copper is preferred. The conductor used should have sufficient diameter in order to carry the fault current safely. The earthing conductor should be installed in such a way that it should not get damaged or cut accidentally. It can be fixed to the equipment with the help of clamps and saddles. When fuses are used, the earth loop impedance should be low enough so as to allow 3 times the current on short circuit and 1.5 times the operating current when circuit breakers are used. The earth electrode should make very good contact with the general mass of the earth.

Different methods of earthing are:

1. Wire or strip earthing, 2. Rod earthing, 3. Pipe earthing, 4. Plate earthing

### Wire or strip earthing

Wire or strip earthing is applied at the places (rocky soil) where it is difficult to dig pits of desired depth. Usually a copper wire of 5 SWG of enough length is buried in horizon trenches of depth.

### Rod earthing

Rod earthing is used at sandy soil. Since excavation is not required, it is cheaper. A solid rod of galvanised iron of diameter 1.9 cm is laid vertically into the earth up to a depth of 200 to 300 cm. The conductor is tied to the rod with small clamps.

### Pipe earthing

Pipe earthing is the common method of earthing done using G.I. of diameter 3.8 cm. A pit of about 40 cm square area and 4 to 5 metre depth is dug in the soil. To increase the dampness and moisture, charcoal and salt are filled in the pit in alternate layers up to about two metres from bottom. Earth pipe can be protected from mechanical damage by covering it with cement concrete work. A funnel with mesh can also be provided to pour water.

### Plate earthing

In the plate earthing a pit of about 3 metres depth is dug. The earth electrode used may be copper plate having a dimension 60 cm × 60 cm × 3.18 mm. (In case of G.I. plate, the dimension is 60 cm × 60 cm × 6.36 mm). After placing the electrode in the pit, layers of charcoal and salt are used to fill the space around it. The electrode can be connected to G.I. pipe of 12.7 mm diameter for carrying G.I. earthwire. The pit is covered with an iron plate for periodic check-up. To increase moisture and dampness a pipe is provided for carrying water.

## 7.8. INDIAN ELECTRICITY RULES

The Indian Electricity Rules have been framed by a competent body to ensure a satisfactory operation of equipment and apparatus and also to safeguard the consumers from electric shocks.

Here an effort has been made to discuss some of the important I.E. rules.

**Rule No. 29**: All electric supply lines and apparatus shall be sufficient in power and size and of sufficient mechanical strength for the work they may be required to do, and so far as is practicable, shall be constructed, installed, protected, worked and maintained in accordance with standards for the Indian Standards Institutions as to prevent danger.

**Rule No. 30**: Service lines placed by the supplier on the premises of a consumer which are underground or which are accessible shall be so insulated and protected by the supplier as to be secured under all ordinary conditions against electrical, mechanical, chemical or other injury to the insulation. The consumer shall take precautions for the safe custody of the equipment of his premises belonging to the supplier and also ensure that the installations under his control is maintained in a safe condition.

**Rule No. 31**: The supplier shall provide a suitable cutout in each conductor of every service line other than the earthed neutral conductor.

**Rule No. 33**: The consumer shall take all reasonable precautions to prevent mechanical damage to the earthed terminal and its lead belonging to the supplier.

**Rule No. 34**: Where bare conductors are used in a building, the owner of such conductors shall

(i) ensure that they are inaccessible

(ii) provide switches for rendering them dead whenever necessary.

**Rule No. 45**: No electrical installation, alterations, repairs (except such replacement of lamps, fans, fuses, switches which does not alter the capacity) shall be carried out except by an electric contractor licensed in this behalf by the State Govt.

**Rule No. 46**: Every installation shall be periodically inspected and checked at intervals not exceeding five years either by Inspector or by the supplier.

**Rule No. 56**: A supplier may affix seal or cutout to any meter or apparatus placed upon as consumer's premises and no person other than the supplier shall break any such seal.

**Rule No. 77:** No conductor of an overhead line, including services lines, erected across a street shall at any part thereof be at a height less than 19 feet for low and medium voltages and 20 feet for high voltages.

When erected along a street, the minimum ground clearance shall be 18 feet for low and medium voltages 19 feet for high voltages.

**Rule No. 79**: Clearance from buildings of low and medium voltage lines and service lines: for flat roof.

(i) when the line passes above the building a vertical clearance of (2.439 m) or 8 feet from the highest point and

(ii) when the line passes adjacent to the building a horizontal clearance of (1.219 m) or 4 feet from the nearest point.

**Rule No. 80**: Clearance from buildings of high and extra high voltage lines is around 3.658m or 12 ft. and plus 1 foot for every additional 33 KV.

**Rule No. 85**: The maximum intervals between supports shall not not exceed 220 ft for overhead lines carrying low or medium voltages.

**Rule No. 87**: Lines crossing or approaching each other: Where an overhead line crosses or is in proximity to any telecommunication line, the owner of the overhead line shall protect it in a manner laid down in the code of practice of the power and telecommunication coordination committee.

**Rule No. 89**: No service line or tapping shall be taken off from an overhead line except at a point of support.

## HIGHLIGHTS

- The important accessories of domestic wiring systems are switches, main switch, distribution board, fuse, socket, flexible cord, plug, ceiling rose, lamp holder, cables. etc.
- The purpose of main switch is to control all the subcircuits provided in the building.
- The output of main switch is given to distribution board where the consumer's load branches into smaller ones forming subcircuits.
- **Abbrevations**

  ICDB – Iron clad distribution box

  DPIC – Double pole iron clad switch

  G.I. – Galvanised iron

  SWG – Standard wire gauge

  VIP – Vulcanised Indian Rubber

  PVC – Polyvinyl chloride

  TRS – Tough rubber sheathed

  CTD – Cab tyre sheathed

  TW – Teak wood

  MS – Mild steel
- The equipment that are to be connected to earth are metal frame of motors, generators; earth terminal of three pin lighting and power plug socket; metal casing of all portable apparatus; metal parts of electric installations.

## REVIEW QUESTIONS

1. What are the various wiring materials and accessories used in domestic wiring?
2. What are the different types of cables used in domestic wiring?
3. Give the ratings of different wiring materials used in domestic wiring.
4. Explain the different types of wiring system.
5. Explain how a stair case wiring is done.
6. Explain a simple domestic wiring layout.
7. What are the different methods of earthing? Explain them briefly?
8. Specify some of the relevant Indian Electricity Rules.

## TWO MARKS QUESTIONS AND ANSWERS

1. *What are the three types of iron clad switches ?*

    1. Double pole iron clad switch (to control single phase circuit)
    2. Triple pole iron clad switch (to control three phase 3 wire circuit)
    3. Triple pole iron clad switch with neutral link (to control three phase 4 wire circuit)

2. *What is the purpose of a fuse ?*

    The main purpose of a fuse is to isolate the circuit in the event of any short-circuit or overloading or fault.

3. *What are the types of lamp holder ?*

    1. Batten holder
    2. Pendant holder
    3. Angle holder
    4. Bracket holder

4. *What is a cable ?*

    A cable is made of copper or aluminium surrounded by insulation and sheath. The cross sectional area of the cable depends on the current capacity and the thickness of insulation depends upon the operating voltage.

5. *What are the various cables used for domestic wiring ?*

    1. Vulcanised Indian rubber insulated cables
    2. Polyvinyl chloride insulated cables
    3. Tough rubber sheathed cable
    4. Cab tyre sheathed cable
    5. Lead sheathed cable
    6. Weather proof cable

6. *What are the accessories used in domestic wiring ?*

    Switches, distribution board, fuse, socket outlet, flexible cords, plug, ceiling rose, lamp holders, cables etc.

7. *Expand the following abbreviations.*

    ICDB – Iron clad distribution box

    DPIC – Double pole iron clad

    SWG – Standard wire gauge

    TRS cable – Tough Rubber Sheathed cable

8. *What are the different types of wiring ?*

    1. Cleat wiring
    2. Wooden casing-capping wiring
    3. PVC/CTS/TRS wiring
    4. Lead sheathed wiring
    5. Conduit wiring

9. *List five additional accessories used for conduit wiring.*
    1. Junction boxes
    2. Elbows, bends and tees
    3. Saddles
    4. Earth clips
    5. Hooks
10. *What are the methods of earthing ?*
    1. Wire or strip earthing
    2. Rod earthing
    3. Pipe earthing
    4. Plate earthing.

Chapter 8

# GENERATION, TRANSMISSION AND DISTRIBUTION OF ELECTRICAL ENERGY

The electrical energy is generated using the thermal, hydel, nuclear energies. Diesel is also used to generate the electrical energy. The electrical energy can be easily converted from one form to other form. (A heater converts electrical energy into heat energy. A motor converts the electrical energy into mechanical energy. An electrical bulb converts the electrical energy into light energy.) The electrical energy can be transmitted from the generating station to the load end with the help of transmission lines (conductors). The electrical energy can be controlled easily with the help of controlling devices.

The three important components of electrical supply systems are listed below:

(i) Generation
(ii) Transmission
(iii) Distribution

**Generation of electric energy**

The various methods employed in generating electric energy are listed below.

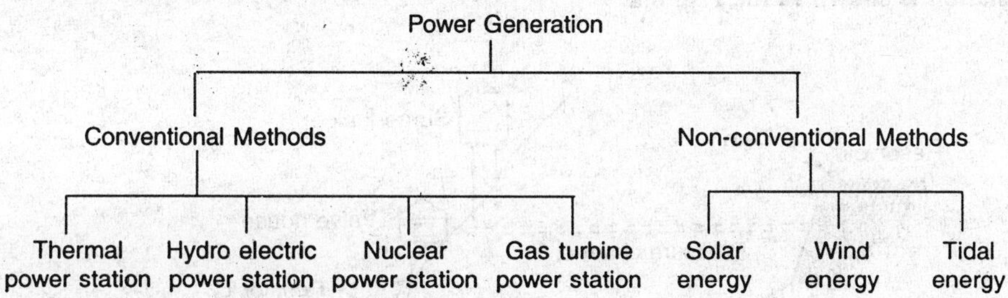


**Thermal power station:** In the thermal power station, heat energy is converted into electrical energy. The heat generated due to the combustion of coal is used to produce the steam. This steam is used to operate a steam turbine which in turn drives an alternator. The alternator converts the mechanical energy of the turbine into the electrical energy. The voltage generated in the alternator is stepped up with the help of a step-up transformer and is then used for transmission purposes.

The schematic diagram of a thermal power station is shown in Fig. 8.1.

The steam after giving the heat energy to the turbine is sent to condenser where it gets condensed and reused as feedwater to the boiler. The thermal efficiency of boiler can be improved by using the feed water from a water source like river after its chemical treatment in the water treatment plant.

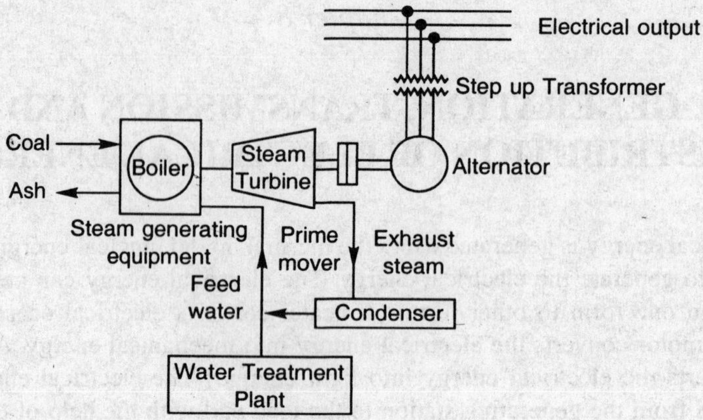


Fig. 8.1

### Hydro electric power station

In the hydro electric power station, the potential energy of water head is used to generate electrical energy. The water head is created by constructing a dam across a river. The water from the dam is taken to water turbine through valve house with the help of steel pipe known as penstock. The surge tank protects the penstock from bursting, in case the turbine gates suddenly gets closed. The turbine converts hydraulic energy into mechanical energy. The alternator connected to the turbine converts the mechanical energy into electrical energy. The schematic of hydroelectric power station is shown in the Fig. 8.2.

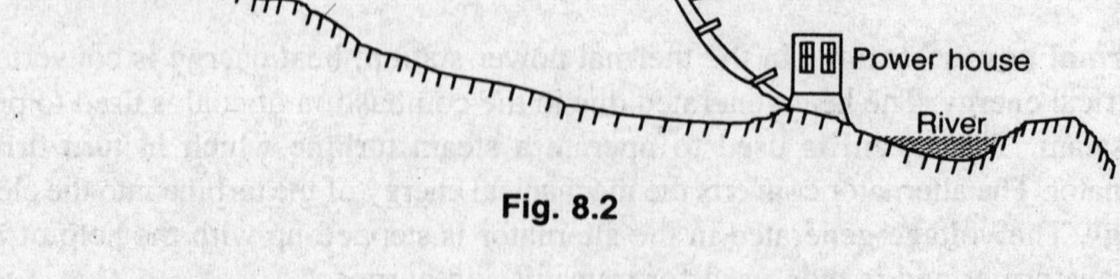


Fig. 8.2

### Nuclear power station

In the nuclear power station, nuclear energy is converted into electrical energy. The heat energy released during nuclear fission (breaking up of nuclei of heavy atoms like uranium, $U^{235}$ or thorium $Th^{232}$ with release of large amount of energy) is used to generate the steam. The steam thus generated is used to run the steam turbine, which converts steam energy into mechanical energy. The alternator coupled to the turbine, converts mechanical energy into electrical energy. The schematic diagram of nuclear power station is shown in the Fig. 8.3.

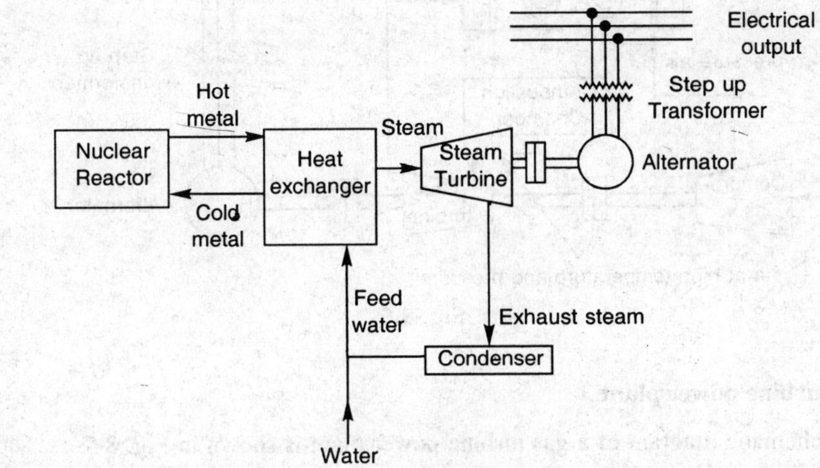


**Fig. 8.3**

The nuclear fission takes place in the nuclear reactor. The nuclear reactor consists of uranium, moderator and control rods as shown in the Fig. 8.4.

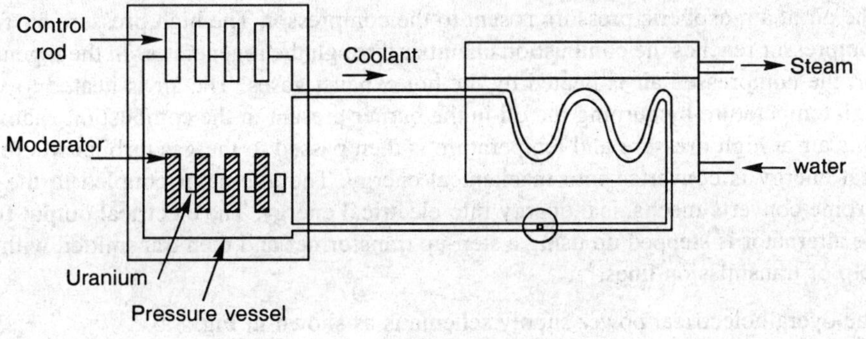


**Fig. 8.4**

The moderator (graphite) slows down the neutrons before they bombard the uranium rod. The control rods (cadmium) regulate the supply of neutrons for fission. The heat produced in the reactor during fission is carried by a coolant (sodium). The heat carried by the coolant is given up in the heat exchanger to generate steam from the water. The steam thus generated is used to drive the steam turbine. The alternator connected to the turbine converts the mechanical energy into electrical energy.

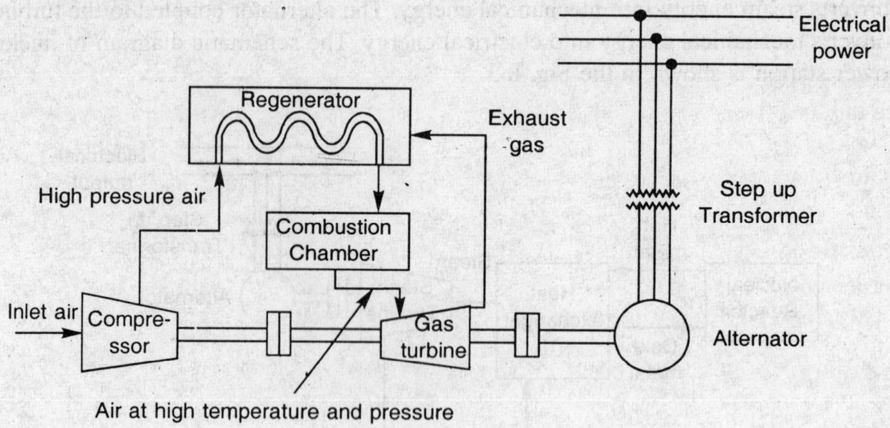


**Fig. 8.5**

### Gas turbine power plant

The schematic diagram of a gas turbine power plant is shown in Fig. 8.5.

The main components of this plant include:

(a) Compressor
(b) Combustion Chamber
(c) Gas turbine
(d) Alternator
(e) Regenerator

The air at atmospheric pressure is sent to the compressor. The high pressure air from compressor reaches the combustion chamber through the regenerator. In the regenerator, the compressed air is heated by the hot exhaust gases. The air is heated to very high temperature by burning the oil in the burner present in the combustion chamber. This air at high pressure and temperature is then passed to the gas turbine where the heat energy is converted into mechanical energy. The alternator coupled to the gas turbine converts mechanical energy into electrical energy. The electrical output from the alternator is stepped up using a step-up transformer and then transmitted with the help of transmission lines.

The overall electrical power supply scheme is as shown in Fig. 8.6.

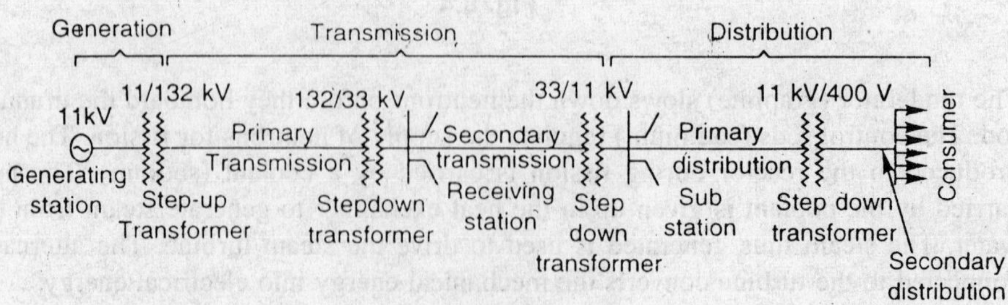


**Fig. 8.6**

**Transmission of electrical energy**

The electrical power is generated in the generating station using thermal or hydel or nuclear energies. The generated voltage may be of the magnitude 6kV/11kV/33kV. Since the location of generating stations are far away from the consumers, the generated voltage has to be transmitted to the consumer end. This process incurs lot of transmission losses. To reduce the loss during transmission (Transmission loss $\propto \frac{1}{(kV)^2}$ ) the generated voltage is stepped up to 132 kV or more with the help of a 3 phase step-up transformer. During the primary transmission, the electrical power at 132 kV is transmitted to the receiving station at the city outskirts with the help of 3 phase 3 wire system. At the receiving station, the voltage (132 kV) is stepped down to 33 kV with the help of step down transformer.

During the secondary transmission, electrical power is transmitted from receiving station to various substations located at the strategic locations in the city. At the substations, the voltage in stepped down to 11 kV and is supplied to bulk consumers. The voltage is further stepped down to 400V and is supplied to the domestic consumers.

The transmission of electrical power can be carried out by means of overhead lines or underground cables. The overhead line transmission consists of the following components:

(a) Poles or towers to support the conductors

(b) Conductors to carry the electric power

(c) Insulators to insulate the conductors from the ground

(d) Cross arms to provide support to the insulators.

The line supports used to carry the transmission lines may be wooden poles or steel poles or RCC poles or steel towers depending on the distance of transmission and the magnitude of the voltage.

The insulators employed in the overhead line transmission are listed below

(a) Pin type insulator

(b) Suspension type insulator

(c) Strain insulator

(d) Shackle insulator

The following are the commonly used conductors for the overhead line transmission.

(a) Copper

(b) Aluminium

(c) Aluminium Conductor Steel Reinforced (ACSR)

(d) Galvanised steel

(e) Cadmium copper.

Classification of overhead transmission lines.

The overhead transmission lines are classified into three categories, namely,

(a) Short transmission lines (for a transmission length upto 50 km with a line voltage < 20 kV)

(b) Medium transmission lines (for a transmission length above 50 km 150 km with a line voltage above 20 kV and below 100 kV)

(c) Long transmission lines (for a transmission length above 150 km with a line voltage above 100 kV)

**Underground cables:** Underground cables are also used for the transmission of electrical power. The following are the advantages of using underground cables.

(i) Move safe, especially in thickly populated areas

(ii) Less affected by storms and lightning

The underground cable consists of one or more conductors surrounded by insulation and a protecting cover.

The various insulating materials used in cables are as listed below:

(a) Rubber

(b) Vulcanised India Rubber

(c) Impregnated Paper

(d) Varnished Cambric

(e) Polyvinyl Chloride (PVC).

**Classification of cables:** Depending on the operating voltage, the cables are classified as follows:

| | | |
|---|---|---|
| 1000V | — | Low tension cables |
| 1000V to 11 kV/22kV | — | High tension cables |
| 22 kV to 33 kV | — | Supertension cables |
| 33 kV to 66 kV/132 kV | — | Extra high tension cables |
| Above 132 kV | — | Extra super voltage cable. |

**Distribution of electrical energy**

In the distribution system, the electrical energy is distributed to various consumers. The important components of a distribution system includes (i) feeders (a conductor which connects the sub-station to the area where electrical energy has to be distributed) (ii) distributor (a conductor from which tappings are taken for supply to the consumers) and (iii) service mains (a case which connects the distributor to the consumers).

The classification of distribution system is presented below.

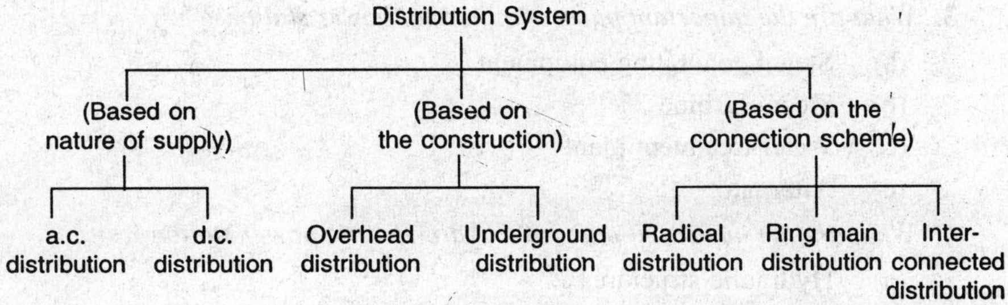


In the a.c. distribution system, the electrical power is distributed using a 3 phase, 3 wire system (11 kV/6.6 kV, primary distribution) or using a 3 phase, 4 wire system (400/230V, secondary distribution). In the d.c. distribution system, the a.c. electrical power is converted into d.c. power and then distributed in the form of 2-wire/3-wire system.

The overhead distribution system employs wooden/concrete/steel poles to carry the distribution transformers and the conductors. Whereas the underground distribution system uses cables, conduits under the earth surface.

The radical distribution system is the simplest distribution circuit. It causes serious fluctuations in the voltage for the consumer at the far end of the distributor. This problem is allievated to some extent in the ring main distribution system. In the case of inter-connected system, the feeder ring is energised by two or more than two sub-stations.

## REVIEW QUESTIONS

1. Explain how the electrical energy is generated in thermal power stations?
2. Write a short note on hydro electric power station.
3. Explain how the electrical energy is generated in the nuclear power stations?
4. Write a short note on:

   (a) Electrical energy transmission (b) Electrical distribution energy.

## TWO MARKS QUESTIONS WITH ANSWERS

1. *What are the conventional ways of generating electrical power ?*

   (a) Thermal power station

   (b) Hydro electric power station

   (c) Nuclear power station

   (d) Gas turbine power station

2. *Give the different non-conventional energy sources for generating electrical power.*

   (a) Solar energy

   (b) Wind energy

   (c) Tidal energy

3. *What are the important parts of a thermal power station ?*
   - (a) Steam generating equipment
   - (b) Steam turbine
   - (c) Water treatment plant
   - (d) Alternator
4. *What are the important parts of a hydro electric power station ?*
   - (a) Hydraulic structures
   - (b) Water turbines
   - (c) alternator
5. *What are the important parts of a nuclear power station ?*
   - (a) Nuclear reactor
   - (b) Heat exchanger
   - (c) Water treatment plant
   - (d) Steam turbine
   - (e) Alternator
6. *What are the important parts of a gas turbine power plant ?*
   - (a) Compressor
   - (b) Combustion Chamber
   - (c) Gas turbine
   - (d) Regenerator
   - (e) Alternator
7. What are the important components of overhead line transmission?
   - (a) Conductors
   - (b) Poles/towers
   - (c) Insulators
   - (d) Cross arms
8. *What is meant by ACSR conductor ?*

   ACSR means "Aluminium Conductor Steel Reinforced" conductor.
9. *List the different types of insulators used in the overhead line transmission.*
   - (a) Pin type insulator
   - (b) Suspension type insulator
   - (c) Strain insulator
   - (d) Shackle insulator
10. *What are the different types of insulator used in cables ?*
    - (a) Rubber
    - (b) Vulcanised India Rubber
    - (c) Impregnated paper
    - (d) Varnished Cambric
    - (e) Polyvinyl Chloride (PVC)

# Chapter 9

# ELECTRONIC CIRCUIT COMPONENTS

Any complicated electronic circuit essentially consists of two basic components, namely, (i) passive components and (ii) active components. These electronic components can further be classified as follows:

## ELECTRONIC COMPONENTS

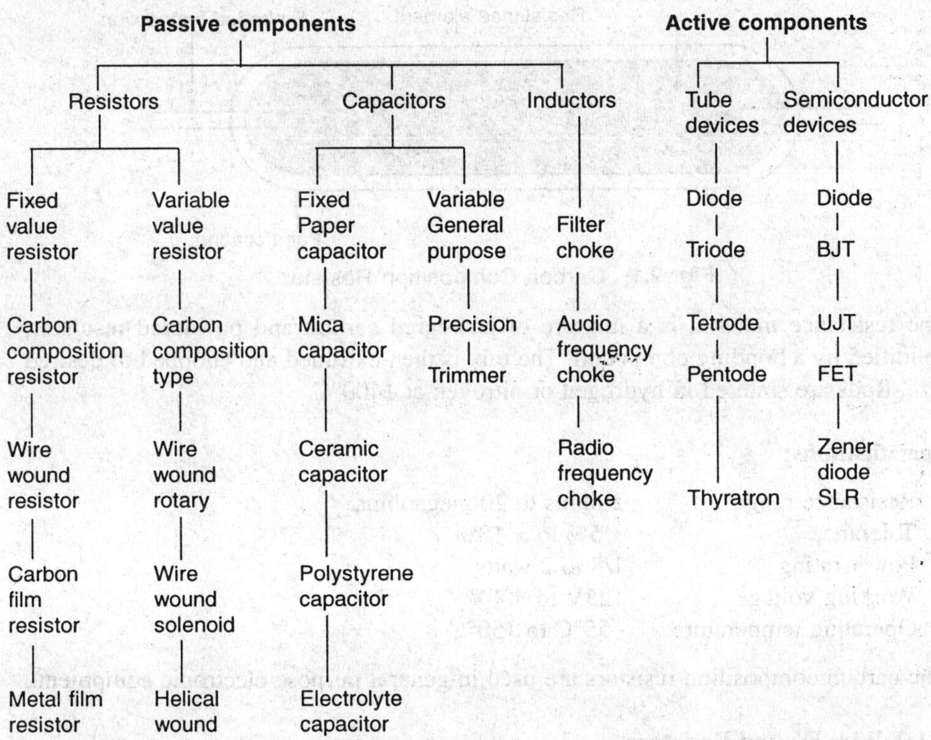


## 9.1. RESISTORS

The resistors are integral part of electronic circuits. Resistance is the ability of a material to oppose the current. Each material has got some resistance. The resistance of the material depends upon its shape, size and temperature. The resistance is measured in ohms. An ohm is defined as the amount of resistance that allows one ampere of current to flow when one volt is applied. Resistors are classified into two general categories: **Fixed value** and **Variable value.**

A fixed value is one whose value remains constant and cannot be varied by the user. Variable resistors are those, whose value can be varied by the user. The values can be varied by making a mechanical adjustment. There are three major types of fixed resistor:

carbon composition wire wound, carbon film and metal film resistors. Selection of resistors is made based on the ohmic value, size, shape, leads, power rating, tolerance, maximum operating voltage etc. The manufacturing process involves (1) substrate preparation (2) Preparation of resistive elements (3) Cap and terminal fitting (4) Protective coating and (5) Colour coding etc.

### 9.1.1 Carbon Composition Resistors

The carbon composition resistor consists of a resistive carbon composition material with leads embedded in its opposite ends as shown in Fig. 9.1 and the whole structure is surrounded by an insulating paint coating and moulded into a cylinder.

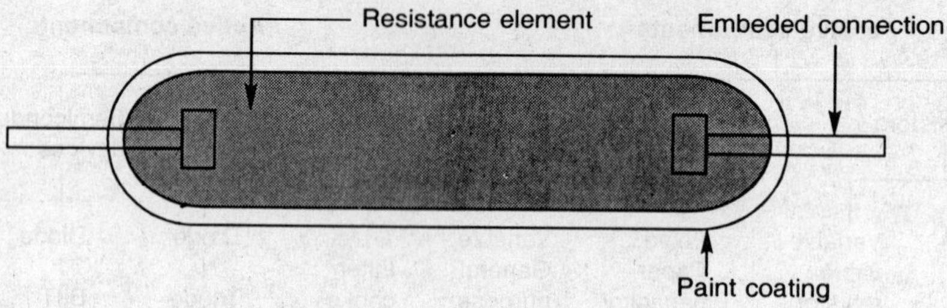


**Fig. 9.1** Carbon Composition Resistor

The resistance material is a mixture of powdered carbon and powdered insulator, solidified by a bonding compound. The mix is then extruded and chopped to desired size. Rods are sintered in hydrogen or nitrogen at 1400°C.

**Specifications:**

| | |
|---|---|
| Resistance range | 2 ohms to 20 megaohms |
| Tolerance | ± 5% to ± 10% |
| Power rating | 1/8 to 2 watts |
| Working voltage | 125V to 800V |
| Operating temperature | –55°C to 150°C |

The carbon composition resistors are used in general purpose electronic equipment.

### 9.1.2 Wire Wound Resistors

The wire wound resistors are constructed by winding a length of wire made from special alloys on an insulating cylindrical ceramic core. The wire is chosen according to its resistivity. The actual required resistance can be varied during winding by varying thickness and length of the wire. The wire is tightly wound around the ceramic substrate. The end leads are soldered to end card and the whole assembly is coated with a protective material such as enamel to prevent moisture penetration as shown in Fig. 9.2.

**Specifications:**

| | |
|---|---|
| Resistance range | 0.1 ohm to one mega ohm |

| | |
|---|---|
| Tolerance | ± 0.1% to ± 5% |
| Power rating | 10 to 75 watts |
| Working voltage | < 150V |
| Working temperature | 55 to 375°C |

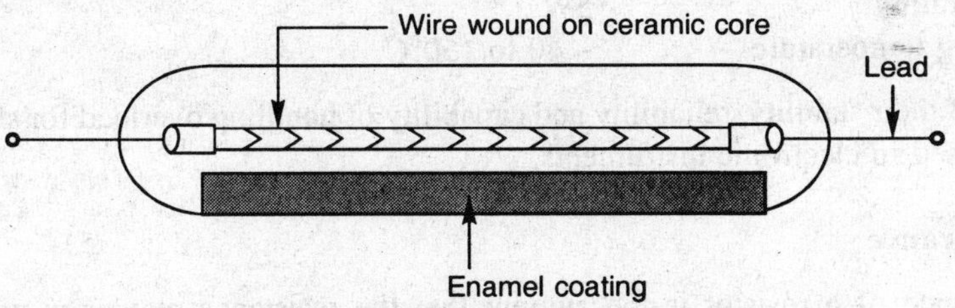


**Fig. 9.2** Wire Wound Resistor

Thes wire wound resistors are suitable for low resistance and low noise applications. They are also used when high power handling capacity is required in small size.

### 9.1.3 Carbon Film Resistors

Pure carbon is deposited on ceramic substrate by thermal decomposition of hydrocarbons at 1000°C. Lead wires are attached to the film at each end and the whole assembly is surrounded by an insulating material. The sheet resistance of the film is controlled by the thickness of carbon film. The manufacturing details are shown in Fig. 9.3.

**Fig. 9.3** Carbon Film Resistor

**Specifications:**

| | |
|---|---|
| Resistance range | 1 ohms to 10 megaohms |
| Tolerance | ± 1% to ± 5% |
| Working voltage | 500V |
| Power rating | 5 watts. |

The carbon film resistors are used in measuring instruments where close tolerances are required. They have better stability compared to carbon composition resistors. For the same resistance valve, their size is larger than carbon composition resistor. They cannot withstand electric overloads.

### 9.1.4 Metal Film Resistors

Nickel film is deposited on the ceramic substrate by electrolytic decomposition of nickel in a chemical bath containing hypophosphate. Metal film resistor value is almost stable. It varies slightly as the temperature changes.

**Specifications:**

| | |
|---|---|
| Resistance range | 0.5 to 10 kilo-ohms |
| Tolerance | ± 2% to ± 3% |
| Working voltage | 300V |
| Power rating | 5W |
| Working temperature | – 40 to 150°C. |

Because of their stability, reliability and capability of handling overload for short time they are used in electronic instruments.

### 9.1.5 Tolerance

The tolerance of a resistor is the amount that the resistance may vary within the acceptable range. For instance a 100 ohm resistance with 5% tolerance can have resistance 5% above or below the coded value.

### 9.1.6 Resistance Colour Code

In case of small sized resistance, instead of printing the value, a colour coded strip system is used to display the resistance value as shown in Fig. 9.4. Reading from left to right, the first band close to the edge gives the first digit in the numerical value. The next band marks the second digit. The third band marks the number of zeros after two digits. Fourth band gives the tolerance value. Fig. 9.5 and Table 9.1 show how a 15 kilo ohm resistance with 10% tolerance is being read.

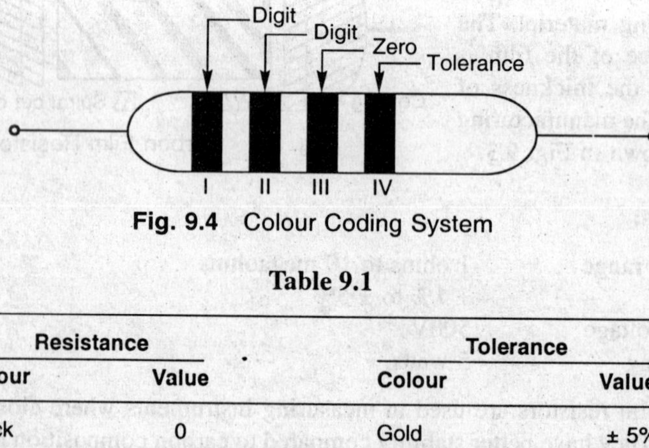


**Fig. 9.4** Colour Coding System

**Table 9.1**

| Resistance | | Tolerance | |
|---|---|---|---|
| **Colour** | **Value** | **Colour** | **Value** |
| Black | 0 | Gold | ± 5% |
| Brown | 1 | Silver | ± 10% |
| Red | 2 | No colour | ± 20% |
| Orange | 3 | | |
| Yellow | 4 | | |
| Green | 5 | | |
| Blue | 6 | | |
| Violet | 7 | | |
| Grey | 8 | | |
| White | 9 | | |

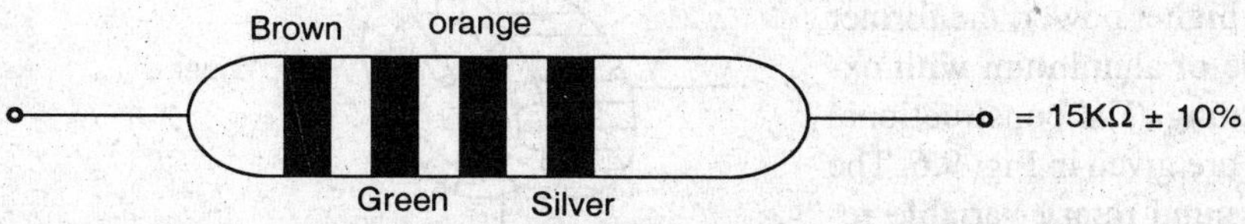


**Fig. 9.5** Colour Code Reading

## 9.2. POTENTIOMETERS

The potentiometers are variable resistors that deliver an output representing some function of an input voltage. A variable resistor can be set at any position between zero and its maximum resistance value.

The different types of variable resistor are: (1) carbon composition potentiometer and (2) wire wound resistors. The characteristics of variable resistors include (i) resistance law (relation between change in resistance and movement of wiper), (ii) tolerance (iii) insulation resistance (must be high) (iv) minimum effective resistance (v) effective angle of rotation (vi) operating torque (vii) speed of operation and (viii) life and performance under given conditions.

### 9.2.1 Carbon Composition Potentiometer

The carbon composition potentiometer can be manufactured in two ways.

**Coated film:** Here a mixture of carbon, filler (silica) and binder is coated on a ring of insulating material. The contact is of brass or phosphor bronze. The abration of the film by the sliding contact tap is minimised by processing the film surface. They are used as preset potentiometers in T.V. (brightness and contrast control), radio and also in measuring instruments.

| | |
|---|---|
| Resistance range | 100 to $10^7$ ohms |
| Power | 1/2 w to 2 1/4 w |
| Tolerance | ± 20% for 1 to $10^6$ ohm |
| | ± 30% for above $10^6$ ohm |

**Moulded tract**: The carbon composition mixture is moulded into a cavity in a plastic base, or a mixture of carbon is coated on a ring of an insulating material. Moving contact is a carbon brush and by varying position of the brush, the resistance value can be varied. ON-OFF switch also can be incorporated with this potentiometer. They are used in servo systems, computers, industrial and defence applications. Since the associated inductance and capacitance is low, these can be used for high frequency applications.

### 9.2.2 Wire Wound Rotary Variable Resistor

Here a flat strip of bakelite or paper is taken and nichrome wire is wound by maintaining proper gap between the turn. Then the strip is bent in the form of arc and fixed in a bakelite mould with end plates and screws. The sliding contact moves on one edge of the element. For dissipating higher power, the former is made of aluminium with oxide coating. The constructional details are given in Fig. 9.6. The wire wound rotary variable resistors are used in radio and T.V. receivers for volume control.

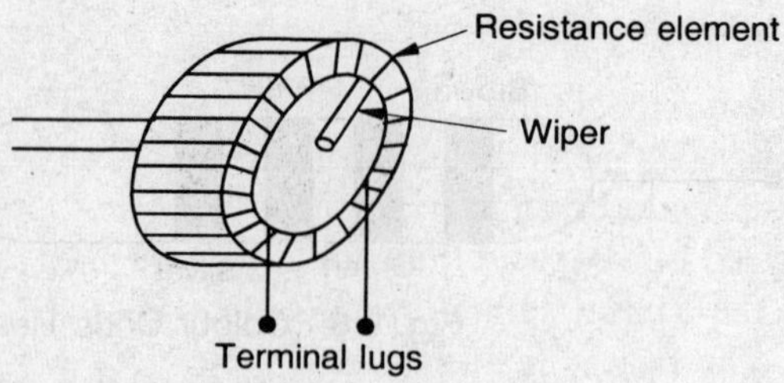


**Fig. 9.6** Wire Wound Rotary

### 9.2.3 Wire wound solenoid

These are mainly used in laboratories and industries where large power has to be dissipated. The constructional details are given in Fig. 9.7. Resistance winding of nickel copper in oxidised form is wound to the former made of ceramic or steel in the form of hexagonal or circular shape. The resistance can be varied by varying the sliding contact.

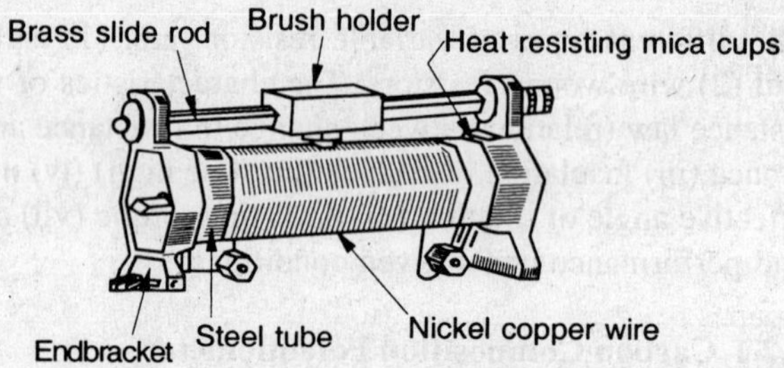


**Fig. 9.7** Wire Wound Solenoid

Copper or graphite is used as brushes. The value of resistance ranges from 500 to 10000 ohms. The current capacity ranges from 0.1 to 20 amperes.

### 9.2.4 Helical Wound Variable Resistor

Here resistance winding is wound on helical former with circular or rectangular cross section. The contacts are then welded. These resistors provide linearity and also very large angle of rotation and high resolution.

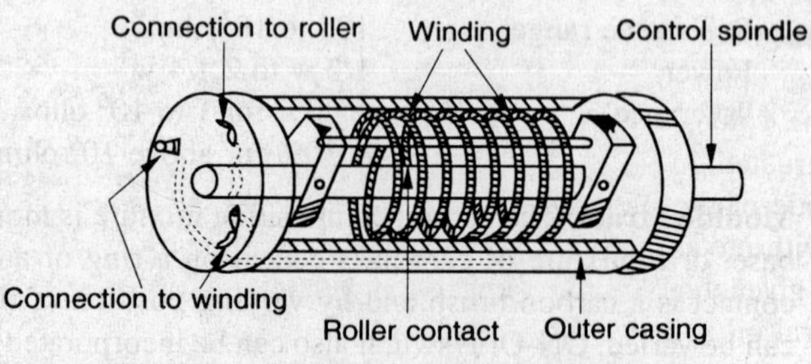


**Fig. 9.8** Helical Wound Variable Resistor

**Specifications:**

| | |
|---|---|
| Resistance | 1 to 125000 ohm |
| Power rating | 100 W to 200 W |
| Tolerance | ± 2% |
| Linearity | ± 0.5% to ± 2% |

The constructional details are shown in Fig. 9.8.

## 9.3. CAPACITORS

Capacitance is the ability to store electrical energy in an electrostatic field. It consists of basically two metal plates separated by an insulating material, such as paper, air, aluminium oxide, ceramic etc, Farad is the unit of capacitance. When a voltage source is connected to a capacitor, a current flows until the capacitor is charged. Once it is charged the current stops flowing and the capacitor voltage is equal to the source voltage. The factors that determine the capacitance are: the area of the plates, the distance between the plates and the dielectric material. Capacitance is directly proportional to the area of the plates and inversely proportional to the distance between the plates. Capacitors are generally of two types: fixed value and variable value.

**Fixed capacitors**: The various types of fixed capacitors are paper capacitor, mica capacitor, ceramic capacitor, polystyrene capacitor and electrolytic capacitor. The important characteristics to be considered while selecting fixed capacitors include value of capacitance, working voltage, power loss, power factor, loss factor, dielectric strength, leakage current, permittivity and the effect of the frequency.

### 9.3.1 Paper Capacitor

Paper capacitors are constructed by rolling paper between metal electrodes. This is called impregnated paper capacitor shown in Fig. 9.9. The thickness of the aluminium foil metal electrode used is 22 microns and that paper is 7.5 microns to 25 microns. In general, two papers are used to avoid short-circuit.

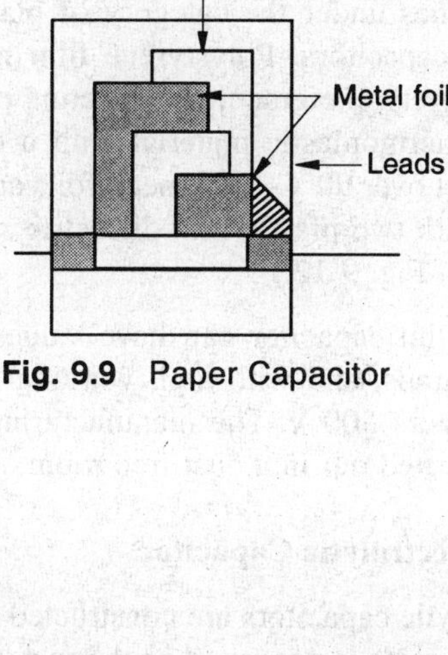


**Fig. 9.9** Paper Capacitor

The metal disc pressed on to the foil edges is followed by ceramic disc. Two leads are taken out for connection purpose. the values upto 1000 PF to 1 micro farad with the voltage rating 400 to 2000V are constructed. In metalised paper capacitor, one side of the impregnated paper is sprayed with metal to give higher capacitance for a given dimension. Impregnation with mineral oil is done to fill the pin holes in the paper.

### 9.3.2 Mica Capacitor

A mica capacitor consists of a stack of thin metal plates alternating with thin layer of mica as shown in Fig. 9.10.

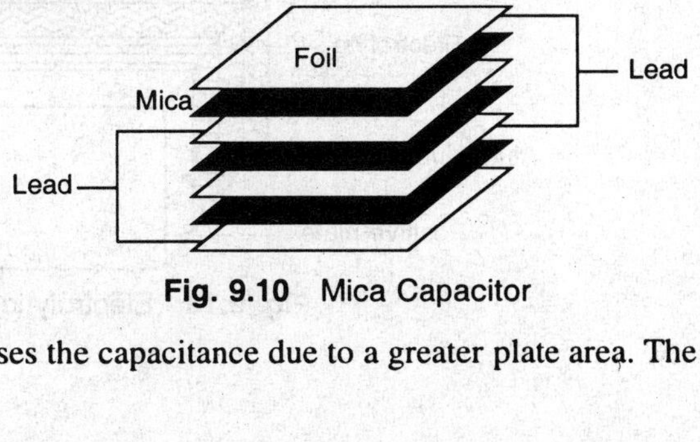


**Fig. 9.10** Mica Capacitor

The multilayer construction increases the capacitance due to a greater plate area. The whole assembly is sealed by moulding equipment. The mica capacitors value ranges from five pico farad to about 10,000 pico farad with a voltage rating of 500 V.

### 9.3.3 Ceramic Capacitor

A ceramic capacitor consists of a ceramic dielectric on which a thin metallic film is fixed at a high temperature. The terminal leads are attached to the electrodes by a pressure contact or by soldering as shown in Fig. 9.11.

Ceramic capacitors are encapsulated to protect the dielectric from the environment and to insulate the capacitor. They have very low leakage currents. The capacitance value ranges from 3 pico farad to 2 micro farad and the working voltage ranges from 3 volts to 6000 volts.

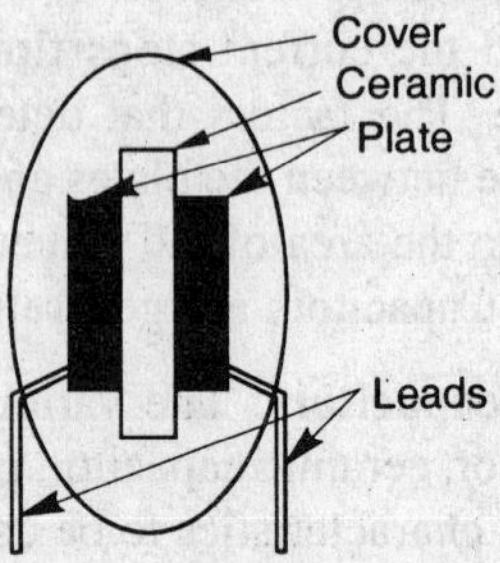


**Fig. 9.11** Ceramic Capacitor

### 9.3.4 Polystyrene Capacitor

This comes under the category of plastic dielectric capacitors. Polystyrene film is made from polystyrene granules by heating process. It is a thermoplastic material with a melting point just over 90°C. Two metal foils are alternated with two plastic-film dielectric strips as shown in Fig. 9.12.

Plastic film capacitor can have values of 10 micro farads, and with high working voltage rating about 500 V. The manufacturing process is carried out in a dust free room.

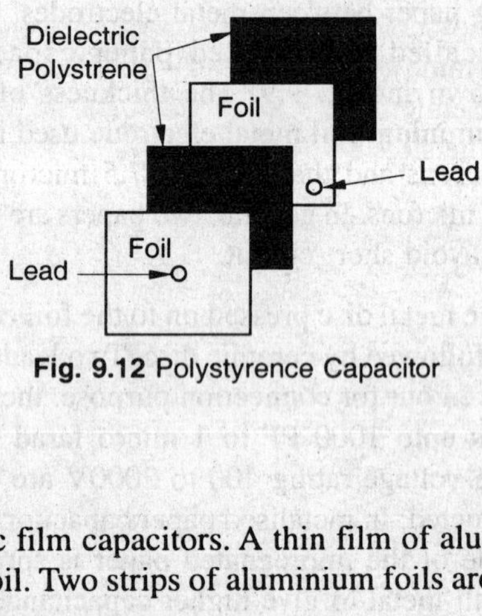


**Fig. 9.12** Polystyrence Capacitor

### 9.3.5 Electrolytic Capacitor

Electrolytic capacitors are constructed like plastic film capacitors. A thin film of aluminium oxide is deposited on the surface of the foil. Two strips of aluminium foils are

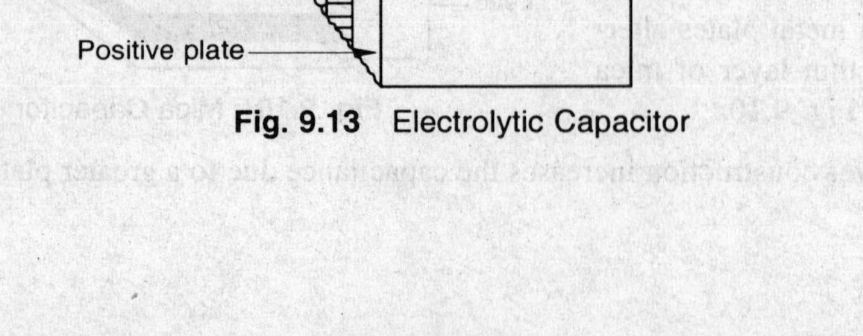


**Fig. 9.13** Electrolytic Capacitor

separated by two layers of porous papers soaked with electrolyte as shown in Fig. 9.13. The electrolyte reacts chemically with the inside aluminium foil to form a layer of aluminium oxide on the surface of the foil and it becomes dielectric medium.

The reaction is electrochemical and the chemical change occurs only at the positive electrode. By connecting the positive terminal of the voltage source to the inside foil and negative terminal to the outside foil, an oxide layer is formed on the inside foil. After this action the capacitor is ready for use in the circuit as an electronic component.

**Variable Capacitors**

In the case of tuning circuits, it is necessary to vary the value of capacitance. This is achieved by means of a variable capacitor. The different types of variable capacitors used are (1) General purpose variable capacitor (2) precision variable capacitor capacitor and (3) Trimmer capacitors.

### 9.3.6 General Purpose Variable Capacitors

The different parts of variable capacitors are (1) Frame (2) Rotor stator (3) Spindle and bearing. The frame may be built up type or bent type or die cast type. The built up type frame has a rigid construction with front and back plates held together by rigid tie bars. For gang units, number of sections can be easily added whereas in the bent frame type, the two end plates are integral with the base plate carrying the stator. Semicircular stator and rotor vanes punched from aluminium strip are assembled in the slots in the stator mounting brackets and in the grooved spindles respectively. The capacitance can be varied by changing the vane spacing. The constructional details of built up type and bent frame type variable capacitor is shown are Fig. 9.14.

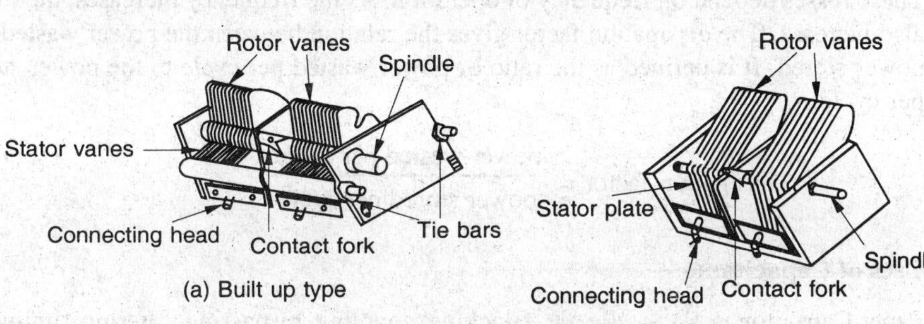


**Fig. 9.14** General Purpose Variable Capacitor

### 9.3.7 Precision variable capacitor

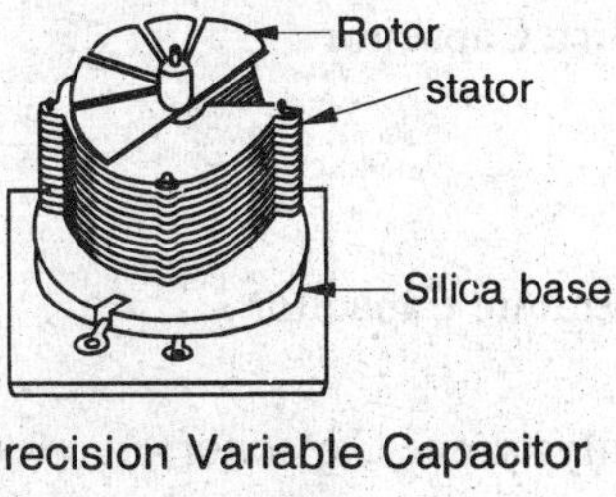


Precision Variable Capacitor

**Fig. 9.15**

It has a stator and a rotor with aluminium plates. Quartz pillars are used to insulate the light alloy end plates carrying the stator plates. The rotor plates are mounted on a duralium shaft. The drive to moving assembly is provided by spring load worm wheel. The capacitors are also provided with inner and outer screens. The capacitance value ranges from 40 pico farads to 1000 pico farads, with maximum working voltage of 1000 V. The constructional details are given in Fig. 9.15.

### 9.3.8 Trimmer capacitors (with ceramic dielectric)

These capacitors can be constructed in two ways as shown in Fig. 9.16. In the rotary type construction, steatite (with low loss, low permittivity) is used as the base of the capacitor. The silver stator plate and balancing plate are fixed on the ceramic dielectric. The rotatable plate made of high permittivity material is silvered (to half circular area) and then soldered to central pivot. The intimate contact between the plates is obtained by making the bottom surface of rotor and top surface of stator flat. The capacitance value of these capacitors ranges from 2 pico farad to 120 pico farads. In the concentric tube construction, a long metal screw running inside a ceramic tube silvered half its length on outside, is used as a trimmer. Here the capacitance value ranges from 0.5 pico farads to 10 pico farads.

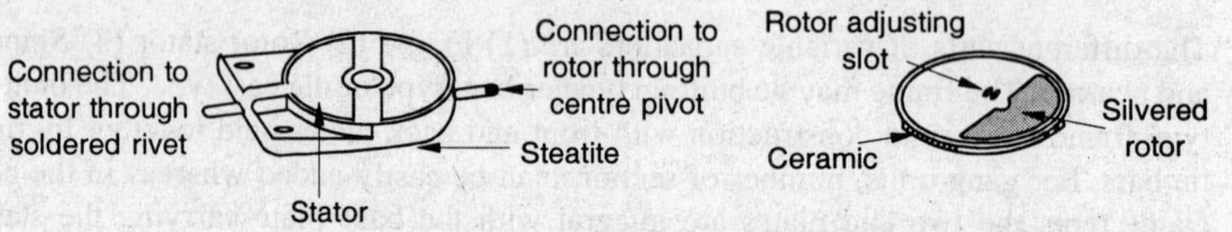


**Fig. 9.16** Trimmer Capacitors

### 9.3.9 Dissipation Factor

The losses in the capacitor are due to the current leakage and dielectric absorption. These losses depend on frequency of operation. As the frequency increases, the losses also increase. The dissipation factor gives the relation between the power wasted and power stored. It is defined as the ratio of power wasted per cycle to the power stored per cycle.

$$\text{Dissipation factor} = \frac{\text{power wasted per cycle}}{\text{power stored per cycle}}$$

**Uses of Capacitors**

| | |
|---|---|
| Paper Capacitor | Blocking, coupling, by passing, filtering, timing circuits, motor starting |
| Mica Capacitor | Coupling, by passing and filtering in audio frequency transmitter circuits, high voltage circuits, padding of large capacitors, resonant and measuring circuits. |
| Ceramic Capacitor | Temperature compensation, blocking, coupling, by passing, filtering, amplifiers and resonant circuits. |
| Polystyrene Capacitor | Radio frequency tuned circuits, digital equipment, dosage measurement in X-ray therapy, measurement of ionisation current in radioactive materials. |

| | |
|---|---|
| Electrolytic Capacitor | Radio circuits, filtering, decoupling, bypassing. |
| General purpose variable Capacitor | Tuning capacitors in broadcast receivers, test equipment. |
| Precision variable Capacitor | Measuring instruments as laboratory standards. |
| Trimmer Capacitor | To balance the stray capacitance in T.V. tuners. |

## 9.4. INDUCTORS

The property of a coil by which it opposes change in the value of the current or flux through it due to the production of self induced emf is called inductance measured in henry. The electronic component producing inductance is called an inductor. Basically there are two types of inductors, namely, **fixed inductors** and **variable inductors.** The other types of inductor available are (i) Filter chokes (ii) Audio-frequency chokes and (iii) Radio-frequency chokes.

### 9.4.1 Filter Chokes

These are used for smoothing pulsating current output from a rectifier. They make use of a laminated core (Fig. 9.17) wound with many numbers of turns. Lamination is done to reduce eddy current loss.

### 9.4.2 Audio frequency Chokes

These are used to provide high impedance to audio frequencies. Their size and inductance values are less than that of filter choke.

### 9.4.3 Radio frequency Chokes

Chokes having still lesser inductance value are used as radio frequency chokes to block the radio frequency.

Variable inductors are used for turning circuits. The permeability-tuned variable coil with movable ferromagnetic shaft is shown in Fig. 9.17. The inductance is varied by varying the core in the coil.

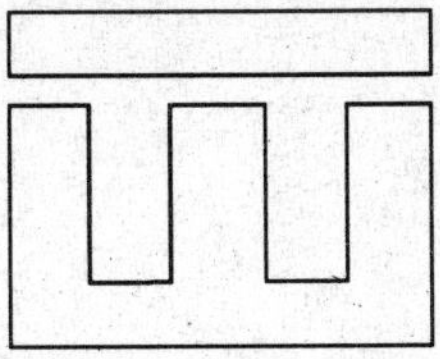

**Fig. 9.17** Laminated Core for Filter Choke

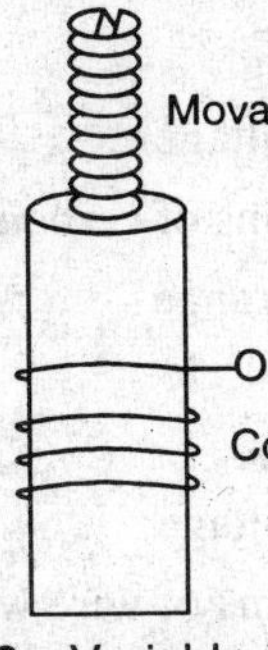


**Fig. 9.18** Variable Inductor

## 9.5. ACTIVE COMPONENTS

The active components of electronic circuits are broadly classified into tube type components (both vacuum and gas filled) and semi-conductor components.

### 9.5.1 Tube devices

A vacuum diode consists of two electrodes, namely, anode and cathode enclosed in a highly evacuated glass envelope. The anode is a hollow cylinder made of nickel or molybdenum which surrounds the cylindrical nickel cathode coated with barium and strontium oxides. When the cathode is made positive, the electrons move towards the plate. A vacuum triode consists of three electrodes, namely, anode, cathode and control grid. It can be used as an amplifier. A vacuum tetrode consists of four electrodes namely, anode, cathode, control grid and screen grid. The inter-electrode capacitance and lower amplification of the triode is overcome by using a tetrode. A vacuum pentode consists of five electrodes, namely, anode, cathode, control grid, screen grid and suppressor grid. The secondary emission in the tetrode is overcome by using a pentode.

A gas filled tube is a vacuum tube with small amount of inert gas at low pressure. The purpose of addition of inert gas is to improve conductivity. A hot cathode gas triode is known as thyratron. It has three electrodes, namely, anode, cathode and grid. A thyratron can be used as controlled rectifier and also as an amplifier.

### 9.5.2 Semiconductor devices

The various semiconductor devices are semiconductor diode, zener diode, Bipolal Junction transistor (BJT), Field Effect Transistor (FET), Unijunction Transistor (UJT), Silicon Controlled Rectifier (SCR). These are dealt in detail in chapter 10.

## HIGHLIGHTS

- The two general categories of resistors are: 1. Fixed value resistors and 2. Variable value resistors.
- The types of fixed resistors are: 1. Carbon composition resistors 2. Carbon film resistors 3. Wire wound resistors 4. Metal film resistors.
- Specifications of carbon composition resistor:

| | |
|---|---|
| Resistance range | 2 ohms to 20 mega ohms |
| Tolerance | ± 5% to ± 10% |
| Power rating | 1/8 to 2 watts |
| Working voltage | 125 V to 800 V |

- Specifications of carbon film resistor:

| | |
|---|---|
| Resistance range | 1 ohm to 1 mega ohms |
| Tolerance | ± 1% to ± 5% |
| Power rating | 5 watts |
| Working voltage | 500 V |

- Specifications of wire wound resistor:

| | |
|---|---|
| Resistance range | 0.1 ohm to 1 mega ohms |
| Tolerance | ± 0.1% to ± 5% |
| Power rating | 10 to 75 watts |
| Working voltage | < 150 V |

- Specifications of metal film resistor:

| | |
|---|---|
| Resistance range | 0.5 ohm to 10 Kilo ohms |
| Tolerance | ± 2% to ± 3% |
| Power rating | 5 watts |
| Working voltage | 300 V |

- Resistance colour code

| | | |
|---|---|---|
| First band | – | First digit |
| Second band | – | Second digit |
| Third band | – | No. of zero's after first two digits |
| Fourth band | – | Tolerance value |

| Resistance | | Tolerance | |
|---|---|---|---|
| **Colour** | **Value** | **Colour** | **Value** |
| Black | 0 | Gold | ± 5% |
| Brown | 1 | Silver | ± 10% |
| Red | 2 | No colour | ± 20% |
| Orange | 3 | | |
| Yellow | 4 | | |
| Green | 5 | | |
| Blue | 6 | | |
| Violet | 7 | | |
| Grey | 8 | | |
| White | 9 | | |

- The different types of potentiometers are
  1. Carbon composition potentiometer
  2. Wire wound potentiometer
  3. Wire wound solenoid potentiometer
  4. Helical wound potentiometer
- The different types of fixed capacitors are
  1. Mica capacitor
  2. Ceramic capacitor
  3. Polystyrene capacitor
  4. Electrolytic capacitor
- The different types of variable capacitors are
  1. Precision type
  2. Trimmer

Paper capacitor is used as bypass and coupling capacitor.

Ceramic capacitor is used as bypass, blocking and filtering capacitor.

Polystyrene capacitor is used as tuned circuit capacitor.

Electrolytic capacitor is used as filtering, decoupling and bypass capacitor.

- The different types of inductors are (i) Filter chokes (ii) Audio-frequency chokes (iii) Radio-frequency chokes.
- The active components of electronic circuits are broadly classified into (i) Tube type components (ii) Semiconductor components.

## REVIEW QUESTIONS

1. Explain the manufacturing process of different types of fixed resistors. Also give their specifications.
2. Explain the colour coding in resistors.
3. What are the different types of variable resistors? Give the details of their construction with sketches and also their specification.
4. Explain the different types of variable capacitors with neat sketches. Also give their specifications.
5. Give the applications of various types of capacitors.
6. What are the different types of inductors?
7. Write a short note on active components.

## TWO MARKS QUESTIONS AND ANSWERS

1. *What is a carbon composition resistor ?*

   It consists of a mixture of powdered carbon and powdered insulator solidified by a bonding compound.

2. *What is a wire wound resistor ?*

   It is constructed by winding a length of wire on an insulating cylindrical ceramic core. The end leads are soldered to end cap and the assembly is coated with enamel.

3. *What is a carbon film resistor ?*

   It is obtained by depositing pure carbon on ceramic substrate by thermal decomposition of hydrocarbons. Lead wires are attached to the film at each end and the whole assembly is surrounded by an insulating material.

4. *How do you get a metal film resistor ?*

   It is obtained by electrolytic decomposition of nickel or ceramic in a chemical bath containing hypophosphate.

5. *What is Tolerance ?*

   It is the amount that resistance may vary within the acceptable range. For example, 100 ohms resistance with 5% tolerance can have resistance 5% above or below the coded value.

6. *What do you understand by resistance colour code ?*

   In case of small size resistance, its ohmic value as well as tolerance can be specified with the help of coloured strip. From left to right, the first band gives first digit and the second band gives the second digit in the numerical value. Third band gives number of zeros after two digits. Fourth band gives tolerance.

7. *What is a potentiometer ?*

   It is a variable resistor that delivers an output representing some function of input voltage.

8. *List the different types of potentiometers.*

   1. Carbon composition potentiometer

2. Wound rotary type
3. Wire wound solenoid type
4. Helical wound

9. *List the types of fixed capacitors.*

1. Paper Capacitor
2. Mica Capacitor
3. Ceramic Capacitor
4. Polystyrene Capacitor
5. Electrolytic Capacitor

10. *What is dissipation factor ?*

It is the ratio between the power wasted per cycle and the power stored per cycle.

# Chapter 10

# TRANSDUCERS

## 10.1. INTRODUCTION

A transducer is an element which converts one form of energy into another. An instrumentation system generally consists of three components, namely, an input device, a signal conditioning device and an output device as shown in Fig. 10.1. The input device with transducer in it, senses the quantity under measurement and changes it to a proportional electrical signal. In the signal conditioning device, the signal is amplified, filtered or otherwise modified to a level accepted to the output device. The output device may be an indicator or a storage medium. The input measurement quantities for most instrumentation systems are non-electrical. The non-electrical quantity is converted to an electrical signal by a device called transducer and is used for measurement and control. In general, the energy transmission by a transducer may be mechanical, electrical, magnetic, thermal, radiant or chemical.

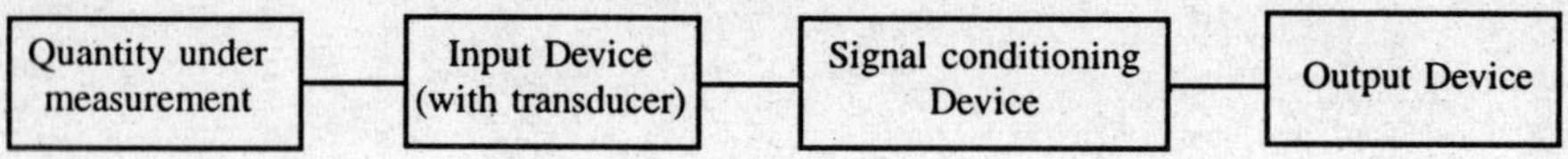


**Fig. 10.1**

## 10.2. TRANSDUCER CLASSIFICATION

There are two basic types of transducers, namely, active transducers and passive transducers.

### Active Transducer

The active or self generating transducers convert energy directly from one state to another, without the need for an external power source or excitation.

### Passive Transducer

A passive transducer does not convert energy directly but derives the power required for energy conversion from an external source.

### 10.2.1. Types of Active Transducers

**1. Thermocouple:** In a thermocouple an emf is generated across the junction of two dissimilar metals, when the junction is heated. Typical applications are: measurement of temperature, heat flow and radiation.

**2. Moving coil generator:** Here voltage is generated when a coil is rotated in a magnetic field. This is used in measuring velocity and vibration.

**3. Photovoltaic cells:** In this case an emf is generated in a semiconductor junction device, when radiant energy stimulates the cell. Typical applications are in light meters and solar cells.

**4. Piezo electric pickup:** Here an emf is generated when an external force is applied across a crystalline material. Typical applications are vibration, acceleration and sound measurement devices.

### 10.2.2. Types of Passive Transducers

**1. Potentiometer:** In the potentiometer the contact position of the slide wire is varied by an external force causing the change in resistance. These are applied in measuring pressure, displacement, etc.

**2. Resistance thermometer:** Here the resistance of the metal varies with the temperature. It is used in temperature and radiant heat measurements.

**3. Strain gauge:** In this type, resistance of a coil wire changes when external stress is applied. They are used in measuring instruments of stress, strain, force, torque, displacement.

**4. Photo conductive cell:** Here the resistance of the cell varies with incident light. They are used in photosensitive relays.

**5. Thermistor:** A thermistor is a non-metallic resistance (semi-conductor of the ceramic material) having a negative coefficient which varies with temperature. This is used in temperature measurement.

**6. Resistance hygrometer:** In this case, the resistance of the conductive strip changes with moisture content. It is used in measuring the relative humidity.

**7. Capacitor transducer:** Here, variation of capacitance is produced by varying the distance between the plates by an external force. It is used in measuring pressure, displacement, etc.

**8. Capacitor microphone:** In the capacitor microphone, the capacitance between the fixed plates and movable diaphragm varies due to the sound pressure. It is used in recognising noise and speech.

**10. Dielectric transducer:** Here variations in dielectric changes the capacitance. It is used in measuring the liquid level and thickness of a material.

**10. Differential transformer:** Here the differential voltage of the two secondary winding of a transformer is varied by varying the position of the magnetic core by an external force. This is also used in measuring the pressure, displacement, etc.

**11. Reluctance pickup:** Here, reluctance of the magnetic circuit is varied by changing the position of the iron core of a coil. It is used in measuring displacement, position etc.

**12. Magnetic transducer:** Here, inductance of the alternating–current excited coil is varied by changing the magnetic circuit. It is also used in measuring the displacement.

**13. Hall effect pickup:** In this type, voltage is generated across a semiconductor plate, when magnetic flux interacts with an applied current. It is used to measure the magnetic flux and current.

**14. Photo emissive cells:** Here, electron emission takes place due to radiations on photosensitive surface. It is used in measuring the radiation and light.

## 10.3. BASIC REQUIREMENTS OF TRANSDUCERS

Some of the basic requirements of a transducer are listed below:

**1. Range:** The transducer must be operable over the minimum to maximum values of the parameters to be measured.

**2. Accuracy:** It is the conformity of an indicated value to an accepted value. A transducer should be accurate.

**3. Repeatability:** The closeness of the output value, among a number of consecutive measurements for the same value of the input is called repeatability. A transducer should have better repeatability.

**4. Sensitivity:** The ratio of change in output to the change in input should be high enough for the transducer for better resolution of the system.

**5. Environmental effects:** The influence of temperature, acceleration, shock, vibration and corrosion should not affect the performance of a transducer.

**6. Noise:** The output signal from the transducer should not be affected by noise.

**7. Loading effect:** It is determined by the mass exterior size, geometric configuration of the transducer. All transducers absorb some energy because of these factors. So the loading effect should be less.

**8. Output impedance:** This should be matched with the rest of the measuring systems.

**10. Power requirements:** Proper voltage should be applied for the externally excited transducers.

**10. Frequency response:** The transducer system must have an accurate response to the maximum rate of change of the system. The change of output with input frequency should be flat over the measurement range.

**11. Linearity:** The input and output characteristics of a transducer should be linear.

**12. Ruggedness:** The transducer should be rugged enough to withstand the overloads.

## 10.4. DISPLACEMENT TRANSDUCERS

The displacement transducers make use of both primary and secondary transducers. Here the primary transducers are also called force summing devices. They convert the mechanical force into displacement with the help of mechanical elements like diaphragm, bellows, bourdon tube and single or double suspension cantilever etc., as shown in Fig. 10.2.

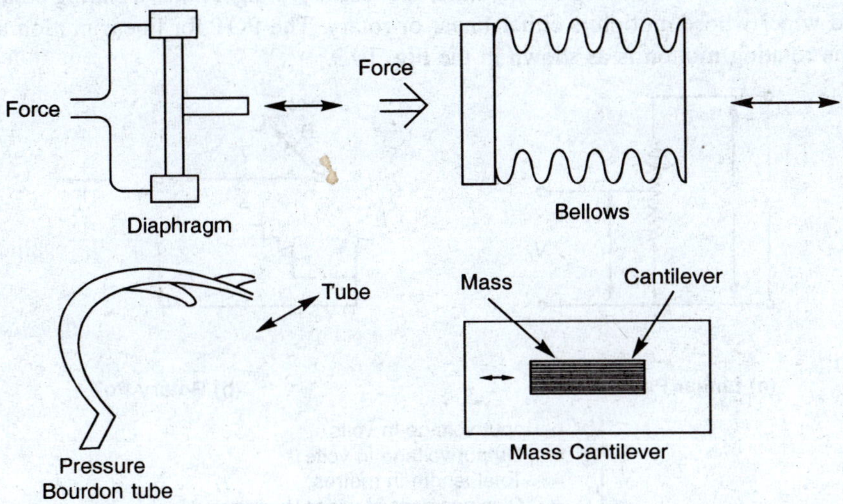


**Fig. 10.2**

The displacement activated by the force-summing devices is converted into electrical signals, using secondary transducers like resistive transducer, potentiometer, resistance strain gauge, capacitive transducers, LVDT, piezo-electric and photoelectric etc.

Thus, the above-mentioned transducers fall under the category of displacement transducers. They are dealt in detail in the later part of this chapter.

## 10.5. PASSIVE TRANSDUCERS

The definition and the types of passive transducers are already dealt under 10.2 and 10.2.2. The details of some of the important passive transducers are presented below.

**10.5.1. Resistive transducer:** Here a resistive element is used to measure several non-electrical quantities. The resistance of a material is given by

$$R = \frac{\rho l}{A} \text{ ohms}$$

where R is the resistance in ohms

ρ is the specific resistance in ohm-metre

l is the length of the material in metres

A is the area of cross section in square metres.

By causing change in displacement (linear or angular), pressure (strain) and temperature, we can change the values 'l', 'A' and 'ρ' respectively. Potentiometer resistance strain gauge, resistance strain gauge, resistance thermometer and thermistor are some of the examples of resistance transducers.

**10.5.2 Potentiometer (POT):** It is a passive transducer with a thin wire of platinum or nickel alloy of 0.01 mm diameter carefully wound on an insulated former. The resistive element can be energised by either d.c. or a.c. voltage. It has a sliding contact called wiper whose motion is either linear or rotary. The POT for linear motion and for the rotating motion is as shown in the Fig. 10.3.

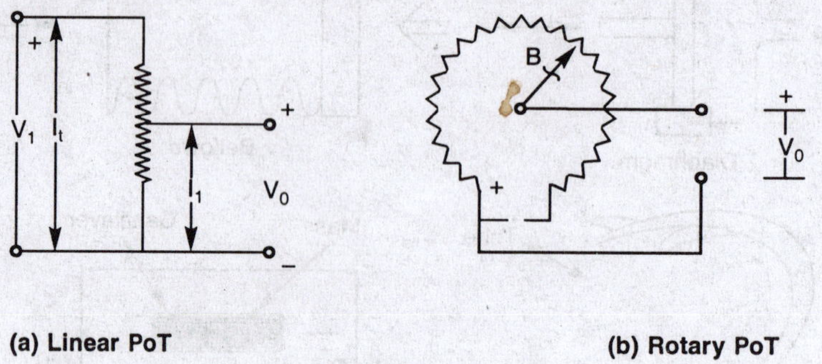


$V_i$ = Input voltage in volts
$V_o$ = Output voltage in volts
$l_t$ = Total length in metres
$l_i$ = Displacement of wiper in metres
$q_i$ = Angular displacement in degrees.

**Fig. 10.3**

**10.5.3 Resistance strain gauge:** When a gauge is subjected to a positive strain, its length increases whereas its area of cross section decreases. Since the resistance is a function of length and area of cross section, it also changes. The resistance-wire strain gauges are available in two forms. 1. Unbonded strain gauge and 2. Bonded strain gauge.

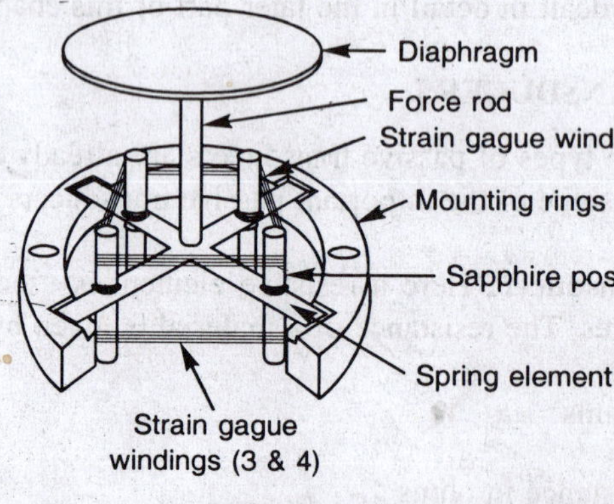


**Fig. 10.4**

**10.5.3(a) Unbonded strain gauge:** It consists of four posts mounted on a star spring structure as shown in Fig. 10.4 below. The four saphire posts hold four equal lengths of tungsten-platinum wire of 5μ diameter. The temperature compensation is obtained by the Wheatstone bridge circuit formed by these four wires. When the star spring is subjected to the force under measurement, the strain gauge elements on the opposite sides of the spring gets strained in opposite polarity. The unbalanced voltage of the bridge circuit is proportional to pressure (due to the applied force) on the diaphragm.

**10.5.3(b) Bonded strain gauge:** There are four types of bonded strain gauge. They are (1) Linear strain gauge, (2) Rosette, (3) Torque gauge, (4) Helical gauge as shown in Fig. 10.5.

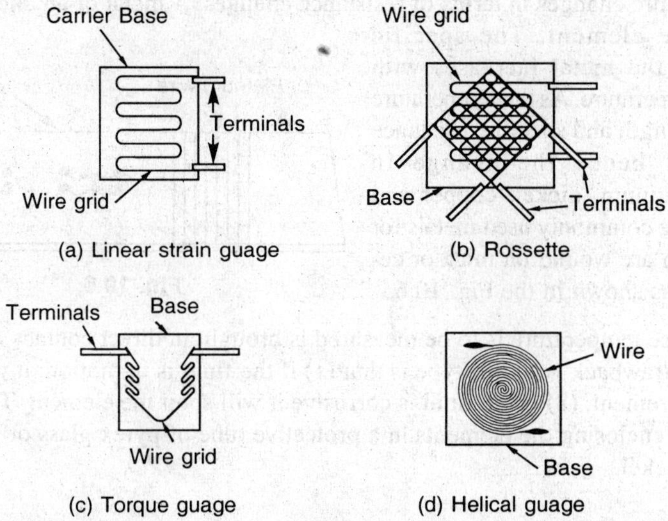


Fig. 10.5

The bonded strain gauge consists of fine resistance wire made of nichrome or constantan or nickel or platinum in the form of a grid of 25 micrometer diameter cemented to a carrier made of thin paper or bakelite or teflon sheets. The spreading of wire ensures uniform distribution of stress. The carrier is bonded to the structure under test by means of an adhesive materials like epoxy, cement or bakelite cement or ethylcellulose cement or nitrocellular cement etc. If the strain gauge is stretched or compressed, the resistance of the conductor changes. This change in resistance is proportional to the applied strain and is measured using bridge circuit. Whenever the bridge circuit balances, no current flows through the meter, the meter reads zero. When strain gauge subjected to strain, resistance of the strain gauge changes, affecting the balance of the circuit. Hence the metre shows some reading which is proportional to the applied strain. Dummy strain gauge is used to cancel the temperature effect of the active gauge.

**Gauge Factor**

Sensitivity of the strain gauge is called gauge factor (K).

$$K = \frac{\Delta R/R}{\Delta l / l} \quad \text{...(10.1)}$$

where R is the nominal unstrained resistance

$\Delta R$ is the change in resistance due to strain

$l$ is the nominal length

$\Delta l$ is the change in length due to strain.

For better performance, the strain gauge should have low temperature coefficient of resistance, high value of gauge factor, high resistance and linear relation between strain and resistance.

**10.5.4 Resistance thermometer:** It is a primary electrical transducer used for measuring temperature changes in terms of resistance changes. A metal or an alloy is used as a resistive element. The specific resistance of the metal increases with increase in temperature. As the temperature changes, the length and specific resistance changes and hence the change in resistance. Platinum, nickel, copper and tungsten are the commonly used metals for the wire which are wound on mica or ceramic former as shown in the Fig. 10.6.

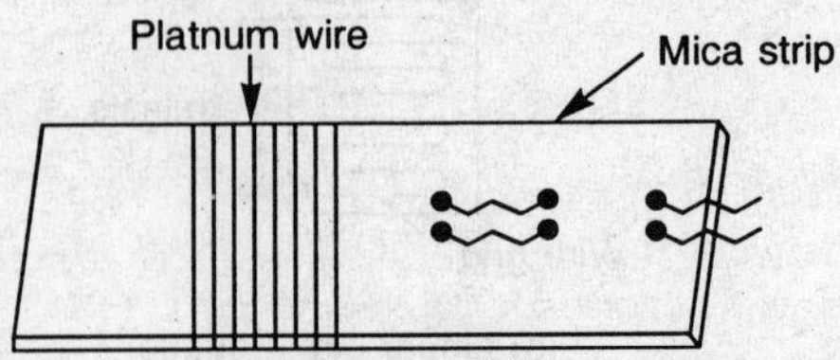


Fig. 10.6

The fluid whose temperature is to be measured is brought in direct contact with open element. The drawback with this type is that (1) if the fluid is in motion, it will cause error in measurement. (2) If the fluid is corrosive it will spoil the element. This could be avoided by enclosing the elements in a protective tube of pyrex glass or porcelain or quartz or nickel.

**10.5.5 Thermistor:** The thermistor has the following advantages over the wire resistance elements used for temperature measurements.

1. Large resistance value
2. High temperature co-efficient
3. Low thermal capacity
4. High speed of response
5. Smaller size
6. Low cost

Thermistor makes use of semiconductor compounds consisting of sintered mixtures of sulphides, silicates, oxides and selenides of metals such as nickel, manganese, cobalt, copper, zinc, iron, aluminium and uranium as resistance elements. These materials are very brittle and hence the elements are in the form of discs, beads and rods.

The drawback with a thermistor is that the reproductivity and stability is not satisfactory and hence frequent calibration is needed. However, stability can be improved by exploring them to a temperature slightly above its rated value. Since a temperature change of 1°C changes the resistance to nearly 75Ω to 80Ω, high resolution is possible in temperature measurement under dynamic conditions.

**10.5.6 Capacitive transducer:** It is used to measure mechanical displacement without causing any additional mechanical loading on the vibrating object. The most commonly used capacitive transducer is a parallel plate capacitor with variable gap. The capacitance of a parallel plate capacitor is given by

$$C = \frac{\varepsilon_0 \varepsilon_r A}{d} \text{ farads} \qquad ...(10.2)$$

where C is the capacitance in farads

$\varepsilon_0$ is the $8.854 \times 10^{-12}$ farads/metre

$\varepsilon_r$ is the Relative permittivity

A is the Area of each plate in metre$^2$

d is the distance between the plates in metres.

From equation 10.2, it is clear that capacitance is inversely proportional to the spacing between the parallel plates and is directly proportional to the plate area and the relative permittivity of the dielectric medium. Thus the capacitance can be varied by varying d (or) 'A' or '$\varepsilon_r$' accordingly.

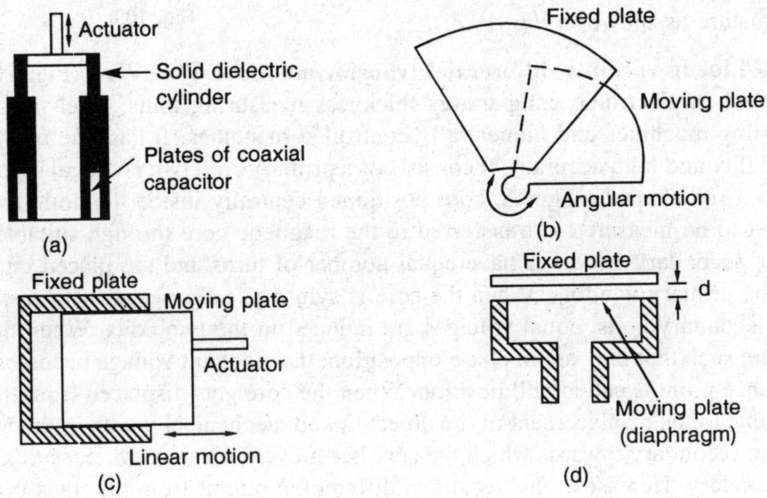


Fig. 10.7

**10.5.6(a) Variable dielectric capacitive transducer:** Here a solid dielectric cylinder connected to the actuator is moved between the plates of a co-axial cylindrical capacitor as shown in Fig. 10.7 (a).

**10.5.6(b) Variable plate area capacitive transducer:** Variation of plate area is achieved with the help of linear or angular movement of the actuator connected to the plate as shown in Fig. 10.7 (b). This in turn varies the capacitance of the transducer.

**10.5.6(c) Variable space capacitive transducer (Fig. 10.7 (c) & (d)):** In the case of variable case capacitive transducer, the diaphragm acts as a moving plate of the parallel plate capacitor. When the pressure increases due to the displacement, the diaphragm moves towards the fixed plate. The distance between the plates decreases and hence capacitance increases. The capacitor plates are mechanically linked to the object whose displacement is to be monitored. Alternating current of specific frequency applied converts the displacement of the plates into an electrical signal. It is measured by the voltmeter attached in the circuit. The change in the voltmeter reading is the measure of displacement. These transducers have high stability, good linearity and compactness.

**10.5.7 Inductive transducer:** It is used to measure quantities such as pressure, acceleration, force and displacement or position. The inductance of a coil depends on the magnetic flux linking with it. A change in the inductance proportional to the quantity to be measured is obtained by changing the flux linkage. A bridge or an oscillatory circuit can be used to measure the change in inductance. The variation of inductance (flux linkages) can be obtained by the movement of an armature as shown in Fig. 10.8.

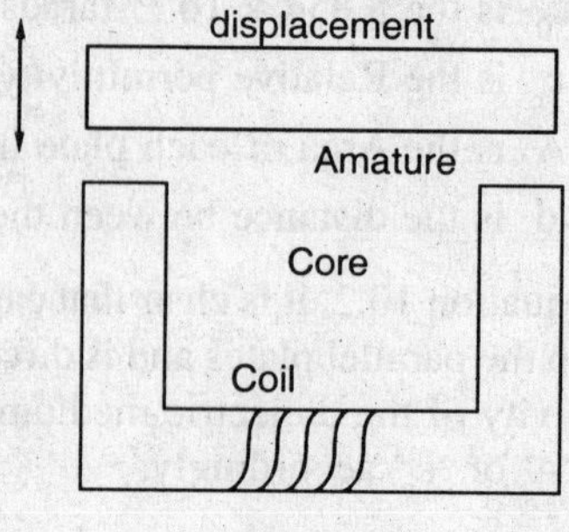


Fig. 10.8

**10.5.7(a) Linear variable differential transformer (LVDT):** LVDT (Fig. 10.9) is widely used in electronic comparators thickness measuring units, level indicators, creep testing machines and numerically controlled machines. It has fine resolution, good stability and high accuracy. It consists of a primary coil, two identical secondary coils and a rod-shaped magnetic core positioned centrally inside the coil. The displacement to be measured is transferred to the magnetic core through suitable linkages. The secondary windings have equal number of turns and are placed on either side of the primary winding. When the core is symmetrically placed with respect to the two secondary coils, equal voltages are induced in the two coils. When the two outputs are such that they are in phase opposition, the resultant voltage becomes zero. This balance point is called null position. When the core gets displaced from the null position due to the displacement of the object linked mechanically with it, the voltage induced in secondary towards which the core has moved increases whereas that in the other secondary decreases. This results in differential output from the transformer.

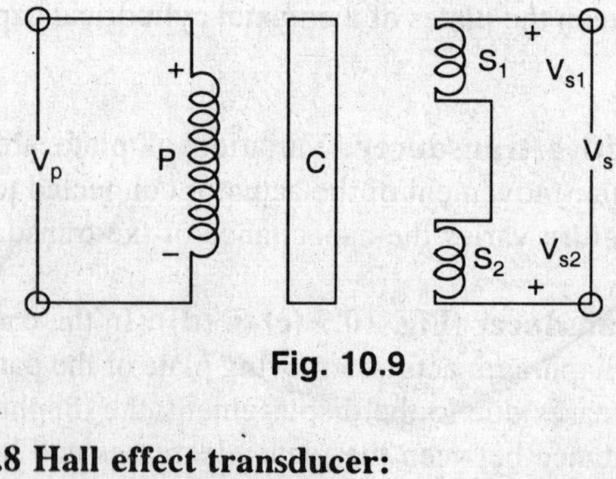


Fig. 10.9

$V_p$ = primary voltage

P = primary winding

C = movable core

$S_1$ = secondary winding 1

$S_2$ = secondary winding 2

$V_{s1}$ = voltage induced in $S_1$

$V_{s2}$ = voltage induced in $S_2$

$V_s = V_{s1} - V_{s2}$

**10.5.8 Hall effect transducer:**

Hall effect transducer (Fig. 10.10) is used for the detection of changes in the magnetic field to which it is exposed. It can be used as displacement transducer alongwith the test object which can distort the magnetic field due to its motion. The advantages are (1) high sensitivity (2) smaller size. According to Hall effect, the interaction between moving charges and the magnetic field results in Lorentz force which alters the motion of charge. The Hall effect is prominent in semiconductor materials. As the number of free charge carriers in semiconductors are far less when compared to metals, they have large Hall coefficients. The advantages with a semiconductor are (i) they require very little space (ii) they are very fast. But there is a limitation with respect to current as the passage of current creates noise. Also semiconductors are highly sensitive. When an n-type germanium carrying current is subjected to magnetic field normal to its surface, the magnetic field exerts a force on the electrons drifting them towards the edges. The potential between the edge surfaces is called Hall potential and the electric field due to build up of charges on the edges is called Hall field.

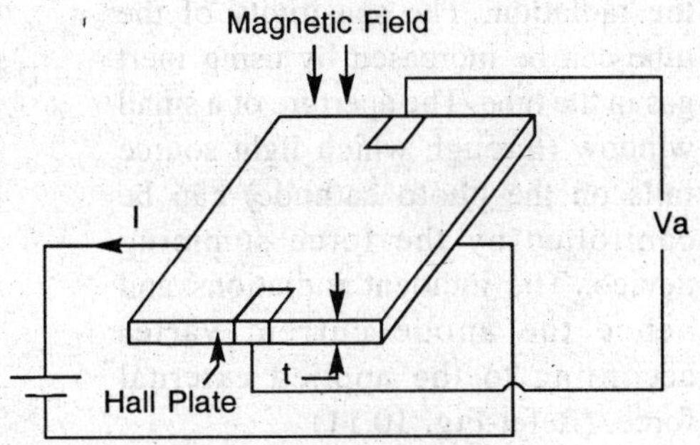

**Fig. 10.10**

Hall voltage $V_0 = R_H I B/t$ ...(10.3)

where t is the thickness of the semiconductor plate

B is the flux density

$R_H$ is the Hall constant

I is the current

Hall constant $R_H = \frac{1}{Nq}$ ...(10.4)

where, N is the concentration of electron and q is electron charge.

**10.5.9 Photoconductive transducer:** Here the electrical resistance of the material varies with the quantum of light energy interacting with it. All semiconductors are photoconductive in nature and their resistivity falls when light falls on them.

The basic materials used for photoconductive cells are lead sulphide, activated polycrystalline cadmium sulphide and cadmium sulpho selenide. The material is deposited on a ceramic substrate. Tin or indium electrode is embedded on the material making ohmic contact with the deposit. The resistance of the cells depends on dimensions of the cell (1 mm$^2$ to 35 mm$^2$), electrode configuration and the properties of photoconductive material. The resistance can be measured with the help of potentiometer or a bridge circuit. The photo conductive cells are used in illumination measurements, detection of optical radiation in spectrophotometers etc.

**10.5.10 Photoemissive transducer:** It consists of a metallic cathode and an anode kept in an evacuated tube. When the radiation falls on the cathode, emission of electrons takes place. These electrons are attracted towards the anode resulting in photocurrent which depends on the wavelength of the radiation. The sensitivity of the tube can be increased by using inert gas in the tube. The aperture of a small window (through which light source falls on the photo cathode) can be controlled by the force summing device. The incident radiations and hence the anode current varies according to the applied external force. (Refer Fig. 10.11)

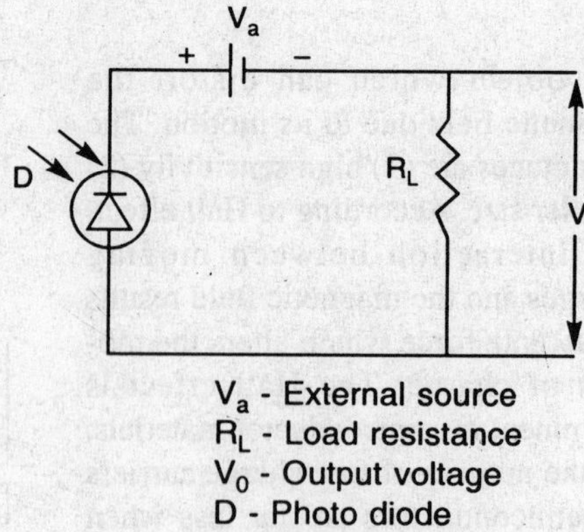


**Fig. 10.11**

## 10.6. ACTIVE TRANSDUCERS

The definition and the types of active transducers are already dealt under 10.2 and 10.2.1. The details of some of the important active transducers are given below:

**10.6.1 Thermocouple:** When two wires of dissimilar materials are joined to make a closed circuit and if one junction is held at a higher temperature than the other, an emf is generated which causes a current flow through the circuit (Seedeck effect). This principle is used in thermocouple. Thus a thermocouple consists of two dissimilar wires insulated from each other but jointed at one end. The net emf and the current in the circuit is a function of difference in temperature between hot and cold junctions. The thermocouple is used for temperature measurement. The common circuit of thermocouple is shown in the Fig. 10.12. Copper wires are run from the thermocouple terminals to the instrument. The thermocouple (metal A and metal B) are hard-soldered or spot-welded to the center of the heater. For low current measurements of order of 2 milliamperes to 500 milliamperes, the heater consists of a small piece of resistance wire mounted on a evacuated glass tube. The vacuum mounting is done to minimize the heat losses. This type of thermocouple is called vacuum thermocouple. The loading effect on the circuit is less in this method of measurement. Because of their negligible inductive effect, they can be used for measurement upto high frequencies. The power consumption is relatively low. But they have limited overload capacity. To get greater output voltage, bridge type thermocouple can be used. Voltmeters can be constructed using low current vacuum thermocouples in series with resistors.

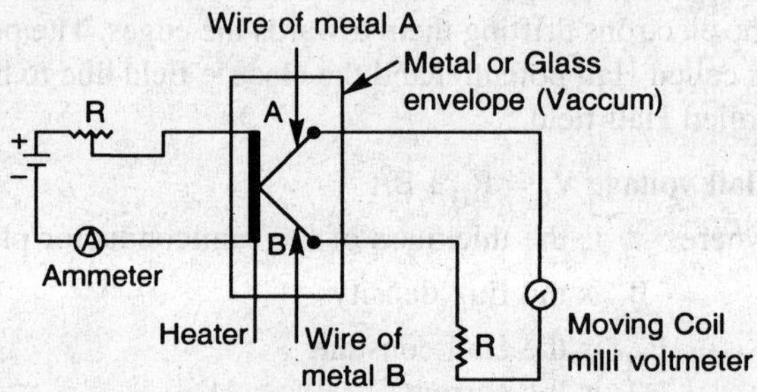


**Fig. 10.12**

**10.6.2 Photovoltaic transducers:** The photovoltaic cell consists of three layers namely, (1) base plate – $S_1$ (2) Semiconductor layer – $S_2$ and (3) thin transparent metal layer - $S_3$ as shown in the Fig. 10.13. A thin film of gold or platinum is deposited on the crystalline selenium with an iron base plate.

When the light is incident on the cells it is absorbed by the barrier layer forming the electron-hole pair. These carriers are separated by the electric field in the barrier. Hence a charge is generated which can cause current flow in the external circuit. Though the emf is generated within a micro-second after exposure to light, due to the presence of internal capacitance of barrier layer, the building of output voltage is delayed. These cells are affected by temperature hence for a stable operation, the temperature of the environment is to be held constant.

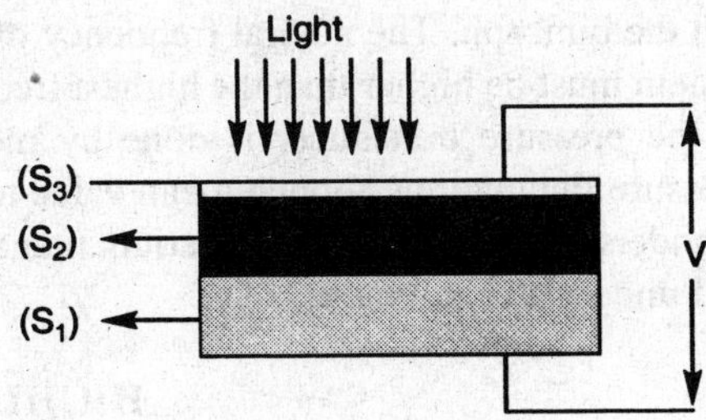


Fig. 10.13

**10.6.3 Piezo-electric transducer:** A piezo-electric material is one in which a voltage appears across the surface of a crystal, if the dimensions of the crystal are changed by the application of a mechanical force. The piezo-electric materials that are commonly used are ammonium dihydrogen phosphate, dipotassium tartarate, potassium dihydrogen phosphate, lithium sulphate, rochelle salts etc. The piezo electric effect is sensitive to direction. A compressive force produces voltage of one polarity whereas tensile force produces voltage of opposite polarity. The magnitude of the induced surface changes are proportional to applied force. The basic equivalent circuit of piezo-electric transducer is as shown in Fig. 10.14.

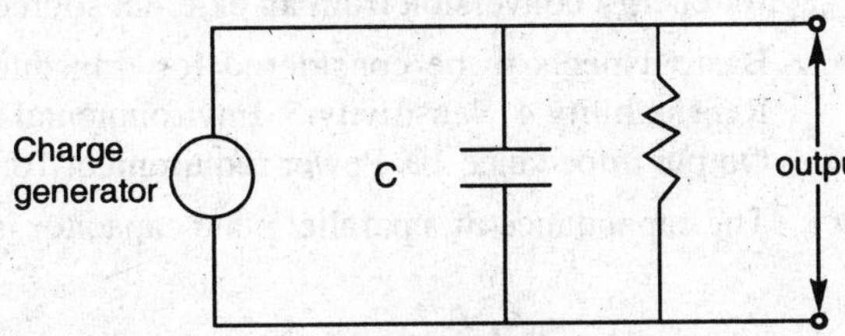


Fig. 10.14

The different modes of utilizing the piezo-electric transducer effect are (i) volume expander (ii) thickness shear (iii) face shear. The various piezo-electric transducers used are (i) piezo-electric force transducer (ii) piezo-electric straitransducer (iii) piezo-electric torque transducer (iv) piezo-electric pressure transducer and (v) piezo-electric acceleration transducer.

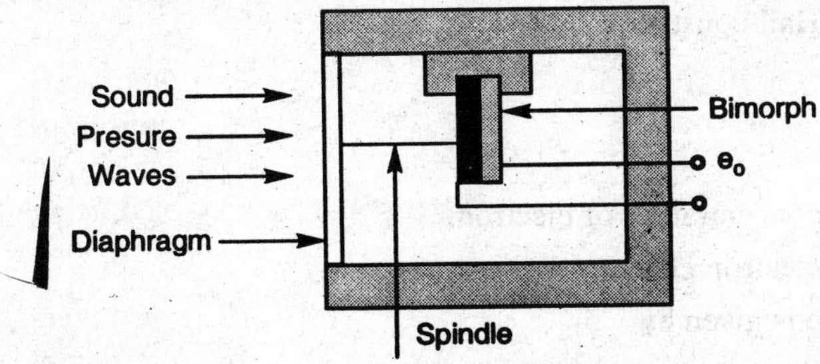


Fig. 10.15

**10.6.3(a) Piezo-electric pressure transducer:** There are suitable pressure measurements under dynamic conditions and are used as microphones, hydrophones, and pressure indicators. The piezo-electric microphone (Fig. 10.15) consists of diaphragm, bimorph and a spindle. The spindle connects the diaphragm and the bimorph. The natural frequency of diaphragm, bimorph and other associated system must be higher than the highest frequency to be responded to. The prestressing of the pressure transducer is done by means of a thin walled tube, to enable the pressure fluctuations about a mean value to be measured. Hollow spheres and hollow cylinders of ceramic material (Barium titanate) are used for measuring air blast pressure and underwater pressure.

## HIGHLIGHTS

- A transducer converts one form of energy into another.
- An active transducer converts energy directly from one state to another without the need for any external power source or excitation.
- Passive transducer does not convert energy directly but derives the power required for energy conversion from an external source.
- Basic aspects to be considered for transducers are 1. Range 2. Accuracy 3. Repeatability 4. Sensitivity 5. Environmental effects 6. Noise 7. Coding effect 8. Output impedance 10. Power requirement 10. Frequency response.
- The capacitance of a parallel plate capacitor is given by

$$C = \frac{\epsilon_o \epsilon_r A}{d} \text{ farads}$$

where A is the Area of each plate in square metres

d is the Plate spacing in metres

$\varepsilon_r$ is the Relative permittivity

$\varepsilon_o$ is the $8.854 \times 10^{-12}$ F/m

- LVDT is a magnetic displacement transducer. The magnitude of voltage induced in secondary would be the indicative of the amount of displacement.
- Hall Voltage $V_o = \frac{R_H . I . B}{t}$ volts

where t is the thickness of semiconductor plate

B is the flux density

I is the current

$R_H$ is the Hall constant.

where $R_H = \frac{1}{Nq}$

where N is the concentration of electron.

q is the electron charge

Sensitivity of strain gauge is given by

$$K = \frac{\Delta R / R}{\Delta L / L}$$

where R is the nominal unstrained resistance

$\Delta R$ is the change in resistance due to strain

l is the nominal length

$\Delta l$ is the change in length due to strain.

- The Mechanical elements that are used to convert the applied force into a displacement are called force summing devices. The examples are diaphragm, bellows, bourdon tube, single or double suspension cantilever etc.
- In a displacement transducer, the displacement activated by the force-summing devices is converted into electrical signals using secondary transducers.

## REVIEW QUESTIONS

1. What is meant by a transducer ? How they are classified?
2. What is meant by an active transducer? Give example.
3. What is meant by a passive transducer? Give example.
4. What are the basic requirements of a transducer?
5. What is meant by forced running device? Explain with neat sketch.
6. What is a displacement transducer? Explain with example.
7. Explain the working principle of
   (a) Resistive transducer
   (b) Resistance strain gauge

## TWO MARKS QUESTIONS AND ANSWERS

1. *What is a transducer ?*

   The broader definition of transducer is that, it is an element which converts one form of energy into another.

2. *What are two basic types of a transducer ?*
   1. Active transducer
   2. Passive transducer

3. *What is an active transducer ?*

   The active or self generating transducer converts energy directly from one state to another without the need for an external power source or excitation. For example, thermocouple.

4. *What is a passive transducer ?*

   A passive transducer does not convert energy directly but derives the power required for energy conversion from an external source. For example, potentiometer.

5. *Give four examples for active transducers.*
   1. Thermocouple
   2. Moving coil generator
   3. Photovoltaic cells
   4. Piezo-electric pick up

6. *Give four examples for passive transducers.*
   1. Potentiometer
   2. Strain gauge
   3. Photoconductive cell
   4. Thermistor
7. *List four basic requirements of transducers.*
   1. **Range:** Must be operable over minimum to maximum values of the parameter to be measured.
   2. **Accuracy:** Confirmity of indicated value to an accepted value.
   3. **Repeatability:** The closeness of the output value among a number of consecutive measurements.
   4. **Sensitivity:** Should be high enough
8. *What is an LVDT ?*

   Linear variable differential transformer is a magnetic displacement transducer. The magnitude of voltage induced in secondary would be the indicative of the amount of displacement that had taken place.
9. *What is Hall effect ?*

   When a thin piece of semiconductor is placed in a magnetic field and a current is passed through it such that an electric field is at right angles to the magnetic field, then a voltage will appear across the remaining traverse face of the material.
10. *What is a strain gauge ?*

    It is an example of a resistance changing passive transducer used for measuring strain. When the gauge is stretched or compressed the resistance of the wire in the strain gauge changes.

*Chapter 11*

# SEMICONDUCTOR DEVICES

## 11.1 INTRODUCTION

It is that field of science and engineering which deals with the study of electron devices and their utilization. An electron device is one in which movement of electrons takes place through vacuum or gas or a semiconductor. Electrons have a very wide range of applications in various fields such as communication systems, generation of power, microprocessors, aerospace, computers, consumer electronics etc. Initially vacuum tubes dominated the field of electronics, later transistors created revolution in the electronic industry. Since last 20 years, miniaturization of electronic equipment has been gaining momentum. In this chapter various semiconductor devices, their working principle, characteristics and applications are dealt.

**11.1.2 Theory of semiconductors:** To understand the theory of semiconductors, one should get acquainted with the keywords like valence electrons, energy band, valence band, conduction electrons, conduction band, forbidden energy gap and fermi level etc.

*Valence electrons*

Electrons present in the outermost orbit is called valence electrons.

*Energy band*

The range of energy possessed by the electrons in an atom is known as energy band.

*Valence band*

It is the range of energy possessed by the electrons present in the outermost orbit.

*Conduction electrons*

The valence electrons get detached themselves from the nucleus on the application of small electric field. These free electrons constituting the flow of current is called conduction electrons.

*Conduction band*

The range of energy possessed by the conduction electrons is called conduction band.

*Forbidden energy gap*

The gap between valence band and conduction band is called forbidden energy gap.

**Fermi level**

It is the energy corresponding to the centre of gravity of conduction electrons and holes weighted according to their energies.

## 11.2. CLASSIFICATION OF MATERIALS

Depending on the conduction property, the materials can be classified into conductors, insulators and semiconductors. Conductors allow the flow of electricity whereas as an insulator is a poor conductor of electricity. The conducting property of semiconductors lies between conductor and insulator.

**11.2.1 Energy band theory:** The classification of materials can also be done with the help of energy band theory.

**11.2.2 Conductors:** In terms of energy band, good conductors are those which have overlapping of valence bands and conduction band as shown in Fig. 11.1. Here plenty of free electrons are available for electronic conduction.

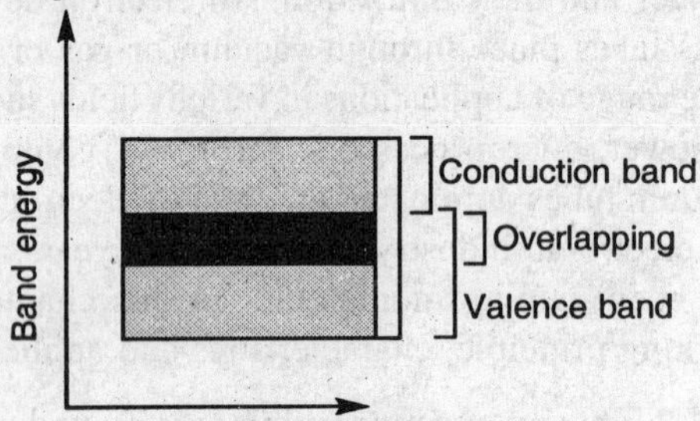


Fig. 11.1

**11.2.3 Insulators:** Here the valence electrons are bound very tightly to their parent atom. The forbidden energy gap is very large. Thus insulators have full valence band and empty conduction band as shown in Fig. 11.2. Because of this, it is impossible for an electron to jump from a valence band to reach the conduction band at room temperatures (without any additional energy).

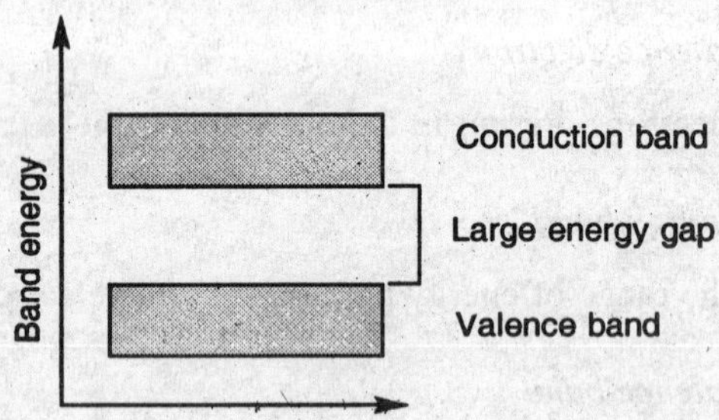


Fig. 11.2

**11.2.4 Semiconductors:** The properties of semiconductor materials lie between conductors and insulators. In terms of energy band theory they have almost an empty conduction band and almost filled valence band with a very narrow energy gap between them as shown in Fig. 11.3. At room temperature, some electrons cross over to conduction band from valence band. As the temperature increases the conduction increases.

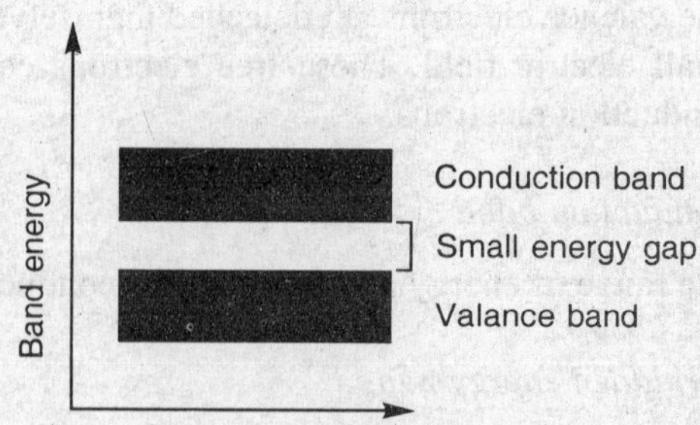


Fig. 11.3

## 11.3. CLASSIFICATION OF SEMICONDUCTORS

- Semiconductor
  - Intrinsic (pure type)
  - Extrinsic (impure type)
    - N-type
    - P-type

**11.3.1 Intrinsic semiconductors:** An intrinsic semiconductor is one which is available in its pure form. Example of an intrinsic semiconductor is silicon with a forbidden energy gap of 0.72 eV and germanium with a forbidden gap of 1.1 eV.

**11.3.2 Properties of intrinsic semiconductors**

1. They have four valence electrons.
2. Their properties lie between that of conductors and insulators.
3. Their conduction property can be varied by varying the temperature.
4. They have negative temperature coefficient of resistance.
5. Their properties can be varied by adding impurities to semiconductor.
6. The resistivity of a semiconductor is greater than a conductor and less than an insulator.
7. The current in a semiconductor consists of movement of electrons and holes.

**11.3.3 Hole formation:** In intrinsic semiconductors even at room temperature, some of the valence electrons may acquire enough to cross over to conduction band from valence band thereby becoming free electrons. As the electrons leave the valence band it creates a vacant space in it. This is known as 'hole'. When an electric field is applied, both the electrons as well as holes constitute current. Thus the total current through the semiconductor will be the sum of electron current and hole current. However the current in the external circuit will be only that due to electrons. As the holes being positive they move towards the −ve terminal of the supply. Meanwhile the electrons enter the semiconductor near the terminal N and combine with holes, thus cancelling them. At the same time, the loosely held electrons near the positive terminal are attracted away from their atoms into the +ve terminal. This causes creation of new holes near +ve terminal which again drift towards −ve terminal as shown in Fig. 11.4.

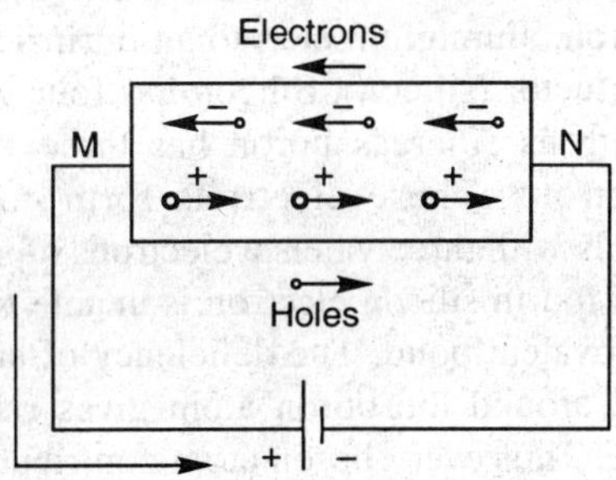

Fig. 11.4

**11.3.4 Extrinsic semiconductors:** As the conductivity of intrinsic semiconductors is poor at room temperature, it is not used in electronic devices. The conduction in the intrinsic semiconductors can be improved by adding impurities to it (about 1 part in $10^6$ intrinsic atoms).

**Doping**: The process of adding impurities deliberately to a semiconductor is called doping. A doped semiconductor is called an extrinsic semiconductor.

**Doping agent**: The added impurity is called doping agent.

**Acceptor:** A trivalent impurity when doped with a semiconductor accepts one electron to achieve stable state. Such a doping agent is called an acceptor. For example, Aluminium, Boron.

**Donor**: A pentavalent impurity when doped with a semiconductor donates one electron to the conduction band. Such a doping agent is called donor. For example, Phosphorus, Antimony.

**11.3.5 N-type Semiconductor:** This is obtained by adding a pentavalent (phosphorus) impurity to intrinsic a semiconductor (silicon). Silicon has four valence electrons where as phosphorus has five valence electrons. Four of these electrons form covalent bond with four valence electrons of silicon and the fifth valence electron is left free. It is loosely bound, as it is away from the nucleus. This electron can be excited from valence band to conduction band by the application of electric field or thermal energy. Thus every phosphorus atom contributes one conduction electron without creating a hole. Therefore the number of free electrons becomes so far greater than the number of holes thus resulting in a N-type semiconductor. The formation of covalent bond is shown in Fig. 11.5.

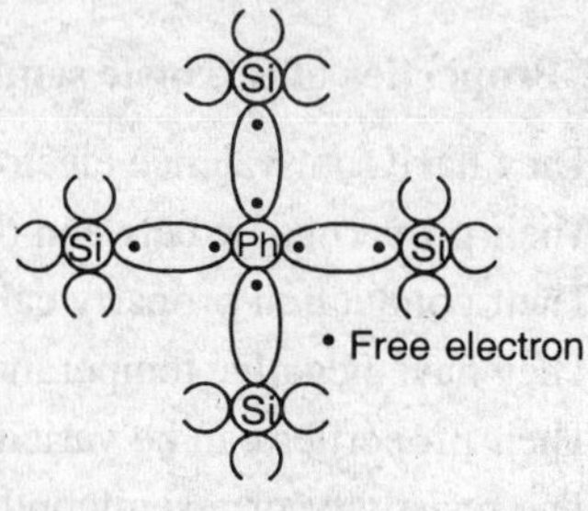


Fig. 11.5

**11.3.6 P-type semiconductor:** This is obtained by adding a trivalent impurity (boron, aluminium etc.) to an intrinsic semiconductor (silicon). Silicon has four valence electrons whereas boron has three valence electrons. These electrons form covalent bonds with three valence electrons of silicon. The fourth silicon electron is unable to form a covalent bond. The deficiency of an electron around the boron atom gives rise to a hole. Thus every boron atom contributes one hole. Therefore the number of holes becomes far greater than the number of electrons thus resulting in a P-type semiconductor. The formation of covalent bond is shown in Fig. 11.6.

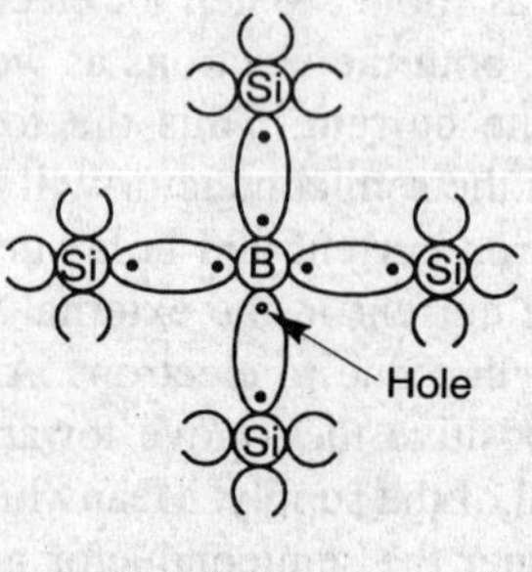


Fig. 11.6

## 11.4. PN JUNCTION

P-type semiconductor and N-type semiconductor materials individually find very limited use. Hence PN junction is formed by a special fabrication technology. The important characteristic is that it conducts current only in one direction. Fig. 11.7 shows the formation of PN junction.

The P-region has holes and negatively charged impurity ions whereas N-region has free electrons and positively charged impurity ions. Holes and electrons are mobile charges whereas the ions are immobile. As soon as the PN junction is formed, the holes in the P-region diffuse into N-region and the electrons in the N-region diffuse into P-region. This process is called diffusion, which occurs for a very short time. After a few recombinations of holes and electrons, a restraining force is developed. This force is called barrier which prevents further diffusion of holes and electrons.

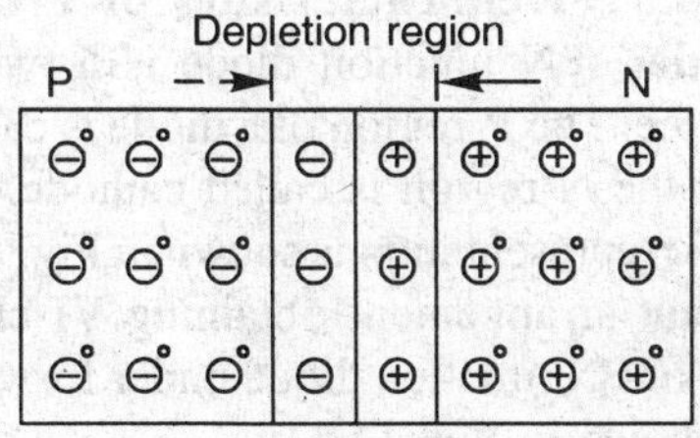

Fig. 11.7

The development of barrier force can be explained as follows. Each recombination of hole and electron eliminates hole and electron. During this process the –ve acceptor ions in the P-region and +ve donor ions in the N- region are left uncompensated. The additional holes trying to diffuse into N-region and the additional electrons trying to diffuse into P-region are repelled by these –ve and +ve charges respectively. The region containing this uncompensated acceptor and donor ions is called depletion region.

**11.4.1 PN Junction with forward bias:** When an external voltage is applied across the PN junction such that positive terminal of the battery is connected to P-region and negative terminal of the battery is connected to N-region is shown in the Fig. 11.8.

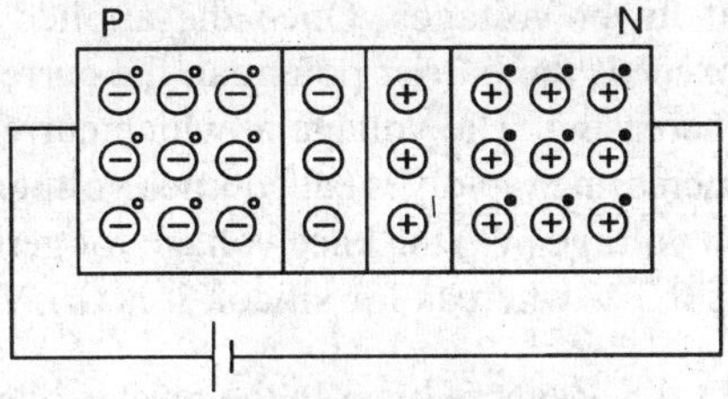

Fig. 11.8

During the forward bias, the electrons are repelled by the –ve terminal of the battery whereas the holes are repelled by the +ve terminal of the battery and both move towards the junction reducing potential barrier. This causes forward current to flow through the circuit.

**11.4.2 PN Junction with reverse bias:** When an external voltage is applied across the PN junction such that positive terminal of the battery is connected to N-region and negative terminal of the battery is connected to P-region as shown in the Fig 11.9.

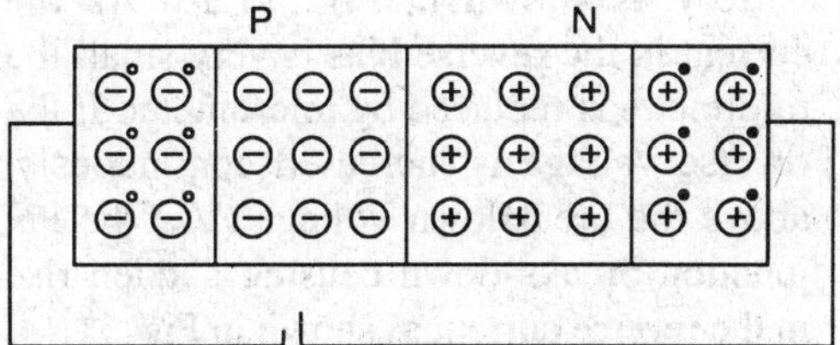

Fig. 11.9

During the reverse bias, the electrons in N region are attracted towards the positive terminal of the battery whereas the holes in P-region are attracted towards the negative terminal of the battery thus widening the depletion layer and barrier potential. This barrier potential makes it difficult for the majority carriers to diffuse across the junction. For all practical purposes the current due to the majority carriers is zero. However there will be current due to minority carriers called reverse saturation current (in the order of nano-amperes for silicon and micro-amperes for germanium).

**11.4.3 VI characteristics of PN junction diode:** PN junction diode is a two-terminal device. The P-region of a diode is called anode and the N-region is called cathode. The symbolic representation is shown in Fig. 11.10. The circuit arrangement obtaining VI characteristics of PN junction diode under forward bias is as shown in Fig. 11.11.

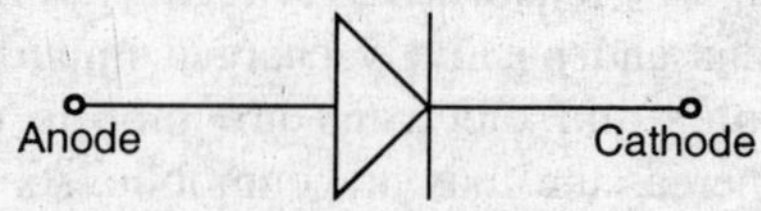


Fig. 11.10

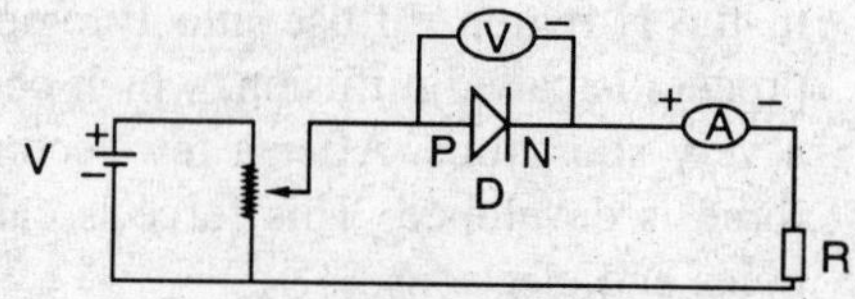


V - Supply voltage
D - PN junction Divide
R - Current limiting resistance

Fig. 11.11

**11.4.4 Forward bias:** In the forward bias, the anode is connected to the +ve terminal of the battery (v) and the cathode is connected to –ve terminal of the battery (v) through a potentiometer. With the help of a potentiometer voltage applied to the diode can be varied. The millammeter measures the anode current and the voltmeter measures the voltage across the diode. The forward bias characteristics are shown in Fig. 11.12. From the figure it is clear that, initially the forward current is very small at lower voltages. Once the applied voltage exceeds the barrier potential, the current starts increasing. The voltage at which current starts increasing rapidly is called **knee voltage** or **cut-in voltage** ($V_0$) the knee voltage for germanium is 0.3 V whereas for silicon it is 0.7 V.

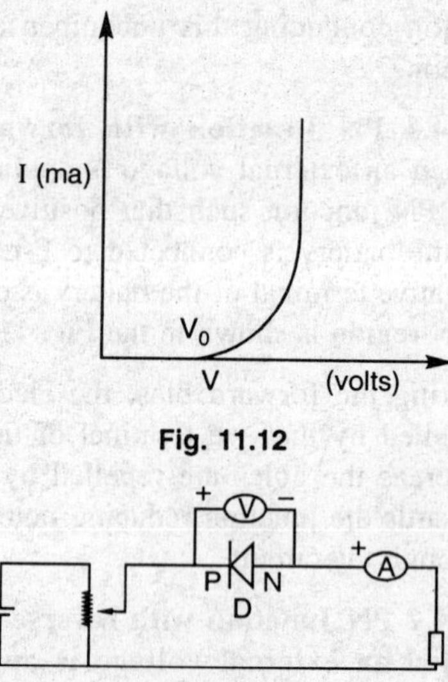


Fig. 11.12

**11.4.5 Reverse bias:** In the reverse bias, the anode is connected to the negative terminal of the battery (v) and the cathode is connected to the positive terminal of the battery as shown in Fig. 11.13. As the current in the reverse bias is very small the millimetre is replaced by micrometer. If the reverse voltage is increased continuously, above the breakdown voltage ($V_B$) the PN junction breaks down causing sudden rise in the reverse current as shown in Fig. 11.14.

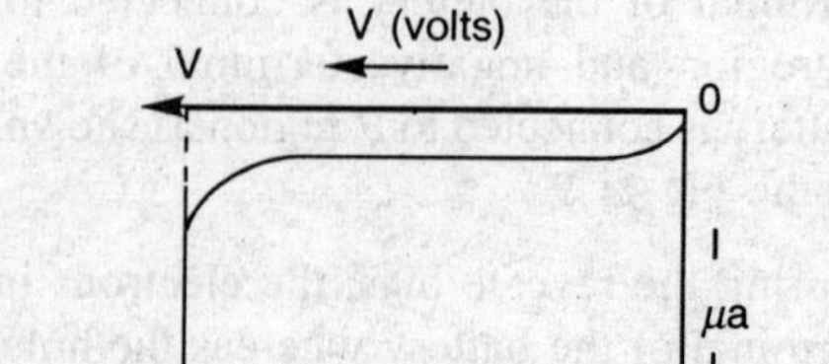


Fig. 11.13

Fig. 11.14

### 11.4.6 Ratings of PN junction diode

(i) **Maximum forward current:** The highest instantaneous value of current that can flow through the forward biased PN junction is called maximum forward current.

(ii) **Peak inverse voltage:** The maximum reverse voltage that can be applied to PN junction without damaging the junction is called peak inverse voltage.

(iii) **Maximum power rating:** The maximum power that can be dissipated at the junction without causing damage to the junction is called maximum power rating.

The PN junction diode will operate satisfactorily, only if it is operated within the limiting values.

**11.4.7 Rectifiers:** A rectifier is an electronic device which converts alternating quantity into unidirectional quantity. The unidirectional conducting property of the diode is being utilised in rectifiers.

Rectifier
- Half wave rectifier
- Full wave rectifier
  - Two diodes with centre-tap transformer
  - Bridge rectifier

The general block diagram of power supply with rectifier is as shown in Fig. 11.15 below.

The a.c. input after rectification is smoothened with the help of filter circuit and given to the regulator, which gives the regulator d.c. power supply.

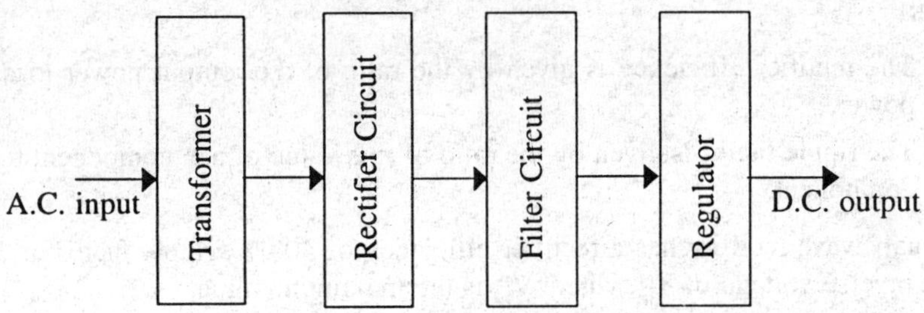


**Fig. 11.15**

**11.4.8 Half wave rectifier:** The circuit arrangement for the half wave rectifier is shown in Fig. 11.16.

| | | |
|---|---|---|
| $V_i$ | - | a.c input |
| T | - | Transformer |
| $i_L$ | - | Load current |
| $R_L$ | - | Load resistance |
| D | - | Diode |
| $V_m$ sin wt | - | voltage across transformer secondary |
| $V_0$ | - | d.c output |

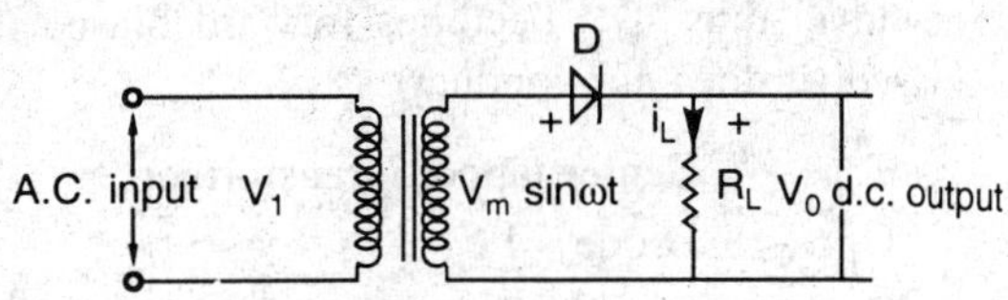


**Fig. 11.16**

The purpose of a transformer is that (i) it provides isolation from the power line (ii) we can use step up or step down transformers depending on the requirement of the a.c voltage. the primary ends of the transformer is connected to the a.c. input. The voltage across the transformer is given by $V_m$ sin wt where '$V_m$' is the maximum value.

During the positive half cycle of the input signal, the anode of the diode becomes positive with respect to cathode. Here the diode becomes forward biased and offers very low resistance. Thus the whole input voltage appears across the load $R_L$.

During the negative half cycle of the input signal, the anode of the diode becomes negative with respect to cathode. Diode becomes reverse biased and offers very high resistance. Thus no voltage is developed across the load $R_L$. The whole input voltage will appear across the diode itself. The input and output voltage waveforms of half wave rectifier is shown in Fig. 11.17.

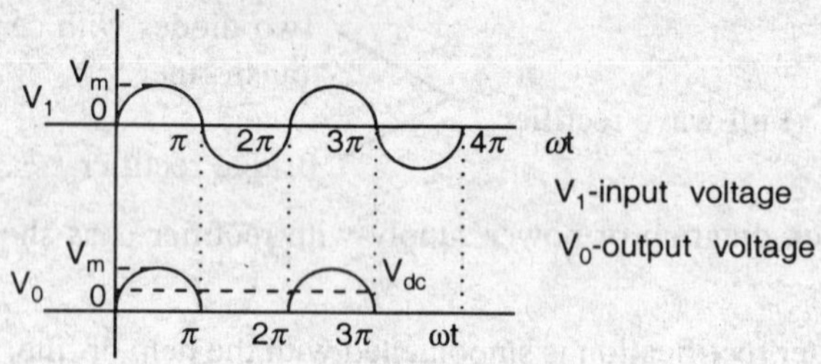


Fig. 11.17

**Note:**

1. The rectifier efficiency is given by the ratio of d.c. output power to a.c. input power.
2. The ripple factor is given by the ratio of rms value of a.c. component to the d.c. component.

The half wave rectifier has a rectifier efficiency of 40.6%, ripple factor of 1.21 and peak inverse voltage of $V_m$, where $V_m$ is the maximum value.

**11.4.9 Full wave rectifier (two diodes with centre tap transformer):** The half wave rectifier uses only one half cycle of input whereas full wave rectifier uses both the half cycles. The circuit arrangement for full wave rectifier using centre tap transformer and two diodes is shown in Fig. 11.18. During the positive half cycle of the input signal, the anode of diode '$D_1$' becomes positive and that of '$D_2$' becomes negative. thus '$D_1$' becomes forward biased it conducts and '$D_2$' becomes reverse biased (it does not conduct).

| | | |
|---|---|---|
| T | - | Center tapped transformer |
| $D_1$ | - | Diode - 1 |
| $D_2$ | - | Diode - 2 |
| $R_L$ | - | Load resistance |
| $V_i$ | - | a.c. input |
| $V_0$ | - | a.c. output |

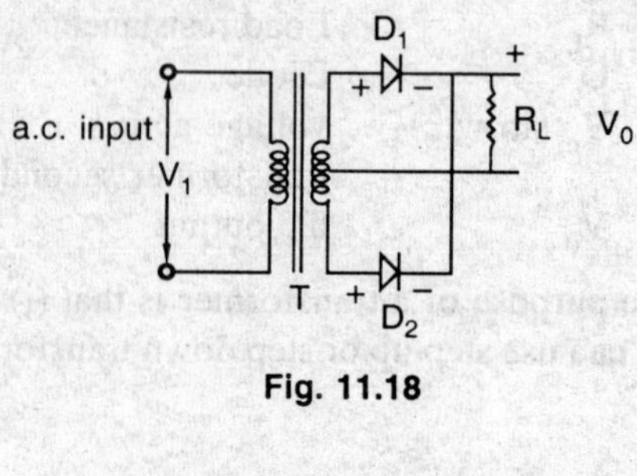


Fig. 11.18

As the diode 'D' conducts, the load current flows through 'D' and the input voltage appears across '$R_L$'.

During the negative half cycle of the input signal, the anode of '$D_1$' becomes reverse biased and '$D_2$' becomes forward biased. As the diode '$D_2$' conducts, the load current will now flow through '$D_2$' and the input voltage appears across $R_L$. The input and output voltage wave forms of full wave rectifier is shown in Fig. 11.19.

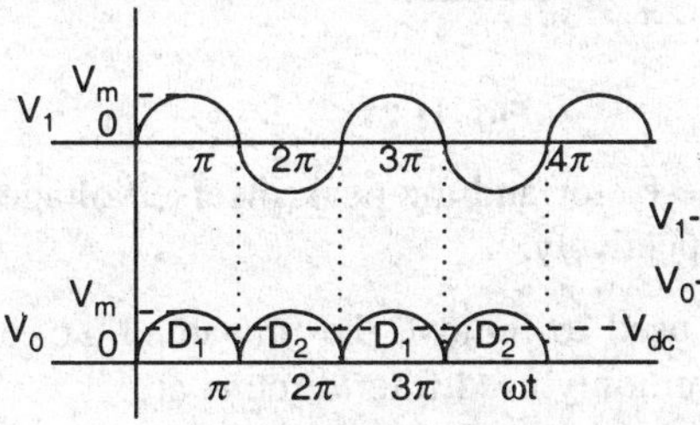


**Fig. 11.19**

The rectifier efficiency, ripple factor and the peak inverse voltage of a full wave rectifier are given by 81.2%, 0.48 and 2 $V_m$ respectively.

**11.4.10 Bridge rectifier:** The bridge rectifier is widely used as full wave rectifier. It offers the following advantages.

1. No centre tapped transformer is necessary.
2. The peak inverse voltage of each diode is less.
3. It can be used for high-voltage applications.

The circuit arrangement for the bridge rectifier without the use of centre tapped transformer is shown in the Fig. 11.20. It makes use of four diodes, namely '$D_1$', '$D_2$', '$D_3$', and '$D_4$'

$D_1$, $D_2$, $D_3$, $D_4$ – diodes
T – Transformer
$R_L$ – Load resistance
$V_i$ – a.c. input
$V_0$ – d.c. output

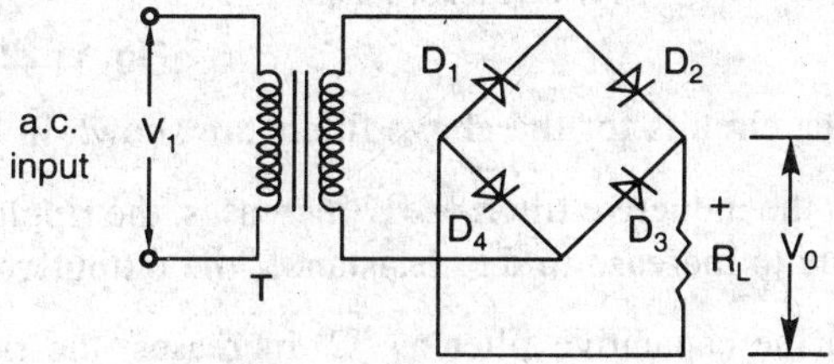


**Fig. 11.20**

During the positive half cycle of a.c. input, the diodes '$D_2$' and '$D_4$' conduct whereas '$D_1$' '$D_3$' do not conduct. Hence current flows through the secondary winding, diode '$D_2$' '$R_L$' and diode '$D_4$'.

During the negative half cycle of the a.c. input, the diodes '$D_1$' and '$D_3$' conduct whereas '$D_2$' and '$D_4$' do not conduct. Hence current flows through secondary winding, diode '$D_1$' '$R_L$' and diode $D_4$. Thus in both the cases current passes through '$R_L$' in the same direction. The input and output voltage wave forms of a bridge rectifier is shown in Fig. 11.21.

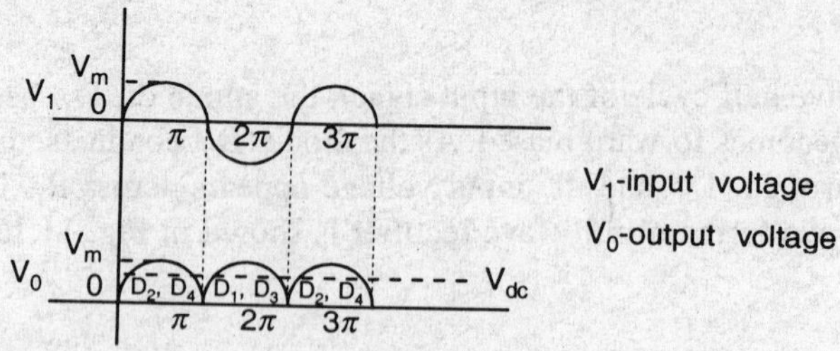


**Fig. 11.21**

The rectifier efficiency, ripple factor and the peak inverse voltage of bridge rectifier are 81.2% 0.48 and '$V_m$' respectively.

**11.4.11 Filters:** Filters are used to remove the unwanted a.c. component (ripples from the d.c. output. The commonly used filter circuits are:

1. Capacitor filter
2. Inductor filter
3. LC filter
4. CLC or π filter

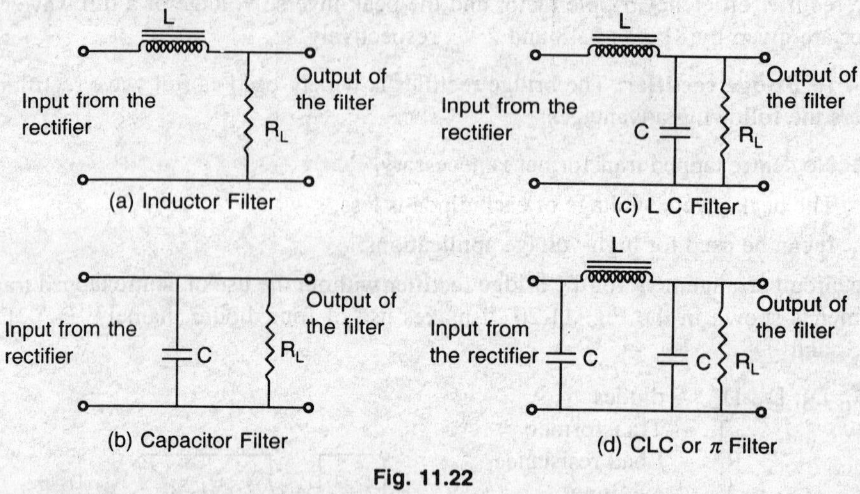


**Fig. 11.22**

The circuits for the above filters are shown in Fig. 11.22.

In the inductive filter, as 'L' increases, the ripples in the d.c. output decrease, however due to increase in d.c. resistance, the output voltage decreases.

In the capacitive filter as 'C' increases, the ripples decrease. In the 'LC' filter the ripple factor is independent of '$R_L$'. The π filter is the combination of 'C' and 'LC' filter.

**11.4.12 Zener diode:** A properly doped diode with adequate power dissipation capabilities to operate in the breakdown region is known as zener diode. The symbolic representation of zenner diode is as shown in the Fig. 11.23.

A zener diode is specified by its breakdown voltage and the maximum power dissipation. The voltage rating varies from 3V to 100 V and the power rating varies from few

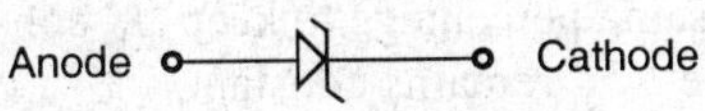


Fig. 11.23

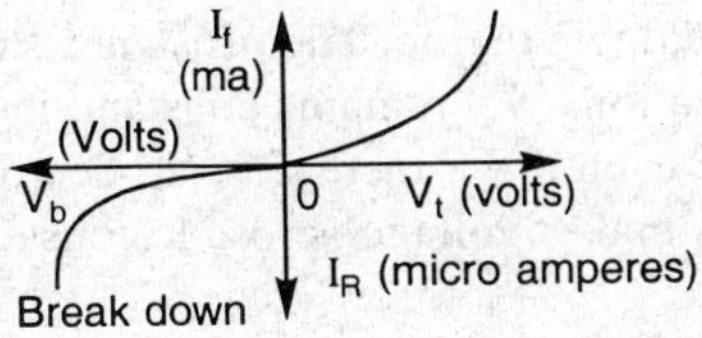


Fig. 11.24

milliwatts to 50 watts. A larger doping will yield a smaller breakdown voltage. Higher heat dissipation capability yields large power rating. Zener diodes are designed to operate in the break region without damage. The V I characteristics of zener diode are as shown in the Fig. 11.24.

The large current during the breakdown is due to (i) Avalanche breakdown and (ii) Zener breakdown. When diode is doped heavily, the depletion layer becomes narrow. Now, if reverse bias voltage is increased, under higher electric field, the electrons are pulled out of covalent bonds. Thus a large number of electron hole pairs are formed, increasing the reverse current sharply. This is called Zener breakdown.

**Avalanche breakdown**

When an external voltage is applied (reverse bias), it accelerates the minority carriers in the depletion region. When these carriers attain sufficient kinetic energy, they disrupt the covalent bond and create new electrons by collision. This action is cumulative and thus generates an avalanche of charged carriers in a short time and hence the reverse current increases sharply.

**Zener diode as a stabiliser**

Zener diode can be used as constant voltage source (voltage stabilizer or regulator) particularly when there is a change in load voltage due to change in the input supply voltage or due to change in load current. The circuit arrangement consists of resistance R in series with input voltage and zener connected in parallel with the load as shown in the Fig. 11.25.

R – Resistance at the input end
$V_i$ – Input voltage
$V_o$ – Output voltage
$R_L$ – Load resistance
$I_i$ – Input current
$I_t$ – Input through zener
$I_L$ – Load current
$V_z$ – Zener breakdown voltage

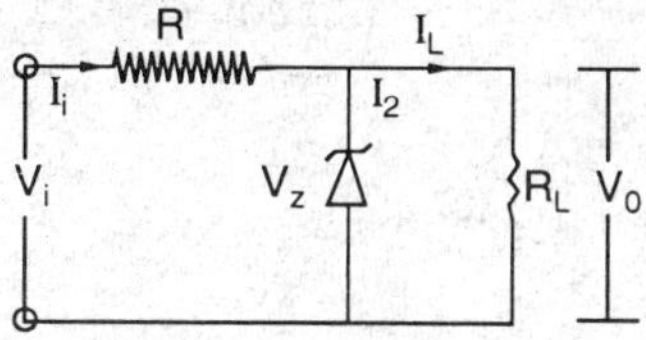


Fig. 11.25

In case '$I_L$' decreases, $I_t$ correspondingly increases to keep $I_s$ constant and $V_o$ remains constant.

Zener starts conducting only when voltage across '$R_L$' becomes more than '$V_z$'. Once '$V_i$' increases, voltage across '$R_L$' becomes more than '$V_z$'. Zener starts operating in breakdown region. The resistance 'R' limits the current through the zener. During this operation, '$V_z$' remains constant, in spite of changes in the value of '$I_z$'. Since $I_i = I_z + I_L$, even if '$I_L$' increases, '$I_z$' decreases by the same percentage to keep '$I_i$' constant. This makes voltage across R constant and hence '$V_0$' remains constant.

## 11.5. BIPOLAR JUNCTION TRANSISTOR

A transistor is a three-terminal semiconductor device consisting of two PN junctions formed by sandwitching thin layer of N-type semiconductor between two layers of P-type semiconductor. This type of transistor is known as PNP transistor. On the other hand, a layer of P-types semiconductor is sandwitched between two layers of N-type semiconductor, it is called NPN transistor. The two types of transistor are shown in Fig. 11.26.

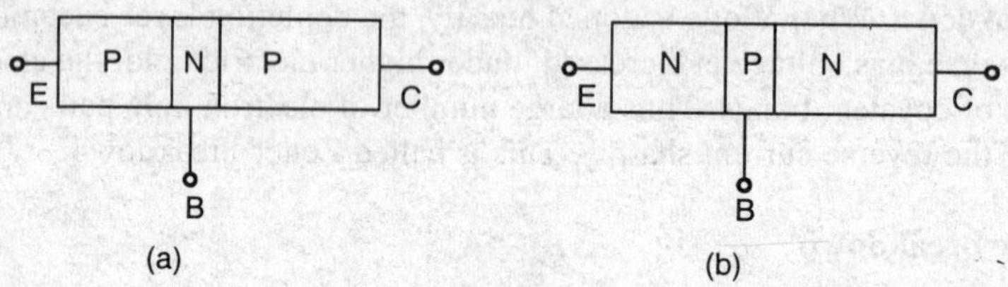


**Fig. 11.26**

The two junctions of transistor (i) one between emitter and base junction and (ii) the second between base and collector are called base junction or collector junction. Thus a transistor is nothing but two PN junction diodes connected back to back. The three regions in the transistor are named as emitter, base and collector (middle region–base, two outer regions–emitter and collector respectively. The base is lightly doped, the collector moderately doped whereas the emitter is heavily doped. The collector region is made physically larger than emitter region, to dissipate the heat. The function of emitter is to inject charge carriers to the base which in turn passes them to the collector. The collector collects the charge carriers from the base. The circuit symbols of PNP and NPN transistors are shown in Fig. 11.27.

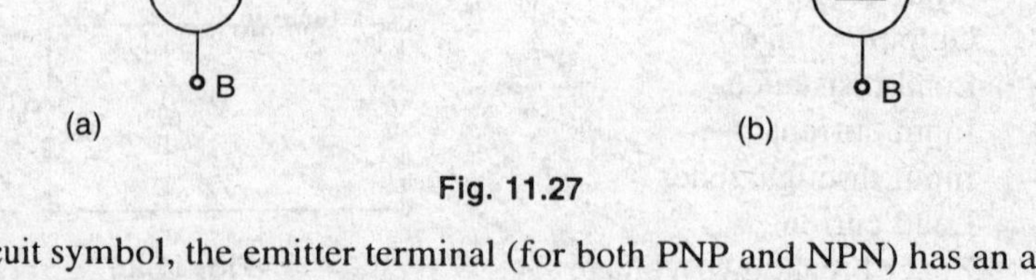


**Fig. 11.27**

In the circuit symbol, the emitter terminal (for both PNP and NPN) has an arrowhead pointing from P-region to N-region.

**11.5.1 Transistor biasing:** For better performance of a transistor, voltage of correct polarity has to be applied to its junctions. For normal operation, the emitter to base junction is forward biased and the collector to base junction is reverse biased as shown in Fig. 11.28.

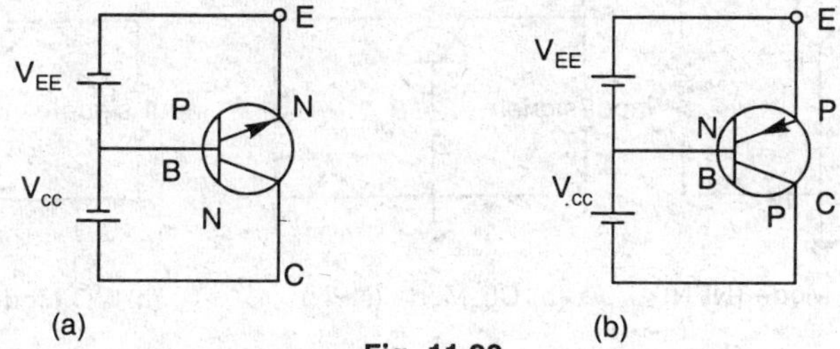


Fig. 11.28

### 11.5.2 Operation of transistor

**11.5.2 (a) NPN transistor:** When the emitter to base junction is forward biased, the electrons from emitter region diffuse towards base region, and small amount of holes from base to emitter region as shown in Fig. 11.29. Since base region is lightly doped (in this case with P-type impurity) a few electrons will combine with holes forming base current '$I_B$'. The remaining electrons crossover to collector region constituting collector current, $I_c$. Thus, the emitter current $I_E$ can be given by

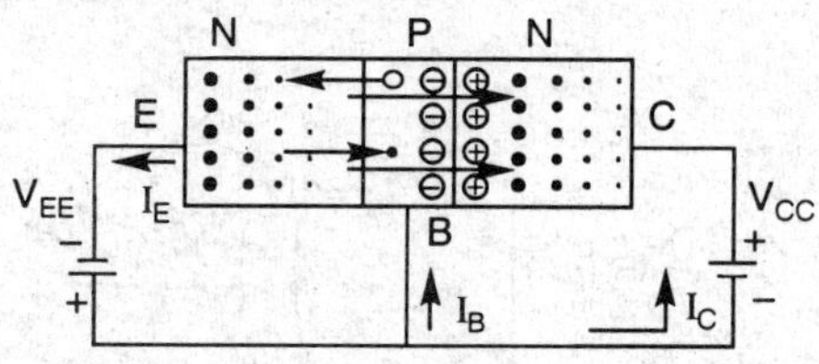


Fig. 11.29

$$I_E = I_B + I_c$$

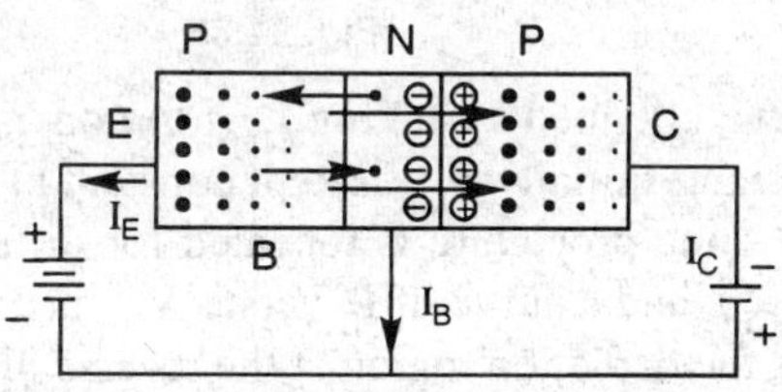


Fig. 11.30

**11.5.2(b) PNP transistor:** When forward bias is applied to emitter base junction of a PNP transistor large number of holes diffuse from emitter to base and small amount of electrons from base to emitter as shown in Fig. 11.30. Since base region is lighty doped (in this case with N type impurity), a few holes will combine with electrons forming base current '$I_B$'. The remaining holes crossover to collector region constituting collector current '$I_c$'.

**11.5.3 Transistor configuration:** While connecting the transistor in a circuit, any of its three terminals may be made common to input and output. In the remaining two terminals, one terminal can be used as input terminal and the other as output terminal. Depending on the terminal connected common to both input and output, the transistor configuration can be classified into three types, namely, (i) common emitter configuration (CE) (ii) common base configuration (CB) and (iii) common collector configuration (CC) or emitter follower. The various configurations are given in Fig. 11.31.

In the common emitter configuration, base acts as input terminal and collector acts as output terminal. In the common collector configuration, base acts as input terminal

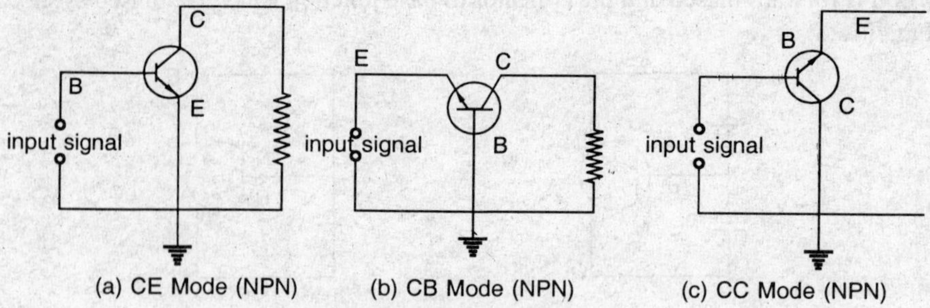


Fig. 11.31

and emitter acts as output terminal. Similarly in common base configuration, emitter acts as input terminal and collector acts as output terminal.

**11.5.4 Transistor characteristics:** The circuit arrangement for obtaining input and output characteristics of a NPN transistor in CE configuration is shown in Fig. 11.32

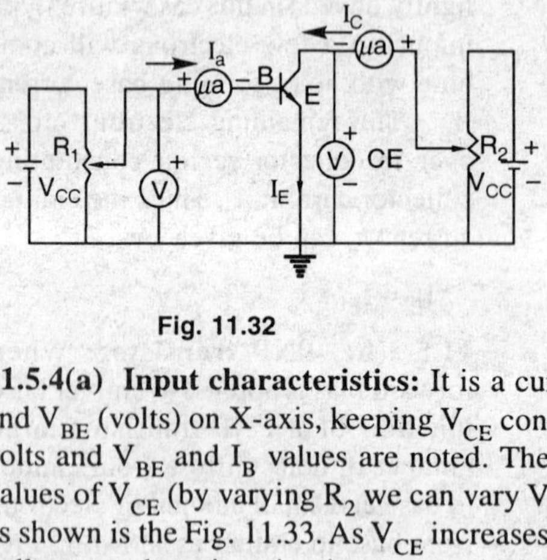


Fig. 11.32

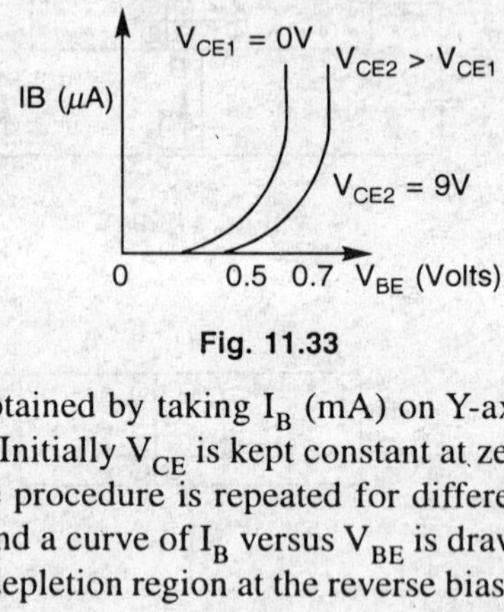


Fig. 11.33

**11.5.4(a) Input characteristics:** It is a curve obtained by taking $I_B$ (mA) on Y-axis and $V_{BE}$ (volts) on X-axis, keeping $V_{CE}$ constant. Initially $V_{CE}$ is kept constant at zero volts and $V_{BE}$ and $I_B$ values are noted. The same procedure is repeated for different values of $V_{CE}$ (by varying $R_2$ we can vary $V_{CE}$), and a curve of $I_B$ versus $V_{BE}$ is drawn as shown is the Fig. 11.33. As $V_{CE}$ increases, the depletion region at the reverse biased collector to base junction increases which reduces the width of base region thus resulting in decrease in the value of $I_B$.

**11.5.4(b) Output characteristics:** The output characteristics of a NPN transistor can be obtained by taking $I_c$ (mA) on Y-axis and $V_{CE}$ (volts) on X-axis, keeping $I_B$ (μA) constant. Initially $I_B$ is kept constant at zero μAmps and $V_{CE}$ is increased in steps by varying $R_2$. The corresponding $I_c$ values are noted and a curve of $I_c$ versus $V_{CE}$ is drawn as shown in Fig. 11.34. Same procedure is repeated for different values of '$I_B$'.

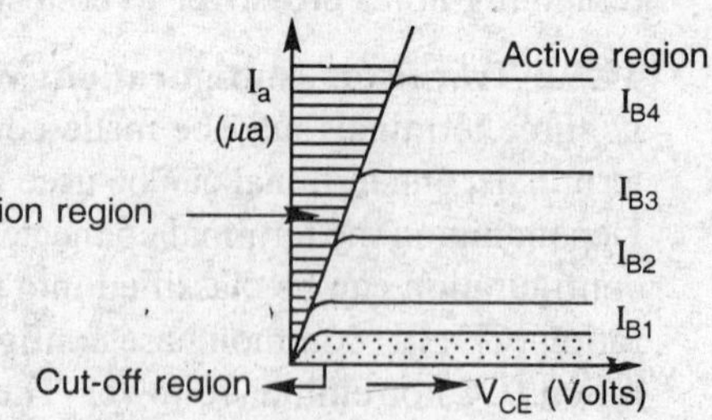


Fig. 11.34

The output characteristics have three regions, namely, (i) saturation region (ii) cut off region and (iii) active region.

In the saturation region both the junctions are forward biased. Also an increase in 'I$_B$' does not yield a corresponding large change in 'I$_c$'.

The region below the curve for $I_B = 0$ is called cut off region, where both the junctions are forward biased.

The middle portion of the characteristics is called active region, here the emitter to base junction is forward biased and the collector base junction is reverse biased.

**Note:** The transistor has to be operated in the active region in case if it has to be used as an amplifier.

**11.5.5 Parameters of Transistor:** The various parameters of transistor are:

1. Input resistance ($r_i$)
2. Output resistance ($r_o$)
3. Current gain ($\alpha$, $\beta$)

**Input resistance: ($r_i$)**

*For CE configuration*

$$r_i = \frac{\Delta V_{BE}}{\Delta I_B} / V_{CE} \text{ is constant}$$

when $\Delta V_{BE}$ = change in base to emitter voltage
$\Delta I_B$ = change in base current.
$V_{CE}$ = collector to emitter voltage.
CE = configuration has very large input independence.

*For CB Configuration*

$$r_i = \frac{\Delta V_{EB}}{\Delta I_E} / V_{CB} \text{ is constant}$$

$\Delta I_E$ = change in emitter current
$V_{CB}$ = collector to base voltage.

**Output resistance ($r_o$)**

*For CE configuration*

$$r_o = \frac{\Delta V_{CE}}{\Delta I_C} / I_B = \text{constant}$$

where $\Delta V_{CE}$ = change in collector i emitter voltage
$\Delta I_C$ = change in collector current
$I_B$ = base current.

*For CB configuration*

$$r_o = \frac{\Delta V_{CB}}{\Delta I_C} / I_E = \text{constant}$$

where $\Delta V_{CB}$ = change in collector to base voltage

$\Delta I_C$ = change in collector current

$I_E$ = emitter current

**Current amplification factor (α)**

The relation between $I_E$, $I_B$ and $I_C$ in a transistor is given by

$$I_E = I_B + I_C$$

where $I_B$ – base current

$I_E$ – emitter current

$I_C$ – collector current.

$$I_C = I_{CBO} + \alpha I_E$$

where α is the current amplification factor

$I_{CBO}$ is collector to base current with emitter open.

From the above equation we have

$$\alpha = \frac{I_C - I_{CBO}}{I_E}$$

But $I_{CBO}$ is very small compared to $I_C$ and hence can be neglected.

$$\alpha = \frac{I_C}{I_E}$$

Thus current amplification factor α is given by the ratio of collector current to emitter current (used in CB configuration. $I_C$ is output current and $I_E$ is input current).

**Current amplification factor (β)**

When a transistor is used in CE configuration, $I_B$ becomes input current and $I_C$ becomes output current. The current amplification factor (β) relates $I_B$ and $I_C$.

Thus, $$\beta = \frac{I_C}{I_B}$$

Relationship between α and β

we have $I_E = I_B + I_C$

dividing the equation on both sides by $I_E$

$$\frac{I_E}{I_E} = \frac{I_B}{I_E} + \frac{I_C}{I_E}$$

$$1 = \frac{I_B}{I_E} + \frac{I_C}{I_E}$$

But $\frac{I_C}{I_E} = \alpha$

$$\therefore \quad 1 = \frac{I_B}{I_E} + \alpha$$

also $I_E = I_B + I_C$

$$\therefore \quad 1 = \frac{I_B}{I_B + I_C} + \alpha$$

Dividing both neumerator and denominator of by '$I_B$' on right hand side, we get

$$1 = \frac{I_B / I_B}{I_B / I_B + I_C / I_B} + \alpha$$

$$= \frac{1}{1 + I_C / I_B} + \alpha$$

But $\frac{I_C}{I_B} = \beta$

$$1 = \frac{1}{1+\beta} + \alpha$$

$$1 = \frac{1 + \alpha(1+\beta)}{1+\beta}$$

$$(1 + \beta) = 1 + \alpha + \alpha\beta$$

$$\beta - \alpha\,\beta = \alpha$$

$$\beta(1 - \alpha) = \alpha$$

$$\therefore \quad \beta = \frac{\alpha}{1-\alpha}$$

Also we have

$$\beta(1 - \alpha) = \alpha$$

$$\beta - \alpha\,\beta = \alpha$$

$$\beta = \alpha\,(1 + \beta)$$

$$\therefore \quad \frac{\beta}{1+\beta} = \alpha$$

Alternate expression for $I_C$

we have, $I_C = \alpha \,.\, I_E + I_{CBO}$

$$= \alpha\,(I_B + I_C) + I_{CBO}$$

$$I_C = \alpha I_B + \alpha I_C + I_{CBO}$$

$$I_C - aI_C = aI_B + I_{CBO}$$

$$I_C(1 - \alpha) = \alpha I_B + I_{CBO}$$

$$I_C = \left(\frac{\alpha}{1-\alpha}\right) I_B + \left(\frac{1}{1-\alpha}\right) I_{CBO}$$

$$I_C = \beta I_B + (\beta + 1) \,.\, I_{CBO}$$

### 11.5.6 Comparison among the three configurations

| Parameter | CE | CB | CC |
|---|---|---|---|
| Input resistance | low | very low | high |
| Output resistance | high | very high | low |
| Current gain | high | less than 1 | high |
| Voltage gain | high | high | less than 1 |
| Application | audio frequency applications | high frequency applications | impedance matching |

### 11.5.7 Advantages of a transistor:

1. Longer life
2. Low power consumption
3. Higher efficiency
4. Smaller in size
5. Light in weight
6. Does not require filaments

### 11.5.8 Applications

1. Transistors are used as switches.
2. They are used in amplifiers to enhance the weak signals.
3. They are also used in oscillator circuits.

## 11.6. FIELD EFFECT TRANSISTOR (FET)

The two main drawbacks of a bipolar transistor are, namely, 1) low input impedance (due to forward bias emitter junction) and 2) considerable noise level, can be overcome using a FET. Depending on the construction, the FET can be classified into two types.

- FET
  - JFET (Junction FET)
    - N-Channel JFET
    - P-Channel JFET
  - MOSFET (Metal Oxide semiconductor FET)

In the N-channel JFET, the electrons are the majority carriers whereas in P-channel JFET, the holes are the majority carriers, whereas in bipolar junction transistor both majority and minority carriers constitute the current flow. Hence FET is also known as unipolar device.

Thus FET is a three-terminal semiconductor device in which the conduction is due to any one type of majority carriers i.e. either electrons or holes. The three terminals are 1. Source (S) 2. Drain (D) and 3. Gate (G). The current conduction is controlled by the electric field between the gate and the conducting channel and hence the name FET. Fig. 11.35 below shows the symbol of N-channel FET and P-channel FET respectively.

In the N-channel FET, the arrow on the gate points inwards as shown in Fig. 11.35(a) whereas in the P-channel FET, the arrow on the gate points outwards as shown Fig. 11.35(b).

a) b)

**Fig. 11.35**

### 11.6.1 Constructional details

**N channel JFET**: It consists of n-type silicon bar forming the conducting channel for the charge carriers. The heavily doped P regions introduced on both sides of the bar form the 'gate'. This is used to control the flow of electrons from source to drain.

**P channel JFET**: It consists of p-type silicon bar forming the conducting channel for the charge carriers. The heavily doped N regions introduced on both sides of the bar form the gate. This is used to control the flow of holes from source to drain. The construction of JFET is shown in Fig. 11.36.

**Source:** At this terminal the majority carriers enter the bar.

**Drain**: At this terminal the majority carriers leave the bar.

**Gate:** The heavily doped P regions introduced on both the sides of the N type bar (in N channel JFET) is called gate.

**Channel:** The space between source and drain (between the two gates) is called channel which allows the movement of majority carriers from source to drain.

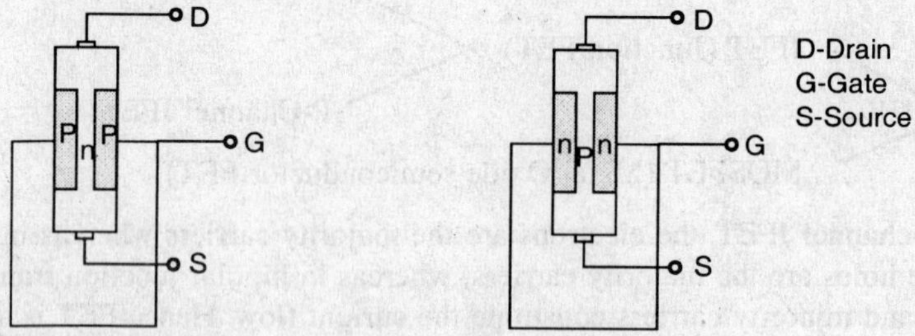


(a) N-Channel JFET (b) P-Channel JFET

**Fig. 11.36**

**11.6.2 Working principle or JFET:** Consider a N-channel JFET with an applied voltage ($V_{DS}$) as shown in Fig. 11.37 (positive terminal to the drain and negative terminal to source). The majority carriers, namely, electrons start flowing from the source to the drain, causing a drain current '$I_D$'. This '$I_D$' passes through the space between two P regions. This width and hence '$I_D$' can be controlled by changing the reverse bias voltage applied to the gate. When the reverse bias voltage ($V_{GS}$) is applied, the width of depletion layer increases, which reduces the channel width and hence causing decrease in '$I_D$'.

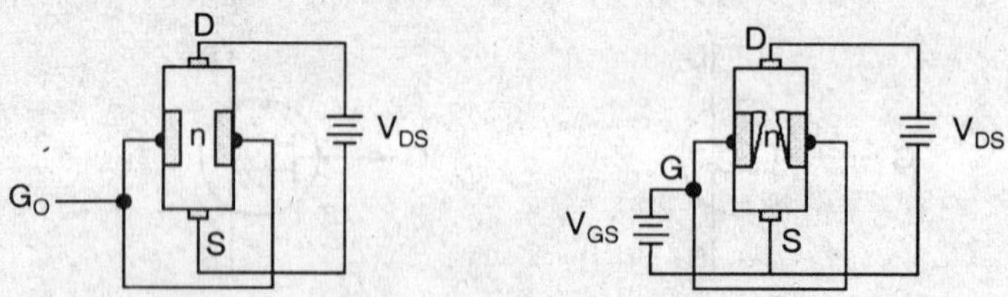


(a) Gate with no-bias (b) Gate wtih reverse bias

**Fig. 11.37**

The operation of P-channel FET operates on the same lines except that the polarity '$V_{GS}$' or '$V_{DS}$' are to be reversed and the current carriers will be holes.

**11.6.3 Characteristics of JFET:** It is a curve drawn taking drain current '$I_D$' on Y-axis and drain-source voltage '$V_{DS}$' on X-axis as shown in Fig. 11.38.

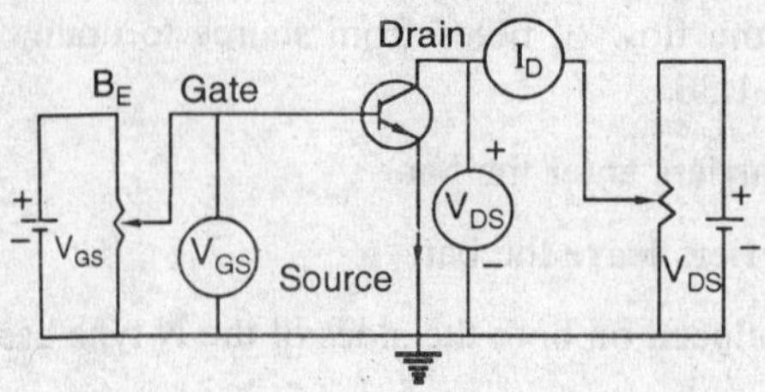


**Fig. 11.38**

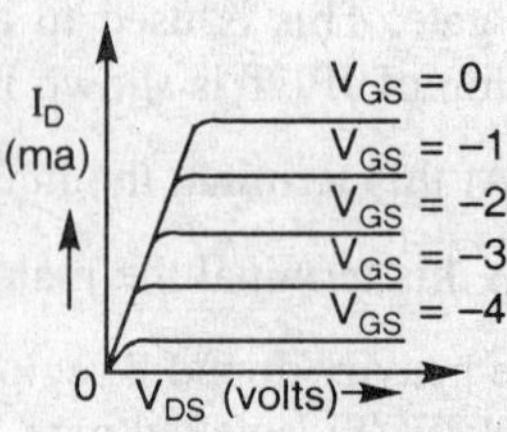


**Fig. 11.39**

The circuit arrangement for obtaining the characteristics is shown in Fig. 11.39. Initially the gate is kept at zero bias ($V_{GS} = 0$). When '$V_{DS}$'is zero, '$I_D$' is also zero (because the drain does not have any force to attract the majority carriers). Now as '$V_{DS}$' is increased, '$I_D$' increases linearly. When the '$V_{DS}$' exceeds certain value called pinchoff voltage, '$I_D$' remains constant. (The value of voltage applied across drain and source, where all the free charges from the channel are removed is called pinch off voltage.) This is because, after the pinch off voltage, the channel width becomes so narrow that the depletion layers almost touch each other. As the '$V_{GS}$' increased, the curve shifts downward because pinch off voltage occurs at lower values of '$V_{DS}$'.

### 11.6.4 Advantages of FET

1. It has very high input impedance enabling high degree of isolation between input and output.
2. The operation is noiseless.
3. There is no risk due to thermal runaway.
4. Longer life.
5. High power gain.
6. Small size.
7. High efficiency.

### 11.6.5 Applications of FET

1. Because of its high input impedance, FET can be used as a buffer amplifier for isolating the two stages.
2. Due to the same reason (i.e. high input impedance), FET can be used in phase shift oscillator to minimise the loading effect.

**11.6.6 JFET Parameters:** There are three important parameters, namely, dynamic drain resistance($r_d$), mutual or transconductance ($g_m$) and amplification factor ($\mu$).

**Dynamic drain resistance** ($r_d$): It is the ratio of small change in drain-source voltage to the small change in drain current, at constant gate-source voltage.

$$\therefore r_d = \frac{\Delta V_{DS}}{\Delta I_D} \text{ at constant } V_{GS}$$

**Transconductance** ($g_m$): It is the ratio of small change in drain current to small change in gate-source voltage at constant drain-source voltage.

$$\therefore g_m = \frac{\Delta I_D}{\Delta V_{GS}} \text{ at constant } V_{DS}$$

**Amplification factor** ($\mu$): It is the ratio of small change in drain-source voltage to small change in gate source voltage at constant drain current.

$$\therefore \mu = \frac{\Delta V_{DS}}{\Delta V_{GS}} \text{ at constant } I_D$$

## 11.7. MOSFET

It is nothing but metal oxide semiconductor field effect transistor. It is available in two forms.

MOSFET
- Enhancement MOSFET
- Depletion MOSFET

Due to very small leakage current, the input impedance of MOSFET is much higher than that of FET. By applying an electric field across the insulator deposited on the semiconductor material, the width of the conducting channel can be controlled. MOSFET is also known as insulated gate field effect transistor (IGFET). The two special features of MOSFET are (i) small chip area and (ii) low power consumption.

Depletion Mode N-channel MOSFET: The circuit symbol and structure is given in Fig. 11.40

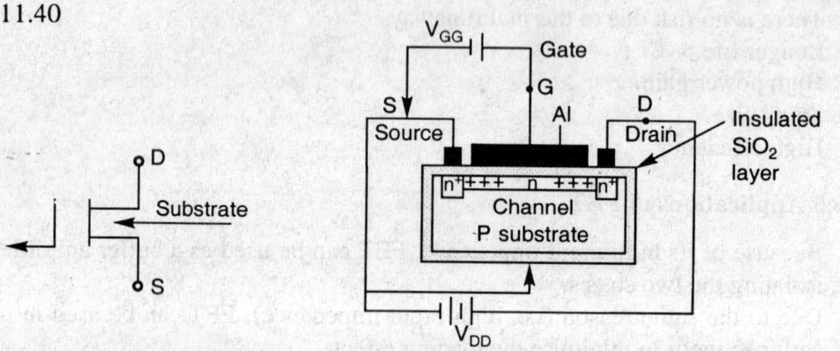


(a) Symbol Fig. 11.40 (b) Structure

Here a lightly doped P-type semiconductor is taken as substrate. The two highly doped $N^+$ regions formed, act as source and drain respectively. Between these two, a shallow N region called 'channel' is diffused. A thin aluminium metallic film deposited over the N region acts as the gate. An insulated layer of $SiO_2$ is deposited overlaping $N^+$ and N regions. Here the important point to note is that, the gate does not form a junction with the source and the drain unlike JFET.

**11.7.1 Characteristics:** When, drain is mode positive with respect to the source, and when $V_{GE} = 0$ then due to presence of electrons a current will flow from drain to source through the N-region. The P-substrate is connected to the source. Now when gate is kept at negative potential with respect to source, the gate and the N-channel acts as a parallel plate capacitor as they are separated by an insulating material. Thus a +ve charge is induced on N-channel whereas a −ve charge at the gate. This positive charge

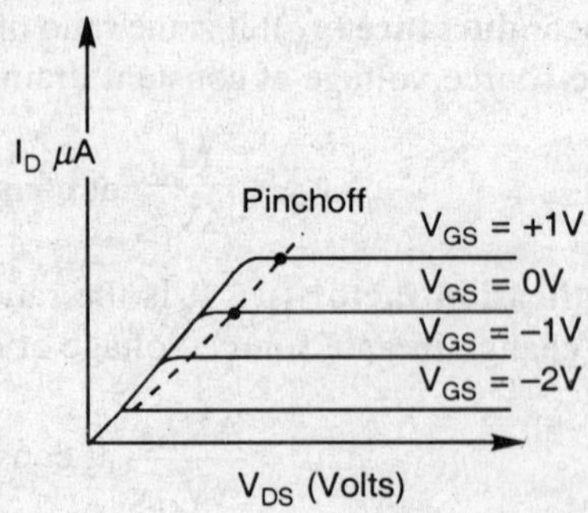


Fig. 11.41

depletes the channel and reduces con-ductivity. Thus by adjusting the negative potential at the gate, the current flow through the channel from drain to source can be varied.

In the enhancement mode of operation. $V_{GS}$ is made positive. With a positive voltage on the gate, negative charge is induced in the channel and the conductivity increases.

## 11.8. SILICON-CONTROLLED RECTIFIER (SCR)

SCR is the most important family member of thyristor. It is a power semiconductor device which can handle currents of several hundred amperes and voltages of several thousand volts. Because of its compactness, reliability and low loss, it is employed in almost all the power controlled devices. The other members of thyristor family include triac, diac, silicon-controlled switch and programmable unijunction transistor etc.

**11.8.1 Constructional details:** SCR is a four-layer, three-terminal, three-junction, unidirectional switching device. The three terminals are anode, cathode and gate. The four layers are of alternate P-type and N-type silicon semiconductors forming three junctions as shown in Fig. 11.42. the layers and junctions are formed by gaseous diffusion and alloying techniques.

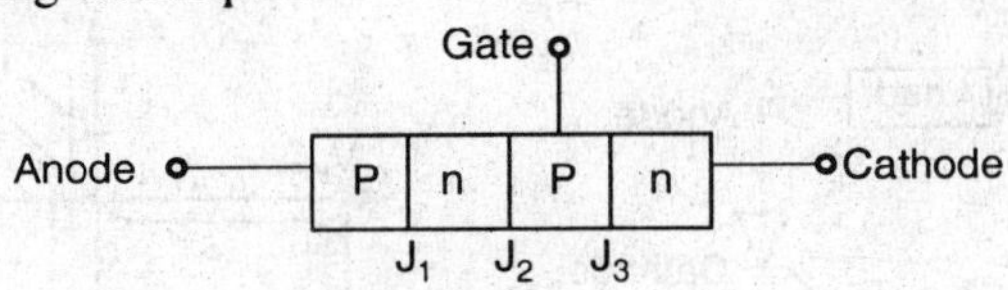


**Fig. 11.42**

The circuit symbol for SCR is shown in Fig. 11.43 and the internal constructional details are shown in Fig. 11.44.

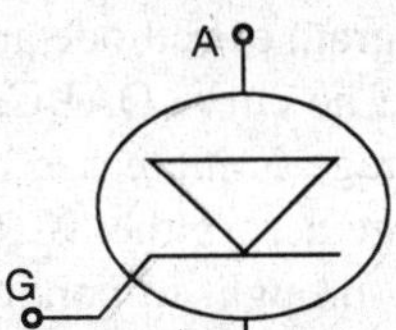


**Fig. 11.43**

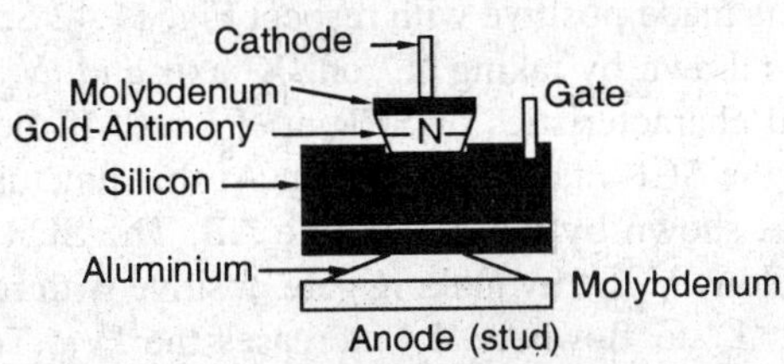


**Fig. 11.44**

The PNP silicon pellet is formed by diffusion. An aluminium wire connected to the top P-layer acts as 'gate'. The upper N-region is made by alloying gold-antimony into the P-type silicon. To minimize the mechanical stresses and the thermal expansion, molybdenum disk is employed both at the top and bottom.

**11.8.2 Operation of SCR:** SCR can be brought to on state by two ways. In the first method, gate terminal is kept open and the supply voltage is made equal to the break over voltage and then turning it on by applying small voltage to the gate. Once the SCR starts conducting the gate loses the control i.e. even if the gate pulse is removed, SCR will not stop conducting. The only way to stop conduction is to reduce the applied voltage to zero.

The important terms that are related to the study of SCR are:

1. **Break over voltage:** Gate terminal being kept open. The minimum forward voltage at which SCR starts conducting is called break over voltage.
2. **Peak reverse voltage:** The maximum reverse voltage that can be applied to SCR in the reverse direction (with conducting) is called peak reverse voltage.
3. **Holding current:** The minimum value of anode current below which it must fall to bring the SCR to OFF state from ON state is called holding current.
4. **Forward current rating:** The maximum anode current that an SCR is capable of withstanding without getting damaged is called forward current rating.
5. **Latching current:** It is the minimum value of anode current which the SCR must attain during turn-on, to maintain conduction, when the gate signal is removed.

**Note:** Latching current is associated in the turn-on process whereas holding current is associated with turn-off process. Latching current is greater than holding current.

**11.8.3 Characteristics of SCR:** The circuit diagram for obtaining V-i characteristics of SCR is as shown in the Fig. 11.45. The characteristics are shown in Fig. 11.46.

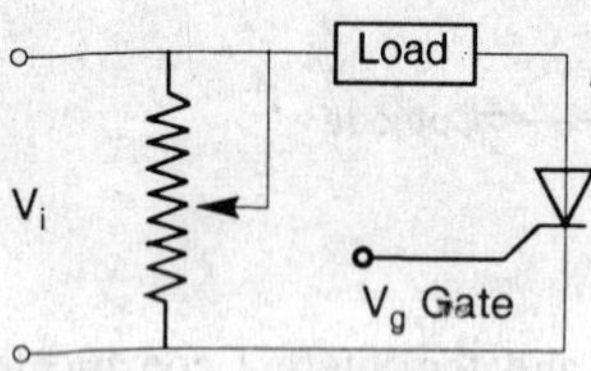


Fig. 11.45

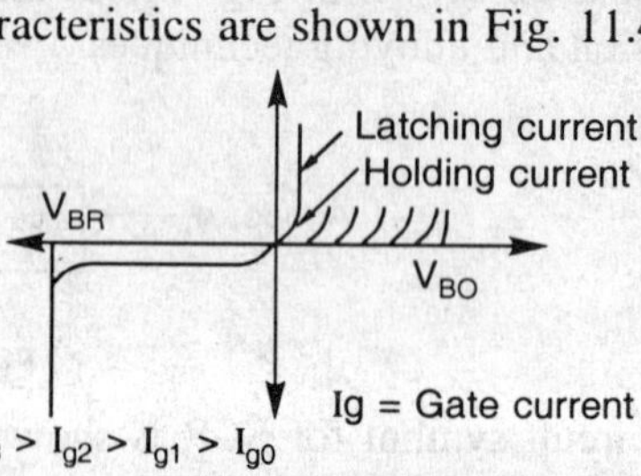


Fig. 11.46

Anode is made positive with respect Fig. 11.42 Schematic diagram to cathode and the curve is drawn by taking '$I_a$' on 'X' axis and '$V_a$' on Y-axis. The curve OABC gives forward characteristics of SCR at '$I_g$' = 0. If the supply voltage is increased above '$V_{BO}$', the SCR starts conducting. At this juncture, the voltage across the SCR falls down as shown by the dotted line AB. The SCR can also be brought to conducting state below '$V_{BO}$', by making gate positive with respect to cathode. This causes a gate current '$I_g$' to flow. As '$I_g$' increases the '$V_{BO}$' decreases. Once the SCR is turned 'ON' the gate loses control. (SCR cannot be turned off using gate.) One method to turn off the SCR is that by reducing '$I_a$' below '$I_h$'.

**11.8.4 Two-transistor model of SCR:** Here the SCR can be considered as NPN and a PNP transistor connected with collector of one transistor coupled to the base of the another resulting a positive feedback action as shown in the Fig. 11.47.

When the voltage applied between anode and cathode is less than '$V_{BO}$' with gate open, there is no base current i.e. $I_{B2} = 0$. Hence no current flows through '$T_2$' and '$T_1$'. Thus SCR is in OFF state. Now if a small gate current is allowed, '$I_{B2}$' and '$I_{C2}$' increases. Hence '$I_{B1}$', and '$I_{C1}$' increase. But as IC increases '$I_{B2}$' increases. This action becomes cumulative as a result the two transistors are driven to saturation. Large current flows through the SCR thus switching to conducting state.

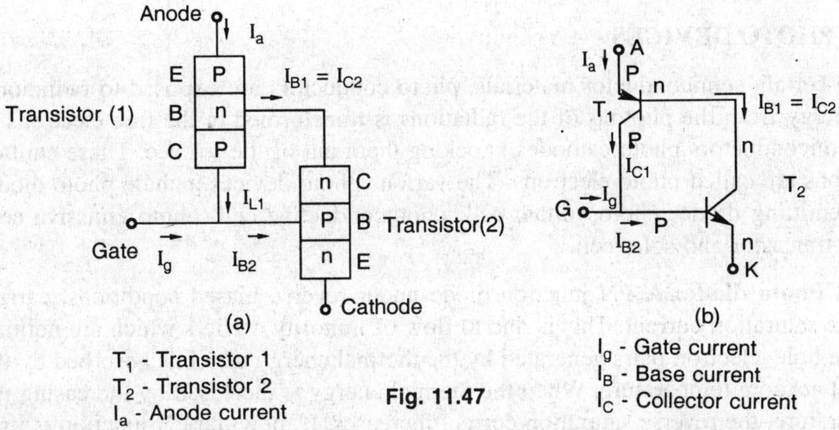


Fig. 11.47

### TURN ON

SCR is turned ON i.e. switched to conducting state by increasing the forward voltage beyond '$V_{BO}$'. It can also be turned on by applying a positive gate signal (d.c. gate signal or a.c. gate signal or by pulsed signal) when the device is forward biased.

### TURN OFF

SCR is turned OFF i.e. brought to off state by reducing the forward current below the level of holding current. This is done by using commutation circuit like resonate commutation auxiliary commutation, complementary commutation, external pulse commutation etc.

### 11.8.5 Advantages of SCR

1. High efficiency due to low loss (For example, when used as a switch)
2. Less maintenance and longer life due to the absence of moving parts. Also it gives noiseless operation
3. Small size
4. High reliability
5. High switching speed
6. High voltage and current rating

### 11.8.6 Applications of SCR

1. It can be used as electronic switch
2. As a.c. to d.c. converter
3. As a.c. voltage controller
4. As d.c. to a.c. inverter
5. As d.c. to d.c. converter (chopper)
6. As a.c. to a.c. converter (cyclo converter)
7. HVDC transmission

It is also used in a.c., d.c. electric drives, uninterrupted power supplies, transformer tap changers, frequency converters, battery charging, illumination control, static power compensation etc.

## 11.9. PHOTO DEVICES

When certain semiconductor materials, photo conductors are exposed to radiations, the energy from the photons of the radiations is transformed to the free electrons in the semiconductors photo cathodes knocking them out of the surface. These emitted electrons are called photo electrons. The various photo devices include photo diode, light emitting diode, photo voltaic cell: photoconductive cell, photo emissive cell, photo transistor and solar cell.

**11.9.1 Photo diode:** A PN junction diode under reverse biased conditions, carries reverse saturation current. This is due to flow of minority carriers which are nothing but the hole–electron pairs generated by the thermal energy which is absorbed by the crystal at room temperature. When the thermal energy is increased by increasing the temperature, the reverse saturation current increases. If, now the PN junction is irradiated by light, instead of thermal energy, the reverse current through the diode increases. The circuit symbol and the biasing is shown in Fig. 11.48.

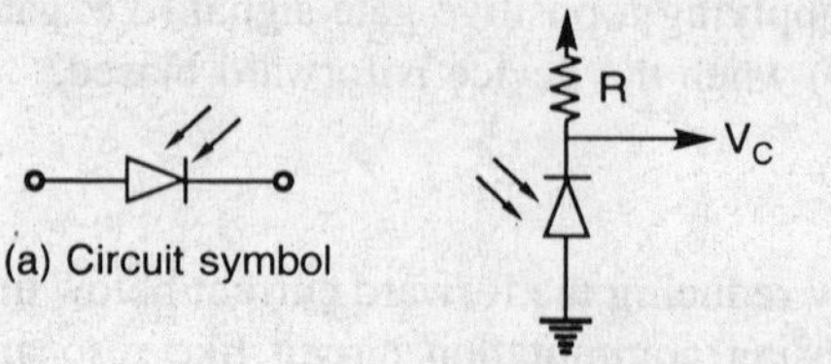

(a) Circuit symbol

(b) Biasing of photo diode

Fig. 11.48

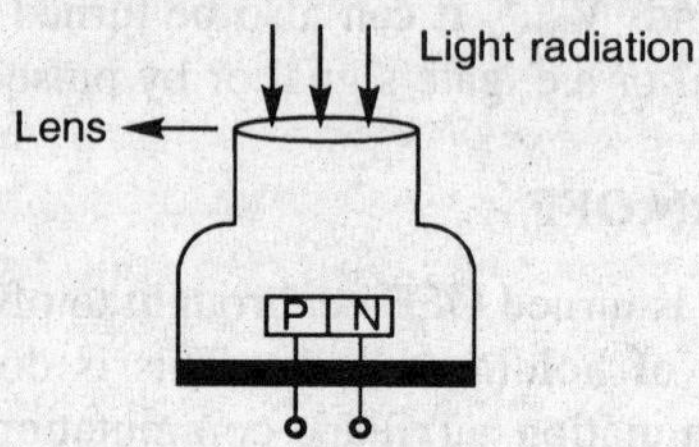

Fig. 11.49

For maximum activity, sometimes, a lens is placed on the junction to focus the incident light as shown in Fig. 11.49. The changes in the output voltage is proportional to the incident light. This output signal is amplified and sent for further processing. These photo diodes are used in industries, process control and automation, instrumentation and communication.

**11.9.2 Light emitting diode:** Some PN junction diodes using gallium arsenide or gallium phosphide release energy in the form of light when an electron falls from the conduction band to the valence band. PN diodes having such a property are called light emitting diodes (LED). The circuit symbol of LED is shown in Fig. 11.50(a).

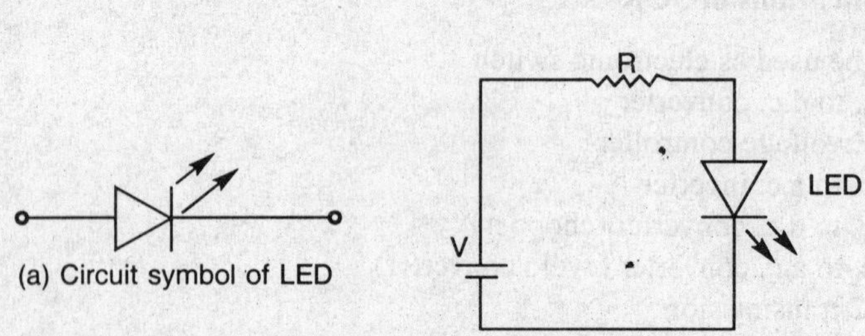

(a) Circuit symbol of LED

(b) Biasing of LED

Fig. 11.50

Since radiations occur due to recombinations of electrons and holes, the majority carriers are required to cross the junction. Hence the LED is forward biased as shown in the Fig. 11.50(b) to produce the radiation. The radiation is concentrated near the junction. The intensity of radiation depends on diode current (varies linearly) and the temperature (varies inversely). Dark red or green are the colours of radiations that are commercially available. Compared to incandescent light sources, LED consumes less power and has longer life. LEDs are used in 1) digital displays 2) as pilot light 3) watches 4) calculators 5) instrument panels 6) movie cameras to convert sound to light and 7) optical communication.

**11.9.3 Photo multiplier:** These photo multiplier tubes are used for detecting very weak light intensities especially in T.V. pickup devices, astronomy and nuclear–radiation measurements. It makes use of secondary emission principle. The important parts are photo cathode, dynode and collector. When light falls on a photo cathode, it emits electrons. These electrons are electrostatically focussed on to the dynode ($D_1$). The dynode uses a cathode material which can emit electrons more in number than that of the incident electrons. These resulting secondary electrons are focussed on $D_2$ and so on. If there are 'N' dynodes then the overall current gain will be $\Delta^N$ where '$\Delta$' is the ratio of secondary electrons to incident electrons. The electrons are finally collected by an output electrode called collector. The schematic arrangement of photo multiphier is shown in the Fig. 11.51.

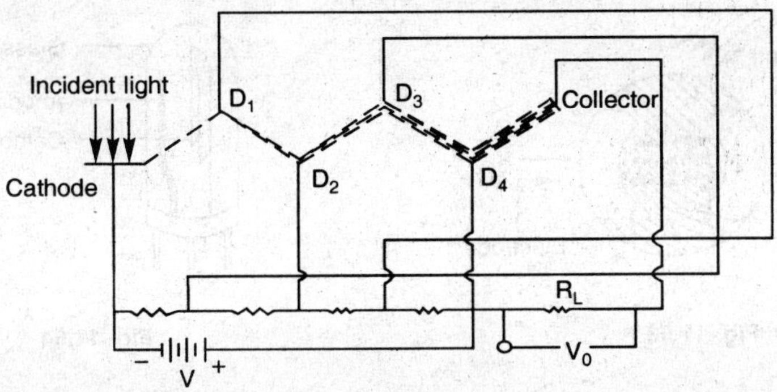


Fig. 11.51

**11.9.4 Photo voltaic cell:** The commonly used photo voltaic cells are of barrier type like iron-selenium cells. It has iron base over which selenium layer is placed. A very thin layer of gold or silver is formed on the selenium which acts as a front electrode. The barrier is formed by the cathode sputtering the transparent film on selenium. When light falls on such a combination, an emf is generated proportional to the incident light. The constructional details of photo voltaic cell is given in Fig. 11.52

Due to the incident light, the selenium semiconductor ejects electrons which travel from selenium to the silver electrode, through the barrier film. The barrier film opposes the flow of current in opposite direction. These are used in reading illumination meters, portable exposure meters etc.

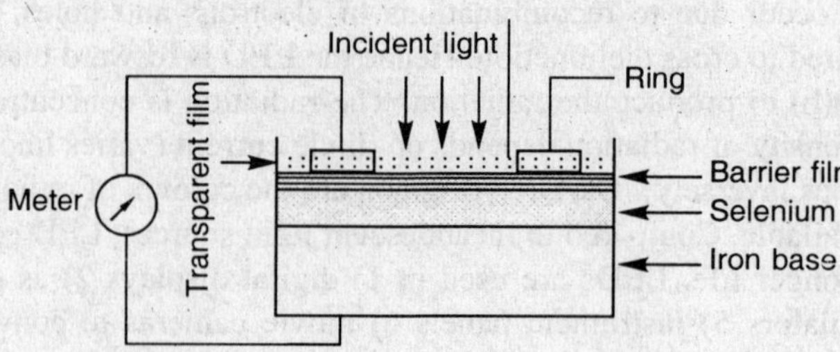


Fig. 11.52

When certain semiconductor materials like selenium, lead sulphide, cadmium sulphide etc. are exposed to radiations, their specific resistance changes. This property is used in the operation of photoconductive cell. The most commonly used photoconductive cells are the cadmium sulphide cells as they possess very high dark/light ratio. The photoconductive cell consists of a semiconductor material with two electrodes attached to as shown in the Fig. 11.53. When the cell is illuminated, its resistance decreases and the circuit current increases, a large ratio of dark to light resistance can be obtained by selecting suitable shape of semiconductor material. The photoconductive cells are used for detecting the location of aircrafts and ships with the help of the radiations coming out from their exhausts.

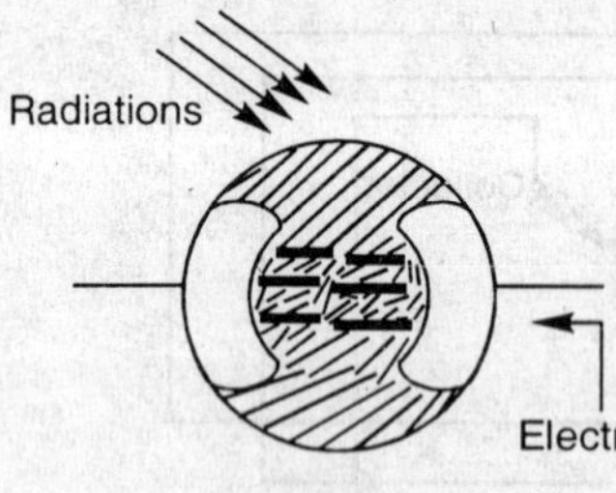


Fig. 11.53

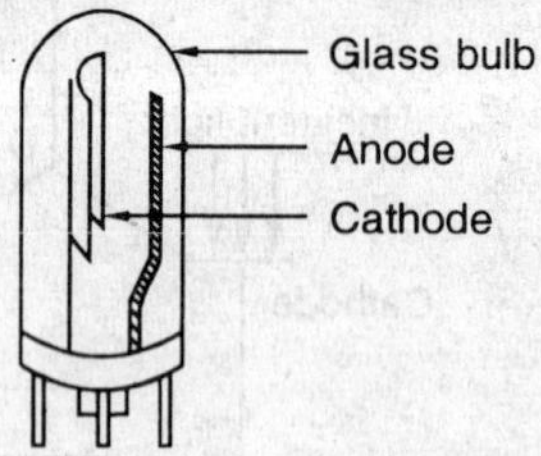


Fig. 11.54

**11.9.6 Photo emissive cell:** These cells are used in photometry, calorimetry, automatic door opening, fire alarms, objects sorting etc. Its working depends on the emission of electrons from a metal cathode when exposed to light or other radiations. The constructional details of the cell are given in Fig. 11.54. It consists of an evacuated glass bulb with semicylindrical metal cathode and an anode in the form of thin wire. The cathode is coated with an emissive material. The metal employed for the cathode depends upon the radiations used. For ultra violet radiations zinc, nickel or aluminium metals are used. For visible light alkali metals are used. Composite cathodes are used for infra-red radiations. When the cathode is illuminated, the electrons are emitted, and these electrons move towards anode thus causing current flow. The magnitude of current depends on the intensity of incident radiations.

**11.9.7 Photo transistor:** The most commonly used photo transistor is the NPN-photo transistor. The circuit symbol and the schematic presentation is shown in Fig. 11.55.

A lens is placed on the junction to focus the incident light for maximum activity. When there is no incident light falling on the junction, then

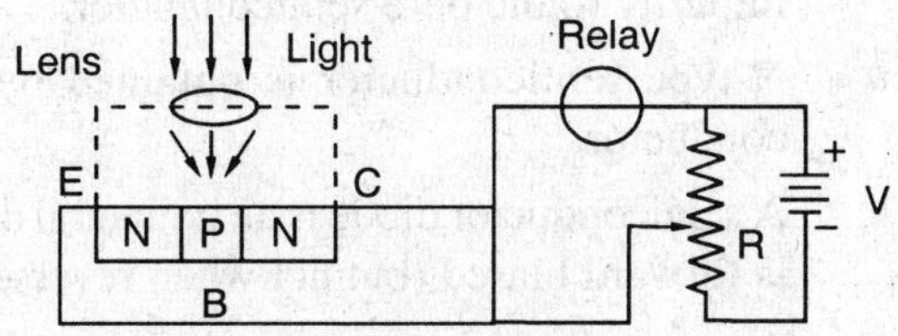


Fig. 11.55

$I_C$ is the $(1 + \beta)\, I_{CO} + \beta I_B$

where $I_C$ is the collector current

$I_{CO}$ is the reverse saturation at the collector junction

$\beta$ is the current gain

$I_B$ is the base current

when $I_B$ is the 0, the above equation can be rewritten as

$I_C$ is the $(1 + \beta)\, I_{CO}$

'$I_{CO}$' is due to thermally generated electron hole pairs. If now, a light is made to focus on the collector junction, additional electron hole pairs are generated, constituting photo transistor current $I_L$. Hence the new collector current is given by

$$I_C = (1 + \beta)\, I_{CO} + (1 + \beta)\, I_L$$

**11.9.8 Solar cell:** The photo voltaic effect can be observed when sunlight is incident on certain semiconductors, the incident sunlight is converted into electrical energy. Such a cell is called solar cell or solar battery which are widely used in satellites to provide the necessary electrical power. The configuration of solar cell is shown in Fig. 11.56. The PN junction is formed by keeping P-type base material into a diffusion furnace containing N-type dopant. The positive and negative charges formed due to the absorption of photons are made to drift into the front where it is collected by fine grid of narrow metallic fingers and to the back where it is collected by metallic contact. Each cell can produce a voltage of 0.5V. To increase the power output, series parallel combination of large banks of cells are used.

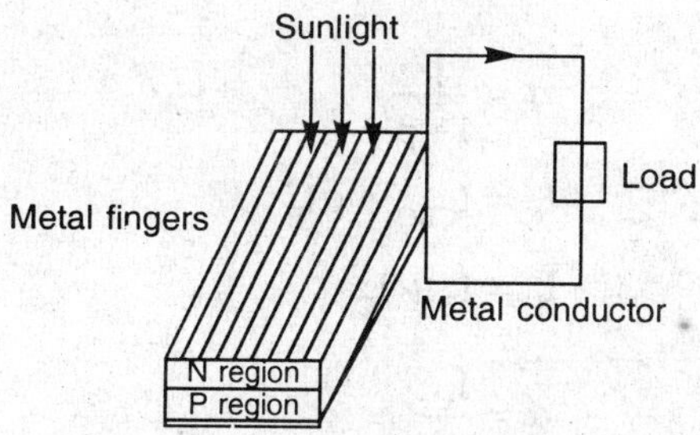


Fig. 11.56

## HIGHLIGHTS

- In the conductors, valence band and conduction bands overlap.
- In semiconductors there will be a small energy gap between almost filled valence band and almost empty conduction band.
- In the insulators, there will be a large energy gap between full valence band and empty conduction band.
- An intrinsic semiconductor is made of semiconductor material in its purest form with equal number of condution electrons and holes.

- An extrinsic semiconductor is obtained by adding an extremely small amount of impurity to the pure semiconductor.
- N-type semiconductor is obtained by adding trivalent impurity to the semiconductor.
- A semiconductor diode is an unilateral device. It conducts only where P-N junction is forward biased (but not when reverse biased).
- A zener diode is a reverse biased silicon or germaium P-N junction which is operated in the breakdown region.
- A semiconductor diode can be used as rectifier.
- A transistor is made of semiconductor material with three different doped regions, namely, emitter base and collector.
- Common emitter configuration.

$$\beta = \frac{I_C}{I_B}$$

$$\beta = \frac{\alpha}{1-\alpha}$$

$$\alpha = \frac{\beta}{1+\beta}$$

$$I_C = I_{CBO} + \alpha I_E$$

$$I_E = I_B + I_C$$

$$\alpha = \frac{I_C}{I_E}$$

- FET is a semiconductor device in which current conduction is either by electrons or holes and is controlled by means of an electric field between the gate electrode and conducting channel of the device.
- SCR is a four layer, three terminal semiconductor device which can act as a switch and also as a controlled rectifier.
- Photo electric devices convert light energy into electrical energy. For example, photo diode, light emitting diode, photo multiplier, photo voltaic cell, photo conductive cell, photo emissive cell, photo transistor and solar cell.

## REVIEW QUESTIONS

1. Explain the following terms

(a) Valence electrons (b) Energy band
(c) Valence band (e) Conduction electrons
(f) Conduction band (g) Forbidden energy gap
(h) Fermi level

2. Explain the classification of materials using energy band theory.
3. What are the types of semiconductors?
4. What are the properties of a semiconductor?
5. Explain the process of hole formation.
6. Explain the following terms:
   (a) Doping (b) Doping agent
   (c) Acceptor (d) Donor
7. Explain the formation of PN junction.
8. Explain the VI characteristics of PN junction.
9. Explain the working of
   (a) Half wave rectifier (b) Full wave rectifier (c) Bridge rectifier
10. Write a short note on filters.
11. Explain the working of Zener Diode. Also write its applications.
12. Explain the operation of NPN transistor.
13. What are the different configurations of a transistor? Compare their parameters.
14. Explain the input and output characteristics of a transistor.
15. What are the advantages and applications of a transistor?
16. Explain the construction and working principle of JFET.
17. What are the advantages and applications of FET.
18. Explain the construction and working principle of MOSFET.
19. Explain the working principle and operation of SCR.
20. Explain the characteristics of SCR.
21. What are the advantages and applications of SCR?
22. What are the various photo devices?
23. Write short notes on
   (a) Photo diode (b) LED
   (c) Photo multiplier (d) Photo voltaic cell
   (e) Photo conductive cell (f) Photo emissive cell
   (g) Photo transistor (h) Solar cell

## TWO MARKS QUESTIONS AND ANSWERS

1. *What is a semiconductor, give examples* ?

   A semiconductor is one whose property lies between conductor and insulator. In terms of energy bands, semiconductor is one which has almost an empty conduction band and an almost filled valence band with a very narrow energy gap, e.g. silicon and germanium.

2. *What is meant by doping* ?

   The process of adding impurity to the semiconductor is called doping. If a pentavalent impurity is added we get n-type semiconductor. On the other hand if a trivalent impurity is added we get p-type semiconductor.

3. *What are the types of semiconductors ?*

   1. Intrinsic semiconductor (pure)
   2. Extrinsic semiconductor (impure)

   The extrinsic semiconductor is further classified into n-type semiconductor and p-type semiconductor.

4. *What is a rectifier ?*

   A rectifier is one which converts alternating quantity into unidirectional quantity. A semiconductor diode can be used as rectifier.

5. *Give two advantages of bridge rectifier ?*

   1. Peak inverse voltage rating per diode is less.
   2. Centre tapped transformer is not required.

6. *What are the applications of Zener diode ?*

   Zener diode can be used as a voltage regulator, peak clipper and also used for meter protection.

7. *What are the three configurations of a transistor. Which is the most commonly used one ?*

   The three configurations in the transistor are

   1. Common emitter configuration
   2. Common collector configuration
   3. Common base configuration

   The commonly used configuration is common emitter configuration because of large gain in voltage, current and power.

8. *What is a FET ?*

   Field effect transistor is a three-terminal, unipolar, solid state device. The three terminals are source, drain and gate.

9. *What is meant by firing and commutation of thyristor ?*

   Firing means bringing the SCR from OFF state to ON state. Commutation means making the SCR to go to OFF state from ON state.

10. *What is a photo electric device ? Give two examples.*

    It is a device which converts light energy into electrical energy. The examples are photo voltaic cell and solar cell.

*Chapter 12*

# INTEGRATED CIRCUITS

## 12.1 INTRODUCTION

An integrated circuit (IC) is an electronic assembly built in such a way that all the components in the circuit are fabricated together in a small container called "chip". These IC chips have become very important in the computer industry. They are also used in home appliances, communication and control systems, etc., where superior performance and reduction in size are the important requirements. It may not be possible to achieve all these characteristics with discrete components. They provide long, trouble-free services. Since they are produced in large scale, economy is achieved.

The other advantages of ICs over discrete components are simple design, low power consumption, high reliability, increased speed of operation and standard packaging. On the other hand ICs have certain limitations like power dissipation, difficulty in the intervention of inductors, limitations with respect to maximum value of capacitors at higher voltage, etc.

There are two types of ICs. First one is Linear/Analog ICs. These are discrete circuits which need external components like resistors and capacitors for satisfactory performance apart from the input. They work on analog signals rather than digital signals. Operational amplifier and modulator circuits come under this category.

Specific codes are assigned to linear ICs like LM, LH, CA etc. LM741 (operational amplifier), LM 117, LM 217, LM 317 (regulated d.c. power supplies), ADC0800, (analog to digital converter), DAC 0800 (digital to analog converter), NE 555 (timer) are some of the commonly used linear ICs for various applications.

The other category is Digital ICs which are complete functioning logic circuits. They require only digital input and not any other component for operation. All ICs like logic gates, adders, comparators etc., used inside a computer are digital ICs.

Specific codes are assigned to the digital ICs like LS, CD by the manufacturers. Motorola, Taxes Instruments are some of the well known manufacturers. 8080, 8085, 8086, 80286. 80386, 80486, 68000 are the ICs used as central processing units in microprocessors. Similarly we have various ICs like 74 L5 138 (Demultiplexer), 8255 (programmable peripheral interface), 6116 (Random access memory), 2732 (Read only memory), CD 4051 (multiplexer) etc., are used for various applications.

## 12.2 FABRICATION OF INTEGRATED CHIPS

There are two types of fabrication techniques. They are monolithic and hybrid techniques.

"**Monolithic**" is a Greek word meaning "**one stone**". In monolithic type, all the transistors and passive components (resistors and capacitors) are fabricated together on a single piece of silicon semiconductor material. Initially all the components are formed by diffusion process. Then materialisation process is used to interconnect these components. Electrical isolation is achieved by dielectric, beam-lead, or PN-junction method. PN-junction isolation is most economical and hence used widely.

Low cost mass production of ICs is possible in this process. Also monolithic ICs have a good thermal stability, since all the components are integrated on the same chip very close to each other. However, large volumes of resistances and capacitances cannot be formed by this method.

In the hybrid techique, passive components (resistors and capacitors) and the active components such as transistors and diodes are connected insulating substrate (foundation). Then along with this the active components and other circuits are connected to form the complete IC. Depending upon the thickness of the substrate, hybrid ICs are classified as thin film or thick film ICs. This technique is best suited for low-volume production,

**Monolithic IC manfacturing process**

This process involves substrate preparation, epitaxial layer formation, oxide layer growth, photographic process, diffusion process and evaporation of aluminium. Important process used in monolithic technology are discussed in detail below.

**12.2.1 Preparation of substrate:** Silicon is obtained by reducing silicon dioxide with carbon in a furnace. Zone refining is done to achieve maximum purity level. To convert the polycrystalline form into a single crystalline form the material is melted in a crucible. A seed crystal with desired orientation is kept in contact with the melt. Molten material solidifies as it touches the seed crystal (seed crystal is kept below the melting point). As the solidified portion is pulled out of the melt, more and more material solidifies thus forming a cylindrical silicon crystal form which we can cut the substrates. For IC fabrication, P type impurities are doped in the substrate. Then the crystal rod is sliced into wafers and polished mechanically or chemically to get good finish.

**12.2.2 Epitaxial growth:** It is a chemical reaction in which silicon is precipitates from a gaseous solution and made to grow on the silicon wafer as a thin film of single crystal silicon. The epitaxial layer is formed by heating the silicon wafer with radio frequency energy in an epitaxial reactor. (Fig. 12.1). The vapours containing silicon and desired doping impurities are passed over the slice. The chemical reaction describing the epitaxial growth is given by

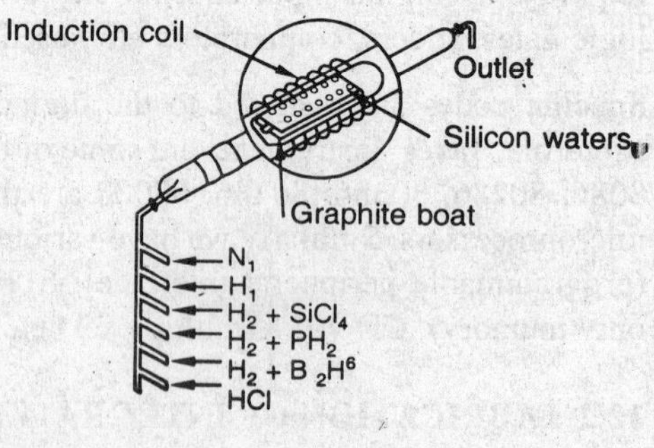


Fig. 12.1

$$SiCl_4 + 2H_2 \underset{}{\overset{1200°C}{\rightleftharpoons}} Si + 4\,HCl$$

**12.2.3 Diffusion:** Initially, to bring the proper number of dopant atoms on to the surface of the slice, a light concentration of dopant atoms is brought in contact with the slice for a short time. Now the dopant surface is removed and the dopant atoms are made to penetrate through the slice under the influence of high temperature. The diffusion apparatus is as shown in the Fig. 12.2.

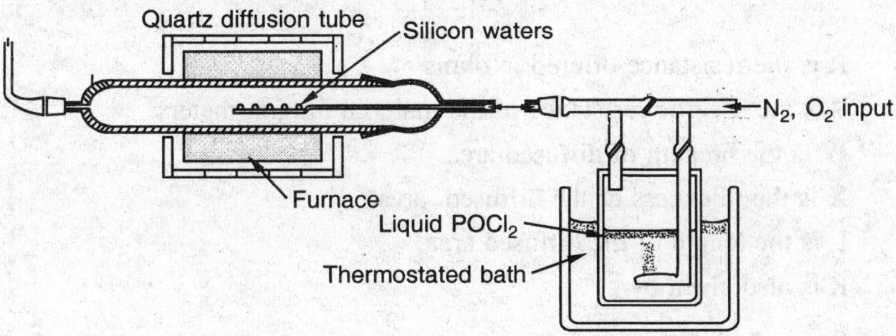


**Fig. 12.2**

Liquid $POCl_3$ is used as a source of phosphorus (dopant). Nitrogen after passing through the bubbler, carries the diffusant atoms to the silicon wafers. The temperature of the furnance is kept at 1200°C (close to the boiling point of silicon). Thus the silicon atoms are replaced by dopant atoms by substitution.

**12.2.4 Photolithography:** The purpose of photolithography is to selectively remove the oxide from silicon wafer. Hence the silicon wafer is coated with an uniform film photosensitive emulsion called Kodak photo resist. The black and white layout of desired pattern called mask is placed over the wafer coated with photoresist. Photoresist under transparent regions of the mask becomes polymerised when exposed to ultra-violet light. The mask is removed and the wafer is developed using chemical like trichloroethylene that removes the unexposed portion of photoresist film. The poly-merised region is cured to make it corrosion resistant. The chip is immersed in hydrofluoric acid (etching solution) to remove the oxide layer (not protected by poly-merised photoresist). Through these openings the dopants can be diffused. After the diffusion the photoresist mask is removed with sulphuric acid and by mechanical abrasion process. Different steps in photolithography are shown in Fig. 12.3.

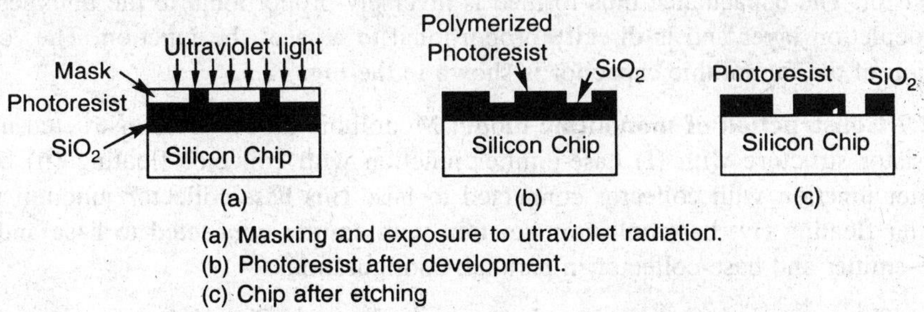


(a) Masking and exposure to utraviolet radiation.
(b) Photoresist after development.
(c) Chip after etching

**Fig. 12.3**

**12.2.5 Construction of monolithic resistors:** The monolithic resistors are fabricated by using either P-type diffusion or N-type diffusion. A resistor in a monolithic integrated circuit is obtained by using the bulk specific resistance of one of the diffused areas. The resistance value is given by

$$R = \frac{\rho l}{WX}$$

Where R is the resistance offered in ohms

P is the specific resistance of the material in ohm-meters

W is the breadth of diffused area

X is the thickness of the diffused area

I is the length of the diffused area.

R is also given by

$$R = \frac{R_s . l}{W}$$

where $R_s = \frac{P}{W}$ called sheet resistance.

The cross section of monolithic resistor is shown in Fig. 12.4.

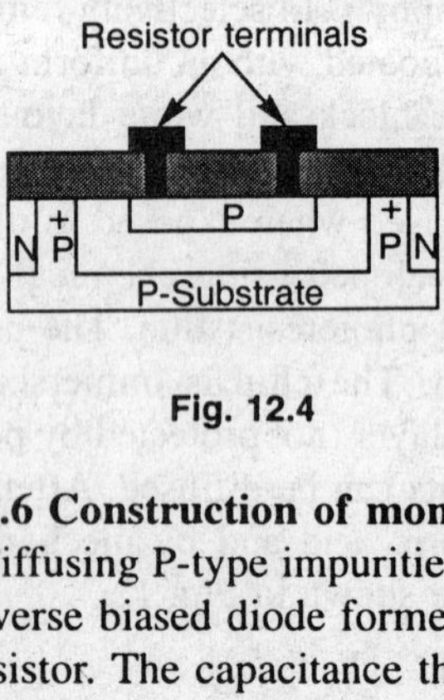


Fig. 12.4

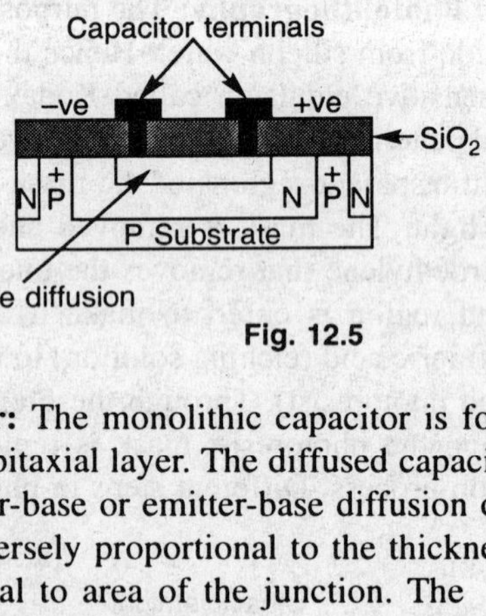


Fig. 12.5

**12.2.6 Construction of monolithic capacitor:** The monolithic capacitor is formed by diffusing P-type impurities into a N-type epitaxial layer. The diffused capacitor is a reverse biased diode formed by the collector-base or emitter-base diffusion of the transistor. The capacitance thus formed is inversely proportional to the thickness of the depletion layer and is directly proportional to area of the junction. The cross section of the monolithic capacitor is shown in the Fig. 12.5.

**12.2.7 Construction of monolithic diode:** Monolithic diodes are constructed using transistor structure with (I) base-emitter junction with collector floating (ii) base-emitter junction with collector connected to base (iii) base-collector junction with emitter floating (iv) base-collector junction with emitter connected to base and (v) base-emitter and base-collector in parallel, configurations.

The cross section of first configuration is shown in Fig. 12.6.

**12.2.8. Construction of monolithic bipolar transistor (NPN type):** A single P-type silicon wafer is doped with arsenic. After removing the oxide by etching, the N-type islands are produced by the $P^+$-isolation diffusal process. After isolation diffusion, P-type base is diffused. Now $N^+$ type emitter diffusion is carried out in the base keeping sufficient base width. The aluminium layer is formed after etching the holes in oxide mask. Then aluminium is removed selectively leaving bonding pads and interconnection. Chip is bonded to the final enclosure whereas the wires are bonded to the aluminium pads. The cross section of monolithic NPN transistor is shown in Fig. 12.7.

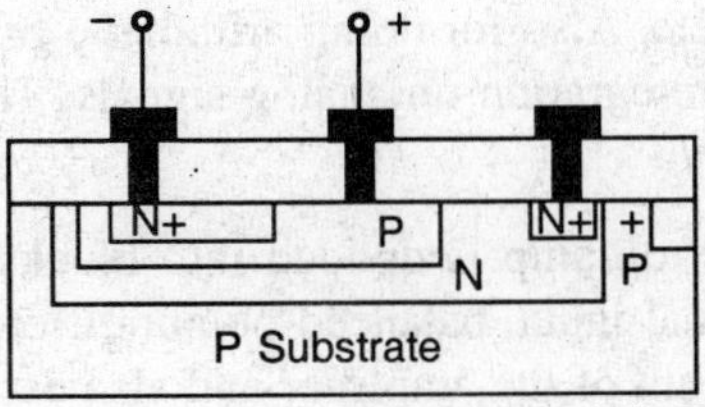


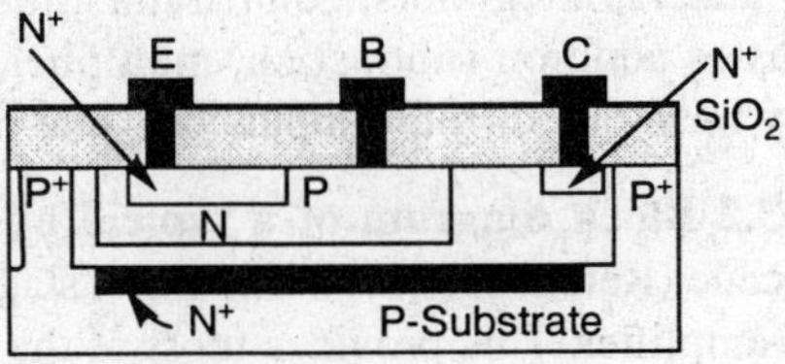


E—Emitter ($N^+$) B—Base (P) C—Collector ($N^+$)

Fig. 12.6

Fig. 12.7

**12.2.9 IC package types** (SSI MSI LSI VLSI packages): ICs are classified according to the number of components integrated on the same chip, as listed below:

| | | |
|---|---|---|
| Small-scale integration (SSI) | < | 10 components |
| Medium-scale integration(MSI) | < | 100 components |
| Large-scale integration (LSI) | < | 1000 components |
| Very large-scale integration (VLSI) | < | million components |

There are three types of IC packages.

1. **Flat pack:** In this case the chip is enclosed in a rectangular ceramic case with terminal leads (pins for input and output) extending through the sides and ends. Small ICs with 8,10, 12, 14, or 16 leads can be packed like this (Refer Fig. 12.8)
2. **The metal can or transistor pack**: Here the ICs are encapsulated in a metal or plastic case. The number of leads my be 3,5,8,10,12.
3. **Duel-in-line packages:** The IC is mounted in a plastic or ceramic case. For ICs with more number of leads, even up to 64 pins, this method is suitable.

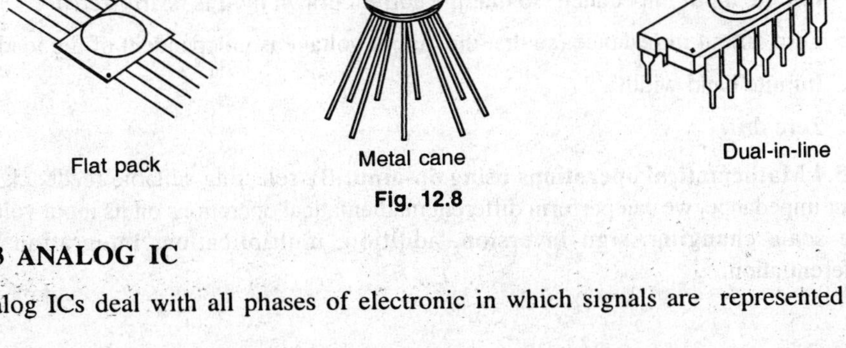

Flat pack

Metal cane

Dual-in-line

Fig. 12.8

## 12.3 ANALOG IC

Analog ICs deal with all phases of electronic in which signals are represented by analog or continuous variable. The operational amplifiers, voltage regulator, camparators, times, oscillators etc. belong to analog ICs.

**12.3.1 Operational Amplifiers:** An operational amplifier (normally called as op-amp) as a direct coupled high gain amplifier usually consisting of one or more push-pull or push-pull symmetry pair. They are used to perform a wide variety of both linear and non-linear operations.

Op-amps are used to amplify DC as well as AC input signals. They are used in designing adders, integrators, comparators, multipliers etc. Also for doing arithmetic functions as addition subtraction, multiplication and integration on analog signals. They may have one or more inputs but, one output only.

**12.3.2 Block diagram of a typical op-amp:** An op-amp is divided into blocks in cascade (Refer Fig. 12.9). The input stage is the dual-input, balanced-output differential amplifier. This provides most of the voltage gain of the amplifier and also establishes the input resistance of the op-amp. The intermediate stage is usually another differential amplifier, which is driven by the output of the first stage. Since direct coupling is used, DC voltage at the output stage is well above the ground level.

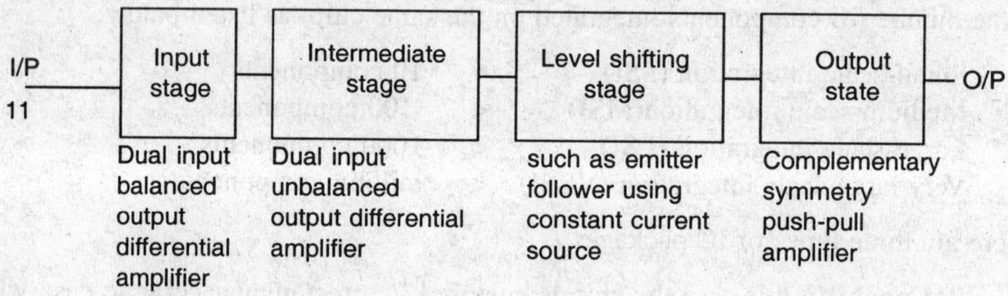


Fig. 12.9

Therefore the level translator (shifting) circuit is used after this stage to shift the DC level at the output of the intermediate stage downward to 0 volts with respect to ground. The final stage is usually a push-pull complementary amplifier output stage. The output stage increases the output voltage swing and raises the current supplying capability of op-amp. A well designed output stage also provides low output resistance.

**12.3.3 Ideal op-Amp:** An ideal op-amp has the following characteristics

1. Infinite input impedance (so that the current drawn by it is nearly zero)
2. Zero output impedance (so that the output voltage is independent of the load)
3. Infinite band width
4. Zero drift

**12.3.4 Mathematical operations using op-amp:** By selecting suitable feedback and input impedance, we can perform different mathematical operations on its input voltage like scale changing, sign inversion, addition, multiplication, integration and differentiation.

### 12.3.5 Scale changing

$R_i$ is the input resistance
$R_f$ is the feedback resistance
$e_i$ is the voltage input
$e_o$ is the 0 voltage

The Fig. 12.10. given an op-amp set up for a scale changer. The output

$$\text{voltage } `e_o' = \frac{-R_f}{R_i} e_i = -KC_i$$

where 'K' is a scalar whose value can be changed by manually adjusting the value of '$R_i$'.

**12.3.6 Sign inversion:** In the above set-up (Fig. 12.10) if $R_f = R_i$, then K becomes =1. Thus $e_o = - e_i$. Hence in a sign inverter, the output is equal to the input in magnitude but opposite in sign (phase).

The sign inverter is shown in Fig. 12.11

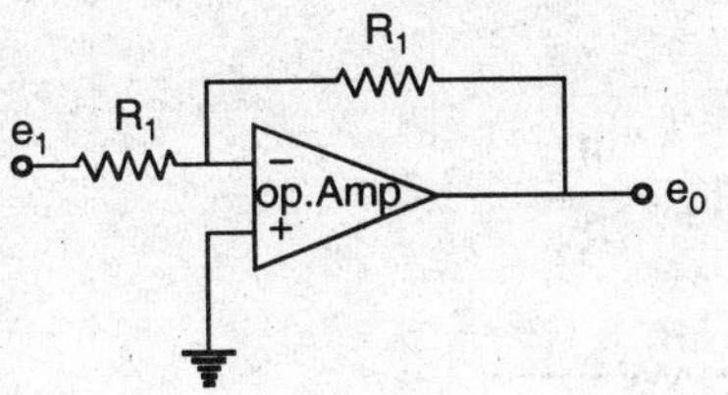


Fig. 12.10.

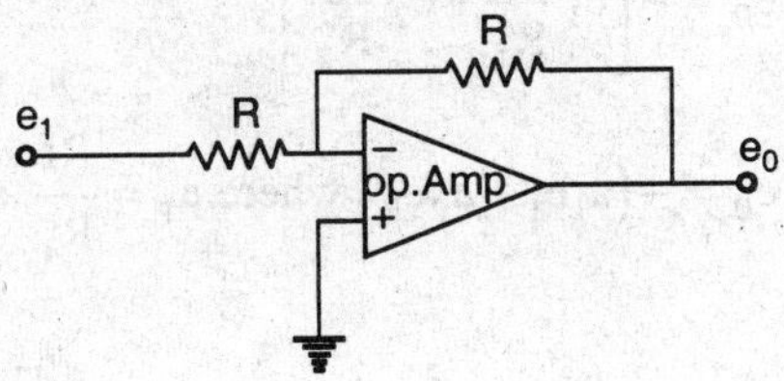


Fig. 12.11

$$eo = \frac{R}{R} \cdot ei = -ei$$

**12.3.7 Adder (summer):** Here the output of op-amp is the sum of voltages at the input terminals. Fig. 12.12 given the circuit for op-amo adder.

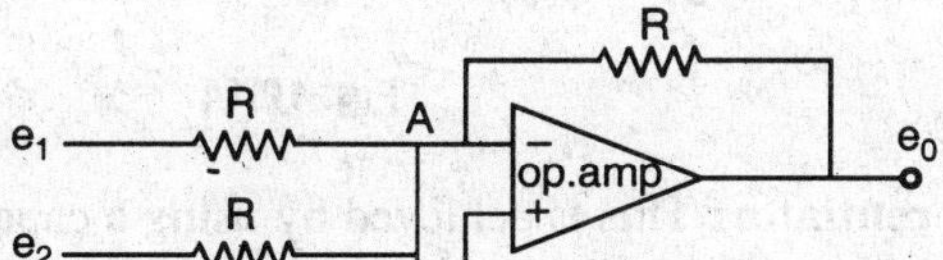


Fig. 12.12

$e_1$, $e_2$, $e_3$, $e_4$, are the voltages at the input terminals.

$e_o$' is the voltage at the output terminal.

At the point A, the nodal equation is

$$\frac{e_1}{R} + \frac{e_2}{R} + \frac{e_3}{R} + \frac{e_4}{R} + \frac{e_0}{R} = 0$$

$$\frac{e_0}{R} = -\left[\frac{e_1}{R} + \frac{e_2}{R} + \frac{e_3}{R} + \frac{e_4}{R}\right]$$

$$e_0 = -\left[e_1 + e_2 + e_3 + e_4\right]$$

**12.3.8 Subtraction:** This is achieved with the help of an inverter and a summer combination (Fig. 12.13). The voltage to be subtracted say '$e_2$' is first inverted into '$-e_2$' and then added to '$e_1$' through a summer. The output of summer '$e_0$' will be $-(e1 - e_2)$.

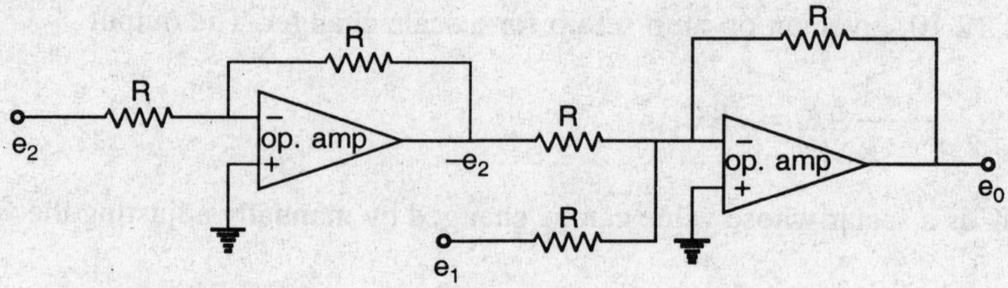


Fig. 12.13

**12.3.9 Multiplication-cum-summation:** A summer can be used for multiplying the input voltage by some constant and then adding them (Fig. 12.14).

$$e_0 = -\left[e_1 \frac{Rf}{R_1} + e_2 \frac{Rf}{R_2}\right]$$

$$e_0 = -\left(a_1 e_1 + a_2 e_2\right) \text{ where } a_1 = \frac{Rf}{R_1} \text{ and } b_1 = \frac{Rf}{R_2}$$

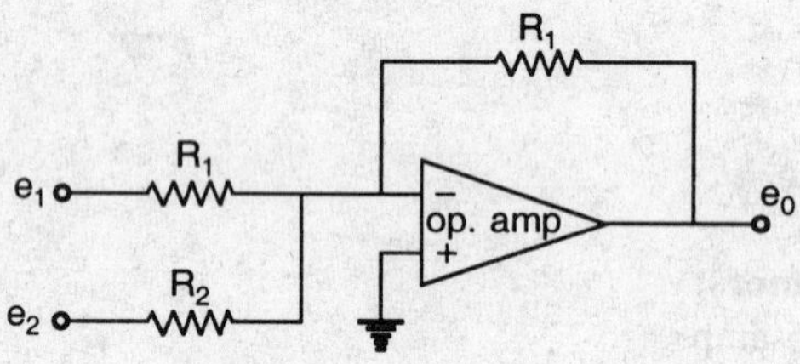


Fig. 12.14

**12.3.10 Differentiator:** This is achieved by using a capacitor 'C' as input impedance and a resistor 'R' as feedback impedance as shown in Fig. 12.15.

At junction A, $i_1 + i_2 = 0$

$$i_1 = \frac{dq}{dt} = \frac{d}{dt}(C.e_i)$$

$$= C\frac{de_i}{dt}$$

$$i_2 = \frac{e_0}{R}$$

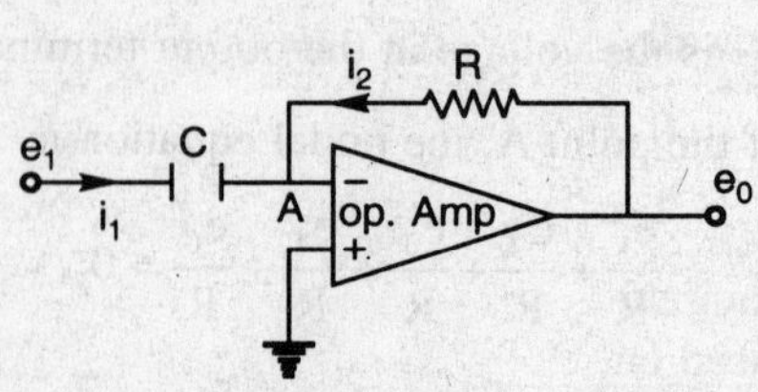


Fig. 12.15

$$i_1 + i_2 = C\frac{de_i}{dt} + \frac{e_0}{R} = 0$$

$\Rightarrow$

$$\frac{e_0}{R} = -C\frac{de_i}{dt}$$

$$e_0 = -R.C\frac{de_i}{dt}$$

Thus the output voltage is proportional to the derivative of input voltage.

**12.3.11 Integrator:** This is achieved by using resistor 'R' as input impedance and capacitor 'C' as feedback impedance as shown in Fig. 12.16.

At junction A, $i_1 + i_2 = 0$

where $i_1 = \frac{e_i}{R}$  $\quad i_2 = \frac{dq}{dt} = \frac{d}{dt}(C.e_0) = C.\frac{de_0}{dt}$

$$i_2 = C\frac{de_0}{dt}$$

$$\frac{e_i}{R} + C\frac{de_0}{dt} = 0$$

$$de_0 = -\frac{1}{RC}\int e_i dt$$

$$e_0 = -\frac{1}{RC}\int e_i dt + k,$$

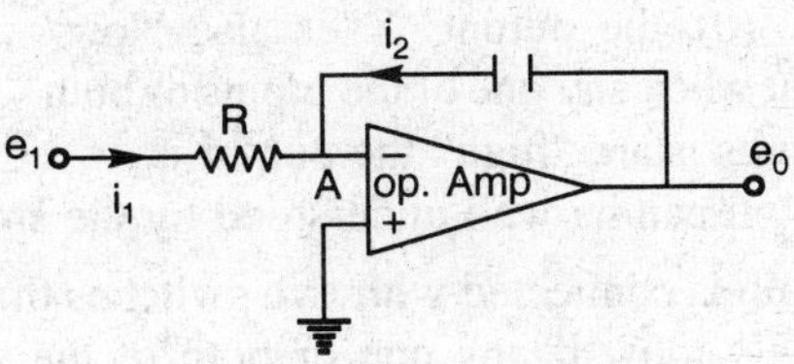


Fig. 12.16

where $K = e_0(0)$ (i.e.) the output voltage '$e_0$' at $t = 0$.

## 12.4. DIGITAL IC

The logic gates, adders and comparators employed in computers fall under the category of digital ICs.

**12.4.1 Introduction to Logic Gates:** Digital logic or binary logic is the fundamental principle of computers. Numerically, this involves only two symbols: 0 and 1, but logically, they can be specified as:

0 = false = no = off = low voltage

1 = true = yes = on = high voltage

Computers are designed to understand only 0s and 1s. All operations are performed based on the binary number system. One important reason for using the binary logic is that it is easy to design stable electronic circuits that can switch back and forth between two clearly defined states. It is also possible to design circuits that will remain indefinitely in one state unless and until they are deliberately switched to the other state. This makes it possible to construct a computer, which can remember sequences of events and adjust its behaviour accordingly. The electronic circuits perform various operations like addition, subtraction, multiplication, etc. based on the Boolean algebra. The following section discusses about the Boolean logic and the basic circuits built for binary operations.

**12.4.2 Boolean Algebra:** Boolean algebra deals with the construction and simplification of expressions using binary logic, i.e. using 0s and 1s. It has three basic operations.

1. Conjunction or logical sum known as OR operation.
2. Intersection or logical product known as AND operation
3. Negation or logical inverse known as NOT operation.

Conjunction operation is expressed as X=A+B. Here both input and output are binary digits and not decimal digits. A and B are inputs and X is the output.

We must understand that it is not adding the two values 1+ 1 or 1+0, but adding the two logical values. So when A and B are "low" (0), the output 'X' is also "low" (0). But when any one of the inputs or both the inputs is/are "high" the output is "high". It can be well understood by the small circuit shown below:

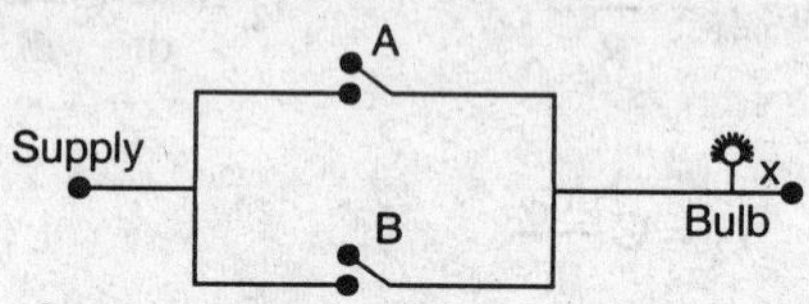

Fig. 12.17

The bulb is connected with two switches that are connected in parallel. The bulb will definitely glow if any one or both of the switches were in "ON" state (Refer Fig. 12.17).

Intersection is the product of two logical values. It is expressed as Y =A.B. It is quite obvious that the output Y can be "high" when both the inputs A and B are "high". The output is always "low", if any one of the inputs were "low". This can be easily understood as a bulb connected with two switches in series. The bulb will glow only when both the switches are closed (refer to Fig. 12.18).

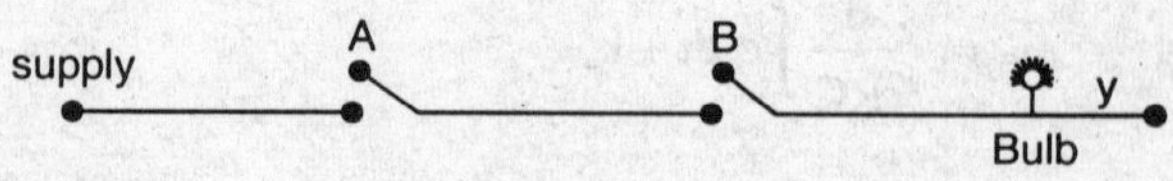

Fig. 12.18

Negation operation is represented Z = A. In this case, Z is "high" only when A is "low", Z is "low" when A is "high".

These three operators OR, AND and NOT are called logic connectives. Any boolean function can be represented by these logic connectives.

**12.4.3 Boolean Postulates**

| | | |
|---|---|---|
| $A + 0 = A$ | $A \,.\, \overline{A} = 0$ | |
| $A \,.\, 0 = O$ | $A + A = A$ } | Identity Law |
| $A + 1 = 1$ | $A \,.\, A = 0$ } | |
| $A \,.\, 1 = A$ | $A + B = B + A$ } | |
| $A + \overline{A} = 1$ | $A \,.\, B = B \,.\, A$ } | Commutative Law |

Binary Arithmetic

- Addition
  - 0 + 0 = 0
  - 0 + 1 = 1
  - 1 + 0 = 1
  - 1 + 1 = 10
- Subtraction
  - 0 − 0 = 0
  - 1 − 0 = 1
  - 1 − 1 = 0
  - 10 − 1 = 1
- Multiplication
  - 0 × 0 = 0
  - 0 × 1 = 1
  - 1 × 0 = 0
  - 1 × 1 = 1

### 12.4.4 Boolean Theorems

| | | | |
|---|---|---|---|
| 1. $\overline{\overline{A}}$ | = | A | (Negative Law) |
| 2. A + $(\overline{A}\,.\,B)$ | = | A + B | |
| 3. A + $(\overline{A} + B)$ | = | A . B | |
| 4. A . (B . C) | = | (A . B) C | (Associative Law) |
| 5. A + (B + C) | = | (A + B) C | (Associative Law) |
| 6. A . (B + C) | = | A . B + A . C | (Distributive Law) |
| 7. A + (B . C) | = | (A + B) . (A + C) | (Distributive Law) |

### 12.4.5 Demorgan's Theorem

1. $\overline{A+B} = \overline{A}.\overline{B}$
2. $\overline{A.B} = \overline{A}+\overline{B}$

The above two laws can be verified as follows:

| Col. No. 1 | 2 | 3 | 4 | 5 | 6 | 7 | 8 | 9 | 10 |
|---|---|---|---|---|---|---|---|---|---|
| A | B | $\overline{A}$ | $\overline{B}$ | A+B | A.B | $\overline{A+B}$ | $\overline{A.B}$ | $\overline{A}+\overline{B}$ | $\overline{A}.\overline{B}$ |
| 0 | 0 | 1 | 1 | 0 | 0 | 1 | 1 | 1 | 1 |
| 0 | 1 | 1 | 0 | 1 | 0 | 0 | 1 | 1 | 0 |
| 1 | 0 | 0 | 1 | 1 | 0 | 0 | 1 | 1 | 0 |
| 1 | 1 | 0 | 0 | 1 | 1 | 0 | 0 | 0 | 0 |

Thus from Column No. 7 and 10, we have $\overline{A+B} = \overline{A}.\overline{B}$ and from Column No. 8 and 9 we have $\overline{A.B} = \overline{A}+\overline{B}$

**12.4.6 Number systems:** The different number systems we come across in a computer are (i) Decimal System (ii) Binary System (iii) Octal system and (iv) Hexadecimal system.

In the decimal system, there are 10 characters, namely, 0, 1, 2, 3, 4, 5, 6, 7, 8, and 9, and the base is 10.

$(0.5)_{10}$ and $(45)_{10}$ are examples of decimal numbers. In the binary system, there are 2 characters, namely, '0' and '1' and the base is 2. $(110.10)_2$ and $(11010)_2$ are examples of binary numbers. In the octal system there are 8 characters, namely, 0, 1, 2, 3, 4, 5, 6, 7, and the base is 8. $(236.5)_8$ and $(655)_8$ are examples of octal numbers.

In the hexadecimal system, there are 16 characters, namely, 0, 1, 2, 3, 4, 5, 6, 7, 8, 9, A, B, C, D, E and F and the base is 16. $(1\ A\ 2.\ 8)_{16}$ $(B\ 8\ D)_{16}$ are examples of hexadecimal numbers.

**Relation among different number systems**

| Decimal | Binary | Octal | Hexadecimal |
|---|---|---|---|
| 0 | 0000 | 00 | 0 |
| 1 | 0001 | 01 | 1 |
| 2 | 0010 | 02 | 2 |
| 3 | 0011 | 03 | 3 |
| 4 | 0100 | 04 | 4 |
| 5 | 0101 | 05 | 5 |
| 6 | 0110 | 06 | 6 |
| 7 | 0111 | 07 | 7 |
| 8 | 1000 | 10 | 8 |
| 9 | 1001 | 11 | 9 |
| 10 | 1010 | 12 | A |
| 11 | 1011 | 13 | B |
| 12 | 1100 | 14 | C |
| 13 | 1101 | 15 | D |
| 14 | 1110 | 16 | E |
| 15 | 1111 | 17 | F |

The method of conversion of binary to decimal and decimal to binary is dealt here.

**Decimal to binary conversion**

Here the decimal number given is divided successively by the base of binary number i.e. 2, until quotient becomes '1'. The binary equivalent will be set of remainders and residuals with the first remainder as least significant bit and the last quotient as most significant bit.

Example: Find the binary equivalent of $(36)_{10}$

| | | |
|---|---|---|
| 2 | 36 | |
| 2 | 18 | – 0 |
| 2 | 9 | – 0 |
| 2 | 4 | – 1 |
| 2 | 2 | – 0 |
| 2 | 1 | – 0 |

$$(36)_{10} = (100100)_2$$

**Binary to decimal conversion**

**Example**: Find the decimal Equivalent of $(100100)_2$

1 0 0 1 0 0

$0 \times 2^0 = 0$

$0 \times 2^1 = 0$

$1 \times 2^2 = 4$

$0 \times 2^3 = 0$

$0 \times 2^4 = 0$

$1 \times 2^5 = 32$

$(100100)_2 = (36)_{10}$ **36**

## 12.5. LOGIC GATES AND TRUTH TABLES

The Boolean expressions can be realised by circuits made up of diodes and/or transistors. These circuits performing the Boolean operations are called logic gates.

The digital or binary logic is dealt in two types:

Combinational logic, in which the logical outputs are determined by the logical function being performed on the logical input states at that particular moment. The logic gates can have one or more inputs but only one output. There are three basic gates: AND, OR, and NOT, and three combinational gates built using these basic gates: NOR, NAND and XOR.

Sequential logic, in which the outputs not only depend on the input states, but also on the prior states of those outputs. The gates are designed to actually remember the past states of their inputs, and to produce outputs based on those past states as well as the current inputs. The circuits that can act according to a sequence of input signals are therefore known as sequential logic circuits. Actually, flip-flops, counters, shift registers, etc. come under this category.

Before proceeding further about gates, we must understand what is a truth table. A table that gives the values of output for the given inputs for a gate is called a truth table. The following section discusses about the circuit diagrams, symbolic diagrams and the truth tables of different gates.

### 12.5.1 Basic Gates

**OR Gate:** It is constructed using diodes or transistors as shown is Fig. 12.19 (a) & (b). If both A and 'B or any one of A and B were "high". The output is also "high". Fig. 12.19(c) is the truth table for OR gate and Fig. 12.19(d) is the symbolic representation of the same.

**AND Gate:** The following circuit shows the AND gate built with diodes. Only when both A and B are "high" the output Y will be "high". Also Fig. 12.20 gives the truth table and symbolic representation for AND gate.

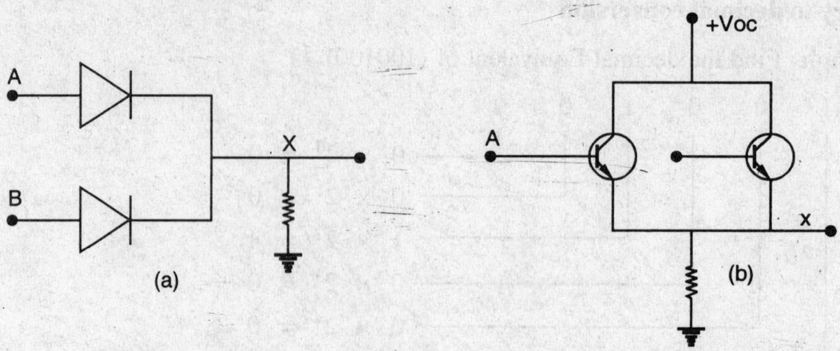


(a) (b)

| A | B | X |
|---|---|---|
| 0 | 0 | 0 |
| 0 | 1 | 1 |
| 1 | 0 | 1 |
| 1 | 1 | 1 |

(c)

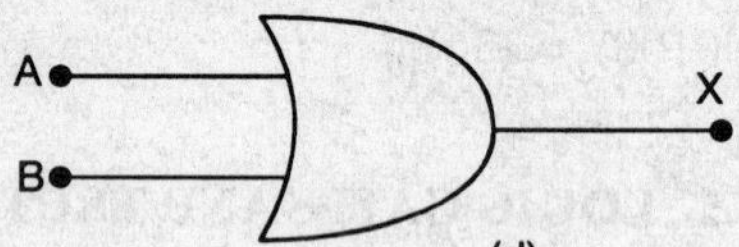


(d)

**Fig. 12.19**

(OR and AND gates can have any number of inputs but only one output)

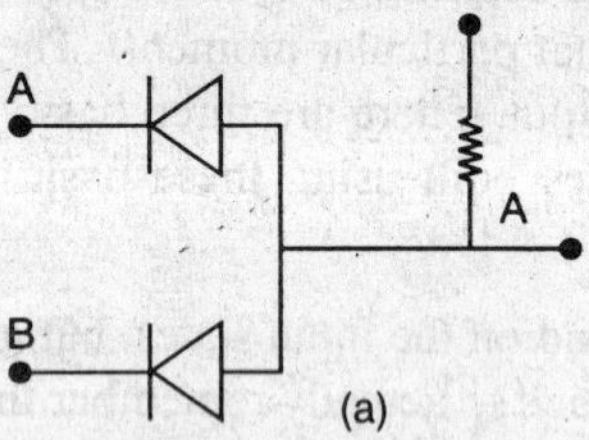


(a)

| A | B | Y |
|---|---|---|
| 0 | 0 | 0 |
| 0 | 1 | 0 |
| 1 | 0 | 0 |
| 1 | 1 | 1 |

(b)

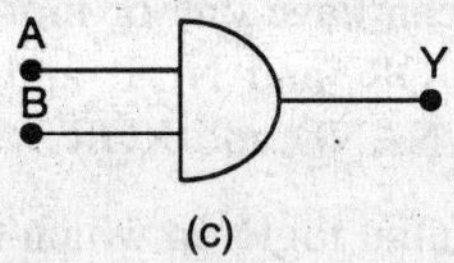


(c)

**Fig. 12.20**

**NOT Gate:** The inversion operation is realised using NPN transistor as shown below in Fig. 12.21

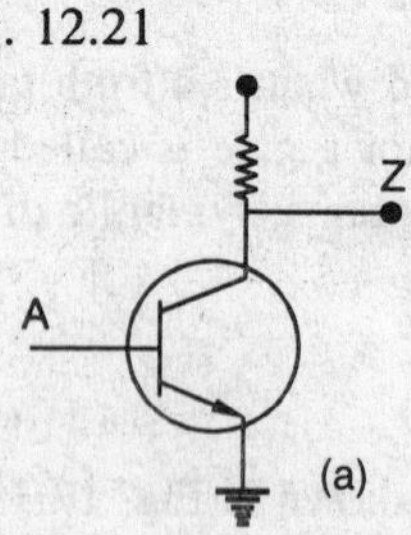


(a)

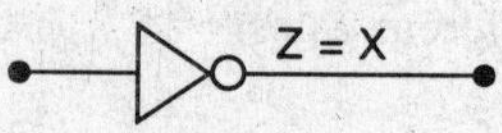


(b)

| A | Z |
|---|---|
| 1 | 0 |
| 0 | 1 |

(c)

**Fig. 12.21**

If the input A were at 0 volt i.e. at "low", there is no base current and hence no collector current. That means, the transistor is in "cut off" condition,. So the output point Z has the potential of V, say 1 volt. The value of R is such as to drive the transistor into saturation. When the input is at "high", the transistor will be in saturated condition and hence Z will be at 0 volts ("low"). This gate has only one point.

**12.5.2 Combinational Logic Gates:** The basic gates can be combined to make combinational gates. NOR, NAND and XOR are the important gates designed using combinational logic. Here, NOR and NAND gates are called universal gates, since all the OR, AND and NOT operations can be performed using these two gates.

**NOR Gate:** The symbolic representation and truth table are shown in Fig. 12.22

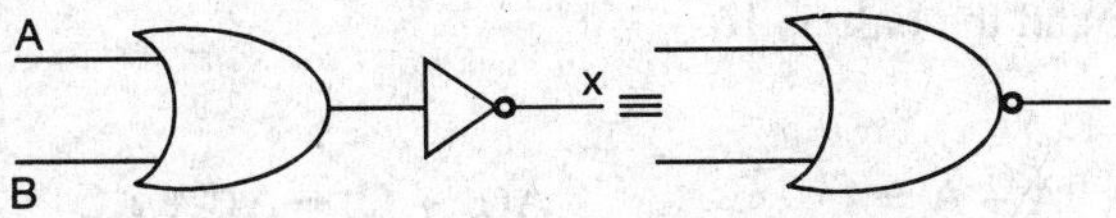


(a) (b)

| A | B | X |
|---|---|---|
| 0 | 0 | 1 |
| 0 | 1 | 0 |
| 1 | 0 | 0 |
| 1 | 1 | 0 |

(c)

Fig. 12.22

**NAND Gate:** The symbolic representation and truth table are shown in Fig. 12.23

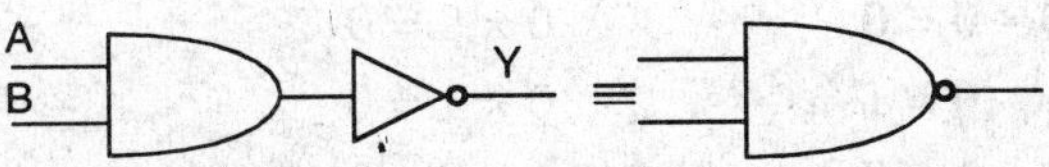


(a) (b)

| A | B | Y |
|---|---|---|
| 1 | 1 | 0 |
| 1 | 0 | 1 |
| 0 | 1 | 1 |
| 0 | 0 | 1 |

(c)

Fig. 12.23

XOR Gate: The XOR gate can be designed using all the three basic gates as given below:

The symbolic representation and truth table are shown in Fig. 12.24

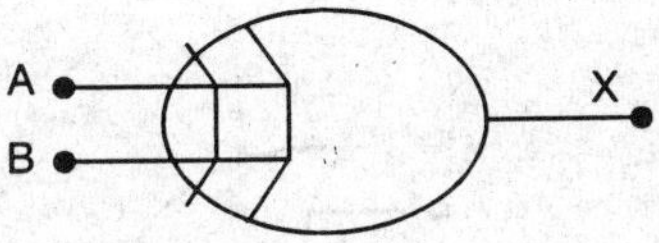


| A | B | $X = \bar{A}B + A\bar{B}$ |
|---|---|---|
| 0 | 0 | 0 |
| 0 | 1 | 1 |
| 1 | 0 | 1 |
| 1 | 1 | 0 |

Fig. 12.24

## HIGHLIGHTS

- An IC is an electronic assembly built by fabricating together all the components in the circuit in a small container called chip.
- An ideal OP - Amp. has 1) Infinite input impedance 2) Zero output impedance 3) Very high voltage gain 4) 180° phase shift between input and output.
- An OP-Amp. can be used as 1) Inverting amplifier 2) Scale changer 3) Adder 4) Multiplier 5) Differentiator and 6) Integrator.

- A binary number system comprises of only two digits, namely, '0' and '1' and the base is 2.
- A decimal number system comprises of ten digits, namely, 0, 1, 2, 3, 4, 5, 6, 7, 8, 9. and the base is 10.
- In the octal system there are 8 characteristics, namely, 1, 2, 3, 4, 5, 6, 7 and the base is 8.
- In the hexadecimal system there are 16 characters, namely, 0, 1, 2, 3, 4, 5, 6, 7, 8, 9, A, B, C, D, E, and F and the base is 16.
- Boolean algebra:

$A + A = 0$ $\qquad$ $A + A = 1$ $\qquad$ $A(B + C) = AB + AC$

$A + 0 = A$ $\qquad$ $A + A = 1$ $\qquad$ $A + AB = A + B$

$A = A$ $\qquad$ $A.A = 0$

$A + AB = A$ $\qquad$ $A.0 = 0$

$A.1 = A$ $\qquad$ $A.B = BA$

$A.A = A$ $\qquad$ $A + B = B + A$

$1 + 1 = 10$ $\qquad$ $0 - 0 = 0$ $\qquad$ $0 \times 0 = 0$

$1 + 0 = 1$ $\qquad$ $1 - 0 = 1$ $\qquad$ $0 \times 1 = 0$

$0 + 1 = 1$ $\qquad$ $1 - 1 = 0$ $\qquad$ $1 \times 0 = 0$

$0 + 0 = 0$ $\qquad$ $10 - 1 = 1$ $\qquad$ $1 \times 1 = 1$

**Demorgan's theorems**

(1) $\overline{A + B} = \overline{A} \cdot \overline{B}$

(2) $\overline{A \cdot B} = \overline{A} + \overline{B}$

Basic Gate Symbol $\qquad$ Truth Table

**OR** Gate

| A | B | Y |
|---|---|---|
| 0 | 0 | 0 |
| 0 | 1 | 1 |
| 1 | 0 | 1 |
| 1 | 1 | 1 |

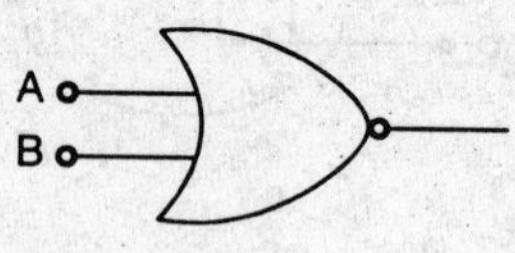


AND Gate

| A | B | Y |
|---|---|---|
| 0 | 0 | 0 |
| 0 | 1 | 0 |
| 1 | 0 | 0 |
| 1 | 1 | 1 |

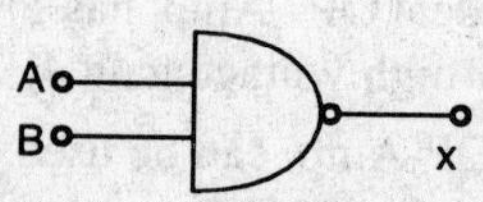

Basic Gate Symbol — Truth Table

NOT Gate

| A | Y |
|---|---|
| 0 | 1 |
| 1 | 0 |

NOR Gate

NOR Gate

| A | B | Y |
|---|---|---|
| 0 | 0 | 1 |
| 1 | 0 | 0 |
| 0 | 0 | 0 |
| 1 | 0 | 0 |

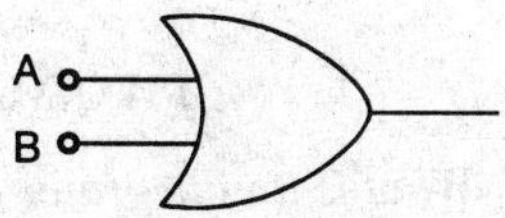


NAND Gate

| A | B | Y |
|---|---|---|
| 0 | 0 | 1 |
| 0 | 1 | 1 |
| 1 | 0 | 1 |
| 1 | 1 | 0 |

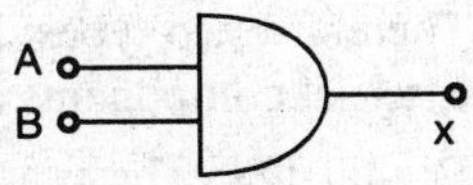


XOR Gate

| A | B | $X = \overline{A}B + A\overline{B}$ |
|---|---|---|
| 0 | 0 | 0 |
| 0 | 1 | 1 |
| 1 | 0 | 1 |
| 1 | 1 | 0 |

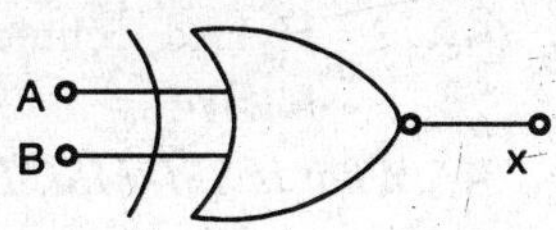


## REVIEW QUESTIONS

1. What are the types of ICs?
2. Explain the monolithic IC manufacturing process.
3. Explain the construction of
   a) Monolithic resistor  b) Monolithic capacitor
   c) Monolithic diode  d) Monolithic transistor.
4. What are the types of IC packages?
5. What are the characteristics of ideal op-amp?
6. Explain how an op-amp can be used for
   a) Scale changing  b) Inversions
   c) Addition  d) Subtraction
   e) Multiplication  f) Differentiation
   g) Integration

7. Write short notes on the following:
   a) Boolean postulates   b) Boolean theorems
   c) Number systems   d) Logic gates
8. Write the truth tables for the following logic gates
   a) OR - gate   b) AND - Gate
   c) NOT - gate   d) NAND - gate
   e) NOR gate   f) XOR - gate

## TWO MARKS QUESTIONS AND ANSWERS

1. *What is an integrater circuit ?*

   It is an electronic assembly built in such a way that all components in the circuit are fabricated together in a small container called chip.

2. *What are the two basic types of ICs ?*

   There are two types: Linear Analog ICs: These are discrete circuits which need external components apart from input for satisfactory performance.

   Digital ICs: These are complete functioning logic circuits which require only digital input and not any other component for operation.

3. *What are the methods of fabrication of ICs ?*

   1. Monolithic technique: Here both active and passive components are fabricated together.
   2. Hybrid technique: Here active and passive components are fabricated separately.

4. *What is SSI, MSI, LSI and VLSI with respect to ICs ?*

   ICs are classified according to the number of components integrated on the same chip, as

| | | |
|---|---|---|
| Small scale integration | (SSI) | < 10 components |
| Medium scale integration | (MSI) | between 10 and 1000 components |
| Large scale integration | (LSI) | between 100 components and 1000 components |
| Very large scale integration | (VLSI) | Million components |

5. *What are the types of IC packages ?*

   1. Flat pack: Here the chip is enclosed in a rectangular ceramic case with terminal leads extending outside.
   2. Metal can pack: Here the IC is encapsulated in a metal or plastic case.
   3. Dual-in-line package: Here the IC is mounted in a plastic or ceramic case.

6. *What is an operational amplifier ?*

   It is a direct coupled high gain amplifier used to amplify d.c. as well as a.c. signals. It is also used in designing address, integrators, comparators, multipliers etc., for performing arithmetic operations.

7. *Give the truth table for OR Gate.*

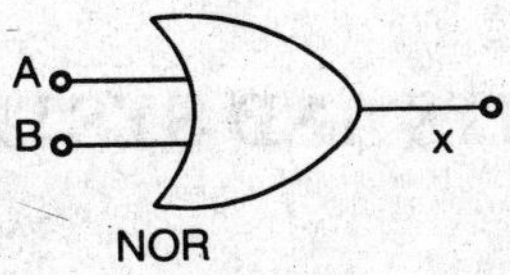


| A | B | X |
|---|---|---|
| 0 | 0 | 0 |
| 0 | 1 | 1 |
| 1 | 0 | 1 |
| 1 | 1 | 1 |

8. *Give the truth table for AND Gate.*

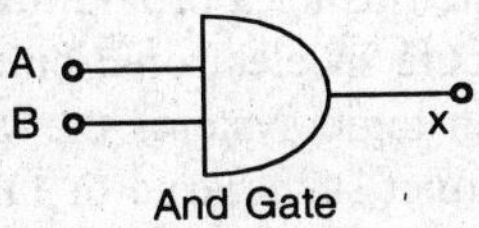


| A | B | X |
|---|---|---|
| 0 | 0 | 0 |
| 0 | 1 | 0 |
| 1 | 0 | 0 |
| 1 | 1 | 1 |

9. *Give the truth table for NOR Gate.*

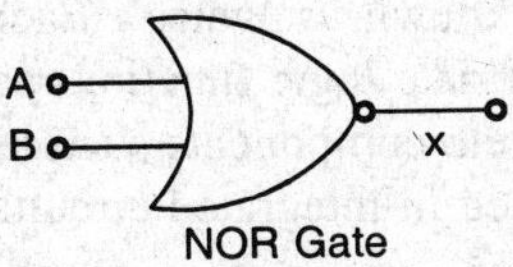


| A | B | X |
|---|---|---|
| 0 | 0 | 1 |
| 0 | 1 | 0 |
| 1 | 0 | 0 |
| 1 | 1 | 0 |

10. *Give the truth table for NAND Gate.*

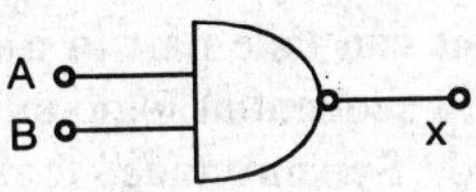


| A | B | X |
|---|---|---|
| 0 | 0 | 1 |
| 0 | 1 | 1 |
| 1 | 0 | 1 |
| 1 | 1 | 0 |

## Chapter 13

# SEQUENTIAL LOGIC ELEMENTS AND SYSTEMS

### 13.1. INTRODUCTION

A computer is a machine that executes instructions, called 'software', using electronic circuits, called 'hardware'. The software is written using a programming language, which is translated so that it can run, or execute in electronic circuit. The hardware is made from 'digital electronics' circuits. In logic systems the variables, circuits, statements, etc., can be in one of the two distinct states: true or false, conducting or not conducting, on or off, energized or not energized, yes or no and so on.

Logic system deals with two state variables. It is also referred as switching algebra. There are three basic logic operations called AND, OR and NOT. In practice the logic operations are implemented using specific circuits known as 'gates'. Each gate is represented by a symbol corresponding to the appropriate logic function realized by the specific gate. Gate can be constructed from discrete components such as transistors, resisters and diodes, but now-a-days implemented in integrated circuits.

A digital logic circuit is practically made up of combinational elements like gate circuits and memory elements using flip-flops, shift registers and counters. Logical operations can be performed sequentially. Information being stored in a memory and released at some particular instant later, and so that it can take part in a sequential operation. The circuits operating in this way are called sequential logic circuits. The circuits, which are controlled by clock signal is called "Synchronous" logic controller. The circuits, which are controlled by random events is called "Asynchronous" logic controller.

All logic circuits can be classified as either combinational or sequential. The outputs of the combinational circuit are determined totally by its external inputs. The outputs of the sequential circuits are determined not only by its external inputs but also by the past history of the circuits.

### 13.2. FLIP-FLOP

The devices used to remember the state of the circuit are called bistable or flip-flops. They are capable of storing one bit of information which may be of logic "1" or "0". Different types of flip-flop available are designed using discrete components or standard gates or they may be obtained on chips.

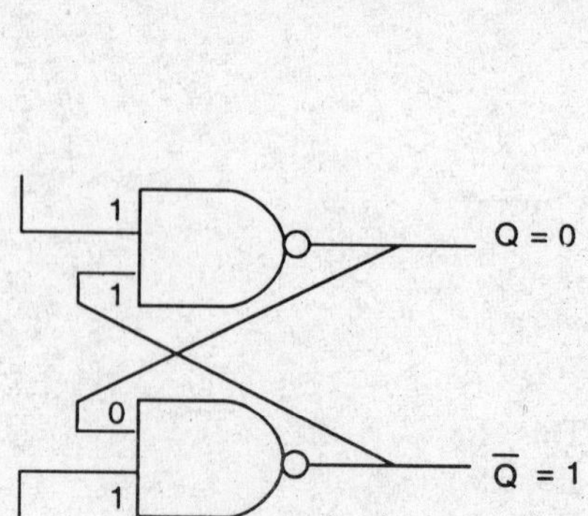


Fig. 13.1

There are two possible states as shown in Fig. 13.1 & 13.2. Initially when the circuit is switched on the bielement will take up one of these two states and remain in that state permanently until the power has been removed.

The general transfer characteristics are shown in Fig. 13.3. In figure the characteristic "I" is ideal and characteristic "p" is practical characteristic. The transition is taken place from state 1 to 0 almost in middle of practical characteristic.

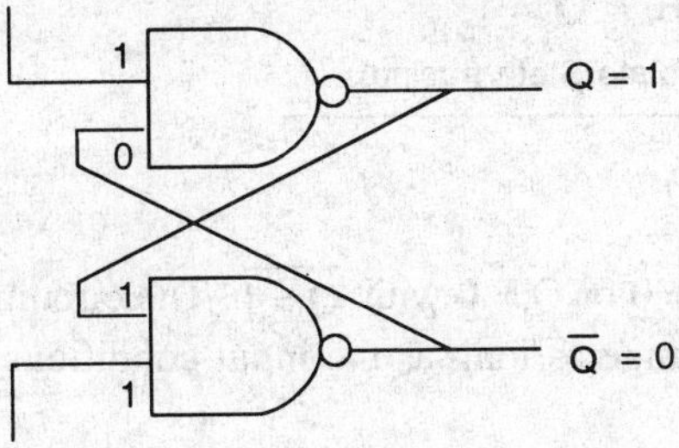


Fig. 13.2

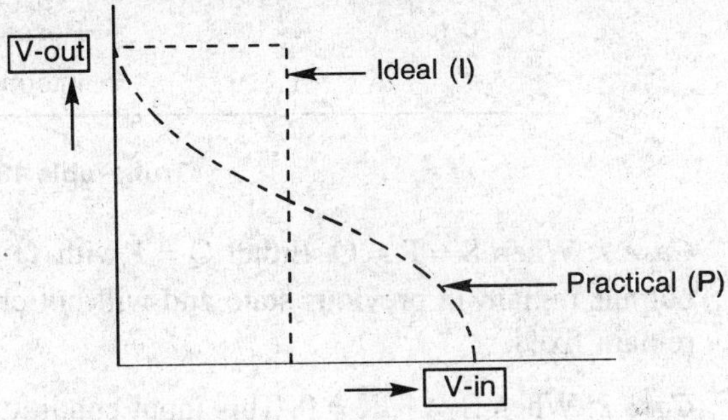


Fig. 13.3

## 13.3. SET-RESET FLIP-FLOP

This is the most simple sequential circuit element and is commonly referred as S-R flip-flop. This circuit is implemented in so many ways. S-R flip-flop implemented using 'nand' gates is shown in Fig. 13.4, and the flip-flop implemented using 'nor' gates is shown in Fig. 13.5. The general block diagram or symbol is shown in Fig. 13.6.

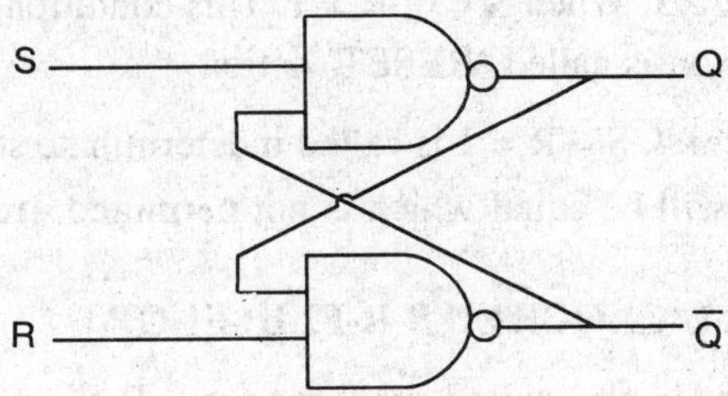


Fig. 13.4

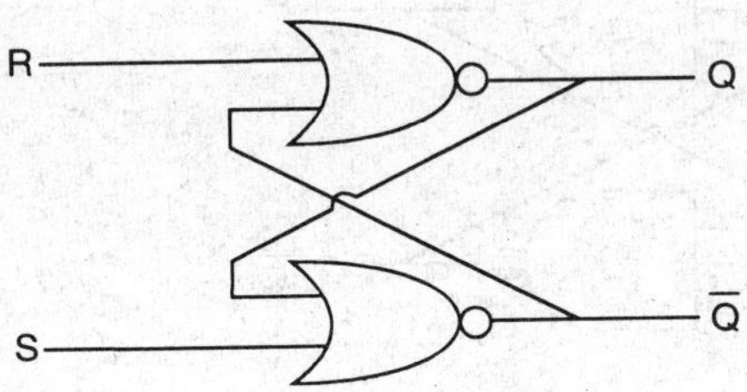


Fig. 13.5

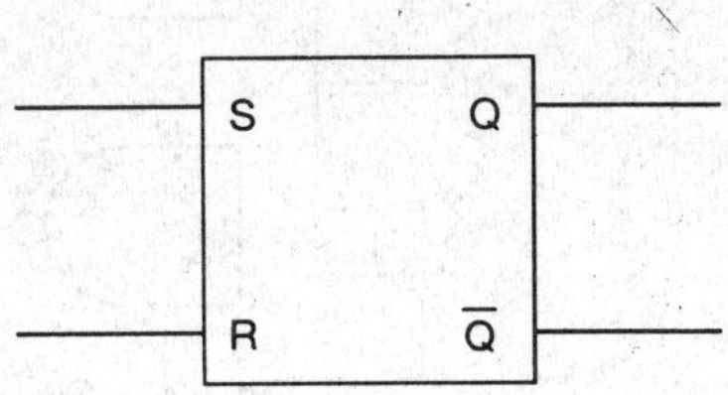


Fig. 13.6

This circuit in Fig. 13.5 (usng nor gates) can be analyzed using all four possible cases along with truth Table 13.1.

| Input | | Output |
|---|---|---|
| S | R | Q |
| 0 | 0 | No change |
| 1 | 0 | Set(s) Q = 1 |
| 0 | 1 | Reset (R) = $\overline{Q}$ = 1 |
| 1 | 1 | Intermediate State (racing) |

**Truth Table 13.1**

*Case 1*: When S = R = O. Either Q = 1 with $\overline{Q}$ = 0 or Q = 0 with $\overline{Q = 1}$. The circuit outputs remain in previous state and will not change as long as the input conditions remain fixed.

*Case 2*: When S = 1; R = 0. This input condition forces the output Q becomes 1 and $\overline{Q}$ = 0. This action Q = 1 is called 'SET' condition.

*Case 3*: When S = 0; R = 1. This condition forces the output $\overline{Q = 0}$ and $\overline{Q}$ = 1. This action is called 'RESET' action.

*Case 4*: S = R = 1 is called indeterminate state; because if R = S = 1, then both Q and $\overline{Q}$ will be equal which is not permitted. (racing condition)

## 13.4. CLOCKED S-R-FLIP-FLOP

This is also called synchronous S-R flip-flop or gated flip-flop. This is achieved by means of simple modification to asynchronous flip-flop as shown in Fig. 13.7 using Nand gates and 13.8 using Nor gates. The block diagram is shown in Fig. 13.9. The clock or enable input is added to provide additional capability.

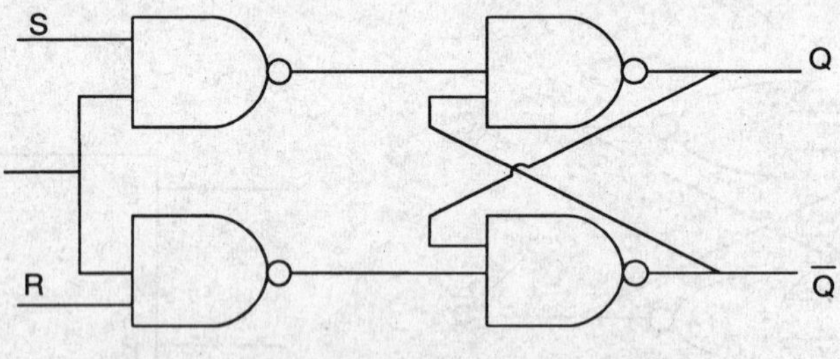


**Fig. 13.7** Clocked SR Flip-flop Using Nand Gates

When clock signal C = 0; the signals applied to the S or R input cannot affect the circuit. The output is latched on its last stage. When the clock signal C = 1, then the signals applied to the S or R input can affect the circuit. The circuit will set if S is high or reset if R is high. The truth Table for the clocked SR flip-flop is shown in Table 13.1.

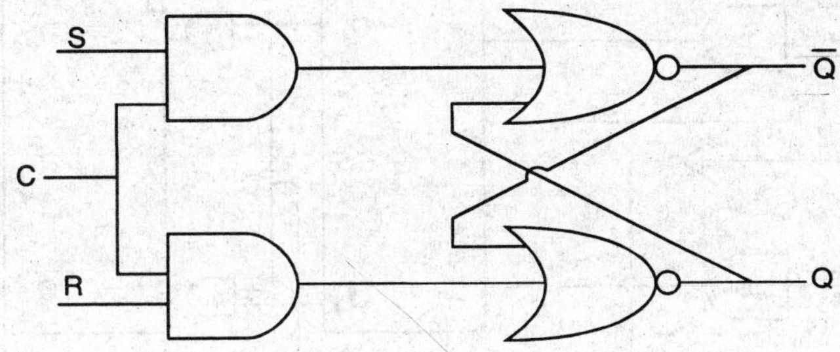


**Fig 13.8** Clocked SR Flip-flop Using Nor Gates

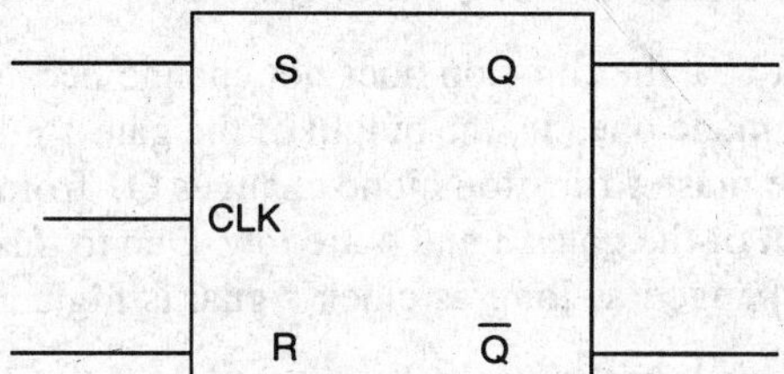


**Fig. 13.9** Block Diagram

**Table 13.1: Truth Table**

| CLK | R | S | Q |
|---|---|---|---|
| 0 | 0 | 0 | NC (No change) |
| 0 | 0 | 1 | NC |
| 0 | 1 | 0 | NC |
| 0 | 1 | 1 | NC |
| 1 | 0 | 0 | NC |
| 1 | 0 | 1 | 1 |
| 1 | 1 | 0 | 0 |
| 1 | 1 | 1 | Indeterminate State |

## 13.5. MASTER SLAVE S-R FLIP-FLOP

The clock pulse must remain high enough to allow the state of the flip-flop to change. If the flip-flop is the part of a sequential circuit, the change of the other flip-flops may cause further changes on S or R. If the clock is still high when changes occur, then further unwanted changes could result. To prevent this, the width of the clock pulse must be carefully controlled to allow just one change for each clock pulse.

Master-Slave flip-flop is constructed by cascading two SR flip-flops as shown in Fig. 13.10. It consists of two flip-flops, which can be clocked alternatively and hence isolates the change on the input and prevents it from simultaneously changing the input.

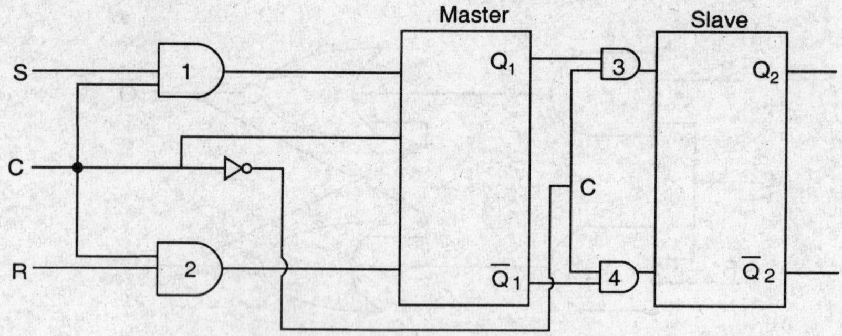


**Fig. 13.10** Master Slave SR Flip-flop

Consider an initial condition C = 0, Q1 = 0, Q2 = 0.

If S = 1, R = 0, Clock = 0, the flip-flop does not change because output of gate 1 and gate 2 are low. If C is made one (1), the output of the gate 1 goes high and gate 2 goes low. The output of the master flip-flop alone changes Q1 from 0 to 1. For this condition (C = 1) the output of the gates 3 and 4 are low. Due to this the output of the slave flip-flop remains unchanged as long as clock signal is high.

If the clock signal goes low then gate 1 and gate 2 of the Master flip-flop getting disabled and gate 3 and gate 4 of slave flip-flop getting enabled which causes the output Q2 to change its state.

## 13.6. SR FLIP-FLOP WITH ASYNCHRONOUS INPUTS

Some flip-flop have inputs called 'preset' (set) and 'clear' used for setting the flip-flop to 1 state or resetting it to zero state by applying appropriate signal to the preset and clear inputs. These inputs can change the state of the flip-flop regardless of the synchronous input or the clock. The symbol is shown in Fig. 13.11a and Fig. 13.11b.

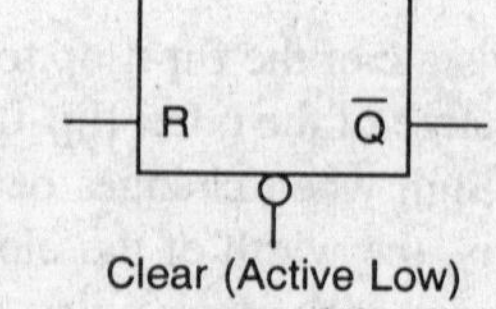


**Fig. 13.11a**

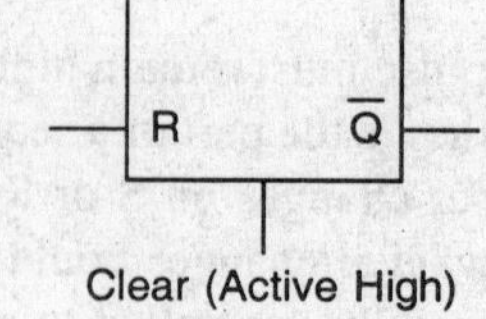


**Fig. 13.11b**

## 13.7. J-K FLIP-FLOP

It is very similar to the SR flip-flop except that a JK flip-flop accepts a logic 1 on both the J and K inputs. The J-K flip-flop made from SR flip-flop is shown in Fig. 13.12a and 13.12b. The truth Table is shown in Table 13.2.

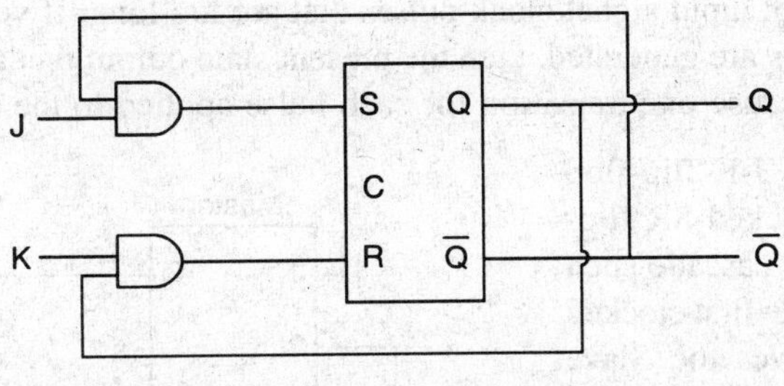


**Fig. 13.12a** J.K. Flip-Flop

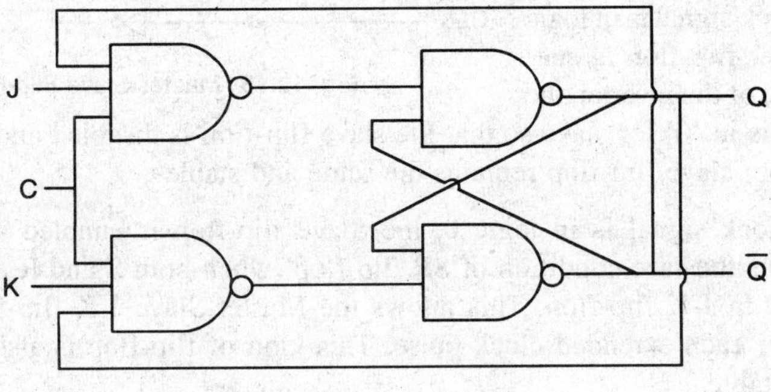


**Fig. 13.12b** J.K. Flip-Flop

When J and K are low, both the input gates are disabled and the circuit is inactive i.e. the O/P remains in the previous state.

When J = 1 and K = 0, forces Q into high state. This is called 'Set' action.

When J = 0 and K = 1 forces Q to become low. This is called 'Reset' action.

When J = 1 and K = 1, the output toggles. Q changes to the complement of the existing state.

**Table 13.2: Truth Table**

| CLK | J | K | Q |
|---|---|---|---|
| 1 | 0 | 0 | No change |
| 1 | 1 | 0 | 1 |
| 1 | 0 | 1 | 0 |
| 1 | 1 | 1 | Toggle |

## 13.8. MASTER-SLAVE J-K FLIP-FLOP

If CLK pulse is of longer period, then in JK FF for J = K = 1, continuous toggling occurs and is called Racing. To overcome the drawback master slave JK flip-flop is used.

The Master-Slave flip-flop is evolved as a result of trying to solve the problem associated with control input signal clock pulses that are too long. If very narrow control input signal pulses are generated, then the present state output that are fed back to the inputs will only cause one transition for each pulse applied to the control input.

The Master slave J-K flip-flop is simply two clocked SR flip-flop connected in cascade such that the Master (the first clocked SR flip-flop) drives the Slave (the second clocked SR flip-flop) as shown in Fig. 13.13.

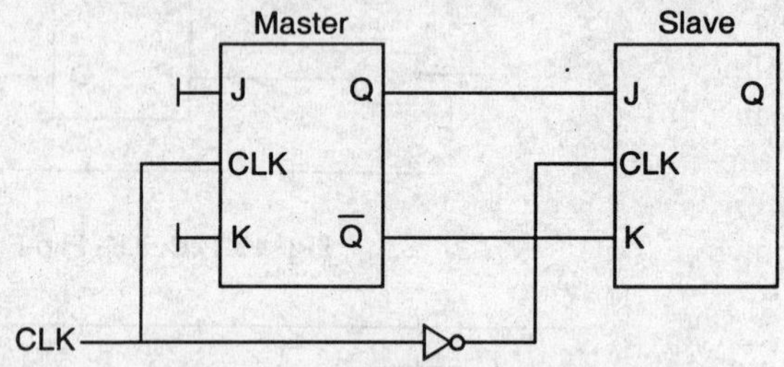


**Fig. 13.13** Master Slave Flip-Flop

When the clock signal is in logic 1, The Master flip-flop is enabled. Because of the inverter, the clock signal is in '0' for slave so that the slave flip-flop is disabled and present state of output from slave flip-flop remains the same and stable.

When the clock signal is in logic 0, the Slave flip-flop is enabled and Master is disabled. Thus the race condition of SR flip-flop (when both S and R are in logic 1) is eliminated in J-K flip-flop. This allows the Master-Slave J-K flip-flop to toggle only once for each extended clock pulse. This kind of flip-flop is also called pulse triggered bistable.

## 13.9. D-FLIP-FLOP

It is totally different from SR and JK flip-flop, because it has only one input. But S-R flip-flop can be converted into D-flip-flop by the simple addition of an inverter as shown in Fig. 13.14a and Truth Table is shown in Table 13.3.

The inverter in D-flip-flop serves two purposes. The inverter provides a latch circuit with only one input called the data input and also insures that the S-R inputs are complimented to avoid S = 1 and R = 1 condition. To 'set' the output, C = 1, D = 1 logic is to be applied. To 'reset' the output C = 1 and D = 0 should be applied.

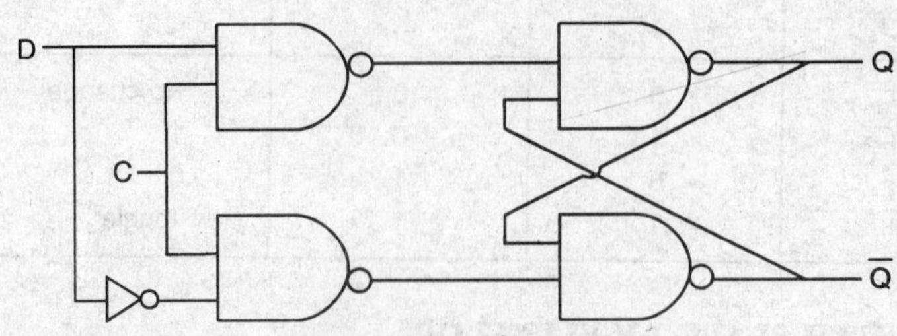


**Fig. 13.14a** D Flip-Flop

**Table 13.3: Truth Table-D-Flip-Flop.**

| Input | Out-put |
|---|---|
| D | Q |
| 0 | 0 |
| 1 | 1 |

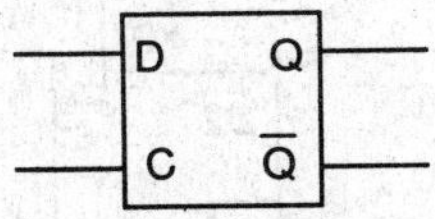


Fig. 13.14b

## 13.10. T-FLIP-FLOP

T-flip-flop can be obtained by connecting both J and K (of J-K flip-flop) to logic 1, as shown in Fig. 13.15. The truth table is shown in Table 13.4.

The state of the device changes state (toggles) each time an input pulse is received.

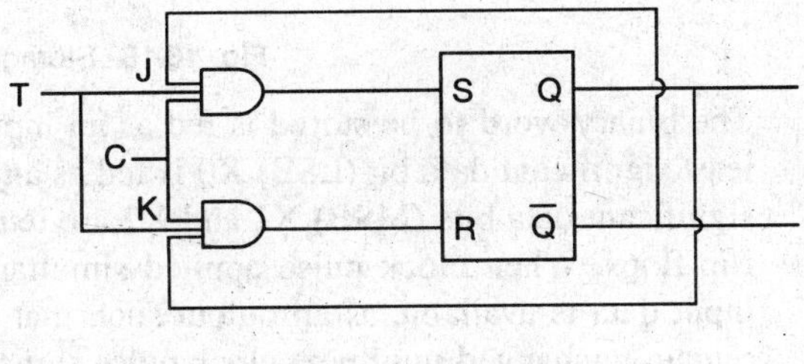


Fig. 13.15 T Flip-Flop

**Fig. 13.4: Truth Table T-FF**

| Input | Present Value | Next Value |
|---|---|---|
| T | $Q_P$ | $Q_N$ |
| 0 | 0 | 0 |
| 1 | 0 | 1 |
| 0 | 1 | 1 |
| 1 | 1 | 0 |

## 13.11 REGISTERS

### 13.11.1 Introduction

All digital system requires "registers" for practical application to store binary-information. A single flip-flop can store one bit binary information in either logic 1 or in logic 0, which is also referred as one bit register. If more than one bit information is required to be stored, an array of flip-flop is to be used. This is referred as register. A register, which stores information, is called 'buffer register'. Registers which moves information to the right or left is called 'shift registers'. The register is a group of flip-flop that operates together as a unit.

### 13.11.2 Storage Register

Storage register is one, which stores each bit of a digital word. This is called 'buffer register' or 'latch register'. Digital word can have one bit to several bits according to the requirements. Fig 13.16 shows a storage register using D-flip-flop for three bit binary word.

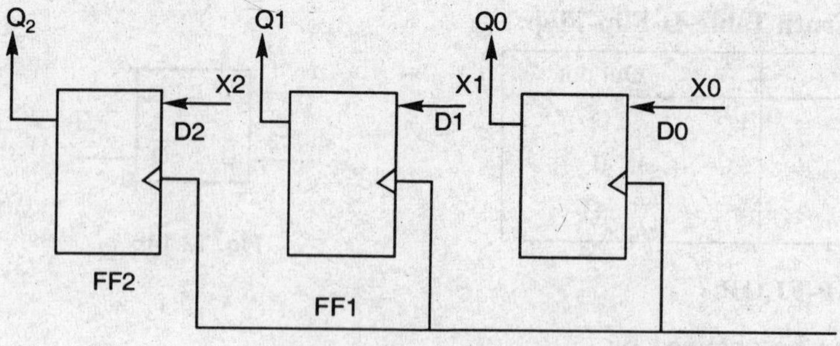


**Fig. 13.16** Storage Register

The binary word to be stored is fed as an input to the corresponding flip-flops. The least significant data bit (LSB) X0 is fed as an input to the first D-flip-flop. The most significant data bits (MSB) X1 and X2 are fed as an input to the second and third D-flip-flops. When clock pulse applied simultaneously to all the flip-flops, the given input data is available as an output such that Q2Q1Q0 = X2X1X0. The stored data remain unchanged until next clock pulse signal along with new data is applied to the flip-flops.

### 13.11.3 Controlled Storage Register

The storage register can be controlled, by using combined sequential logic system. The one bit storage register is shown in Fig. 13.17. When clear signal goes high, the flip-flop gets reset and the register output Q0 becomes zero. After resetting, the clear signal is made low and the register is now ready for operation. The control action can be made by means of combined logic using AND/OR gates. When load signal is high (logic 1), the data X0 is applied to the register through AND gate G1 and OR gate G3. When the load signal is low (logic 0), the existing output data is fed back to input and the existing data is retained. If the word of several bits is used, the same control system is implemented for all the flip-flops used according to the requirement.

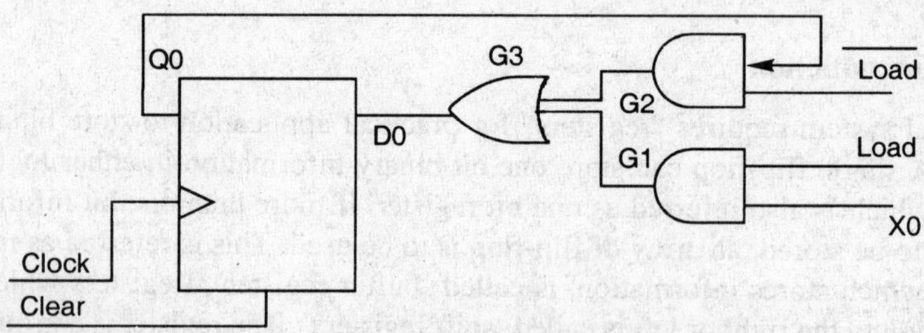


**Fig. 13.17** Controlled Register

### 13.11.4 Shift Register

The registers which are used to shift data to right hand side is called 'shift right register' and which are used to shift to the left hand side is called 'shift left register'. The registers used to shift both left and right are called bi-directional register.

### 13.11.5 Shift Left Register

Fig 13.18 shows the shift left-register using D-flip-flop.

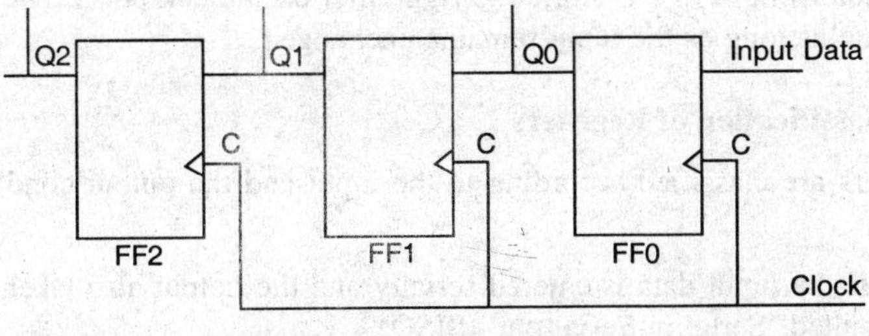


**Fig. 13.18** Shift Left Register

Consider initially all the outputs Q2, Q1 and Q0 are at their 0 state. The input data is applied to the first flip-flop.

After first clock pulse the output Q2Q1Q0 = 001;

After Second clock pulse the output Q2Q1Q0 = 011;

After third clock pulse the output Q2Q1Q0 = 111.

Thus the data "1" from Q0 is shifted to the left after each clock pulse. And the output data stay at same state as long as the input remains unchanged.

### 13.11.6 Shift Right Register

The 13.19 shows the shift right register using D-flip-flop.

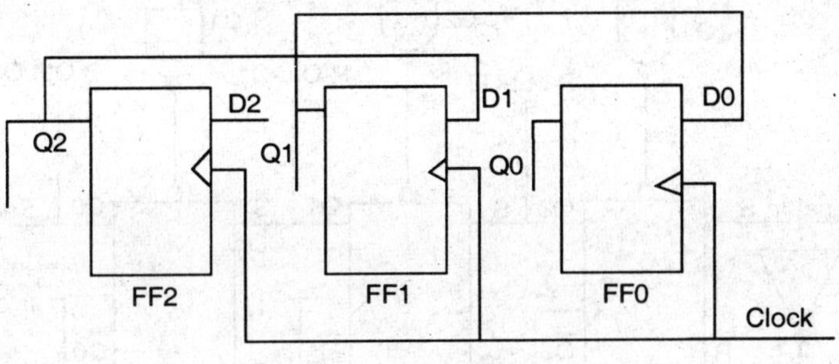


**Fig. 13.19** Shift Right Register

The data input is applied to flip-flop # 2. The output of flip-flop # 2 is connected to the input of the flip-flop # 1 and the output of the flip-flop # 1 is connected to the input of the flip-flop # 0. Initially the output Q2Q1Q0 are made to zero by resetting all flip-flops i.e. Q2Q1Q0 = 000.

When high input (logic 1) is applied to flip-flop # 2;

After first clock pulse, the output Q2Q1Q0 = 100;

After second clock pulse, the output  Q2Q1Q0 = 110;

After Third clock pulse, the output  Q2Q1Q0 = 111;

Thus the data from FF # 2 is shifted to right after each clock pulse. The output stays in same state as long as the input remains unchanged.

### 13.11.7 Classification of Registers

The registers are classified according to the input and the output conditions as follows:

**13.11.7.1**: If the input data is entered serially and the output also taken serially, the register is called 'Serial in-Serial out' (SISO).

**13.11.7.2**: If the input data is entered serially and the output is taken out simultaneously, the register is called 'Serial in-Parallel out' (SIPO).

**13.11.7.3**: If the data is entered simultaneously to all the flip-flop and taken out one be one, the register is called 'Parallel in-Serial out' (PISO).

**13.11.7.4**: If the data is entered in all the flip-flops simultaneously and also the output is taken out simultaneously, the register is called 'Parallel in Parallel out' (PIPO).

**13.11.7.5**: If the data is shifted from left to right and also from right to left with the aid of sequential logic circuits, the register is called 'Bi-directional shift register'.

Fig. 13.20 illustrates the different classifications of the registers.

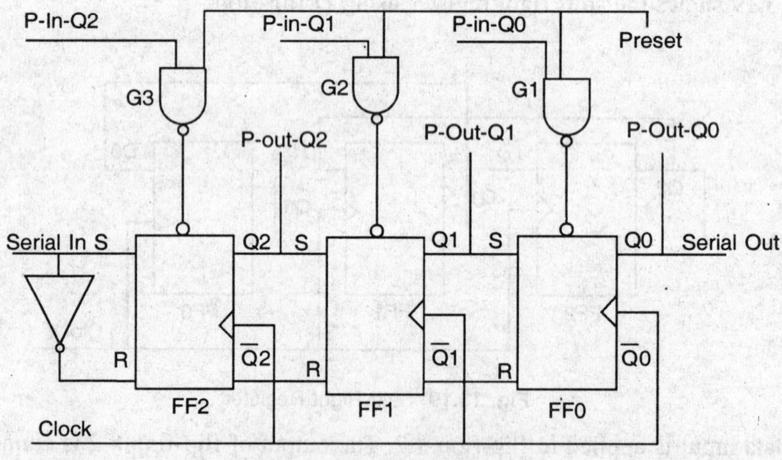


**Fig. 13.20** Universal Register

**SISO operation:**

When input data is applied to FF2,
After first clock pulse, the output from FF2 is available as Q2,
After second clock pulse, the output from FF1 is available as Q1,

After third clock pulse, the output from $FF_0$ is available as $Q_0$,
This data transfer is referred as Serial-in-Serial out mode.

**SIPO operation:** After all binary inputs are transferred serially, the stored data is available at the output of each flip-flop as Q2Q1Q0 and remain unchanged until new data along clock pulse is applied. The stored output data can be read simultaneously.

This is referred as Serial in Parallel out mode.

**PISO operation:** When both P-in data along with preset enable signal are available to the nand gates G1, G2 and G3 simultaneously, then all the flip-flop are set to a preset value at a time. This is referred as 'parallel in' data transfer. This data can be read serially by applying successive clock pulses. This is referred as Parallel in Serial out mode of operation.

**PIPO operation:** When all the data are entered simultaneously in parallel in mode, the stored data can be read from all the flip-flop as Q2Q1Q0 without any clock pulse. This is referred as Parallel in-Parallel out mode of operation.

### 13.11.8 Bi-Directional Shift Register

The bi-directional shift register can be achieved by using shift register along with combination logic system as shown in Fig. 13.21.

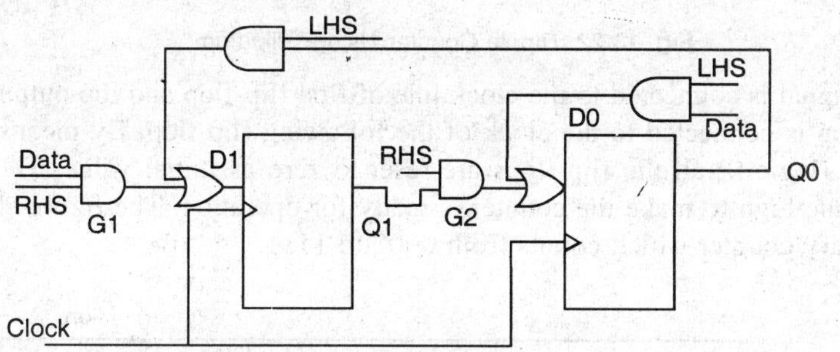


**Fig. 13.21** Bi-directional Shift Register

When data and RHS enable signal both are available for the respective AND gates, the register will function as shift right register. When data and LHS enable signal both are available for the respective AND gates, the register will function as shift left register.

## 13.12. COUNTERS

### 13.12.1 Introduction

All digital logic circuits in practical field of application require counters. Digital instruments use counters to control the precise measurements of the number of events per unit time. Digital computer uses counters to control both the sequence and execution of programming steps. The counting circuits when they are clock driven is called "Synchronous Counters" and when they are event driven (each flip-flop is triggered by the previous flip-flops) are called "Asynchronous or Ripple counter".

### 13.12.2 Asynchronous Counter

Asynchronous sequential logic circuits are not dependent on a system clock. For example, when two independent systems such as computer and a printer must communicate without a common system clock, an asynchronous design is often used.

### 13.12.3 Asynchronous Binary Counter (Ripple Counter)

Ripple counter using T-flip-flop is shown in Fig. 13.22, and using J-K flip-flop is shown in Fig. 13.23.

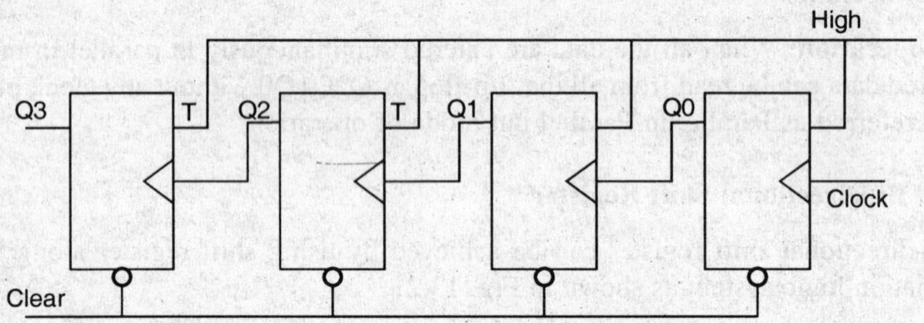


**Fig. 13.22** Ripple Counter Using T-flip-flop

The clock signal is connected to the clock line of first flip-flop and the output Q0 of each flip-flop is connected to the clock of the following flip-flop. By means of low clear signal (logic 0) all the flip-flops are reset to zero as initial value. Then clear signal is made high to make the counter is ready for operation. The figure shown is four bit binary counter which counts from 0000 to 1111.

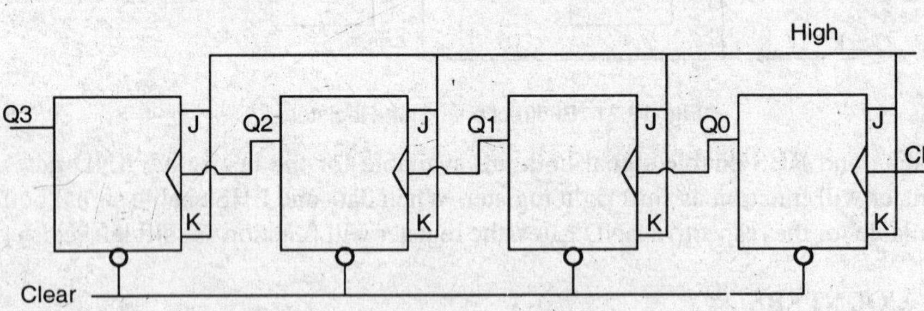


**Fig. 13.23** Ripple Counter Using K-K flip-flop

Initial output count is 0000

After first clock pulse, Q0 becomes 1, then the output will be 0001,

After second clock pulse, Q0 = 0, Q1 = 1, then the output will be 0010,

After third clock pulse, the output will be 0011 and so on,

After fifteenth clock pulse the output will be 1111

After sixteenth clock pulse all the flip-flops reset to 0000 and the cycle repeats. This counter is also called "Modulo 16 counter". The change of state ripples through the counter from input to output.

The state diagram is shown in Fig. 13.24.

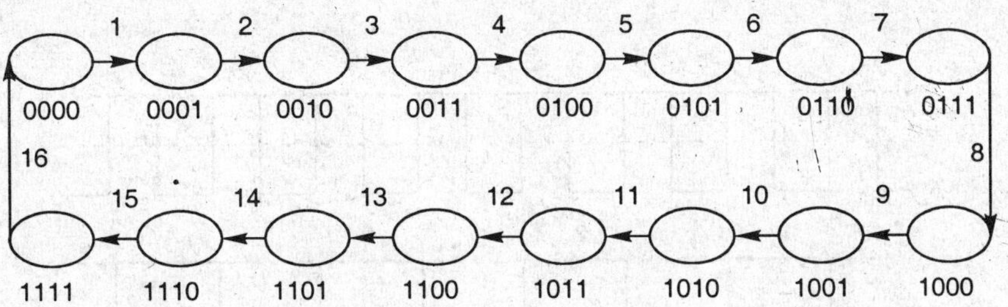


**Fig. 13.24** State Diagram

### 13.12.4 Down Counter

In this counter the output decreases with the application of the successive clock pulses. Since the counting is done in down direction it is called "Down Counter". The circuit is constructed with some modification (clock signal is taken from $\overline{Q}$ instead of Q) to ripple up counter dealt earlier as shown in Fig. 13.25a with T-flip-flop and 13.25b with J-K flip-flop.

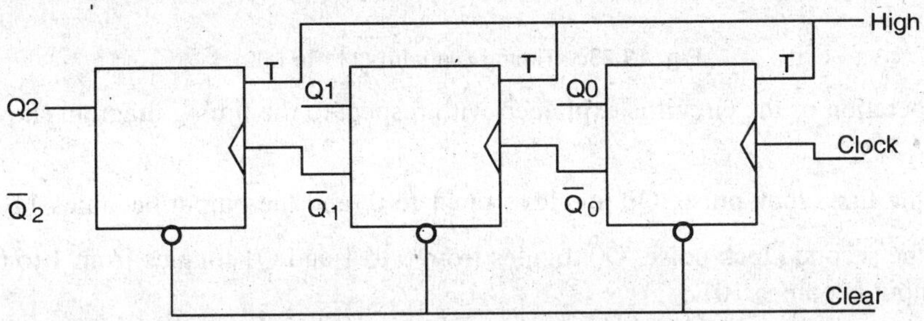


**Fig. 13.25a** Down Counter Using T-flip-flop

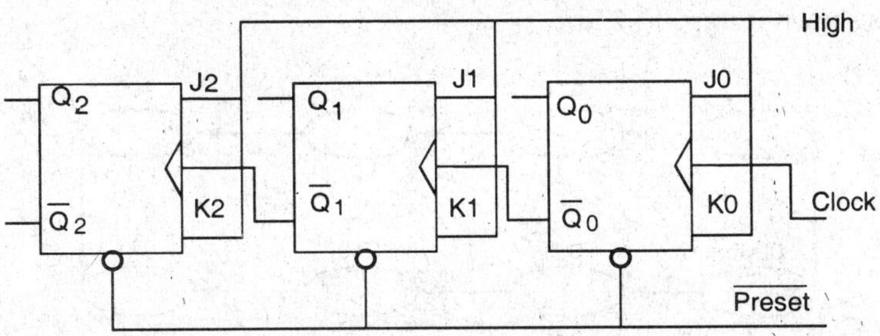


**Fig. 13.25b** Down Counter Using J-K Flip-flop

In this counter the clock signal is connected to the clock line of the first flip-flop. The output $\overline{Q}$ (Q) of each flip-flop is connected to the clock of the following flip-flop. The output is read from $Q_2$ $Q_1$ $Q_0$ terminal only.

Consider when preset signal goes low the output is made to set such that Q2Q1Q0 = 111. When preset goes high, the counter is ready for operation.

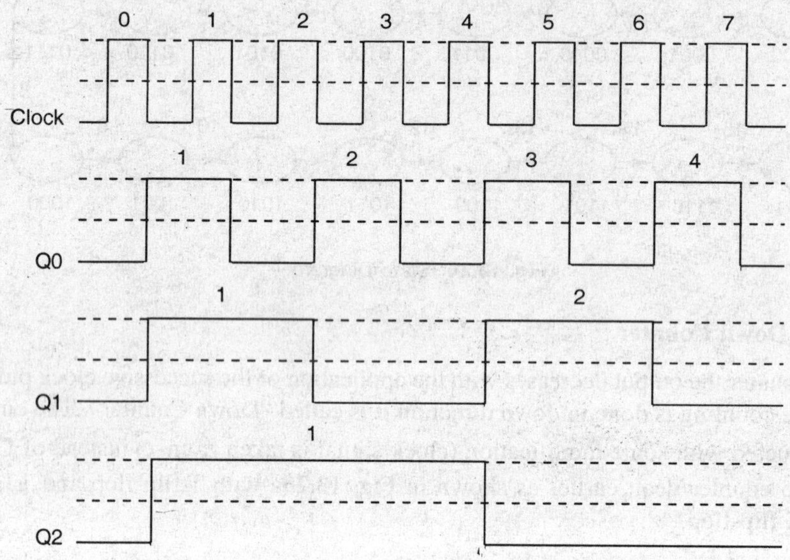


**Fig. 13.25c** Timing Diagram (111 to 000)

The operation of the circuit is explained with respect to the timing diagram shown in Fig. 13.25c.

After the first clock pulse, Q0 toggles from 1 to 0 and the output becomes 110.

After the second clock pulse, Q0 toggles from 0 to 1 and Q1 toggles from 1 to 0 and the output becomes 101.

After third clock pulse, Q0 toggles from 1 to 0 and the output becomes 100.

Thus the counting process will be continued up to 000 and the cycle repeats. The state diagram is shown in Fig. 13.25d.

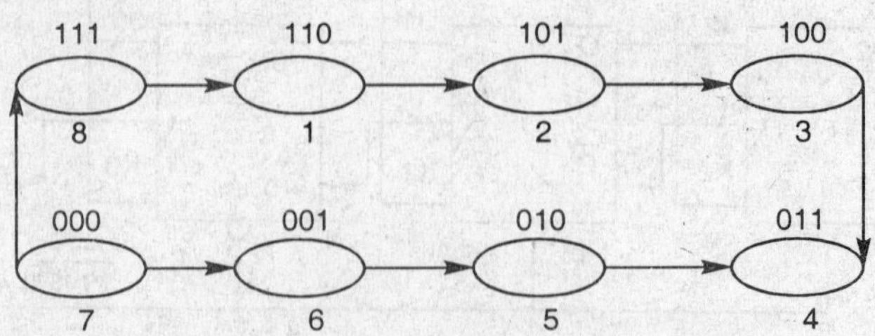


**Fig. 13.25d** Down Counter State Diagram

### 13.12.5 Synchronous Counter

When all the flip-flops are clocked simultaneously in the counter circuit, it is referred as 'Synchronous Counter'. It can be made to operate at any count sequence. Fig. 13.26 shows the synchronous counter using J-K flip-flop.

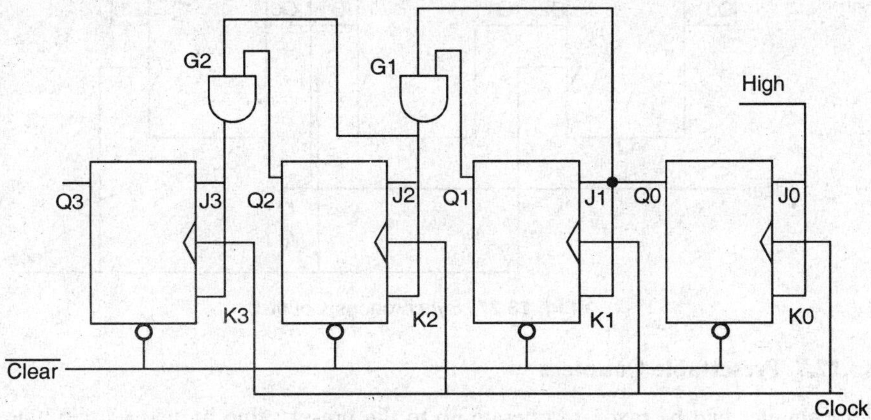


**Fig. 13.26** Synchronous Counter

The first flip-flop J-K signal is always made high.

Q0 – toggles for every clock pulse.

Q1 – toggles only when Q0 = 1

Q2 – toggles only when both Q1 and Q0 are 1 (through gate G1).

Q3 – toggles only Q2, Q1, Q0 = 1.

Initial value of the output = 0000,

After first clock pulse, the output = 0001,

After second clock pulse, the output = 0010,

After third clock pulse, the output = 0011. Thus the counter, counter counts up to 1111 and the cycle repeats.

### 13.12.6 Ring Counter

This counter is used for rotating the data among the registers. By connecting the output of the least significant flip-flop stage to the input of the most significant flip-flop stage, a ring counter is formed. Final stage output is fed back to the input. A three stage ring counter is formed using D-flip-flop is shown in Fig. 13.27. When one stage of flip-flop is at logic 1, while other stages are at logic 0. The logic 1 will be circulated around the register.

Preset of the first flip-flop is connected to the clear low signal. Clear low signal is connected to the second and third flip-flops. When clear low signal is applied, the output will be 001. Then clear signal is made high to make the counter is ready for operation. After first clock pulse Q0 is shifted to Q 1 and the output will be 010. After second clock pulse Q1 is shifted to Q2, and the output will be 100. After fourth clock pulse Q2 shifted to first flip-flop and the cycle repeats as ring circuit.

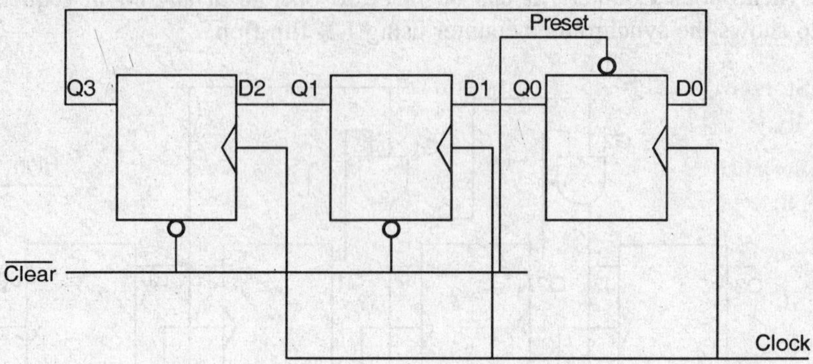


**Fig. 13.27** Synchronous Counter

### 13.12.7 Presettable Counters

This counter can be made to operate up to the preset value by using logic gate systems. Consider Fig. 13.28 which is a presettable counter used as divide-by 10 or a decade counter. The input to the nand gate is taken from Q1 and Q3. The output from the nand gate is applied to all flip-flops as low clear signal, which is used to reset the counter. The counter starts from 0000 onwards up to 1010. When the output reaches 1010 the Nand gate will be enabled and the output from the gate will reset the counter to 0000. Thus counter will reset on every ten clock pulse. The preset can be made set to any value according to the requirement.

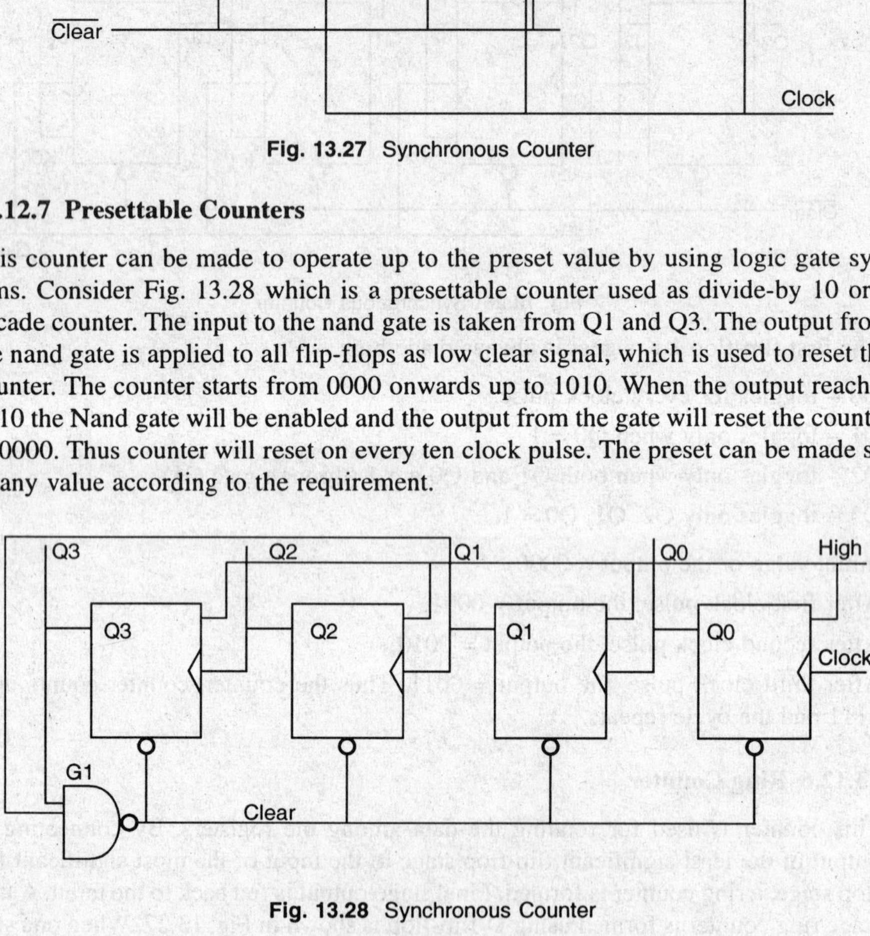


**Fig. 13.28** Synchronous Counter

## HIGHLIGHTS

- Flip-flop—An electronic circuit that has two stable states.
- Race condition—In RS flip-flop of both R and S inputs are in high state simultaneously is referred as race condition.
- D-flip-flop—A modification to R-S flip-flop to eliminate race condition.

- Master-Slave flip-flop—It is a combination of two clocked flip-flops. The first flip-flop is called master and the second is called slave.
- Toggle—Changing of the output to the opposite state of the existing state.
- Register—A register is a group of flip-flop operating together as a unit.
- Storage register—It is also called buffer or latch, which stores each bit of a digital word.
- Serial shift—Contents of the register is circulated to other register at each clock pulse in a serial fashion.
- Parallel shift—Data bit is simultaneously shifted with a single clock transition.
- SISO—Data transmission takes place in serial in and serial out fashion.
- SIPO—Data transmission takes place in serial in and parallel out fashion.
- SIPO—Data transmission takes place in parallel in and serial out fashion.
- PISO—Data transmission takes place in parallel in and serial out fashion.
- PIPO—Data transmission takes place in parallel in and parallel out fashion.
- Bi-directional shift—Data will be shifted both the directions using logic circuits.
- Asynchronous counter—These counters are event driven and do not depending on system clock.
- Synchronous counter—These counters are clock driven.
- Ripple counter—An asynchronous counter in which each flip-flop is triggered by the output of the previous flip-flop.
- Up Down counter—This counter is capable of counting in either direction.
- Presettable counter—The counter can be made to start with any preset value instead of zero.

## REVIEW QUESTIONS

1. What is the necessity of clocking? Explain clocked R-S flip-flop.
2. Compare J-K flip-flip with master slave J-K flip-flop.
3. Write short notes on the following:
   (a) D - flip-flop.
   (b) T - flip-flop.
4. Explain how the data is transferred to the left or right using the shift registers.
5. What are the classifications of the registers and how it can be achieved?
6. Explain the bi-directional register.
7. Explain Up Down counters.
8. Explain the presettable counter.

9. Write short notes on the following:
   (a) Ring counter.
   (b) Ripple counter.
   (c) Synchronous counter.

## TWO MARKS QUESTION AND ANSWERS

1. *What is R-S flip-flop ?*

   The R-S flip-flop is a device with two stable states.

2. *What does racing mean ?*

   It is an unpredictable state when S and R inputs are in high state simultaneously in R-S flip-flop.

3. *What is D - flip-flop ?*

   It is a modification of R-S flip-flop, to eliminate the race condition.

4. *What is truth Table ?*

   The truth Table is a summarizing Table of the output corresponding to the input.

5. *What is clocking ?*

   Clocking is a signal that coordinates the action of the flip-flop.

6. *What are 'set' and 'clear' signals ?*

   The set signal sets the flip-flop to 1 state and clear signal resets the flip-flop to zero state.

7. *What are sequential circuits ?*

   In the sequential circuits, the outputs are determined not only by its external inputs but also by the past history of the circuits.

8. *What is meant by 'hold time' ?*

   The minimum time the input signals must be available after the clock pulse is applied is called hold time.

9. *What is register ?*

   The register is a group of flip-flop that operate together as a unit.

10. *What is a buffer register ?*

    A register that stores the information is called buffer register.

11. *What are shift registers ?*

    The register that moves the information is called shift register.

12. *What are the classifications of the registers ?*

    Serial in serial out, serial in parallel out, parallel in serial out, parallel in parallel out are the classifications of the registers.

13. *What is bi-directional shift registers ?*

    The bi-directional shift register is used to shift the data in both the directions.

14. *What is counter ?*

    Counter is a device that counts the events per unit time.

15. *What is asynchronous counter ?*

    The counting circuits that are not dependent on system clock are called asynchronous counters.

16. *What is ripple counter ?*

    The change of state that ripples through the counter from input to output is called ripple counter.

17. *What does the down counter mean ?*

    The output that decreases with the applications of the successive clock pulse is called down counter.

18. *What does the synchronous counter mean ?*

    When all the flip-flops are clocked simultaneously in the counter circuit is called synchronous counter.

19. *What is ring counter ?*

    The counter that rotates the data among the registers is called ring counter.

20. *What is presettable counter ?*

    The counter which is made to operate up to a preset value is called presettable counter.

*Chapter 14*

# INTRODUCTION TO DIGITAL COMPUTERS

## 14.1. INTRODUCTION

Computers have done wonders so far. The need for computers in our day-to-day life is being intensified. Recruitment of personnel for any job is based on the individual's computer handling abilities. Computers predict the weather and give warnings. They take pictures of the solar system and send them to the earth. Everybody talks about, computerization of everything. World Wide Web—a network of computers has made the entire globe a virtual marketplace. Any one can buy anything from anywhere through a computer. An electronic device is creating such an impact in the world, and it is essential that everyone acquires atleast some basic knowledge about computers. Though dealt briefly, this chapter will definitely lay a good foundation for beginners.

## 14.2. HISTORY OF COMPUTERS

Generally speaking, the word "computing" means "calculating". Computer is an electronic device, which is able to accept data in a prescribed form, process data, and supply the results as information. Nowadays we are using highly sophisticated computers, but there lies a long history behind the evolution of such computers.

If we trace the history back, abacus is the earliest known computing device, which originated in China around 3500 B.C. It is a wooden frame with 10 wires across it carrying colored beads. Counting is done by shifting the beads from one side to the other. Even now, it is used by our children to learn decimal number system.

The next invention in computing was made only in 1622 by an English mathematician William Oughtred. He invented the Slide rule, which uses the idea of Logarithms and it represents numbers by lengths.

A French mathematician Blaise Pascal invented an adding machine in 1641, which was a major breakthrough in computing technology. He was a young inventor with multifarious interests. He had invented Barometer, wheel barrow, hydraulic press etc. His father was a tax collector. To help his father in calculation he invented a machine called **Pascaline**. It consisted of dials and toothed wheels. The movement of one complete round of a wheel made next wheel to move 1/10th of its position. The number to be added is to be dialed and the result of the addition appears through a window. Pascal could not improve it since his interest of invention was diverted to other fields and he died at the young age of 39. To pay tribute to him one of the programming languages has been named after him—**Pascal** Leibniz was another mathematician who made some more improvements in Pascal's machine to make it perform multiplication and division.

Charles Babbage is the greatest figure in the history of computer science. He attempted to mechanise sequences of calculations. The machine designed by him used cardboard cards with holes punched in them to introduce both instructions and necessary data (numbers) into the machine. The machine was to perform the instructions dictated by the cards automatically, not stopping until entire sequence of instructions had been completed. To do the research work in this field he got funds from the British government. Although the technology prevalent in his time was a limiting factor to improve his machine further, Babbage succeeded in establishing the basic principle on which modern computers are built.

It was only through Ada Augusta, attempts of Babbage were known to the world. She was the daughter of the famous English poet Lord Byron. Lady Ada is considered to be the first computer programmer of the world. In recognition of her services one of the programming languages has been named after her—**ADA**.

By 1930s, punched cards were in wide use in large businesses, and various types of punched-card-handling machines were available. In 1937 Howard Aiken, at Harvard, proposed to IBM (International Business Machines) that a machine could be constructed, which would automatically sequence the operations and calculations performed. This machine used a combination of electromechanical devices. The machine was in operation for some time, generating many tables of mathematical functions, and was used for trajectory calculations in world war II.

In 1943 S.P. Eckert and J.W. Mauchly, of the Moore School of Engineering of University of Pennsylvania devised the ENIAC-Electronic Numerical Integrator and Calculator, which employed vacuum tubes. This first generation computer was very big, and generated too much of heat. But it was capable of computing 300 times faster than the human brain. This initially used decimal system for computing.

A year later, John Van Neuman, at the Institute of Advanced Study (IAS) in Princeton, improved computing with the help of the Binary system.

The UNIVAC-I was the first commercially available electronic digital computer and it was designed by Eckert and Mauchly at their own company, which was first bought by the U S Board of Censes. Later IBM stated having done R & D work in this field. No wonder, now IBM is one of the biggest computer manufacturing companies in the world.

## 14.3. CLASSIFICATION OF COMPUTERS

Computers can be classified according to

(i) Generation
(ii) Technology
(iii) Size, and
(iv) Application.

**(i) Generations of computers:** Initially computers were built with only vacuum tubes i.e. diodes and triodes. These computers were very large, slow, heat dissipating and very costly. They were called **first generation computers**. These computers were built around vacuum tubes, and they were big, expensive and finicky.

In the late 1950s, electronic industry introduced transistors to the world. So, the transistors replaced all vacuum tubes, and hence the size of the computer reduced, speed improved, and the cost also came down. This was the **second generation**. These second-generation computers were smaller and less expensive.

Then came the concept of integration. Many transistors and other circuits were fabricated together and assembled in small containers called integrated chips (ICs). But the number of components in an integrated chip was less than ten. They were called small scale integration (SSI). They were called **third generation computers**. These third-generation computers were again smaller, less expensive and much more powerful.

As the integrated circuit technology developed rapidly, millions of components can be packed in a single IC. The **fourth-generation** came about with the invention of the first microprocessor (the critical components of a complete computer housed on a tiny silicon chip), which further surpassed the invention of the vacuum tube, the transistor and silicon chips. This brought about a radical change in the capability, appearance, and the availability of computers. The speed increased and cost came down. Large-scale integration circuits (LSI) and very large scale integration circuits (VLSI) were built.

The computer industry has already set its goal to make **fifth generation computers**. The only difference between a computer and a human being is—it cannot think. But the world is already on the move, of making the computers think. These fifth generation computers are based on **artificial intelligence** and **natural language processing**. The main objective is to make the computers think, which will resemble human intelligence and decisions.

**(ii) Technology:** According to the technology used, computers are classified as **Analog computers** and **Digital computers**. The computers which perform operations on analog signals i.e. varying voltage signals are called analog computers. These are also called measuring devices. Whereas digital computers perform operations on discrete signals which will represent binary digits. They will have two discrete values to represent a 0 and a 1. They are also called counting devices. In this chapter we are going to discuss only digital computers.

**(iii) Size:** Computers are available in a wide range of sizes and capabilities. According to the memory capacity, speed, cost, and other capabilities, computers are classified into four types. In chronological order, they are: **mainframe computers**, **mini computers**, **microcomputers**, and **super computers**. Let us discuss these one by one.

**Mainframe Computers:** In the early days computers were very large, about the size of the room, and the engineers referred to that as **mainframe**. They were also costly. However the development in electronics engineering have helped to build powerful, low cost, small sized mainframe computers.

On a single mainframe computer more than ten people can work at a time. It is called multi-access or multi-user system. Mainframe computers are now built with large, high speed memory, very sophisticated CPU, and I/O devices. They are used in places where large volumes of data should be processed and multi-access is necessary. Insurance companies, banks, scientific laboratories and universities use mainframe computers. They are used to store international databases which can be produced from anywhere in the world.

**Mini computers:** Developments in IC technology have helped us to pack more and more components into smaller and smaller sizes. This has led to the development of mini computers. They are smaller in all respects and cheaper than the mainframe computers. They are multi-access systems. They are widely used in control systems, scientific applications and business data processing for small business firms, schools and laboratories. Mini computers find a potential application in local area networks.

**Microcomputers:** Now, we find computers everywhere. It is a microcomputer that has made it possible. A microcomputer is built using microprocessor chips, which are single chips on which all the major components of a computer are fabricated. Microcomputers are very small in size. Notebook size computers are center of attraction in today's market. There are a wide range of microcomputers depending upon their usability, memory size, speed and capabilities. Before the microcomputer revolution people were reduced to using immobile room sized computers. The evolution of computers has come about rapidly and accommodates almost all people. Today people can choose to work with mainframe computers, embedded computers, supercomputers, workstations, notebook computers, subnotebook computers, palmtop computers, laptop computers, and personal computers.

Computers can be made even in our homes with our television. By converting TV screen into a display screen, adding a microprocessor chip and a keyboard, we can make home computers.

There is no field where we can avoid computer applications. Traffic signals, communication controls, automatic milk vending machines, automatic checkouts in airport, wristwatches, washing machines, and countless other applications use microprocessor based machines.

**Super computers:** These computers hold the world record for their computing speed and power. Today's super computers can do their calculations at a rate of a few billion operations per second. They are relatively specialised in the sense that very few applications need such a high speed. But for super computers we would not have enjoyed the spectacular achievement in space technology. Super computers are used for massive scientific and engineering calculations. They are needed for aircraft, missile and spacecraft designing, weather forecasting, seismological studies etc.

**(iv) Application:** According to the applications they can be classified as **special purpose/real time computers** and **general purpose computers**.

Those systems where an immediate response is needed against the inputs, are termed real time systems. These normally have dedicated connections to a process or system. The elapsed time between sensing of input and directing the output is a critical factor in these systems. Examples are: flight control systems on-board aircraft, systems for control of power generation in a nuclear power plant, process control systems for production lines in textile mills etc.

As opposed to these, processing in the **general purpose computers** is not time critical and they are stand-alone systems. They could be used for any purpose inclusive of general software development etc. Their role would change accordingly. Examples are: computer systems used for preparation of payrolls, invoice generation, and systems at computer centers of different organisations inclusive of educational institutions.

## 14.4. COMPONENTS OF A COMPUTER SYSTEM

A computer system is divided into two parts as shown in Fig. 14.1.

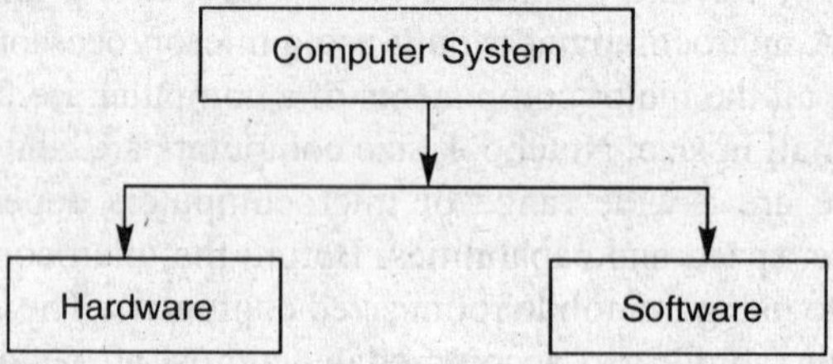


Fig. 14.1

**1. Hardware:** Electronic and mechanical components of a computer put together is called hardware. We will be discussing about this in detail in the next section.

**2. Software:** A computer system with hardware components alone cannot do a particular task unless it is instructed properly. The set of instructions or programs used to make a computer to do different operations is called **software**. We will be discussing about this later.

## 14.5. BASIC ORGANISATION OF A DIGITAL COMPUTER

The block diagram of a digital computer is given in Fig. 14.2. This shows how different hardware components of a computer are organised together.

A digital computer has the following hardware components:

**Central Processing Unit (CPU):** This component is based on an integrated circuit called 'microprocessor'. Its function is to act as the brains of the computer. It interprets and executes, the instructions given by manipulating the data. The CPU contains two sub-components: the Control Unit (CU) and the Arithmetic Logic Unit (ALU).

The Control Unit is used for the interpretation of instructions or programs. These instructions might be used, for example, to send information to and from memory or to control the operation of other components, etc. The ALU is primarily used for data manipulation using mathematical techniques, for example, addition or multiplication of two numbers.

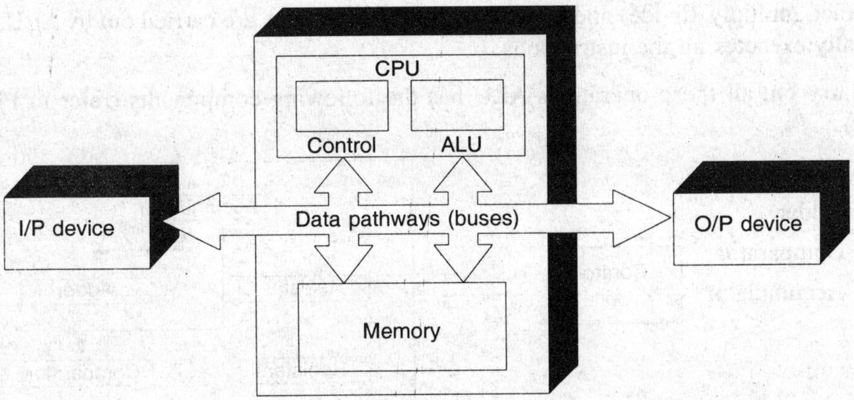


**Fig. 14.2**

**Main Memory:** This is used to store data, instructions, programs and results during computation. CPU accesses the memory whenever it requires data to execute a particular operation. The types of memory units are discussed later.

**Input/Output (I/O) Devices:** These devices are used for user-control of the computer and generally consist of a keyboard, visual display unit, printer, and mouse. A computer should always be instructed to do any operation. These instructions and the data required are fed into the computer with the help of a keyboard. The output devices are used to record the results obtained by the computer and present them to the outside world. The visual display unit acts as a common output unit to display the information. Some other I/O devices used to enhance the user interaction with the computer are discussed later.

**Computer Bus:** The computer bus is the communication pathway for the components of the computer. Its function is similar to the central nervous system. The bus carries the information between different components like I/O devices, memory, ALU, CPU, etc. The speed of a computer is dependent on the speed at which the bus works.

We will be discussing the functions of each unit in detail in the subsequent sections.

## 14.6. FUNCTIONS OF CENTRAL PROCESSING UNIT (CPU)

Central processing unit or the CPU is considered as the **'brain'** of a computer system. It performs the following functions:

1. It co-ordinates the functions of different hardware units;
2. It supervises the flow of data between input devices, main memory, the output devices, and other units;
3. It takes each instruction in sequence, interprets correctly and executes it by moving the required data to the appropriate units.

There are two different units inside the CPU. They are: **1. Arithmetic Logic Unit (ALU)** and **2. Control unit**.

**14.6.1. Arithmetic Logic Unit:** As we discussed earlier, all the arithmetic (viz. add, subtract, multiply, divide) and logic (compare) instructions are carried out by ALU. It actually executes all the instructions.

To carry out all these operations ALU has the following components (refer to Fig. 14.3).

1. Registers
2. Adder
3. Comparator
4. Accumulator

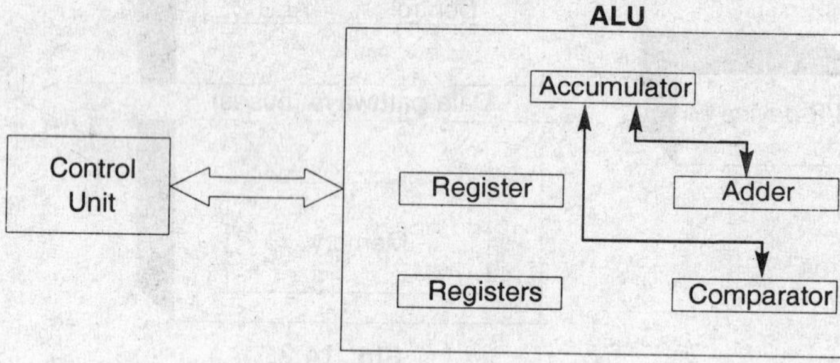


Fig. 14.3

**A register** is a temporary storage which can hold a limited number of bits (say 8 or16 or 32 bits) for some time. **Accumulator** is an important register which is used to receive the input data and place the result, before and after execution of any instruction.

**Comparator** is used for comparing two binary numbers. All the four basic arithmetic operations, viz. addition, subtraction, division and multiplication are carried out by the **adder** circuit only. It is made up of the logic gates which we discussed in Chapter 13. All the operations can be performed as some form of addition.

For example, 27 – 13 is nothing but 27 + (–13)

Similarly, repeated addition is multiplication.

For example, 3 × 4 is nothing but 3 + 3 + 3 + 3

And repeated subtraction is division.

For example, consider 12/3, here 3 can be subtracted from 12, 4 times, so 12/3 = 4.

**14.6.2. Control Unit:** As we already mentioned **registers** are temporary storage units. There are a number of registers in control unit also. Each performs a specific function by holding the data temporarily while processing. There may be different number of registers in different names according to the organisation of the computers. But generally speaking the following registers are very important:

1. Program counter (PC)
2. Instruction register (IR)
3. Address register (AR)
4. Decoder register (DR)

A computer program is nothing but a set of instructions doing different operations. This program is initially stored in the memory. Each instruction has a unique address in the memory. The function of the **Program counter** is to receive the address of the first instruction, when the program needs to be executed. Further, PC always holds the address of the next instruction to be executed. Accordingly for instructions like add, subtract, etc., it gets incremented by 1.

**Instruction register** stores the instruction being executed. Each instruction consists of two parts: one is **operation** part which specifies the operation to be done. The other is **operand** part which specifies the memory location or the register which contains the data to be operated upon. There may be one or two operands in an instruction.

From the IR, the operation part is sent to the **decoder register** and the address part is sent to the **address register**. The decoder interprets the operation and the signals are sent to the Arithmetic Logic Unit (ALU) to perform that operation. CPU then sends the data from the address locations specified in the instruction, to the ALU and the operation (addition, subtraction, multiplication, division, etc.) is performed.

To clarify the functions of the CPU (both control unit and ALU), let us take a simple example.

Assume that the following are two instructions in a program encountered by the CPU for execution.

MOV ACC, 5000 – Move the contents of the memory location 5000 to the Accumulator (ACC).

ADD ACC, 5001– Add the contents of the location 5001 in the memory to the Accumulator contents.

These two instructions are stored in the memory as shown in Fig. 14.4.

Let us now follow the functions of various registers for these two instructions one by one. For the first instruction

**MOV ACC 5000**

1. Initially the program counter (PC) holds the address of the instruction 2000, which is then moved to the address register (AR).
2. Next, the control unit accesses the location 2000 in the memory and moves the instruction "MOV ACC 5000" to the instruction register. Meantime, as the address of the instruction is already sent to AR, the PC gets incremented by 1.

| IR | MOV ACC 5000 |
|---|---|

| PC | 2001 |
|---|---|

3. From the instruction register, the operation part of the instruction is sent to the decoder register (DR) and the address part is sent to the AR.

| DR | MOV |
|---|---|

| AR | 5000 |
|---|---|

4. Decoder register interprets the meaning of the instruction to the control unit. Immediately the control unit sends the signals to ALU and makes all the registers in the ALU ready.
5. The control unit then goes to location 5000 and moves 99 (refer Fig. 14.4) to the

accumulator. So now by the "MOV" operation the value "99" is moved to the accumulator from the memory.

| ACC | 99 |
|---|---|

After the execution of move instruction.

Memory

| Address | contents |
|---|---|
| 2000 | MOV ACC, 5000 |
| 2001 | ADD ACC, 5001 |
| | : |
| | : |
| 5000 | 99 |
| 5001 | 100 |
| | : |

**Fig. 14.4**

Same sequence of operations are performed for the next instruction "ADD ACC 5001" also.

1. PC which is holding the address 2001, sends the same to the AR.

   | PC | 2001 |
   |---|---|

   | AR | 2001 |
   |---|---|

2. Control unit moves the instruction in this location 2001 to IR

   | IR | ADD |
   |---|---|

   | ACC | 5001 |
   |---|---|

3. From this the operation part is sent to the DR and the address part is sent to AR.

   | DR | ADD |
   |---|---|

   | AR | 5001 |
   |---|---|

4. DR interprets the instruction to the control unit and since this is an "ADD" operation once again the signals are sent to the ALU. Now the ALU activates its adder circuit.
5. The control unit goes to location 5001 and moves the value 900 to the ALU which is in turn sent to the adder circuit. The adder circuit now adds this value with the accumulator. So the accumulator now holds the result 999.

| ACC | 99 |
|---|---|

Before executing the add instruction.

| ACC | 999 |
|---|---|

After executing the add instruction.

In this way the CPU continues its function. These operations can be performed within one millionth of a second by the CPU.

We notice that there are two phases in processing each instruction:

1. Execution phase done by ALU where actual operation is carried out and
2. Instruction fetching phase done by control unit, in which movement of data and instruction and interpretation of the instructions are carried out. These two phases go on alternatively. Each phase is carried out within one millionth of time.

So it is now clear that the ALU and the control unit put together is called CPU.

## 14.7. MEMORY

No computer can work without a memory to store data, programs, instructions etc. A memory unit in a computer consists of a large number of binary storage cells. The main characteristic of a cell is, it must have two stable states, one to store a '0' and another to store a '1'. There are two broad classifications of memory and different technologies are used to build these. They are

1. Main memory or primary memory
2. Secondary memory or auxiliary memory

**14.7.1. Main Memory:** This is the memory always residing inside the computer connected with the CPU. This is relatively large and fast memory used to store programs, data, etc. during the computer operations. We already discussed about the instruction and data being taken from the memory by the CPU while executing a program. It is this memory which is accessed by the CPU whenever necessary. In earlier days, **core money** was used as main memory. Now, it has been replaced by the low cost semiconductor memory. Let us discuss the different technologies used, one by one in this section.

**Core memory:**

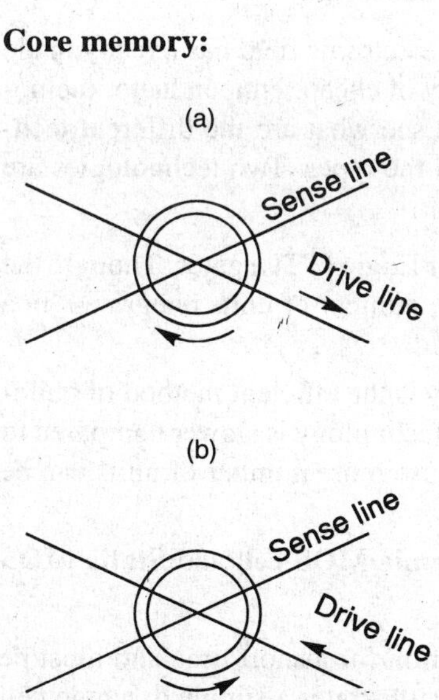


Fig. 14.5

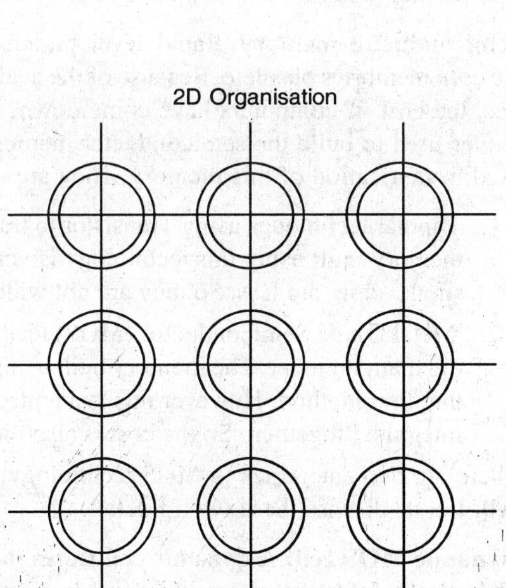


Fig. 14.6

Until the advent of semiconductor memory ICs in the 1970s most computers employed core memory only. The main principle used here is magnetising a small core (refer to Fig. 14.5a & b). Actually current is passed through a tiny piece of ferrite core . This current called **drive current** magnetises the core in either clockwise or anti-clockwise direction depending upon its direction. These two directions of magnetisation are used to represent a logical 0 and 1 state. The direction of the current determines the direction of magnetisation. The property of this ferrite material is such that, even if the current is reduced to zero, the core is capable of retaining its previous magnetised state. Number of such cores are grouped together in 2 dimensional or 2½ dimensional forms.

To do both read and write operation on the ferrite core, two conductors: **drive line** and **sense line**, are required. Drive line is used to write either a 1 or a 0 into a core a as mentioned above. For example when current I is passed in the drive line in the direction as shown in Fig. 14.5a, magnetic flux will be produced in the direction shown in the same figure. This can be taken to represent a 0 state. When the current is reversed, the flux direction also reverses as shown in Fig. 14.5b. This can be taken to represent a 1.

To read the core, current I is passed through the drive line as in Fig. 14.5a. If the core is already in zero state, there will not be any change in the direction of the magnetic flux. However, if it were in 1 state, since the current is flowing in the opposite direction the flux will reverse and come to a 0 state. This induces a voltage in the sense line according to the Faraday's law. This is detected by a sense amplifier and transferred to the CPU. Since this method is destructive while reading a 1, after reading it should be restored.

More number of cores can be arranged in 2 dimensional or 2½ dimensional, so that more number of bits can be stored. Fig. 14.6 shows a 2 dimensional organisation of core memory. Core memories have already become obsolete.

**Semiconductor memory:** Rapid development in the electronic field has already made the core memories obsolete. Because of the availability of cheap semiconductor memories, the cost of computers have come down. Let us see what are the different techniques used to build the semiconductor memory and the types. Two technologies are used in fabrication of this memory. They are:

1. Bipolar techniques using Transistor to transistor Logic (TTL) gates. Though the memory built using this technology is very fast, number of units integrated in a single chip are less. So they are not widely used.
2. Metal Oxide Semiconductor (MOS) technology is the efficient method of building main memory. The memory built using this technology is slower compared to the first method. However this is adapted because more number of units can be integrated together. So the cost is also reduced.

There are two categories in MOS technology: **Dynamic MOS cell** and **Static MOS cell**. Let us discuss these two in detail.

**Dynamic MOS cell:** A dynamic cell stores information for a short time and must be periodically refreshed to retain its contents. Fig 14.7 illustrates a simple dynamic cell using charge storage. It incorporates MOS transistor T, which acts as a switch line and a capacitor C, which stores the data. It is connected with an address line and a data line. To write a 1 into this cell a voltage V is applied to the data line. The address line is also connected to voltage V. This switches T on and a charge is transferred to C. This can represent a 1. If there is no supply, then the capacitor will not be charged, which can represent a 0.

To read the contents of the cell the address line is again connected to V volts which turns on the data line. If C was in 1 state (i.e. charged state) then this charge discharges on the data line and is detected by a sense amplifier connected to it. If C is in 0 state, then no charge flows through the data line.

But, reading the data in this way is destructive as the capacitor starts discharging, rewrite operation should follow a read operation. Besides this, periodic replenishment of charge stored in the capacitor stored in the capacitor should be done to avoid destruction of memory.

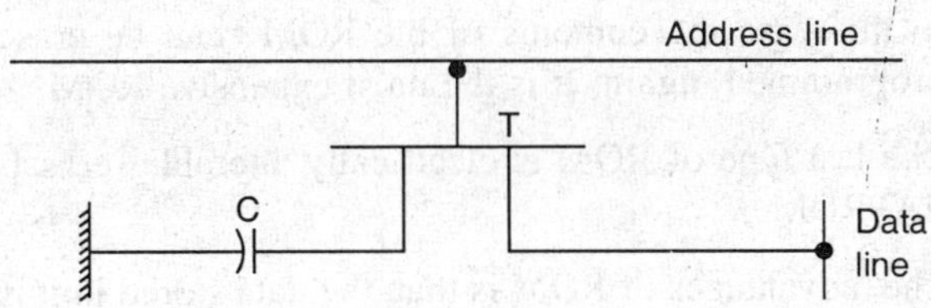


Fig. 14.7

**Static MOS cell:** A static memory cell stores the data indefinitely. The working of static cell is explained with the help of its circuit diagram as in Fig. 14.8. There are two transistors connected which can be in two stable states. One stable state (say 1) is with $T_1$ conducting and $T_2$ non-conducting. Other state is with $T_2$ conducting and $T_1$ non-conducting. When voltage V is applied at the gate of $T_2$ (corresponding circuit not shown), the voltage at the point P is zero since $T_1$ is conducting. Voltage at Q is V volts. This can represent a 0. When voltage at P is V volts, i.e. when $T_2$ is conducting it can be taken as a 1.

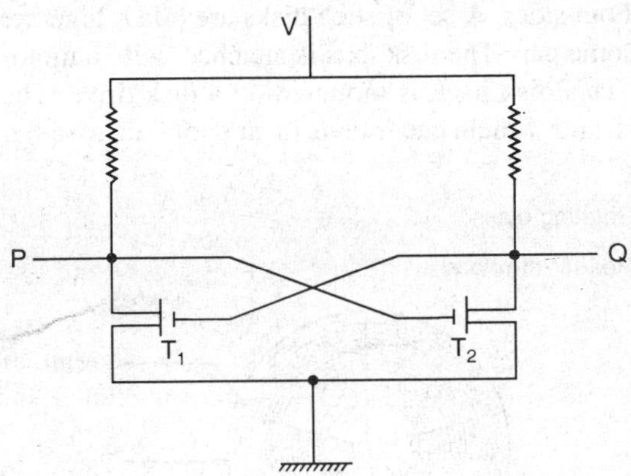


Fig. 14.8

As core memory, semiconductor memory can also be organised in 2, and 2½ dimensions. The main memory is supposed to be large and so, millions of these memory cells are integrated together. This integrated memory can store millions of bytes as data, information, instruction etc.

It is possible to read from or write into any memory location "at once", that is, without delay in identifying the particular part of the memory. The memory having such success is called **random access memory (RAM)**. The memories organised as Integrated semiconductor cells are RAMs.

**Read only memory (ROM):** ROM has a unique characteristic that the contents from it can be read out, but we cannot write anything into it. The data is permanently or semi-permanently stored inside a ROM. When there is a mass production of identical programs, ROMs are the ideal medium of storage. They can be constructed using diodes or transistors. Many ready-made programs are sold in ROMs. The ROM memory can also be accessed as fast as in RAM made with similar storage cells.

There are four types of ROMs: Manufacturers provide a type of ROM in which a user can electrically write something other than what is already stored. This memory is called programmable ROM or PROM.

Next type of ROM is called ultraviolet erasable programmable ROM or UVEPROM. In this case the contents of the ROM can be erased by the ultraviolet light, and programmed again. It is the most expensive ROM.

The last type of ROM is electrically alterable (erasable and reprogrammable) called EAPROM.

The advantages of ROM is that, the data stored in it is never lost and large volume of memory cells can be packaged.

**14.7.2. Secondary Memory: Secondary or auxiliary memory is the memory which is not directly accessed by the CPU.** Whenever the data in this storage is to be used, it will be transferred to the main memory and referred. A large volume of data can be stored using different secondary memories available. This also helps to avoid overloading of the main memory. There are different types of secondary memories. We are going to discuss some of them.

**Magnetic disk memory:** Magnetic disks, also called hard disks, provide large storage capabilities with moderate speed. These disks are smooth metal plates coated with a thin of magnetic material on both sides. A set of such disks are piled together in an axis one below the other with some gap. The disk axis is attached with a motor so that it can rotate to 360 degrees. This disk pack is mounted on a disk drive. The drive has a set of read/write heads and which can move in and out in a radial

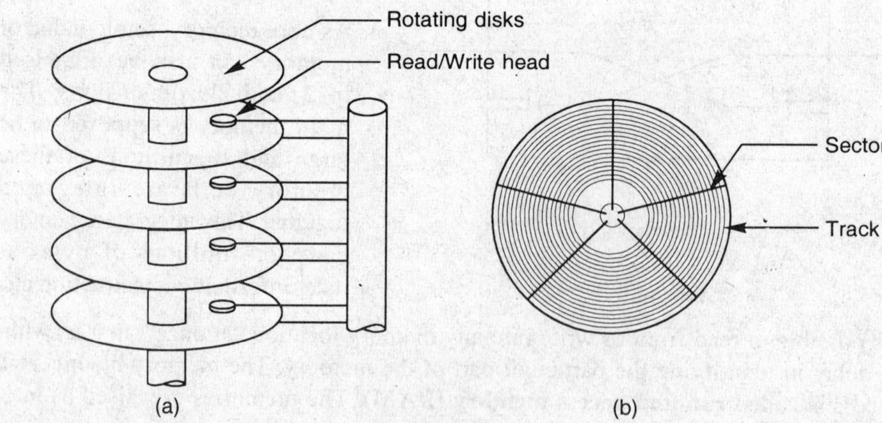


**Fig. 14.9**

direction as shown in Fig. 14.9a. The disk is divided into different tracks and sectors and sectors as shown in Fig. 14.9b.

To write the data on the disk, a current is passed through a coil wound round the head. This current magnetises the coating on the disk surface. The magnetisation can be either in the clockwise or anti-clockwise direction (depending upon the direction of the current). These two directions represent a 0 and a 1 respectively. The read operations is done the same way. When the disk rotates the magnetised spot below the head induces a current in the coil.

An improved version of this hard disk is **Winchester disk**. In this case the read/write heads are light weight. Also the heads are sealed inside the disk pack so that no foreign particles can affect the disk surface.

**Magnetic tape memory:** The magnetic tapes used here are the same as the tapers used as audio/video cassettes. They are made up of plastic material coated with a ferromagnetic material. The data is stored in the same way, by magnetising spots as magnetic disks. There are a number of lengthwise tracks on the tape.

Writing on or reading from a tape is done using **tape drive**. The drive consists of motors, a tape transport unit and read/write heads (refer Fig. 14.10). Each track will have a read/write head. The movement of a tape is similar to that of a film in a film projector. It moves from one reel to another over capstan and rollers and slides over the read/write heads at a speed of about 5 meters a second.

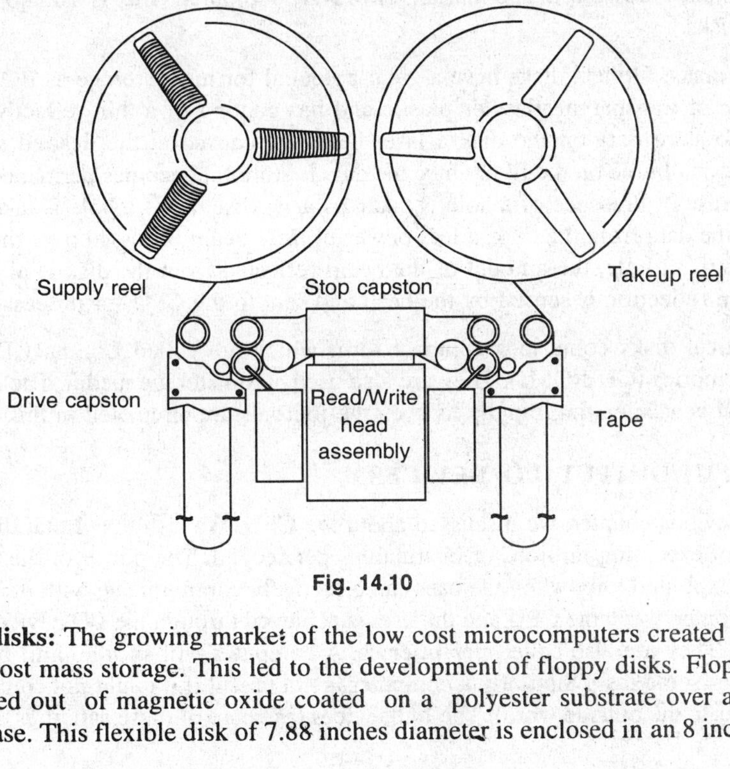


Fig. 14.10

**Floppy disks:** The growing market of the low cost microcomputers created the need for low cost mass storage. This led to the development of floppy disks. Floppy disks are created out of magnetic oxide coated on a polyester substrate over a flexible plastic base. This flexible disk of 7.88 inches diameter is enclosed in an 8 inch square jacket. This gives protection to the disk. The envelope has a long slit for read/write had access, a hole in the center for mounting the disk drive hub and a hole for index mark sensing as shown in Fig. 14.11. The floppy is inserted into the floppy disk drive, and the read/write operations are done similar to that of the hard disk.

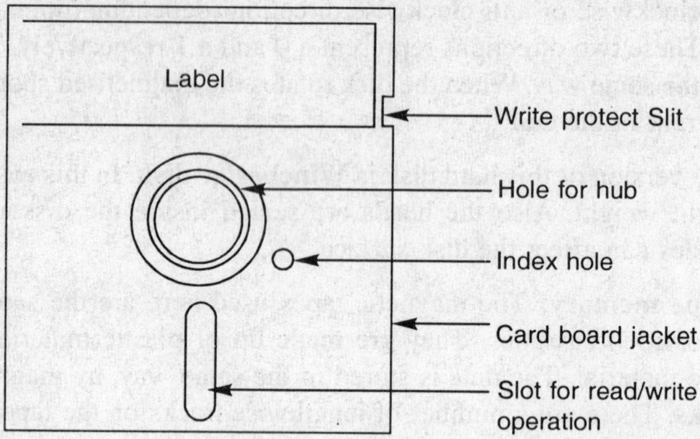


The disk surface is divided into many tracks and sectors similar to that of the magnetic disk as shown in Fig. 14.9b. The data is stored on the tracks. The sectors are used to divide the whole area of the disk. Since floppy disks are portable and cheaper, large volumes are sold in the market. However, computer virus is a major threat to floppy disks.

**Optical disks:** Optical disks have a great potential for mass storage as ROMs. They are made of transparent glass or plastic and has coating of a thin reflective film of metal. To store data on the disk a laser beam is focused at the desired spot. This creates a small hole on the film. Once the data is stored it becomes permanent and we cannot erase it. Presence of a hole is taken as a 1. Absence of a hole is taken as a 0. To read the data from the disk, a less powerful laser beam is passed over the surface. If there was a hole, the amount of the beam reflected from the disk is altered. The change in reflection is sensed by the head and sent to the CPU for processing.

Now optical disks come in a compact form which are called Compact Disk-Read Only Memories (CD-ROMs). They are also used audio storage media. The market of CD-ROM is accelerating rapidly as even the journals are circulated in this form.

## 14.8. INPUT/OUTPUT (I/O) DEVICES

In the previous chapter, we discussed about the CPU. We also noted that the CPU is capable of executing millions of instructions per second. The power of the CPU will be fully exploited only when the user can effectively communicate with it. The communication between the CPU and the user is achieved through the I/O devices and the memory. They are also called **peripherals**. A computer will sit idle until input activates it for some task. Similarly a computer is not useful if it could not communicate the results to the outside world. The I/O devices take care of these activities. There are many such devices, adapting different methods to input and output data. In this section, we are going to discuss some of them and their functions.

**1. Input**

- card reader
- keyboard
- mouse
- tough technology
- light pen
- digitizer
- scanners
  - * OCR
  - * MICR
- image scanners

**2. Output**

- video display units
- printers
- plotters
- voice generators

### 14.8.1 Input Devices

**Card readers:** In the past, from the first generation to third generation computers, punched cards were used extensively to input the data to computers. It is a rectangular thin card of size 18.8 × 8.3 cm as shown in Fig. 14.12. It is divided into 80 columns and 12 rows. Rows from bottom to top are numbered 9 to 0. Rows 11 and 12 are above row 0. A punching machine is used to punch holes on these cards. The machine is just a key typewriter with additional control keys to feed a card, release a card, duplicate a card etc. When a key is pressed on a card, it punches a set of holes along column and prints the character on top of the column.

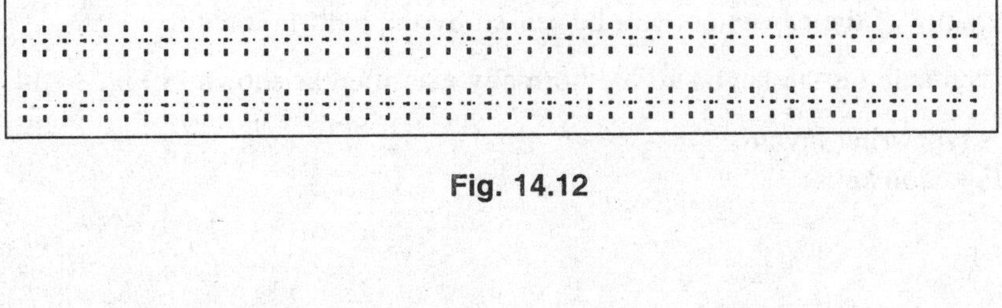

Fig. 14.12

Those punched cards are read by a card reader attached to the computer. There is a reading station on the card reader on which the cards are moved past. Photoelectric mechanism is used to sense the holes. The reading station is mounted with photo-sensors. Light is passed through the holes in the cards and is picked up by the photo-sensors. The cards are normally read columnwise. The photosensors then send the corresponding bits to a decoder which stores the values in the computer.

To avoid errors in reading, the cards are read twice by sending through two reading stations and the results are compared. If both results are same, then the values are sent to the computer. On an average 800 cards can be read in a minute. However it has become obsolete now.

**Keyboards:** Keyboards are the most widely used input devices. The principle of a keyboard is straightforward and they are fairly easy to design and implement. Key-boards use key switch technology coupled with electronic circuitry, to identify the data that is entered by pressing the key. When a key is pressed, electric signals are generated which will enable the computer to determine the particular key. This is called encoding. This encoding is done with the help of key-switch technology (refer to Fig. 14.13).

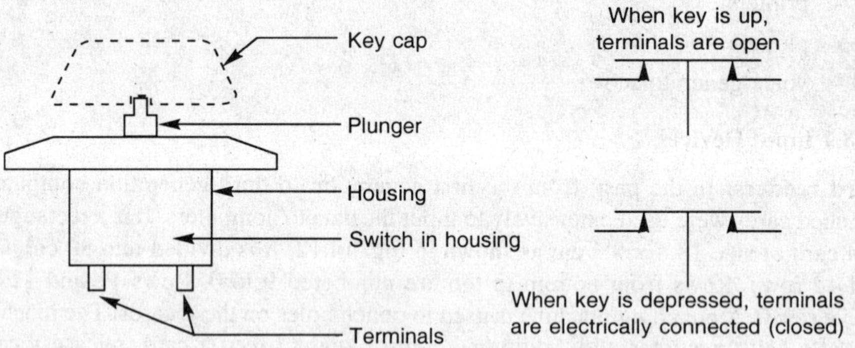


Fig. 14.13

There is a push button switch, which is mounted on a plunger. This plunger is kept over another switch, which is in housing. There are two terminals below the housing. When push button is pressed, the plunger also gets depressed and it contacts the switch in the housing. This switch in turn contacts the two terminals, which creates a signal in the circuit. When the plunger is up, the terminals are not electrically con-nected. The signals sent to the CPU and is sent to the display unit.

There is another type of keyboard called solid-state key-board. In this case a capacitor is used with all the keys, which will be charged when the key is pressed. Variations in the capacity of the capacitors will be sensed by the built-in circuitry.

Keys available on the keyboard are normally classified as shown in Fig. 14.14.

1. A typewriter layout
2. Function keys

3. Special control keys.
4. Cursor movement keys.

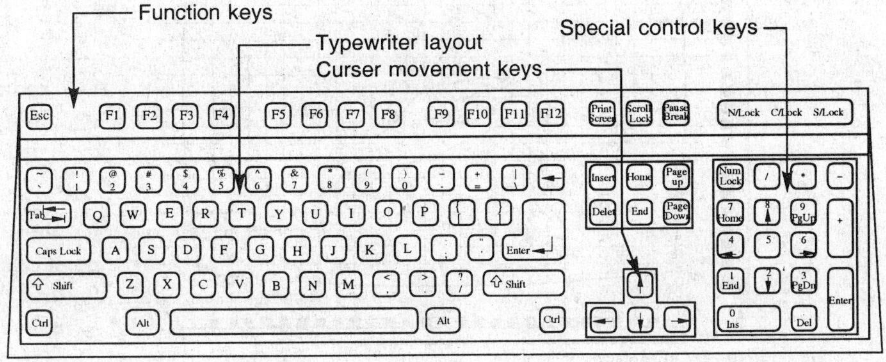


Fig. 14.14

**Mouse:** It is a pointing device used to select an object on the display screen. It can sometimes be used instead of the keyboard. The working principle of the mouse is as follows: Mouse is a small box, which has a rolling ball on the underside. As the mouse rolls up, down left and right on a flat surface, a signal is sent to the computer which will move the cursor up, down, left or right according to the motion of the mouse. When the cursor is moved to the object to be selected on the screen, a button on the upper side (refer in Fig. 14.15) of the mouse can be pressed to select that. It is one of the fastest, simplest and easier-to-learn methods of manipulating a sophisticated computer program.

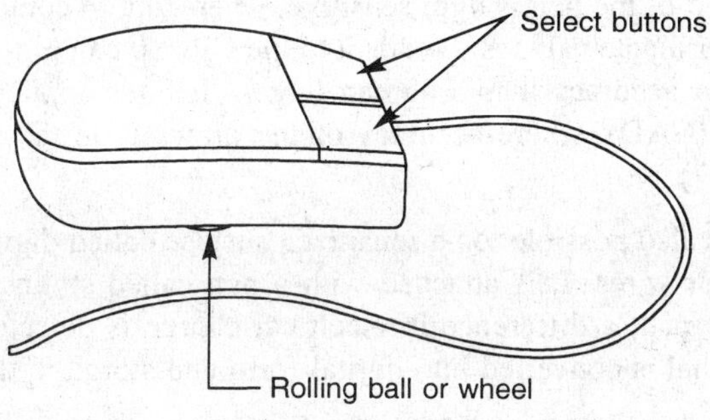


Fig. 14.15

**Tough Technology:** The most natural of all pointing devices is our finger. Pointing with finger is used in two methods: tough screens and tough pads. This technology makes the computer system easy to use. When a finger nears or touches the screen, that part of the display will be sensed by the sensor attached with the screen. For example, a touch screen might contain a menu with several selections. When a particular choice is to be activated, it can merely be touched by a finger (refer to Fig. 14.16).

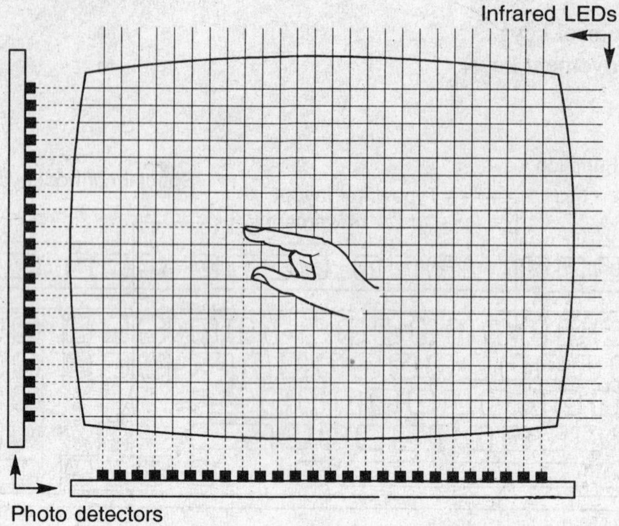


**Fig. 14.16**

This can be implemented by criss-crossing the display screen with invisible beams of infrared light. When we touch a point on the screen the finger interrupts the vertical and horizontal beams, which can be sensed by the CPU.

Another method involves overlaying the screen with a thin layer of plastic that has a sensing grid built into it. The same way touch pads, which can be kept on the table and used. For quicker information retrieval this technology is the best suitable.

**Light pens:** It also has the principle of touch sensitivity but here instead of finger, a pen is used. The tip of the pen is light sensitive, when kept in contact with the screen it receives the co-ordinate value and sends it to the CPU. It can pin-point a spot on the screen with greater accuracy than a human finger. It finds application in Computer Aided Designing (CAD), where accuracy of the drawing on the screen is essential (refer to Fig. 14.17).

**Digitizer:** CAD is also possible on a sensitized surface called digitizer. This is a pad with grid of sensor wires. It is attached with a pen called stylus. When the trip of stylus touches the pad, a difference in electrical charge is detected by the sensors. This electrical signal is converted into digital form and stored in the computer.

**Optical character recognition (OCR):** This technique enables the computer to directly read a source document. The document may be handwritten or printed. Here a scanner, which will convert the text or picture on a page into a digital form with the help of optical technology, is used. These digital values will be processed and stored in a computer OCR input devices are capable of reading 120 characters pre second.

**Magnetic ink character recognition (MICR):** This technique was originally invented for the banks. MICR is used to speed up the draft clearance. On each draft, the account number and the bank code number are written in one corner with a magnetic ink containing iron oxide. When the cheque is issued to a person, the amount of the draft is written in the same way on the other corner of the draft as shown in Fig. 14.18.

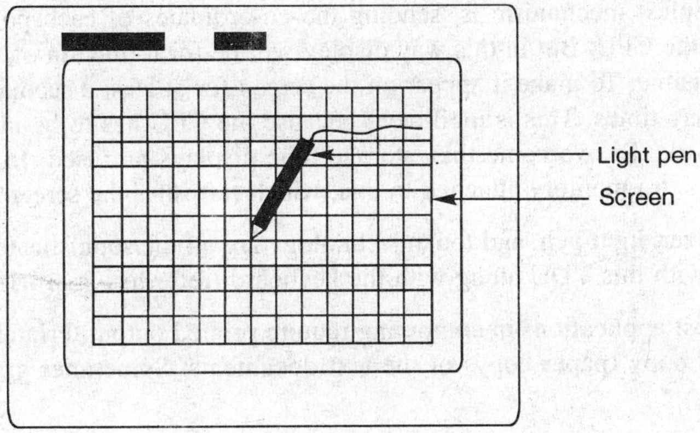


Fig. 14.17

When another person who received the draft taker it for clearance, it is fed to a reader. This reader has magnetic field which magnetics the ink. Because of this the account number, bank code and the amount are read by the computer. MICR speeds up the clearing operation and even if the cheque was damaged, the reader can read the data.

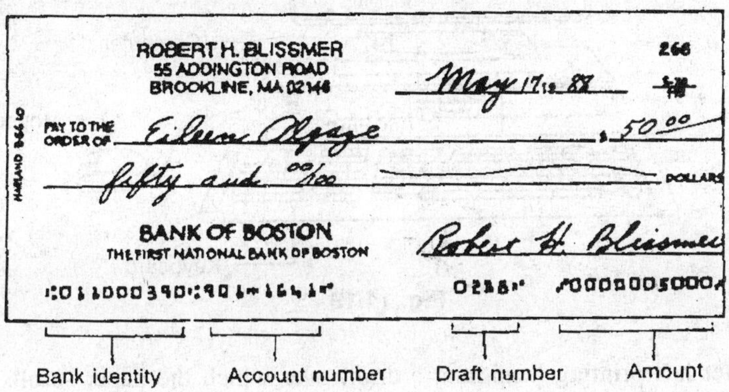


Fig. 14.18

**Image scanners:** Image scanners convert real images rather than one on a paper or document, which are optically focused, into digital images. Here a photoreceptor is used for this purpose. These digital images are then processed by the computer. The images stored in the computer can later be retouched, resized or cropped. This technique is used for computer aided publications.

### 14.8.2 Output Devices

**Video display unit:** VDU is nothing but the Cathode Ray Oscilloscope (CRO) which is used in television. It is the most widely used output device. It is a fast and inexpensive device, but only drawback is that it does not deliver a hard copy.

Here the simplest mechanism is, sending the co-ordinates of each point to be displayed from the CPU. But in this way display will be for a fraction of a time, which will not be visible. To make it appear on the screen for at least a second, it has to be refreshed many times. This is inefficient because the CPU has to be involved in the refreshing work. To overcome this, storage tube displays are used. In this case the VDU has an extra memory attached to this, which refreshes the screen.

Mouse, digitizer, light pen, and touch technology are all the sophisticated input techniques used with this VDU along with the keyboard (refer to Fig. 14.19).

**Printers:** Most applications in computing require printed output. Printers are used to take the hard copy (paper copy) of the text documents. Sometimes graphs are also taken.

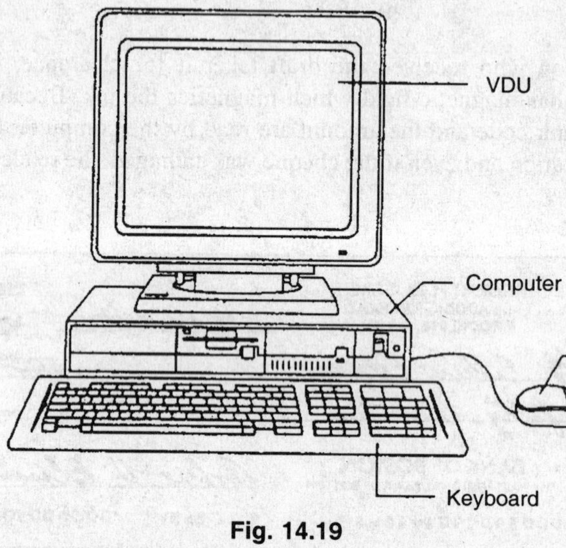


**Fig. 14.19**

Each printer has printing head, and a drum over which the paper scrolls when the characters are printed.

There are two types of printers:

1. Character printer
   - dot matrix printer
   - daisy wheel printer
2. Line printer.

**Dot matrix printer:** Here the printing head will have a set of pins arranged as a matrix (normally 7 × 5). The character is formed by selecting appropriate set of pins from this matrix. For example characters A & O can be formed as shown in

Fig. 14.20 and the paper will be kept on a rolling drum on which the head will make Impressions. Between the paper and the head, there will be an inked ribbon, when the character to be printed is sent from the computer, the printer will select the appropriate pins for that character and the head will strike the ribbon, which in turn will touch the paper and make the impression. This is shown in Fig. 14.21b.

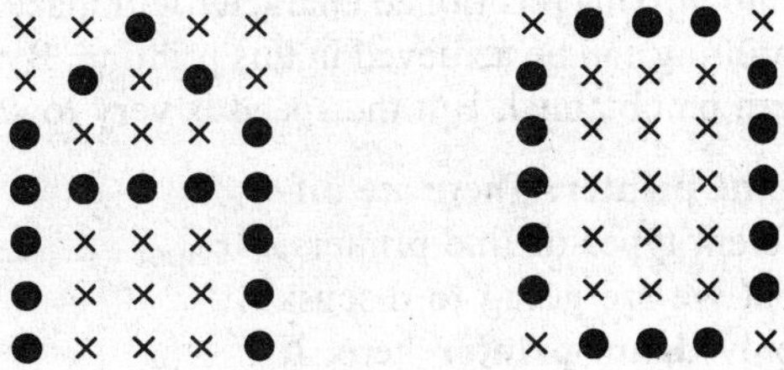

Fig. 14.20

This is to print a single character. Let us see how the whole line will be printed,. The printer will have a temporary storage attached with it, called buffer. The CPU will send the line to be printed to this buffer from this buffer the whole line will be sent to the printer head, character by character. After printing one character the head will move one position to the right on the paper and the next character will be printed from here. In this way the head will print up to 80 characters. After printing the 80th one, the printer carriage advances the paper up by one line, so that next line could be printed. Meanwhile the next line to be printed would have been sent to the buffer by the CPU. Now the head is at the 80th position, and the printer head will start printing from the last character to the first. This is called bi-directional printing. There are 132 character printers also (refer to Fig. 14.21a).

Varying sizes and styles of the letter can be achieved with the help of different facilities built inside a printer.

Fig. 14.21

**Daisy wheel printer:** In this case the print head is a plastic disk on whole edge all the characters are embossed as shown in Fig. 14.22. This disk is called a daisy wheel. This moves from left to right. The characters to be printed will be sent to the buffer as discussed earlier. When these characters are sent to the print head one-by-one, the wheel is rotated, so that the character to be printed is positioned right against the ribbon. This positioned character will make an impression on the paper. High quality printing can be achieved in this printing. By changing the daisy wheel, different fonts can be obtained. But the speed is very low.

**Line printer:** There are different types of line printers, but we are going to discuss only **drum printer** here. It consists of a cylindrical drum whose length equals the length of a printed line. Normally, there are 132 characters in a print line. The drum has 132 parallel tracks along its circumference (refer to Fig. 14.23). Each track has all the characters (normally 64) embossed on it. A set of 132 print hammers one per track are positioned so that the printer ribbon and the paper are sandwiched between the drum and hammers. The line to be printed is sent from the buffer. All the 132 tracks will be activated so that the correct character comes to the corresponding track hammer. When all the characters are aligned, the drum is activated and the hammers strike the paper through the ribbon and the characters get printed. The problem with this is synchronisation of the hammers. It might look wavy if not synchronised.

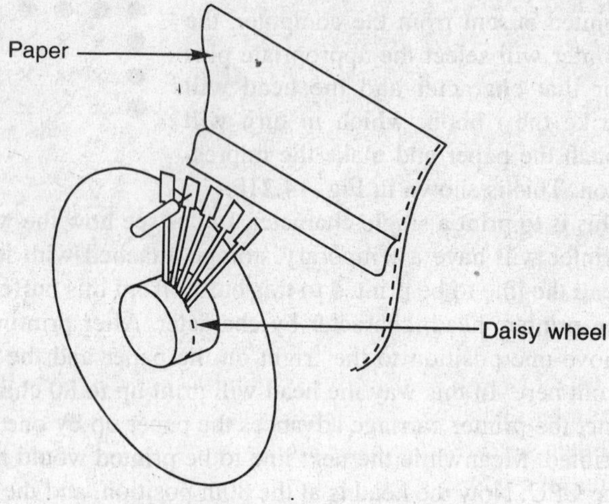


Fig. 14.22

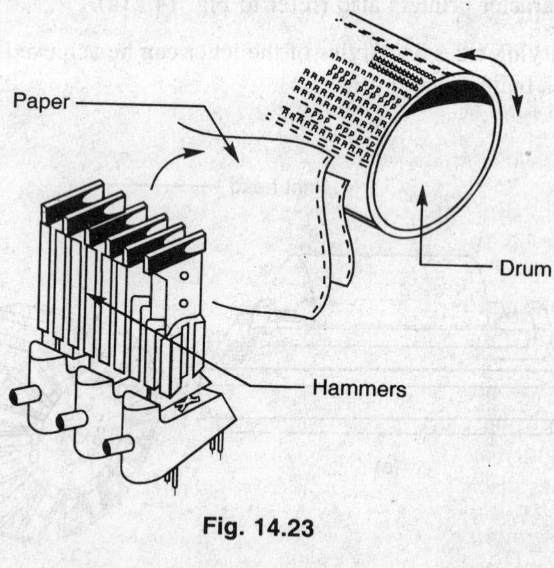


Fig. 14.23

**Plotters:** Printers are best suited for printing texts. In order to take the hard copy of graphs, plotters are used. The plotters are in different sizes. A plotter has a flat board on which paper is kept for drawing. There is an arm connected to a stepper motor, which moves across the flat surface. Multicolour pens are kept in a row, on one side of the board. According to the program written in the computer, the stepper motor gets activated and the arm moves across. It picks up the required color pen and draws the graph on the paper. Plotters are used for Computer Aided Drawings for machine design, civil engineering etc.

**Voice generator:** We can find computer voices being used in television serials. This is achieved with voice generators. Initially the computer is trained for a particular voice and vocabulary. Then the input voice signals are converted to digital form and stored in a computer. Whenever necessary, appropriate sentences are formed and given as output.

## 14.9. SOFTWARE

So far we discussed about different parts of a computer. We also know that these components, CPU, ALU, memory, input/output devices, all put together is called **hardware**. So hardware is nothing but electronic and mechanical parts of the computer. A computer merely with this hardware alone cannot function unless, it is instructed to do something.

The set of instructions or programmes which instruct the computer to do different operations is called **software**. It is a collection of programmes which instruct the computer what to do and when. On the whole software controls the operations of a computer system.

Nowadays computers are built in such a way that they are similar in functioning: Software written for one may also run on the other. Software industries are taking care of providing important programmes, which can run on wide range of machines or they provide different versions of the same software with slight modifications, so that it runs on other types of computers.

The illegal copying of software is also done; which is known as **piracy**.

**14.9.1. Binary System:** In early days, computer designers tried to use different voltage levels to represent different numbers. For example, 1 volt for the number 1, 2 volts for 2, 3 volts for 3, and so on up to 9. This did not work well because in a complicated electronic circuit, the voltage levels tend to deviate, and so what starts out as a 6 may end up looking like 5 or 7.

So, it was necessary to think of an efficient way of representing the numbers. Later it was felt that only a "low" and a "high" voltage levels could be used to reduce the ambiguity and thus the Binary system was developed. Since this electronic device handles discrete digital numbers it is called a digital computer.

We all might have learnt this binary arithmetic in our school level. Just to brush up the memory, let us briefly discuss about that. In binary arithmetic, 0 and 1 are the only digits. These 0 and 1 can easily be represented by a "low" and "high" voltage respectively in a computer. The binary numbers for the 9 decimal digits are shown in the following table.

| Decimal | Binary |
|---|---|
| 0 | 0 |
| 1 | 01 |
| 2 | 10 |
| 3 | 11 |
| 4 | 100 |
| 5 | 101 |
| 6 | 110 |
| 7 | 111 |
| 8 | 1000 |
| 9 | 1001 |

**ASCII Code:** The most important thing about the binary system is not the details; it is the mere fact that any number can be represented by using just 0s and 1s. Not only numbers but also symbols, punctuation marks and alphabetic characters can be represented. Since the technique of representation is known, individual programmers may start coding numbers and characters in their own way. This will lead to ambiguity in programming. Unless these codes are standardised, programming languages cannot be standardised. So a standard set of codes for the numbers, symbols, punctuation marks and the alphabets were generated by American Standards Institute in binary form, which is called ASCII, American Standard Code for Information Interchange. The following table gives the ASCII values for the alphabets.

| Letter | ASCII | | Letter | ASCII | |
|---|---|---|---|---|---|
| A | 0100 | 0001 | N | 0100 | 1110 |
| B | 0100 | 0010 | O | 0100 | 1111 |
| C | 0100 | 0011 | P | 0101 | 0000 |
| D | 0100 | 0100 | Q | 0101 | 0001 |
| E | 0100 | 0101 | R | 0101 | 0010 |
| F | 0100 | 0110 | S | 0101 | 0011 |
| G | 0100 | 0111 | T | 0101 | 0100 |
| H | 0100 | 1000 | U | 0101 | 0101 |
| I | 0100 | 1001 | V | 0101 | 0110 |
| J | 0100 | 1010 | W | 0101 | 0111 |
| K | 0100 | 1011 | X | 0101 | 1000 |
| L | 0100 | 1100 | Y | 0101 | 1001 |
| M | 0100 | 1101 | Z | 0101 | 1010 |

These codes are written in 8 digits, because computers are organised to work with sequences of 1s and 0s of a definite length, called **word length**. Typical word lengths are 8,16,32. In most computers the length is 8. A single binary digit, 0 or1 is called a **bit**; a sequence of 8 bits is called a **byte**. There are 256 possible combinations or bytes from 00000000 to 11111111.

We already discussed about instructing a computer to do a particular function with the help of a software. As the computers are designed to understand the signals 1s and 0s only, the software also should be written with the help of these binary numbers. In the next chapter the main aspects of software are discussed.

**14.9.2. Classification of Software:** As we have already seen, merely the computer hardware components put together cannot do a particular function unless it is instructed to do so, by a software. In this chapter we discuss about the classification of software and the revolution in software technology.

Software is broadly classified as shown in Fig. 14.24.

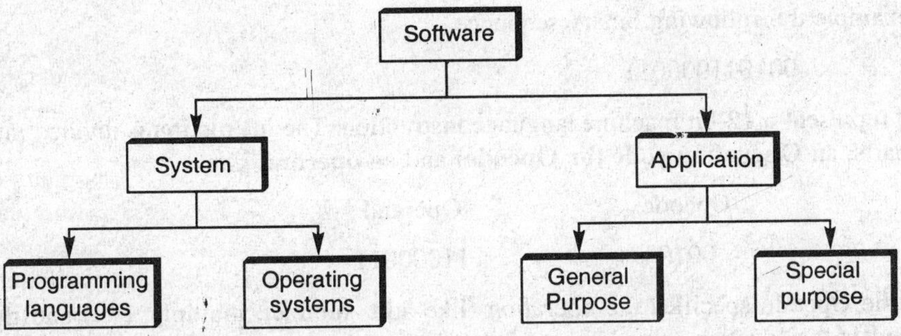


**Fig. 14.24**

1. System software
   - operating system
   - programming languages
2. Application software
   - general purpose
   - special purpose

## SYSTEM SOFTWARE

**Operating system (OS):** OS is the set of programmes or modules that **manages** the overall operations of a computer. The major functions of OS are:

1. It acts as mediator between the user and the computer system i.e. hardware components.
2. It allocates users the required resources (memory, CPU time, input/output devices and system software).
3. It assigns priorities to different jobs.

Operating systems have improved tremendously. Earlier they used to be command driven, but now Microsoft has revolutionised the OS market by introducing graphical user interface based Windows operating system.

Examples : MS-DOS, Windows 95, Windows NT, Unix, Linux, MacOS, OS/2, MVS, OS/400, Novell Netware, etc.

**Programming languages:** Initially the computers were instructed directly with the help of binary codes. But now constant efforts by the programers have led to a massive development in software. Let us see what are the different programing languages that were adapted from the time computers were introduced.

**Hierarchy of languages**

**1. Machine Language:** On the bottom rung is the machine language. Every computer has its own machine language, which is the only language understood by the computer. As we already know, a computer can understand only 0s and 1s. Writing the programs with the help of this binary logic, so that the computer is instructed directly, is nothing but machine language programing.

For example the following binary sequence

001011000011

could represent a 12-bit machine language instruction. The instruction is divided into two parts, an **Operation code (or Opcode)** and an **operand like**

| Opcode | Operand |
|---|---|
| 0010 | 11000011 |

Here the Opcode specifies the operation (like add, subtract, multiply, etc.) and the operand is the location (or address) of the data in the computer memory, which is operated upon.

Originally the computers were only instructed in this way. The problems with this machine language are:

1. A programer not only has to remember all the operation codes, but also the addresses or memory locations of all the data he uses.
2. Programing is highly complicated and error prone.
3. Program is machine-dependent, i.e. since different machines use different machine languages, programs written for one machine may not be used on another machine.

Because of all these drawbacks, a vast development in software technology took place in 1950s.

**2. Assembly Language:** In this case the operation codes represented as 1s and 0s in machine language are replaced by alphabetic codes for the benefit of programers. These alphabetic codes are called **mnemonics**. These memory aiding words may not be exact English words, but one can easily make out.

For example, in 8086/88 family assembly language,

"Add" is for Addition

"Sub" is for Subtraction

"Mul" is for Multiplication.

Obviously these mnemonics are far easier to use than opcodes. Along with mnemonics, symbolic addresses in place of actual storage addresses can be used in the operand part. Data items can be assigned with comfortable names and used in the instruction. For example,

ADD PAY, TOTAL

Is an instruction, meaning, add the basic pay to the total salary. Here PAY and TOTAL refer to the memory locations, where basic pay and the total salary respectively, are stored. It is also called symbolic programing.

All right, we have already stressed that a computer can understand the instructions written in 1s and 0s only, but how can it understand these mnemonics and symbolic addresses?. Obviously there must be a way of converting these assembly language instructions into machine language instructions. This is achieved by another program called **ASSEMBLER**.

The assembly language and the machine language have a one-to-one correspondence, i.e. each assembly language instruction gets translated into an equivalent machine language instruction with the help of this assembler program.

Though writing programs may be slightly easier, in this case also, all the rules concerning the instructions, input, output, machine level etc. have to be scrupulously observed. It is also machine-dependent. For these reasons, both machine language and assembly language are called **low-level languages.**

### 3. High-level Languages

Initially when the computers were introduced, one has to write programs only in the low-level language. As it was very difficult to write complicated programs, many programers started working in this software field. As a result, in 1950's there was a major breakthrough in computer programing with the instruction of **high-level Language**.

It is also a symbolic language as assembly language, but it has many advantages. The instructions developed are almost "English-like", and use conventional mathematical notations to make programing easier and quicker. The important factor is, it is machine-independent and hence the programer need not worry about learning the hardware aspects deeply. Just as the assembly language being converted into machine language by an assembler, these high-level language instructions are also converted into machine language by another sophisticated program called **COMPILER**.

Software technology has developed so vastly that, one can see a large number of such compilers in the market. Depending upon the applications these high-level languages are developed. For example,

FORTRAN (FORmula TRANslation) is a high-level language for scientific applications.

BASIC (Beginners All purpose Symbolic Instruction Code) for training the beginners in programing.

COBOL (Common Business Oriented Language) for business applications.

Object oriented programing concepts have evolved and quite a few powerful languages have been introduced worldwide. C and Pascal were considered sophisticated in the early 80s, but now, C++, VC++, VB, etc. are much more sophisticated and powerful for developing object oriented, graphical user interface based applications. The languages were machine dependent, meaning, for different operating systems, different compilers have to be written. For example, a C++ written for Windows 95 will not run on Unix. But, now, Java, a new language is introduced in such a way that, programs can be written on any OS and run on a different OS. The famous phrase about Java is "write once and run anywhere".

We should never forget that each language has its own compiler. Along with operating systems, assemblers and compilers are also called **system software**.

## APPLICATION SOFTWARE

The programs which are already written in any one of the above languages and tested for a particular application are called **packaged application software**. These are meant to solve specific problems. Even in India, most of the software industries are involved in developing such application software packages and exporting them. There are two categories.

**1. General purpose programs:** These are ready-made packages which are adaptable to a wide variety of applications. For example, WordStar is a famous package used for office automation. AutoCAD is an excellent package for drawing; Lotus 1-2-3 is for accounting; and there are many such packages available in the market. With the help of these, one can develop special purpose application programs.

**2. Special purpose programs:** As already mentioned, these are developed for specific applications. These are dedicated to perform certain tasks such as payroll, accounting education, computer games, library, statistical analysis etc. They contain built-in problem solving features specially designed for tasks.

**12.9.3. Programing: Programing is nothing but a way of instructing the computer to do a particular task or solve a problem with the help of a set of instructions.** This set of instructions (for example, for a problem to find the biggest number in a given array) is called a program. A program can be developed in any one of the languages or packages available.

We all know the power of computers in this information era: present-day massive military build-up, space exploration, weather forecasting, mass media communication, and various other fields have undergone a spectacular change-over with the advent of computers. One can never deny that, it is all because of man's creativity in programing.

Programs are developed for different purposes, in different ways and in different languages. As the applications grow wider, the complications in developing programs become deeper and deeper. Unless proper planning is done it many be difficult to reduce the complications in programing. For example, before constructing a building, one should know, what it is being constructed for. How should it be constructed i.e. plan of the building? What are the requirements etc.? Similarly, before developing a program, a programer must know the application of the program, procedure to develop the program, resources (like memory, I/O devices software etc.). Only then he can be efficient.

First step is to write the procedure to solve the particular problem. The procedure written step-by-step in English before writing it in any one of the computer languages is called **algorithm**. For big problems the algorithms may be complicated and ambiguous. In such situations, it would be effective to write the algorithm as a **flow chart.**

**Flow charts:** Flow charts are the pictorial representation of an algorithm. These are drawn with the help of standard symbols accepted worldwide. The standard symbols used to prepare flow charts are given in Fig. 14.25:

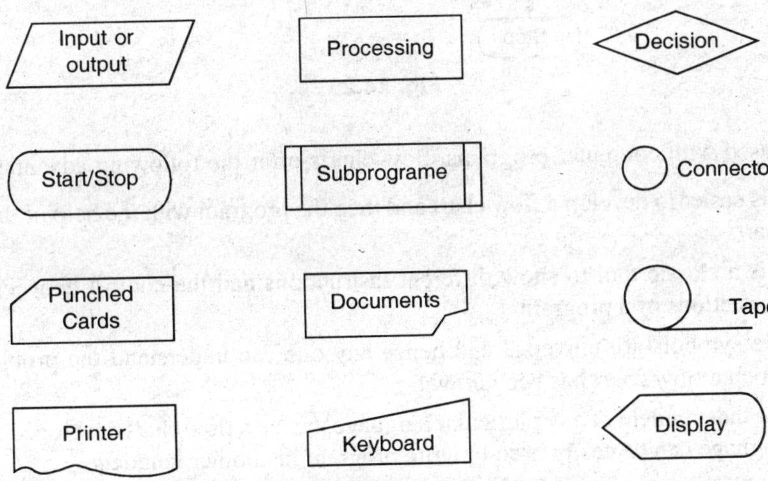


**Fig. 14.25**

Let us consider an example. For easy grasping, let us take a BASIC program. The following program is to print the number and its square value, for all the numbers starting 1 to 100.

```
10    LET N = 1
20    PRINT N, N × N
30    IF N = 100 THEN STOP
40    LET N = N + 1
50    GOTO 20
60    END
```

Even though it is a simple program for those who already know BASIC programing, it may be difficult for the beginners, and those who do not know the language. In that case it is better to have a flow chart drawn for the problem. It may help the beginner to code the program, or it may help another programer who wants to solve the same problem in some other language. The flow chart is as shown is Fig. 14.26.

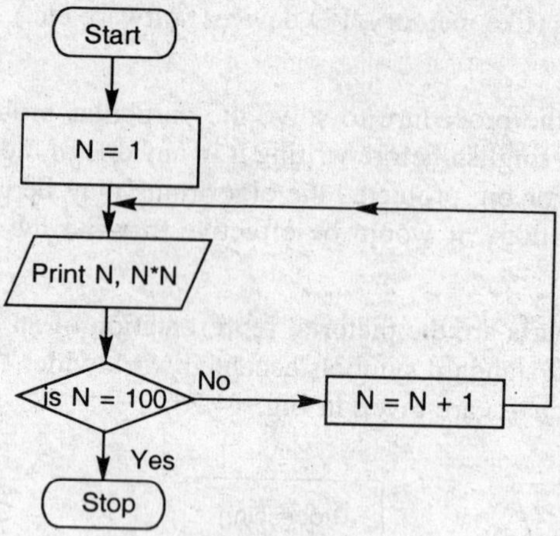


**Fig. 14.26**

When used with computer programs, flow charts offer the following advantages:

1. It is easier to develop a flow chart and then the program with the help of that flow chart.
2. It is a classic tool to show different instructions and the control between these instructions of a program.
3. The symbols are universal and hence any one can understand the problem for which a flow chart has been drawn.
4. It is independent of any particular language, hence a flow chart developed for one language can be easily used to write program in another language.

## 14.10. INTRODUCTION TO MICROPROCESSOR

A microprocessor is a single integrated chip, in which all the important components of a computer viz. ALU, control unit, and other circuits are fabricated together. The microprocessor age began in 1970s, when IC technology (refer Chapter 11) had advanced enough to make a single chip CPU. Because of the low cost and higher speed qualities of a microprocessor it is used as a controller for almost all the design equipment. Microprocessor chips are very good examples for VLSI chips. No wonder, the computer technology is vastly improved because of the development of microprocessors.

There are varieties of microprocessor chips with different capabilities. The main factor here is, the number of bits they can handle. For example, microprocessors are made to handle 8 bit, 16 bit or 32 bit operations. An 8 bit chip can handle addition of two 8 bit numbers only. To make this chip perform 16 bit operations then special registers are needed. We are going to discuss 8088 microprocessor, which normally handles 8 bit operations, in this section.

**12.10.1 Architecture of 8088 Microprocessor:** This microprocessor is nothing but a single chip used as CPU in personal computers. The block diagram of 8088 is given in Fig. 14.27. It is actually 8 bit microprocessor capable of handling 16 bit operations with the help of some special registers and circuits. Since we have already discussed about the functions of CPU in detail let us discuss the functions of these special registers alone.

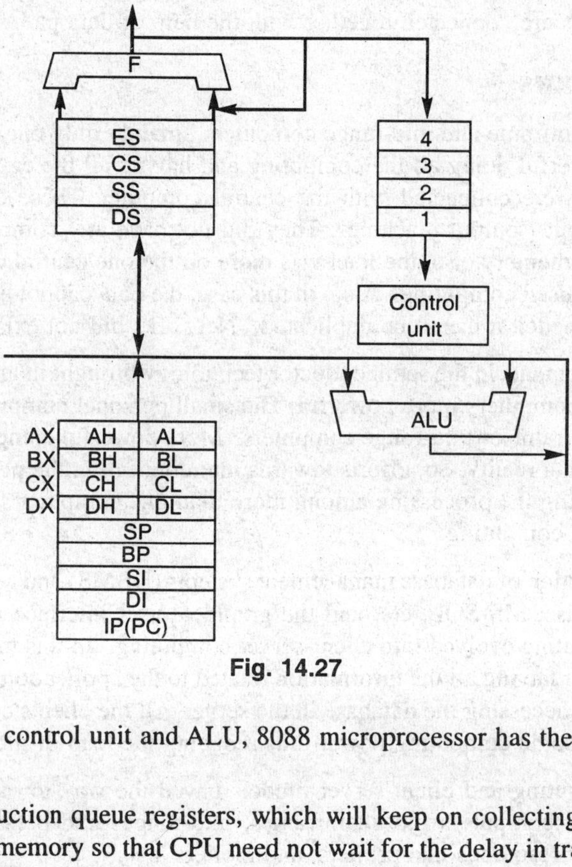


**Fig. 14.27**

Apart from the control unit and ALU, 8088 microprocessor has the following registers.

1. Four instruction queue registers, which will keep on collecting the instructions from the memory so that CPU need not wait for the delay in transfer of instructions from the memory.
2. Fours pairs of general purpose registers viz. **AH & AL, BH & BL, CH** and **CL**, and **DH & DL**. They are used by the ALU while executing the Instructions. These registers independently can hold 8 bits of data, at the same time, together as a pair can hold 16 bits of data.
3. Processor Status Word (PSW), is used to identify the status of different registers and signals.
4. Segment registers viz. **ES, CS, SS**, and **DS** are used to find the address locations, when a big program is stored in different memory locations.

5. Pointer registers **SP, BP SI, DI** and **IP**. Among these **Stack pointer (SP)** is an important register. A stack is special group of storage locations in the memory. It is organised like the trays arranged one above the other, in such a way that, the data stored last is drawn first. So it is called **Last In First Out (LIFO)** memory. SI and DI are used by the control unit to find address of an array element. SP is the register always holding the address of the top of the stack. BP, base pointer is used to access the stack. **Instruction pointer (IP)** is same is the **program counter (PC)** discussed in the functions of CPU.

All these registers are connected together with the help of data pathways or buses.

## 14.11. NETWORKS

In the case of mainframe and mid range computers, mainly only one central computer was very powerful doing all the computing and having all the data. One or more dumb terminals were connected with the central computer. These dumb terminals acted only as input / output machines. They did not have any computing power in terms of CPU or memory. So, the load was more on the one central computer and it was called centralised computing. Also, in this case, the data cannot be used by other applications, if needed it has to be duplicated. Networks did not exist.

Later, the developments in the semiconductor technology brought in amazing changes and made small computers more powerful. The small personal computers became as powerful as mainframe or mid-range computers. More powerful computers at affordable costs became a reality. So, efforts towards interconnecting the personal computers and distributing the processing among more than one computer succeeded. It is called distributed computing.

After the introduction of database management systems (DBMS) and relational DBMS like Oracle, Sybase, MS-SQL, etc. and the graphical user interface technology, the distributed computing evolved into client-server computing. In this model, a computer acts as a server having all the information related to the application in the database and many clients accessing the database in the server. All the clients connected to the server also have some computing power thus reducing the load of the central server.

Distributed computing and client-server models paved the way towards networking different types of computers like mainframes, mid-ranges and personal computers and sharing other resources like printers, and plotters also.

A Network is defined as a set of communication links between different devices like computers, telephones, printers, plotters and data-communication devices. Some of the data-communication devices are switches, hubs, routers, bridges and gateways. An excellent example for a network is the World Wide Web—the Internet. Today, the whole world is witnessing the power of Internet, connecting to any computer from anywhere at anytime and accessing the information in it. Internet is a reality, mainly because of the evolution of the networking technology.

Depending upon the geographical areas covered by a network, there are three types of networks:

1. Local Area Network (LAN) which connects the computer system within a building

or within 10 kilometers. Air/rail/bus ticket reservation system is a good example for a LAN.

2. Metropolitan Area Network (MAN) which connects the people across the city.
3. Wide Area Network (WAN) which connects the people across the country.

**14.11.1 Local Area Networks:** LANs are local area networks. LAN can cover only a 5-mile geographical area. It may consist of a few computers in a small office, or several hundred units spread across different floors in a multi-story building. LANs are the most common networks. They are the building blocks of the other networks.

LAN is a network connecting computers and associated devices, which are used to interchange information within a limited geographical area. Along with mini- or microcomputers, LANs are commonly linked with:

Keyboards, PC terminals and VDUs
Printers and plotters
Mass storage devices (magnetic disks and tapes)
Various computer-controlled machines.
Facsimile (FAX), telex machines.

For that matter, any office equipment which has some form of computer connections can be connected in LAN. The ultimate aim of this is resource sharing.

Figure 14.28 shows as simple LAN connection.

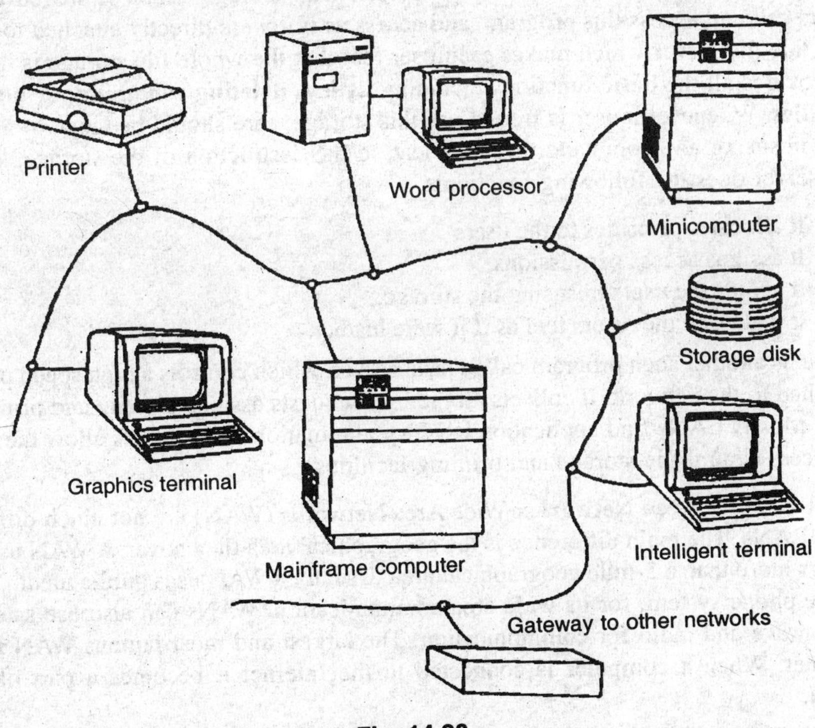


Fig. 14.28

The components of a LAN are

1. Hosts
2. Switches
3. Routers
4. Bridges
5. Gateways and
6. Communication paths or buses.

**Hosts** are the computing devices in which a database (collection of different computer files) is stored which will be addressed by different people connected on the network. Hosts can be either mainframe computers, minicomputers or microcomputers.

A **node** is the point or device from where the hosts are accessed. A PC or PC-XT or PC-AT can act as a node.

Hosts, nodes and other devices are connected together with either twisted pair cables or coaxial cables or optical fibers. This connection is called a **bus.**

**File server:** Even though all the machines are connected together, it is the software which makes a LAN work. Since, everyone on the network can access all the devices attached, there should be an efficient program which can monitor the whole network. These software include, file server, print server, electronic messaging, distributed processing facilities, teleconferencing, electronic mailing, Internet browsing, etc.

File server is a computer with a program residing inside it on the network. The main function is to control the users to access the main storage which is shared by all. Users call and access this program, and access as if it were directly attached to them. It is this file server which makes each user feel that the whole file storage is his/her. It provides all the basic functions including **listing, deleting renaming, or altering the files**. Whenever a user is free to use this storage, care should be taken to avoid a user misusing any command that may lead to the destruction of the storage. So the file server does the following functions:

1. It allocates priorities to the users
2. It assigns access permissions.
3. It avoids the users misusing the storage.
4. It makes all the users feel as if it were his/her.

There is another such program called print server, which controls a high speed printer attached to the network. It collects all the user requests assigns priority and prints the data. Mostly LANs find application in office automation. Here LANs allow the users to access central file storage and printing facilities.

**14.11.2. Wide Area Networks:** Wide Area Networks (WAN) are not much different from LANs. The main difference is the geographical area they cover. A WAN usually covers more than a 5-mile geographical area. Usually a WAN uses public media, such as the phone system, for its wide area communication. WANs can also use satellite, microwave and radio for communication. The largest and most famous WAN is the Internet. When a computer is connected to the Internet it becomes a part of that WAN.

**14.11.3. Internet:** Internet or the World Wide Web (WWW) or the Web is the greatest achievement in the 20th century. Anyone can access any computer anywhere in the world through Internet. Functionality of the Internet is based on a client-sever model. It is made possible with Internet server holding the data/information, and clients worldwide accessing the information on the server using a browser. There are different types of Internet servers available like Microsoft Internet Information Server, Java Web Server, Netscape Suitspot, etc., which help to configure a computer as Internet server. Internet Explorer and Netscape Communicator are some of the client programs (called browsers) that help to access the information on the Internet Server. There are billions of Internet servers available throughout the world connected with the help of standard communication protocols.

Internet technology has also been deployed for organizational purposes through Intranets and Extranets. Intranet is the Internet within an organization. Actually the organization can provide the common information on an Intranet server that can be accessed by all the employees inside the organization. An Intranet can make paperless office a reality. For example, policies, leave applications, employee details, and other information that can be shared by all the employees can be made available in an Intranet server, which can be browsed by all the employees. The information will be protected from being accessed by outsiders through security software.

Similarly, an Extranet is an Internet established between select customers of an organization. Only those who have the permission to access can view the information in the Extranet server of an organization. Extranets are useful to share marketing information with valuable customers, or purchase information with selected vendors, or any communication with only a select group.

E-commerce is an important milestone in the Internet evolution. Conducting business through Internet is called E-commerce or E-business. With the advent of Internet, the whole world has become boundaryless, anybody can buy anything from anywhere. Today, someone from India can order a book from America through Internet by providing just the credit card number.

Computers have revolutionized the entire human society. The impacts of computers are much more than what is discussed in this book. But, one can be rest assured that computers have made wonders so far and will continue to make wonders in the coming years too!!

Chapter 15

# COMMUNICATION SERVICES

## 15.1. INTRODUCTION

The communication services are developed to send information from a source to one or more destinations. Distribution of data, message or information from one location to another is the roll of communication systems. The general functional block diagram is shown in Fig. 15.1.

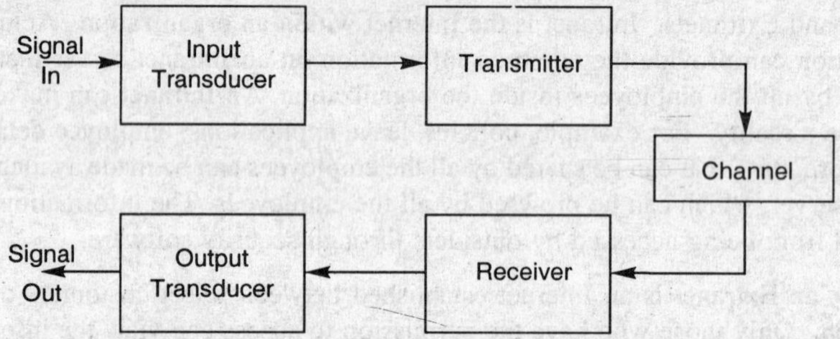


**Fig. 15.1** General functional block diagram

In the communication system the sending end input signal may be of the form of voice, a picture or text of any shape. This signal is fed into the transducer. Transducer is a device, which is used to convert the signal into a suitable form for the transmission systems. The signal from the transducer is fed into the transmitter. The transmitter converts the signal into a form, which is further suitable for transmission medium. This process is called 'modulation'. The modulated signal is fed into the channel, which is a physical medium that is used to send the signal from transmitter to receiver. After reaching the receiving end, the signal is recovered as a message signal through a device called receiver. This process of recovering the signal is called 'demodulation'. The demodulated signal is fed into the output transducer that converts the signal according to the requirements of the user.

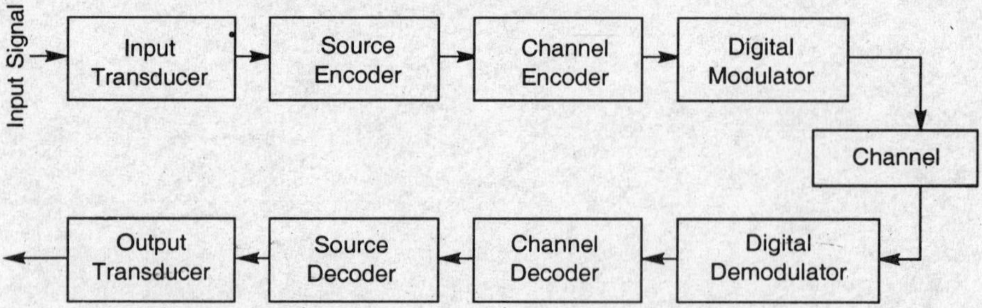


**Fig. 15.2** General block diagram of a digital communication system

The general block diagram of a 'Digital' communication is shown in Fig. 15.2. The input signal may be of analog or digital is fed into the input transducer that converts the signal, which is suitable to the source encoder. The source encoder then converts the incoming signals into a sequence of binary digit. This process is called source encoding. The sequence of binary digit is passed to the channel encoder which will pass the signal in a controlled manner to the digital modulator. Main purpose of digital modulator is to map the binary information sequence into a signal wave forms. This signal is transmitted to the channel (which is a medium to send the signal from transmitter to the receiver).

At the receiver end the signal is demodulated to recover the data. The demodulated information is fed into decoder, which will reconstruct the original information sequence as per the input data. The decoded output data will be made available to the user through the output transducer.

## 15.2. ANALOG AND DIGITAL SIGNALS

Signaling is the way the information is transmitted across the medium. The information for the communication system can be of Analog or Digital form. The characteristics of an analog signal are that it changes continuously. The characteristics of a digital signal consists of discrete states like 'on or off', 'logic 1 or logic 0', 'yes or no', 'open or close' and so on.

**15.2.1 Analog Signaling:** An analog signal consists of an electromagnetic waves which is changing continuously from maximum value to minimum and minimum to maximum and so on. Three characteristics are used to describe the analog signals, which are amplitude, frequency and phase. The three characteristics are shown in Fig. 15.3.

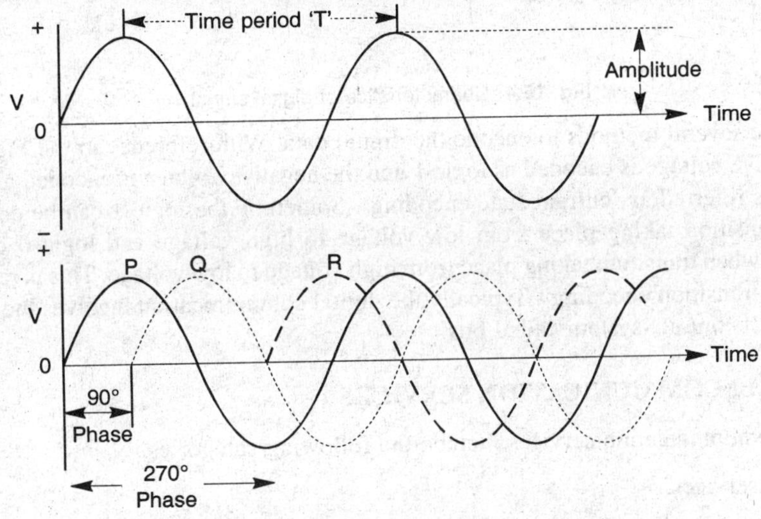


**Fig. 15.3** Three characteristics of an analog signal

The amplitude measures the capacity of the analog signal or the height of the wave, which is expressed in volts, current, watts and so on.

The frequency is in the amount of time it takes for a wave to complete one cycle and is measured in cycles per second or hertz.

The phase sequence is the relative state of one wave when compared to another reference wave, which is measured in degrees.

In Fig. 15.3 the signal 'P' is taken as a reference, then signal 'Q' is 90 degrees phase difference from 'P' and the signal 'R' is 270 degrees phase difference from 'P'.

Analog signals include the amplitude of a human voice, frequency of a radio signal, the amplitude of an electrical voltage or current and so on. In an ordinary telephone loop, the signal consists of an electrical current which varies in amplitude in step with the variation of the intensity of sound that are impinging upon the microphone in the handset at the transmitting end. The variation of the electrical current amplitude is converted back to sound at the receiving end.

**15.2.2 Digital Signaling:** The digital data consists of two discrete states, logic 0 or 1, on or off, close or open, yes or no and so on. Most of the computer networks use digital signaling. In digital the state of change is practically instantaneous as shown in Fig. 15.4.

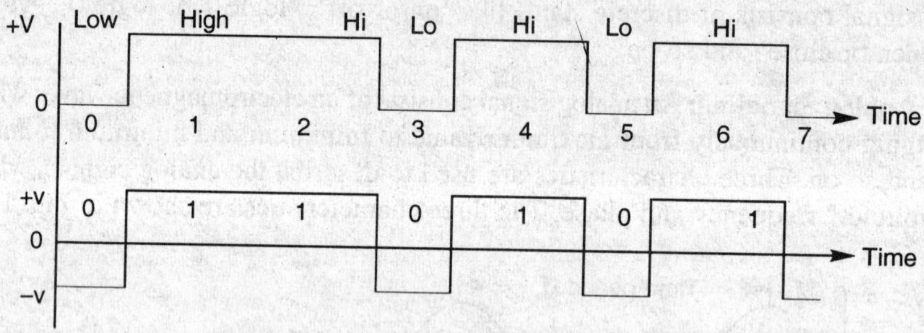


**Fig. 15.4** Characteristics of digital signal

There are several methods to encode the digital data. With reference to the Fig. 15.4 the positive voltage is encoded as logic 1 and the negative voltage is encoded as logic 0. This is referred as 'current state encoding'. Sometime the logic 1 can be encoded when transition taking place from low voltage to high voltage and logic 0 can be encoded when transition taking place from high voltage to low voltage. This is referred as 'State transition encoding'. Typically the digital communication involves the transmission of 'on/off' system called bits.

## 15.3. TELECOMMUNICATION SERVICES

The telecommunication services include the following categories.

- Cable services.
- Broadcast services.
- Phone services.
- Video services.

- Wireless services.
- Local area network services.
- Wide area network services.
- Internet services.
- Microwave services.

## 15.4. TRANSMISSION PATH (MEDIA)

The physical path through which communication networks send and receive signals is called transmission media. The signals may be of electrical current, radiowaves, microwaves, light spectrum etc. The path is divided into two categories.

- Cable medium normally used in local area networks (LAN).
- Wireless media normally used in wide area networks (WAN).

The consideration of the path depends on the cost, installation procedure, capacity, attenuation and electromagnetic interference.

**15.4.1 Open Wire Pairs:** This path is used in telephone services. A pair consists of two open wires of steel or coated copper suspended on the poles. It is used up to maximum of 50 km distance. since this medium is exposed to sun and rain, severely affected by atmospheric conditions and also is now obsolete.

**15.4.2 Twisted Pair Cable:** Twisted pair cables are insulated pairs of copper wire that are bundled together and insulated to form a single cable. Individual pair is twisted together to minimize cross talk as shown in Fig. 15.5.

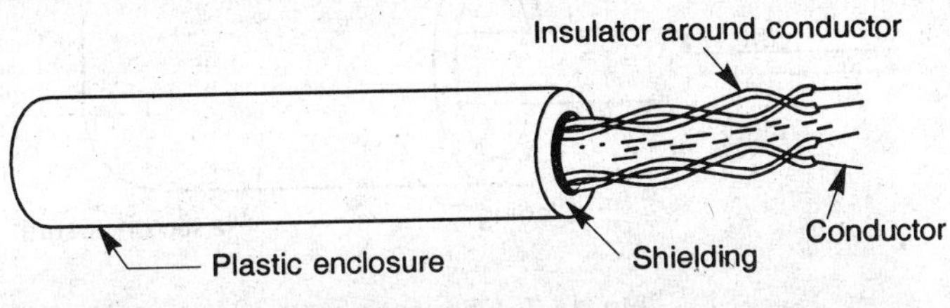


**Fig. 15.5** Twisted pair cable

Cable can contain several hundreds of twisted pairs, ranging from 16 to 18 gauge copper wire. It can be used in underground systems. Repeaters are necessary to boost the signal strength when used in long distance systems. Shielding is used around the cable and connected to the ground to reduce electromagnetic interference.

**15.4.3 Coaxial Cable:** Normally for the frequencies above the range of 1 KHz, it is considered to use coaxial cables. Coaxial shielding eliminates radiation losses and adjacent channel interferences. The cables are manufactured with a hollow cylindrical copper tube used for the shield. The insulating material separates the conductor tube. A solid or stranded wire runs down the center of the cable and this wire is surrounded by the plastic insulation. This is again surrounded by a second conductor, and further surrounded by a mesh tube called shield to protect from electromagnet interference to avoid signal distortion. The generalized diagram is shown in Fig. 15.6. Initial cost will be high but installation is easy. Band-width capacity is around 10 megabits per second.

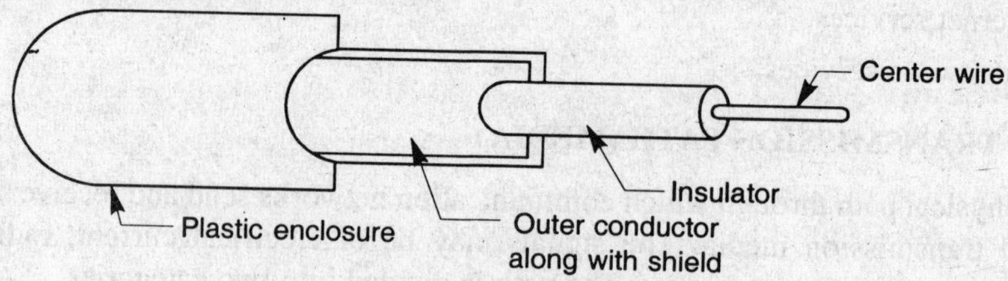


**Fig. 15.6** Coaxial cable

**15.4.4. Fiber-Optic Cable:** It is more efficient than other cable network systems. Fiber optic cable transmits light signal. It has an inner core that conducts light. Cladding, a layer of glass that reflects light back to the core, surrounds the inner core as shown in Fig. 15.7. A plastic sheath that provides strength against weather conditions and breaking surrounds each fiber. Optical fibers are smaller and lighter, approximately same diameter as human hair. The fiber optic cables are more expensive than copper cables. Installation cost is also more and difficult. It can provide higher bandwidth since it is using light. It can support 100 megabits per second over several kilometers and not subjected to electromagnetic interference.

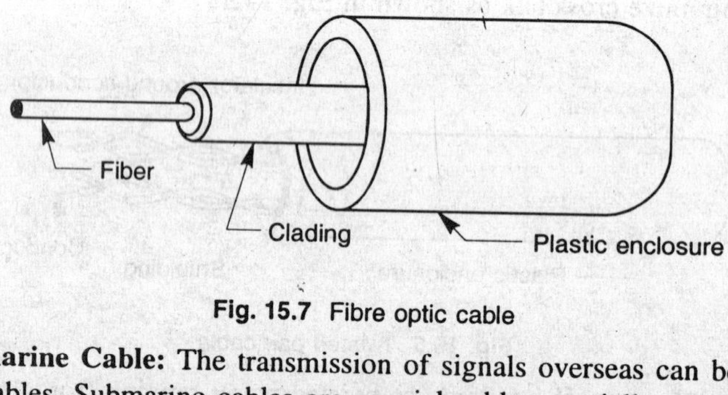


**Fig. 15.7** Fibre optic cable

**15.4.5 Submarine Cable:** The transmission of signals overseas can be done using submarine cables. Submarine cables are coaxial cables specially designed to withstand the rugged oceanic conditions. The construction of the cable includes several layers of insulations and armored steel reinforcement surrounding the conductor to protect it from corrosion, temperature changes and leakages. There are several types of communication technologies developed with electronics system using light and sound.

**15.4.6 Polivinyl Chloride Cable (PVC):** This is used in coaxial system, because it is flexible and less expensive. It is very well used in the exposed areas, due to its insulating property. But proper care should be taken, when it is used in high temperature and fire environment due to its chemical property.

**15.4.7 Radio Wave Transmission Path:** Radio frequency has the range of electromagnetic spectrum between 10KHz and 1GHz. The radio waves can be of short waves (SW), very high frequency waves (VHF) and ultra high frequency waves (UHF). Antennas are used to broadcast radio signals. Transmitters and receivers are used to transmit and receive signals.

**15.4.8 Microwave Transmission Path:** There are two types of microwave transmission system which are 'Terrestrial' and 'Satellite'.

**15.4.8a Terrestrial system:** The terrestrial microwave systems use directional parabolic antennas to send and receive the signals. The physical path must be in line of sight and focused properly as shown in Fig. 15.8. If necessary the relay towers are also used to extend signals. It uses the frequency range between 4 to 6 GHz and 21 to 23 GHz. The installation cost is more and also line of sight between two antennas is required.

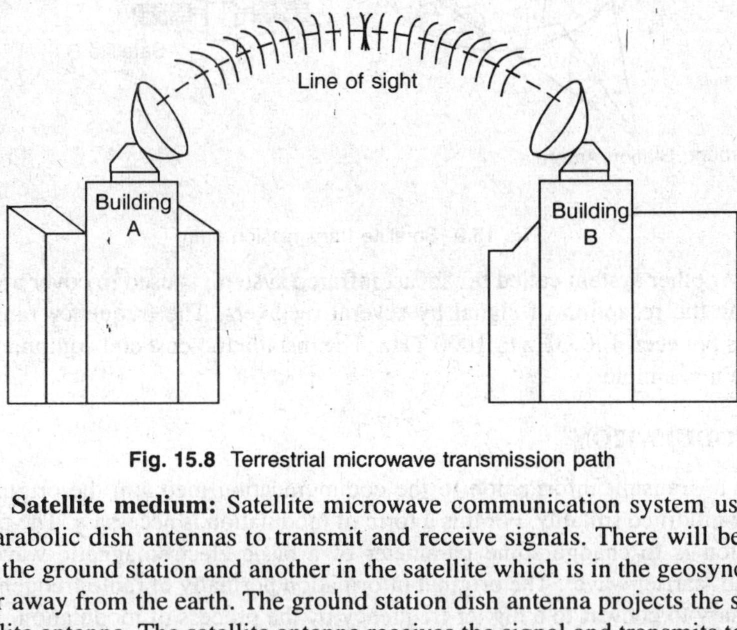


**Fig. 15.8** Terrestrial microwave transmission path

**15.4.8b Satellite medium:** Satellite microwave communication system uses directional parabolic dish antennas to transmit and receive signals. There will be one antenna in the ground station and another in the satellite which is in the geosynchronous orbit far away from the earth. The ground station dish antenna projects the signals to the satellite antenna. The satellite antenna receives the signal and transmits to another station antenna on the earth. The satellite antenna can also transmit the signal to other satellite antenna, which will be used to retransmit to the other part of the earth station antenna as shown in Fig. 15.9.

Since the signal is traveling long distance, there will be a small delay between transmission and reception. This is called 'propagation delay time' which could be around 0.5 to 5 seconds. The operating frequency ranges between 11 and 14 GHz. The cost of the medium is extremely high.

**15.4.9 Infrared Path:** In this medium, the infrared signal is used for transmission purpose. Infrared signals are in the terahertz range. Infrared beams are made to focus at a specific target. The focused signals are received by the receiver and conditioned in accordance to the requirements of the user. This is referred as point-to-point

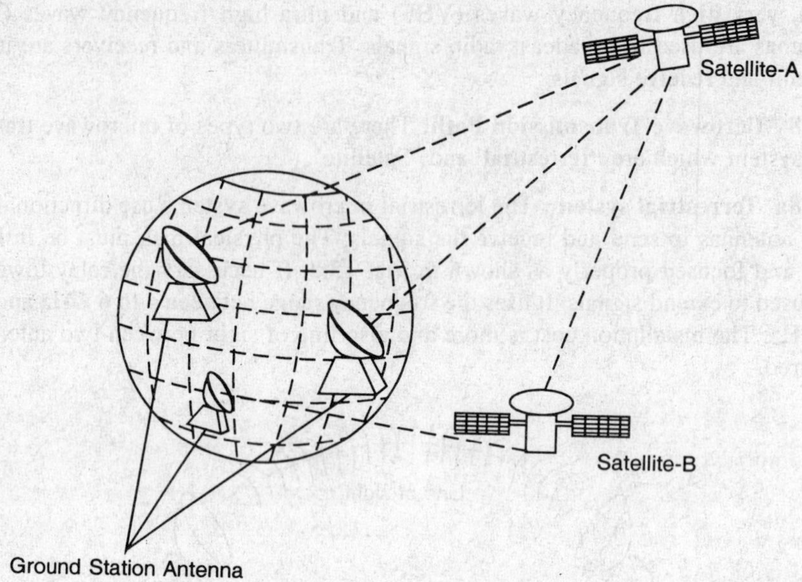


**Fig. 15.9** Satellite transmission path

system. Another system called broadcast infrared system, is used to cover a wide area and allow the reception of signal by several receivers. The frequency range of the system is between 100 GHz to 1000 THz. The installation cost and equipment cost of the system is simple.

## 15.5. MODULATION

In order to transmit information to the communication medium, the original signal has to be modified suitably. For this a form of modulation is necessary. The process of modulation is to change some parameter of a basic electromagnetic wave usually called the 'carrier wave'. The original information normally of radio frequency signal is necessary to convert to a higher frequency by the process of modulation. In analog method, analog carrier is used for modulation. In pulse method, a digital carrier signal comprising a pulse train is used for modulation. In digital method, digital data signal is used to modulate a sine wave carrier.

**15.5.1 Amplitude Modulation:** The processes of varying the amplitude of the radio frequency carrier wave by a modulating voltage is called amplitude modulation. This is shown in Fig. 15.10.

Consider,

A radio frequency carrier wave = $\upsilon_c = V_c \sin \omega_c t$ where $\omega_c = 2\Pi f_c$ and $f_c$ is the carrier frequency. A modulating signal $\upsilon_m = V_m \sin \omega_m t$ where $\omega_m = 2\pi f_m$ and $f_m$ is the audio frequency.

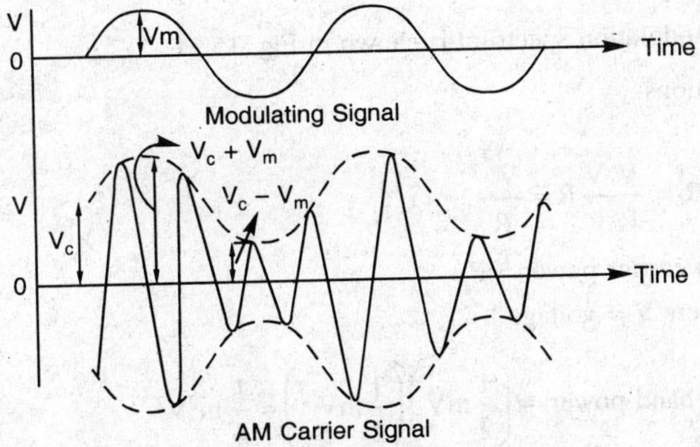


**Fig. 15.10** Amplitude modulation

The amplitude of the modulated carrier is varying from $(V_c + V_m)$ to $(V_c - V_m)$.

The modulation index is the degree of modulation, which is considered as an important parameter. It is the ratio of the peak amplitude of the modulating voltage $V_m$ to the peak amplitude of the carrier voltage $V_c$.

Modulation index = $V_m/V_c = m$, which lies between 0 and 1.

$V_m$ and $V_c$ are peak values

$\upsilon_m$ and $\upsilon_c$ are instantaneous values

Modulated carrier wave $\upsilon_c$

$$\therefore \quad \upsilon_c = (V_c + V_m \sin \omega_m t) \sin \omega_c t$$

$$\upsilon_c = V_c \sin \omega_c t + V_m \sin \omega_m t \,.\, \sin \omega_c t$$

$$\frac{V_m}{V_c} = m \therefore V_m = mV_c$$

$$\therefore \quad \upsilon_c = V_c \sin \omega_c t + mV_c \sin \omega_c t \,.\, \sin \omega_m t$$

$$\sin \omega_c t \,.\, \sin \omega_m t = \frac{1}{2}[\cos (\omega_c - \omega_m)t - \cos (\omega_c + \omega_m)t]$$

$$\therefore \quad \upsilon_c = V_c \sin \omega_c t + \frac{m V_c}{2} \cos (\omega_c - \omega_m)t - \frac{m V_c}{2} \cos (\omega_c + \omega_m)t$$

From the above expression we can conclude the following:

$V_c \sin \omega_c t$ = carrier frequency

$\frac{1}{2} mV_c \cos (\omega_c - \omega_m) t$ = Lower Side Frequency [LSF]

$$\frac{1}{2} mV_c \cos(\omega_c + \omega_m) t = \text{Upper Side Frequency [USF]}$$

The amplitude modulation spectrum is shown in Fig. 15.11.

Power considerations:

$$\text{Power} = I^2R = \frac{V}{R}\frac{V}{R}R = \frac{V^2}{R}$$

If $R = 1$ Then carrier power $= P_c$

$\therefore$ $P_c = V^2$ where V = voltage

$\therefore$ $$\text{Lower side band power} = \left(\frac{1}{2}mV\right)\left(\frac{1}{2}mV\right) = \frac{1}{4}m^2V^2$$

where m = modulating Index

$$\text{Upper side band power also} = \frac{1}{4}m^2V^2$$

$\therefore$ Total power = Carrier Power + LSB power + USB power

$$= V^2 + \frac{1}{4}m^2V^2 + \frac{1}{4}m^2V^2$$

$$= V^2\left[1 + \frac{1}{2}m^2\right]$$

$\therefore$ we can conclude,

The carrier power is proportional to the amplitude of the signal.

The side band power is proportional to $m^2$

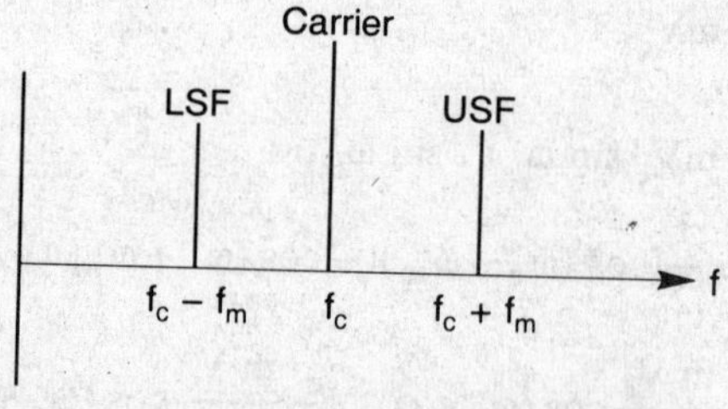


**Fig. 15.11** Amplitude modulation spectrum

**15.5.2 Frequency Modulation:** The process of varying the frequency of the carrier wave in proportion to the modulating signal is called frequency modulation. The carrier frequency increases when modulating voltage increases positively. The carrier wave frequency decreases when modulating voltage decreases negatively as shown in Fig. 15.12.

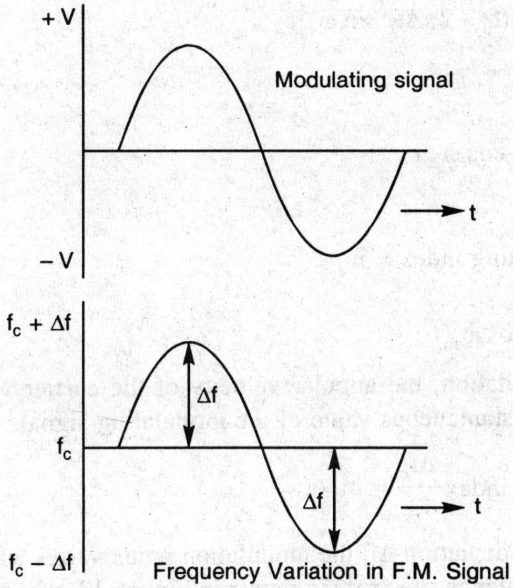


**Fig. 15.12** Frequency modulation

when modulating signal is zero the output frequency of the modulated signal = $f_c$.

when the modulating signal is at positive maximum, the output frequency of the modulated signal = $f_c + f_m$.

when the modulating signal is at negative maximum, the output frequency of the modulated signal = $f_c - f_m$

∴ The deviation from the centre frequency = ± Δf

The instantaneous carrier $\upsilon_c = V_c \sin \omega_i t = V_c \sin 2\pi f_i t$

when $f_i$ = instantaneous frequency.

Considering "Positive" increases in frequency,

$$f_i = f_c + \Delta f_c \sin \omega_m t$$

where $f_c$ = carrier frequency, $\Delta f_c$ = deviation of the carrier, due to modulating signal frequency fm.

$$\text{Angular velocity} = \frac{d\phi_i}{dt} = \omega_i = 2\pi f_i$$

∴ where $\phi_i$ is instantaneous carrier phase

$$\therefore \quad \frac{1}{2\pi}\frac{d\phi_i}{dt} = f_i = f_c + \Delta f_c \sin \omega_m t$$

$$\frac{d\phi_i}{dt} = 2\pi f_i = 2\pi f_c + 2\pi \Delta f_c \sin \omega_m t$$

By integrating

$$\phi_i = \omega_c t - \frac{\Delta f_c}{f_m} \cos \omega_m t$$

$$\frac{\Delta f_c}{f_m} = \text{Modulating index} = m_f$$

$$\therefore \quad \phi_i = \omega_c t - m_f \cos \omega_m t$$

After frequency modulation, the angular velocity of the carrier wave is varying in proportion with the instantaneous value of the modulating signal.

$\therefore$ The modulation index $\frac{\Delta f_c}{f_m} = m_f$

For a given frequency deviation $\Delta f$, the modulation index varies with the modulating frequency $f_m$. The frequency spectrum is shown in Fig. 15.13, when $m_f$ is small, a few vs small, a few side-band frequency of large amplitude, and when $m_f$ is large, there are many side-band frequencies with smaller amplitude are present.

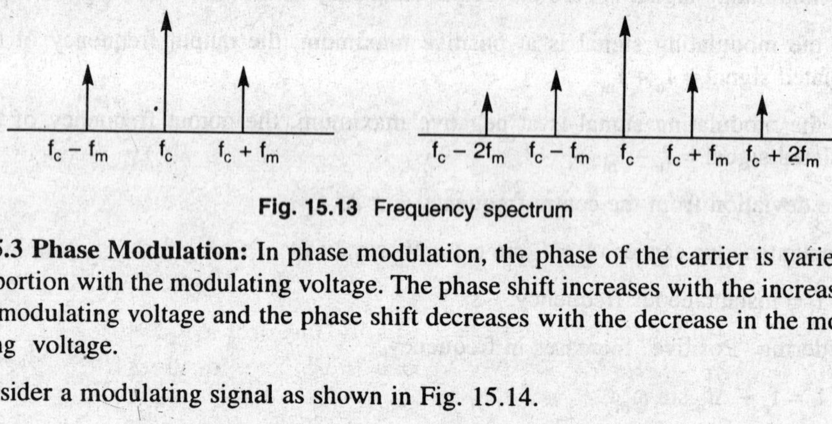


**Fig. 15.13** Frequency spectrum

**15.5.3 Phase Modulation:** In phase modulation, the phase of the carrier is varied in proportion with the modulating voltage. The phase shift increases with the increase in the modulating voltage and the phase shift decreases with the decrease in the modulating voltage.

Consider a modulating signal as shown in Fig. 15.14.

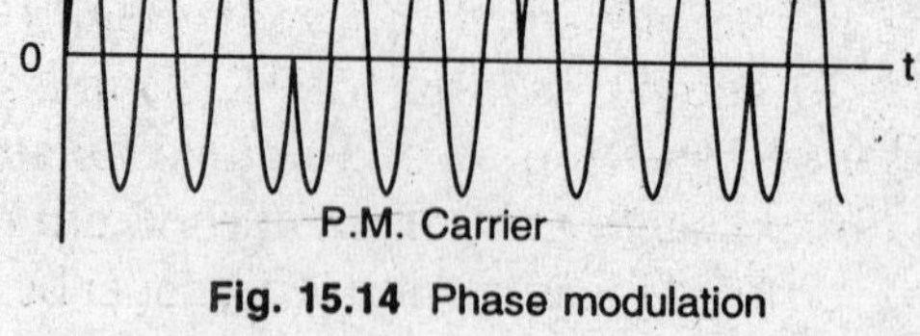


**Fig. 15.14** Phase modulation

It $\upsilon_i$ is the instantaneous value of the unmodulated carrier voltage, then let

$\upsilon_i = V_c \sin(\omega_c t + \phi)$ where $\phi$ is phase of the carrier.

The modulating signal $\upsilon_m = V_m \sin \omega_m t$,

where $\omega_m = 2\pi f_m$ and $f_m$ = modulating audio frequency

Let the carrier phase varies with a peak phase deviation $\Delta\pi$, then the phase modulated carrier wave is

$$\upsilon_c = V_c \sin[\omega_c t + \pi + \Delta\pi \sin \omega_m t]$$

If = initial '$\phi$' is assumed to be zero

then $\upsilon_c = V_c \sin[\omega_c t + \Delta\pi \sin \omega_m t]$

The Fig. 15.14 shows the square wave as modulating signal. When square wave changes from positive to negative (or) negative to positive, the carrier wave shifts it phase by 180°.

### 15.5.4 Pulse Modulation

In pulse modulation, the digital signal (instead of analog) is modulated by an analog-modulating signal. This may be achieved in several ways as discussed below.

**15.5.4.1 Pulse Amplitude Modulation:** The amplitude of the train of digital pulses is varied in proportion to the amplitude of the modulating signal as shown in Fig. 15.15.

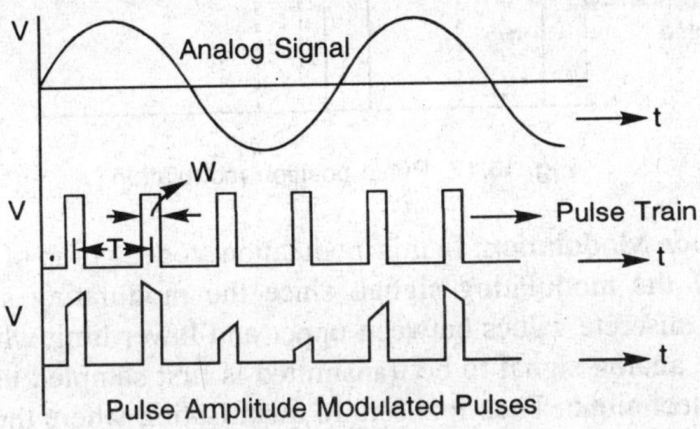


**Fig. 15.15** Pulse amplitude modulation

**15.5.4.2 Pulse Duration Modulation:** This is achieved by varying the width of the pulse by the modulating signal. This is also called pulse width modulation. Amplitude of the modulating signal determines the width as shown in Fig. 15.16.

**15.5.4.3 Pulse Position Modulation:** The process of varying the position or the time occurrence of a pulse due to the modulating signal is called pulse position modulation (PPM). This is also referred as pulse time modulation (PTM) shown in Fig. 15.17. This is achieved by shifting each pulse from its unmodulated position by an amount proportional to the modulating signal when the modulating signal is maximum positive, the deviation of the pulse from its reference is maximum and for negative it is minimum. The amplitude and width remain constant.

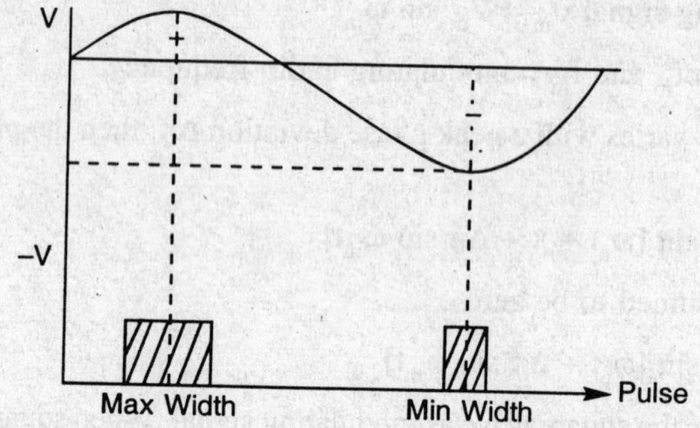


**Fig. 15.16** Pulse duration modulation

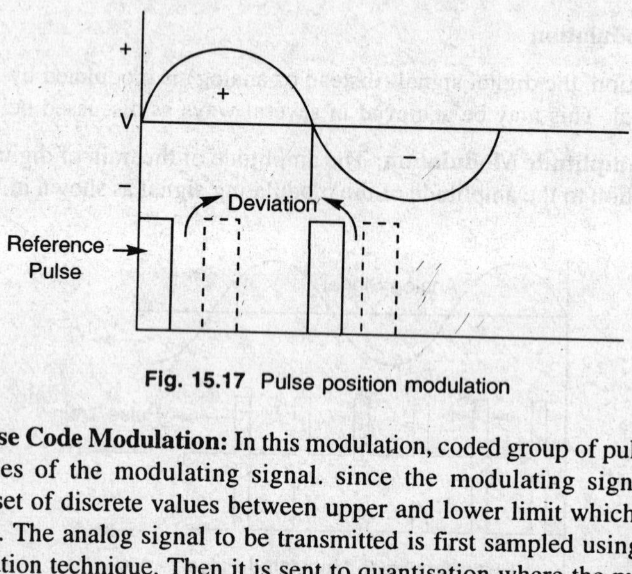


**Fig. 15.17** Pulse position modulation

**15.5.4.4 Pulse Code Modulation:** In this modulation, coded group of pulses, represents certain values of the modulating signal. since the modulating signal consists of continuous set of discrete values between upper and lower limit which is referred as quantisation. The analog signal to be transmitted is first sampled using pulse amplitude modulation technique. Then it is sent to quantisation where the pulse amplitude signals are rounded off to the nearest levels. Then the pulses are coded into groups according to the binary code. Each pulse group is represented as a binary number. The same is transmitted to the communication path. At the receiving end the signal is recovered by using decoder. The block diagram for the user is shown in Fig. 15.18.

### 15.5.5 Digital Modulation

Digital signal consists of logic 1 or logic 0, which is transmitted by varying the amplitude, frequency or phase of a sinusoidal carrier wave. Using the following methods the digital modulation is carried out amplitude shift keying (ASK), frequency shift keying (FSK), and phase shift keying (PSK).

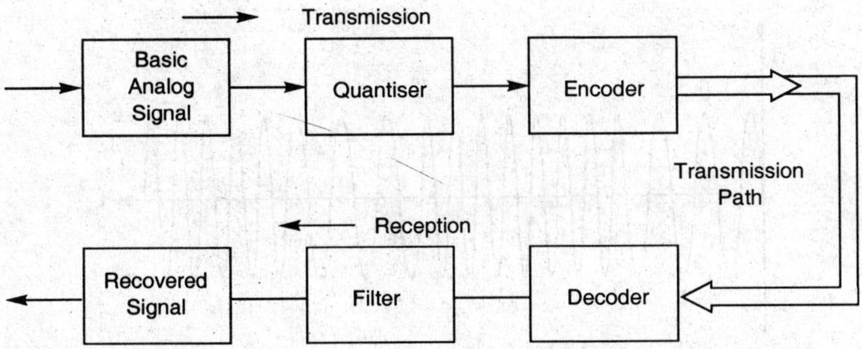


**Fig. 15.18** Pulse code modulation

**15.5.5.1 Amplitude Shift Keying:** This is achieved by varying the amplitude of the signal. A carrier wave is switched on and off by the binary signals. The on and off is corresponding to logic 1 and logic 0. During logic 1, the carrier wave is transmitted and during logic 0 the carrier wave is suppressed. Sometimes stronger amplitude of the signal referred as logic 1 and weaker amplitude is referred as logic 0 as shown in Fig. 15.19.

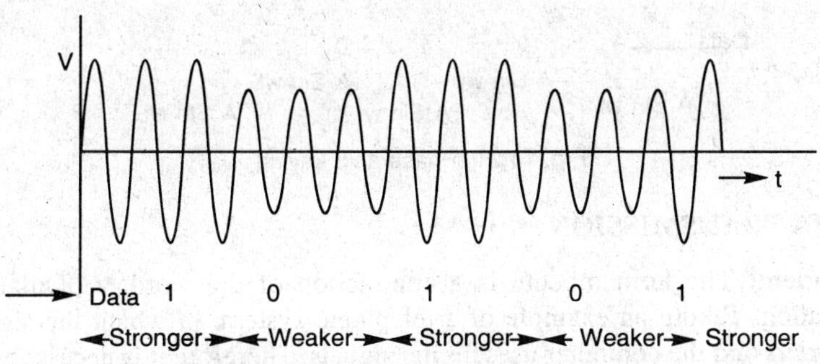


**Fig. 15.19** Amplitude shift keying

**15.5.5.2 Frequency Shift Keying:** In this method two different carrier frequencies are used and they are switched on and off by the binary signals. Logic 1 can be identified with respect to one carrier frequency and logic 0 can be identified with respect to another carrier frequency as shown in Fig. 15.20.

**15.5.5.3 Phase Shift Keying:** In this method the binary signals are used to switch the phase of a carrier wave between two values 0 and 180. The positive phase is referred as logic 1 and the reverse phase is referred as logic 0 as shown in Fig. 15.21 Logic 1 = A sin $\omega_t$ and logic 0 = –A sin $\omega_t$.

**15.5.6 Demodulation:** The modulated signal is transmitted through transmission path, and the signal is received through the receiver and the data or message is recovered. The process of recovering the signal is called 'Demodulation'.

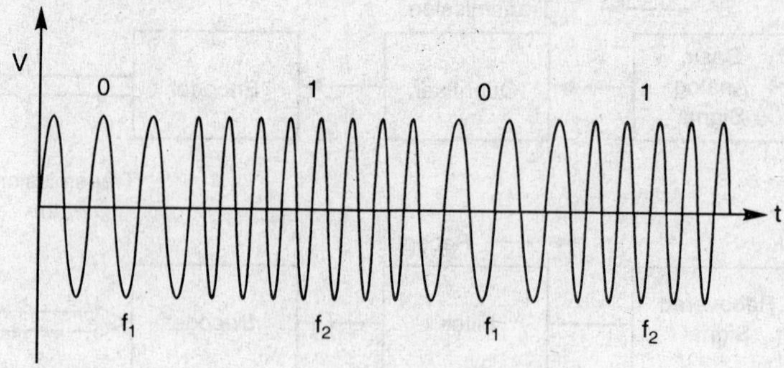


Fig. 15.20 Frequency shift keying

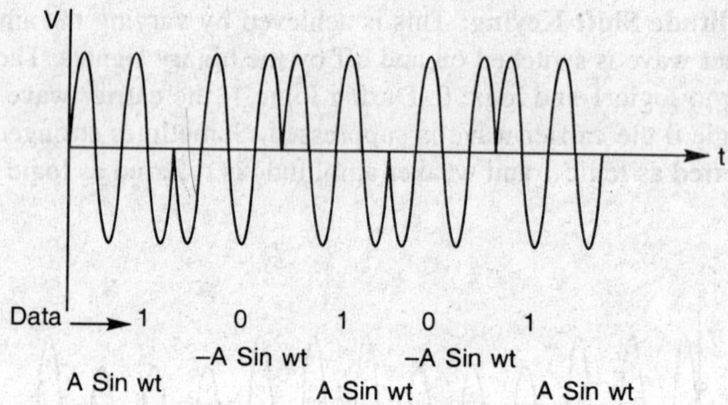


Fig. 15.21 Phase shift keying

## 15.6. DATA TRANSMISSION

**15.6.1 Modem:** The term modem is a contraction of the word MODulation and DEModulation. Taking an example of a telephone system, in which the signals are analog carriers and the computer uses digital signals. Therefore it is necessary to have a device to interface these two systems. This device is called modem. There are two main factors that the modem performs. The computer's digital serial bit stream is used by the modem to modulate a carrier signal suitable for transmission over the phone lines. The modem at the receiving end demodulates the signals to recover the signal to its original digital form.

There are two types of modem available: asynchronous and synchronous. Asynchronous modem is generally used in telephone lines. In asynchronous type, at the end the data to be transmitted is first divided into bytes. The bytes are sent bit by bit serially along with an identification bit for 'start' and 'stop' purpose as shown in Fig. 15.22. At the receiving end the start and stop bit is identified and followed by this, the data is recovered. The method of identification of start and stop bit is referred as hand shaking process.

In synchronous method, identification of start and stop bit is avoided. Data is directly sent and received by the use of careful timing. Special type of clocking mechanism is used at the sending end modem and the receiving end modem. Both the clocks are synchronized. The clock synchronization will be in such a way that the receiver recovers the correct data at the predetermined and programmed interval.

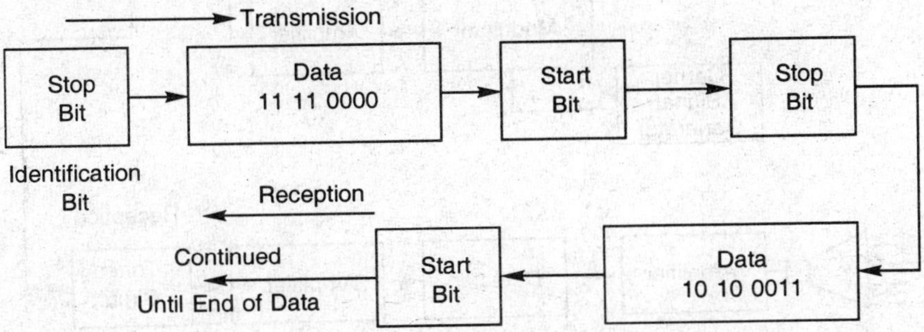


**Fig. 15.22** Asynchronous modem

Frequency shift keying method of modulation is used in low speed asynchronous transmission for 300 to 1800 bits per second. The carrier frequency of the modem is shifted between two discrete frequencies in accordance with the logic levels of the digital signal. The higher frequency is referred as logic 1, and the lower frequency is referred as logic 0.

According to the requirement other modulation like, amplitude shift keying (ASK), phase shift keying (PSK) may also be used. Quadrature amplitude modulation which is a combination of ASK and PSK is used to achieve for higher transmission rate.

If the modem is used to send and receive the signals in one direction only, then it is referred as 'Simplex' mode operation.

In 'half duplex' mode of operation, the communication is shared between transmission and reception. While transmitting, the receiver is switched off and while receiving the transmitter is switched off.

In 'full duplex' operation the modem can transmit and receive data simultaneously.

**15.6.2 Radio Transmission:** The radio transmission system transmits radiowaves. The signal to be transmitted is modulated using amplitude or frequency or phase modulation methods and transmitted to the communication medium. The received data is recovered after demodulating the signal at the receiver end. The general block diagram of radio transmitter and the receiver is shown in Fig. 15.23. The basic data called modulating signal is amplified. The carrier frequency wave is generated using high frequency oscillator. Both the modulating and carrier waves are fed into the modulator. The modulated signal is further amplified using power amplifier and transmitted to the communication medium. The radio receiver is a device that picks up the signals from the receiver antenna. The tuning circuit selects the desired frequency range. The signal from the tuner is amplified and fed into the detector (demodulator) where the data is recovered and fed into the power amplifier. The amplified audio signal is then fed into the speaker.

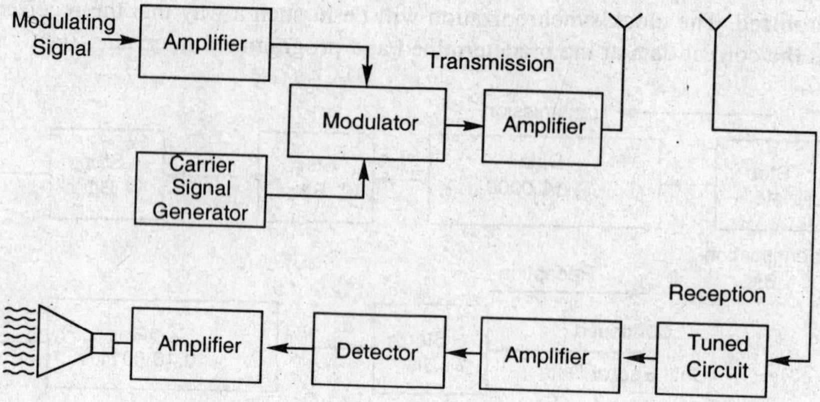


Fig. 15.23 The radio transmitter and receiver

**15.6.3 Television Transmission:** A television system is used for transmission and reception of visual and audio information by electronics medium. The general block diagram of T.V. transmitter and receiver is shown in Fig. 15.24 and 15.25. At the transmitter end, the camera converts the picture signal into electrical signals. The conversion is carried out by image 'orthicon' or 'vidicon' or 'plumbicon' methods operated using the principle of photoconduction. Video amplifier amplifies the electrical signal from the camera. The amplified picture signal is amplitude modulated, filtered and further amplified.

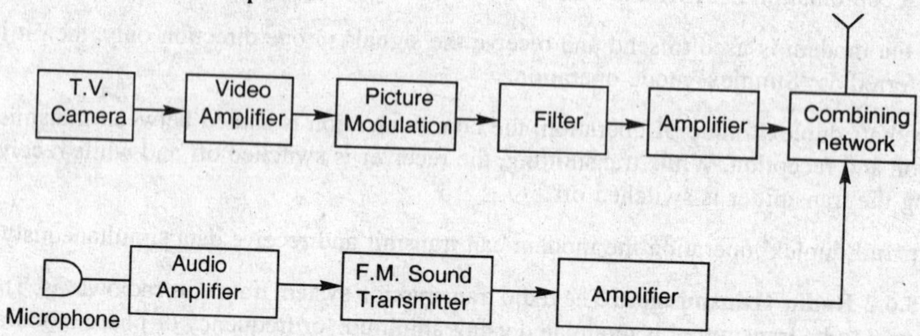


Fig. 15.24 T.V. transmitter

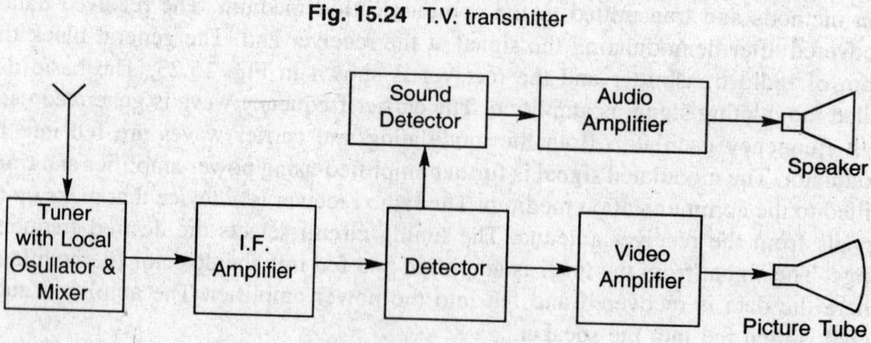


Fig. 15.25 T.V. receiver

The audio signal is separated from video signals. It consists of microphone, audio amplifier, transmitter and power amplifier. The amplified signal from microphone is applied to the modulator, which changes the radio frequency in accordance to the audio signal and produces the frequency-modulated wave. This signal is further amplified. Both the video and audio signals mixed in a combining network and transmitted through the same antenna.

In the tuner, the section function is accomplished, which selects one particular channel and rejects other channels. The turner section consists of local oscillator and mixer to convert the RF signal to an intermediate frequency signal (IF). This signal is amplified using IF amplifier. The signal is demodulated in detector section. The detected video and audio signals are amplified using separate video and audio amplifiers. Finally the video signal is fed into the picture tube and the audio signal is fed into the speaker. The received signals are synchronized with the transmitted signals using synchronization pulses.

**15.6.4 Microwave transmission:** Several signal channels are modulated into microwave carrier frequencies and transmitted to the repeater stations spaced 50 to 70 km apart. Repeater antennas are placed on towards, and hilltops so that there will not be any obstruction in the line of sight between the repeater antennas. This system is called 'Line of sight microwave link'.

The general block diagram of line of sight transmission system is shown in Fig. 15.26. The base signal is first conditioned using conditional circuits. The conditioned signal is amplified using amplifiers to increase the signal strength. The signal is fed into modulator to produce a frequency-modulated wave. This signal is mixed with local oscillator signal. The output from the mixer is intermediate frequency (IF) wave and is fed into the transmitter where the IF wave is transferred into microwave range using microwave carrier. Then it is transmitted through the antenna after amplification. The

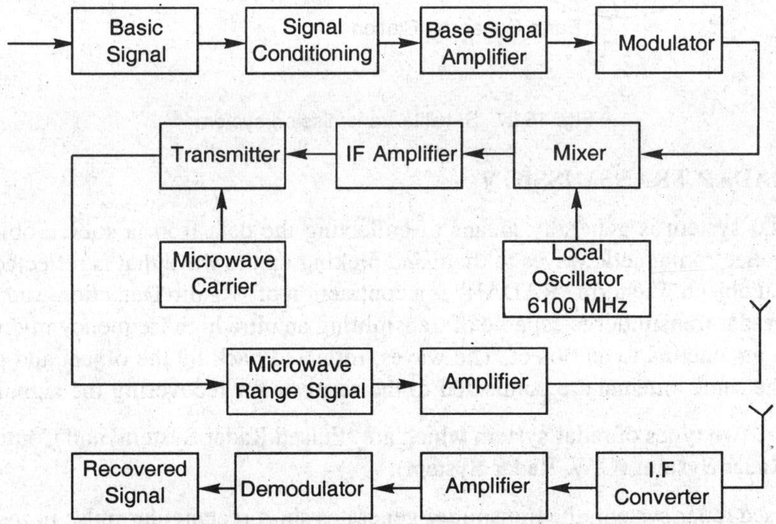


**Fig. 15.26** General block diagram of microwave transmission system

receiver separates the IF signals and demodulates to recover the original data or message.

**15.6.5 Satellite Transmission:** The satellite is essentially a microwave station placed in orbital space. The broadcast signals are beamed up to the satellite from an earth station through the directional dish antenna that is synchronized to the position of the satellite. a device called transponder is used in the satellite to receive the weak signal, amplify, condition it and further retransmit the signal back to another earth station in a different location on the earth. The earth stations typically transmit their signals to satellites on carrier frequencies ranging from 5.92 to 6.43 GHz band called the uplink frequency. The satellite transponders convert these signals to a range from 3.7 to 4.2 GHz band. These frequencies are referred to as downlink frequencies. The modern satellites are positioned in an orbit at an elevation very far away from the equator. This is referred as geosynchronous or geostationary orbit. In this orbit, the satellite is made to travel at a velocity equal to rotation of earth in order to maintain a fixed position relative to a point above equator. The general diagram is shown in Fig. 15.27.

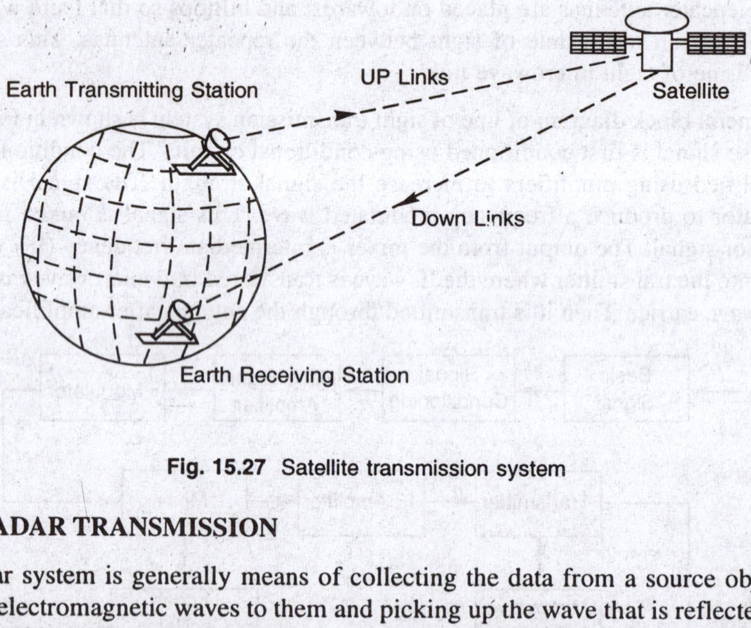


Fig. 15.27 Satellite transmission system

## 15.7. RADAR TRANSMISSION

The radar system is generally means of collecting the data from a source object by sending electromagnetic waves to them and picking up the wave that is reflected back from that object. The term "RADAR" is a contraction of "RAdio Detection And Ranging". A radar transmitter is capable of transmitting an ultra high frequency microwave through an antenna to an object. The waves, reflected back by the object and picked up by the same antenna are connected to the receiver for recovering the signal.

There are two types of radar system which are 'Pulsed Radar System' and Continuous Wave Radar System (C.W. Radar System).

In a pulsed radar system, the transmitter generates short rectangular pulse in response to an internally generated trigger pulse. This pulse is fed into a device called 'duplexer', which disconnects the receiver from the antenna and connects to the transmitter. At a time either transmitter or receiver is connected by the use of duplexer. Once the pulse is transmitted to the source, the duplexer disconnects the transmitter and reconnects the receiver in order to get the reflected signal. The received signal is recovered by the use of demodulator. The distance of the object can be calculated from the time taken by the pulse to travel from the radar to the object and back to the receiver.

C.W. Radar system transmits continuous wave instead of pulse through the transmitting antenna to the object. The reflected signal received by the receiver by a separate antenna and recovered using demodulator. The demodulated signal is amplified using video amplifier and fed into the oscilloscope to read the information. The block diagram is shown in Fig. 15.28.

The radar that is used to cover all round the area and made to search the unknown object is called 'Search radar'. After locating the object by the search radar, the object is tracked by the 'Tracking radar'. The map of the object area is made to be displayed using cathode ray tube CRT, which is called 'Plan Position Indicator'.

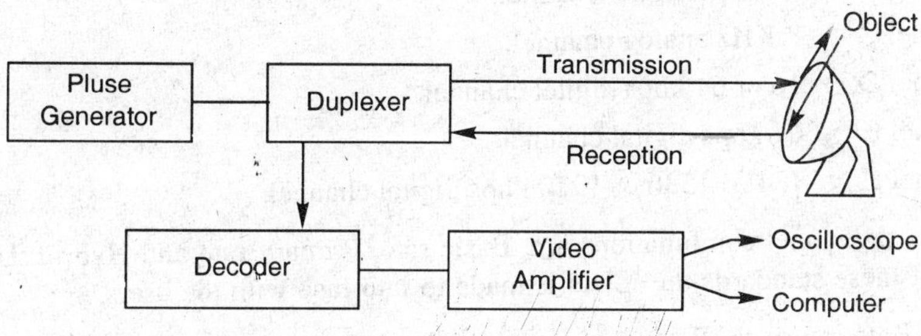


**Fig. 15.28** General block diagram of radar system

**15.7.7 Optical Transmission:** Optical fiber is used as a channel, which transmits light signals. Optical fiber consists of a core material whose refractive index is greater than that of surrounding medium known as cladding.

In optical communication, the transmitter is a light source whose output acts as a carrier wave. This carrier wave modulated with digital signal by using ON and OFF technique called as 'on-off keying' or 'amplitude shift keying'. In optical system this is achieved by varying the source drive current directly causing a proportional change in optical power. The most common light source used are 'Semiconductor Laser Diodes (SLD)' and 'Light Emitting Diodes (LED)'.

At the receiving end, a photo diode is used to convert the modulated light back to electrical signal. The photo diode current is directly proportional to the incident optical power. Normally the output of the photo diode will be of small amplitude and the same is amplified according to the requirement of the user. The block diagram is shown in Fig. 15.29.

**15.6.8 Integrated Service Digital Network (I.S.D.N):** In general the data from the computer is transferred to analog signal using modem and then transmitted to the

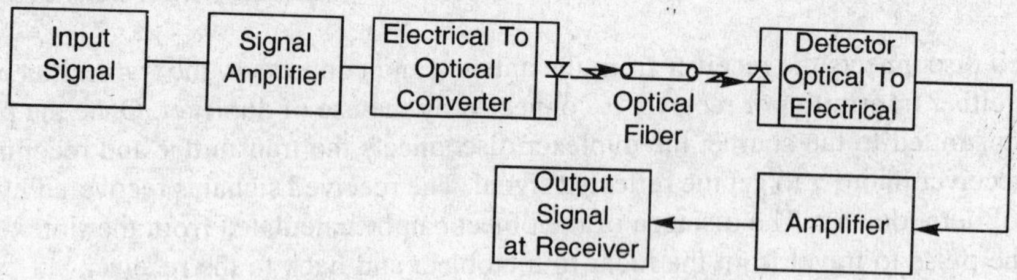


**Fig. 15.29** Optical transmission system

communication system. The modem at the receiving end reconverts the analog data to digital form to be used by the other end computer. As an improvement to this, a set of standard developed to provide a data transfer over a digital telephone network, the way of introducing ISDN network. In ISDN system, the signal originating from the digital source remains digital throughout the network. The ISDN is connected through communication channels. There are several communication channels available.

Channel A : 4 KHz analog channel.

Channel B : 64 kbps digital channel.

Channel C : 8 KHz analog channel.

Channel D : 16 or 64 kbps digital channel.

Channel E : 64 kbps digital channel.

Channel H : 134 or 1536 or 1920 kbps digital channel.

The standard channel combinations are, Basic rate, Primary rate and Hybrid. Using any one of these standards the ISDN is made to interface with the users.

The Basic Rate Interface (BRI) carrier, two B channels (Bearer) 64 K bits per second (kbps) for carrying the users voice, audio, video and data. Also it carries one D channel (Delta) 16 kbps capacities to exchange the signaling messages necessary to request services on the B channel. The Basic rate interface is mostly used for residential applications with limited bandwidth.

The Primary rate interface (PRI) delivers ISDN services used for digital PBX (Private Branch Exchange), host computers and local area networks. It uses 23 or 30 B-channels each at 64 Kbps for signaling and one D-channel for messaging at 64 kbps. The primary rate interface is normally used for large business applications with a Private Branch Exchange (PBX). The general diagram is shown in Fig. 15.30.

The hybrid rate interface uses one A channel with 4 KHz analog and one D channel with 16 kbps digital.

Local area networks and wide area networks must fulfill the demand for the very high-speed data delivery. A new bandwidth—intensive services such as high definition television (HDTV), and ultra high-speed computers are developed. In order to meet this need a BROAD BAND ISDN (BISDN) has been developed and mostly used with fiber optic communication links, which is capable of transmitting at the speed ranging from 150 megabits per second (Mbps) to 2.5 gigabits per second (Gbps).

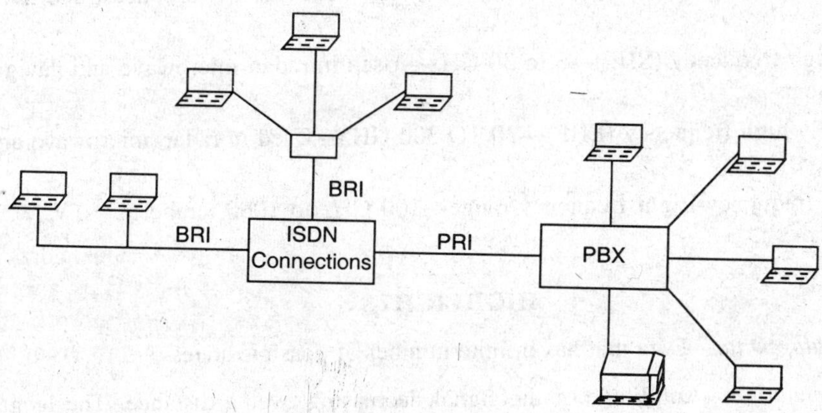


Fig. 15.30 ISDN interface

**15.7.9 Applications:** In general the factors to be considered for the applications of the transmission systems are cost, installation, capacity, attenuation and immunity from electromagnetic interference.

Modem is used in computers and telephone systems. It is a device that converts the digital signal from computer to an analog signal to the telephone system, and vice versa.

I.S.D.N system, a basic rate interface is used for the residential applications and the primary rate interface is used in business applications with PBX.

Infrared system uses infrared light as a medium, which uses the lower range of light frequencies. In general it is used in remote control operation of TV, VCR, and CD player to receive and send signals. This is called point-to-point system.

Microwave system uses lower GHz frequency range of electromagnetic spectrum, which are other than the radio frequency. The terrestrial system used in lower GHz range at 4 to 6 GHz is used to connect separate building where cable would be too expensive. The satellite system uses the frequency range 11 to 14 GHz and applied to transmit signals from one earth station to another earth station.

Fiber optic light signals used in laser instruments, defense communications etc.

The electromagnetic spectrum is given below.

Very low frequency (VLF)—10 to 30 KHz—Used in Point to point systems

Low frequency (LF)—30 to 300 KHz—used in Point to point, marine, navigation and broadcast.

Medium frequency (MF)—300 to 3000 KHz—Used in marine, navigation, and broadcast.

High frequency (HF)—3 to 30 MHz—used in Local and Wide area network.

Very high frequency (VHF)—30 to 300 MHz—Used in TV, radar, FM broadcast and navigation.

Ultra high frequency (UHF)—300 to 3000 MHz—Used in TV, broadcast and radar systems.

Super high frequency (SHF)—3 to 30 GHz—Used in radar, microwave and navigation systems.

Extremely high frequency (EHF)—30 TO 300 GHz—Used in radar, microwave and navigation.

Infrared frequency-Light frequency range—100 GHz to 1000 terahertz.—TV, VCR and broadcast.

## HIGHLIGHTS

- *Analog Data*—Data that has infinite number of possible states.
- *Attenuation*—Amplitude of the signal decreasing over a distance. The length and resistance of the cable can affect the amount of attenuation.
- *Angle modulation*—Frequency modulation and Phase modulation are referred as angle modulation.
- *Bits per second*—The amount of data transferred in a second.
- *Baud rate*—The rate at which signal is modulated is referred as Baud rate.
- *Cladding*—In fiber optic, a layer of glass that surrounds the inner core and reflects the light back into the core.
- *Decoding*—The process of translating a data from transmittable form to original form.
- *Digital data*—The data that uses logic 1 or 0 to store the information.
- *Digital modulation*—Digital signal used to modulate a sine wave carrier.
- *Electromagnetic interference*—A type of low voltage, high frequency signal that interferes with the normal transmission that is mainly caused by improper insulation or insufficient grounding.
- *Fiber optic*—One of the mediums used for communication. It uses glass or plastic fiber and sends signal through it.
- *Frequency Modulation (FM)*—The carrier frequency is varied in proportion to the instantaneous amplitude of the modulating signal.
- *Frequency shift keying (FSK)*—The carrier frequency is shifted between two discrete frequencies in accordance with the binary serial data.
- *Hand shaking*—the exchanges of codes between two devices in order to negotiate the transmission and reception of data.
- *Laser*—Light amplification by stimulated emission of radiation.
- *Local Area Network (LAN)*—The data communication link that shares resources

within local area. LAN can be of a single room, building, or a group of buildings generally with less than a few km of each other.

- *Modem*—A device that converts the digital data of a computer into an analog signal for the telephone line and vice versa.
- *Modulation*—The process of modifying a carrier signal to transmit information.
- *Pulse Amplitude Modulation (PAM)*—A modulation technique that produces a serial of pulses whose amplitude are in proportion to the modulating voltage at the time of sample.
- *Pulse Coded Modulation (PCM)*—The process of converting an analog signal into an encoded digital values for transmission.
- *Photo detector*—A device used to convert light energy into electrical energy, which is used in fiber optic systems.
- *Pulse Modulation (PM)*—An angle modulation technique in which the carrier's phase is made to vary as a function of the instantaneous value of the modulating signal.
- *Pulse Position Modulation (PPM)*—A modulation technique in which the position of the pulse relative to its time of occurrence is varied in accordance to the modulating signal.
- *Primary rate interface (PRI)*—An ISDN linking technology that delivers ISDN services to digital PBX, host computers, and LANS.
- *Phase Shift Keying (PSK)*—A modulation technique in which carrier frequency remains constant and its phase is shifted in accordance with the binary serial bit stream.
- *Pulse Width Modulation (PWM)*—Also called Pulse Duration Modulation (PDM). In this the width of the pulse carrier is made to vary the modulating voltage.
- *Repeaters*—A communication device that amplifies the signals to extend the distance they can travel.
- *Synchronous transmission*—A type of transmission that uses a clock to control the timing of bits being sent.
- *Twisted path*—A type of insulated pairs of twisted wires used for connecting the users. It minimizes the cross talk interference.

## REVIEW QUESTIONS

1. Explain analog and digital signaling used in communication systems.
2. Explain the principle of analog modulation.
3. Explain the technique used in digital modulation.
4. Explain various types of pulse modulation.
5. Explain various kinds of path used in the communication systems.
6. Explain the basic principle of radar and how it is used in the communication system.

7. Write short notes on the following:
   (a) Modem.
   (b) TV and Radio transmitter and receiver.
   (c) Microwave communication.
   (d) Fiber optic communication.
   (e) ISDN.

## TWO MARKS QUESTIONS AND ANSWERS

1. *What are communication systems ?*

   The communication systems are developed to send and receive the information from a source to one or more destinations.

2. *What is analog and digital signal ?*

   The analog signal is one that changes continuously. The digital signal consists of discrete signals either logic 1 or 0.

3. *What is analog modulation ?*

   The modulation is carried out using analog carrier.

4. *What is digital modulation ?*

   A form of modulation, that uses a digital data to modulate a sine wave carrier.

5. *What is modulation index ?*

   It is a degree of modulation.

6. *What is phase modulation ?*

   The phase of the carrier is varied proportionally by the modulating voltage.

7. *What is ISDN ?*

   ISDN is Integrated Service Digital Network.

8. *What is a radar ?*

   It is radio detection and ranging system.

9. *What is meant by path ?*

   The physical path through which the signals are sent and received.

10. *How many types of cable media are available ?*

    There are three types of cable media available. Twisted pair, coaxial, and fiber-optic are the three types of cable media.

11. *How many types of wireless media are available ?*

    There are three main types of wireless media: radiowave, microwave, and infra-red.

12. *What is fiber-optic ?*

    Fiber-optic transmits light signals rather than electrical signals.

13. *How many types of radiowaves are available ?*

    Short wave, high frequency wave and FM radio wave are the three types available.

14. *How many types of microwave communication available ?*

    Terrestrial and satellite are the two types of microwave system.

15. *What is infrared ?*

    Infrared media uses infrared light to transmit signals.

16. *What is ISDN modem ?*

    It is an interconnectivity device that connects a network to an ISDN line.